Matthew Through the Centuries

Wiley Blackwell Bible Commentaries

John Through the Centuries
Mark Edwards

Revelation Through the Centuries
Judith Kovacs and Christopher Rowland

Judges Through the Centuries
David M. Gunn

Exodus Through the Centuries
Scott M. Langston

Ecclesiastes Through the Centuries
Eric S. Christianson

Esther Through the Centuries
Jo Carruthers

Psalms Through the Centuries: Volume I
Susan Gillingham

Galatians Through the Centuries
John Riches

Pastoral Epistles Through the Centuries
Jay Twomey

1 & 2 Thessalonians Through the Centuries
Anthony C. Thiselton

Six Minor Prophets Through the Centuries
Richard Coggins and Jin H. Han

Lamentations Through the Centuries
Paul M. Joyce and Diana Lipton

James Through the Centuries
David Gowler

The Acts of the Apostles Through the Centuries
Heidi J. Hornik and Mikeal C. Parsons

Chronicles Through the Centuries
Blaire French

Isaiah Through the Centuries
John F.A. Sawyer

Psalms Through the Centuries: Volume II
Susan Gillingham

Matthew Through the Centuries
Ian Boxall

Matthew Through the Centuries

Ian Boxall

WILEY Blackwell

This edition first published 2019

Registered Office(s)
John Wiley & Sons, Inc., 111 River Street, Hoboken, NJ 07030, USA
John Wiley & Sons Ltd, The Atrium, Southern Gate, Chichester, West Sussex, PO19 8SQ, UK

Editorial Office
9600 Garsington Road, Oxford, OX4 2DQ, UK

For details of our global editorial offices, customer services, and more information about Wiley products visit us at www.wiley.com.

Wiley also publishes its books in a variety of electronic formats and by print-on-demand. Some content that appears in standard print versions of this book may not be available in other formats.

Library of Congress Cataloging-in-Publication Data

Names: Boxall, Ian, author.
Title: Matthew through the centuries / Ian Boxall.
Description: First Edition. | Hoboken : Wiley, 2018 | Series: Wiley Blackwell Bible commentaries | Includes bibliographical references and index. |
Identifiers: LCCN 2018035610 (print) | LCCN 2018038137 (ebook) | ISBN 9781118588819 (Adobe PDF) | ISBN 9781118588802 (ePub) | ISBN 9781118588864 (hardcover)
Subjects: LCSH: Bible. Matthew–Commentaries.
Classification: LCC BS2575.53 (ebook) | LCC BS2575.53 .B69 2018 (print) | DDC 226.2/0709–dc23
LC record available at https://lccn.loc.gov/2018035610

Cover Image: Wikimedia Commons
Cover Design: Wiley

Set in 10/12.5pt Minion by SPi Global, Pondicherry, India
Printed in Singapore by C.O.S. Printers Pte Ltd

10 9 8 7 6 5 4 3 2 1

In memory of Br. Saúl Soriano Rodriguez OFM Cap (1986–2018)
inspirational student, friar, and human being

Contents

List of Illustrations

Series Editors' Preface

The Wiley Blackwell Bible Commentaries series, the first to be devoted primarily to the reception history of the Bible, is based on the premise that how people have interpreted, and been influenced by, a sacred text like the Bible is often as interesting and historically important as what it originally meant. The series emphasizes the influence of the Bible on literature, art, music, and film, its role in the evolution of religious beliefs and practices, and its impact on social and political developments. Drawing on work in a variety of disciplines, it is designed to provide a convenient and scholarly means of access to material until now hard to find and a much-needed resource for all those interested in the influence of the Bible on Western culture.

Until quite recently this whole dimension was for the most part neglected by biblical scholars. The goal of a commentary was primarily if not exclusively to get behind the centuries of accumulated Christian and Jewish tradition to one single meaning, normally identified with the author's original intention.

The most important and distinctive feature of the Wiley Blackwell Commentaries is that they will present readers with many different interpretations of each text, in such a way as to heighten their awareness of what a text, especially a sacred text, can mean and what it can do, what it has meant and what it has done, in the many contexts in which it operates.

The Wiley Blackwell Bible Commentaries will consider patristic, rabbinic (where relevant) and medieval exegesis as well as insights from various types of modern criticism, acquainting readers with a wide variety of interpretative techniques. As part of the history of interpretation, questions of source, date, authorship, and other historical-critical and archaeological issues will be discussed, but since these are covered extensively in existing commentaries, such references will be brief, serving to point readers in the direction of readily accessible literature where they can be followed up.

Original to this series is the consideration of the reception history of specific biblical books arranged in commentary format. The chapter-by-chapter arrangement ensures that the biblical text is always central to the discussion. Given the wide influence of the Bible and the richly varied appropriation of each biblical book, it is a difficult question which interpretations to include. While each volume will have its own distinctive point of view, the guiding principle for the series as a whole is that readers should be given a representative sampling of material from different ages, with emphasis on interpretations that have been especially influential or historically significant. Though commentators will have their preferences among the different interpretations, the material will be presented in such a way that readers can make up their own minds on the value, morality, and validity of particular interpretations.

The series encourages readers to consider how the biblical text has been interpreted down the ages and seeks to open their eyes to different uses of the Bible in contemporary culture. The aim is to write a series of scholarly commentaries that draw on all the insights of modern research to illustrate the rich interpretative potential of each biblical book.

John F.A. Sawyer
Christopher Rowland
Judith Kovacs
David M. Gunn

Preface

Writing a reception-historical commentary on arguably the most influential of the canonical Gospels has been both daunting and exhilarating in almost equal measure. Tracing the complex journey by which a text of a minority Jewish breakaway group came to serve as foundation document for an empire-wide, and, eventually, a worldwide religion with a predominantly Gentile membership, has been a fascinating experience. What has made it particularly fascinating has been the opportunity to explore 'roads less-travelled,' less familiar trajectories of interpretation preserved by other Christian communities (and, in some cases, by non-Christians), opening up new vistas, and enabling me to view well-known texts and their interpretations with fresh eyes. Yet the sheer volume of possible receptions of Matthew's Gospel, and their effects on individuals and communities across centuries and cultures, has at times been overwhelming. Matthew's impact has been enormous, not simply in the commentary tradition, but also in liturgy, hymnody, preaching, spirituality, political discourse, music, drama, film, and visual art.

This diversity is attributable in no small measure to the tensions inherent in the Gospel text itself. Matthew has functioned as an effective weapon in apologetic and theological controversy; as word of comfort and of prophetic warning and challenge; as a text justifying the political and ecclesial status quo and as advocating a radical path of discipleship directed toward a 'higher righteousness.' The First Gospel contains some of the most sublime words in the whole of scripture, and some of the bitterest, all of which have added to the complexity of its reception and the diversity (both positive and negative) of its effects.

As a consequence of such an *embarras de richesses*, as well as the constraints of this commentary series, what is contained here is a tiny, representative selection of this Gospel's extraordinary history and impact. Priority is given to so-called 'pre-critical' interpretation (which in reality is far from 'uncritical'), and to showcasing the different, and not necessarily mutually exclusive, effects that the same text can provoke. Matters more typically found in modern critical commentaries are less in evidence; when they do appear, they are largely presented as relatively late examples of the Gospel's reception, and often dependent on what has gone before.

I owe a huge debt of gratitude to so many people who, in their different ways, have contributed their insights or opened up new perspectives on the Gospel attributed to the tax-collector from Capernaum, or who have supported this project through their encouragement. The School of Theology and Religious Studies at the Catholic University of America has been a marvellous context within which to write this commentary. I am grateful for the support of our Dean, Mark Morozowich, and the Faculty and Staff of the School. I am also indebted to the University's Institutional Grants Committee for financial support toward permissions for images produced in this commentary.

Many colleagues and friends, both at CUA and elsewhere, have generously given of their time to answer specific questions related to their areas of expertise, and offer encouragement for the project. Worthy of special mention are Stefanos Alexopoulos, Regis Armstrong OFM Cap, Mark Clark, Juliette Day, Rebekah Eklund, David Gowler, Bill Mattison, Paul McPartlan, Michael Root, Kevin Rulo, Sean Ryan, Dominic Serra, Josh Shepperd, and Tarmo Toom. I am particularly grateful to my colleagues in the Biblical Studies Area (Chris Begg, David Bosworth, Brad Gregory, Jack Heil, and Bob Miller) for their support and encouragement, and to our students with whom I have had the privilege of studying this fascinating Gospel. I am especially appreciative of the wisdom and insights of budding Matthean scholars Brian Carrier, Sung Cho, Brian Main, and Tim Rucker, and to my research assistants, Eric Trinka and Xi Li, for their invaluable work in the final stages of this project.

The staff at Wiley Blackwell have been unfailingly helpful and encouraging. Particular mention should be made of Rebecca Harkin, Catriona King, Elisha (Benji) Benjamin, Jake Opie, and Vimali Joseph, as well as my copyeditor, Louise Spencely. Of the 'extended family' of the Wiley Blackwell Bible Commentaries, I have valued the regular authors' meeting at SBL, and the insights and encouragement from fellow authors. My fellow 'Synoptic' authors, Chris Joynes and Mark Bilby, deserve a special mention for making the writing exercise a truly collaborative as well as enjoyable experience. The series editors, John Sawyer, David Gunn, Judith Kovacs, and Chris Rowland, have been models of kindness, critical insight, and wisdom. Judith and Chris have been truly inspirational, with their enthusiasm for the project, their careful, detailed, and incisive feedback on drafts of chapters (more often than not introducing me to even more material!), and their provoking me to deeper reflection on the hermeneutical issues at stake. This commentary would have been severely impoverished without their contribution. Any remaining deficiencies are, of course, my own.

The support of family and countless friends has, as always, been foundational. Particular mention should be made of Pam Boxall, William Whittaker, Jackie and Doug Wall, Robin Johnson, Emily and Matt Chapman, Toby Wall, Isobel Wall and Ashley Laker, and Michael Johnson.

This commentary is dedicated to the memory of one of my students, Br. Saúl Soriano Rodriguez OFM Cap, who died suddenly as I was bringing the manuscript to completion. Saúl's warm humanity, Franciscan simplicity, and passion for social justice made him an inspiration to many. In a very tangible way, he exemplified St. Francis of Assisi's radical, joyful reception of Matthew's Sermon on the Mount. May he rest in peace.

Ian Boxall
Washington, DC

Abbreviations

1 Apol.	Justin, *First Apology*
1 Clem.	*1 Clement*
1 En.	*1 Enoch*
1QS	Qumran *Community Rule*
2 Bar.	*2 Baruch*
2 En.	*2 Enoch*
4Q525	Qumran *Beatitudes* (4QBeat)
4QpPs	Qumran *Pesher* on the Psalms
$11QT^{a}$	Qumran *Temple Scroll*^{a}
AB	Anchor Bible
ABRL	Anchor Bible Reference Library
ACCS	Ancient Christian Commentary on Scripture
Acts Thom.	*Acts of Thomas*
Adv. Eunom.	Basil, *Adversus Eunomium*

Adv. Haer.	Irenaeus, *Adversus haereses*
Adv. Iud.	*Adversus Iudaeos*
Adv. Jov.	Jerome, *Adversus Jovinianum*
Adv. Marc.	Tertullian, *Adversus Marcionem*
Adv. Prax.	Tertullian, *Adversus Praxeam*
ANF	*Ante-Nicene Fathers*
Ant.	Josephus, *Antiquities of the Jews*
Apoc. Ab.	*Apocalypse of Abraham*
Apol.	Tertullian, *Apology*
Appian, *B. Civ*	Appian of Alexandria, *Bellum civile*
Arab. Gos. Inf.	*Arabic Gospel of the Infancy*
ASE	*Annali Di Storia Dell' Esegesi*
As. Mos.	*Assumption of Moses*
ATR	*Anglican Theological Review*
Augustine, *De Trin.*	Augustine, *De Trinitate*
AV	Authorized Version (also King James Version = KJV)
b. Ḥul.	Babylonian Talmud, Tractate *Ḥullin*
b. Sanh.	Babylonian Talmud, Tractate *Sanhedrin*
b. Šabb.	Babylonian Talmud, Tractate *Šabbat*
BDF	F. Blass, A. Debrunner, and R.W. Funk, *A Greek Grammar of the New Testament*. Chicago: University of Chicago Press, 1961.
BETL	Bibliotheca Ephemeridum theologicarum Lovaniensium
BGBE	Beiträge zur Geschichte der biblischen Exegese
Brev. prin. tyr.	William of Ockham, *Breviloquium de principatu tyrannico*
BZNW	Beihefte zur Zeitschrift für die neutestamentliche Wissenschaft
Catech.	Cyril of Jerusalem, *Catechetical Lectures*
CBQ	*Catholic Biblical Quarterly*
CBQMS	Catholic Biblical Quarterly Monograph Series
CD	Cairo Genizah copy of the *Damascus Document*
C. Diat.	Ephrem the Syrian, *Commentary on the Diatessaron*
CCC	*Catechism of the Catholic Church*. London: Geoffrey Chapman, 1994.
CCCM	Corpus Christianorum, Continuatio Mediaevalis
CCSL	Corpus Christianorum, series latina
CEB	Common English Bible
Cels.	Origen, *Contra Celsum*
CFS	Cistercian Fathers Series
Civ. Dei	Augustine, *City of God*

Conf.	John Cassian, *Conferences*
CSCO	Corpus scriptorium christianorum orientalium
CSEL	Corpus scriptorum ecclesiasticorum Latinorum
CSS	Cistercian Studies Series
CUP	Cambridge University Press
CWS	Classics of Western Spirituality
De Bapt.	Tertullian, *De Baptismo*
De fid.	Ambrose, *De fide*
De fug.	Tertullian, *De fuga in persecutione*
Dem. ev.	Eusebius, *Demonstratio evangelica*
De orat.	Tertullian, *De oratione*
De praesc.	Tertullian, *De praescriptione haereticorum*
De Princ.	Origen, *De Principiis*
De Pudic.	Tertullian, *De Pudicitia*
De unitate	Cyprian, *De catholicae ecclesiae unitate*
De vir. illus.	Jerome, *De viris illustribus*
Dial. contra Pel.	Jerome, *Dialogi contra Pelagianos*
Did.	*Didache*
Did. apost.	*Didascalia apostolorum*
EBR	H.-J. Klauck et al. (ed.), *Encyclopedia of the Bible and Its Reception*. Berlin and New York: de Gruyter, 2009–.
EKK	Evangelisch-Katholischer Kommentar
Ep.	*Epistulae*
Ep. apost.	*Epistula apostolorum*
Ep. Arist.	*Epistle of Aristeas*
Ep. Barn.	*Epistle of Barnabas*
ETL	*Ephemerides Theologicae Lovanienses*
ExpTim	*Expository Times*
FC	Fathers of the Church
Frag.	*Fragment*
GCS	Griechischen christlichen Schriftsteller
Gos. Bart.	*Gospel of Bartholomew*
Gos. Pet.	*Gospel of Peter*
Gos. Thom.	*Gospel of Thomas*
Gos. Truth	*Gospel of Truth*
H.E.	Eusebius, *Historia ecclesiastica*
Herm. *Mand.*	Shepherd of Hermas, *Mandate*
Hilary, *De Trin.*	Hilary, *De Trinitate*
Hom.	*Homily*
HTR	*Harvard Theological Review*
ICC	International Critical Commentary
Ign., *Eph.*	Ignatius of Antioch, *To the Ephesians*

Ign., *Magn.*	Ignatius of Antioch, *To the Magnesians*
Ign., *Pol.*	Ignatius of Antioch, *To Polycarp*
Ign., *Smyrn.*	Ignatius of Antioch, *To the Smyrneans*
Ign., *Trall.*	Ignatius of Antioch, *To the Trallians*
Inf. Gos. Thom.	*Infancy Gospel of Thomas*
Instit.	Lactantius, *Institutiones Divinae*
JBL	*Journal of Biblical Literature*
JETS	*Journal of the Evangelical Theological Society*
JSHJ	*Journal for the Study of the Historical Jesus*
JSNT	*Journal for the Study of the New Testament*
JSNTS	Journal for the Study of the New Testament Supplement Series
JTS	*Journal of Theological Studies*
Jub.	*Jubilees*
KJV	King James Version (also Authorized Version = AV)
LCL	Loeb Classical Library
Leg.	Athenagoras, *Legatio pro Christianis*
LNTS	Library of New Testament Studies
LXX	Septuagint
Mart. Pol.	*Martyrdom of Polycarp*
m. ʾAbot	Mishnah, Tractate *ʾAbot*
m. Giṭ	Mishnah, Tractate *Giṭṭin*
m. Ned.	Mishnah, Tractate *Nedarim*
m. Sanh.	Mishnah, Tractate *Sanhedrin*
m. Šabb.	Mishnah, Tractate *Šabbat*
m. Šeb.	Mishnah, Tractate *Šebuʿot*
m. Soṭa	Mishnah, Tractate *Soṭa*
Monog.	Tertullian, *De Monogamia*
MT	Masoretic Text
NA	Nestle-Aland Novum Testamentum Graece
NABRE	New American Bible Revised Edition
NEB	New English Bible
NIV	New International Version
NJB	New Jerusalem Bible
NLT	New Living Translation
Novatian, *De Trin.*	Novatian, *De Trinitate*
NovT	*Novum Testamentum*
NPNF	*Nicene and Post-Nicene Fathers*
NRSV	New Revised Standard Version
NTS	*New Testament Studies*
Od. Sol.	*Odes of Solomon*
OED	Oxford English Dictionary

Orat.	Gregory of Nazianzus, *Orations*
OUP	Oxford University Press
Paed.	Clement of Alexandria, *Paedagogos*
Pan.	Epiphanius of Salamis, *Panarion*
PG	Patrologia Graeca [= Patrologiae Cursus Completus: Series Graeca]. Edited by Jacques Paul Migne. 161 volumes. Paris, 1857–1866.
PIBA	*Proceedings of the Irish Biblical Association*
PL	Patrologia Latina [= Patrologiae Cursus Completus: Series Latina]. Edited by Jacques Paul Migne. 217 volumes. Paris, 1844–1864.
PLS	Patrologia Latina Supplementum [= Patrologiae Cursus Completus: Series Latina Supplementum]. Edited by Adalbert-G. Hamman. Paris, 1958–1974.
Pliny, *Nat.*	Pliny the Elder, *Historia Naturalis*
P. Oxy.	Oxyrhynchus Papyri
Prot. Jas.	*Protevangelium of James*
Ps.-Clem. Hom.	*Pseudo-Clementine Homilies*
Ps.-Clem. Rec.	*Pseudo-Clementine Recognitions*
Pss. Sol.	*Psalms of Solomon*
QJRAS	*Quarterly Journal of the Royal Astronomical Society*
Quis dives	Clement of Alexandria, *Quis dives salvetur*
Ref.	Hippolytus, *Refutation of All Heresies*
SBLDS	Society of Biblical Literature Dissertation Series
SBLMS	Society of Biblical Literature Monograph Series
SBLSymS	Society of Biblical Literature Symposium Series
SC	Sources chrétiennes
Scorp.	Tertullian, *Scorpiace*
Sib. Or.	*Sibylline Oracles*
ST	Thomas Aquinas, *Summa Theologiae*
Str-B	H.L. Strack and P. Billerbeck, *Kommentar zum Neuen Testament aus Talmud und Midrasch*. Munich: Beck, 1922.
Strom.	Clement of Alexandria, *Stromata*
T. Ab.	*Testament of Abraham*
T. Ash.	*Testament of Asher*
T. Ben.	*Testament of Benjamin*
T. Naph.	*Testament of Naphtali*
TLZ	*Theologische Literaturzeitung*
Trypho	Justin, *Dialogue with Trypho*
TS	*Theological Studies*
UBS	United Bible Societies Greek New Testament
VC	*Vigiliae Christianae*

Vit. phil.	Diogenes Laertius, *Vitae philosophorum*
War	Josephus, *The Jewish War*
WUNT	Wissenschaftliche Untersuchungen zum Neuen Testament
ZNW	*Zeitschrift für die neutestamentliche Wissenschaft und die Kunde der älteren Kirche*
ZThK	*Zeitschrift für Theologie und Kirche*

Introduction

Matthew Among the Gospels: A 'Harmonious and Gentle Fullness'

> For, indeed, the Gospel which the publican wrote for us, with its perfect Sermon on the Mount, and mostly more harmonious and gentle fullness, in places where St. Luke is formal, St. John mysterious, and St. Mark brief – this Gospel according to St. Matthew, I should think, if we had to choose one out of all the books in the Bible for a prison or a desert friend, would be the one we should keep. (Ruskin 1904: 139–140)

Matthew Through the Centuries, First Edition. Ian Boxall.

These words of Victorian art critic John Ruskin (1819–1900) express the sentiments of many readers of the Gospel according to Matthew across the centuries. Presuming that this Gospel was written by Christ's apostle Matthew, the 'publican' or tax-collector (Matt 9:9; 10:3), Ruskin is impressed by its 'mostly more harmonious and gentle fullness,' i.e. its sense of inner coherence, and its more comprehensive coverage of the Jesus story. As New Testament scholars frequently note, Matthew overlaps with more than 90 percent of Mark, yet also contains so much more: a family tree, narratives about Jesus' origins, substantial teaching discourses, and post-resurrection appearances. Not for nothing did Augustine of Hippo (354–430), who spent a whole year studying that 'perfect Sermon on the Mount' highlighted by Ruskin, describe the evangelist Mark as Matthew's mere 'acolyte and summarizer' (*Agreement of the Evangelists* 1.2.5; Augustine 2014: 140). There is also a practical, 'down-to-earth' dimension to Matthew's concentration on the teaching of Jesus, presented as an invitation to a radical 'higher righteousness.' As the Dominican scholar Benedict Viviano has commented, Matthew is 'a gospel for "do-ers," activists, people who are incensed about big problems in the world like genocide, ethnic cleansing, institutionalized racism, systemic rape practices, child abuse, sweatshop labor conditions, unemployment, war and peace, and clean water and air' (Viviano 2010: 344). This might explain in part Ruskin's preference for Matthew over the formality of Luke, or the mystical character of John.

Other 'friends' of Matthew across the centuries have found that friendship cemented by aspects of the text different from those which Ruskin highlights. The thirteenth-century Franciscan John of La Rochelle, when teaching in Paris, began his lectures on Matthew with a quotation from the prophet Isaiah which, he claimed, perfectly encapsulated the intention of the Gospel: "The Lord our judge, the Lord our lawgiver, the Lord our king, he it is who will save us" (Isa 33:22; Kealy 1997: 1/156). Whereas Ruskin emphasizes narrative fullness and the sublimity of its teaching, John of La Rochelle prioritizes the Gospel's Christology, articulated in terms that reflect its emphasis upon prophetic fulfillment. His chosen Isaianic passage brilliantly summarizes Matthew's Christological emphases: Jesus the Lord as judge (coming Son of Man), as lawgiver (new Moses), and as king (Son of David), who will save his people (implied in the name 'Jesus,' 1:21).

Readers of Matthew have also prioritized its call to radical discipleship, its appeal to ecclesial order, or its openness to Gentiles. Alternatively, they have been moved by specific narratives, from the adoration of the outsider Magi, through the dramatic conversion of Matthew the tax-collector ('a contemptible little quisling official,' according to Dorothy L. Sayers in the introduction to her 1940s radio drama *The Man Born to Be King*: Sayers 2011: 41), to the quaking events surrounding both crucifixion and resurrection, and the climactic 'Great

Commission' on a mountain in Galilee. What they share in common with Ruskin is a desire to retain Matthew's narrative as a familiar and cherished 'desert friend.'

This widespread popularity begins to explain the particular challenge of a reception-historical study of the First Gospel. Writing a reception history of *any* biblical book is a daunting task. It has been likened to viewing the tip of a very deep iceberg, the bulk of which remains hidden below the surface of the water (Bockmuehl 1995: 66). If this applies to biblical reception generally, then writing a reception history of Matthew borders on the realm of impossibility. For the Swiss New Testament exegete Ulrich Luz, who has contributed more than anyone else to our understanding of Matthew's *Wirkungsgeschichte* or 'effective history,' such a study only serves to highlight the limited knowledge and perspective of each individual practitioner: 'the material … is nearly infinite. However, the knowledge of every commentator is finite' (Luz 2007: 62; see also Luz 1994, 2005b). It is only the slightest of exaggerations to claim that everyone who has written about Jesus of Nazareth, contemplated his teaching, or presented his life, ministry, or passion in other media (whether the visual arts, music, literature, drama, or film), has had something to say about Matthew's Gospel.

The task is further compounded by the richness and multivalency of Matthew's text, and its 'Janus-like' tension between particularism and universalism, judgment and mercy (Riches 2000: 228). This makes even the 'plain sense' of the text often subtle and complex, whether one is concerned, as historical criticism has generally been, with authorial intention, or something more like the story-level meaning. There is always more to be said. When reading one of Matthew's many narrative units, the reader is confronted with a host of interpretative options: the prioritization of specific words or phrases in a given passage to guide overall meaning; communal memories attached to named locations, whether Bethlehem, the River Jordan, Jericho, or Jerusalem; possibilities opened up by complex Old Testament allusions; the dynamic interplay between characters; the specific function of the passage in the narrative as a whole. Even before one moves to the more contested 'spiritual sense,' then, the question of a passage's meaning is complex.

For believers (and the majority of interpreters explored in this volume would place themselves in this category), there is also the 'Author' (with a capital A), i.e. the divine Author. For what has driven so much of the fascination with and attention to Matthew's Gospel across the centuries is the conviction – though commentators will disagree vehemently over an appropriate model for inspiration – that these frail human words convey the divine *Logos*. It is a story of Jesus and his teaching which demands action on the part of the reader, or what Jonathan Pennington calls 'the disciple-making, virtue-forming emphasis' of the text (Pennington 2012: 34). Indeed, the preponderance of Jesus' teaching preserved in this Gospel foregrounds its catechetical aspects. This already moves us beyond the precise concerns of Matthew the evangelist into the diverse contexts, theological concerns, and ideological commitments of those who have read the First Gospel for inspiration and enlightenment.

To these may be added those beyond the Christian church who also read Matthew for spiritual nourishment, or who are impressed by its immense influence on human culture. Matthew's Sermon on the Mount, for example, profoundly affected the Hindu Mahatma Gandhi, while the Gospel as a whole so captivated the Italian communist poet, intellectual, and film director Pier Paolo Pasolini that it provided the subject-matter and script for his classic 1964 film *Il Vangelo secondo Matteo*, dedicated to Pope John XXIII (see Testa 1994; Pasolini 2012: 70–83). Echoing the sentiments of Ruskin, Pasolini explained his preference for Matthew by dismissing John as 'too mystical, Mark too vulgar, and Luke too sentimental' (Testa 1994: 185). But above all, he was captivated by the figure of the Matthean Jesus:

> Deep down there was something still more violent stirring me. It was the figure of Christ as Matthew sees him. Nothing seems to me more opposed to the modern world than that figure. That Christ, gentle at heart, but 'never' so in mind, who never gives up for a moment his own terrible freedom as the will to continually test his own religion – a continual contempt for contradiction and scandal. (Pasolini 2012: 74)

The Approach of This Commentary

As the diversity across volumes in the Wiley Blackwell Bible Commentary series reveals, reception history, and the closely related *Wirkungsgeschichte* or 'effective history' (derived from the philosophical hermeneutics of Hans-Georg Gadamer: Gadamer 2012), can be undertaken in a variety of different ways and with different goals in view (see e.g. Luz 1994; Parris 2009, 2015; Crossley 2010: 117–163; Morgan 2010; Rowland and Boxall 2013). Some concentrate on the 'big players,' significant commentators whose readings of the text have become foundational for specific communities of readers. Others are more attentive to marginal voices, or readings which might once have been significant but which have been forgotten with the passing of the ages. For some reception historians, especially those who are Christian believers, the task is undertaken out of a desire better to understand where they have come from, i.e. the learned reading habits of specific ecclesial traditions, and the influential figures within those traditions. Alternatively, or in a complementary fashion, attention to a wider range of voices exposes reception historians to different ways of reading, or different types of questions, in other faith communities or cultural contexts, as well as challenging voices from outside the Christian churches. Thus reception history can have an important ecumenical dimension, fostering greater understanding and changed perceptions across traditional denominational divides. In the process, it can lead to surprises which undermine received wisdom. Examples from the reception of Matthew might include the discovery that Roman Catholics in the Middle Ages espoused a range of interpretations regarding the 'rock' on which Christ builds the church (16:18), rather than the one now widely regarded as '*the* Roman Catholic view,' or that the early Reformers were staunch upholders of the perpetual virginity of Mary.

Still others engage reception history, especially early reception, out of a primary interest in the first audiences of the text, i.e. in order to do historical criticism better (e.g. Bockmuehl 2006; Allison 2008). On the one hand, the interests of pre-critical commentators in textual multivalency can challenge the historical-critical assumption that there is one, univocal 'original meaning.' On the other, it raises the possibility that earlier interpreters, with their much richer 'memory-bank' of scriptural texts and scriptural narratives, especially from the Hebrew Bible, might be closer in their intertextual sensitivities to the evangelist Matthew, whose book is shot through with the conviction of prophetic fulfillment. In addition, in exposing exegetes to 'forgotten' interpreters, it can be a humbling reminder that so-called 'new discoveries' by critical scholars are sometimes very ancient readings of the text. Reception history can thereby function as a remedy for 'exegetical amnesia' (Allison 2008: 5).

The approach of this present commentary is deliberately broad, broad enough to encompass the likes of Gandhi and Pasolini as well as the 'classic voices' of Origen, Jerome, Aquinas, Calvin, and Cornelius a Lapide, and that late strand of Matthew's reception history, i.e. critical biblical scholarship, which normally dominates accounts of Matthew's 'history of interpretation' (*Auslegungsgeschichte*). Thus a range of voices will be heard, reflecting a diversity of chronological periods, geographical locations, and theological positions. Sometimes, they will be singing in harmony; at other times, a stronger discordant note will be audible. In line with the broad parameters of the Wiley Blackwell series, this commentary also seeks to expose the reader to the rich receptions of Matthew's Gospel outside the commentary genre: in homilies, liturgy, drama, literature, visual art, film, and Christian praxis. Historical-critical commentary is also included among the various voices, although primarily as an example of late, post-Enlightenment reception rather than as foundational to the Gospel's meaning (on this issue, see e.g. Gadamer 2012; Joyce and Lipton 2013: 11–12). The exception is in the 'Ancient Literary Context' section at the beginning of each chapter or chapter-group, which attempts to locate the passage within the broader literary flow of Matthew, alert the reader to parallels in the other Gospels, and provide brief comments on genre and historical context.

The particular challenge for the First Gospel, as noted above, is that the material for potential inclusion is vast. The size constraints of this commentary series mean that what follows is merely indicative of the range of possible receptions. As with any reception-historical work, moreover, what is included is shaped by the perspectives, interests, and knowledge of the author: in this present case, a white male British Roman Catholic, whose teaching experience has been limited to the United Kingdom and the United States. Another commentator may well have selected a very different range of receptions entirely. For other possibilities, and in some cases more detailed exposition, readers should consult the excellent EKK commentary by Ulrich Luz (Luz 2001, 2005a, 2007), and other works referenced in what follows (in addition, useful articles and book chapters on the reception of Matthew include Turner 1911; Widdicombe 2013; Williams 2014).

The influence of Luz is particularly evident in this commentary, as is his "ecumenical" concern to expose the reader to a diversity of receptions from different traditions, although my aim has been to complement his significant groundwork rather than repeat what he has already described far more eloquently. His approach, at least in his EKK commentary, is somewhat different from mine, though this is determined in part by the aims of our respective commentary series. Although the amount of attention Luz devotes to *wirkungsgeschichtliche* matters increases in the later volumes of his Matthew commentary, the EKK format means that what the text has effected often appears as an 'add-on' to the foundational meaning of the text established by more traditional historical-critical and literary-critical 'analysis' (attention to structure, sources, followed by verse-by-verse interpretation; for various assessments, see e.g. Gnilka 2003; Elliott 2010). The format of the Wiley Blackwell Bible Commentaries, by contrast, allows me to examine earlier receptions, or receptions in other media, as directly related to a semantic or hermeneutical issue provoked by a reading of the text in specific contexts, rather than supplementary to a prior, 'original' meaning established through the application of historical-critical tools. This is complemented, in this introduction, by an attempt to describe 'the big picture': the main trends in the reception of Matthew across the centuries, and in different ecclesial and cultural contexts. The differences, however, should not be overplayed. Luz's other writings (especially Luz 1994, 2005b) offer a more nuanced perspective on *Wirkungsgeschichte*, challenging a somewhat artificial distinction between meaning and significance, and revealing a particular appreciation of the multivalency of patristic exegesis, as well as its philological and cultural proximity to the worldview of the First Evangelist which give certain of the Fathers' specific readings particular hermeneutical weight (on this, see Luz 2005b: 295–303).

Although Luz is an obvious major player, many others have also contributed to laying the rock-like foundation on which this commentary is built (among them, Smith 1925–1929; Kealy 1997; Simonetti 2001, 2002; Clarke 2003; Allison 2005; Jorgensen 2016). With such predecessors, one cannot help but recall the tiny figure of St. Matthew, straddling the shoulders of the prophet Isaiah in the famous stained-glass window in Chartres Cathedral. Like the Chartres St. Matthew, this volume too stands on the shoulders of giants.

In what sense does what follows constitute a reception history of the Gospel according to Matthew? How has the constructive task of doing reception history been undertaken? My approach has been twofold. In the remainder of this introduction, I attempt to sketch a broad historical narrative from the first century to the twenty-first, identifying key emphases, important figures, and important texts in broadly chronological sequence. That historical 'story' is a somewhat artificial construct, reflecting my own attempt to give manageable shape to what is inevitably complex and unwieldy. Chronological divisions are not hard and fast, and what might hold for the Latin West may be wholly inappropriate for the different Christian communities of the East. Identifying what is 'typical' of a particular period risks minimizing common features shared with other generations. Moreover, interpretations may be as much genre-related as chronological or geographical. Thus the same author might read a text very differently when giving a homiletic exposition to a Christian congregation than in a polemical treatise directed at a theological opponent. Alternatively, two receptions separated by centuries might be reading Matthew in a very similar way, without any obvious genealogical connection.

Therefore the introductory sketch is complemented in the commentary proper by an attempt to identify commonalities across diverse receptions. An effort is made to present different effects in a broadly chronological sequence, not least to illuminate clear or potential relationships between earlier and later exemplars. However, chronology is not always the most useful organizing principle. Thus similar types of reading are frequently brought together, including receptions in non-commentary genres, in order to highlight commonalities. This even affects the presentation of visual exegesis throughout the commentary. There are instances (e.g. on the Beatitudes, Salome's dance, or the Transfiguration) where the reception of Matthew in visual art is coherent enough to allow separate treatment. In other cases, particularly where different elements of the story are highlighted by different visual treatments (as in the Magi story, where artists might prioritize the identity of the Magi, the star which guided them, or their presentation of gifts), it seemed more fitting to integrate examples into the wider discussion.

Any reception-historical approach has its limitations. Some readers may find that the wide range of receptions offered here has sacrificed depth on the altar of breadth. Attempts have been made to mitigate this danger, not least through the narrative framework which seeks to identify *how* the text is being read rather than simply providing an anthology of receptions. A decision for breadth, moreover, seems more appropriate for a narrative work such as Matthew, whose rich stories, complex characters, and developing plot invite a diversity of readings and responses. Others may feel that the long list of interpreters, some of whom are introduced only fleetingly, rules out what Hans Robert Jauss, the literary critic and pupil of Gadamer who particularly shaped the concept of reception history or reception criticism (*Rezeptionsgeschichte*) in literary studies, calls the *Gipfeldialog* or 'summit dialogue': bringing into conversation with each other those key interpreters who represent the 'summits' or 'peaks' of the text's interpretation (see Parris 2009: 216–222).

That is not necessarily the case. Significant attention is given to the most influential interpreters of the patristic, medieval, and early modern periods. Yet the broader approach potentially highlights the fact that different reading communities have their own significant 'peaks' and key interpreters (Ephrem the Syrian, Rufus of Shotep, Gregory of Narek, and Isho'dad of Merv are some obvious examples from non-Byzantine eastern Christian communities). It also proposes that some of the most interesting and illuminating readings of Matthew might be happening, not on the mountain's summit, but somewhere closer to the foothills.

Nor does this commentary attempt to cover every verse. Priority has often been given to passages unique to Matthew, or elements within shared passages which most obviously betray Matthean influence. In the discourse material (Matt 5–7; 10; 13; 18; 24–25), where sayings often depend closely on each other, I have attempted fairly full coverage (though some readers will be disappointed that, on occasion, I have glossed certain verses, and passed others over entirely). In sections of Matthew where there is substantial overlap with another Gospel, notably in the passion narrative, I have combined a broad-sweep overview with detailed focus on characters and scenes unique to the First Gospel (notably, the suicide of Judas, the dream of Pilate's wife, and Pilate washing his hands).

Much of the time, I have been willing to allow these different readings of the same text to sit side by side, without adjudicating between them, much in the manner of medieval commentaries where 'authorities' from the past are juxtaposed as alternative or even complementary readings. In part, this reflects the conviction that, insofar as one can speak of a text's 'original sense,' even that is far from univocal. But it also marks a recognition that texts, especially sacred texts, are open to new possibilities when 'performed' in new circumstances and by new audiences (on Scripture as 'performance,' see e.g. Lash 1986: 37–46). Very occasionally, however, I have been more forthright in identifying 'better' or 'worse' readings, or suggesting how unfamiliar readings might be especially illuminative. At these points, I come closest to what Paul Joyce and Diana Lipton describe as 'reception exegesis,' that is, critical analysis of receptions, in order to 'yield exegetical fruit' (Joyce and Lipton 2013: 18). On the other hand, I am also aware that the very task of 'cataloguing' receptions is itself a critical and constructive exercise, far more than a mere list or anthology, much in the way that a catalogue for an art exhibition incorporates careful and sophisticated selection, organization, and critical evaluation (see Boxall 2013: 208–212).

The First Gospel as the Church's Gospel

If there is one feature which binds together diverse receptions of Matthew from at least the second century through to the modern period, it is its popularity, reflected in the dual titles 'the First Gospel' and 'the Church's Gospel.' The former descriptor, although largely rejected by modern scholars as a true statement about chronological priority (see e.g. Brown 1997: 216–217), remains valid in terms of this Gospel's prestige. Its canonical position at the beginning of the New Testament (even in codices where the order of the other three is reversed, as Bezae and Washingtonianus) allows Matthew's Gospel to function as a bridge between Old and New Testaments. This befits its strong emphasis on the continuity of Christ's teaching with the Law and the prophets (e.g. 5:17–20). This is underscored visually in the frontispiece to Matthew by Donald Jackson in the Saint John's Bible, a modern revival of the medieval illuminated manuscript tradition, which is dominated by a Jewish menorah, combined with names of Christ's ancestors in Hebrew characters (Patella 2005: 225–227; Calderhead 2015: 163–165). Equally, this Gospel functions as 'the prologue, an interpretive key for the rest of the New Testament' (Wanke 2015: 60).

Matthew's canonical priority also reflects early convictions about its apostolic authorship. Hence the fourfold Gospel begins and ends with narratives attributed to apostles, Matthew and John 'embracing' the Gospels written by non-apostles, Mark and Luke. Moreover, the Gospel which most stresses Christ's Jewish credentials, and believed at an early stage to be specifically composed for converts from the synagogue, is appropriately placed prior to those more amenable to Christians from pagan backgrounds (notably Mark and Luke, though also John, given its more mystical and 'philosophical' feel).

However, the decision to place Matthew at the head of the New Testament canon is the result of more than convictions about authorship and concern for scriptural continuity. Content and subject matter seem also to have come into play. As both Augustine and John Ruskin recognized, who would not prefer a Gospel which contains almost all the content of Mark, and so much more besides? By contrast, moreover, the 'rough and ready' style of Mark made Matthew's text far more appealing to those early patristic authors who had received rhetorical training (see Schildgen 1999: 56–60).

For much of Christian history, of course, Matthean priority also meant that Matthew was considered the first to be written. Our earliest witness, Papias, who claims that Matthew composed 'the oracles in the Hebrew language' (or 'style,' *hebraidi dialektō*), is ambiguous about order. Indeed, as cited by Eusebius, his comments about Mark precede those on Matthew (Eusebius, *H.E.* 3.39.16). The chronological priority of Matthew is, however, supported by Irenaeus, Clement of Alexandria (who places 'the Gospels containing the genealogies,' i.e. Matthew and Luke, prior to Mark: in Eusebius, *H.E.* 6.14.6), Origen, Eusebius, Jerome, and Augustine (see Kealy 1997: 1/21). A possible exception is Tertullian, who may imply that John precedes Matthew: 'Of the apostles, therefore, John and Matthew first instil faith into us; whilst of apostolic men, Luke and Mark renew it afterwards' (*Adv. Marc.* 4.2; *ANF* 3:347). Whether this near consensus on the priority of Matthew is the result of precise historical knowledge, or a deduction from Matthew's canonical position, remains a moot point.

As for dating, this too was generally presumed to be early, consonant with belief in authorship by an apostle. For Irenaeus, Matthew 'issued a written Gospel among the Hebrews in their own dialect, while Peter and Paul were preaching at Rome and laying the foundations of the Church' (*Adv. Haer.* 3.1.1; *ANF* 1:414), i.e. c. 61–64 CE. The influence of Papias' *hebraidi dialektō* is evident in Irenaeus' phrasing. Even earlier dates are subsequently attested. The ninth-century monk Christian of Stavelot dates the Gospel to the reign of Gaius, i.e. 37–41 (*Liber Generationis* 1; CCCM 224: 59). In the eleventh century, the Greek exegete Theophylact, bishop of Ochrid in Bulgaria, is even more precise, dating Matthew to eight years after the Ascension, i.e. c. 41. An early modern proponent of a similar early dating is the Dutch Protestant scholar Hugo Grotius (1583–1645), who argues for 40–50.

In the modern period, the scholarly consensus has been very different. While a scholarly minority continues to support Matthean priority (e.g. Farmer 1994; Dungan 1999) and/or authorship by Matthew the apostle (e.g. Gundry 1994), most exegetes regard Matthew as later than Mark, and non-apostolic. Mark's relationship to Matthew is now explained as the exact opposite of Augustine's 'abbreviator.' Indeed, in many individual stories, it is Matthew who appears to be abbreviating Mark (e.g. compare Mark 5:1–20 with Matt 8:28–34). This new conviction of Markan priority is bolstered by the substantial body of material, both narrative and teaching, absent from Mark but present in Matthew, as well as evidence for Matthean 'fatigue' in using Mark as a source text (e.g. compare 8:1–4 with Mark 1:40–45; 14:1–12 with Mark 6:14–29; see Goodacre 1998). Other scholars represent a modified version of Papias, whereby our Greek Matthew incorporated a sayings collection compiled by the apostle into a Markan framework (e.g. Allen 1907: lxxix–lxxxiii).

The expansive character of the First Gospel, its overt Christology, and its attention to Christ's teaching also explains Matthew's description as 'the Gospel of the Church.' Christians soon found it much more useful than the ambiguous and enigmatic Mark in defending the doctrine of the Trinity (e.g. 28:19), the sinlessness of Christ (e.g. 3:14–15), or the continuity between the Old and New Testaments (e.g. 1:2–17). Thus the First Gospel soon comes to the fore in theological debate, exegetical commentary, and homiletic exposition, as 'the most annotated, exposited, and sermonized Gospel of the four throughout the patristic era' (Williams 2014: 83). This early popularity is evidenced by frequent pre-Nicene citations from this Gospel, especially from the Sermon on the Mount (e.g. Smith 1925–1929; Massaux 1990–1993; Köhler 1987), and by a succession of patristic commentaries and homilies (see Kealy 1997; Simonetti 2001, 2002; Sim 2009: 479–480). It is also the most popular Gospel in church lectionaries, meaning that Matthew's functions as the default version in the minds of both exegetes and ordinary Christians.

Moreover, compared to the other Gospels, Matthew is most striking for its interest in ecclesiology. Not only is it the only one of the four to use the term 'church' (*ekklēsia*: 16:18; 18:17), it also provides blueprints for the structures of settled ecclesial life (e.g. resolution of community disputes, 18:15–20; communal prayer, 6:9–13; liturgical formulae for the Eucharist and Christian baptism, 26:26–28; 28:19). The prominence this Gospel gives to Peter, and its saying about the 'keys of the kingdom' (16:19), have been important for the developing institution of the papacy. Unsurprisingly, therefore, according to the medieval legend (reflected in the 12 apostle columns in the Liebfraukirche, Trier) whereby the Apostles' Creed was jointly composed by the apostles after the resurrection, it was Matthew who contributed the phrase 'I believe in the Holy Catholic Church.'

Equally important is this Gospel's attention to Christ's moral teaching. Its well-organized discourses, together with its repetitions and numerical patterns, made it easy to memorize, and it came to be a popular source both for lay catechesis and monastic formation (on the latter, see Olsen 2015: 22–23). As Erasmus so eloquently put it, the First Gospel 'teaches heavenly philosophy, which was given to the race of mortals by the heavenly teacher Jesus Christ' (Erasmus 2008: 29).

However, one should not assume that the title 'Gospel of the Church' made it the preserve of church hierarchies. On the contrary, Matthew's vision of the *ekklēsia* gives centrality to 'the little ones' (18:6, 10; 19:14; 25:40, 45), while the Matthean Jesus' uncompromising demands call for a distinctly rigorous form of discipleship. Hence this Gospel has provided especial inspiration for radical figures and groups who have pricked the consciences of the ecclesiastical establishment, such as Antony of Egypt, the 'father of monasticism,' Francis of Assisi and the early Franciscans, the visionary Hildegard of Bingen, or the sixteenth-century Anabaptists. On the other hand, its distinctive parables such as the Wheat and the Tares (13:24–30, 36–43) have also laid the foundation for a more nuanced ecclesiology of the *corpus permixtum*, the church as comprised of both saints and sinners, indistinguishable until the last judgment.

The Gospel with the Human Face

One further title for Matthew is also worthy of note: the 'Gospel with the human face.' This moniker is ultimately traceable to Irenaeus of Lyons (c. 180 CE). In his defense of the fourfold Gospel against Marcionite and gnostic alternatives, Irenaeus appeals to Ezekiel's vision of the heavenly throne supported by four cherubim (Ezek 1), together with John's reworked version in Revelation 4. Each creature is linked to a specific Gospel: John the lion, Luke the ox, Mark the eagle, and Matthew the creature with a human face:

> Matthew, again, relates His generation as a man, saying, 'The book of the generation of Jesus Christ, the son of David, the son of Abraham;' and also, 'The birth of Jesus Christ was on this wise.' This, then, is the Gospel of His humanity; for which reason it is, too, that [the character of] a humble and meek man is kept up through the whole Gospel. (Irenaeus, *Adv. Haer.* 3.11.8; *ANF* 1:428)

Jerome is one of many who concur with Irenaeus' assessment of Matthew as the human figure, setting the trend for the traditional image of the evangelist, albeit often transformed into an angel (e.g. the *Book of Kells* f. 32v). In later art, the angel often accompanies the writing evangelist as his inspiration and guide, as in Simone Cantarini's *Saint Matthew and the Angel* (Figure 1). Augustine is a rare dissenter, maintaining that Matthew corresponds to the lion, not the man. Nonetheless, even he understands Matthew's book as the Gospel of Christ's humanity: leonine, in that his opening genealogy presents Christ's life 'according to the royal lineage,' yet balancing Christ's words and deeds 'as they relate to the present human life' (*Agreement Among the Evangelists* 1,2,4; 1,6,9: Augustine 2014: 140, 143).

Similarly, for the author of the *Opus imperfectum* (a now-incomplete fifth-century Latin commentary misattributed to John Chrysostom), Matthew

Figure 1 Simone Cantarini (1612–1648). *Saint Matthew and the Angel*. c. 1645–1648. Oil on canvas, 1168 × 908 mm. Gift of James Belden in memory of Evelyn Berry Belden. National Gallery of Art, Washington, DC. Source: Photo courtesy National Gallery of Art, Washington.

intended 'not only to set forth the history of Christ's life but also to teach the disposition of an evangelical life' (Kellerman and Oden 2010: 1). He does this through his careful ordering of Christ's life, which also parallels the Christian life: birth; baptism; temptation; doctrine; miracles; passion; resurrection and ascension. The Benedictine monk Smaragdus of Saint-Mihiel (c. 760–843) goes further, offering a moral interpretation of all four evangelists, with Matthew's man signifying the humble, Mark's lion those strong in faith, Luke's calf the merciful, and the Johannine eagle the mystics (PL 102:33C; see Kealy 1997: 1/22).

There is, however, a more problematic side to the First Gospel, which has particularly come under the spotlight in the modern period. One aspect of this relates to the origins of this Jewish-Christian Gospel in the cut-and-thrust of first-century intra-Jewish debates. This is reflected in its prophetic critique of the 'scribes and Pharisees' (23:13–36), language of differentiation such as 'their synagogues' (e.g. 10:17), and the words attributed to 'all the people' at the trial of Jesus: 'His blood be on us and on our children' (27:25). These words, understandable as the protests of a threatened Judeo-Christian minority (see e.g. Johnson 1989; Sim 1998), effected something very different once Matthew's Gospel came to be read by a Gentile church as a 'foundation' document for a new religion. At times, the effects have been devastating, particularly when 27:25 has provoked violence against Jewish people on the grounds of deicide. Greater awareness of the darker strands in this Gospel's history of effects is increasingly evident in Christian discourse, particularly in light of the Holocaust and subsequent Jewish–Christian rapprochement. The changed circumstances are eloquently expressed by the American Jesuit scholar Daniel Harrington, whose 1991 *Sacra Pagina* commentary prioritizes Matthew's historical origins in Judaism, and seeks to correct unhistorical caricature:

> Besides my academic concern with Judaism in antiquity, I have also experienced the vitality of modern Judaism, continue to admire it, and seek to be sensitive and sympathetic toward it as I interpret early Christian writings. (Harrington 1991: 1)

Other modern readers problematize the strong emphasis on eschatological judgment, reflected in the Gospel's moral dualism, a heightened role for the Son of Man as judge, and warnings about being cast into Gehenna (regularly translated as 'hell'). Sermonic condemnations across the centuries, with preachers apparently relishing Matthew's words about 'weeping and gnashing of teeth,' have undoubtedly left their toll on troubled Christian consciences. Such emphasis risks obscuring Matthew's focus on divine and human mercy (Hos. 6.6, quoted at 9.13 and 12.7), and fierce denunciation of those who 'bind heavy burdens' (23:4; see e.g. Byrne 2004). Nonetheless, squeamishness about judgment can be more prominent among comfortable readers of Matthew, while the poor, persecuted, and marginal more easily locate judgment closer to the heart of the Gospel, as salvation from injustice and wickedness (see e.g. Cardenal 2010).

Key Interpreters Across the Centuries

Much has been said already about the early application of Matthew in apologetics and doctrinal disputes, its popularity in liturgy and commentary, and its central place for reflection on the Christian moral life, as well as darker effects resulting from its polemical language against specific Jewish character groups within its narrative. This diversity is an indication that the Gospel has been used for very different purposes, sometimes within the same time period and even by the same interpreters, according to target audience and perceived need. Nonetheless, it is possible to highlight particular emphases in specific periods or within specific communities across the centuries.

Early Church

The polemical and apologetic use of the Gospel according to Matthew is evident already in the early centuries, as exegetes respond to theological opponents and hostile outsiders. The particular issue of debate inevitably affects the Matthean passages discussed, though questions of Christology are frequently to the fore. However, over-emphasis on the apologetic and polemical risks obscuring evidence for less defensive uses of the Gospel: in liturgy (e.g. Justin Martyr's reference to public reading from the 'memoirs' of the apostles: e.g. *1 Apol.* 67), homiletic instruction (e.g. John Chrysostom; Leo the Great), and moral education (e.g. the frequent citation from Matthew's Sermon on the Mount). The Christian need to 'fill in the gaps,' whether for entertainment or devotional purposes, is well-represented in imaginative apocryphal embellishments (e.g. the *Protevangelium of James*, the *Gospel of Peter*, and the *Acts of Pilate/Gospel of Nicodemus*).

This period sees the beginnings of Christian methods of scripture interpretation. Non-literal, allegorical readings occur already in the second century, and different communities will develop their own exegetical habits. Some give greater weight to the letter, others to the spiritual sense (though the oft-cited distinction between Alexandrian allegory and Antioch's preference for the literal obscures the similarities between exegetes of both traditions: see Young 2002: 161–185). Though some patristic interpretations appear obscure or even forced to the modern reader, they have their own inner logic. In particular, the regular emphasis in figurative exegesis on ecclesial readings (e.g. the 'boat,' the 'field,' or the 'temple' as symbols of the church) has strong roots in the evangelist's own reworking of the Jesus tradition, which is 'transparent' to the life of the post-Easter community (see Luz 2005b: 115–142). Moreover, given their immersion in the biblical texts of both Testaments, early commentators are often valuable and insightful conversation partners for contemporary scholars interested in Matthew's intertextuality (Allison 2008).

At this point, a brief word is appropriate concerning terminology. Scholars are increasingly aware that commentators in the first few centuries are frustratingly inconsistent in their use of the ancient equivalents of 'allegorical,' 'spiritual,' and 'typological,' or, in the case of Latin exegetes, 'figural' exegesis (see e.g. Dawson 1992, 2002; O'Keefe and Reno 2005; Martens 2008). The technicalities of the debate need not concern us here. My practice in this commentary is to use 'allegorical' and 'figurative' of the 'spiritual sense,' where an interpreter moves beyond the 'letter' to explore a less obvious, symbolic meaning. Indeed, I generally restrict 'allegorical' to complex figurative interpretations, where all or most details required explaining or 'decoding.' (I am aware that this does not solve all the problems, not least because Matthew almost certainly understands the parables of Jesus as complex allegories, i.e. in such instances the allegorical is the 'literal' sense of the text.) I also use 'typology' in a very precise sense, to describe those 'patterns' (*tupoi*) in Old Testament narratives which re-emerge in Matthew's Gospel, normally in relation to Jesus (e.g. Moses–Christ typology; Israel–Christ typology; Joseph–Christ typology).

The earliest receptions of Matthew are difficult to identify with certainty. Some would locate them within the New Testament itself, whether in Luke (Franklin 1994), John (e.g. Austin Farrer: see Muddiman 1983), or the Epistle of James, with its strong echoes of the Sermon on the Mount (see Jas 3:12; 5:2–3, 12). Scholars are also divided as to the extent to which the Apostolic Fathers are directly dependent on Matthew's Gospel. Some detect direct dependence in the *Didache*, *1 Clement*, the *Epistle of Barnabas*, and the letters of Ignatius of Antioch (e.g. *Did.* 1:3; 6:5; 7:1–2; 8:2–3; *1 Clem.* 15:2; 27:5; 46:7–8; *Ep. Barn.* 4:14; 5:9; Ign., *Magn.* 8:2; *Eph.* 5:2; *Pol.* 2.2: Köhler 1987; Massaux 1990–1993), while others attribute the similarities to independent use of shared traditions (e.g. Koester 1957, 2005; for mediating positions, see e.g. Schoedel 1991; Tuckett 2005), or, in the case of the *Didache*, Matthew's dependence on the latter (Garrow 2004). The case of Ignatius is especially complex, given that the overlap is with Matthew's special material ('M'; see Smit Sibinga 1966; Trevett 1984; Foster 2005). Perhaps the strongest evidence in favor of Matthew as a direct source is *Smyrn.* 1:1, where Ignatius asserts that Christ was baptized 'in order that all righteousness might be fulfilled by him' (Holmes 2007: 249; see Matt 3:15).

The use of Matthew is much clearer by the mid- to late second century, where it is widely used by both the proto-orthodox and gnostics (on the influence of Matthew on Nag Hammadi writings, see e.g. Tuckett 1986: 149–150). Many of the references are scattered across polemical writings, or theological treatises. The influential philosopher and exegete Clement of Alexandria (c. 150–215) can skillfully exegete Matthew's text to critique the extreme asceticism of the Basilidians (on 'eunuchs for the sake of the kingdom,' 19:12: *Strom.* 3.1), and engage Matthew's version when interpreting Mark's story of the rich man in his *Quis dives salvetur?* (on Clement, see e.g. Kovacs 2001, 2009). Justin Martyr (100–165) draws extensively from Matthew (possibly from memory) in his *Dialogue with Trypho*, and his *1 Apology* 33–53 shows a close following of Gospel narratives, Matthew included. The defense of the fourfold Gospel by Irenaeus of

Lyons (c. 180) is but one example of Irenaeus' widespread use of Matthew as a weapon in polemical disputes against Marcion and gnostic opponents. He also deploys the First Gospel to prove continuity between Old and New Testaments (Bingham 1998).

As will become clear in the commentary proper (e.g. on Matthew 13, 21–22, and 25), the interpretation of the parables is a particular battleground, with Valentinian exegetes such as Ptolemy arguably pioneering allegorical interpretation which is then appropriated by Irenaeus. Indeed, for some, the similarities between Valentinian and proto-orthodox exegesis are as striking as the differences (Jorgensen 2016: 270–271). Although interpreters like Irenaeus are generally more restrained in their allegory than Valentinians, especially in terms of cosmological speculation, there are examples to the contrary. For example, while the Valentinian *Interpretation of Knowledge* interprets the parable of the Wheat and Tares about the 'world,' in line with Matthew's text (13:38), Tertullian's *Prescription Against Heretics* reads it as justification for rooting out heretics from the church (Jorgensen 2016: 272).

There is a paucity of extant exegetical commentaries from the early patristic period (see e.g. Turner 1911; Reuss 1957; Glover 1985; Romero Pose 1992; Simonetti 2001: xlii–l; Williams 2014). Although Jerome knows of one written by Victorinus of Pettau, who was martyred in 304, this is now lost, while fragments from other commentaries he uses (Apollinaris of Laodicea, Theodore of Heraclea) only survive in *catenae* or 'chain' collections (texts in Reuss 1957). The picture is brighter from the mid-third century onwards, with the appearance of important patristic commentaries which will feature regularly in this commentary.

One significant shift in the early reception of Matthew, which will have far-reaching repercussions, is that of readership: from predominantly Jewish Christian to predominantly Gentile Christian. Thus patristic commentators often highlight those aspects of this Gospel which prioritize the faith of non-Jews, or find the transition from Israel to the Gentiles present in less obvious passages (e.g. in the ass and colt of Christ's triumphal entry, 21:1–9).

However, this is not the whole story. This 'Gospel for Jewish converts' did not entirely lose its gloss for subsequent groups of Jewish Christians (or Judeo-Christians, to incorporate those from a Gentile background who observed aspects of Mosaic Law). *5 Ezra* (2 Esdras 1–2), probably dependent on Matthew, provides evidence for the survival of Matthean-type Christianity well into the second century (see Stanton 1992: 256–277). Irenaeus claims that the Jewish-Christian sect known as the Ebionites used only Matthew's Gospel (*Adv. Haer.* 1.26.2), while other Church Fathers refer to a variety of Jewish-Christian gospels in circulation, though without consistency in the titles attributed to them. Scholars often identify three different texts: the *Gospel of the Hebrews* (a Greek text almost as long as canonical Matthew, of which only a few quotations have survived), the *Gospel of the Ebionites* (a Greek harmony of the Synoptic Gospels) and the *Gospel of the Nazareans* (an Aramaic translation of Greek Matthew, with some non-canonical additions: Koester 2005: 35–36; see also e.g. Frey 2015: 22–25).

The first significant commentary on Matthew is by ORIGEN (184/5–253/4), the giant of the Alexandrian church, composed in the 240s, toward the end of his life (Text: PG 13: 829–1800; GCS 28, 1–299; 40/1, 1–703; 4; ANF 9). Of the 25 books of the original, 8 books survive in Greek (covering Matt 13:36–22:33), together with an anonymous Latin translation (covering Matt 16:36–27:63) and a large number of fragments. His interpretation is sophisticated, and although he regularly gives allegorical interpretations, he often does so tentatively, and with attention to the literal sense.

EPHREM THE SYRIAN (303–373), deacon, theologian, and hymnwriter of the Syriac church, is an important witness to reception in Syriac Christianity. Although his Gospel commentary (Text: SC 121; Harris 1895) is on Tatian's *Diatessaron* rather than Matthew directly, he comments inter alia on the Matthean genealogy, 'He shall be called a Nazorean' (2:23), the Beatitudes, and the bread petition in the Lord's Prayer (6:11).

HILARY OF POITIERS (c. 315–367/8) wrote a Latin commentary on Matthew between 350 and 355, complete except for the preface and the commentary on the last seven verses (Text: PL 9:917–1076; SC 254 and 258; Hilary of Poitiers 2012). Born in Gaul, Hilary became bishop of Poitiers before being forced into exile in Asia Minor in 356. His commentary is highly allegorical, anti-Arian in places, and exegetically sophisticated (Simonetti 1969), suggesting a literate, perhaps episcopal, readership. At the same time, it anticipates modern narrative criticism in its care to connect Matthean passages to their wider literary context (e.g. drawing conclusions from the juxtaposition of the healings of the ruler's daughter and the two blind men in Matthew 9).

FORTUNATIANUS OF AQUILEIA (d. 368), an African who became bishop of Aquileia in northern Italy, wrote a commentary on the Gospels in the mid-fourth century, the majority of which is a commentary on Matthew (Text: CSEL 103; Fortunatianus of Aquileia 2017). This is one of the sources used by Jerome, who described its style as terse and rustic (*De vir. illustr.* 97). Thought to have been lost for centuries, apart from a few fragments (published in PLS 1: 216–219; CCSL 9: 365–370), it was recently rediscovered in a manuscript in Cologne Cathedral Library. Fortunatianus' approach is highly allegorical, encouraging decoding (he prefers the Latin terms *figura* and *figurare*: see Houghton, 'Introduction,' in Fortunatianus of Aquileia 2017: XIX–XXIII).

JOHN CHRYSOSTOM (c. 347–407), monk, presbyter of Antioch, and later patriarch of Constantinople, preached a series of 90 homilies on the Gospel of

Matthew in the Great Church in Antioch in 390 (Text: PG 57–58; *NPNF* 1st series, 10). His approach, reflecting his exegetical training under the Antiochene Diodore of Tarsus, shows a concern for the literal sense, and is 'full of moral and ascetical exhortation' (Kelly 1995: 92). The latter reflects his homiletic genre: his focus is on the needs of his congregation, many of whom were comfortable and uncommitted, listening to his sermons as examples of rhetoric (see Pelikan 1967: 12–19; Widdicombe 2013: 109–112).

Jerome (c. 345–420), the great biblical exegete of the western church, wrote his commentary on Matthew for his friend Eusebius of Cremona in March 398 (Text: PL 26: 15–218; SC 242, 259; Jerome 2008). In the preface, Jerome lists his sources, including the commentaries of Origen, Fortunatianus of Aquileia, and Hilary (see Turner 1911; Widdicome 2013: 105–109). Eusebius had asked for a 'historical' commentary on the Gospel of Matthew for his impending journey to Rome. Written hastily, in the space of two weeks (accounting for its brief coverage of many passages, and errors in quotations: see Kelly 2000: 222–225), it nonetheless reflects Jerome's training in both Alexandrian and Antiochene exegetical methods. His literal, historical approach is liberally sprinkled with what he calls 'the flowers of the spiritual understanding' (*Preface* 5; Jerome 2008: 58). Whole phrases from Origen are reproduced verbatim, despite his claim that he had not read Origen's commentary for many years. Jerome's commentary would become very influential in the Latin West (commended inter alia by Cassiodorus, Bede, Bonaventure, and Thomas Aquinas).

Augustine of Hippo (354–430) did not write a commentary on Matthew. Nonetheless, several of his works provide insight into his interpretation of the First Gospel (Texts: PL 34: 1071–1216, 1229–1308; 35: 1323–1335, 1365–1376; CSEL 43: 81–393; Augustine 2014). *On the Lord's Sermon on the Mount* (written in 398) is an important systematic commentary on Matthew 5–7. His *Agreement Among the Evangelists* (*De consensu evangelistarum,* written in 400) sets out to defend the truth of the Gospels against charges of discrepancy or inconsistency, either within each Gospel narrative or with the other Gospels. Augustine also wrote *Questions on the Gospels* (*Quaestiones evangeliorum*) c. 400, addressing a series of questions related to Matthew and Luke, posed to him when reading the Gospels with one of his disciples, and *Seventeen Questions on Matthew* (*Quaestiones XVII in Matthaeum*).

Chromatius of Aquileia (d. c. 407) preached a series of homilies on Matthew (Text: PL 20: 327–68; CCSL 9A: 185–498; excerpts in Kraszewski 1999). He is now known to have been influenced by the commentary of his episcopal predecessor Fortunatianus (though without attribution).

The Opus Imperfectum or 'Incomplete Work' on Matthew is an important fifth-century Latin witness (Text: PG 56: 611–946; CCSL 87B; Kellerman and Oden 2010). As its title suggests, it has not survived in its entirety (it currently lacks Matt 8:11–10:15 and 13:14–18:35, and breaks off at 25:46). Due in large part to its misattribution to John Chrysostom, it was widely cited in the Middle Ages and beyond. Thomas Aquinas reportedly said that he would rather have a complete copy of this commentary than be mayor of Paris (Kellerman and Oden 2010: xvii). Its actual author is uncertain, though he knew Greek, and was familiar with Origen's exegetical method. A plausible candidate is an Arian priest called Timothy, writing c. 430, though the text's Arian sympathies are restricted to a small number of passages (Kealy 1997: 1/56; Kellerman and Oden 2010: xvii–xx).

The Middle Ages

The 'Middle Ages' broadly describes the thousand years or so from the collapse of the Western Roman Empire through to the eve of the Reformation. Describing the reception of Matthew over such a long period risks major simplification, and is inappropriate in the case of eastern Christian communities (for eastern Orthodox exegesis, see Blowers 2009). Nonetheless, a broad brush-stroke description is possible, especially for the Latin West. Patterns established in the early period are continued and developed, often with a greater degree of systematization, and key interpreters continue to emerge (see e.g. Gibson 1993; Kealy 1997: 1/83–188; de Lubac 1998–2009; Mayeski 2009; Ocker 2009).

Liturgical use of Matthew continues to be hermeneutically significant in both East and West, in at least three ways. First, meaning is affected by the selection and rearrangement of passages from Matthew in different church lectionaries (for reflection on the similar process in modern lectionaries, see Lee 2010). Second, the juxtaposition of the Gospel with Old Testament texts underscores certain Old Testament allusions in Matthew's text, as well as inviting new intertextual possibilities. Third, the association of Matthean texts with specific Christian feasts prioritizes certain dimensions of the text (e.g. the Feast of the Holy Innocents, interpreting 2:16–18 as a story of Christian martyrs).

Liturgical reading is complemented by monastic meditative reading of Scripture, though the latter is equally directed toward growth in holiness and contemplation of the vision of God. Homilies expound the moral implications of Matthew, often using allegorical interpretations as a springboard for making connections with contemporary experience. Some homilies are specifically for monastic or clerical audiences, others for general Christian congregations.

Exegetical commentary on Matthew's Gospel also continues apace, though its particular genre depends on context and usage. Classic patristic commentaries become major authorities to be cited and juxtaposed (see e.g. Olsen 2015: 74).

Systematic exposition occurs in the later Middle Ages, where the *Glossa ordinaria*, an evolving project containing comments from mainly Latin patristic and earlier medieval commentators and prioritizing the allegorical meaning, is widely used in the cathedral schools and the new universities such as Paris and Oxford (see Gibson 1993; Ocker 2009). The *Glossa* also functions as a valuable resource for bishops and senior clergy, and will be more widely disseminated at a later period through its incorporation into printed editions of the Vulgate Bible. The *Glossa* on Matthew is believed to be the work of Ralph of Laon, drawing heavily on Jerome and Paschasius Radbertus.

The Middle Ages, particularly in the West, witness a greater systematization of patristic distinctions between the literal and figural or allegorical, developing into the 'four senses' of Scripture. As the famous distich of the thirteenth-century Dominican Augustine of Dacia has it:

> *Littera gesta docet, quid credas allegoria,*
> *quid agas tropologia, quo tendas anagogia.*

According to this definition, the 'letter' or 'literal sense' teaches facts, the allegorical meaning what one is to believe, the tropological or moral how one is to act, and the anagogical what one is to aim for, i.e. the ultimate goal of the vision of God (de Lubac 1998–2009; Ocker 2009: 265; for a critique, see Fitzmyer 2008: 94). An illustration of how the four levels might work is the interpretation of Matthew's version of Christ's entry into Jerusalem (21:1–9). On a literal level, Christ enters into terrestrial Jerusalem in the week before his passion. Allegorically, 'Jerusalem' is sometimes understood as a figure of the church. However, the journey also has a moral application: describing the journey of sinners to salvation. Finally, 'Jerusalem' describes the heavenly Jerusalem that Christians hope for. Latin medieval exegesis was not monochrome, however. Certain exegetes (e.g. Thomas Aquinas; Nicholas of Lyra) place greater emphasis than others on the priority of the literal sense.

The imaginative expansion and harmonization of Matthean narratives, found in early apocryphal texts, also persists. Reworkings of Matthew's infancy narratives appear in the (probably seventh-century) *Gospel of Pseudo-Matthew*. Its influence re-emerges in the visual art of the Renaissance and early modern period (e.g. in paintings of *The Rest on the Flight into Egypt*). Other popular reworkings include *The Golden Legend*, a collection of saints' lives produced c. 1260 by the Italian Dominican Jacobus de Voragine, the fourteenth-century Franciscan *Meditations on the Life of Christ*, misattributed to Bonaventure, which invites the reader to enter into the Gospel story and contemplate Christ's humanity, and *The Book of Margery Kempe* (1436–1438), containing imaginative accounts of Gospel-related scenes by an English female mystic.

Eastern Christian communities manifest different trajectories from those of the West. Such diversity is evident both in liturgical and iconographic practice, and in the commentary and homiletic tradition. From the Byzantine tradition, important exegetes include Theophylact of Ochrid and Euthymius Zigabenus. Examples from other eastern communities include Rufus of Shotep (Coptic), Isho'dad of Merv (the Church of the East), and Dionysius bar-Salibi (Syriac Orthodox). Brief descriptions of these, and of other significant medieval commentators on Matthew are provided in what follows.

GREGORY THE GREAT (c. 540–604) was a Roman patrician and monk, who was elected pope in 590. His *Homilies on the Gospels* include several on passages from Matthew, including the temptation of Jesus, and the parables of the Treasure, the Dragnet, and the Marriage Feast (Text: Gregory the Great 1990). His exegesis is widely repeated by later medieval Latin exegetes (see Wailes 1987).

RUFUS OF SHOTEP (late sixth century), bishop of Shotep in Upper Egypt, is an important witness to the interpretation of Matthew in Coptic Orthodox Christianity. His homilies in Coptic on Matthew 1–5 have survived (Text: Rufus of Shotep 1998). These are firmly allegorical, in the tradition of Origen, Didymus the Blind, and Cyril of Alexandria.

The Saxon RABANUS MAURUS (c. 780–856), was a pupil of Alcuin at Aachen, who subsequently became abbot of the Benedictine Abbey of Fulda, then archbishop of Mainz. Maurus wrote commentaries on most of the Bible, including Matthew (Text: PL 107:727–1156). He drew on a large number of patristic exegetes, including the lost commentary of Victorinus of Pettau, though also clarified them with his own interpretation, marked in the text by his initial 'M' (Gibson 1993: 6). He was one of Aquinas's sources for his *Catena Aurea*.

PASCHASIUS RADBERTUS (785–865), abbot of Corbie in northern France, wrote a commentary on Matthew in 12 books (Text: PL 120: 31–994; CCCM 56–56B). Though his monastic context is evident in his exposition, Radbertus's *Expositio* became an important source for the *Glossa ordinaria*.

ISHO'DAD OF MERV (ninth century), bishop of Hdatta on the Tigris, and theologian of the Church of the East, commented widely on the Bible, Matthew included, c. 850 (Text: Isho'dad of Merv 1911). His exposition is an attempt to meld together the historical-grammatical focus of the Antiochene Theodore of Mopsuestia, typical of exegesis in the Church of the East, with the allegorical method favored by Jacobites (see Kealy 1997: 1/114–115).

THEOPHYLACT OF OCHRID (1050–1107), archbishop of Ochrid in Bulgaria, wrote an influential commentary on Matthew (Text: PG 123: 139–92; Theophylact 1992). A Greek who studied in Constantinople, he was steeped in patristic exegesis and was especially influenced by John Chrysostom. The moral application of the Gospel is an important dimension of his commentary.

Euthymius Zigabenus (twelfth century), Greek monastic exegete and close associate in Constantinople of the Byzantine emperor Alexius I Comnenus, wrote a commentary on all four Gospels with a strong emphasis on the literal sense under the influence of John Chrysostom (Text: PG 129: 107–766). Euthymius was widely cited by later Western authors such as Juan de Maldonado.

Hildegard of Bingen (1098–1179), Benedictine nun, abbess, and mystic, was rare among medieval women for exercising a ministry of preaching (see Kienzle 2009). Her *Homilies on the Gospels*, delivered informally to the nuns of her community, cover 27 Gospel lectionary readings. Those from Matthew include parts of the infancy narrative (for Christmas Eve and the Epiphany), the temptation (the First Sunday of Lent), some of the miracles, and the parable of the Workers in the Vineyard (Text: Hildegard of Bingen 2011).

Dionysius bar-Salibi (twelfth century), also known as Jacob bar-Salibi, theologian, exegete, and bishop of the Syriac Orthodox Church, wrote a commentary on Matthew, influenced by Ephrem and Moses bar Kepha as well as John Chrysostom (Text: CSCO, Scriptores Syri, ser. 2, 98). His commentary on the Apocalypse is an important source for the eschatological views of the third-century exegete Hippolytus, which impacted his own interpretation of Matthew 24 (see Gwynn 1889).

Thomas Aquinas (1225–1274), Dominican friar and arguably the most important theologian in the medieval West. Thomas delivered his *Lectures on Matthew* at the University of Paris between 1268 and 1272 (Text: Aquinas 2013a, 2013b). The surviving manuscripts are based on notes by two of his students, unchecked by Thomas himself (Holmes 2005: 74–75). He subsequently compiled his extensive *Catena aurea* (or 'golden chain') of patristic and earlier medieval commentary. (Unless otherwise specified, all references in this commentary are to his *Lectures on Matthew*.)

Peter John Olivi (1248–1298) was a French Franciscan theologian on the radical wing of the Franciscan movement, whose exegesis was strongly influenced by the twelfth-century abbot, Joachim of Fiore, especially his interpretation of the Book of Revelation. Olivi reads Matthew on two levels. The literal speaks of Christ's life, teaching, death, and resurrection. The non-literal speaks of Olivi's own day; in particular, Matthew's strong emphasis on persecution is read as a prophecy of the persecution of Franciscans (see Madigan 2003).

Nicholas of Lyra (c. 1270–1349), a French Franciscan, composed *postillae litterales* on Scripture, Matthew included, based on lectures given in Paris during the 1320s. As their title suggests, they emphasize the literal sense, historical meaning, and philology, and anticipate modern textual criticism. In the fifteenth century, printed Bibles were produced containing both Nicholas's *postillae* and the *Glossa ordinaria* as parallel commentaries on the text.

From the Sixteenth Century

Renaissance humanism's emphasis on return to the sources, philology, and greater historical awareness had its impact on the interpretation of Matthew. The early sixteenth century witnessed new editions of the New Testament, and greater interest in textual criticism. Erasmus's 1516 edition of the New Testament translated the verb in Matt 4:17, not as 'do penance' (*poenitentiam agere*) as had Jerome's Vulgate, but as 'repent' (*resipiscite*: Rummel 2009: 281). This distinction would be fundamental to Martin Luther's critique of Catholic penitential practices in light of his understanding of justification by faith alone.

This Lutheran critique is but one example of the impact on the Gospel's reception of the Protestant Reformation during the early sixteenth century. The use of Matthew was often profoundly polemical, as different sides found this Gospel's warnings against hypocrisy and false prophecy (e.g. 7:15–20; 23:13–36) actualized in their theological opponents, or sought to defend treasured beliefs. Lutheran and Reformed interpreters did battle not only with Roman Catholics but also with Anabaptists, disdainfully dismissed as the 'new monasticism.' Anabaptist sources attest to a radical embrace of Christ's demands, especially in the Sermon on the Mount (see e.g. the 1540 Biblical Concordance of the Swiss Brethren), and contain female as well as male voices (e.g. Anna Jansz of Rotterdam). As a consequence of the Catholic Counter-Reformation, particularly the Council of Trent, there was a renewed emphasis on preaching among Roman Catholics, and a requirement on bishops to establish chairs for the teaching of Scripture (Bedouelle 2009).

The degree of discontinuity from the Middle Ages can be overstated. Particularly in Catholic circles, the four senses of Scripture continued to be espoused (e.g. in the Great Commentary of Cornelius a Lapide). Even Reformers such as Luther stood in significant continuity with their medieval predecessors: Luther's biblical commentaries essentially continue the tradition of the thirteenth- and fourteenth-century *postillae*. Moreover, Matthew was also received in less controversial contexts, especially in worship, prayer, and personal devotion. Generations of Anglican Christians were formed spiritually by the 'Comfortable Words' of Thomas Cranmer's 1549 *Book of Common Prayer*, notably those drawn from Matthew 11:28 ('Come unto me all that travail and are heavy laden, and I will refresh you').

Of the vast number of exegetes who commented on Matthew during the turbulent period of the Reformation and its aftermath, the following will recur in this commentary with greater frequency.

Desiderius Erasmus of Rotterdam (1466–1536), perhaps the most famous Catholic humanist scholar. Erasmus composed both *Annotations* to accompany his text of the New Testament (Erasmus 1986), and a series of *Paraphrases*

(Erasmus 2008), the latter published in March 1522 and undergoing three revised editions. (Unless otherwise stated, references in the commentary are to Erasmus's *Paraphrase on Matthew*.)

Martin Luther (1483–1546), leader of the Reformation in Germany, preached extensive exegetical sermons on Matthew, often interspersed with polemical attacks on theological opponents. Their homiletic genre also prioritizes the moral demands of the passage (Key texts: Luther 1956, 1959, 2014, 2015). Luther's 1522 *Preface to the New Testament* gives a less central place to the Synoptic Gospels, Matthew included, than to John, Paul, and 1 Peter. Matthew, for Luther, is primarily about Christ's deeds than his words (see Becker 2015: 23–24; on Luther's biblical interpretation, see Thompson 2009).

John Calvin (1509–1564), leader of the Reform in Switzerland, was strongly influenced by humanism. A major source for Calvin's interpretation of Matthew is his *Commentary on the Harmony of the Three Evangelists* (1555; Text: Calvin 1949, 1972). Calvin gives attention to philological, textual-critical, and rhetorical questions, as well as the evangelist's first-century historical context, in order to uncover his intention or 'mind,' and the moral or spiritual lessons intended. He cites patristic as well as contemporary exegetes, though often to disagree with them (on Calvin's biblical interpretation, see Flaming 2006; Pitkin 2009).

Juan de Valdés (*c*. 1490–1541), a Spanish Catholic humanist scholar and adviser to Emperor Charles V, wrote a commentary on Matthew which was not published until 1880 (Text: Valdés 1882). Valdés was held in some suspicion for his criticism of papal corruption and friendship with the Italian Reformer Peter Martyr Vermigli, and was later suspected of heresy. His focus was on the literal sense of the text, though he also sought to draw out implications for living the Christian life (Valdés was particularly struck by what Matthew reveals about Christ's humility).

Juan de Maldonado (1533–1583) or Maldonatus, a Spanish Jesuit, wrote a *Commentary on the Holy Gospels*, published posthumously in 1596–1597 (Text: Maldonado 1888). His emphasis on the literal sense, supported by a strong grounding in ancient languages, meant that it was widely read outside Roman Catholic circles (the English translation was by a Victorian Anglican). His use of patristic commentators is judicious, parting from their views when the text suggests otherwise.

Cornelius a Lapide (1567–1637), or Cornelis Cornelissen van den Steen, was a Flemish Jesuit exegete whose commentary on Matthew formed part of his *Great Commentary* on scripture, published posthumously in 1681 (Text: Lapide 1890). Lapide's commentary shows more continuity with pre-Reformation commentaries than that of Maldonado. He addresses the four senses of Scripture, and draws heavily on the Fathers and later medieval exegetes, as well as engaging polemically with Protestants.

Numerous commentaries were published on Matthew during the seventeenth and eighteenth centuries. Besides the *Great Commentary* of Cornelius a Lapide, those worthy of note include the Anglican Henry Hammond's pioneering *Paraphrase and Annotations on the New Testament* (1653), the popular commentary by the Welsh Non-Conformist Matthew Henry (1708–1710), and the *Gnomon Novi Testamenti* by the German Lutheran scholar Johann Albrecht Bengel (1742), whose influence is evident on the founder of Methodism, John Wesley (1703–1791). The Cambridge scholar John Lightfoot illuminated this most Jewish of Gospels through pioneering study of rabbinic literature in his 1658 *Horae Hebraicae et Talmudicae*. Lightfoot also offered a strongly historicist interpretation of the Eschatological Discourse (Matt 24–25), as referring entirely to the first-century Roman destruction of Jerusalem. A similar reading occurs in the 1741 *Commentarius in Novum Testamentum* by the French Jesuit Jean Hardouin. A rare example of a woman exegete is Mary Cornwallis, an evangelical Anglican and wife of the rector of Wittersham, Kent. Her *Observations, Critical, Explanatory, and Practical, on the Canonical Scriptures* include what is probably the first commentary on Matthew by a woman author, published in 1817 (Kealy 1997: 1/365; on her life and work, see Taylor 2007; Taylor in Taylor and Choi 2012: 142–145).

The Enlightenment impacted the scholarly interpretation of Matthew significantly. The publications of Hermann Samuel Reimarus's *Fragments* in 1774–1778 drew a wedge between the Jesus of history and the portraits offered by his evangelist interpreters. Reimarus claimed that Jesus had been a Jewish nationalist, questioned the historicity of Matthew's story of the guard at the tomb (27:62–66; 28:4, 11–15), and argued, contrary to the evangelist, that the disciples stole Jesus' body. The gradual acceptance of Markan Priority in the nineteenth century (after initial questioning of Matthew's position by G.C. Storr in 1786) further tarnished Matthew's reputation as 'the First Gospel,' as pride of place for historical reconstruction was ceded to the shorter but previously neglected Mark. A further consequence was the loss of confidence in Matthew's Gospel as an early work by an apostolic eyewitness.

The Enlightenment brought not simply reassessment of Matthew's dating, authorship, and historical reliability. Rationalist interpretations also critiqued the Gospel's supernatural dimensions. The German biblical critic Heinrich Eberhard Gottlob Paulus (1761–1851) pioneered influential readings of miracles such as the multiplication of the loaves, attributing the proliferation of food to Jesus provoking generosity among the crowd, or highlighting psychological dimensions of Jesus' healings. In the United States, Thomas Jefferson's *The Life and Morals of Jesus of Nazareth* (popularly known as 'Jefferson's Bible') is typical of an anti-supernatural position. Jefferson expunged all supernatural elements from the Gospels, removing from Matthew the infancy narratives, Christ's temptation by the devil in the wilderness, the miracles, and the whole narrative following the burial of the dead Jesus. Jesus emerges as a great moral teacher, but little else.

New interests and concerns would emerge toward the end of the modern period (for a survey of recent Matthean scholarship, see e.g. Boxall 2014). In the United States, the *Woman's Bible* (1895–1898), produced by a team of women scholars chaired by Elizabeth Cady Stanton, anticipated later feminist criticism of the Gospel (Stanton 2002). The section on Matthew provided sympathetic commentary on key women characters (e.g. Salome, Peter's mother-in-law, and the women at the tomb), and reworked such Matthean parables as the Wise and Foolish Virgins (25:1–13) in support of women's education. The Gospel's use in political discourse mirrors its polemical use in earlier centuries. Both sides in the debate over slavery in nineteenth-century America claimed its support. The Protestant scholar Philip Schaff pointed to the healing of the centurion's servant (8:5–13; Schaff 1861) as justification for slave-ownership, while the African-American abolitionist and former slave Frederick Douglass used Matthew 23 to critique 'scribes and Pharisees' within respectable Christian churches, who would shun 'a sheep-stealer' yet think nothing of fellowshipping with 'a man-stealer' (Douglass in Tippens, Walker, and Weathers 2013: 70). In similar fashion, texts from Matthew's Gospel were used by twentieth-century South African Christians both to legitimate apartheid (not least in the Dutch Reformed Church) and to critique it theologically (see Combrink 1994).

The tension in the First Gospel between continuity with Israel's heritage and fierce polemic against specific Jews has also re-emerged as an issue in its modern reception. Given its Jewish-Christian emphasis, the First Gospel was sidelined by nineteenth- and early twentieth-century German scholars advocating for an 'Aryan Christ,' for whom John's anachronistic critique of 'the Jews' was more amenable (Nicklas 2011: 270). Matthew's Sermon on the Mount was also fundamental to the Confessing Church's opposition to the Nazi regime in the 1930s. Yet the detrimental effects of the Gospel's polemic, especially in the light of the Holocaust, have come to shape the concerns of modern critical scholarship (e.g. Levine 1988; Harrington 1991).

Matthew's Gospel in the Arts and Literature

The prominence of Matthew among the Gospels, and the popular imaginative impact of certain of its narratives (especially associated with Christ's birth and infancy), has had a profound impact far beyond the contexts of exegetical commentary, homiletic exposition, theological disputation, and liturgical performance. Scenes from this Gospel have been powerfully conveyed, and reshaped, by visual artists almost from the beginning. Visual art has particular potential for evoking a personal response to the narrative (or, occasionally, non-narrative teaching), conveying the multivalency of the text in a more immediate way, or presenting several moments from a story in a synchronic fashion (see e.g. Berdini 1997: 1–35; O'Kane 2005, 2010). A significant number of paintings and other visual images will be explored in the commentary proper, though publishing constraints permit only a small number of illustrations. Others are readily available on the internet, however, via sites such as https://images.google.com.

The visual impact of Matthew can be felt early (Jensen 2000). Uniquely Matthean scenes appear in early Christian frescoes and on sarcophagi: fresco examples include the adoration of the Magi (2:1–12: e.g. Catacomb of St. Priscilla, Rome, late third/early fourth century) and Jesus and Peter walking on the water (14:28–31: e.g. third-century Christian baptistery, Dura Europos). A famous ivory panel juxtaposes the living Christ on the cross with the dead Judas hanging from a tree (27:3–10: 420– 430, British Museum). Old Testament narratives shaped by Matthew also appear, such as the prophet Jonah as a 'sign' of the resurrection (12:38–40; e.g. Catacomb of St. Callixtus, Rome, third century). Irenaeus' identification of the four evangelists as the four living creatures (Matthew as the human or the angel) is widely represented across the centuries in fresco, mosaic, sculpture, as well on Gospel book covers.

In medieval Europe, the First Gospel's influence appears in the great Gothic cathedrals. The genealogy is an important source for the Tree of Jesse, found in stained glass in Notre Dame, Paris, and Chartres Cathedral, and playing an important political role in legitimating the French kings. Other important Matthean motifs appear in sculpture, whether the Flight into Egypt, the Massacre of the Innocents, the Wise and Foolish Virgins, or the Sheep and the Goats. The emergence of narrative cycles of Christ's life (e.g. Giotto's famous Scrovegni Chapel frescoes in Padua), though tending toward Gospel harmonization, offers visual witness to scenes from Matthew such as the Flight into Egypt. Jacques Joseph Tissot's watercolor series of the Life of Christ (1886–1896, Brooklyn Museum, New York), includes such Matthean details as the earthquake at the crucifixion scene (27:51–52). Many images drawn from Matthew appear as part of altarpieces, thus linking engagement with the image more directly to eucharistic worship, or the more personal reception of holy communion on the part of the viewer. Important examples include allusions to the Beatitudes in Jan van Eyck's *Adoration of the Mystic Lamb* (1430–1432; St. Bavo's Cathedral, Ghent), Gentile da Fabriano's *Adoration of the Magi* (1423; Uffizi, Florence), and the right panel of Matthias Grünewald's Isenheim Altarpiece (1510–1515; Unterlinden Museum, Colmar), featuring the risen Christ hovering over the guards at the tomb. Manuscript illuminations and printed book illustrations can also reflect exegesis of Matthew's text.

A complex system of Old Testament typology occurs in the medieval picture-book *Biblia pauperum* (e.g. British Library Blockbook C.9 d.2). Saul's massacre of the priests of Nob (1 Sam 22:17–18), and Athaliah's murder of the royal princes (2 Kgs 11:1), are presented as foreshadowing Herod's slaughter of the innocents.

In the East, narrative sequences are less prominent. Nonetheless, the liturgical prominence of Matthew has left its mark on the iconographical tradition. Icons of Christ's temptation follow the Matthean order (4:1–11), while Christ's triumphal entry (21:1–9) is visualized with children, an import from 21:15–16. The later *Painter's Manual*, compiled in the early eighteenth century by a monk of Mount Athos, Dionysius of Fourna, gives detailed descriptions for a number of narrative icons, including several of the parables unique to Matthew (Hetherington 1996).

Visual exegesis can often closely parallel theological controversy, or broad social and political trends. Visualization of passages mentioning Peter (14:28–31; 16:17–19; 17:24–27) are often employed in debates over papal authority. Examples include Giotto's *Navicella* (commissioned c. 1305–1313 for Old St. Peter's, Rome), Pietro Perugino's *The Delivery of the Keys* (1481–1482; Sistine Chapel, Rome), and Masaccio's *The Tribute Money* (1425; Brancacci Chapel, Santa Maria del Carmine, Florence). In the twentieth century, the trauma of the First World War, combined with opposition to the Nazis, shaped the 1960 lithograph series *Matthäus Evangelium* by the German Expressionist Otto Dix (e.g. in his *Slaughter of the Innocents*, the executioner wears a German military uniform).

Matthew's Gospel has also been an important source for dramatic performance. In the Middle Ages, a similar process occurred to that in visual art: the tendency to harmonize different Gospels supplemented by the imaginative 'gap-filling' provided by apocryphal texts. Medieval mystery plays, such as those performed in Coventry, Chester, and York (see e.g. Sharp 1825; Mooney 1915; Hussey 1975; Elliott and Runnalls 1978; Reed 2000; Ryan 2001), often incorporated developed versions of Matthean characters (e.g. Joseph as an aged cuckold; the Magi as three kings; Pilate's wife as the recipient of a demonic dream). The actualization of the Gospel story also occurred in passion plays, the version at Oberammergau in Bavaria, still performed in the twenty-first century, being the most famous. In the modern period, Matthew's Gospel has occasionally been dramatized in its entirety (e.g. the one-man performance by the British actor George Dillon).

The genre of Jesus film generally perpetuates the textual and dramatic Gospel harmony (see e.g. Baugh 1997; Reinhartz 1998; Goodacre 2000; Kreitzer 2002), or supplements the canonical text from apocryphal writings, classic art, and devotional texts (in the case of Mel Gibson's *The Passion of the Christ*, the Stations of the Cross and the visions of the early nineteenth-century German mystic Anne Catherine Emmerich). However, most prioritize some Matthean elements (Magi; sermon; earthquake; guards at the tomb). Pasolini's fidelity to Matthew's text in *Il Vangelo secondo Matteo* has been mentioned already. Exclusive focus on Matthew's text is also found in *The Visual Bible: Matthew* (1993), directed by Regardt van den Bergh. The film follows closely the text of the NIV, an elderly Matthew (identified as the apostle of Jesus) dictating as he reminisces about Christ's public ministry decades earlier.

Matthew has long had a musical impact, initially due to its prominence in the liturgy (see Dowling Long and Sawyer 2015). Examples discussed in this commentary include Latin antiphons, some with classic settings (e.g. the versions of *Audivi vocem de caelo,* based on 25:6, by the sixteenth-century English composers Thomas Tallis and John Taverner), Orthodox liturgical hymns, and Bach's *St. Matthew Passion* (composed in 1727). A large number of hymns and carols interpret specific Matthean passages; these will be discussed at the relevant point in the commentary. Recurring examples include the *Olney Hymns,* a collaborative work published in 1779 by the Evangelical Anglicans John Newton and William Cowper (Dowling Long and Sawyer 2015: 178).

The literary effects are also diverse. Matthew's narrative as a whole has been reshaped in various forms, while specific Matthean passages and phrases have impacted novelists, playwrights, and poets. A hexameter version of the four Gospels, drawing substantially from Matthew, was produced by the fourth-century Spanish Christian poet Juvencus. Also in the fourth century, Ephrem the Syrian, poet as well as theologian, offered imaginative explorations of some of Matthew's parables, including the Pearl of Great Price, in his *Hymns on Faith.* The tenth-century Armenian Gregory of Narek's poetic prayers include one which draws on Matthew's story of the Canaanite woman. The ninth-century Old Saxon epic *The Heliand* reworks the Gospel story in language intelligible to its contemporary audience, with Christ and his disciples as warriors. Important modern poets have engaged imaginatively with Matthew's story of the Magi, most famously T.S. Eliot's *Journey of the Magi* (1927) and the brief but evocative *The Magi* by William Butler Yeats (1914). The radical political message of Matthew has also been versified, e.g. by the US political activist Sarah Cleghorn:

> Thanks to St. Matthew, who had been
> At mass-meetings in Palestine,
> We knew whose side was spoken for
> When Comrade Jesus took the floor.
> (in Atwan, Dardess and Rosenthal 1998: 426)

Among the many novelists who have been inspired by the First Gospel, Leo Tolstoy perhaps deserves pride of place. His 1899 novel *Resurrection* includes what is arguably one of the most perceptive commentaries on Matthew's Sermon on the Mount. Very different, though massively influential in terms of book sales in the United States, are the *Left Behind* series of novels (1995–2007), by Tim LaHaye and Jerry B. Jenkins, which offer a distinctive reading of Matthew's eschatological discourse, along with key passages from Daniel, 1 and 2 Thessalonians, and Revelation.

The Afterlife of Matthew the Evangelist

But what of the ongoing story of the evangelist himself, identified from the second century with Matthew the apostle? Listed among the Twelve in all three Synoptics and the Acts of the Apostles (Mark 3:18; Luke 6:15; Acts 1:13), Matthew is explicitly identified as 'the tax-collector' or 'toll-collector' in the Gospel which bears his name (10:3), operative in or near the Galilean border-town of Capernaum, located on the important trade route, the Via Maris. Since the time of Jerome, this Matthew has generally been harmonized with the tax-collector Levi, son of Alphaeus (Mark 2:15; Luke 5:27, 29), albeit with some notable exceptions (e.g. Clement of Alexandria, *Strom.* 4.9; Origen, *Cels.* 1.62; see Romero Pose 1992). As one of the Twelve, this Matthew was among those sent out by Jesus to continue his mission (10:3, 5), thus hinting at a more significant post-Easter role. The New Testament itself, however, fails to complete his story. Matthew's last appearance is alongside the other disciples in Jerusalem in the first days of the church's life (Acts 1:13).

These are not exactly rich pickings for a developed afterlife. Nonetheless, his growing biography exploits these brief references as well as indicators from Matthew's Gospel of what modern narrative critics call 'the implied author' (the author as reconstructed by the reader from the text). His role as tax-collector provoked fruitful speculation about his background and attitudes. In art, he is regularly identified by coins or a money bag (e.g. bronze sculpture by Ian Rank-Broadley, 2009; St. Matthew's, Northampton, UK), or depicted seated at his tax-office (e.g. Caravaggio, *Calling of St. Matthew*, 1599–1600; San Luigi dei Francesi, Rome). The apostle in Carpaccio's *The Calling of St. Matthew* (1507; San Giorgio degli Schiavoni, Venice) is apparently modeled on the Jewish bankers of Venice, his open-air table resembling those of the Ghetto (Böhm 1910).

That Matthew writes a Gospel with an infancy narrative leads to the attribution to him of another infancy text, the so-called *Gospel of Pseudo-Matthew* (or *Liber de ortu beatae Mariae et infantia Salvatoris*). Alternatively, his identification with Levi leads to the conclusion that he came from that tribe and was therefore a priest (e.g. Christian of Stavelot, *Liber Generationis* 1: CCCM 224: 60).

A modern variant, based on this evangelist's concern for Old Testament fulfillment and his knowledge of variant textual traditions, is that he was a scribe rather than a tax-collector (e.g. Cope 1976; Orton 1989).

Matthew the Christian Jew

Fairly consistent across the centuries is the conviction that the evangelist wrote as a Jew for audiences of Jewish origin (see e.g. Mitchell 2005). The alternative view that he was a Gentile (e.g. Clark 1947; Meier 1991:18–22) appears to be largely a modern thesis, the second-century Marcion being a rare ancient proponent (according to Tertullian, *Adv. Marc.* 4.11). Clement of Alexandria's report concerning Matthew's vegetarianism ('Accordingly, the apostle Matthew partook of seeds, and nuts, and vegetables, without flesh,' *Paed.* 2.1; *ANF* 2:241) presents him as a prototypical Jewish-Christian Ebionite, like James the Lord's brother. The earliest statements about Matthew's text and intended audience follow a similar vein. Particularly influential is Papias' ambiguous statement that Matthew compiled 'the sayings' (of the Lord?) *hebraidi dialectō* (Eusebius, *H.E.* 3.39.16). This is normally taken to mean that the Gospel was originally composed in Hebrew (or Aramaic: see John 5:2; 19:17; Acts 21:40; Josephus, *Ant.* 3.10.6; *War* 5.4.2; 5.9.2), although Papias could be alluding to the 'Hebrew style' of Matthew's Greek (so e.g. Kürzinger 1983: 17–22).

Later patristic tradition assumes a Semitic original, as does a sixth-century mosaic in San Vitale, Ravenna, depicting the evangelist transcribing his Gospel in Hebrew letters. Echoes of Papias occur in Irenaeus' claim that Matthew composed his Gospel 'among the Hebrews in their own dialect' (*Adv. Haer.* 3.1.1; *ANF* 1:414), and Origen's similar statement that the first Gospel was 'prepared for the converts from Judaism, and published in the Hebrew language' (Eusebius, *H.E.* 6.25.4; *NPNF* 2nd series, 1:273). Similarly, Jerome states in the preface to his commentary that Matthew wrote 'in the Hebrew language, chiefly for the sake of those from the Jews who had believed in Jesus' (Jerome 2008: 53; see also Eusebius' own comments at *H.E.* 3.24.6). Moreover, he locates the Gospel's composition in Judea itself (so also the *Monarchian Prologue*, Theophylact, and the *Martyrdom of Saint Matthew in Parthia*). Others (e.g. the *Opus imperfectum*) prefer the vaguer Palestine. Even modern scholarship retains this conviction that Matthew was written 'close to the action.' Proposals include Sepphoris or Tiberias in Galilee, a Palestinian coastal city such as Caesarea Maritima, a contiguous area such as Transjordan (see 4:15; 19:1) or southern Syria (see 4:24), as well as the widely cited northern Syrian city of Antioch-on-the-Orontes (e.g. Streeter 1924: 500–523; Slingerland 1979; Viviano 1979; Brown and Meier 1983: 22–27; Saldarini 1992: 661–662).

Early commentators are divided as to how an originally Semitic Gospel came to be translated into Greek. Jerome is unsure of the translator's name, though he claims that a Hebrew version of Matthew was preserved in Pamphilus' library at Caesarea, and that another copy was used by the Nazarenes of Beroea in Syria (*De vir. illus.* 3). Others are more specific, attributing the translation to James the Lord's brother (Athanasius), John (Theophylact), Barnabas, Luke, or Paul (see Lapide 1890: I/xxxvii–xxxviii). The theory of translation by John is widely repeated in a preface attributed to Epiphanius, frequently found in Byzantine Gospel manuscripts:

> The Gospel according to Matthew was written by him in the East with Hebraic language and letters and was published in Jerusalem and translated by John. (Nelson 1980: 18)

Eusebius of Caesarea, meanwhile, knows a tradition that Pantaenus, the teacher of Clement of Alexandria, came across a Hebrew copy of Matthew on a visit to India, supposedly brought there by the apostle Bartholomew (*H.E.* 5.10.3). The Barnabas connection re-emerges in the sixth-century Greek *Ecclesiastical History* of Theodor the Lector, who describes the *inventio* of Matthew's Gospel during the reign of the Byzantine emperor Zeno (491):

> The relics of the apostle Barnabas were found in Cyprus under a carob-tree, and on his breast there was the gospel of Matthew, written by Barnabas' own hand. (Theodorus Lector, *H.E.* II.2; Rose 2009: 177)

Certainly there is a close connection between canonical Matthew and certain 'Jewish-Christian Gospels' circulating in the early centuries. Moreover, a Hebrew translation of Matthew (suitably edited in line with Jewish-Christian sensibilities, including a heightened role for John the Baptist and a downplaying of a mission to Gentiles) is preserved in a fourteenth-century Jewish polemical treatise by Shem-Tob (Howard 1995, 1998). However, our Greek Matthew bears few traces of being a translation from either Hebrew or Aramaic.

Matthew as Apostle and Martyr

Yet Matthew is more than a converted Jewish tax-collector and Gospel writer. His identification as an apostle, one of the Twelve, also has implications for his afterlife (on this, see e.g. Réau 1958; Spadafora 1967; Rose 2009). Christ's post-resurrection commission to the Eleven to 'make disciples of all the nations' (Matt 28:16–20) led to the reasonable conviction that the mission territory was divided up among them. Regions assigned to Matthew in subsequent traditions are impressive in their diversity: Ethiopia, Persia, Pontus, Syria, Macedonia, Spain, and even Ireland (Réau 1958: 927; Spadafora 1967: 120; Rose 2009: 164). The legends associating Matthew with Ethiopia (e.g. Rufinus, *H.E.* 1.9; Socrates, *H.E.* 1.19) are among the most extensive, with cycles of miracles including raising the king's daughter from the dead. Occasionally, Matthew is aided in his missionary endeavors by the Ethiopian eunuch of Acts 8 (e.g. *The Golden Legend*).

Although some thought that Matthew died a natural death (e.g. Heracleon in Clement of Alexandria, *Strom.* 4.9), most identify the apostle as a martyr. This is a reasonable deduction from Christ's teaching, whereby his disciples should take up their cross (16:24–26). Matthew's martyrdom is dated to 21 September in the Roman Martyrology, 16 November in the Greek tradition, and 9 October in a colophon to the Ethiopic *Martyrdom of Saint Matthew in Parthia* (Budge 1935: 114). The precise circumstances and location differ, however. Isidore of Seville (*De ortu et obitu patrum* 75) has Matthew's last resting-place in Parthia, though he makes no explicit mention of martyrdom. A Parthian/Persian martyrdom is explicit in *The Martyrdom of Saint Matthew in Parthia* (by beheading: Budge 1935: 109–114), the Greek *Martyrium Matthaei* (by burning, the fire also consuming the palace of the local king and his idols), and the *Breviarum apostolorum* (see Rose 2009: 168–169, 174). Alternatively, Matthew dies by the sword in Ethiopia, at the instigation of King Hirtacus (e.g. *Passio Matthaei* in Pseudo-Abdias; *Golden Legend;* see McDowell 2015: 226–230). The martyrdom is a consequence of Matthew's thwarting Hirtacus' plan to marry Iphigenia, the Christian daughter of the former king, whom the apostle supported in her desire to embrace consecrated virginity. The martyrdom takes place after Matthew has finished celebrating Mass, as *The Golden Legend* records:

> After the ceremony of the mass was concluded, the king sent a swordsman, who found Matthew standing before the altar with his hands raised to heaven in prayer. He stabbed the apostle in the back, killing him and making him a martyr. The people found this out and thronged to the royal palace, intent on setting it and everything in it afire, but the priests and the deacons restrained them, and they all celebrated Saint Matthew's martyrdom joyfully. (Jacobus de Voragine 1993: II/185)

The martyrdom is a popular scene for Western artists from the late Middle Ages into the early modern period. Examples include Stefan Lochner's panel of the martyrdom from the right wing of his *Last Judgment Altarpiece* (c. 1435, Städel Museum, Frankfurt), Caravaggio, *The Martyrdom of St. Matthew* (1599–1600, San Luigi dei Francesi, Rome), and Claude Vignon, *Martyrdom of*

St. Matthew (1617, Musée des beaux-arts d'Arras). In Caravaggio's version, one of his three canvases painted for the burial chapel of Cardinal Matthieu Cointerel (Matteo Contarelli), the soldier slaying Matthew with the sword is nude apart from a loincloth. The recumbent figure of Matthew is accompanied by three male figures, similarly clad (x-ray photographs reveal these figures to be a major change in the final version of the canvas). One of them lowers his foot into what might be a baptismal piscina. Their interpretation as neophytes underscores the baptismal potential of the painting (Trinchieri Camiz 1990).

The martyrdom is also depicted in earlier cycles of the Life of St. Matthew (see Réau 1958: 929), including the South Rose Window in Notre Dame, Paris (thirteenth century), the stained glass from the Upper Basilica of St. Francis, Assisi (thirteenth century), and Andrea Orcagna and Jacopo di Cione's *Retable of St. Matthew* (1369; Galleria degli Uffizi, Florence).

Traditions about Matthew's final resting place reflect the disagreement over his place of martyrdom. For Isidore, Matthew 'has his resting place in the mountains of the land of the Parthians' (*De ortu et obitu patrum* 75 in Rose 2009: 175). A rival tradition has it that his relics were brought from Ethiopia to Salerno in Italy, known as the 'city of St. Matthew' (the feast of the translation being 6 May). Alternatively, they were taken first to Brittany, where the Abbaye Saint-Matthieu-de-Fin-de-Terres claims his head. His body was subsequently transferred via Paestum to Salerno in 954 (Réau 1958: 927–928; Rose 2009: 165–166). A new cathedral was built there by Archbishop Alfanus in the eleventh century, which remains a place of pilgrimage and Matthean devotion. A hymn for Matthew's feast day (21 September), composed by Alfanus, includes an appeal for the saint's ongoing protection for Salerno's citizens:

> Matthew, apostle, receive now worthily
> The due thanks of your citizens,
> And let them be safe from all sin,
> So that they in future trial will feel
> That they have submitted themselves firmly to such a patron.
> (in Rose 2009: 202)

Matthew the Evangelist as Exemplar

Various dimensions of Matthew's story come to serve a paraenetic purpose for those wishing to imitate the publican-turned-apostle. *The Golden Legend* identifies four as of special note: his prompt obedience in answering Christ's call (9:9); his generosity (exemplified by the feast he gave following his call: 9:10–13); his humility (not being ashamed to describe himself as a despised tax-collector, 10:3); the priority given to his Gospel by the church (which underscores the gifts lavished on him by God, due to the greatness of his conversion from a life of avarice).

Many are particularly impressed by the third of these: the evangelist's humility in publicly associating himself with a disreputable occupation, where Mark and Luke hide his identity behind the name 'Levi' (e.g. Eusebius, *Dem. ev.* 3.5). A related aspect of his call is his status as sinner, who invites fellow sinners to dinner in his house, and writes a Gospel of mercy as one who has received mercy. Matthew as a model for other converted sinners is a popular deduction, as for the author of the *Opus imperfectum*:

> Matthew was an evangelist of saints, but nonetheless especially of those who had been sinners, since he proclaimed the gospel to sinners not only by his words but also by the emendation of his life. (Kellerman and Oden 2010: 1–2)

For Epiphanius of Salamis (c. 310–403), this alone is sufficient justification for Matthew's being the first among the Gospels:

> Because he had repented of many sins, and had risen from the receipt of custom and followed Him who came for man's salvation and said, 'I am not come to call the righteous, but sinners to repentance,' it was Matthew's duty to present the message of salvation <first>, as an example for us, who would be saved like this man who was restored in the tax office and turned from his iniquity. (*Pan.* 51.5.1; Epiphanius 2013: 30)

In a poem for the feast of St. Matthew (21 September) published in his 1827 collection *The Christian Year*, the nineteenth-century Anglican Tractarian John Keble (1792–1866) combines this dramatic transfer of allegiance on the part of 'the meek Publican' with Matthew's description of the scribe 'discipled in the kingdom of heaven' (13:52) and the traditional symbol of the evangelist as the angel:

> At once he rose, and left his gold;
> His treasure and his heart
> Transferred, where he shall safe behold
> Earth and her idols part;
> While he beside his endless store
> Shall sit, and floods unceasing pour
> Of Christ's true riches o'er all time and space,
> First angel of His Church, first steward of His Grace.
> (Keble 1885: 247)

Another way in which interpreters approach the evangelist's exemplary role is to reflect on the meaning of his name. Matthew is an abbreviated form of the name Mattatya or Mattatyahu, meaning 'gift of Yahweh' (Davies and Allison 1991: 99). Patristic and medieval exegetes sometimes start with this etymology, drawn from Jerome's *On Hebrew Names*, though they often then take a different route. The eighth-century Northumbrian monk Bede interprets the name Matthew as 'granted' and Levi as 'added.' The reason why Matthew has both names is that he was 'granted' heavenly grace, and 'added' to the band of apostles (*Homily on the Gospels* I.21; Bede the Venerable 1991: 206). *The Golden Legend* contains several etymological proposals for Matthew, in Latin *Matthaeus*. These include 'hasty gift,' 'giver of counsel,' and two which implausibly merge Latin and Greek words (*magnus*, 'great,' or *manus*, 'hand,' and *theos*, 'God'):

> Saint Matthew was a hasty gift by his speedy conversion, the giver of counsel by his salutary preaching, great unto God by the perfection of his life, and the hand of God by the writing of his gospel. (Jacobus de Voragine 1993: II/183)

Note on References in the Commentary

To avoid unnecessary repetition, references to frequently cited classic commentaries and homilies are simplified in the main text. Where reference is being made to that author's commentary on the passage in question, the name alone is cited (e.g. 'Jerome' refers to Jerome's *Commentary on Matthew* to the passage under discussion, 'Aquinas' to the relevant section of Thomas Aquinas's *Lectures on Matthew*). Edition and page number (e.g. Jerome 2008: 79) are only given when the text is being quoted directly.

Note on Biographies and Glossary

Brief biographies of many of the interpreters of Matthew discussed in this commentary, together with a glossary of less familiar terms, are provided at the end of the book.

Matthew 1

Ancient Literary Context

The evangelists each provide distinctive openings to their Gospels. Matthew's uniquely incorporates a genealogy (Luke locates his at a later point in his Gospel, Luke 3:23–38), while sharing with Luke 1–2 interest in Jesus' origins and early life. Particularly noteworthy is the punctuation of his narrative with 'formula citations' (1:23; 2:6, 15, 18, 23), explaining how the events fulfill

Matthew Through the Centuries, First Edition. Ian Boxall.

biblical prophecy. However, Matthew's opening chapters are equally rich in more subtle allusions to Hebrew Bible narratives and heroes.

Early readers are likely to have detected family resemblances with Jewish 'rewritten Bible' (compare, e.g. Josephus' *Antiquities* or Philo's *Life of Moses*), as well as biblical 'annunciation' stories (e.g. Gen 16:7–12; 17:15–16; 18:9–15; Judg 13:3–5). There are also striking parallels with the ancient motif of 'the announcement, persecution, and rescue of the "royal child"' (Luz 2007: 75). The emphasis then would be less on historicity concerning Jesus' early years, than on illuminating his person and work by recalling key figures and events of salvation history. Thus Christ is presented as another Moses, who leads his people from slavery to freedom (1:21), and as the faithful 'Son of God' who relives the experience of God's 'son' Israel (2:15; see Hos 11:1). The genealogy, of the linear, legitimating type (presenting direct paternal descent: Wilson 1975: 180–182), highlights Christ's royal ancestry and Jewish pedigree.

The Interpretations

The wide divergence between Matthew and Luke was noted by early opponents of Christianity (e.g. Porphyry: Wilken 2003: 146). However, it has often been obscured by the Christian penchant for harmonization (e.g. Tatian's *Diatessaron*; Augustine's *Agreement Among the Evangelists*). This is reflected in dramatic and liturgical reception. Thus, in the medieval Coventry Corpus Christi plays, the annunciations to Mary and Joseph are linked by an imaginary dialogue in which Joseph fears Mary's infidelity; Luke's Presentation in the Temple is slotted in between the Matthean visit of the Magi and the Slaughter of the Innocents (Block 1922). In the western Christian calendar, Luke's adoration of the shepherds on Christmas Day is followed by the appearance of the Magi 12 days later, on 6 January (Epiphany). Thus the difficulties are smoothed over by positing a longer time-frame (though not completely resolved: locating Luke's Presentation in the Temple on 2 February is hard to reconcile with Matthew's urgent Flight into Egypt following the Magi's visit).

Visual artists have sometimes been better at keeping the two Nativity narratives apart. Matthew's Adoration of the Magi is a favorite subject, from which the Lucan shepherds are regularly absent (e.g. Gentile da Fabriano, *Adoration of the Magi*, 1423; Uffizi, Florence), or present only as marginal figures (e.g. Domenico Ghirlandaio, *Adoration of the Magi*, 1485–1488; Ospedale degli Innocenti, Florence). For modern scholarship, the differences between the two Infancy Narratives is often appealed to in support of the Two-Source Theory (i.e. that Matthew and Luke independently drew upon Mark and the Sayings Source 'Q'). Q skeptics, by contrast, highlight their similarities: e.g. virginal conception; birth in Bethlehem; association of the Holy Family with Nazareth. The textual differences reflect divergent theological concerns, Luke being a 'critic of Matthew' (Franklin 1994: 353–364).

The Title (1:1)

The incipit of Matthew's Gospel reworks Mark's 'beginning of the good news of Jesus Christ the Son of God' (Mark 1:1). Recalling the first book of Moses, his is the 'book of genesis (*biblos geneseos*) of Jesus Christ,' evoking Genesis 2:4 and 5:1. *Genesis* here is ambiguous. Scholars debate whether it introduces the genealogy (1:2–17: e.g. Nolland 1996), the 'birth narrative' (Matt 1–2), the Gospel's longer prologue (1:1–4:16: Krentz 1964), or the whole Gospel (e.g. Kingsbury 1976: 9–11; Luz 2007: 69). The lack of a main verb strengthens the latter view, and *liber generationis* has often served as an alternative title for the Gospel in Latin commentators (e.g. the ninth-century Benedictine Christian of Stavelot). For the Dominican theologian Thomas Aquinas, the parallels with Genesis 5:1 ('This is the book of the generation of Adam') is a reminder that 'as in Adam all die, so also in Christ all will be made alive' (1 Cor 15:22).

Matthew's initial identification of his Gospel's protagonist neglects Jesus' divine sonship, despite Matthew's preference for the title 'Son of God' elsewhere (2:15; 3:17; 4:3, 6; 8:29; 14:33; 16:16; 17:5; 26:63; 27:40, 54; 28:19). Rather, Jesus is introduced as 'Son of David' and 'Son of Abraham' (out of chronological sequence, pointing to David's higher rank as king, according to the fifth-century *Opus Imperfectum*). This emphasis on Christ's human descent is appropriate for an evangelist symbolized by the living creature with the human face (so Jerome; see Ezek 1:5, 10; Rev 4:7).

'Son of David' emphasizes Christ's royal messianic status (e.g. 2 Sam 7:14; *Pss. Sol.* 17:21; *b. Sanh.* 97a–98a), and will recur in relation to Jesus' healing ministry (9:27; 12:23; 15:22; 20:30, 31; see Duling 1975; Heil 1993; Willitts 2007). The meaning of 'Son of Abraham' is more ambiguous. This title could emphasize Jesus' Jewish pedigree. However, many (e.g. Chromatius of Aquileia; Theophylact; Juan de Valdés) have found a reference to Abraham the 'father of many nations' (Gen 17:4–5; 22:18; Rom 4:18; Gal 3:8), prefiguring the 'Great Commission' (28:19).

Alternatively, according to the twelfth-century Benedictine exegete Rupert of Deutz, the two titles point to Christ's dual role as king (David) and priest (Abraham, recalling his sacrifice of Isaac in Gen 22; Rupert of Deutz 1979: 7). Aquinas concurs, adding that Abraham was prophet (Gen 20:7) as well as priest, while David was both prophet (Acts 2:30) and king. The Isaac connection is reflected in the 1960 lithograph series *Matthäus Evangelium* by the

German Expressionist Otto Dix, which begins with a depiction of the Akedah. Others seek a common thread linking the two names. For Jerome, David and Abraham are singled out because, alone among Christ's ancestors, promises about the Messiah were made to them (see Gen 22:18; Ps 132:11).

The Genealogy (1:2–17)

Matthew's genealogy has long impressed readers for its structural precision. It presents three sets of fourteen generations (though the last set falls short of fourteen, a point noted by Jerome, Augustine and Theophylact, as well as opponents of Christianity like Porphyry), organizing salvation history around moments of promise, disaster, and fulfillment. Each set marks a change of state for God's people. According to the *Opus imperfectum*: 'From Abraham until David they were under judges; from David to the exile they were under kings; from the exile to Christ they were under priests' (Kellerman and Oden 2010: 23).

In Christian art, the Tree of Jesse brings together Matthew's schematized royal ancestry with his emphasis upon prophetic fulfillment (Watson 1934; Taylor 1980–1981; Sawyer 1996: 74–84). Its roots lie in Tertullian's connection between Matthew's genealogy (which he regards as presenting Jesus' descent through the Virgin Mary: *De carne Christi* 20–22) and Isaiah's prophecy of the messianic branch of Jesse (Isa 11:1–2). In the Latin, Isaiah 11 reads: 'And a rod [*virga*] will emerge from the root of Jesse, and a flower [*flos*] will ascend from his root.' The resemblance of *virga* to *Virgo* led to Mary being identified with the 'rod' of Jesse, while the 'root' was David, and Christ was the 'flower.' Most Jesse Trees locate Jesse at the root of the tree, surmounted by his son David and other royal descendants, with the Virgin and her Son at the top. In the twelfth-century Jesse window at Chartres, the royal ancestors are flanked by prophets (Johnson 1961). The Jesse window in the Abbey of Saint-Denis makes the connection with Matthew explicit by including the evangelist to the left of Jesse (Watson 1934: 112–113). The popularity of the Tree of Jesse in French stained glass particularly reflects the ideology of the French monarchy, who regarded Israel's kings as their spiritual ancestors (Sawyer 1996: 79). Increasing emphasis on patrilineage sometimes leads to the figure of Mary disappearing (though this is countered by visual focus on the 'Holy Kinship,' which prioritizes the female roles of Mary's mother, Saint Anne, and her three daughters: Sheingorn 1990).

In the western liturgical tradition, Matthew's genealogy was sung at the end of Matins on Christmas Eve – with increasingly complexity of musical tone to express its solemn character – matched at the close of the Christmas season by the chanting of Luke's genealogy on the Feast of the Epiphany

(Noble 2001). This is paralleled in the Byzantine tradition on the Sunday before Christmas, the Sunday of the Holy Ancestors, where Matthew's genealogy is the Gospel lection.

Problems in the Genealogy

Yet the Matthean genealogy has also provoked bewilderment for its contradictions with the Lucan version, which traces Joseph's ancestry via David and Abraham back to Adam (Luke 3:23–38). Not only do the two family trees disagree significantly over the number of ancestors between Abraham and Joseph (40 in Matthew, 56 in Luke), there are also substantial discrepancies over their names (e.g. in Matthew the line passes through David's son Solomon, in Luke through Nathan; in Matthew, Joseph's father is Jacob, whilst in Luke he is Heli: 1:6, 16; Luke 3:23, 31).

The artificiality of Matthew's reckoning is variously explained. Jerome notes that Matthew passes over several generations between Joram and Uzziah, omitting ancestors related to Ahab and Jezebel (2 Kgs 8:18; 9:27; 10:30; 15:12). Augustine finds a non-literal explanation for the fact that, by his reckoning, there are only 40 generations in the 3 cycles between Abraham and Joseph, not 42. This symbolizes 'that painful period when we shall be under the discipline of Christ and fight the devil' (*Agreement Among the Evangelists* 2.4.9: Augustine 2014: 173), foreshadowed by the 40-day fasts of Moses and Elijah, Christ's fast in the wilderness, and the risen Lord's 40 days of appearances.

Reconciling the Genealogies

Interpreters have dealt with the contradictions with Luke's genealogy in different ways (Brown 1993: 57–95; Miller 2009). Harmonizations such as Tatian's *Diatessaron* sidestep the difficulties by omitting the genealogies entirely (*ANF* 9:43–47). One intriguing text-critical solution, represented by the fifth-century Codex Bezae (D), 'corrects' Luke's text with names drawn from Matthew's version (Ammassari 1996: 404–407).

However, the commonest explanation is that of levirate marriage, whereby the brother of a Jewish male who died without an heir was obliged to marry his widow so as to continue his lineage (Deut 25:5–10). Julius Africanus (*Letter to Aristides* in Eusebius, *H.E.* 1.7) presents Matthew as preserving the natural and Luke the legal blood-line. Africanus claims that Luke's Heli and Matthew's Jacob were half-brothers, having the same mother (Estha) but different fathers. Heli died without a child; Jacob therefore fathered Joseph in his brother's stead. Moreover, the fact that they had different fathers, Matthan according to Matthew, Melchi according to Luke (Africanus overlooks Matthat and Levi,

Luke 3:24), explains why the two genealogies trace Davidic descent through two different sons of David, Solomon, and Nathan respectively.

Africanus's solution does not solve all the problems (e.g. the presence in both genealogies of Shealtiel and Zerubbabel: see Miller 2009: 18–19). Nonetheless, the levirate explanation is followed by Eusebius, Fortunatianus of Aquileia, Jerome, and the later Augustine (*Revisions* II,16). Augustine originally held that Joseph was adopted into a different family after his father's death, with Matthew preserving the blood-line (*Agreement Among the Evangelists* 2.3.5). The levirate theory is also dominant in medieval Latin commentators (e.g. Aquinas), and a variant, whereby Matthew preserves the legal descent through Jacob, and Luke the natural through Eli, is followed by some modern commentators (see Brown 1993: 503).

A second solution attributes the divergent genealogies to the families of Joseph and Mary respectively. For Ephrem the Syrian, Matthew preserves Mary's lineage, and Luke that of Joseph (Ephrem the Syrian 1993: 55). This explanation is reversed, e.g. by the Lutheran pietist scholar Johann Albrecht Bengel (1687–1752), following a suggestion made c. 1490 by Annius of Viterbo: Matthew's genealogy contains Joseph's line, and Luke's Mary's, Joseph being figuratively the 'son of' Heli through his wife.

Other explanations are focused less on historical reconciliation than on Christology. For Origen (*Homilies on Luke* 28.3), they signify Christ's royal and prophetic roles, David's son Nathan (2 Sam 5:14; 1 Chron 3:5; 14:4) apparently being identified as Nathan the prophet (2 Sam 7:2). According to Hilary, Matthew's genealogy presents Christ as king, Luke's as priest, linking Nathan with the tribe of Levi (cf. Zech 12:12–13). As Eusebius noted, however (*Quaest. ad Stephanum* 4.1), both genealogies are Davidic. Modern critical scholarship also tends to emphasize the evangelists' theological concerns, Matthew's genealogy highlighting Jesus' messianic credentials for a primarily Jewish audience.

The Additions

The genealogy's monotonous rhythm (x was the father of y) is broken at several points (e.g. 'and his brothers,' vv. 2, 11; 'and Zerah,' v. 3; 'the king,' v. 6; 'at the time of the deportation to Babylon,' v. 11; 'the husband of Mary,' v. 16). The precise function of these additions is unclear, although the motifs of exile, forced displacement, and flight connect many of these named characters (see Myles 2013).

Some are given a typological interpretation. The reference to Judah's brothers is taken by the *Opus imperfectum* to prefigure the 12 apostles. Others are read in a fuller allegorical sense. According to Genesis 38:27–30, Zerah had a scarlet thread tied to his hand by the midwife, because he put out his hand first, but then withdrew it so that his brother Perez was born first. Thus, according to Theophylact, Zerah symbolizes the 'life in Christ' which appeared before the Law (i.e. with Abraham), and then withdrew only to re-emerge in the Christian dispensation, 'marked with the scarlet threat, that is, sealed with the blood of Christ' (Theophylact 1992: 15).

Most notable among the additions are the mothers. Surprisingly, as John Chrysostom observes, the great matriarchs of Israel's past (e.g. Sarah, Rebekah) are displaced by more marginal figures: Tamar, Rahab, Ruth, 'the wife of Uriah.' One popular explanation, found in Jerome, is that the women are sinners:

> In the Savior's genealogy it is remarkable that there is no mention of holy women, but only those whom Scripture reprehends, so that [we can understand that] he who had come for the sake of sinners, since he was born from sinful women, blots out the sins of everyone. (Jerome 2008: 59)

Jerome treats as sinners Tamar, Ruth, and Bathsheba, though overlooks Rahab (who was praised by the rabbis, and by early Christians: Str-B 1.20–23; Heb 11:31; Jas 2:25; *1 Clem.* 12.1). Modern commentators often view their sins as sexual, though this is difficult to sustain exegetically in the case of Ruth (Harrington 1991: 32). For Aquinas, by contrast, Ruth's sin was idolatry, given her Gentile origins.

Other interpretations incorporate the sinfulness of Christ's male ancestors. The sixth-century Severus of Antioch points to the 'shocking carnal relations' of Judah and David as revealing Christ's true humanity, and that he came to heal our sinful nature (Severus, *Cathedral Sermons, Homily* 94; in Simonetti 2001: 6). In more contemporary language, the twentieth-century Dominican theologian Herbert McCabe puts it thus, contrasting the Gospel message with Irish and British middle-class standards:

> The moral is too obvious to labour: Jesus did not belong to the nice clean world of Angela Macnamara or Mary Whitehouse, or to the honest, reasonable, sincere world of the *Observer* or the *Irish Times*, he belonged to a family of murderers, cheats, cowards, adulterers and liars – he belonged to *us* and came to help *us*, no wonder he came to a bad end, and gave *us* some hope. (McCabe 1991: 249)

Alternatively, the women are considered Gentiles (e.g. Luther, *Lectures on Genesis* on Gen 38:6–7). Rahab was a Cananite (Josh 2), and Ruth a Moabite (Ruth 1:4), although Scripture is ambiguous about the ethnicity of Tamar (Gen 38:6; according to *Jub* 41:1 she was an Aramean) and Bathsheba (2 Sam 11:2–3; 'the wife of Uriah' may be intended to evoke her husband's Hittite ancestry).

This Gentile interpretation allows the women to be viewed as types of the church (e.g. *Glossa ordinaria*). For the *Opus imperfectum*, the fact that Rahab the harlot received the spies of Joshua (Jesus in Greek) makes her an appropriate representative of the 'whoring' nations that accept the apostles, the 'spies' of Jesus Christ (Kellerman and Oden 2010: 9). Similarly, Theophylact of Ochrid finds the Gentile church's story prefigured in that of Ruth, taken as bride by the seed of Abraham.

Ephrem the Syrian makes a somewhat different salvation-historical point, at least with respect to Tamar and Ruth. Both acted as they did because they were farsighted enough to anticipate the coming of the Messiah from their descendants:

> Since the King was hidden in Judah, Tamar stole Him from his loins;
> Today shone forth the splendor of the beauty whose hidden form she loved.
> Ruth lay down with Boaz because she saw hidden in him the medicine of life;
> Today her vow is fulfilled since from her seed arose the Giver of all life.
> (*Hymns on the Nativity* 1:12–13; Ephrem the Syrian 1989: 65)

Further figurative interpretations focus on the mothers' names. Some of these are clearly etymological in origin. Bathsheba means 'daughter of the mighty one' (*Opus imperfectum*), appropriate for a mother who is a type of the church, married to Christ the new David and therefore the daughter of God Almighty. Christian of Stavelot notes that Tamar means 'palm tree' (*palma*): 'on account of the saints who have been born from her offspring, about whom it is written: "the just man will flourish like a palm tree"' (Christian of Stavelot 2008: 224).

Modern interpreters often posit a third possibility, that the women are linked by some irregularity in their unions, irrespective of personal culpability (Brown 1993: 73–74). According to Johann Bengel, 'Matthew mentions in this list such *women* as were connected with the race of Abraham ... by any peculiar circumstance' (Bengel 1971: 51). This strengthens the link between these four women and Mary, found to be pregnant before completion of the marriage.

Fourteen Generations (1:17)

The number 14 also provokes interest. The *Opus imperfectum* explains it as the sum of ten and four. In Greek, the letter for ten is iota, the first letter of the name Jesus. Four points to the fact that Christ is prefigured in his genealogy three times (as judge, as king, and as priest, each role associated with one set of 14 generations), with the fourth marking his coming in the flesh. Alternatively, for Thomas Aquinas, 4 represents the fourfold Gospel, and 10 the Decalogue, i.e. the Old Testament; thus 14 indicates 'that through the New and the Old Testament we come to Christ in the faith of the Trinity.'

Another solution builds on the Judeo-Christian tradition of dividing history into periods (cf. Dan 9:24–27; *1 En.* 91:11–17; 93:1–10), linked to the six days of creation followed by a Sabbath rest (Gen 1). For Augustine, Matthew's genealogy presents the middle three of seven ages of history from Adam to the End (following the periods from Adam to Noah, and from Noah to Abraham). Christians now find themselves in the sixth age of indeterminate length (Acts 1:7; Augustine, *Civ. Dei* 22.33.5; see Viviano 2009). Alternatively, the triads of 14 are recalculated as 6 sets of 7 (e.g. Clement of Alexandria, *Strom.* 1.21.147; Origen, *Hom. in Num.* 27.3), with all 6 epochs present in the historical period between Abraham and the Messiah.

Modern scholarship finds a solution in *gematria* (the practice of adding together the numerical value of a word's constitutive letters), noting that in Hebrew 14 is the number of David's name (e.g. Davies and Allison 1988: 163–164). The objection that Matthew's Greek audiences would hardly grasp the Hebrew allusion is somewhat ameliorated by a similar gematrial technique at Revelation 13:18 (where the Hebrew calculation of the name Nero Caesar explains both the number of the beast 666 and its variant 616).

The Annunciation to Joseph (1:18–25)

Whereas Luke recounts the more famous annunciation to Mary (Luke 1:26–38), Matthew focuses on Joseph. It is to the sleeping Joseph that the divine announcement is delivered, by an unnamed 'angel of the Lord' (1:20), identified as the Angel Gabriel (Luke 1:26) in the sixth- or seventh-century *History of Joseph the Carpenter*. Joseph is the key player in the events surrounding Jesus' birth in Matthew 1–2, as he names the child, takes the child and his mother to safety in Egypt, and brings them up again following Herod's death.

Following the genealogy, the story introduces a problem. The revelation that Mary is pregnant 'by the Holy Spirit' undercuts Jesus' Davidic ancestry, for the reader discovers that Joseph is not Jesus' natural father (though see the views of the Carpocratians and Cerinthus: Irenaeus, *Adv. Haer.* 1.25.1; 1 2.6.1). One solution is that Mary is also from the tribe of Judah and the family of David (e.g. Jerome; Theophylact). In support, Jerome points to the Jewish law (Num 36:8–9) that a man choose his wife from within his own tribe and lineage.

Alternatively, this annunciation story resolves the dilemma (addressing the 'parentage' of Jesus: see Cantwell 1982). Modern commentators regularly interpret Joseph's 'naming' of Jesus as legal adoption, thus bringing Jesus into the Davidic line (Davies and Allison 1988: 219). Such a reading underlies John Paul

II's 1989 Apostolic Exhortation on St. Joseph, *Redemptoris Custos*: 'In conferring the name, Joseph declares his own legal fatherhood over Jesus, and in speaking the name he proclaims the child's mission of Savior' (John Paul II, *Redemptoris Custos* 12 in Stramare 1997: 28). However, the evidence that Jews, as opposed to Romans, allowed inheritance on the basis of adoption is disputed (see e.g. Levin 2006; Bockmuehl 2011: 478–479).

Matthew's description of Joseph remains skeletal. The only clue to his character is Matthew's statement that he was 'just' or 'righteous.' We learn nothing of his age, his place of origin (though one might surmise from Matthew's narrative than he is a native of Bethlehem), or his ongoing role in the life of Jesus. Even supplementing Matthew by Luke adds little to the picture.

Joseph in Reception History

But subsequent reception has exploited these significant gaps to maximum effect, with a particular explosion of devotion to this shadowy figure in the second Christian millennium (see e.g. Filas 1962; Lienhard 1999; Chorpenning 2011; Jacobs 2016). In the earlier period, he is overshadowed by the Virgin Mary and her Son. Many early interpreters emphasize Joseph's primary role as protector of Mary's virginity. In the *Protevangelium of James* (late second century), Joseph is an elderly widower with sons from a previous marriage (one explanation of 'the brothers' of Jesus at 13:55 and parallels). He is selected as spouse for the 12-year-old Mary by the high priest, when a dove emerges from his rod and flies onto his head (*Prot. Jas.* 9). This scene, expanded in the thirteenth-century *Golden Legend* to include the budding of Joseph's rod (Jacobus de Voragine 1993: II/153), is a popular subject in Christian art (e.g. Giotto, *The Marriage of the Virgin,* 1304–1306, Scrovegni Chapel, Padua). Joseph's great age, and therefore the lack of sexual relations in the marriage, becomes more explicit in later texts. According to the *Gospel of Pseudo-Matthew* (possibly early seventh century), even Joseph's grandsons are older than Mary (*Pseudo-Matthew* 8). In the *History of Joseph the Carpenter*, Joseph is 91 when Mary is betrothed to him, and dies at the age of 111 (*History of Joseph the Carpenter* 10; 14). Echoes of this remain in the fifteenth-century *Cherry Tree Carol*: 'Joseph was an old man, and an old man was he, He married sweet Mary, the Queen of Galilee.'

Joseph's advanced age is often combined with hints of incompetence. In the *Infancy Gospel of Thomas*, his shortcomings as a carpenter (he cuts one beam shorter than the other in making a bed for a rich client) are overcome by the miracles of his foster-son Jesus (*Inf. Gos. Thos.* 13). The image of Joseph the aged cuckold, rather than Joseph the Just, recurs regularly in the western dramatic tradition. In the Coventry Corpus Christi cycle, Joseph laments his fate on returning home to find his betrothed with child:

> Alas Alas my name is shent
> aƚƚ men may me now dyspyse
> *and* seyn olde cokwold þ*i* bow is bent.
> (Block 1922: 110)

A more positive reception of Joseph can be found in the second millennium, especially in the West. Joseph the bumbling great-grandfather gives way to Joseph the super-hero, the protector of and provider for the Holy Family (the salvific role implied by the Flight into Egypt, 2:13–15). Joseph's role as 'nourisher' of Christ (*nutritius*) is emphasized in the twelfth-century treatise *Jesus at the Age of Twelve* by the English Cistercian Aelred of Rievaulx (Aelred of Rievaulx 1987: 116), and becomes enshrined in late medieval Latin liturgy, which commemorates Joseph as *nutritor Domini*, 'the Lord's guardian,' 'foster-father,' or 'provider' (see e.g. Schwartz 1975: 58–63). This role requires a more youthful, often handsome Joseph, reflected in Renaissance and early modern art: e.g. Raphael, *Marriage of the Virgin* (1504; Pinacoteca di Brera, Milan); Philippe de Champaigne, *The Dream of St. Joseph* (1642–1643; National Gallery, London). His main western feast is celebrated on 19 March (on liturgical commemoration, see e.g. Bertrand 1954; Burkey 1971; Wilson 2001: 7–9). A second feast of St. Joseph the Worker on 1 May was introduced by Pope Pius XII in 1955, apparently as a Catholic alternative to the Socialist International Workers' Day. More recently, St. Joseph's name was added to that of Mary his spouse in the Roman rite of the Mass: to Eucharistic Prayer I (the Roman Canon) by Pope John XXIII in 1962, and subsequently to Prayers II, III, and IV by Pope Francis in 2013.

For Bernard of Clairvaux (1090–1153), devotion to Joseph parallels his intense Mariology. As the protector of the Lord's human body and spouse of the Virgin, Joseph is also the church's protector and spouse:

> I tell you, he was the wise and faithful servant whom his Lord set to be the comfort of his mother and the bread-winner for his body. He was God's only and most faithful coadjutor in his great plan on earth. (*Homiliae ad laudibus Viriginis Mariae* 2:16: Saïd and Perigo 1979: 29)

Alternatively, Joseph's role as protector demands that he be a figure of intelligence. He is sometimes portrayed in typical philosopher pose, head in hand, or engaged in intellectual pursuits, as in Joos van Cleve's *The Holy Family* (1540–1541; National Gallery, London) or Gerrit van Honthorst's *St. Joseph Reading by Candlelight* (c. 1615; Convent of S. Francesco a Ripa Grande, Rome).

Joseph's Dilemma (1:19)

Matthew's description of Joseph as 'just' or 'righteous' creates tension with his decision to release Mary quietly (Bulbeck 1948; Sottocornola 1957; Sicari 1971). Is he righteous according to the Mosaic Law (so Brown 1993: 127–128)? If so, as Theophylact notes, Joseph's actions undercut his righteousness, for Moses decreed that adultery should be punished by stoning (Deut 22:21–24). Or did he presume an alternative explanation for Mary's surprising pregnancy, in which case his 'justice' relates to his compassion for his betrothed? The English poet W.H. Auden relocates this dilemma to a modern setting in his 'The Temptation of St. Joseph,' part of his 1942 Christmas Oratorio *For the Time Being* (Auden 1991: 362–368).

For Justin Martyr (followed by Ambrose, Augustine, and Peter Chrysologus), Joseph assumes Mary to be pregnant through 'fornication' (Justin, *Trypho* 78). Thus the angelic appearance reveals to him the true cause of Mary's conception. His desire to divorce Mary 'informally' is a reflection of his goodness, which mitigates his strict observance of the Mosaic Law. A similar characterization of Joseph is given by the Anglican scholar Henry Hammond: it indicates that Joseph is a 'merciful pious man' (Hammond 1845: 3). According to Pseudo-Bonaventure's *Meditations on the Life of Christ*, this misapprehension about Mary's pregnancy provoked in Joseph considerable anguish, though he 'virtuously restrained himself from accusing her, patiently disregarding the injury and not seeking revenge; but overcome by pity he wished to leave her secretly' (*Meditations* 6; Ragusa and Green 1961: 27–29).

In the late medieval Chester Mystery Plays, performed in the days after Pentecost, Joseph's advanced age is used to explain Mary's presumed infidelity:

> Three months she hath been from me
> And now she has gotten, as I see,
> A great belly for her fee
> Since she went away.
> And mine it is not, I make so bold
> For I am both old and cold;
> This thirsty winter though I would
> I have played no such play.
>
> (Hussey 1975: 43–44)

A second explanation emphasizes Joseph's suspension of judgment. In the *Protevangelium of James*, Joseph is unsure whether Mary has committed adultery or the child she is carrying is 'from the angels' (*Prot. Jas.* 14; Elliott 1993: 62).

The *Opus imperfectum* imagines Joseph's internal wrestling which exemplifies his character as a 'just man':

> What therefore am I to do? I will send her away secretly because in an uncertain matter it is better that an adulteress should escape than an innocent woman die. (Kellerman and Oden 2010: 15)

Alternatively, Joseph had some knowledge of Mary's special status prior to the annunciation (Sicari 1971; e.g. *Glossa ordinaria*). Matthew's statement at 1:18 that Mary 'was found' to be with child by the Holy Spirit is understood to mean that Joseph so 'found' her, and therefore knew the charge of adultery to be false (Theophylact; also e.g. Eusebius, *Quaest. ad Stephanum* 1.6; a modern example is Cantwell 1982). The angel's message then assuages Joseph's 'fear' to touch the woman who has been made holy by God (Luz 2007: 94).

Joseph's Dream

Revelation by dream is well-attested in the Jewish tradition, although more regularly linked to miraculous births in Egyptian, Greek, and Roman mythology (Mussies 1990; a notable exception is the father of Moses: Josephus, *Ant.* 2.210–18). In Matthew, the Gentile Magi and Pilate's wife share this privilege with the Jewish Joseph (2:12; 27:19).

Modern commentators often draw parallels between the dreaming Joseph and his Old Testament namesake, a connection already made by Bernard of Clairvaux, who cites their chastity, their journey to Egypt, and their dreams (Saïd and Perigo 1979: 28–29; see also Haimo of Auxerre, *Hom.* 12; Lapide). However, this connection is rarely made by patristic commentators, for whom a Joseph–Christ typology dominates (e.g. Justin, *Trypho* 36; Tertullian, *Adv. Marc.* 3:18; Ambrose, *De Patriarcha Joseph* 14; see Argyle 1956). Both Joseph and Jesus suffer rejection by those called their 'brothers,' and are handed over at the instigation of Judah/Judas (Gen 37:18–20, 26; Matt 12:49; 26:47–56); both go down into Egypt (Gen 37:28; Matt 2:13–15). If there is an Old Testament prefigurement of the New Testament Joseph, it is found in Jacob's dream at Bethel (Gen 28:10–19; see Origen, *Adnotationes in Genesim* 37.10; Rabanus Maurus).

Alternatively, Joseph the dreamer functions as exemplar. The Carmelite Jerónimo Gracían de la Madre de Dios, in his 1597 *Summary of the Excellencies of St. Joseph, Husband of the Virgin Mary*, interprets Joseph's sleep as the sleep of contemplation: his habitual state, 'contemplation in action' as advocated by Gracían's associate Teresa of Avila (Chorpenning 2011: 121).

A Virgin Shall Conceive (1:22–23)

The angelic message is accompanied by the first of Matthew's formula citations, from Isaiah 7:14. It is quoted in the LXX version, which translates the Hebrew *almah* (young woman) as *parthenos* (virgin). The original purpose of the formula citations was probably to teach early Christian audiences about the continuity between Christ and the Hebrew Scriptures (so Brown 1993: 97–99). Nonetheless, they soon come to be used apologetically, both in Christian debates with Jews (Justin, *Trypho* 84; for the charge that Mary conceived Jesus by a Roman soldier, Panthera, see Origen, *Cels.* 1.32) and in defending Christianity against charges of borrowing from pagan myths. For Justin, Isaiah 7:14 signifies that 'a virgin should conceive without intercourse', thus ruling out parallels being draw with pagan parallels such as those associated with Jupiter who 'went in to women through lust'" (Justin, *1 Apol.* 33; *ANF* 1:174).

The title Emmanuel does not occur again in Matthew's narrative. However, it forms the first part of an *inclusio* bracketing the whole Gospel, completed by Jesus' final words 'I am with you always …' (28:20), a connection already known to Thomas Aquinas. Aquinas, believing that Matthew wrote in Hebrew, presumes that the translation 'God-with-us' was provided by the Greek translator.

Until She Bore a Son (1:25)

For the fourth-century Christian author Helvidius, 1:25 is evidence that Joseph and Mary had sexual relations after Christ's birth, a view vehemently opposed by Jerome, keen to promote the virtues of virginity above marriage (Jerome, *Against Helvidius*). Jerome's critique is two-pronged. First, he points out the ambiguity of the verb 'know,' which could refer to intellectual knowledge. This interpretation is followed by the *Opus imperfectum*, which rejects the view that Joseph would have dared take possession of the one he now knew to be God's temple. Second, Jerome refutes the argument that 'until' (Greek *heōs*) implies a change after the event (support can be found from Matthew's Gospel itself: 5:25; 16:28; 28:20; but cf. 2:9, 13; 5:26). Remigius, ninth-century monk of Auxerre, comes to the same position by a different route: he interprets Mary and Joseph's 'coming together' in verse 18 as a reference to their nuptial rites (Remigius in Aquinas 1995: 44).

Jerome's view of Mary's perpetual virginity is widely accepted by the Fathers. Chromatius of Aquileia (d. c. 407) notes a parallel with her namesake, Moses' sister Miriam who 'remained a virgin unsullied by man' after beholding the Lord's glory (Chromatius, *Tractate on Matthew* 3.1: Simonetti 2001: 19; also e.g. Chrysostom; Ambrose, *Concerning Virgins* 2.2; Augustine, *Sermon* 186; see Beattie 2007). This view is remarkably resilient until the modern period, being accepted by Luther, Calvin (who called Helvidius 'ignorant'), and Zwingli (despite its lack of direct attestation in scripture: MacCulloch 2004: 191–217; Williams 2007b: 317), Thomas Cranmer and Hugh Latimer (Williams 2007a: 250–251), and John Wesley (e.g. his 1749 *Letter to a Roman Catholic* 7).

Jerome also promotes belief in Joseph's virginity to parallel Mary's perpetual virginity:

> You can say that Mary did not remain a virgin; as for me, I claim more emphatically that Joseph himself was also a virgin through Mary (*per Mariam*), so that a virgin son might be born of a virgin wedlock. For if fornication ill befits a holy man, and it is not written down that he had a second wife, but was the guardian rather than the husband of Mary whom he supposedly possessed as his own, the conclusion follows that he, who was deemed worthy to be called the father of the Lord, remains a virgin with Mary. (Jerome, *Against Helvidius* 19; Jerome 1965: 38–39)

This motif will re-emerge in later Catholic devotion to Joseph, as in the writings of Jean Gerson, chancellor of the University of Paris in the late fourteenth century. Gerson presents Joseph as young and celibate, the ideal model for priests (McGuire 2011).

Matthew 2

Ancient Literary Context

This second chapter again reflects Matthew's distinctive infancy traditions, which fill in the gaps left by Mark's silence about Jesus' birth and upbringing. In contrast to Luke's humble shepherds, Matthew has the infant Christ being adored by oriental Magi (2:1–12). The wider narrative, in which Herod the Great (37–4 BCE) is cast in the role of duplicitous ruler and fierce persecutor, a second Pharaoh, prefigures Matthew's passion story. The motif of threat is

Matthew Through the Centuries, First Edition. Ian Boxall.

prominent: the flight of the holy family into Egypt and their subsequent return after Herod's death, framing a tragic story of a massacre of children (2:13–23). Early Christian audiences would probably have recalled the biblical narratives of Balaam (the star, Num 22–24) and Moses (Exod 1–2, with Herod as another Pharaoh), as well as contemporary embellishments of the Moses story (e.g. Pseudo-Philo, *Biblical Antiquities* 9.9–15; Josephus, *Ant.* 2.205–37). Further scriptural interest is provided by additional 'formula quotations,' of which there is a particular concentration in this chapter (2:15, 18, 23; cf. 2:5).

The Interpretations

The Magi (2:1–12)

The significant gaps in Matthew's story have given the Magi a particularly rich reception history, even greater than that of Joseph (e.g. Marsh-Edwards 1956; Schulze 1975; Trexler 1997; Witakowski 1999, 2008; Hegedus 2003; O'Kane 2005; Luz 2007: 106–111; Landau 2008, 2010). Interpreters are faced with ambiguity about the Magi's origins, identity, number, and the purpose of their unusual gifts. As the Dominican friar Giordano da Rivolto observed in a sermon for the Epiphany preached in Florence in 1305:

> The Fathers had many questions to ask about these Magi. They wanted to know what motivated the Magi to come on their journey, who these Magi were and where they came from, what was their status, and how many of them there were, and how long their journey had taken them. (in Lubbock 2006: 8)

The question of their role – whether magicians, kings, ambassadors, or wise men – is regularly connected to their place of origin. The original Magi were Persian priests (Herodotus, *Hist.* 1.101.132), and the Persian provenance of Matthew's Magi is often assumed (e.g. Fortunatianus of Aquileia; Jacob of Edessa; *Maronite Chronicle* 55; Theophylact; *Glossa ordinaria*). Indeed, it has some historical plausibility at the story level, given that the Parthians/Persians were a challenge to Roman dominance, and thus their appearance in Jerusalem would explain Herod's concern. The Flemish Jesuit Cornelius a Lapide (1567–1637) rejects their Persian provenance, given the distance between Persia and Bethlehem (he presupposes the tradition that the Magi arrived on the Feast of the Epiphany, 13 days from the birth).

The Persian interpretation is reflected in early Christian art, where the Magi often wear the distinctive Phrygian cap, e.g. the fifth-century door panels at Santa Sabina, Rome, and the sixth-century mosaic in Sant' Apollinare Nuovo,

Ravenna (Figure 2). The *Arabic Gospel of the Infancy* 7 even claims that their arrival in Jerusalem had been predicted by Zeraduscht (i.e. the Persian prophet Zarathustra or Zoroaster).

A less positive view is that they are workers of magic or astrologers, perhaps Chaldaeans (for negative connotations of *magos*, see Acts 8:9; 13:6, 8; LXX Dan 2:2, 10; Philo, *Life of Moses* 1.92, 276). Ignatius of Antioch regards the Magi's star as heralding the defeat of magic and ignorance: 'Hence every kind of magic was destroyed, and every bond of wickedness disappeared; ignorance was removed, and the old kingdom abolished' (Ign., *Eph.* 19:3; *ANF* 1:57). Similarly, Justin Martyr sees them as being delivered from demonic powers through the worship of Christ (*Trypho* 78). Peter Chrysologus describes their transformation from 'standard-bearers of the devil' into Christ's 'most faithful servants' (*Sermons* 150.9: Simonetti 2001: 32). John Milton (1608–1674) calls them 'Star-led Wizards' (Milton, 'On the Morning of Christ's Nativity,' line 23; Buhler 1997: 44), while his contemporary Henry Hammond (1605–1660) describes them, more sympathetically, as 'the Chaldean or Arabian astronomers' (Hammond 1845: 4).

FIGURE 2 *The Three Magi on Their Way*. Sixth century. Mosaic. Sant' Apollinare Nuovo, Ravenna. Source: Photo Erich Lessing/Art Resource, NY.

A third option (partially hinted at in Hammond's Arabian suggestion) is that the Magi come from the south, and are kings in their own right. Such a view arises from reading Matthew's story intertextually with Psalm 72:10b–11 ('may the kings of Sheba and Seba bring gifts. May all kings fall down before him, all nations give him service,' NRSV), and taking such intertextual connections to imply identification (Powell 2000a: 471). The exegetical justification for this lies in Matthew's description of the Magi worshipping the infant Christ as they offer him gifts (2:11). The connection is further strengthened by Isaiah 60:6, which prophesies that, among the Gentiles participating in the eschatological pilgrimage to Jerusalem will be pilgrims from Sheba, bringing gold and frankincense. Tertullian notes that the Magi were often regarded 'almost' (*ferē*) as kings in the East (*Adv. Marc.* 3.13), while Caesarius of Arles explicitly calls them 'the three kings' in the early sixth century (*Sermon* 139).

Their legendary character could support a more mythical provenance. In the Syriac *Revelation of the Magi*, they are 12 wise kings belonging to 'an ancient mystical order' and descended from Adam's son Seth, who come from the land of Shir located in the East on the shore of the Great Ocean (*Revelation of the Magi* 2; Landau 2010: 7; for Shir as China, see Witakowski 2008: 811). Their number allowed them to prefigure the 12 apostles and their successors, the bishops, thus proving useful in the church's de-legitimatization of secular powers (who might otherwise claim the Magi-kings for themselves). A similar assertion of ecclesiastical over secular authority is found in the triumphal arch in Santa Maria Maggiore, Rome (commissioned by Pope Sixtus III in the early fifth century: Trexler 1997: 30). By contrast, rulers often use the Magi cult to claim their royal, magian power over the church, though even this is undercut, or parodied, by more popular festivities in which the poor or children play the kings (see Trexler 1997: 170–185; Luz 2007: 111).

Eventually, their number comes to be fixed at three (*Pseudo-Matthew* 16), a deduction from the number of gifts (according to John Calvin, a 'childish error' of the papists: Calvin 1949: 1/128). The *Syriac History of the Blessed Virgin Mary* combines both traditions, by having the three Magi-kings accompanied by a retinue of nine (Witakowski 2008: 820). The Magi also gain names and individuality. Most popular in the West are Caspar (Gaspar or Jaspar), Melchior, and Balthazar. Ephrem the Syrian knows them as Hormizdadh, king of Persia, Yazdegerd, king of Saba, and Perozadh, king of Sheba (see also *Cave of Treasures*), while the Syrian *Book of Adam and Eve* has the names Hor, Basantor, and Karsudas (Marsh-Edwards 1956: 6). They also come to represent different ages (youth, maturity, and old age) and races, as descendants of all *three* sons of Noah (Gen 6:10; O'Kane 2005: 355). In the fourteenth-century collection of traditions about the Magi produced by the Carmelite John of Hildesheim, they are rulers of different Indian kingdoms, prompted by local astronomers to follow the star: Melchior king of Nubia and Arabia; Balthasar, ruler of the kingdoms of Godolia and Saba; Jaspar, a black Ethiopian (cf. Ps 68:32), king of Tharsis and its isles (John of Hildesheim 1955: 10–13). More commonly, the triad of Magi signify the three known continents (Asia, Europe, and Africa, a point made in the early ninth-century commentary of Pseudo-Bede = PL 92:13), though explorations of the New World would lead some to posit four Magi as a better symbol of Christ's universal reign. By the seventeenth century, one of the Magi is a Native American ruler (Trexler 1997: 140).

The kingly interpretation undergoes critique in the early modern period, especially from the Reformers. John Calvin calls it 'the most ridiculous contrivance of the Papists' (Calvin 1949: 1/129). Even the Jesuit exegete Juan de Maldonado acknowledges that their kingly status is only 'a probable opinion,' and not 'a certain article of the Catholic faith' (Maldonado 1888: 1/50). A popular sixteenth-century alternative, that the Magi are wise men, is anticipated in Pseudo-Bede, who claims that they are named not for their magical arts but on account of philosophy (PL 92:12), and by the Irish exegete Frigulus, for whom the Magi represent 'the three sciences of physics, ethics and logic' (Kealy 1997: 1/110). For Erasmus, the Magi are 'those recognized for the public profession of philosophy' (Erasmus 2008: 48), a view reflected in Luther's 1522 translation of the New Testament ('*die weysen*'), the statement of the Spanish humanist scholar Juan de Valdés (c. 1490–1541) 'that "magi" is the same as learned men' (Valdés 1882: 22), and the preference for 'wise men' in English translations from Tyndale onwards (the 1582 Catholic Rheims New Testament has 'sages'; Eugene Peterson's 2002 *The Message* opts for 'a band of scholars'). Treating the Magi as scholars – philosophers, astronomers, scientists – had become popular during the Renaissance, paralleling its own quest for learning. But the royal and scholarly interpretation of the Magi were not necessarily mutually exclusive. Preaching before King James I at Whitehall in 1620, Bishop Lancelot Andrewes (1555–1626) describes them as both 'Great Persons' and 'Wise Men' (Andrewes 1632: 130), a reference in part to the king's own scholarly reputation, in part to the Anglican church's university-trained clergy (Buhler 1997: 50).

Such traditions may be imaginatively far removed from Matthew's text and the expected readings of implied readers, for whom Magi would have been perceived as socially ambiguous royal servants rather than kings, and 'fools' rather than 'wise' (see e.g. Powell 2000a, 2000b). Nonetheless, they preserve a fundamental element of that text: namely, that the adoration of the Magi signifies the worship of the Gentiles (Isa 60:6), just as Luke's shepherds symbolize the Jews (e.g. Fulgentius; Augustine; see Brown 1999: 86–92). As the audiences of Matthew shift from a primarily Christian-Jewish minority to a predominantly Gentile-Christian majority, this dimension, and the appeal of the Magi, will become more prominent. It requires just a small step to view these Gentile worshippers as symbolizing the whole church, gathered from among the Gentiles (Pseudo-Bonaventure, *Meditations* 9).

Following the Star (2:2, 9)

Balaam's prophecy of the star arising from Jacob (Num 24:17) was an important messianic text (e.g. 4Q175; CD 7:19–20; cf. *Targum Onkelos* on Num 24:17; Rev 22:16). Although Matthew does not quote it explicitly, several interpreters make that connection (e.g. Justin, *Trypho* 106.4; Irenaeus, *Adv. Haer.* 3.9.2), even to the extent of presenting the Magi as spiritual heirs to Balaam who had personally discovered his oracle (e.g. Eusebius, *Dem. Ev.* 9.1; Origen, *Cels.* 1.60; Theophylact; Romanos the Melodist, *Kontakion on the Nativity of Christ* 5; Nicholas of Lyra; Erasmus; Lancelot Andrewes, 1622 *Nativity Sermon*). As Mary puts it in the medieval York Cycle of mystery plays:

> For Balaam told full long before
> How that a star should rise full high,
> And of a maiden should be born
> A son that shall our saving be
> from cares keen.
> (Mooney 1915: 34)

Balaam sometimes appears in scenes of the adoration of the Magi in early Christian art, pointing to his star overhead (Hegedus 2006: 214).

Christian commentators note the unusual, supernatural character of the star of Bethlehem, 'specially created for the service of Christ' (Aquinas 2013a: 55). In the *Protevangelium of James*, the Magi themselves comment on its unprecedented size: 'We saw how an indescribably greater star shone among these stars and dimmed them, so that the stars no longer shone; and so we knew that a king was born for Israel' (*Prot. Jas.* 21:2; Elliott 1993: 65). According to the *Revelation of the Magi*, this star had originally shone over the tree of life in Eden, and its reappearance had been prophesied by Adam's son Seth (Landau 2010: 8–9).

The star's ability to descend over a specific house in Bethlehem (2:9), and to shine during the day as well as the night, leads many to conclude that it was no mere astronomical phenomenon. As Theophylact of Ochrid puts it: 'When you hear "star," do not think that it was a star such as we see, but a divine and angelic power that appeared in the form of a star' (Theophylact 1992: 24). In the *Arabic Gospel of the Infancy* 7, the star is an angel who will also lead the Magi back home. Ephrem's reading through the interpretative lens of John's Prologue (following Tatian's *Diatessaron*) leads him to connect the star with the 'true light' which was coming into the world, a hypostasized agent of the Word (Crawford 2015; on angels and stars, see also Hegedus 2003: 94–95; Allison 2005: 17–41).

Similarly, the *Revelation of the Magi* identifies the star with Christ himself, who appears in different guises to each of the Magi: as an infant, a youth, a humble human being, crucified, descending to Sheol, and ascending (*Revelation of the Magi* 14). The *Opus imperfectum* and *The Golden Legend* emphasize one particular manifestation of the star, 'appearing as a small body and having the image of the cross above itself' (Kellerman and Oden 2010: 32). This motif is popular in art, such as Rogier van der Weyden's *Bladelin Altarpiece* (1445–1450; Staatliche Museen, Berlin).

More recent interpretations, by contrast, often impose modern astronomical presuppositions onto the ancient narrative (see Kidger 1999; Molnar 1999), overlooking the fact that the astronomer Johannes Kepler held it to be 'a special miracle' (in Molnar 1999: 24). Some propose that the star of Bethlehem was a comet (e.g. Humphreys 1991), a possibility already anticipated by Giotto in his 'Adoration of the Magi' fresco in the Scrovegni Chapel, Padua (1302–1304). It is possible that Giotto has depicted Halley's Comet which appeared in 1301 (Kidger 1999: 82–84; though see Hughes, Yau, and Stephenson 1993). However, ancient Romans tended to regard comets as presaging disaster, rather than the birth of a new ruler (Molnar 1999: 17).

A second option, as in Arthur C. Clarke's 1955 short story 'The Star,' is a supernova, a 'new star' (now understood by astronomers as a dying star) which appears suddenly and lasts for weeks or months (Clark, Parkinson, and Stephenson 1977). Such a view had been anticipated, e.g. by Origen, who also speaks of the star of Bethlehem as a 'new star' (Origen, *Contra Celsum* 1.58). A third proposal explains the star as the result of a conjunction of planets (e.g. the conjunction of Jupiter and Saturn in 7/6 BCE: in Luz 2007: 105), on the grounds that the Greeks often called a planet a 'star' (*astēr*). Kidger argues for a complex combination of events between 7 and 5 BCE: a triple conjunction of Jupiter and Saturn in Pisces (the constellation associated with the Jews), a massing of planets in Pisces, a pairing of Jupiter and the Moon, and of Mars and Saturn in Pisces, the appearance of a nova (Kidger 1999).

The star also fulfills a symbolic function. For Hilary, it symbolizes the forthcoming profession of faith by the pagans. Thomas Aquinas explains how this is so, by referencing God's promise to Abraham that his descendants would be as numerous as the stars (Gen 15:5). The martyred El Salvadorean archbishop Óscar Romero (1917–1980) also treats it as a metaphor of faith: 'As the magi from the East followed their star and found Jesus, let us too, … not fail to follow that star, the star of our faith' (Romero 2003: 41).

The Adoration of the Magi (2:10–11)

The brief reference to the Magi prostrating themselves before the Christ child has particularly fired the human imagination. The adoration of the Magi is one of the earliest Christian motifs to be depicted visually (e.g. Catacomb of St. Priscilla, Rome). The scene is also found on early Christian sarcophagi, where the (wealthy) deceased are depicted offering their own gifts (Trexler 1997: 24–25). Their royal status and representative role means that they are increasingly envisaged as having a large entourage (cf. Isa 60:3, 6), traveling 'with mules and camels and horses loaded with treasure and with a great multitude of people in the best array that was possible for them' (John of Hildesheim 1955: 13).

In visual representations, the multitude often includes the patrons and their families. In Benozzo Gozzoli's 1459 frescoes in the Medici Chapel of the Magi, Florence, Piero and Cosimo de' Medici can be identified behind Caspar, whose horse is decorated with the Medici coat of arms (Luchinat 1994: 43). The vast accompanying throng in the *Adoration of the Magi* by Fra Angelico and Fra Filippo Lippi (c. 1440/1460; Figure 3) may be modeled on Florence's annual procession in honor of the three kings, in which the adoration was 'actualized' among the Florentine populace, and in which the Medici played a prominent role (Boskovits and Brown 2003: 21–30; Sale 2007).

The Florentine procession is one relatively late example of a widespread practice of dramatic re-enactment. In medieval Besançon in France, for example, three clergy dressed as the kings joined the Gospel procession, accompanied by attendants carrying gifts, after the reading of Matthew's narrative. They would then deposit their gifts and crowns at the high altar (Young 1933: II/37–42).

The significance attached to the Magi's gifts (see Exod 23:34; Isa 60:6; Song of Songs 3:6) by Irenaeus becomes widely accepted: '*myrrh,* because it was He who should die and be buried for the mortal human race; *gold,* because He was a King; and *frankincense,* because He was God ...' (Irenaeus, *Adv. Haer.* 3.9.2; *ANF* 1:423). This interpretation has been popularized in Christian poetry (e.g. Juvencus, *Poem on the Gospels* 1.250–251) and hymnody, most famously in the English translation by Edward Caswall (1814–1878) of Prudentius' fourth-century hymn *O sola magnarum urbium*:

> Solemn things of mystic meaning:
> incense doth the God disclose,
> gold a royal child proclaimeth,
> myrrh a future tomb foreshows.

FIGURE 3 Fra Angelico (c. 1395–1455) and Fra Filippo Lippi (c. 1406–1469). *The Adoration of the Magi*. c. 1440–1460. Tempera on poplar panel, diameter 1373 mm. Samuel H. Kress Collection, National Gallery of Art, Washington, DC. Source: Photo courtesy National Gallery of Art, Washington.

The same interpretation is found in the popular carol 'We Three Kings of Orient Are' written by John Henry Hopkins Jr. in 1857: gold is 'to crown Him again,' incense 'owns a Deity nigh,' and myrrh's 'bitter perfume | Breaths a life of gathering gloom.' It also appears in Franco Zeffirelli's 1977 film *Jesus of Nazareth*: Balthazar presents incense 'to perfume the halls of the mighty,' Gaspar interprets gold 'for kingly rule,' while Melchior hints at the passion when he describes myrrh as the 'most precious herb of the east … and the most bitter' (in Kreitzer 2002: 35–36). Anselm of Canterbury (c. 1033–1109) deduces from this symbolism that the Magi presented all three gifts together rather than offering one each, since Christian faith requires acknowledging Christ's kingship, divinity, and humanity simultaneously (Anselm in Ford 1859: 25).

The Assyrian Isho'dad of Merv provides additional interpretations. Gold signifies Christ's purity as well as his kingship; myrrh his role as healing physician, and 'the preciseness and difficulty of His commandments'; frankincense, being a 'mixed substance,' symbolizes both his divinity and humanity (Isho'dad of Merv 1911: 20). The Syriac tradition frequently links the myrrh to Christ's identity as doctor (e.g. *Cave of Treasures*; *Teaching of Addai*: Witakowski 2008: 815). Maximus of Turin also finds the frankincense appropriate to Christ's role as high priest (Maximus of Turin, *Hom*. 21; PL 57:270). By contrast, Bernard of Clairvaux provides a more mundane, literal interpretation (rejected by Lapide as 'undignified'): gold 'to succour their poverty, myrrh to strengthen Christ's infant limbs, frankincense to prevent the unpleasant odors of the stable' (Lapide 1890: 1/67).

According to John of Hildesheim, gold, frankincense, and myrrh were only some of the vast array of gifts brought by the kings (a plausible reading of 2:11), which comprised 'all the ornaments that Alexander of Macedonia left in India and Chaldea and Persia and all the ornaments that the Queen of Saba offered in Solomon's temple.' Each king brought a gift appropriate to his own kingdom, thus acknowledging Christ's universal reign: Melchior Arabian gold; Balthasar Sabian incense; Jaspar myrrh from the isles of Tharsis (John of Hildesheim 1955: 12, 23). The *Revelation of the Magi* claims that these gifts had been deposited by the Magi's ancestors in the Cave of Treasures of Hidden Mysteries (*Revelation of the Magi* 16:2; by Adam, according to Isho'dad of Merv). In some eastern traditions, the Magi offered three gifts in order to classify the child by the gift he chose, not at all expecting that he would take all three (Monneret de Villard 1952: 70, 90).

The costly nature of the gifts is sometimes viewed as inappropriate for the poverty of the child of Bethlehem. In Pseudo-Bonaventure, reflecting the Franciscan attitude to worldly riches, Mary gives away the valuable gifts to the poor (*Meditations* 10). Alternatively, according to Henry Hammond, the gift of gold comes at just the right time, to defray the substantial costs of the journey to Egypt. In the *Arabic Gospel of the Infancy* 7–8, the Magi also receive a gift from Mary, anticipating the salvation her son will bring: one of Christ's swaddling-bands, which becomes a prized possession in their own country after it is thrown into a fire but not consumed.

Returning by a Different Way (2:12)

The Magi disappear as suddenly as they arrived, returning to their own country 'by another way.' While Matthew's primary concern is geographical, his statement is often given a figurative interpretation, with a moral application. For Hilary, the Magi's circuitous return route provides a warning against reliance on the Law as opposed to its fulfillment in Christ: 'we are admonished to refrain from following the "route" of our former life by placing all our salvation and hope in Christ' (Hilary of Poitiers 2012: 46). Gregory the Great finds an allegory of his Christian audience's return to its own country, paradise. Humanity left paradise due to pride, disobedience, and the pursuit of what is visible. Knowing Jesus, it cannot return by the same route, but must travel the path of repentance: 'And so we return to our country by another way: pleasure led us away from the joys of paradise, sorrows summon us to return' (Gregory the Great 1990: 59).

There is much speculation concerning their subsequent story. In the Syriac *Revelation of the Magi*, they perform a 'missionary role' in telling their own people about the star-child who remains present with them, even before their baptism by an apostle, St. Thomas (a possible addition to the text to make it more orthodox: Landau 2010: 12–13). Their transformation from non-Christian worshippers of the true God (probably Zoroastrians) to fully fledged Christian figures is complete by the time of John of Hildesheim, who speaks of Thomas subsequently consecrating them as archbishops (John of Hildesheim 1955: 41). The sense of dislocation from their former world caused by their encounter with Christ is well expressed by T.S. Eliot in his *Journey of the Magi*, published two months before his own decision to be baptized (see Kreitzer 2002: 26–31; Birns 2008):

> We returned to our places, these Kingdoms,
> But no longer at ease here, in the old dispensation,
> With an alien people clutching their gods.
>
> (Eliot 1965: 101)

Eliot's poem takes as its starting-point a sermon on the Nativity by Bishop Lancelot Andrewes, preached before King James I on Christmas Day 1622. Andrewes's original sermon challenges his wealthy, establishment congregation to embrace the more demanding journey undertaken by the Magi.

The end of the Magi's earthly journey is also of interest. In Western medieval tradition, the three kings died within days of each other, having witnessed the reappearance of the star, and were buried in a shared tomb. Their bodies were only separated years later, and taken to their own countries, where they were rediscovered by the Empress Helena and brought to Constantinople (John of Hildesheim 1955: 44–51). The relics were subsequently transferred to Milan at the request of Archbishop Eustorgius (c. 344), where they remained until they were transferred to Cologne Cathedral in 1164. Their shrine in Cologne remains a place of pilgrimage to this day. An alternative tradition is attested by Marco Polo, who claimed to have seen the bodies of the Magi, intact with hair and beards, in the city of Saba in Persia (Williams Jackson 1905).

The Flight into Egypt (2:13–15)

Matthew recounts the flight of the holy family to Egypt in bare outline only, emphasizing how 'the plan and hand of God stand over Jesus' destiny' (Luz 2007: 120), paralleling Jewish traditions about the birth of Moses, Israel-Jacob's journey to Egypt, and Israel's return at the Exodus (see Soares-Prabhu 1992). The latter connection is made explicit by the formula citation from Hosea, originally referring to the Exodus: 'Out of Egypt I have called my son' (2:15, citing Hos 11:1, in a form closer to the Hebrew than the LXX, as Jerome noted). There are also pagan parallels to Jesus' fugitive status: e.g. Odysseus, Aeneas, and Romulus and Remus (O'Kane 2002: 16).

The brevity of Matthew's narrative presents multiple gaps: the route taken, mode of transport (generally a donkey or ass) and journey's length, as well as the final destination and duration of the sojourn. The *Gospel of Pseudo-Matthew*, *Arabic Gospel of the Infancy*, and *The Golden Legend* supply many of the missing details. Unsurprisingly, the Coptic Orthodox Church has its own distinctive traditions, identifying specific locations visited by the Holy Family (e.g. Farid 1965; Meinardus 1986; Cowan 2013; Good 2013; Nicklas 2016).

The journey itself is provoked by persecution. Joseph is told in another dream to 'flee' (v. 13); he takes the child and his mother 'by night' (v. 14, a possible allusion to the Exodus: Soares-Prabhu 1992: 236–240; *Arabic Gospel of the Infancy* 9 specifies 'towards cockcrow') and 'withdrew' (a verb which Matthew associates with escape from danger, leading to prophetic fulfillment: e.g. 2:12, 22; 4:12; 12:15; see Good 1990). For Theophylact, this very human drama confirms Christ's humanity. Yet underlying Matthew's narrative is the protecting hand of providence, as well as the memory of Egypt as a place of refuge for Jews (e.g. 1 Kgs 11:17, 40; 2 Kgs 25:26; Jer 26:20–23; 41:16–18; 43:5–7; Josephus, *Ant.* 12.387–388; 14:21, 374; 15:42–49; *War* 7.410: Luz 2007: 120, n. 22). In the *Gospel of Pseudo-Matthew* 20, the divine Christ ensures the survival of the Holy Family, causing a palm-tree to bend down so that the starving Mary can eat some of its dates, and a spring of water to emerge miraculously from its roots (*Pseudo-Matthew* 20). The same motif is present in the legends of Christ being worshipped by dragons, lions, and panthers (*Pseudo-Matthew* 18–19, 35). Coptic tradition has an alternative story about a sycamore tree near Heliopolis, which miraculously opens to conceal Mary and the child from Herod's troops (a variation has a spider spin a web to hide them from view: Farid 1965: 75–76).

The date palm story from *Pseudo-Matthew* inspired a popular motif in northern European art. In *The Rest on the Flight into Egypt* by the Flemish artist Gerard David (c. 1510; Figure 4), the palm-tree has become a chestnut more appropriate to David's northern European context, from which Joseph is extracting nuts (the Christ child has already supplied his mother with a bunch of grapes, perhaps symbolizing the Eucharist). Joseph's action reflects the greater prominence given him as *nutritor Domini* (see Schwartz 1975; Mundy 1981/1982; Hand and Wolff 1986: 63–67; for the Rest motif in Scandinavian folk art, see Bringéus 2003).

The preferred route of the journey ('by the way of the desert' rather than the quicker coastal route, *Pseudo-Matthew* 17) recalls Israel's Exodus journey which Christ recapitulates. Alternatively, as for John Chrysostom, it parallels the journey of the patriarch Jacob (Gen 45–46). Moreover, their fugitive status also has a tropological dimension, as Chrysostom reminds his congregation in Antioch:

> Instead you may keep in mind the long-suffering example of the mother of the Child, bearing all things nobly, knowing that such a fugitive life is consistent with the ordering of spiritual things. You are sharing the kind of labor Mary herself shared. (*Homily on Matthew* 8.2; Simonetti 2001: 31)

FIGURE 4 Gerard David (c. 1460–1523). *The Rest on the Flight into Egypt*. c. 1510. Oil on panel, 419 × 422 mm. Andrew W. Mellon Collection, National Gallery of Art, Washington, DC. Source: Photo courtesy National Gallery of Art, Washington.

The exemplary character of Jesus, Mary, and Joseph as exiles has found particular significance in the modern period (e.g. Soares-Prabhu 1992; Melanchthon 2015). Pope Pius XII's 1952 Apostolic Constitution *Exsul Familia* presents the holy family as the 'type' of all refugee families, while the Flight into Egypt is the subject of Irish and Vatican City postage stamps commemorating the international Year for World Refugees in 1959/1960. Carolyn Winfrey Gillette's hymn for immigrants, 'Abraham Journeyed to a New Country,' also explores this theme.

The arrival in Egypt often takes precedence over the journey itself, emphasizing Christ's revelation to the Gentiles ('an undeveloped secondary accent in the story': Luz 2007: 121). The story of the Flight thus mirrors the Magi narrative in having Egypt as well as the Orient submit to Christ, a parallel not lost on Photius of Constantinople (c. 810–893): 'Christ flees into Egypt, in order that he might sanctify her, just as he sanctified Babylon through the Magi who came to worship him' (Reuss 1957: 272; also Theophylact). The arrival of the Son of God in Egypt marks the defeat of demons, the destruction of idols (e.g. *Arabic Gospel of the Infancy* 10–11; Eusebius, *Dem. ev.* 6:20; 9:2; *Pseudo-Matthew* 22–23) and the conversion of the Egyptians (*Pseudo-Matthew* 24). By contrast, according to rabbinic tradition, Egypt is the place where the young Jesus learned magic (*b. Sanh.* 107b; *b. Šabb.* 104b).

According to the *Gospel of Pseudo-Matthew*, the holy family ends its journey at Sotinen near Hermopolis, where the Roman governor Aphrodisius pays Jesus homage, and where 365 idols fall (*Pseudo-Matthew* 22–23). This victory over Egyptian idolatry is widely interpreted as the fulfillment of Isaiah: 'See, the Lord is riding on a swift cloud and comes to Egypt; the idols of Egypt will tremble at his presence' (Isa 19:1 NRSV; e.g. *Pseudo-Matthew* 23; *Opus imperfectum*). It reverses the wickedness of Egypt at the Exodus (Chromatius, *Tractate on Matthew* 6.1). John Chrysostom sees in the Christian Egypt of his day the fruits of the first-century acceptance of the Christ Child:

> And now, shouldest thou come unto the desert of Egypt, thou wilt see this desert become better than any paradise, and ten thousand choirs of angels in human forms, and nations of martyrs, and companies of virgins, and all the devil's tyranny put down, while Christ's kingdom shines forth in its brightness. (*Homily on Matthew* 8.6; *NPNF* 1st series, 10:53)

Sotinen occurs regularly in Western art (e.g. Santa Maria Maggiore, Rome). Other Egyptian destinations for the holy family include Cairo (Abu Sergis church), Memphis (where they encounter Pharaoh, *Arabic Gospel of the Infancy* 25), On or Heliopolis (Pseudo-Bonaventure, *Meditations* 12), and Kuskam (Farid 1965: 53–54).

The Slaughter of the Innocents (2:16–18)

Sandwiched between Matthew's narrative of the Flight and Return is the troubling story of Herod's revenge. Modern scholars frequently note how well this action fits Herod's ruthless character, even as they dispute its historical value due to its absence from non-Christian records, echoing the ancient skepticism of Celsus (Origen, *Cels.* 1.58; e.g. Davies and Allison 1988: 265; though see France 1979).

The parallels between Herod and Pharaoh in the time of Moses (Allison 1993a; Brown 1993: 214–216) are sometimes noted by earlier commentators. Indeed, according to Theophylact, the massacre of the innocents was permitted to reveal Herod's wickedness. The *Biblia Pauperum* (British Library Blockbook C.9 d.2) finds other Old Testament types: Saul's slaughter of the priests of Nob (1 Sam 22:17–18), and Athaliah's murder of the royal princes (2 Kgs 11:1: Labriola and Smeltz 1990: 21, 105, 152). Medieval sermons for the western Feast of the Holy Innocents on 28 December explain Herod's own death, or that of one of his own sons killed along with the Bethlehem children (following Macrobius, *Saturnalia* 2.4.11), as divine punishment for his actions (e.g. *The Golden Legend*). That Herod's brutality could be replicated by tyrants is exemplified in the regularity with which even Christian princes were called 'Herods' (e.g. Henry VIII of England; Philip of Spain; Ivan the Terrible; Henri III of France: see Kunzle 2001: 55). In a homily on the passage, preached to her nuns on the eve of the Epiphany, the twelfth-century German mystic Hildegard of Bingen allegorized Herod: he is the devil, who 'will toil to destroy the knowledge that is in the human' (*Homily* 11; Hildegard of Bingen 2011: 65).

The fact that children had to die in order to ensure the safety of God's Son raises issues of theodicy (Aichele 1978; Erikson 1996; Luz 2007: 121–122), a problem compounded by the *Protevangelium of James*, which claims that John the Baptist was also spared the massacre by Elizabeth's taking him into the hill country, where a mountain miraculously opened up to hide them (*Prot. Jas.* 22). It is possible that Matthew himself draws back from attributing Herod's action to the divine will, replacing his usual purpose clause with an awkward 'Then' (2:17; Brown 1993: 205). Peter Chrysologus sees the difficulty, asking rhetorically how Christ could have abandoned his 'standard-bearers' to their fate. His solution is that they are martyrs: far from leaving them behind, Christ 'sent his soldiers ahead' of him, allowing them to 'attain heaven before earth and share in the divine life immediately' (Peter Chrysologus, *Sermons* 152.7: Simonetti 2001: 34).

Innocent Martyrs

Martyrdom, indeed, is a common explanation of the children's fate, putting them ahead of Stephen (Acts 7:54–60) as 'the first martyrs of Christ'

(Chromatius, *Tractate on Matthew* 6.2: Simonetti 2001: 35; also e.g. Irenaeus, *Adv. Haer*. 3.16.4; Leo the Great, *Sermon* 37.4; Theophylact). Indeed, Cyprian of Carthage uses their martyrdom to warn fellow Christians that no one is exempt from persecution (Cyprian, *Ep*. 58.6). The Preface for the Octave of Christmas in the medieval Leofric Missal likewise sees their deaths as anticipating Christ's: 'the little ones through their passion were crowned with glory' (in Olsen 2015: 110). Their martyr status is implicit in the designation of their feast as 'the Holy Innocents' ('Childermas' in medieval England). The *Golden Legend* proposes that they are 'innocent' for three reasons: their life (too young to commit sin), their death (unjustly killed), and the innocence they gained (as martyrs, they achieved 'baptismal innocence,' i.e. 'the baptism of blood': Jacobus de Voragine 1993: I/56–58). This idea of the massacre as a 'baptism of blood' is visualized in Giotto's fresco in the Scrovegni Chapel, Padua (c. 1305), where the children are slaughtered in front of a baptistery. In poetry, it shapes the reflection on the feast by the Anglican priest-poet, John Keble (1792–1866):

> Baptised in blood for Jesus' sake,
> Now underneath the Cross their bed they make,
> Not to be scared from that sure rest
> By frighten'd mother's shriek, or warrior's waving crest.
> (Keble 1885: 34)

Their martyr status is reflected in their vast number in some traditions: 144 000, the number of the martyrs in Revelation 14:1–5 (a text which served as the Epistle at Mass for the feast: Flanigan 1992: 336). Other numbers include 3000 (*Martyrdom of Matthew*), 14 000 in the Byzantine and Ethiopic liturgies, and 64 000 in the Syriac (Brown 1993: 205; Lapide 1890: 1/83), far exceeding the total population of Bethlehem in the first century (Saintyves 1928: 234). Their perfection is expressed in one of the liturgical texts for the western feast, *ex ore infantium et lactentium perfecisti laudem* ('out of the mouths of infants and sucklings you have perfected praise,' Ps 8:3). A hymn by Prudentius presents them as types of Christ, the Paschal Lamb, living out their childhood eternally in the heavenly court:

> You, tender flock of lambs, we sing,
> First victims slain for Christ your King:
> Before the Altar's heavenly ray.
> With martyr palms and crowns ye play.
> (in Lapide 1890: 1/85)

Figure 5 William Holman Hunt (1827–1910). *The Triumph of the Innocents.* 1883–1884. Oil paint on canvas, 1562 × 2540 mm. Acquisition presented by Sir John Middlemore Bt 1918. Tate Gallery. Source: Photo © Tate, London/Art Resource, NY.

William Holman Hunt's *The Triumph of the Innocents* (1883–1884; Figure 5) underscores their close connection to Christ by depicting these new martyrs surrounding the holy family in their flight to Egypt, treading a stream of water sourced by the 'fountain of the water of life' (Hunt 1885: 10). One infant playfully touches a tear in his shirt, the mark of a sword whose flesh-wound is now healed. The 'full-blooded healthiness' of the children presents Hunt's conviction that the resurrection life, in which they now participate proleptically, is more substantial than the life they have left behind (Forsyth 1905: 176–177).

Augustine finds a wider reference to martyrdom in their age: two years and under. Thus for him they symbolize 'the humble who have twofold charity' (i.e. love of God and neighbor: see 22:34–40), which enables them to die for Christ (*Seventeen Questions on Matthew* 1; Augustine 2014: 431).

Weeping Mothers (2:18): Ecclesial and Individual Grief

The formula citation connected to this event (Jer 31:15) is a surprising one. It originally referred not to the deaths of children but the gathering of the exiles at Ramah. Jerome, who spent many years living in Bethlehem, is troubled by the linkage of the slaughter with Jeremiah's reference to Rachel weeping, on the grounds that Rachel's offspring belonged to the tribe of her son Benjamin rather than Judah. His solution is that, because the two tribes bordered each other, the 'surrounding regions' (2:16) include portions of Benjamin.

Rachel weeping for her children is often interpreted as a type of the church, following a common typological reading of her story in Genesis (e.g. Justin, *Trypho* 134; Irenaeus, *Adv. Haer.* 4.21.3; Hilary; Fortunatianus of Aquileia). For the sixth-century Coptic bishop Rufus of Shotep:

> Rachel is the church, the little sister of Lea, that is, the synagogue, whose womb was shut up and she did not bring forth all this long while (cf. Gen 29:31). It is she who is weeping for these little children whom Herod killed, that is, the blood of the martyrs which has been shed. (*Homilies on Matthew* 7: Rufus of Shotep 1998: 131)

Hilary, by contrast, views Rachel-as-church not as weeping out of sorrow for the innocents (who have gained the martyrs' crown) but because they were being killed 'by those whom she had wanted to preserve as her firstborn sons,' that is the Jewish people, symbolized by Herod (Hilary of Poitiers 2012: 47).

The *Opus imperfectum* has a greater sensitivity to the grief of the mothers, hidden behind Rachel's voice in Matthew's narrative: they 'lamented loudly because they were bereft of their sons and separated from them, as if their own heart had been torn out' (Kellerman and Oden 2010: 41). They take center stage in medieval art and drama. They are prominent on the west portal of Chartres Cathedral, defending their children from Herod's soldiers whom they equal in size and number. The juxtaposition of this Chartres image to the Flight, where Mary's baby is spared, anticipates Christ's own future death which will vindicate their children's blood. For twelfth-century mothers of the city, there may be a further reference to Mary, Virgin of Chartres, given that several of the miracle stories associated with her cult involved dead children restored to life (Nolan 1996). In the medieval Mystery Plays, the women find their own voice to protest the injustice done to them and their children, chanting defiantly in the faces of Herod's soldiers (on a modern rendition of the York Cycle version, see Reed 2000). In the Chester play, the slanderous and ridiculing language employed by the mothers functions to assert their moral superiority over the soldiers (Ryan 2001). Their voices in the sixteenth-century Pageant of the Shearmen and Tailors in Coventry have been preserved in the popular 'Coventry Carol':

> Herod, the king, in his raging,
> Chargid he hath this day
> His men of might in his owne sight
> All yonge children to slay,—

That wo is me, pore child, for thee,
And ever morne and may
For thi parting nether say nor singe,
By by, lully, lullay.
(Richard Croo 1534; Sharp 1825: 113–114)

Pieter Brueghel the Elder's *Massacre of the Innocents* (c. 1565–1567; Royal Collection, Windsor Castle) locates the massacre in a snow-covered Netherlandish village, the soldiers wearing the armor of the ruling Spaniards and their German mercenaries. In the Nicaraguan *Gospel in Solentiname* (1980s), a series of congregational dialogues on the Sunday readings, the illustration for the Massacre of the Innocents portrays the mothers and babies as Nicaraguan peasants, and Herod's soldiers as Somocista guards (see Kunzle 2001: 52–53; Scharper and Scharper 1984: 19).

From Egypt to Nazareth (2:19–23)

Matthew is silent about the length of the sojourn in Egypt. Suggestions range from between one to eight years, seven being a popular figure (e.g. Pseudo-Bonaventure, *Meditations* 12). Hippolytus speaks of three-and-a-half years, the length of the woman's stay in the wilderness at Revelation 12:14 (GCS 1/2.201), perhaps underscoring the Exodus-like character of the Flight. Celsus presumes a lengthy stay, claiming that Christ worked as a laborer in Egypt (Origen, *Cels.* 1.38).

The details of the return are sometimes fleshed out: according to Pseudo-Bonaventure, they meet John the Baptist at the edge of the desert, where he is already doing penance (*Meditations* 13). Though it is understandable that the holy family move on from Judea due to the threat posed by Archelaus (2:22), Matthew fails to explain why Joseph chose to settle in Galilee, a territory governed by Herod Antipas (a problem noted by John Chrysostom).

The command to return echoes the return of Moses from Midian to Egypt in Exodus 4:19: 'for *those* seeking the child's life are dead' (only Herod's death has been mentioned). This may be another foreshadowing of the Passion. The Passion motif is prominent in a rare visual depiction of this scene, by Nicolas Poussin (*Return of the Holy Family from Egypt*, c. 1628–1638; Dulwich Picture Gallery). The holy family are crossing the river in a boat, the boatman resembling Charon ferrying passengers across the Styx. The Christ Child is transfixed by a vision of a bright, triumphant cross held by cherubs, whilst Joseph is distracted by the dark cross on the back of the accompanying donkey (Mitchell 1938; Francis 1953).

Rufus of Shotep finds in the return to Judea on Herod's death an allegory of the human struggle with sin, following a common etymological explanation of 'Herod' as 'skin' (see e.g. Origen, *Hom. in Lev.* 5):

> If the man of skin is reigning with his works in the flesh, let the reason take the mind and your thought and flee with it (or him) to hidden places. If the old man dies (Rom 6:6) and the flesh becomes powerless, rise up from the hidden places in which you have hidden yourself and walk to the land of revelation. (*Homilies on Matthew* 9; Rufus of Shotep 1998: 132)

Hilary interprets Joseph, crossing over from Judea into 'Galilee of the Gentiles' (4:15), figuratively as an image (*species*) of the apostles in their preaching first to 'the lost sheep of the house of Israel,' then to the pagans.

'He Shall Be Called a Nazorean' (2:23)

The provenance of this formula citation has puzzled interpreters across the centuries, and Matthew's vague 'through the prophets' may suggest his own uncertainty. Several of the solutions proposed by modern scholars (see Luz 2007: 122–123) are already anticipated in the patristic period.

Jerome takes the plural 'through the prophets' as an indication that Matthew has drawn 'the sense' rather than the precise words from Scripture (Jerome 2008: 67). Nonetheless, he also notes that the translation of 'Nazarene' is 'holy' (*sanctus*: a possible allusion to the *nazir* or 'consecrated one' of Num 6:1–21 and Judg 13:5, 7; 16:17). Eusebius comes to the same conclusion via Leviticus 21:12, which refers to the 'consecration' of the high priest (*Dem. ev.* 7.2). The Judges reference is explicit in the fourth-century Latin commentary of Fortunatianus of Aquileia, one key source for Jerome: 'So Samson the Nazirite, a man of great power, was a figure of the Saviour to come' (Fortunatianus of Aquileia 2017: 28). In the sixteenth century, it is adopted by Martin Bucer, and cited approvingly by John Calvin. This etymological explanation may also underlie the figurative interpretation of Rufus of Shotep, for whom Christ's 'dwelling in Nazareth' can be actualized in the lives of believers: 'For whoever will dwell in purity, it is he who will be called "the Nazorean"' (*Homilies on Matthew* 11; Rufus of Shotep 1998: 133). Secondly, Jerome cites the testimony of 'the Hebrew truth' in Isaiah 11:1, prophesying the messianic 'branch' (Hebrew *nētzer*) from Jesse's root: 'A shoot shall arise from the root of Jesse, and a Nazarene shall ascend from the root' (Jerome 2008: 67; also e.g. Ephrem in Harris 1895: 40–41; *Glossa ordinaria*).

Alternatively, the reference is understood to be to a prophecy not contained in the prophetic canon. The *Opus imperfectum* suggests that the reference is to non-canonical prophets, such as Nathan or Ezra. John Chrysostom notes that many prophetic writings were lost (so also Isho'dad of Merv 1911: 21). According to the early nineteenth-century Anglican commentator Mary Cornwallis, Matthew is referring 'to the general declaration of the prophets, that the Messias should be despised and rejected' (Cornwallis 1820: 9), symbolized by the town's poor reputation (John 1:46).

Matthew 3

Ancient Literary Context

Mark's narrative opens with the preaching of John the Baptist, an ascetic Jewish figure also known to Josephus (*Ant.* 18.116–119), understood by the Gospels as the forerunner to Jesus. Matthew parallels Mark closely at this point, albeit providing greater detail about the content of John's preaching (3:7–10, 12; see Luke 3:7–9, 17), and avoiding Mark's misattribution of a prophecy from Malachi to Isaiah (Mark 1:2, citing Mal 3:1; cf. Matt 11:10; Luke 7:27). He also gives

Matthew Through the Centuries, First Edition. Ian Boxall.

prominence to an 'unholy alliance' of Pharisees and Sadducees attending John's baptism (3:7; cf. Luke 3:7), anticipating later opposition to Jesus by a range of Jewish groups. All this accentuates John's complex role as wilderness preacher and fiery eschatological prophet as well as forerunner of Christ. The chapter climaxes with the baptism of Jesus by John, a story shared by all three Synoptic Gospels (and alluded to by John 1:32). Classified form-critically as a legend, though one with a historical foundation (Bultmann 1968: 247–248), it shifts the focus from the baptismal act itself to the Christological significance of what follows (the opening of the heavens, the descent of the Spirit and the declaration of Jesus's divine sonship). Thus the various pericopae in this section combine to underscore the close relationship between John and Jesus, and to present Jesus' baptism as a necessary preparatory event for his public ministry.

The Interpretations

John the Baptist's Ministry (3:1–6)

John the Baptist begins his ministry of preparation in the wilderness. Matthew underscores John's relationship to Jesus by having them preach an identical message ('Repent, for the kingdom of the heavens has drawn near': 3:2; 4:17), thus turning the Baptist into a 'preacher of Christian repentance' (Meier 1980: 388). This is reflected in Rembrandt's *Preaching of St. John the Baptist* (c. 1634–1635; Gemäldegalerie, Berlin), where John resembles Christ preaching his Sermon on the Mount. Luke will go even further in positing a blood relationship between John and Jesus on their mothers' side, with names for John's parents (Luke 1:5, 36).

The length of John's wilderness preaching is not spelt out. Matthew's solemn 'In those days' is probably meant to emphasize the new stage in salvation history inaugurated by John's ministry (e.g. Davies and Allison 1988: 286–287; though see e.g. Stock 1994: 43–44). However, it could be read as locating the beginning of John's ministry in close chronological proximity to the holy family's aforementioned arrival in Nazareth (2:22–23; Luz 2007: 134). Caravaggio, following a lead set by Raphael, paints John the Baptist in the wilderness both as a prepubescent boy (*St. John the Baptist in the Wilderness*, 1601–1602; Pinacoteca Capitolina, Rome) and as a teenager (*St. John the Baptist in the Wilderness*, c. 1610; Galleria Borghese, Rome: see Townsend and Ward 1995: 10–11, 15). Alternatively, harmonizing Matthew with Luke 3:1, 'in those days' refers to the fifteenth year of the Emperor Tiberius (Lapide 1890: 1/98). The Orthodox Office of the Conception of the Forerunner (24 September) traces John's wilderness ministry even earlier: 'Angel, you came out of barren loins,

O Baptist! From your very swaddling clothes you lived in the desert' (Bulgakov 2003: 36, n. 4). Nicephorus asserts that he was taken there by Elizabeth at the age of 18 months (in Lapide 1890: 1/100).

John Prepares the Way in the Wilderness (3:1–3)

John's presence in the wilderness is interpreted by all four evangelists in light of Isaiah 40:3 (Mark 1:3; Luke 3:4–6; John 1:23). The wilderness evokes multiple associations, from the Exodus wanderings to the place of retreat and struggle, populated by wild animals and demons (e.g. Exod 13:18–20; 16:1; 1 Sam 23:14; Jer 2:1–2; 4 Macc 18:8; Mark 1:12–13). Matthew's earlier Mosaic and Israel typology (e.g. 2:1–12, 15, 16–17) underscore the Exodus dimension here. Nonetheless, Matthew clarifies that John's location is the wilderness *of Judea* rather than Sinai (3:1; cf. Mark 1:4), allowing Hilary of Poitiers to connect the deserted terrain with the people of Judea, 'deserted by the visitations of God' (Hilary of Poitiers 2012: 49).

More positively, many have followed John into the wilderness in search of monastic solitude (e.g. the Desert Fathers: Ryrie 2011). For Gregory of Nazianzus, being 'seduced' by John's desert is one of those marks of authentic Christians despised for their lowliness and poverty (Gregory of Nazianzus, *Orat.* 33). Figuratively, the wilderness symbolizes the church of the Gentiles, once deserted but now watered by the river of life (Eusebius, *Dem. ev.* 9.6; similarly Aquinas).

The application of the Isaiah passage to John transforms an oracle anticipating the return from exile into a job description for the Baptist. John has been divinely commissioned as the prophetic 'voice' who prepares the Lord's way. In an early sixteenth-century French Passion play (Harvard Theater Collection MS Thr 262), this commissioning takes place in the heavenly throne-room, John kneeling before God the Father:

> From this day forward you shall preach
> Baptism and holy penance,
> Peace, goodness, meekness and mercy,
> Among men of good will.
> (*Harvard Passion Play*, lines 13–16; Elliott and Runnell 1978: 55)

John Calvin allows a wider application: Isaiah 40:3 is not exclusively about John, 'yet he is one of the number of those to whom it certainly refers,' including the prophets Zechariah, Haggai, and Malachi (Calvin 1949: 1/181).

In its Matthean context, the 'way' is clearly metaphorical. Jerome takes it to mean John's preparing human souls to receive Christ. In a full-blown allegory which ignores the Hebrew parallelism of Isaiah's original, Theophylact distinguishes between the 'way' and the 'paths.' The former refers to the Gospel, while the 'paths' are the ordinances of the Mosaic Law which are to be made 'straight,' i.e. interpreted spiritually. Thus the Baptist narrative is recast as a commentary upon biblical hermeneutics, contrasting the Christian 'spiritual' interpretation with Judaism's attention to the 'letter.'

Sixteenth-century debates over John's preaching reflect a return *ad fontes*, emphasizing the original Greek's 'Repent' (*metanoeite,* which invites a change of heart or mind) rather than the Vulgate's 'Do penance' (*paenitentiam agite*, e.g. Erasmus 1986: 18; Martin Luther, 'Letter to John Staupitz,' 1518). The Reformers thus reject medieval penitential practices. According to Johann Albrecht Bengel, John invites his hearers to 'put on a disposition worthy of the kingdom of heaven, royal, heavenly' (Bengel 1971: 85).

John's Clothing (3:4)

John's distinctive clothing foregrounds his likeness to Elijah, who was similarly attired (2 Kgs 1:8 LXX; see also the clothing of a prophet at Zech 13:4). Jerome makes explicit the connection between Elijah and John's leather girdle. According to the fourth-century *Life of John the Baptist*, attributed to the Coptic bishop Serapion, the camel hair came from Elijah and the leather belt from his successor Elisha. Both items of clothing were brought from heaven by the Angel Gabriel and entrusted to John's father Zechariah (Mingana 1927: 241).

Many also find in John's manner of dress a reflection of his ascetical lifestyle (cf. Bannus in Josephus, *Life* 11), supported by traditions that John remained celibate (Tertullian, *Monog.* 8). For Jerome, John's camel hair points to his austerity, his belt to his mortification (also Cyril of Jerusalem, *Catech.* 3:6). The fifteenth-century English *Life of St. John the Baptist* treats both John's clothing and his diet as signs of his poverty and asceticism: 'And there he lived in the humblest poverty and asceticism, to such an extent that his clothes were made of camel's hair, which is rough and of little value, his drink was water, and his food was wild honey and other poor foods of the desert' (Waters 2008: 95). The Jesuit scholar Cornelius a Lapide uses John's example polemically, contrasting it with the flowing robes of the German Lutheran David Chytraeus 'and those luxurious innovators, who magnificently adorn themselves in the pulpits like the suitors of Penelope' (Lapide 1890: 1/103). In the modern period, Ulrich Luz suggests that the inherited description of John would have 'sounded ascetic in the large Syrian city where Matthew lived' (Luz 2007: 136).

For Luz, John's asceticism underscores his uniqueness. By contrast, earlier commentators interpreted it as an example for others to imitate: in Clement of Alexandria's words 'an example of simple, frugal living' (*Paed.* 2.10: Clement of

Alexandria 1954: 186). John Chrysostom finds in John's meager clothing an invitation to return to Adam's simplicity in Eden, before he had need of clothes. For Theophlyact, John's camel-hair is 'the garb of mourning' (Theophylact 1992: 33; sackcloth was often made from camel hair: Taylor 1997: 35–37). In seventeenth-century art, following the Council of Trent, the Baptist is regularly depicted in the company of Christian saints also known for their asceticism, such as Mary Magdalen, Jerome, and Francis (Townsend and Ward 1995: 36). He is thus appropriately called 'the prince of monks and anchorites' (Lapide 1890: 1/99).

Locusts and Wild Honey (3:4)

John's peculiar diet parallels his striking clothing. Given that Jews were permitted to eat locusts or grasshoppers (e.g. Lev 11:20–23; *Ep. Arist.* 145; 11QT*a* 48:3–5; CD 12:14–15), this could reflect his concern for ritual purity (Davies 1983). According to Serapion's *Life of John the Baptist*, John was fed this diet by his mother, after their flight into the wilderness to escape Herod, out of a concern to avoid unclean food (Mingana 1927: 242).

On the other hand, Matthew's implication that John's *total* diet consisted of locusts and wild honey (3:4; cf. Mark 1:6) may emphasize John's asceticism (Kelhoffer 2005: 5–6; but see Andersen 1961–1962: 61 for evidence that some considered locusts a delicacy). Alternatively, it exemplifies his trust in divine providence for his food supply (like Josephus' mentor Bannus: Taylor 1997: 32–42). Both foods would have been readily available in the Judean desert (e.g. Josephus, *War* 4.468). 'Honey' (see e.g. Deut 32:13; Judg 14:8; 1 Sam 14:25; Ps 81:16) could refer not just to honey from bees, but to a wide range of sweet substances, including dates or sap from trees (Kelhoffer 2005: 81–89). The Syriac tradition emphasized its bitterness, to show that the honey eaten by John was no delicacy (Brock 1970).

The desire to present John as the archetypal ascetic may partly explain early claims about his vegetarianism, perhaps inspired by the description of Judas Maccabeus at 2 Maccabees 5:27 (Brock 1970). The *Gospel of the Ebionites* reads 'locusts' (*akrides*) as 'cakes' (*egkrides*): 'And his food was, it said, wild honey, of which the taste was that of manna, like cakes in olive oil' (Epiphanius, *Pan.* 30.13.4–5, in Klijn 1992: 67; see Num 11:8). John then parallels the Israelites who were fed with heavenly food in the wilderness. According to Isho'dad of Merv, Tatian's *Diatessaron* had the alternative reading 'honey and milk of the mountains' (Isho'dad of Merv 1911: 23–24; see Kelhoffer 2005: 141–143). Cornelius a Lapide knows the reading *achrades*, 'wild pear trees,' as well as 'certain innovators' who interpret the locusts as 'sea-crabs' (*acharides* or *karides*: Lapide 1890: 1/105).

Other interpreters retain the reading 'locusts,' but interpret it in a vegetarian sense. Athanasius of Alexandria (c. 296–373) finds justification in Ecclesiastes 12:5b ('The almond tree will blossom, and the locust will become thick') for interpreting the 'locust,' like the almond tree, as a type of plant (Athanasius, *Fragmenta in Matthaeum* 8A: Kelhoffer 2005: 172). For Isidore of Pelusium (c. 350–435), the locusts are 'twigs of herbs or plants' (Isidore, *Ep.* 1.132 in Kelhoffer 2005: 173). Similarly, according to the Syriac Jacob of Serugh (c. 451–521), John 'lived off herbs and plants and flowers' (in Brock 1970: 117). Theophylact knows the interpretation of 'locusts' as the fruit of a pod-bearing tree, or 'St. John's bread' (Theophylact 1992: 33).

John Calvin rejects this ascetical interpretation of the Baptist, and its subsequent use to bolster Christian monasticism. He emphasizes that John's diet was nothing remarkable for a 'man of the mountains' who adapted his diet to his environment (Calvin 1949: 1/183–184).

John's diet also invites allegorical interpretations. For Origen, the locusts symbolize John's preaching of 'a word that traveled high aloft in the air and had not yet passed over the earth,' while the honey (which cannot be obtained through purely human efforts) symbolizes the spiritual meaning of the Law and the prophets inaccessible to the 'superficial' reading of Judaism (see Simonetti 2001: 41; Kelhoffer 2005: 150). Cyril of Jerusalem interprets the honey as John's words which were 'sweeter than honey,' while his diet of winged locusts caused him to grow wings on his soul (Cyril of Jerusalem, *Catech.* 3.6; Kelhoffer 2005: 150). By contrast, for Arnobius the Younger, the 'locusts' are a figure of the many people who came to John for baptism, while the 'honey' signifies 'the fruit of the sweetness of those with whose trust and faith John was satisfied' (Arnobius the Younger, *Expositiunculae in Matthaeum* 3; Kraszewski 1999: 262).

The Preaching of John (3:7–12)

Matthew and Luke both give substance to the preaching of John, presenting his baptism as a challenge to Jewish presumption of covenant status (see Luke 3:7–9). What surprises many is Matthew's 'unholy alliance' of Pharisees and Sadducees (poles apart religiously and politically) coming to John's baptism. The *Gospel of the Ebionites* smooths this out by having only Pharisees appear (Epiphanius, *Pan.* 30.13.4).

Their fleeing 'from the coming wrath' might suggest genuine repentance on their part. However, this is undermined by John's description of them as a 'brood of vipers' (v. 7; also 12:34; 23:33). The *Opus imperfectum* notes its appropriateness for such ambiguous figures seeking baptism, given that a viper runs to water once it has bitten someone, 'in order to avoid the danger of death' (Kellerman and Oden 2010: 48).

Some attempt to negotiate this tension in the narrative by differentiating between good and bad individuals. In the *Harvard Passion Play*, for example, Joseph of Arimathea and Nicodemus are examples of penitent 'Pharisees and Sadducees' who request baptism at the hands of John (lines 183–186; Elliott and Runnalls 1978: 71). Yet this is hard to justify given the universal condemnation these two groups receive in Matthew's text. More focused is John Calvin's actualization of the Pharisees and Sadducees in the 'mitred Bishops, Abbots, Canons, Monks, Sorbonnists, and every description of Priests' of his own day, who glory in their clerical titles and hold the laity in contempt (Calvin 1949: 1/191).

Raising up Children for Abraham (3:9)

Reliance on physical descent from Abraham is no defense, given that God can raise up children for Abraham from the stones. Exploiting the ambiguity of 'son of Abraham' at 1:1 (cf. Rom 4:12; Gal 4:28), many find in these transformed stones a reference to the Gentiles, children for Abraham by faith (e.g. Ign., *Magn.* 10; Theophylact). Irenaeus finds John's words fulfilled in Christ's 'drawing us off from the religion of stones, and bringing us over from hard and fruitless cogitations, and establishing in us a faith like to Abraham' (*Adv. Haer.* 4.7.2; *ANF* 1:470). Theophylact finds an additional intratextual allusion to the earthquake at Jesus' crucifixion (27:51), 'when many believed upon seeing the stones which were sundered' (Theophylact 1992: 34).

While identifying Abraham's children as Gentiles acknowledges the universal thrust of Matthew's narrative (28:19), such an interpretation often lapses into unwarranted anti-Judaism. This overlooks Matthew's clear distinction between the negatively portrayed Pharisees and Sadducees on the one hand, and the pious Jews who come in repentance to John's baptism on the other (Luz 2007: 137). Moreover, as the author of the *Opus imperfectum* acknowledges, John's warning is equally severe for those who 'think that they must be saved because of the fact alone that they are Christians' (Kellerman and Oden 2010: 49). Presumption of all kinds is excluded.

Baptism in Holy Spirit and Fire (3:11)

Matthew's narrative distinguishes sharply between John's water baptism for repentance, and Jesus' baptism with 'the holy spirit and fire,' apparently a fiery judgment (v. 12). Thus John is urging his hearers to submit to his call to repentance, so as to escape the harsher baptism of the mightier one who follows him. 'Spirit' and 'fire' could be synonymous, a possibility raised by Jerome, on the basis of Acts 2:3. Cornelius a Lapide similarly recognizes the phrase as a hendiadys, referring to 'the Holy, Fiery, and Inflaming Spirit' (Lapide 1890: 1/121).

Or the Baptist's words may describe separate dimensions of Christ's baptizing activity. For Hilary, Christians baptized in the Holy Spirit in the present will be perfected by fiery judgment, apparently judgment according to their deeds on the last day. Others interpret the fire as a 'purgatorial' fire (e.g. Origen, *Hom. in Luc.* 24), or the fire of Hell (Basil the Great, *On Isaiah* 4; John Damascene, *de Fide* 4.10), or sufferings and temptations (Strabo 82; see Luz 2007: 138).

The distinction between John's water baptism and Christian baptism is underscored by the sixteenth-century Council of Trent: 'If anyone says that the baptism of John had the same effect as the baptism of Christ: let him be anathema' (Trent, Session 7, *Decree on the Sacraments: Canons on the Sacrament of Baptism* 1; Tanner 1990: II/685).

The Baptism of Jesus (3:13–17)

Matthew presents Jesus' baptism as a public event, in which the heavenly voice declares 'This is my Son, the beloved' (anticipating the Transfiguration, 17:5; cf. Mark 1:11; Luke 3:22, 'You are my Son, the beloved'). Matthew's is also the only canonical account to contain the dialogue between Jesus and a reluctant John, who tries to 'prevent' him. This reflects early embarrassment over Christ submitting to a baptism of repentance, also attested in the *Gospel of the Nazarenes* (Jerome, *Dial. contra Pel.* 3.2). Artists sometimes attempt to convey this sense of reserve on John's part, as in Lorenzo Ghiberti's bronze for the cathedral baptistery in Siena (1427), in which the Baptist recoils and draws his clothing close to him with his left hand even as he baptizes Jesus with his extended right hand (see Masseron 1957: fig. 89). Another example is Paris Bordone's *The Baptism of Christ* (c. 1535/1540; Figure 6). John reaches for the tree behind him with his left hand, thus emphasizing the distance between him and Christ as he pours water over his head.

In the Orthodox tradition, John has full knowledge of Christ's divinity: 'Even though you are the child of Mary, I know who you are, supra-eternal God. You walk on the earth glorified by the seraphim, and the servant is not authorized to baptize the Master' (Office of Baptism: Bulgakov 2003: 53). That Jesus says 'let it be so *now*' leads some to conclude that the concession is only temporary: Christ would later remedy things by baptizing John (e.g. Gregory of Nazianzus, *Orat.* 39.15; *Opus Imperfectum*; Aquinas; Lapide). Thus, in the *Harvard Passion Play*, John is baptized by Christ in the name of the Trinity immediately after baptizing Jesus (lines 352–360: Elliott and Runnalls 1978: 83).

FIGURE 6 Paris Bordone (1500–1571). *The Baptism of Christ.* c. 1535–1540. Oil on canvas, 1295 × 1320 mm. Widener Collection, National Gallery of Art, Washington, DC. Source: Photo courtesy National Gallery of Art, Washington.

The baptism takes place in the River Jordan, full of historical and soteriological significance (Bertrand 1973: 127). Readers may recall the Israelites crossing the Jordan to enter the promised land (Josh 1–4), Elijah parting the river's waters (2 Kgs 2:8), or Naaman the Syrian washing seven times in the Jordan at Elisha's behest (2 Kgs 5:10, 14). Christ in the Jordan is sometimes interpreted as 'another Joshua, leading his people through the waters of Jordan, to the land of promise' (Cornwallis 1820: 13). The Elijah link is found in the Byzantine Troparion for the Afterfeast of the Theophany of Christ (6 January):

> The River Jordan receded of old by the mantle of Elisha when Elijah ascended into heaven; and the water was separated to this side and that, the wet element turning into a dry path for Him, being truly a symbol of Baptism, by which we cross the path of transient age. Christ appeared in the Jordan to sanctify its waters.[1]

1 http://orthodoxwiki.org/Theophany#Hymns.

In the *Biblia Pauperum* (British Library Blockbook C.9 d.2), Christ's baptism is juxtaposed with the Israelites crossing the Red Sea (Exod 14:21–28), and the scene from Numbers 13, in which the scouts spying out the Promised Land cross the Jordan with a bunch of grapes. The moral is drawn out for the readers: 'This incident shows that if we wish to enter the kingdom of heaven, we must first pass through the waters of baptism' (Labriola and Smeltz 1990: 107).

Equally rich are the possibilities for what Christ's baptism means. Jerome's threefold explanation is widely cited. Christ fulfills 'all the justice and humility of the Law,' shows his approval of John's own baptism, and sanctifies the waters of the Jordan so as to prepare for the baptism of Christian believers (Jerome 2008: 70). In the East, hallowing the waters is presented in icons of the Baptism or Theophany, where Christ raises his right hand in blessing as he is immersed in the Jordan (e.g. Baggley 2000: plate 9). Thomas Aquinas adds two further reasons: confirmation of Christ's true humanity, 'made in the likeness of the body of sin' (see also Irenaeus, *Smyrn.* 1.1; Hilary), and showing how Christ himself submitted to what he would demand of others (also Chromatius, *Tractatus in Matthaeum* 12.1; Kraszewski 1999: 265). This exemplary understanding is dramatized in the sixteenth-century French *Harvard Passion Play*:

> I wish to show them good habits
> And virtuous humility
> In truth,
> To move them to grief
> And to tears
> For their crimes and wickedness.
> So I shall go directly, without delay,
> In righteousness
> To receive baptism, to show
> That washing and cleanness
> And purity
> Must precede all other virtues.
> (lines 203–214; Elliott and Runnall 1978: 73)

The idea that Christ's baptism in the Jordan prepares for, or even institutes, Christian baptism finds justification in Matthew's narrative itself, 'painted with colors drawn from the palate of the Christian theology and practice of baptism' (Boring 1995: 161). This idea plays a key role in later sacramental theology (e.g. *Didascalia Apostolorum* 142; Aquinas, *ST* 3a, q. 66, art. 2) and liturgy. The link is underscored in art by Nicolas Poussin's *The Baptism of Christ* (1641/1642; National Gallery of Art, Washington, DC), one of a series of canvases depicting the seven sacraments.

Fulfilling All Righteousness (3:15)

The primary reason given by Matthew is that Jesus' baptism allows both Jesus and John to 'fulfil all righteousness' (3:15), i.e. 'doing the revealed will of God' (Boring 1995: 160). Although Matthew includes John, many commentators focus on how Christ uniquely fulfills all righteousness in this event, as the only person capable of fulfilling the Mosaic Law (e.g. Hilary). Jerome expands this to include the fulfillment of natural justice.

A second interpretation identifies 'all righteousness' specifically as humility (e.g. Dionysius bar Salibi; *Glossa ordinaria*). Pseudo-Bonaventure's *Meditations on the Life of Christ* has Christ address John the Baptist in these words:

> Remain quiet now; it is so we must fulfill every justice. Do not say this now and publicize me, for my time is not yet manifest or come, but baptize me. Now is the time for humility, and I wish to carry out every humility. (Ragusa and Green 1961: 106–107)

Pseudo-Bonaventure goes on to identify this (following the *Glossa*) as the third and highest degree of humility: submission by a superior to an inferior. Likewise, Aquinas sees in Jesus' baptism a concrete expression of 11:29 ('learn from me, for I am meek, and humble of heart').

A third possibility, espoused by John Calvin as 'a more simple interpretation' (Calvin 1949: 1/202), is that the statement reflects the Son's filial obedience. Modern scholarship tends to be more specific about the nature of Christ's obedience here. Jesus submits to John's baptism to show his solidarity with God's sinful people Israel, as their representative (e.g. France 2007: 120).

Defeating the Powers

Christ's descent into the Jordan also invites consideration of the event's mythological dimensions. Christ, by his baptism, defeats the hostile powers in the waters (Bertrand 1973: 31). This may be implied already in Ignatius' statement about Christ purifying the waters (Ign., *Eph.* 18.2; Schoedel 1985: 84). Possible intertextual echoes include Psalm 114:13 ('Why is it, O sea, that you flee? O Jordan, that you turn back?'), a psalm celebrating God's victory at the Exodus and Israel's crossing the Jordan (e.g. Exod 14:21–22; Josh 3:1–17). This is reflected visually in personifications of the sea and the Jordan in some Byzantine icons of the Baptism of Christ (Martin 2002: 188–189).

Cyril of Jerusalem (c. 313–386) exploits this dimension for catechumens preparing for baptism: 'Since, therefore, it was necessary to break the heads of the dragon in pieces, He went down and bound the strong one in the waters, that we might receive power to tread upon serpents and scorpions'

(*Catech.* 3.11: *NPNF* 2nd series, 7:17). Similarly in the West, the German Carthusian Ludolphus of Saxony (c. 1295–1378) notes that Christ is baptized so 'that He might bruise in the water the serpent's head' (Ludolphus, *Vita Christi* 21; Ford 1859: 42). This victory over the powers sometimes extends to Christ's followers. In Spenser's *Faerie Queene,* being baptized into Christ gives Redcrosse Knight extraordinary prowess against the dragon (1.11.36; Greco and Jeffrey in Jeffrey 1992: 75). The motif is common in Christian art. The early sixth-century dome mosaic of the Baptistery of the Arians, Ravenna, shows a personified Jordan, raising his hand as if acknowledging Christ's divinity (Schiller 1971: 133, fig. 355). In an eleventh-century Byzantine mosaic in the Monastery of Hosios Lukas, near Delphi, the baptism is linked visually to Christ's descent into Limbo, another event which celebrates his defeat of death and the forces of chaos (Schiller 1971: fig. 362).

The Opening of the Heavens (3:16)

The primary focus of Matthew's account, however, is less on the baptism than on subsequent events. In Matthew, the heavens are opened 'to him,' suggesting an apocalyptic vision (Aquinas calls it a 'vision of the imagination': Aquinas 2013a: 96). This motif, which has strong biblical precedent (e.g. Isa 63:19 LXX; Ezek 1:1), is sometimes given a salvation-historical interpretation. For Theophylact, just as Adam had closed the heavens, now they are opened through Christ. This opening, moreover, is apprehended by believers in their own baptism. Alternatively, as in the *Opus imperfectum*, this refers to a spiritual opening visible to the incarnate Christ alone, anticipating the physical opening of the heavens to be achieved by the cross (27:51–53).

Additional Old Testament echoes suggest themselves. The dove recalls Noah's dove which announced salvation following the flood (Gen 8:8–12; e.g. Hippolytus, *Theophany* 7; Tertullian, *De Bapt.* 8; Theophylact; Lapide), or God's Spirit brooding over the waters at the first creation (Gen 1:2), a connection established in the fifth-century Armenian baptismal catechesis *The Teaching of St. Gregory* 413 (McDonnell 1995: 217–219). The Noachic connection is clear in an eleventh-century mosaic in the Monastery of Hosios Lukas near Delphi, where the dove has a twig in its beak (Schiller 1971: 136, fig. 362). Alternatively, it symbolizes the love that the Spirit brings (*Opus imperfectum*), virtues such as charity, innocence, and simplicity (Aquinas), or the gentleness of Christ (Calvin). Matthew's explicit statement that the dove descending on Jesus was 'the Spirit of God' allows Irenaeus to refute the alternative versions of Cerinthus and the Valentinians, whereby it was Christ himself, or the Savior, who descended on Jesus in the shape of a dove (Irenaeus, *Adv. Haer.* 1.7.2; 1.26.1; 3.9.3).

Similarly, the words of the heavenly voice echo a range of biblical texts (Abraham's 'beloved son' Isaac in Gen 22:2 LXX, the Servant in Isa 42:1; the anointed Davidic King in Ps 2:7). Cornelius a Lapide detects another reference to Noah, 'who alone of his generation pleased God' (Gen 6:9; 8:20; Lapide 1890: 1/138). Matthew's redactional change from 'You are' (Mark 1:11; Luke 3:22) to 'This is' suggests that Christ's identity is revealed either to John (e.g. Calvin), or more publicly to those coming for baptism (Augustine in Aquinas); in the *Harvard Passion Play*, they are addressed by the Father not to human bystanders but to the angels (lines 301–303; Elliott and Runnalls 1978: 79).

The baptism is often understood as a revelation of the Trinity: 'The Lord is baptized, the Spirit descends in the form of a dove, the voice of the Father is heard offering testimony to the Son' (Jerome 2008: 71; see also *Life of St. John the Baptist* 12: Waters 2008: 101–103). Indeed, for Epiphanius, fourth-century bishop of Salamis, Christ's baptism serves as an antidote against Sabellianism, the heresy that Father, Son, and Holy Spirit are different modes or manifestations of the one God (Epiphanius in Ford 1859: 44). For Cornelius a Lapide, it provides additional scriptural warrant, alongside 28:19, for Trinitarian baptism.

Seeing a Great Light

Further significance is attached to Christ's baptism by a minority reading inserted into two Old Latin manuscripts after verse 15: 'And when Jesus was being baptized a great light flashed (a tremendous light flashed around) from the water, so that all who had gathered there were afraid' (Metzger 1994: 8). This motif, sometimes associating the light with fire (3:11: McDonnell 1996: 106), is also found in the *Gospel of the Ebionites* (Epiphanius, *Pan*. 30.13; 30.14; see Elliott 1993: 15), Justin Martyr (*Trypho* 88), and Ephrem the Syrian (*Commentary on the Diatessaron* 4:5). Ishoʻdad of Merv includes additional elements, including the appearance of 'many troops of spiritual beings' singing praises and a sweet odor emanating from the waters (Ishoʻdad of Merv 1911: 27). All this heightens the public and supernatural character of the baptism, and plays into the theme of the sanctification of the waters. Liturgical hymns for the Feast of the Theophany (6 January) also emphasize this theme of light as Christ's divinity is revealed:

> Thou hast appeared today to the whole world, and Thy light, O Lord, hath been signed upon us who hymn Thee with understanding. Thou hast come, Thou hast appeared, the Light unapproachable. The Babylonian furnace which poured forth dew showed forth a most glorious mystery: how the Jordan was to receive the immaterial Fire in its streams and embrace the Creator baptized in the flesh. (Lambertsen 2000: 126)

A similar theme is present in the fourth-century Christian poet Juvencus (see Schiller 1971: 128), and in Gregory of Nazianzus' festal oration 'On the Baptism of Christ':

> For the holy day of lights, to which we have come and which we are deemed worthy to celebrate today, takes its origin from the baptism of my Christ, the true light, which illumines every human being coming into the world, effects my purification, and strengthens the light we received from him from the beginning, which we darkened and blotted out through sin. (*Orat.* 39.1; Gregory of Nazianzus 2008: 79)

Matthew 4

Ancient Literary Context

Matthew's Prologue arguably extends to 4:11 (or even 4:16, Krentz 1964), thus linking Jesus' baptism and temptation to the infancy narrative as preparation for his public ministry. The ministry itself then begins at 4:12 with the 'handing over' of John (or 4:17, as 'from then on' Jesus began to preach), the gathering of the first disciples (4:18–22), and a summary of his actions and the crowds' response (4:23–25).

Matthew Through the Centuries, First Edition. Ian Boxall.

All three Synoptics recount Jesus' temptation or 'testing' in the wilderness (also Mark 1:12–13; Luke 4:1–13; see Gibson 1995), a motif later repeated when religious leaders seek to 'test' him (e.g. 16:1; 19:3; 22:35). Mark's version (Mark 1:12–13) is terse and ambiguous. The 40-day sojourn in 'the wilderness' is probably meant to recall Israel's 40 years in the wilderness, though this is not spelt out. Nor is the identity of 'the Satan' (see Job 1:6) clarified. Matthew's more expansive account addresses such questions. Satan is 'the devil' (4:1, 5, 8, 11) and 'the tempter' (4:3). The connections with the Exodus generation, and Moses specifically, are more explicit (e.g. 4:2, recalling Moses' fasting at Exod 34:28; Deut 9:9, 18, emulated by Elijah at 1 Kgs 9:5, 8). Matthew gives content to Jesus' temptations, as does Luke, albeit with a different order for the last two temptations. Though often attributed to Q, Matthew's version may rather be an imaginative midrash on Israel's wilderness testing in Deuteronomy, from which all three of Jesus' quotations come (Deut 8:3; 6:16; 6:13). Jesus the Son of God thus recapitulates the story of God's 'son' Israel. The climactic temptation in Matthew's version, in which Jesus is shown all the kingdoms of the world from a high mountain, may well recall Mount Pisgah, from which Moses viewed the promised land (Deut 3:2; 34:1).

Echoing the 'withdrawal' of the Magi to escape Herod (2:12), and the holy family's 'withdrawal' to Galilee to avoid Archelaus (2:22), Jesus now 'withdrew' to Galilee in response to John's 'handing over' (see Good 1990). The swift move of Jesus from Nazareth to Capernaum, a fishing town on the Sea of Galilee, is presented as prophetic fulfillment, a favorite Matthean motif. The quotation from Isaiah 9:1–2 originally offered liberation for parts of the land occupied by Assyria, through the birth of a descendant of David (see Luz 2007: 159). Its actualization in Matthew's story of the new Son of David exploits the words 'Galilee of the Gentiles,' anticipating the post-resurrection charge in Galilee to make disciples of 'all the nations' (28:19).

The terse character of the call of the first four disciples (4:18–22; cf. Mark 1:16–20) highlights the urgency of the Kingdom. Both pairs of brothers are fishermen, providing another metaphor for the missionary task they will undertake. Their model will be the ministry of Jesus, a summary of which concludes this chapter. Matthew's version highlights three aspects to that ministry: teaching, preaching, and healing (cf. Mark 1:39).

The Interpretations

The Temptation (4:1–11)

Following his baptism, Jesus is led up into the wilderness by 'the Spirit' (in context, clearly the Holy Spirit received at the Jordan, although Gregory the Great knows of some who posit the action of an evil spirit: *Homily* 14). Matthew's version is given pride of place in Christian lectionaries, and therefore in preaching. In the East, Dionysius of Fourna's influential *Painter's Manual* gives instructions that Byzantine iconographers follow Matthew's order of the temptations (stones–temple–mountain) in depicting the story visually. In the West, Matthew's temptation story has traditionally been read on the First Sunday of Lent, to illuminate the Christian practice of rigorous preparation for Easter and, in the case of catechumens, for baptism. Such liturgical centrality risks obscuring the diverse reasons why many have found the story problematic or challenging, or chosen to omit it in their presentation of Jesus' life (e.g. Thomas Jefferson's 1820 *The Life and Morals of Jesus of Nazareth*, popularly known as *The Jefferson Bible*, passes directly from Jesus' baptism to his arrival in Capernaum).

Typological Interpretations

Modern exegetes often highlight the parallels between Jesus and Moses (e.g. Allison 1993a: 165–172). There are older antecedents for this (e.g. Irenaeus, Hilary, Jerome, Gregory the Great, Cornelius a Lapide, and Henry Hammond note the connection with the 40-day fasts of Moses and Elijah). Conviction of Mosaic typology is also reflected in the Sistine Chapel frescoes, where Sandro Botticelli's *The Temptations of Christ* (1480–1482) is paired with his *The Trials of Moses* on the opposite wall. But sensitivity to the unity of Scripture, particularly in response to Marcionite and Gnostic objections, means that patristic authors find other Old Testament narratives equally illuminating.

The most obvious is the 'temptation' of Adam, which Christ's temptation is regarded as reversing (e.g. Justin Martyr; Hilary; see Steiner 1962; Koppen 1989), anticipating the great reversal on the cross. Irenaeus sees Christ's refusal to turn stones into bread as the undoing of Adam's eating the fruit: 'For as at the beginning it was by means of food that [the enemy] persuaded man, although not suffering hunger, to transgress God's commandments, so in the end he did not succeed in persuading Him that was an hungered to take that food which proceeded from God' (Irenaeus, *Adv. Haer.* 5.21.2: *ANF* 1:549; see Steiner 1962: 44–80). It is as the New Adam, the human one, that Christ replies to the devil: '*Man* does not live on bread alone …' (Pelikan 1951: 253).

Gregory the Great makes a similar connection: the devil tempted both Adam and Christ 'by gluttony, by vain glory, and by avarice' (*Homily* 14; Gregory the Great 1990: 102; also Theophylact; John Cassian has the slight variation of gluttony, vainglory, and pride, the latter regarded as the root of all vices: PL 49: 615–616). Indeed, the ninth-century Benedictine Haimo of Auxerre observes that Matthew's order more closely reflects Adam's temptations (Murdoch 1974: 36): 'for God knows that when you eat of it your eyes will be opened, and you will be like God, knowing good and evil' (Gen 3:5 NRSV). By contrast, John Calvin rejects such interpretations as 'ingenious trifles'; the first temptation, far from mere gluttony, is 'to persuade Christ to depart from the word of God, and to follow the dictates of infidelity' (Calvin 1949: 213).

Christ's temptation as the undoing of Eden is popular in medieval and early modern literature (see Murdoch 1974). According to the *Passio Bartholomaei*: 'Therefore the devil, who won a victory through a man who ate, was condemned by one who fasted' (Murdoch 1974: 32). John Milton expresses it thus in his *Paradise Regained:*

> By one man's firm obedience fully tried
> Through all temptation, and the tempter foiled
> In all his wiles, defeated and repulsed,
> And Eden raised in the waster wilderness.
> (Book I, 1–7; Gorbunov 2006: 47)

The Genesis connection is occasionally made in art, where Christ and the tempter are depicted under a large tree (e.g. Metz School ivory, c. 850; Albani Psalter, 1119–1146; Schiller 1971: fig. 391, fig. 394). The *Biblia Pauperum* (British Library Blockbook C.9 d.2) explicitly juxtaposes Christ's temptation with the Fall of Adam and Eve, as well as with Esau selling Jacob his birthright (Gen 25:29–34; Labriola and Smeltz 1990: 24).

The location in the wilderness leads Tertullian to find an Israel–Christ typology, Jesus reliving the experience of Israel yet victorious where the first Israel failed (Steiner 1962: 81–97):

> For the people, after crossing the sea, and being carried about in the desert during forty years, although they were there nourished with divine supplies, nevertheless were more mindful of their belly and their gullet than of God. Thereupon the Lord, driven apart into desert places after baptism, showed, by maintaining a fast of forty days, that the man of God lives 'not by bread alone,' but 'by the word of God.' (Tertullian, *De Bapt.* 20; *ANF* 3:679)

Many modern exegetes concur (e.g. Davies and Allison 1988: 352, 360–361; but cf. Luz 2007: 150–151). A variant is found in Justin Martyr, who presents Jacob, *alias* Israel, struggling with the angel (Gen 32:23–33) as a type of Christ struggling with Satan (*Trypho* 125). Thus Jesus is both second Adam and true Israel.

Hilary of Poitiers is especially sensitive to the intertextual richness of the temptation story (see Doignon 1975). The 40 days recall the waters of the Flood (Gen 7:11–12), the scouting out of the Promised Land (Num 13:25; Neh 9:21), God's writing the Mosaic Law (Exod 24:18), and the 40-year wanderings in the wilderness (Ps 78:25).

Christological Implications

The temptation story has been treated as Christologically significant, and Christologically problematic, in almost equal measure. Irenaeus' reading presupposes that the episode plays a key role in Christ's defeat of the devil. It also proves polemically advantageous in his battle with Docetism, revealing that Christ was 'a real and substantial man' who suffered genuine hunger (*Adv. Haer.* 5.21.2: *ANF* 1:549). Later Antiochene interpreters emphasize how the event is a test of Christ's filial obedience (e.g. Theodoret of Cyrus, *De incarnatione Domini* 13–15; Chrysosotom). In the West, Leo the Great finds a scriptural defense of Christ's two natures: 'for by His bodily hunger His perfect Manhood was shown, and by the attendant angels His perfect Godhead' (Leo the Great, *Sermon* 40.3: *NPNF* 2nd series, 12: 155).

The ministration of angels *after* the temptation is an important feature of Matthew's account (cf. Mark 1:13). In the *Harvard Passion Play*, the archangels Gabriel, Uriel, and Raphael feed Jesus with a meal prepared by his mother, which they have carried from Nazareth, along with heavenly bread (*Harvard Passion Play* lines 854–972; Elliott and Runnalls 1978: 123–135). In his *Christ in the Desert, Served by Angels* (1608–1610; Berlin), the artist Lodovico Carracci exploits the Eucharistic potential of the scene. Christ stands at an altar-like table, extending his hands to be washed by attendant angels, like a priest at Mass.

Other interpreters struggle with the notion that the divine Son of God could undergo extreme hunger or temptation (Luz 2007: 153–154). For some, Christ's humanity is the veil which leads the devil to be deceived (e.g. Gregory of Nyssa, *Orat. Cat.* 26.1). Hilary understands Christ's hunger figuratively: 'The Lord hungered not for the food of man but for their salvation' (Hilary of Poitiers 2012: 55). Gregory the Great emphasizes how Christ's temptation differed from ours. Temptation takes three forms: suggestion, delight, and consent. Christ, as God, could only be tempted 'by suggestion' or 'in a rhetorical sense' (*per suggestionem,* Kraszewski 1999: 268), 'but no delight in sin took hold of his heart. This whole diabolic temptation then took place from without, not from within' (*Homilies on the Gospels* 14; Gregory the Great 1990: 102). In the sixteenth-century *Harvard Passion Play*, it is Christ's superior intelligence which dooms the devil's temptation to failure. As the demon Asmo warns Satan: 'He is clever | In the face of attack. | Satan, you will never get him!' (*Harvard Passion Play* lines 796–798; Elliott and Runnell 1978: 119).

Modern readers, by contrast, are more interested in Jesus' psychology, assuming that Matthew's narrative is sufficiently historical to provide access to Christ's inner state. As the American Presbyterian minister Andrew Flinn Dickson noted in his 1872 study:

> The true place of conflict was not the desert, or the pinnacle of the temple, or the exceeding high mountain. It was *the soul of Jesus;* his finite, human soul, perplexed and oppressed by the mysteries of his position, and borne down yet more by a suffering and weakened body. (Dickson 1872: 19)

As explored by Nikos Kazantzakis in his 1955 novel *The Last Temptation of Christ* (adapted for film by Martin Scorsese in 1988), this internal conflict between spirit and flesh extends beyond the wilderness period to embrace the totality of Christ's earthly life. Following a lead in Matthew's text, whereby the 'last temptation' comes from the passersby at the cross (27:40, reprising 4:3, 6), Kazantzakis presents this as a temptation to renounce his destiny in favor of domestic bliss with Mary Magdalene. For Fyodor Dostoyevsky's Grand Inquisitor in *The Brothers Karamazov* (1879–1880), Christ's rejection of Satan's three temptations was misguided, opting for a freedom beyond the grasp of ordinary human beings.

That the devil can cite Scripture (4:6) and that Christ three times responds 'It is written' (4:4, 7, 10) has led to the occasional suggestion that Satan appeared to Jesus in the guise of a scribe (e.g. Bengel 1971: 93). This may explain his visual depiction from the fifteenth century as a monk or friar, the contemporary counterparts to a Jewish scribe (e.g. Sandro Botticelli, *The Temptations of Christ*; 1480–1482, Sistine Chapel).

Exemplary Character

In popular reception, the temptation story has been important, not so much for what it reveals about Christ's uniqueness as for its exemplary character. The first temptation, for example, is a reminder that the soul is 'nourished by the Divine Word | And by all its sermons'; the second that one 'should honor one's lord | Wherever one finds him' (*Harvard Passion Play* lines 740–741, 747–748; Elliott and Runnalls 1978: 115). A twelfth-century homily in preparation for Lent makes the point in general terms: 'But he did this as an example for our way of living, because he wished us to understand how easily he overcame the devil – not with his divine power alone, but with human righteousness. So, too, every man can now overcome the devil, if he passes his life in righteousness and in good deeds' (Belfour 1909: 99).

Equally important is Matthew's emphasis on an extended period of fasting. An Old English homily for Quadragesima Sunday takes Christ's fasting as a universal example for all: 'So it is necessary for us to fast; for we are often tempted by the devil after our baptism. The Lord warned us with his fasting and with all his deeds, that we should serve him and overcome the devil' ('Blickling Homilies'; translation from Murdoch 1974: 59). The popular Lenten hymn 'Forty Days and Forty Nights' by George Hunt Smyttan (1822–1870) finds encouragement in Christ's being 'tempted, and yet undefiled' during his 'fasting in the wild' for Christians who emulate his experience during their own Lenten fast:

> Should not we thy sorrow share and from worldly joys abstain,
> fasting with unceasing prayer, strong with thee to suffer pain?
> (*The Hymnal 1982*: 150)

The centrality of Lenten fasting becomes a source of division in Reformation debates. Calvin mocks those who seek to imitate Christ's 40-day fast during Lent. For him, Christ's fasting was unique, 'a distinctive badge of the divine glory,' and observed 'only once' during his life (Calvin 1949: 208–209; see also *Institutes* 4.12.20). In literature, John Milton's *Paradise Regained* (1671) also plays down the exemplary dimensions of Christ's temptation (see Clarke 2003: 51).

By contrast to Calvin and Milton, Christian monastics, and those exercising ministry, have often found Christ's wilderness asceticism a particular model. The sixth-century Coptic bishop Rufus of Shotep offers this homiletic exhortation: 'The Word has been taken to the wilderness. Let the spiritual man flee there with him' (Rufus of Shotep 1998: 141). For the sixteenth-century Jesuit Cornelius a Lapide, Christ's example teaches 'that those who are about to become doctors, preachers, prelates, apostles, must needs be first proved by temptations, and be strengthened by prayer and meditation in solitary retreats, and there drink in a large supply of the Spirit, which they may afterwards pour forth upon others' (Lapide 1890: 1/143).

Allegorical Readings

Many details of this rich narrative have been susceptible to allegorical readings. Some of these are driven by concerns to contemporize the narrative, as well as sensitivity to the wider revelation of Scripture. Thus, for the fifth-century exegete Arnobius the Younger, the 'stones' are humanity, with hardened hearts; the 'temple' Christians, whose pinnacle is love (*Expositiunculae in Matthaeum* 5; Kraszewski 1999: 268). Alternatively, some difficulty in the text challenges the reader to find a more satisfactory allegorical reading. Rufus of Shotep concludes that 'the holy city' to which the devil takes Christ cannot be literal Jerusalem, which stoned the prophets (23:37): 'Rather, the city of each one is his soul,' where the faithful interpreter of scripture constructs a 'temple' with a pinnacle which is 'the height of spiritual interpretation,' the height of virtue (Rufus of Shotep 1998: 146).

Many, like the evangelist himself (e.g. 1:17; 14:17, 20–21; 15:34, 37–38; 18:22), are sensitive to the symbolic significance of numbers. Hence, the meaning of the '40 days' extends beyond the obviously typological. Origen proposes two explanations for the '40 days' (four times ten). The first connects the number to the four elements out of which the world of the senses is formed. The second proposes the fittingness that the time of fasting in preparation for the new creation matches that required for human beings to be formed in the womb (Origen, *Frag.* 61; Simonetti 2001: 57). Gregory the Great explains the number (ten times four) on the grounds that the Mosaic Decalogue finds its fulfillment in the four Gospels (*Homily* 14; Gregory the Great 1990: 104).

To 'Galilee of the Gentiles' (4:12–17)

Matthew's introduction to Jesus' ministry is replete with place-names. The focus of its Galilean phase is Capernaum (Tell Hum), probably derived from *Kephar Nahum* ('the village of Nahum'). Jerome, however, proposes a different etymology, *caphar naim* or 'field of pleasantness,' which for Cornelius a Lapide is indicative of its surpassing 'wealth, luxury, and beauty' (Lapide 1890: 1/168). This seems to give the village greater prestige than is historically probable.

The tribal names Zebulun and Naphthali (Isa 9:1–2) are often taken, following Eusebius' *Onomasticon,* to designate two distinct Galilees: 'Galilee of the Gentiles' in the territory of Naphthali, and a 'Galilee of the Jews' around the Sea of Galilee in the 'land of Zebulun' (see Luz 2007: 158, n. 19). Thus the quotation from Isaiah is understood as prophesying the mission to both groups. Some give the names symbolic significance. Cyril of Alexandria interprets 'Zebulun' as 'a sweet smell and blessing,' and 'Naphthali' as 'a sprouted stump.' Both names describe what Christian believers have become (*Fragment* 37; Simonetti 2001: 74). For Theophylact, they mean 'noctural' and 'a broadening' respectively (Theophylact 1992: 41), signifying the 'dark and broad' life of the Gentiles prior to receiving the 'great light' of the Gospel.

Theophylact's understanding of 'the great light' as the preached good news is plausible, given that Matthew locates the Isaiah quotation in the context of Christ's evangelical preaching. Óscar Romero (1917–1980), El Salvadorian archbishop and martyr, stresses that it is a good news which challenges the complacent: 'A preaching that does not discomfort sinners but lulls them in their sin leaves Zebulun and Naphtali in the shadow of death' (Romero 2003: 46). Alternatively, the light could be Christ himself (John 1:4–5), or the presence in the world of the disciples, who are called 'the light of the world' at 5:14. For Cyril of Alexandria, the great light is both 'Christ our Lord and the brightness of the gospel preaching' (*Fragment* 34; Simonetti 2001: 67).

Four Disciples Called (4:18–22)

The four Gospels diverge in recounting how the first disciples encounter Jesus. Pseudo-Bonaventure is typical in harmonizing the difficulties (*Meditations* 19), identifying three separate calls: the first by the Jordan (John 1:35–42), the second while fishing (Luke 5:1–11), the third while mending their nets (4:18–22; Mark 1:16–20). Thus the dramatic call to 'follow me' is acted upon in light of these earlier encounters. Modern preachers also sometimes presuppose an earlier encounter with Christ, albeit to offer a psychological explanation of the abrupt abandonment of family and trade. Such interpretations, however, fail to do justice to the urgency of the Matthean narrative.

This story is important for the biographies of these four apostles, particularly Andrew, about whom little else is known from the New Testament (John claims he was an early follower of John the Baptist, and that he and his brother were from the city of Bethsaida, John 1:40, 44; see also Mark 13:3; John 6:8; 12:22). On the basis of the Johannine account, the Orthodox East honors him as 'the First-called,' according him a certain primacy to parallel Rome's stress on the primacy of Peter. Various traditions and legends emerge concerning his subsequent career. Origen claims that Andrew preached in Scythia (in Eusebius, *H.E.* 3.1), while the Syriac *Teaching of the Apostles* has him evangelize Nicaea, Nicodemia, Bithynia, and Galatia (McDowell 2015: 179; thus he shared missionary territory with his brother Peter: 1 Pet 1:1). The apocryphal *Acts of Andrew* also connects him with Byzantium, and records his martyrdom by crucifixion at Patras, Greece, where his relics are traditionally preserved. Later tradition has him martyred on an X-shaped cross, hence the saltire Cross of St. Andrew on the Scottish flag. The connection with Scotland is established by traditions that his relics were taken there from Constantinople by Regulus, a monk of Patras; the 1320 Declaration of Arbroath even claims that the apostle had evangelized the Scots. Andrew is also claimed as patron saint by Greece, Luxembourg, Romania, Russia, and Ukraine. His feast is celebrated on 30 November, for which Matthew's story of his call is the Gospel. Peter and the sons of Zebedee have a much higher profile in the New Testament and beyond, especially Peter and John (James will be martyred by Herod Agrippa I in 62 CE: Acts 12:2).

Matthew's sparse narrative is scoured for every scrap of detail. Jerome concludes from their occupation that the four fishermen were illiterate, giving them an exemplary character: 'lest it be thought that the faith of believers comes from eloquence and learning rather than from the power of God' (Jerome 2008: 74). John Calvin similarly views them as 'rough mechanics – persons not only destitute of learning, but inferior in capacity,' ripe for training and renewal by the Holy Spirit (Calvin 1949: 243). Theophylact points to the need of the sons of Zebedee to repair their nets as evidence that they were materially poor. John Chrysostom goes even further: 'For in truth they had nothing to be proud of, being fishermen, poor, ignoble, and illiterate' (*Homily* 15: Pelikan 1967: 42), while Desiderius Erasmus adds that they were young, emphasizing the greater openness of youth to new teaching. In his reflection on the call of Peter and Andrew, Gregory the Great meets head-on a potential objection, that their poverty meant they had given up little to follow Christ:

> The kingdom of God has no assessment value put on it, but it is worth everything you have. To Zacchaeus it was worth half his goods, because he kept the other half to restore fourfold what he had taken unjustly; to Peter and Andrew it was worth the nets and boat they gave up; to the widow it was worth two small coins; to another person it was worth a cup of cold water. (*Homily* 2; Gregory the Great 1990: 11)

This view of the four as poor and uneducated permeates the popular Christian consciousness through devotional texts and hymnody, as in the hymn by William Alexander Percy (1924):

> They cast their nets in Galilee
> Just off the hills of brown
> Such happy simple fisherfolk
> Before the Lord came down.

Modern scholarly study of fishing in first-century Galilee, by contrast, offers a very different assessment of the socio-economic status of Galilean fishermen (e.g. Wuellner 1967).

The urgency of their response reminds both ancient and modern interpreters of Elisha (e.g. John Chrysostom; Nolland 2005: 178), although Elisha was permitted to take leave of his parents rather than leave 'immediately' (1 Kgs 19:19–21). Alternatively, Chromatius of Aquileia thinks of Abraham, who also left his earthly father in response to a divine call (*Tractate on Matthew* 16.2; see Gen 12:1–3). Chromatius also regards Jesus' call to Peter and Andrew as fulfillment of Jeremiah 16:16: 'I am now sending for many fishermen, says the Lord, and they shall catch them …' (also Lapide; France 2007: 147 notes the parallel, though he recognizes that Jeremiah is concerned with sinners being 'caught' for judgment). Rufus of Shotep draws greater significance from the mythological associations of 'the sea' (see above on 3:13–17). Thus he sees in the choice of four fishermen in 'Galilee of the Gentiles' a direct attack on the 'prince of wickedness' who inhabits the sea: these fishermen, who know the craft of the sea so well, will be able to dive to 'the house of the dragon' (Rufus of Shotep 1998: 151).

For Hilary, the call of the first four apostles prefigures the number of the evangelists, who preach the Gospel in writing. Aquinas presents them as types of preachers in the church. However, a more universal interpretation, as applicable to all Christians, is also common. In the *Opus imperfectum*, the apostles are understood as teaching 'us by leaving their nets behind that no one can own anything earthly and come perfectly to heaven' (Kellerman and Oden 2010: 78). Katharina Schütz Zell (c. 1498–1562), one of the few women writers of the early Reformation, hears this passage as addressed directly to her as part of the priesthood of all believers. Hence she calls herself a 'fisher of people' in assisting the male reformers in her native Strasbourg (Zell 2006: 16, 226). A similar broad application appears in the hymn 'Dear Lord and Father of Mankind' by the Quaker John Greenleaf Whittier. Recalling the episode 'beside the Syrian sea,' the hymn urges a similar 'simple trust' on the part of the contemporary believer: 'Let us, like them, without a word | Rise up and follow Thee.'

The Sermon on the Mount: An Overview

> All this sermon-on-the-mount-but-no miracle business is most saddening. Because it's about impossibilities. You can receive a sacrament, and you can find salvation, but you can't live the sermon on the mount. So of course it makes people discontented. (Macaulay 1921: 52)

So comments 'Grandmama,' a character in Rose Macaulay's 1921 novel *Dangerous Ages*, extolling the advantages of Roman Catholicism and the Salvation Army over her unhappy daughter's Unitarianism. Grandmama articulates a common reaction to what is probably the most famous block of Jesus' teaching (marked

Matthew Through the Centuries, First Edition. Ian Boxall.

out as a single chapter in the 'Old Greek Divisions' found in the fifth-century Codex Alexandrinus: Edwards 2010: 422). Known at least since Augustine as the Lord's 'Sermon on the Mount,' a title which was adopted by sixteenth-century English translations such as the Coverdale Bible and the Catholic Rheims New Testament (McArthur 1960: 11), it contains memorable material: the Beatitudes, the Lord's Prayer, and the Golden Rule. Form-critically, it could be categorized as a 'compendium' or *epitome,* a proposal already made in the sixteenth century by Erasmus, 'presenting the theology of Jesus in a systematic fashion' (Betz 1985: 14–15; but see Carlston 1988). Parallels with Luke's 'Sermon on the Plain' (Luke 6:20–49) have suggested to interpreters both ancient and modern that the two Sermons are variants of the same. Modern redaction critics often conclude that Matthew is responsible for shaping disparate teachings of Christ into the coherent discourse we now possess, albeit drawing on existing traditions including a shorter sermon in Q. A similar solution was already proposed by John Calvin, who urged his pious readers to be 'satisfied with having a brief summary of the doctrine of Christ placed before their eyes, collected out of his many and various discourses' (Calvin 1949: 259). A variant is that of Hans Dieter Betz, who holds that the Sermon is a pre-Matthean product of anti-Pauline Jewish-Christian circles, incorporated by the evangelist into his narrative (Betz 1995: 80–88).

The conviction that the Matthean Sermon is an artificial construct of teachings delivered on separate occasions seems to have influenced Pier Paolo Pasolini in his 1964 film *Il Vangelo secondo Matteo*. Pasolini presents the Sermon through a series of headshots of Jesus against a changing sky to suggest variation in time (see Aichele 2002: 529–530; on Pasolini's reworking of Matthew, see Goodacre 2000: 35–36). Augustine, by contrast, after weighing the options, concludes as 'probable' that Matthew's was delivered on the mountain to the disciples; Christ then descended 'to a level place' where he provided an abridged version for the sake of the crowds, preserved by Luke (Augustine, *Agreement Among the Evangelists* 2.19.47; see Tholuck 1834: 2). A modern variant is that of the Hindu Swami Prabhavananda: Jesus, like every spiritual teacher, has two sets of teaching, one for the crowds (Luke's), the other for his disciples (Matthew's: Swami Prabhavananda 1964: 17–18).

Whatever its sources, the Sermon is internally coherent and structured (Luz 2007: 172–174). It contains favorite Matthean concepts (e.g. 'fulfill'; 'righteousness'; a moral dualism focused on the 'two ways'). It is also the first of five major discourses which punctuate Matthew's narrative of Christ's ministry (also Matt 10; 13; 18; 24–25), drawing the audience into the ongoing significance of Jesus' teaching for Christian life.

Contested Meaning

Yet the meaning of the Sermon on the Mount is as contested as it is famous. In part, this is due to a profoundly Jewish text – in W.D. Davies' words, 'the Christian answer to Jamnia' (referring to the so-called rabbinic 'council' in that city: Davies 1964: 315) – being reread in the very different circumstances in which later Christians found themselves (see Pelikan 2001: 41–45). Thus some of its teachings (e.g. plucking out one's eye, 5:29) might be examples of Semitic hyperbole rather than commands to be observed literally. But there are other reasons for profound disagreement over its interpretation. The relationship of the Sermon's teaching to the Law of Moses is open to debate (what precisely does Jesus mean by 'fulfill,' 5:17?). Its specific audience, and contemporary referents, are also disputed. Is it addressed only to the disciples, or also the crowds? If the former, do they represent all followers of Christ, or specifically the apostles and those believed to be their successors, the bishops or ministers? If the latter, then does this extend the Sermon's strictures to the whole church, laity ('crowds') as well as clergy ('disciples'), or do 'the crowds' signify non-Christians?

Furthermore, is the teaching of the Sermon meant to provide wisdom for individual believers only, or does it set down a pattern to be adopted by whole societies? Is it applicable for all time, or only for specific circumstances? The 1909 *Scofield Reference Bible*, for example, treats the Sermon as 'pure Law,' for the future dispensation of the millennial Kingdom, and therefore not directly applicable to the church living in the dispensation of grace (Scofield 1917: 999–1000; Turner 2010: 703–705; for the range of Dispensationalist interpretations of the Sermon, see Martin 1986). Albert Schweitzer, following Johannes Weiss, famously viewed it as presenting an 'interim ethic,' radical demands for disciples in preparation for the supernatural Kingdom that Schweitzer's apocalyptic Jesus believed to be imminent (Schweitzer 1914). In Jeremias' immortal words, this presents 'a form of "martial law" declared in the last decisive phase of a total war' (Jeremias 1961: 14). Others, like Macaulay's 'Grandmama,' have wondered whether the rigorous demands of the Sermon are even possible, or, in the words of the Grand Inquisitor in Fyodor Dostoyevsky's *The Brothers Karamazov*, whether Jesus has 'judged humanity too highly' (in Davies and Allison 2004: 76).

There are early indications that the Sermon was perceived as presenting demands which, if not completely impossible, were too demanding for the average Christian. The *Didache* clearly presents the Gospel message as the 'narrow path' in a Two Ways theology, addressed to all Christians. Nonetheless, it acknowledges that this 'higher righteousness' may not be attainable for some: 'For if thou canst bear the whole yoke of the Lord, thou wilt be perfect, but if thou canst not, do what thou canst' (*Did.* 6:2: Lake 1912: 319; compare Matt 5:48). The textual history of Matthew 5–7 also evidences scribal attempts to soften its demanding character. Thus some manuscripts insert the phrase 'without cause' at 5:22, rather than have Jesus condemn all cases of anger against brother or sister (Metzger 1994: 11). Hence Chromatius of Aquileia can speak of the Gospel forbidding 'causeless wrath' (*irascendum sine causa:* Kraszewski 1999: 273). This is the reading underlying the KJV: 'But I say unto you, That whosoever is angry with his brother without a cause shall be in danger of the judgment.' In the sixteenth century, John Calvin appeals to a canonical principle when interpreting Matthew 5:33–37 to avoid a total prohibition of oath-taking. In Calvin's reasoning, since God commands oaths at Exodus 22:10–11, the Sermon should only be interpreted as banning oaths that 'abuse and profane the sacred name' (Guelich 1987: 120; Calvin, *Harmony* I, 295; *Institutes* I, 391).

A Sermon for All Christians

Nonetheless, the dominant view from the early patristic period onwards has been that the Sermon lies at the center of the Christian message, and presents a call to perfection addressed to all Christians (on its history of interpretation and reception, see e.g. Tholuck 1834; Jeremias 1961; Kissinger 1975; Beyschlag 1977; Grant 1978; Bauman 1985; Guelich 1987; Allen 1992; Betz 1995: 5–44; Clarke 2003: 61–94; Luz 2007: 177–181; Greenman, Larsen, and Spencer 2007). It is one of the most widely cited sections of the Gospels in the early centuries, when we find the Christian apologist Athenagoras (c. 133–190) seeking to persuade Emperor Marcus Aurelius that the Sermon reveals the superiority of Christ's teaching over paganism (*Embassy* 32). Ephrem the Syrian commented extensively on the Sermon, albeit as mediated through Tatian's harmonized version (see McCarthy 1991; Hogan 1999). Ten of John Chrysostom's 90 homilies on the Gospel of Matthew are devoted to Matthew 5–7, presenting the Sermon as a 'greater philosophy' which makes the Christian life superior to others (see Pelikan 2001: 67–80; Mitchell 2007). Augustine's early work *De Sermone Domini in monte*, composed between 392 and 394 during a sabbatical following his ordination as priest, offers a sustained account of his own interpretation (Augustine 2014: 23–114), although he continued to return to this subject at various points throughout his career (see Pelikan 2001: 53–66; Wilken 2007).

Augustine well summarizes the dominant Christian view. The Sermon embodies 'the perfect summary of all those precepts necessary for leading the Christian life' (Augustine 2014: 23). Augustine's view will hold firm throughout the Middle Ages and beyond. 'Read it often and diligently,' Pseudo-Bonaventure exhorts his late medieval readers, 'and commit to memory the things said in it, for they are spiritual' (*Meditations* 21; Ragusa and Green 1961: 152). The Anglican priest-poet John Donne expresses it even more eloquently in a Lenten sermon from 1629:

> All the articles of our religion, all the canons of our Church, all the injunctions of our princes, all the homilies of our fathers, all the body of divinity, is in these three chapters, in this one sermon in the Mount. (quoted in McArthur 1960: 12)

Similarly, in a journal entry from 1771, John Wesley describes the Sermon as 'the noblest compendium of religion which is to be found even in the oracles of God' (quoted in Noll 2007: 153).

Apologetic and Polemical Use

But the Sermon on the Mount has also functioned as a storm-center of Christian controversy. It was widely cited in the Ante-Nicene period, both by Gnostic groups who sought to penetrate its deeper significance (see Grant 1978: 219–225) and by their orthodox opponents, stressing the continuity of Christ's teaching with the Old Law against Gnostics and Marcionites (e.g. Irenaeus, *Adv. Haer.* 4.12–13; Tertullian, *Adv. Marc.* 4.14–17). Origen is forced to confront head-on the objections of Celsus, that Jesus' teaching merely plagiarizes Socrates and Plato (*Cels.* 7: 58). At a later period, Augustine engages the Sermon on the Mount against the Manicheans, who read it as supporting their radical dualism (Betz 1995: 46). Augustine emphasizes the Sermon's continuity with the Old Testament. He also finds resources to refute the Donatists (the distinction between suffering persecution and doing so 'for the sake of righteousness,' Matt 5:10) and Pelagians (the necessity of praying for the forgiveness of debts, Matt 6:12). John Chrysostom also seeks to combat Manichean tendencies; as important for him, however, is the Sermon's capacity to shine a penetrating light on the lukewarm commitment of many who listened to his homilies in Antioch (Pelikan 1967: 12–19).

The use of the Sermon is particularly pronounced in Reformation polemics. Martin Luther is remembered for his two-pronged attack on both Catholic and Anabaptist readings. On the one hand, he objected to a 'monastic' distinction used by some Catholic theologians, probably emerging with the Benedictine Rupert of Deutz (c. 1075–1129), between 'precepts' binding on all Christians and 'counsels of perfection' or 'evangelical counsels' for those wishing a more perfect imitation of Christ (see e.g. Kissinger 1975: 17–18; Pelikan 1997: 119–121). This distinction between *praecepta* and *consilia* is classically expressed in Thomas Aquinas's *Summa Theologiae* (*S.T.* 2.1. q. 107–108), which presents Christ's invitation to the rich man (Matt 19:21), and the call to some to be 'eunuchs' for the sake of the Kingdom (Matt 19:12), as examples of the latter. However, it seems to have been far less central to medieval Catholic thought than the Protestant polemic suggests (Luz 2007: 178). Aquinas himself emphasizes the Sermon's function as a New Law, written on human hearts, which reveals not so much what we can do, but rather 'what the Holy Spirit wants to accomplish in our lives' (Pinckaers 1998: 16).

On the other hand, Luther critiques the 'new monasticism' of the Anabaptists. Their radical interpretation, which emphasized the supremacy of the New Testament over the Old, viewed the Sermon as providing the norms for a new kind of Christian society, i.e. to be observed literally by whole communities. In some cases (e.g. the Swiss Brethren and Mennonites) complete separation from state structures is envisaged (Kissinger 1975: 29–34; Guelich 1987: 119). Early Anabaptist sources reveal the centrality of the Sermon on the Mount for community praxis. The *Biblical Concordance of the Swiss Brethren, 1540*, an Anabaptist compilation of biblical texts in a form lending itself to memorization by those who were illiterate, has several sections rooted in the Sermon: Prayer; Fasting; Almsgiving; Righteousness; Mercy; Treasure; Do Not Worry; No One Can Serve Two Masters; Swearing (Fast and Peters 2001).

Luther's contemporary John Calvin also opposes the Anabaptists, though by emphasizing the continuity between the Mosaic Law and Jesus' teaching, the latter understood as cleansing and correcting distortions of the former (*Institutes* 1.26), and the former providing the key to correct interpretation of the Sermon's precepts such as oath-taking (Kissinger 1975: 26–29; Spencer 2007). Calvin's position equally critiqued the medieval tendency to treat the Sermon as a 'new Law.' Similar is that of the English Reformer William Tyndale (c. 1494–1536). In his 1532 'Exposition Uppon the V. VI. VII. Chapters of Mathew,' Tyndale understands the Sermon as the 'restoring agayne' of the Law of Moses corrupted by the scribes and Pharisees, actualized in the sixteenth century through Tyndale's exposition, which marks 'the restoring agayne of Christes Lawe corrupte by the Papistes' (Duffield 1965: 182).

Luther's own pragmatic position, set out in his 1532 commentary (Luther 1956: 3–294), proposes the concept of the two realms. This makes a distinction between an individual Christian's 'person' and his 'office' in secular society, ordained by God to ensure law and order; the distinction between a Christian *coram Deo* or *Christperson* and a Christian *coram hominibus* or *Weltperson*. The Sermon is concerned with the former, not with worldly social and political structures. Thus, for example, Christians may obey Christ's command to 'turn the other cheek' in their personal life, while using violence against an evildoer as a judge or member of the army (see Kissinger 1975: 20–23; Pelikan 1997:

277–279; Pelikan 2001: 81–89, 144–149; Schreiner 2007). On a personal level, therefore, the Sermon plays a positive role in orienting Christian living: it presents a Christ who comes, not with demands or threats, but 'in a very friendly way, with enticements, allurements, and pleasant promises' (Luther 1956: 10). There is little in Luther's interpretation of the 'impossible ideal' associated with later Protestant scholasticism, whereby the Sermon's unbearable demands were meant to expose human sinfulness and the need for justification by faith (see e.g.; Oberdorfer 2015; Grosshans 2015). For him, the Sermon is addressed to those who have already been justified by faith, and concerns the fruit produced in the Christian's life by God's grace (Guelich 1982: 16–17).

The Sermon's Radical Demands

The perspective of the Radical Reformation is arguably closer in spirit to Matthew's own perspective than Luther's pragmatism (Luz, following Troeltsch, finds in both the Gospel and the Anabaptists the perfectionist 'sect' theology: Luz 2007: 178). Moreover, it has its antecedents in earlier centuries. Luther's comment about 'monkish' interpretations, albeit sarcastic, is not far from the truth. Early Christian monasticism (the 'new martyrdom') gave a central place to the demands of the Sermon, as had actual martyrs before them, and this helps explain its central place in the thought of John Chrysostom, himself a monastic. Francis of Assisi (1181/1182–1226) and his 'Lesser Brothers' famously embraced the radical demands of the Sermon, providing a dramatic example of 'actualization': 'Francis wrote little about the Sermon; he preferred to act it out' (Allen 1992: 251). The liturgical Office for the feast of St. Francis, by Julian of Speyer (1228–1232), presents the saint's life of radical discipleship as a perfect expression of the Sermon's fulfillment of Law and prophets (5:17–20):

> Francis, taking up the Gospel,
> Not a single dot or morsel
> Nor a jot did he transgress.
> (Antiphon for First Vespers, in Armstrong, Hellmann and Short 1999: 328)

A similar combination of radical poverty and itinerant preaching is found in Francis's older contemporary Peter Waldo or Pierre Vaudès (c. 1140–1205), founder of the Waldensians. For Waldo, Matthew 6:25–34, which urges radical dependence on God, seems to have been particularly inspirational (Gonnet 1986).

This insistence that the Sermon's uncompromising demands can provide a blueprint for communal living has continued to find supporters in subsequent centuries. The establishment in 1850 of *Taiping Tianguo* or 'the great peace kingdom of heaven' by Chinese Christian convert and rebel leader Hong Xiuquan is one concrete expression, albeit founded on an idiosyncratic reading of the Sermon which did not eschew military conquest and violent destruction of Buddhist temples (see Spence 1996; Yieh 2009; Kilcourse 2016). Yet its peaceable dimensions are often to the fore in attempts to actualize its teaching in concrete communities. The *Foundations of Our Faith and Calling* of the contemporary Bruderhof community reveals the central place of the Sermon in its communal life: 'We must prove our love to [Jesus] in deeds, putting into practice his words in the Gospels, especially the Sermon on the Mount' (Bruderhof 2012: 3). The Russian novelist Leo Tolstoy (1828–1910) also came to view the Sermon as central to his understanding of Christ's message, and the final chapter of his novel *Resurrection* is essentially 'a commentary on the Sermon on the Mount' (Pelikan 1997: 228–229). Tolstoy's character Nehlúdof begins reading Matthew's Gospel, which utterly transforms his life, indeed, causes him to begin to live a new life:

> When he had read the Sermon on the Mount, which had always touched him, he saw in it to-day for the first time not beautiful abstract thoughts, setting forth for the most part exaggerated and impossible demands, but simple, clear, practical laws, which if carried out in practice (and this is quite possible) would establish perfectly new and surprising conditions of social life, in which the violence that filled Nehlúdof with such indignation would not only cease of itself, but the greatest blessing attainable by men – the kingdom of heaven on earth – would be reached. (Tolstoy 1927: 512)

Tolstoy's interpretation would profoundly influence the Hindu Mahatma Gandhi (Pelikan 1997: 229), whose daily reading of the Sermon contributed significantly to his philosophy of non-violence. The demands of the Sermon also weigh heavily on the German Lutheran theologian Dietrich Bonhoeffer (1906–1945). For Bonhoeffer, confronted with a secular realm dominated by Nazi ideology, only a literal engagement with the Sermon as embracing the totality of life will suffice. As he writes in his 1937 book *Nachfolge* (published in English as *The Cost of Discipleship*):

> Humanly speaking, we could understand and interpret the Sermon on the Mount in a thousand different ways. Jesus knows only one possibility: simple surrender and obedience, not interpreting it or applying it, but doing and obeying it. (Bonhoeffer 1963: 218–219)

Matthew 5

Ancient Literary Context

The Sermon's opening section contains a set of 'beatitudes' (5:3–12; cf. Luke 6:20–23). In the Old Testament, beatitudes occur in both prophetic (e.g. Isa 32:20; 56:2; Jer 17:7; Dan 12:12) and wisdom traditions (e.g. Pss 1:1; 32:2; 64:5; 84:5; Prov 8:34; Sir 14:20–27; 25:7–11; 4Q525). They tend to express the good fortune of particular groups in the present, consequent upon God's gracious activity. Matthew's Beatitudes contradict one pervasive strand in Old Testament

Matthew Through the Centuries, First Edition. Ian Boxall.

theology, whereby wealth and health signify divine favor (e.g. Deut 6:1–3; Ps 128). They share with beatitudes in the apocalyptic tradition (e.g. Dan 12:12–13; *1 En.* 58:2; *2 En.* 13:28–35; *Sib. Or.* 3:371–72; *Pss. Sol.* 17:50; 18:7; Rev 1:3; 19:9) an eschatological character, pointing beyond the present to future fulfilment ('for they shall ...').

Matthew 5:17–48 expresses the Matthean concept of fulfillment. Its introduction (vv. 17–20) provides the interpretive lens for what follows, firmly rejecting the view that Jesus abrogated the Jewish Law. Some of the details are contested (e.g. in what sense is 'fulfill' being used? does 'until all is accomplished' in 5:18 simply reiterate 'until heaven and earth pass away,' or qualify it?), but the location of these verses makes it clear that what follows in verses 21–48 provide examples of this 'higher righteousness.'

This final section is often called 'the antitheses,' since it juxtaposes quotations from Moses (Exod 20:12–16; 21:23–24; Lev 19:12, 18; 24:19–20; Num 30:2; Deut 5:16–20; 19:21; 23:21; 24:1–4) with Jesus' own teaching. Yet the explicit claim to fulfilment in verses 17–20 makes 'antitheses' a potentially misleading designation. Others have therefore proposed 'supertheses' (theses which 'go beyond') as a better description of Jesus' more demanding invitation (e.g. Lapide 1986: 45–46).

The Interpretations

Jesus Ascends the Mountain (5:1–2)

Matthew begins by recounting Jesus' ascent 'onto the mountain.' Although some propose a more general 'into the hills' (e.g. France 2007: 156), most interpreters presume that a specific Galilean mountain is meant. Matthew is silent about its location, but this has not stopped readers from filling the gap. A mount called Eremus was identified as the place already in the late fourth century, when it was visited by the pilgrim Egeria (according to the seventh-century monk Valerius: Wilkinson 1981: 176). The twelfth-century monk of Monte Cassino, Peter the Deacon, locates it above Tabgha or Heptapegon by the Sea of Galilee: 'Near there on a mountain is the cave to which the Saviour climbed and spoke the Beatitudes' (Peter the Deacon, *Book on the Holy Places* V.4; Wilkinson 1981: 200). This surprising location in a cave suggests a sermon directed specifically to Christ's disciples, rather than the crowds generally. Jerome prefers Mount Tabor, traditionally associated with the Transfiguration, 'or some other high mountain' (a view followed, e.g. by Pseudo-Bonaventure and Cornelius a Lapide). Jerome is rather dismissive of those 'more simple brothers' who locate it on the Mount of Olives, given that this is not in Galilee but in Judea (Jerome 2008: 75).

However, symbolic geography is often as important as literal. Modern commentators regularly stress the parallels with Sinai (e.g. Allison 1993a) or Zion (e.g. Donaldson 1985). The Mosaic echoes are occasionally found in earlier commentators (e.g. Erasmus), and in visual art. Thus in the Sistine Chapel in Rome, Cosimo Rosselli's fresco *The Sermon on the Mount and Healing of the Leper* (1481–1482) directly faces his *The Giving of the Law*, part of a complex Moses–Christ typology spanning the side walls of the chapel. Eusebius of Caesarea recognizes that the Sermon presents Jesus as the expected prophet like Moses (Deut 18:18), although he also draws a distinction between the two. Moses was leader and lawgiver of only one nation; Christ legislates for the whole human race (*Dem. ev.* 9.11). Other patristic exegetes view the location of the Sermon as a reflection of its heavenly character. Hilary interprets the ascent as an allegory of Christ's ascent to 'the height of the Father's majesty'; from eternity, Jesus speaks about eternity (Hilary of Poitiers 2012: 59). Likewise, for Jerome, the ascent refers to the deeper matters to which the crowds are incapable of ascending. The *Opus imperfectum* finds a fulfilment of Isaiah 40:9, which commands the herald of good tidings to ascend a high mountain.

On reaching the mountain's summit, Jesus sits down, befitting his dignity as a teacher (Augustine, *On the Lord's Sermon on the Mount* 1.1.3). The Franciscan Pseudo-Bonaventure further surmises that Christ's posture is one of humility (*Meditations* 21). Surprisingly, Christ's sedentary posture is often overlooked in artistic representations, which depict him standing so as to heighten his prominence: e.g. the early sixth-century mosaic in Sant' Apollinare Nuovo, Ravenna, Cosimo Rosselli's Sistine Chapel fresco, and Jacques Tissot's *The Sermon of the Beatitudes* (1886–1896; Brooklyn Museum).

Christ's precise audience is unclear from Matthew's text: is the Sermon directed only toward the disciples (v. 1b), or also to the crowds who are impressed by his teaching 'with authority' (v. 1a; 7:28–29)? Fra Angelico understands the former in his fresco of the scene, which depicts the Twelve in a semicircle below the seated Christ (1436–1443; Museo di San Marco, Florence). A similar scenario appears in Jacques Callot's 1635 engraving (Figure 7). John Chrysostom finds evidence here for Jesus' rhetorical strategy of drawing in the larger group by focusing on the smaller, more committed disciples. Chrysostom will employ the same strategy to draw in the less committed members of his own congregations in Antioch. The precise relationship between the crowds and the Sermon has provoked the occasional satirical response. Monty Python's 1979 film *The Life of Brian* presents it from the perspective of those on the periphery of the crowd, leading to such humorous mishearings as 'Blessed are the Cheesemakers' (Chapman et al. 1979: 9; on the Sermon in *Monty Python's Life of Brian*, see Walsh 2013; Taylor 2015).

FIGURE 7 Jacques Callot (1592–1635). *Sermon on the Mount.* 1635. Etching. R.L. Baumfeld Collection (Lieure, no. 1421, State i/ii), National Gallery of Art, Washington, DC. Source: Photo courtesy National Gallery of Art, Washington.

Matthew's statement that Jesus opened his mouth (v. 2) is often passed over in silence by modern exegetes, except to note that it is a familiar biblical idiom for a significant pronouncement (e.g. France 2007: 158). By contrast, early interpreters treat this as no mere figure of speech. For Hilary of Poitiers, it alerts the reader that Jesus is allowing the Spirit to speak through his human mouth. Augustine suggests that it is an indication of Christ's divinity, a statement that the one who opened the mouths of Israel's prophets is now speaking directly (*On the Lord's Sermon on the Mount* 1.1.2). For Luther, Christ's action has an exemplary function. It is aimed at the Christian preacher, who 'should also open his mouth vigorously and confidently, to preach the truth that has been entrusted to him' (Luther 1956: 9).

The Beatitudes (5:3–12)

Bible translators are divided on how best to render the Greek *makarioi* and Vulgate *beati*. While most English translations opt for 'blessed' (e.g. Tyndale, Geneva Bible, Douay-Rheims, KJV, NRSV, and NABRE), others prefer 'happy' (e.g. John Wesley; CEB; Rotherham Bible; see Mattison 2013 on 'happiness' and virtue ethics), while the Jesus Seminar's Scholars' Version has the provocative 'Congratulations to ...' Richard France points to the Australian 'Good on yer,' and the traditional Welsh translation *Gwyn eu byd* (literally 'White is their world') as conveying the idiom most effectively (France 2007: 161).

It is often observed that the Beatitudes run counter to conventional wisdom for, as Cornelius a Lapide observes, 'the world and philosophers place blessedness in wealth, not in poverty, in loftiness, not in humility' (Lapide 1890: 1/180–181). They certainly contradict those who understand Jewish messianism in overtly military terms. This is expressed satirically by Francis, a member of the 'People's Front of Judea,' in *Monty Python's Life of Brian*: 'Well, blessed is just about everyone with a vested interest in the status quo ...' (Chapman et al. 1979: 9). In actuality, the Beatitudes have proved profoundly revolutionary in human history, such that their proponents have frequently experienced persecution, as Matthew's Jesus promises (5:10–12: on this beatitude and the Wycliffites, see Jeffrey 2007: 102).

The placing of the Beatitudes at the head of the sermon is significant, as the French bishop Jacques-Bénigne Bossuet (1627–1704) notes in his Gospel meditations for the Visitation nuns: 'If the sermon on the mount is the précis of all Christian doctrine, the eight beatitudes are the précis of the whole of the sermon on the mount' (in Tugwell 1980: 1). Regularly regarded as the *magna carta* for citizens of the Kingdom, the Beatitudes were read at Mass on the western Feast of All Saints (1 November) as indicative of the universal call to holiness, a theme well-articulated in a sermon for the feast by the tenth-century Benedictine Ælfric of Eynsham (Olsen 2015: 167).

A plain reading of 5:3–12 might suggest nine beatitudes rather than Bossuet's eighth. Ephrem the Syrian knows ten, but he is working with Tatian's *Diatessaron*, which combined Matthew's and Luke's (Hogan 1999: 28), and an interest in the mystical dimensions of the number. Bossuet's calculation may be justified on the grounds that the ninth (vv. 11–12) is set apart from the others by its length, and its shift from the third to the second person. Eight is reflected in the octagonal shape of the Church of the Beatitudes in Galilee (built between 1936 and 1938, ironically under a commission from Mussolini). More controversial is Augustine's preference for seven (a perfect number, appropriate for a sermon which teaches how to be perfect, 5:48): this requires treating the eighth in verse 10 as a repetition of the first and a summary of the rest.

Augustine famously views the Beatitudes sequentially, as seven stages on the path to blessedness (although his Latin text reverses the order of vv. 4 and 5, thus referencing the meek prior to the mourners). He is not the first to do so. Influenced by Genesis 28:10–19, Gregory of Nyssa described the Beatitudes as a ladder, leading the Christian in the ascent of virtue to the summit of the mountain (*Sermon on the Beatitudes* 2; Gregory of Nyssa 1954: 97; see also Eklund 2017: 731). Gregory seems to be the unlikely influence on the Baptist preacher Charles Spurgeon (1834–1892), who describes the Beatitudes as a 'celestial ascent' and a 'ladder of light' (Larsen 2007: 194–195). A twentieth-century example comes from Clarence Jordan's *Cotton Patch Version*, produced against the backdrop of the US civil rights movement, which presents the Beatitudes as 'stages in the naturalization of the kingdom citizen' (in Patte et al. 2003: 67).

Augustine's psychological analysis (see Betz 1995: 107) is the most influential on Western thought. He traces their progression from humility (poverty of spirit) through acquaintance with the scriptures (requiring meekness), knowledge (leading one to mourn for the loss of the ultimate good), toil (the hungering for justice as the soul struggles to extricate itself from worldly attachments), reliance on divine mercy (involving a counsel to be merciful oneself), purification of the intellect (purity of heart), to acquisition of wisdom (contemplating the truth, which brings 'a likeness to God') (*The Lord's Sermon on the Mount* 1.3.10; Augustine 2014: 26–27).

Augustine's precise definitions of each beatitude depend on Isaiah 11 as their hermeneutical key. Latin versions of Isaiah 11:2–3 present seven gifts of the Spirit, which Augustine correlates with his seven Beatitudes, albeit in reverse order, beginning with Isaiah's ultimate 'fear of the Lord' (on the grounds that it is the *beginning* of wisdom, Sir 1:14; *The Lord's Sermon on the Mount* 1.4.11). He thus injects an emphasis on divine grace into a Sermon which might otherwise be interpreted as prioritizing human action. He also attempts to correlate Beatitudes and gifts with the seven petitions of the Lord's Prayer (*The Lord's Sermon on the Mount* 2.11.38). The result is a schema which appears 'somewhat artificial and contrived'; nonetheless, it gives greater depth to the Beatitudes as virtues (an interpretation already found in Clement of Alexandria, *Strom.* 4.6.25–41; see Kovacs 2000), and one which is easily memorable for Christians to apply in their own lives (see Wilken 2007: 48–49).

Augustine's interpretation is expanded by the Augustinian theologian Hugh of St. Victor (c. 1096–1141) in his treatise *On the Five Sevens*, which pairs seven virtues with corresponding vices (Coolman 2007). Hugh's idea reappears in Dante's *Purgatorio* where the Beatitudes are presented as sequential steps to the summit of Mount Purgatory, provoking virtues which expurgate a corresponding vice: hence poverty of spirit counters pride, and peacemaking anger (Twomey in Jeffrey 1992: 79; Jeffrey 2007). Thomas Aquinas (*S.T.* Ia-IIae, q. 69, a. 1) also offers a variation on Augustine's schema. Thomas is uneasy with Augustine's correlation of the Beatitudes with the gifts of the Spirit. Rather the virtues and gifts are *habitus*, habits or dispositions, whereas the Beatitudes describe the *actus*, actions resulting from those dispositions.

Perhaps most famous among those who act out the Beatitudes in their Christian lives is Francis of Assisi, described thus by Gregory IX in the bull for Francis's canonization in 1228:

> And as he had received the sevenfold grace of the Spirit and the help of the eight beatitudes of the Gospels, he journeyed to Bethel, the house of God, on a path which he had traced in the fifteen steps of the virtues mystically represented in the psalter. (in Muessig 2009: 137)

The 'fifteen steps' refer to the fifteen 'Gradual Psalms' (Pss 120–134) which marked the 'steps' of ancient pilgrims to Jerusalem.

The Beatitudes in Music and Visual Art

Musical interpretations of the Beatitudes include those by César Franck, Vladimir Martynov, and Arvo Pärt (see Dowling Long and Sawyer 2015: 26–27). In Edward Elgar's 1903 oratorio *The Apostles*, various characters (John, Peter, Judas, the Virgin Mary, the people) react with citations from the Psalms and Isaiah as Jesus intones each beatitude in turn, providing a musical acknowledgment of Matthew's key scriptural sources (Elgar 1903: vi–vii). In the Russian Orthodox Church, the Beatitudes are chanted during the Divine Liturgy, a fact which impressed the British writer A.N. Wilson: 'Think of the old women in Stalin's Russia, when the men were too cowardly to profess their loyalty to the Church, who stubbornly continued to chant the opening verses of the Sermon on the Mount in defiance of the KJB. "Blessed are they that mourn for they shall be comforted" (5:4)' (Wilson 1998: viii).

More surprising, given their non-narrative character, is their frequent depiction in art. Some attempt to convey their 'essence' by giving each a corresponding angel, as in a set of windows produced by the Tiffany Studios in New York. An eschatological interpretation is present in Theodor Galle's 1601 engraving *The Eight Beatitudes,* depicting eight figures above Christ on the mountain, ascending to the heavenly Jerusalem. Alternatively, each beatitude is linked to human exemplars. The Ghent Altarpiece by Jan van Eyck originally contained texts from the Beatitudes, designating the different categories of *beati* around the Lamb (e.g. apostles as 'poor in spirit,' virgins as 'pure in heart,' hermits and pilgrims as 'meek': Philip 1971: 105–107). This probably reflects their liturgical use on All Saints' Day. The windows in St. Front Cathedral in Périgueux, France (by E. Didron of Paris, 1881) illustrate each beatitude through an appropriate Old Testament character (Job as 'poor in spirit'; Abel offering sacrifice as 'pure in heart'; Abraham and Lot as 'peacemakers'). Sixteenth-century Dutch engravings draw on figures from both Testaments. A series produced c. 1566 by

Harmen Jansz. Muller (after Maarten van Heemskerck) presents the stoning of Stephen as illustrative of the 'persecuted,' and the annunciation to Mary of the 'pure in heart,' alongside Job as 'poor in spirit' and Tobit as 'merciful' (Clifton 2014: 558–560). A variant is the early twentieth-century Beatitudes Rose Window by Charles Connick in the Cathedral of St. Paul, St. Paul, Minnesota. This represents the Beatitudes actualized in the lives of eight saints of the Americas.

The Poor in Spirit (5:3)

The precise meaning of 'poor in spirit' is contested (cf. 'you poor' at Luke 6:20). Modern exegetes often look to the *'aniyim* or *'anawim*, the humble poor among God's people (e.g. France 2007: 165). This is a connection already made by Hilary, who references Isaiah 66:2 in interpreting the 'poor in spirit' as 'those who possess the character of humility,' that is, those who remember their humanity (Hilary of Poitiers 2012: 59; also e.g. Gregory of Nyssa, *Sermon on the Beatitudes* 1; Jerome; Augustine, *The Lord's Sermon on the Mount* 1.1.3; Abba John of the Thebaid, *Saying* 1 in Ward 1975: 106). It is adopted as a paraphrase by the NEB (1970): 'How blest are those who know their need of God.' John Chrysostom equates the 'spirit' with the soul, the 'faculty of choice': thus it refers to 'the humble and contrite in mind' (*Homily on Matthew* 15; Pelikan 1967: 41). Ephrem the Syrian emphasizes that such people have become poor 'of their own volition' (in Hogan 1999: 31).

The early Franciscans interpret 'poor in spirit' as genuine poverty for the sake of Christ. In a sermon to fellow friars, the Franciscan theologian Bonaventure (1221–1274) elucidates:

> *Blessed*, he said, *are the poor in spirit*; and for this reason, poverty, which is fled from in fear by all those living in a worldly way, is accepted or must be accepted by perfect men, because as the primary foundation of evangelical instruction, it completes and leads to perfection in the present life. (Johnson 2008: 522)

For Bonaventure, the greatest exemplar of spiritual poverty, as of the other Beatitudes, is Christ himself (in Ford 1859: 141).

By contrast, Luther reads 'poor in spirit' in terms of his doctrine of the two kingdoms. The Beatitudes are not to do with the secular realm, but only the personal, 'how to live before God, above and beyond the external.' Hence even a man with considerable wealth can be called 'spiritually poor,' if 'he does not covet it or set his comfort and trust upon it as though it were his kingdom of heaven' (Luther 1956: 12, 19). The rich King David was such an exemplar of poverty of spirit. For William Tyndale, for whom God apportions wealth and poverty as he wills, poverty of spirit is 'neither beggary, nor against the possessing of riches, but a virtue contrary to the vice of covetousness, the inordinate desire and love of riches, and putting trust in riches' (Duffield 1965: 194).

Some German exegetes (e.g. Olearius, Michaelis, Paulus) propose taking the qualifier 'in spirit' with 'blessed/happy': i.e. the poor are spiritually happy, thus avoiding a major clash with the Lucan 'Happy are you poor.' This solution is hard to justify given the word-order, however (see Meyer 1877: 157).

Those Who Mourn (5:4)

The second beatitude is third in most Latin versions. It is unique in the list for promising happiness on those who find themselves suffering a particular condition (mourning; cf. Luke 6:21) rather than positively pursuing a specific disposition. Moreover, for much of human history, human misery and bereavement have been integral to everyday life, such that all might be said to mourn at some point. The earliest interpreters see the problems, and generally avoid treating this beatitude as a literal reference to mourning for the dead. Several interpret it as a 'mourning' for sins, whether those of others (e.g. Jerome) or one's own (Hilary; Ephrem; Chrysostom). The *Opus imperfectum* includes both, though finding greater blessedness in the former, 'because those who grieve over other people's sins certainly do not have sins of their own over which to grieve' (Kellerman and Oden 2010: 85).

Gregory of Nyssa knows of this interpretation, but prefers the more profound sorrow of separation from the true good, knowledge of which we once possessed (*Sermon on the Beatitudes* 3; see Eklund 2017: 732–733). Aquinas lists three kinds of mourning: for sins, both one's own and those of others; for our present existence, exiled from our heavenly home; over the joys of the world, which people have relinquished to follow Christ (Aquinas 2013a: 136–137). Davies and Allison, highlighting the reference to Isaiah 61:2, propose that the mourning is caused by the present suffering of God's people, while the wicked prosper; this will be reversed when God's Kingdom comes fully (Davies and Allison 2004: 66–67).

The Meek (5:5)

The 'poor in spirit' and the 'meek' can be regarded as near synonyms (Nolland 2005: 201). For those who regard the Beatitudes as a progression through virtues, however, the two categories are distinct. Thus for Aquinas, poverty needs to be supplemented with meekness, which is capable of restraining anger.

Although Psalm 37:11 ('The meek shall inherit the land/earth') probably references the land of Israel, this beatitude could be taken as promising the whole earth (as reflected in English translations from Tyndale onwards). Nonetheless, it lends itself to non-territorial interpretations. Jerome rejects the idea that it means 'the land of Judea or the land of this world,' which can be possessed by violent warriors. Rather it refers to 'the land of the living' of Psalm 27:13 (Jerome). Augustine appeals to the same phrase in Psalm 142:5, thus finding the promise of an eternal inheritance in heaven (*The Lord's Sermon on the Mount* 1.2.4). For the *Opus imperfectum,* the 'land of the living' is the transformed earth, set free from slavery to corruption (see Rom 8:21). Hilary prefers a figurative interpretation: it is the inheritance of Christ's body, apparently a reference to the resurrection body. By contrast, the Antiochene John Chrysostom rejects merely figurative readings. William Tyndale also understands it in concrete terms, as the promise of 'a hundredfold' here in this present life (Duffield 1965: 198; see Mark 10:30).

Hungering and Thirsting for Righteousness (5:6)

Matthew understanding hunger and thirst figuratively (cf. Luke 6:21), directed toward 'righteousness' or 'justice.' For Matthew, 'righteousness' means 'practical obedience to the will of the Father.' Read in a Pauline light, it might refer to God's righteousness, his gift of justification, or his covenant faithfulness to his people. Alternatively, it could refer to a longing for justice in the social order (NEB: 'those who hunger and thirst to see right prevail').

Interpreters have not always opted for a univocal meaning. The *Opus imperfectum* understand it as the righteousness of God, albeit something human beings can put into practice. For the Franciscan preacher Bernardino of Siena (1380–1444), the 'justice' is threefold: justice toward God, by honoring, loving, and fearing him; justice toward self through purity of heart, guarding the tongue and disciplining the body; justice toward neighbor, which might involve obedience, concord, or beneficence depending on one's social status (Muessig 2009: 144). Mindful of Paul's Gospel, William Tyndale understands the term not as saving righteousness, which is presumed, but rather its fruits: 'Wherefore understand here the outward righteousness before the world, and true and faithful dealing each with other, and just executing of the offices of all manner of degrees, and meek obedience of all that are under power' (Duffield 1965: 200).

Seeing God (5:8)

Modern commentators tend to focus on purity of heart, understood variously as integrity, or singleness of devotion (Luz 2007: 196; Nolland 2005: 204–205; France 2007: 168–169). Tradition connects it especially with Christian asceticism (e.g. Athanasius, *Life of Anthony*). In his treatise *Schola cordis*, the Netherlandish Benedictine Benedict van Haeften (1588–1648) defines it as 'a heart which in every respect, rests entirely content with God alone' (quoted in

Ford 1859: 69). Such an ascetical view is rejected by Martin Luther: having a pure heart is not achieved by those who 'run away from human society into a corner, a monastery, or a desert.' Rather, it is 'completely consistent with being a husband, loving wife and children, thinking about them and caring for them, and paying attention to other matters involved in such a relationship' (Luther 1956: 32).

Older interpreters are often more intrigued by the promise of 'seeing God.' The meaning is highly contested, given the tension within the Bible over this question. On the one hand, it is claimed that 'no one shall see me and live,' such that Moses must content himself with seeing God's 'back' (Exod 33:20–23; cf. e.g. Deut 4:12; John 1:18; 1 Tim 6:16 1 John 4:12). On the other hand, there are accounts of the Lord 'appearing' to humans (e.g. Gen 12:7; 17:1; 18:1; Exod 4:5; 24:9–11; Isa 6:1), including the claim that some saw or spoke to God 'face to face' (Jacob: Gen 32:30; Moses: Exod 33:11; Num 12:8; Deut 34:10; see also Allison 2005: 45, n. 7). Other passages point to the possibility of seeing God or his face in the future, especially the hoped-for experience of God's presence in the temple (e.g. Ps 11:7; 17:15; 42:3; see Smith 1988).

Theological and philosophical presuppositions regularly come into play in understanding Matthew's concept of 'seeing God' (see e.g. Allison 2005: 43–63; Viljoen 2012). Some interpret the vision of God somatically (see Paulsen 1990), a view not improbable given Matthew's dependence on apocalyptic traditions (see e.g. Ezek 1; Dan 7; *1 En.* 14; though see Rowland 1979). Indeed, 18:10 seems to presuppose a corporeal God currently beheld by the angels. The *Pseudo-Clementine Homilies* (probably third-century) assume that God can be seen bodily: 'God has the most beautiful shape on account of humanity, that the pure in heart may be able to see Him' (*Hom.* 17:7: in Viljoen 2012). Tertullian argues against Praxeas that God has bodily substance (*Adv. Prax.* 7.8–9), whilst John Cassian (c. 360–435) knows of 'Anthropomorphite' monks in Egypt (*Conf.* 10.2).

One alternative for those believing that God is immaterial is to interpret the vision of God Christologically. The third-century *Acts of Thomas* combines two Matthean beatitudes: 'Blessed are you meek, because you will see the face of the Lord,' i.e. the face of Jesus (*Acts of Thomas* 94: in Allison 2005: 49–50). A modern variant is that 'seeing God' refers to the vision of Christ at his Parousia (Gundry 1994: 71). However, both are problematic when this beatitude is read in the light of 18:10, which clearly refers to a vision of the Father, as Novatian noted against the Modalists (*Trin.* 28).

A different explanation is that Matthew envisages mystical apprehension of the divine. For the Byzantine mystical theologian Gregory Palamas (1296–1359), it promises a vision of the uncreated light (God's energies, though not his essence), already accessible to the pure in heart (see Lossky 1974). Ephrem the Syrian seems to envisage an indirect vision of God, akin to Moses seeing God's back: 'those whose hearts are pure will see God, like Moses' (*C. Diat.* 6.1: in Allison 2005: 53).

A more common solution understands the verb metaphorically (see 2:16; 8:4; 9:2, 4, 30; 13:14–15; 16:6; 24:6; 26:65; 27:4, 24). For Origen, it refers to intellectual apprehension: 'understanding and knowing Him with the mind' (*De Princ.* 1.1.9: *ANF* 4:245). Erasmus speaks of seeing God 'with the eyes of the mind' (Eph 1:18: Erasmus 2008: 89). Aquinas finds in this intellectual 'vision,' together with an eschatological interpretation of the promise, a solution to the tension with 1 John 4:12 ('no one has ever seen God').

For Luther, 'seeing God' is seeing God's true reality, already in this life and not only as an eschatological hope: 'That is exactly what it means "to see God," not with physical eyes, with which no one can see Him in this life, but with faith, which sees His fatherly, friendly heart, where there is no anger or displeasure' (Luther 1956: 37). The English social reformer Florence Nightingale (1820–1910) also asserts the possibility of seeing God in this mortal life, albeit 'hidden' in suffering: 'in all temptations, trials, and aridities, in the agony and bloody sweat, in the Cross and Passion: this is not the prerogative of the future life, but of the present' (in Stoddart 1914: 39).

Gregory of Nyssa understands the vision of God to be indirect, seeing God in ourselves and our neighbors, like the reflection of the sun in a mirror. His view presupposes the eastern doctrine of *theōsis*, as the image of God, formerly obscured by sin, is once again visible in the restored humanity. Augustine's view is more complex: in the perfected creation, the saints will have the intellectual capacity to 'discern things of an immaterial nature' and thereby to discern the action of the incorporeal God:

> We will then see the physical bodies of the new heaven and the new earth in such a fashion as to observe God in utter clarity and distinctness, seeing him present everywhere and governing the whole material scheme of things by means of the bodies we will then inhabit and the bodies we will see wherever we turn our eyes. (*Civ. Dei* 22.29: Hoffmann in Allison 2005: 56)

The Peacemakers (5:9)

In contrast to Hellenistic and Roman usage, where the term 'peacemaker' often described a conquering ruler (Guelich 1982: 106), here it reflects the Jewish concern for *shalom*, wholeness and wellbeing (e.g. Isa 9:5–6; Zech 9:9–10). This beatitude is probably not directly concerned with brokering peace in warfare, but rather with interpersonal relationships (Davies and Allison 2004: 68; Luz 2007: 198, n. 135). However, it has frequently functioned in the former sense. This is despite Luther's protestation, formulated according to his 'two kingdoms' doctrine, that there is no contradiction between this beatitude and the need of secular society to go to war (Pelikan 2001: 129). In the Middle Ages, it was particularly important for the mendicant friars, mediating peace between warring cities (Muessig 2009: 145). King James I of England adopted it as his personal motto, indicating his success at avoiding war (Stoddart 1914: 40). In more recent times, it functioned as a fundamental text for the pontificate of John Paul II (1978–2005), who sought to re-educate humanity against the inevitability of war (Powers in Walsh 2003: 90).

Salt and Light (5:13–16)

Matthew has transformed Jesus' proverbs about salt and lamps (Mark 4:21; 9:50; Luke 8:16; 11:33; 14:34–35) into job descriptions for Jesus' followers. These would have sounded polemical to first-century Jewish ears, for whom salt and light were descriptions of Israel, the Torah, Jerusalem, or the temple (see Guelich 1982: 122; Davies and Allison 1988: 471–472). Again, decisions about the audience of the Sermon affect interpretation. The *Opus imperfectum* understands the 'you' to refer chiefly to the apostles, and therefore contemporary Christian priests. Cornelius a Lapide extends the reference to include the bishops, while the sixteenth-century Swiss Reformer Heinrich Bullinger applies it to pastors and doctors (in Luz 2007: 209, n. 54). Others (e.g. Chrysostom) find a more universal application.

The point of the salt metaphor is not immediately clear. Hilary seeks an answer in the physical property of salt: composed of water and fire (see Pliny, *Nat.* 31.7). Just as salt preserves that on which it has been sprinkled, so 'the apostles are the preachers of heavenly matters, and sowers of eternity, planting seeds of immortality in all bodies on which their word has been sprinkled and perfected … by the sacrament of water and fire,' i.e. baptism (Hilary of Poitiers 2012: 62).

Salt's preservative quality is widely cited. For the *Opus imperfectum*, this means that the salt and light sayings address two different audiences. Salt can preserve food in the state in which it is found, but cannot make bad meat fresh again. By contrast, light can illuminate things in darkness. Thus the apostles are 'salt' of the land already cultivated by the word of the cross, i.e. preserving the Christian people, but 'light of the world' for the heathen, or those who 'have fallen in the church in the darkness of their sins' (Kellerman and Oden 2010: 90).

Thomas Aquinas lists several additional explanations, including salt's function as seasoning (signifying the wisdom of 'apostolic men'), its ability to preserve from rotting, and its rendering the earth sterile, thus preventing the growth of 'earthly works' (Aquinas 2013a: 147; similarly, Lapide).

The connection with wisdom can be traced to the rabbinic tradition (e.g. *m. Soṭa* 9.15), and is known to Cyril of Alexandria (*Frag.* 41 in Reuss 1957: 165). Aquinas's allowance for the multivocal character of Matthew's metaphor is echoed in some modern commentators (e.g. Davies and Allison 1988: 473). William Tyndale stresses salt's caustic nature; hence true preaching is 'a salting that stirreth up persecution' (Duffield 1965: 209–210).

'Salt of the earth' has entered into popular English discourse, meaning a decent and straightforward person. The British writer Anna Letitia Barbauld (1743–1825) connects both sayings to those who advocate for political change, in her 1797 hymn (see Duquette in Taylor and Choi 2012: 53–57):

> Salt of the earth, ye virtuous few,
> Who season human kind;
> Light of the world, whose cheering ray
> Illumes the realms of mind.
> (Barbauld 2002: 136)

The saying about light also inspired Harry Dixon Loes's 'This Little Light of Mine,' written in the 1920s, which became one of the most influential protest songs of the civil rights movement (Dowling Long and Sawyer 2015: 240–241).

Disciples as light of the world are likened to a city on a hill, possibly a reference to Jerusalem (von Rad 1966: 232–242, on the basis of Isa 2:1–4; 60:1–21). Hilary of Poitiers interprets it Christologically: the city is the flesh that Christ assumes in his incarnation. However, it is most frequently given an ecclesial interpretation: the city is the church, the mountain being Christ (*Opus imperfectum*). It thus becomes an appropriate description of specific Christian communities, as in the 1630 sermon 'A Model of Christian Charity' by John Winthrop, the English Puritan and future governor of the Massachusetts Bay Colony. Winthrop preached this sermon to his fellow colonists while sailing to New England aboard the *Arbella* (it was reprised in political contexts by US Presidents John F. Kennedy and Ronald Reagan: Clarke 2003: 68):

> For we must consider that we shall be as a city upon a hill. The eyes of all people are upon us. So that if we shall deal falsely with our God in this work we have undertaken, and so cause Him to withdraw His present help from us, we shall be made a story and a by-word through the world.[1]

1 http://winthropsociety.com/doc_charity.php.

Fulfilling the Law and the Prophets (5:17–48)

This lengthy section provides six specific examples of the 'higher righteousness' proposed by Jesus (5:21–48), prefaced by an explanatory introduction (5:17–20). The Babylonian Talmud preserves what looks like a rabbinic satire on 5:17, attributed to 'a corrupt philosopher': 'I have not come to take away from the Torah of Moses, but I have come in order to add to it' (*b. Šabb.* 116a; in Betz 1985: 41).

The intimate connection between verses 17–20 and the 'antitheses' of verses 21–48 is widely recognized. Ephrem the Syrian calls the latter the 'perfect commands which our Lord was introducing,' which, far from abolishing the Mosaic commandments, bring them to fullness or perfection (*C. Diat.* 6.3a: Hogan 1999: 94). Ephrem's Jesus is thus like a scribe who completes a child's education, a father who sees his son grow up, or a nurse who weans a baby off milk onto solid food. This link between verses 17–20 and 21–48 is exegetically important, even if it fails to resolve the tension for all interpreters, some of whom point to certain antitheses (e.g. divorce, oaths, and retaliation) as abrogating aspects of the Law (McArthur 1960: 45). The tension is sometimes explained in terms of Christ removing those elements from the Law which were 'rough and imperfect, owing to the weakness of the hearers,' such as wrath, lust, and the *lex talionis* (Jerome 2008: 77–78; cf. 19:8). Alternatively, the saying about lust presents a 'radicalization' of the commandment against adultery ('adultery of the heart'). Thus John Paul II controversially interpreted Jesus' words as a warning that husbands could even commit adultery with their own wives (General Audience, 8 October 1980).

This section served patristic authors well in refuting the radical discontinuity between the Old Testament and Christ advocated by heretical groups. Thus Irenaeus understands the antitheses as extending the Mosaic Law rather than contradicting it: 'For all these do not contain or imply an opposition to and an overturning of the [precepts] of the past, as Marcion's followers do strenuously maintain; but [they exhibit] a fulfilling and an extension of them, as He does Himself declare' (*Adv. Haer.* 4.13.1: *ANF* 1:477). Hilary similarly speaks of Christ surpassing the Law 'by advancement, not by abolition' (Hilary of Poitiers 2012: 66; see also Eusebius, *Dem. ev.* 3.2).

In fact, the Matthean passage is more complex, for it speaks of Christ coming to fulfil *both* Law *and* prophets. John Chrysostom is sensitive to this distinction, relating the latter specifically to the Matthean formula quotations. Thus Jesus fulfills the prophets through specific actions of his life and ministry. Chrysostom also avoids a univocal meaning for fulfilling the Law, given that 5:17–20 references both a fulfillment unique to Jesus ('I have come …') and one possible for his followers ('Unless your righteousness exceeds …'). He posits a threefold fulfilment: by Christ's sinlessness; by granting to his people righteousness by faith (see Rom 3:31; 8:3–4); by his teaching in the Sermon, which represents 'a drawing out, and filling up of' the Mosaic Law, giving the old commandments 'greater security' (*Homily on Matthew* 16; Pelikan 1967: 71–72). Here Chrysostom exploits a particular nuance of Matthew's Greek verb *plēroō*, which can mean 'fill up' as well as 'fulfill' or 'complete.' Christ's teaching reveals the greater capacity, the fuller meaning of the Mosaic commandments. A similar move is made by Theophylact, who likens Jesus to an artist who 'fully painted in' what the Law had only 'sketched in outline,' thus completing the picture (Theophylact 1992: 48). In his *Reply to Faustus* the Manichean, Augustine posits no less than six ways in which Christ fulfils the Law: through his personal obedience to its commands; fulfilling the Law and prophets as messianic prediction; drawing out its true meaning; showing the true significance of Mosaic observances such as Sabbath and circumcision; making its observance possible for his people by grace through the power of the Spirit; providing additional commandments which extend although do not abrogate the Mosaic code (*Reply to Faustus 17–19*; see McArthur 1960: 28–30).

Others are wary of the proposal that Christ's teaching advances or 'adds to' the original Law. For Martin Luther, Christ comes 'to show its real kernel and meaning, and to teach them what the Law is and what it requires, in antithesis to the glosses which the Pharisees have introduced' (Luther 1956: 70). William Tyndale paraphrases 5:17 in a similar fashion: 'I come not to destroy the law, but to repair it only, and to make it go upright where it halteth' (Duffield 1965: 216), to 'only wipe away the filthy and rotten glosses wherewith the scribes and the Pharisees have smeared the law, and the prophets.' Tyndale has in mind here those he regards as contemporary 'scribes,' such as 'our bishops, chancellors, commissaries, archdeacons, and officials' (Duffield 1965: 217).

In context, the 'least of these commandments' (5:19) probably refers back to the Mosaic commandments of verse 18 (Calvin identifies them specifically as the Decalogue), although some find a reference to Jesus' own teaching in verses 21–48 (e.g. Erasmus). For Augustine, Jesus is describing the practice of the Pharisees, 'who taught the law in word, while they broke it in deed' (*Reply to Faustus* 17; see 23:3). This, however, sits uncomfortably with verse 20, which implies that the scribes and Pharisees will not even enter the Kingdom. Those who break such commandments, on the contrary, will be within the Kingdom, albeit as its 'least' (though Luther understands this to mean that they will be expelled from the Kingdom: Luther 1956: 68). Johannes Weiss finds anti-Pauline polemic here: Paul, who teaches others to abandon certain commandments of the Torah, takes his name from the Latin *paulus* meaning 'little' (in Betz 198: 51; Paul describes himself as the 'least' of the apostles, 1 Cor 15:9).

On Anger (5:21–26)

Augustine finds in the command not to become angry the key to the 'higher righteousness': 'The righteousness of the Pharisees consists in refraining from killing. Whereas the righteousness of those who will enter the Kingdom of God consists in not being angry for no reason' (*The Lord's Sermon on the Mount* 1.9.21; Augustine 2014: 34). Augustine here knows the variant reading 'without a cause,' which ameliorates Jesus' harsh words. Cornelius a Lapide appeals to this addition to address the obvious objection that Christ himself became angry with the moneychangers in the temple (21:12–13): Christ's was a just anger, with a very specific cause. Appealing to his doctrine of the two realms, Martin Luther also stresses the necessity of anger in certain circumstances, 'but only in those whose responsibility it is,' for punishing sin and evil (Luther 1956: 76).

The link between murder and being angry with one's brother, in the context of offering a sacrifice at the altar, suggested to many earlier commentators the story of Cain and Abel in Genesis 4:1–16 (e.g. Cyprian, *De unitate* 13; also e.g. Hugh of St. Cher; Albert the Great; Hugo Grotius; Matthew Henry: Allison 2005: 65–78). The disciples are thereby warned to seek reconciliation with estranged brothers, lest they find themselves replaying the role of Cain. This fits better the Matthean context than the modern tendency to interpret the 'altar' as the sacrificial altar in the Jerusalem temple, for only priests would stand at that altar (see Schweizer 1975: 115).

By extension, Jesus' words come to be applied to the Christian Eucharist, increasingly understood as a sacrifice. For Cyril of Jerusalem, it refers to the liturgical kiss of peace (*Catech.* 23.3), an interpretation reflected in some contemporary Eucharistic liturgies (e.g. 5:23–24 is an optional sentence prior to the Peace in Rite One of the *Book of Common Prayer* of the US Episcopal Church). In the modern period, the Colombian priest Fr. Camilo Torres used it as justification for giving up active ministry to join the revolutionary National Liberation Army: 'I have ceased to say Mass, but I will practice love for my fellow man in the temporal, economic, and social spheres. When my fellow man has nothing against me, when he has carried out the revolution, then I will return to offering Mass' (in Clarke 2003: 70).

Verses 25–26 may well refer to literal opponents, and the need for reconciliation to avoid acrimonious legal proceedings and physical imprisonment (so Chrysostom). Nonetheless, after references to Gehenna in the preceding verses, the passage is unsurprisingly read as an allegory of eschatological judgment by Arnobius the Younger:

> The 'adversary' spoken of here is the external man, that is, the body with whom we make our journey. The 'road' travelled upon is this age. Let us therefore treat this adversary well, that is, let us live a pure life with him, so that He should not

> hand us over in our flagrant crimes to the judge, that is, to Christ, and the judge, as He says, pass us on to His 'ministers,' that is, to the angels, who will then toss us in 'prison,' which signifies Gehenna. (*Expositiunculae in Matthaeum* 6: Kraszewski 1999: 275)

Chrysostom knows of some who interpret the 'adversary' as the devil (see Tertullian, *De Anima* 35), though he is suspicious of such allegorical readings, while Aquinas regards this interpretation as 'forced' (*extorta*: Aquinas 2013a: 167). Aquinas does, however, understand the 'prison' to be a reference to Hell, despite the difficulty that Hell is eternal, whereas Jesus' words presume that the imprisonment will only last until the last penny has been paid. His solution is based on the observation that 'until' does not always designate a limited time: 'he will never get out, for he will never repay the last penny' (Aquinas 2013a: 168). Alternatively, the prison is taken as a reference to the temporary state of Purgatory (e.g. Lapide; the marginal note to the 1610 Douay-Rheims Bible), a reading challenged by William Tyndale: 'And that some make purgatory of the last farthing, they shew their deep ignorance' (Duffield 1965: 227). That this passage is at least partly allegorical is mooted also by certain modern commentators: e.g. that the judge is 'perhaps a symbol for God' (Davies and Allison 1988: 519).

The Divorce Exception Clause (5:32)

The two Matthean passages concerning divorce (here and at 19:1–9) presuppose Jewish law whereby only husbands are in a position to divorce wives (though see e.g. Brooten 1982 for evidence that Jewish women could sue for divorce in exceptional circumstances). Many modern scholars understand Matthew's formulation as a particular interpretation of first-century Jewish debate over the interpretation of Deuteronomy 24:1, where a man may divorce his wife for 'something objectionable' (literally 'nakedness of the thing'). Rabbinic tradition records a dispute over this issue between two Pharisee contemporaries of Jesus, Shammai and Hillel (*m. Giṭ* 9:10), with the position of the Matthean Jesus being closer to the cautious Shammai.

Certainly some patristic authors seem to be aware of the deleterious consequences of divorce on wives in a Jewish institution which favored husbands (e.g. Augustine, *The Lord's Sermon on the Mount* 1.14.39). Christ's treating Moses' words as a concession (19:8) reveals his concern that wives not be lightly dismissed. Hilary regards Jesus' teaching as establishing 'equity for all people,' representing an advance on the Mosaic requirement by establishing a man's guilt in forcing his wife into adultery (Hilary of Poitiers 2012: 69).

Both 5:32 and 19:9, moreover, present an exception to Jesus' otherwise uncompromising teaching, on the grounds of *porneia* (see Collins 1992: 184–213; Moloney 2015; attempts to render the Greek differently, e.g. that the question of *porneia* is parenthetical, being left out of Jesus' present discussion, or that it is inclusive, i.e. 'and that includes even the case of *porneia*,' have failed to convince many). The precise meaning of *porneia*, however, is highly contested. Early Fathers regularly presume it refers to adultery (e.g. Tertullian, *Adv. Marc.* 4:34; *De Pudic.* 16; Lactantius, *Instit.* 6.23: Smith 1918), a view which accords with Matthew's portrayal of Joseph, a 'righteous man' who contemplates divorcing Mary for suspected marital infidelity (1:19; see Luther 1956: 96; Allison 1993b; Janzen 2000). The Vulgate reads *excepta fornicationis causa,* and 'fornication' is a regular English translation going back to William Tyndale. Others propose the more general 'unchastity' (e.g. RSV): '*any* kind of obviously unlawful sexual relationship' (Bockmuehl 1989: 295).

In the modern period, Catholic scholars have often interpreted *porneia* as marriage within the forbidden degrees of kinship (Lev 18:6–18; CD 5.7–8; see 1 Cor 5:1; possibly Acts 15:20, 29). Hence Matthew presents a pastoral adaptation for Gentile converts in unions considered illicit by Jews (e.g. Bonsirven 1948; Fitzmyer 1976), an interpretation reflected in contemporary Catholic translations: 'unless the marriage is unlawful' (NABRE); 'except for the case of an illicit marriage' (NJB). Other proposals include a mixed marriage between a Christian and a pagan (the situation envisaged at 1 Cor 7:12–16), and a metaphorical reference to idolatry.

Contested too are the practical consequences of this exception: does it permit divorce *and* remarriage, or only the former? The patristic consensus seems to be that Matthew's exception allowed for separation from 'bed and board,' albeit without the right to remarry (though for Erasmus, this interpretation is 'strained and farfetched': *Apology Against Bedda* in Surtz 1957: 250). For the *Shepherd of Hermas*, a husband ought to dismiss his wife if he becomes aware of 'some adultery,' though not remarry so that he can receive her back should she repent (Herm. *Mand.* 4.1; see Arendzen 1919: 231). The exception clause thus modifies only 'anyone who divorces his wife,' not also 'and marries another' (19:9; also e.g. Justin, *1 Apol.* 1.15; Jerome, *Ep.* 77.3.1; Augustine, *The Lord's Sermon on the Mount* 1.37–50). Indeed, Tertullian and Athenagoras go so far as to rule out remarriage even for the widowed (see Smith 1918).

An alternative patristic view takes the exception to cover remarriage (e.g. Clement of Alexandria, *Strom.* 3.6.50; Lactantius, *Instit.* 6:23; Basil, *Ep.* 188 *ad Amphilochum* 1119, can. 48; for different assessments, see Smith 1918 and Arendzen 1919). Epiphanius has a broad definition of *porneia*, albeit applicable to the laity, but not the clergy:

> But if the man could not be content with the one wife, who had died, <or> if there has been a divorce for some reason – fornication, adultery or something else – and the man marries a second wife or the woman a second husband, God's word does not censure them or bar them from the church and life, but tolerates them because of their weakness. (*Pan.* 59. 4.9; Epiphanius 2013: 31)

The fourth-century Latin commentator on Paul known as 'Ambrosiaster' appeals to the Matthean exception in his commentary on 1 Corinthians 7:10–11, in order to justify a man remarrying (though he fails to extend the same privilege to a wife, on the grounds that 'a man is the head of woman': Ambrosiaster 1968: 75).

Different patristic interpretations are reflected in differing ecclesial practices. Whereas contemporary Roman Catholic teaching allows only separation from 'bed and board,' eastern Orthodox practice permits a second (albeit non-sacramental) marriage following a period of repentance. Many Anglican and Protestant Christians also treat the clause as a genuine exception to the prohibition of divorce *and* remarriage, influenced by the paraphrase of 5:32 by Erasmus:

> For whoever divorces his wife – unless she is an adulteress (for she has stopped being his wife if she has had sexual relations with another man) – forces her into adultery. (Erasmus 2008: 105)

Erasmus goes on to clarify that the exception clause means 'except in the case of unfaithfulness, which contradicts the very nature of marriage,' and makes explicit in his annotation on 1 Corinthians 7:39 that this permits remarriage as well as divorce (see Olsen 1971: 20–27). Nor is Erasmus a lone Catholic voice: the clause is also understood to permit remarriage following adultery by the Dominican theologian Cardinal Thomas Cajetan (in Lapide 1890/1: 229; see Olsen 1971: 33–36).

Among the Reformers, Luther maintains that the exception for adultery permits remarriage, on the grounds that Leviticus 20:10 prescribes death for the adultery. Thus the adulterous partner is already dead in God's eyes, leaving the innocent party free to remarry (Luther 1956: 96). For John Calvin, a woman who has violated her marriage vow 'is justly cast off; because it was by her fault that the tie was broken, and the husband set at liberty' (Calvin 1949: 1/293). Canon 7 of the Session 24 of the Council of Trent (promulgated on 11 November 1563) explicitly rejects the Reformers' view, though the nuanced debate at Trent reflected awareness of patristic divergence, as well as the practice of the eastern churches (see Fransen 1970).

On Oaths (5:33–37)

Jesus' teaching against swearing probably challenges traditional practice whereby only oaths which mentioned God's name were considered binding, whereas swearing by heaven, earth, Jerusalem, or one's own head were not (see *m. Šeb.* 4:13; *m. Ned.* 1.3; *m. Sanh.* 3.2; Talbert 2010: 85). Thus Christ's words are calling for truthfulness in speech, combined with a concern that God's holy Name not be profaned. Thus all oath-taking is to be avoided (e.g. Justin, *1 Apol.* 16.5; Irenaeus, *Adv. Haer.* 2.32.1; Chrysostom; the Pelagians, according to Augustine, *Ep.* 157; Erasmus). According to the *Opus imperfectum*, this forbidding of oaths is aimed at curtailing perjury, citing Sirach 23:9: 'Do not accustom your mouth to oaths, for there are many ways to stumble by it' (Kellerman and Oden 2010: 105).

Yet this literal aversion to oath-taking is regularly softened, in part because oaths are common in the Hebrew Bible, and used by Paul (e.g. Rom 1:9–10; 1 Cor 11:31; Gal 1:20; see Augustine, *Reply to Faustus* 19:23). This is especially the case once the state becomes Christian and imposes oaths of loyalty to the emperor (see Luz 2007: 266–267). One solution is to claim that oaths taken in God's Name are not forbidden, but only the alternative swearing by heaven, earth, Jerusalem, or one's head (e.g. Jerome). Alternatively, the proscription of oaths is restricted to monastics or priests (e.g. *Rule of St. Benedict* 4).

A nuanced position is also found among the magisterial Reformers. Neither Luther nor Calvin regard this antithesis as banning oaths *per se*. Luther finds a resolution in his doctrine of the two kingdoms: Christ forbids, the state commands; but both are right, in their own sphere of influence (see Pelikan 1997: 178). For Calvin, Christ's teaching about oaths needs to be read against the totality of the scriptural revelation, to avoid the suggestion of divine inconsistency. Thus 5:33–37 cannot be a rejection of all oaths, but only those which profane the divine name, thus aimed at restoring 'the true and genuine meaning' of Scripture, corrupted 'by the false glosses of the Scribes and Pharisees' (*Institutes* 2.8.26). Christ's expression 'not at all' refers, not to the verb 'swear,' but to the additional phrases listed in verses 34b–36.

Calvin's position directly challenges the Anabaptists' radical rejection of oath-taking. For the Anabaptist leader Menno Simons (1496–1561), Christ's radical words lead his disciples from the imperfect Mosaic Law to the perfect:

> Behold, beloved reader, before these words of Christ all human laws and regulations concerning swearing must stand back and be abolished; … no matter how they be performed; be it by words, or by raising your hand, or holding your hands upon your breast, or upon a cross, or upon the New Testament, &c. And the truthful yea and nay, ordained of the Lord himself must be restituted, if the magistrates and subjects do not want licentiously to transgress the word of the Lord

> and reject it as vain; for, whatsoever is more than yea and nay (says Christ) cometh of evil.[2] ('The Swearing of Oaths' in *A Fundamental and Clear Confession of the Poor and Distressed Christians*, 1552)

In England, opposition to oath-taking led to imprisonment (e.g. for George Fox, founder of the Religious Society of Friends or Quakers), until the 1689 Act of Toleration permitted 'affirmations' to be substituted (Clarke 2003: 73). Arguments against Christians swearing oaths were also set forward by William Penn in his 1675 *A Treatise of Oaths*.

Love of Enemies (5:43–48)

The gloss – 'and hate your enemy' – to Jesus' quotation from Leviticus 19:18 ('You shall love your neighbor') is not directly attested in the Mosaic Law (though scholars often point to hostile passages such as Deuteronomy 23:3–6, as well as the command to hate the 'sons of darkness' in 1QS 1:9–10). For Matthew's first audiences, 'those who persecute you' may have brought synagogue leaders to mind. Nonetheless, a universal love of enemy becomes a distinguishing feature of Christians. Justin Martyr refers to Jesus' teaching in order to reassure critics that Christians were peaceable: e.g. *1 Apol.* 14.3; *Trypho* 35.8 (see Roukema 2014: 202). The early church's prohibition on Christians joining the army is as much a response to this teaching as to the previous antithesis on not resisting evil (5:38–42). The further call to pray for persecutors ensures the introduction of this antithesis into the Christian liturgy. The fourth-century Syrian *Apostolic Constitutions* includes the following petition:

> Let us pray for our enemies, and those that hate us.
> Let us pray for those that persecute us for the name of the Lord,
> that the Lord may pacify their anger, and scatter their wrath against us.
> (*Apostolic Constitutions* 8.10.16)

Whereas most presume that Christ's teaching broadens love of neighbor to include loving enemies, Origen distinguishes between the two. The command to love neighbor ('as oneself') is more demanding than the command to love an enemy, which simply rules out hating one's adversary (Origen, *Hom. in Canticum* 2.8: Roukema 2014: 201).

Post-Constantine, a less radical interpretation comes to the fore, with Jesus' teaching representing a personal rather than political demand. Both Ambrose

2 http://www.mennosimons.net/ft109-oaths.html.

and Augustine agree that Christian governments can exercise violence against enemies, though they should treat subjected enemies leniently (Roukema 2014: 208–210). This distinction between 'personal enemy' and 'political enemy' is widely made in times of war. During World War I, German exegetes justified Germany's aggressive war tactics on the grounds that the Sermon is only concerned with the former (Meiser 2013: 157).

Matthew 6–7

Ancient Literary Context

The Sermon's central section (6:1–18: see Luz 2007: 295) coheres around the theme of practical piety. It probably presupposes Rome's destruction of the temple in 70 CE and the consequent reinterpretation of temple sacrifices associated with Rabban Johanan ben Zakkai and the rabbis of Jamnia or Javneh (see Davies 1964: 304–307; Allison 2005: 211–212). Like Jamnia, Matthew's Jesus emphasizes 'sacrificial acts' which do not require temple sacrifice: prayer,

Matthew Through the Centuries, First Edition. Ian Boxall.

fasting, and that prominent 'deed of loving kindness,' almsgiving. Nonetheless, this section of the Sermon also betrays the mutual antagonism between synagogue and church within which this Gospel was forged (notably its condemnation of 'hypocrites' in the synagogues, 6:2, 5, 16).

At the very center is the Our Father (6:9–13). Matthew's longer version is more liturgical than Luke's (Luke 11:2–4), an impression enhanced by the concluding doxology found in many manuscripts (see also *Did.* 8:2). Parallels with synagogue prayers, notably the Eighteen Benedictions, may suggest the shaping of Matthew's prayer in close proximity to synagogue liturgy (e.g. Bahr 1965). It is also presented as an alternative to verbose pagan prayers (a caricature revealing the Gospel's Jewish bias). Its eschatological character (urgent prayer that God act to bring in his Kingdom, and rescue his people from the Evil One during the trials of the end time) is widely noted (e.g. Brown 1961; Jeremias 1967).

The next section (6:19–7:12, mainly Double Tradition or Q material) lacks obvious structural and thematic coherence ('an ill-assorted pile of addenda': Bornkamm in Luz 2007: 328). It concludes with the Golden Rule (7:12; see Luke 6:31; *Did.* 1:2), presented as a summary of the Law and the prophets (thus forming an *inclusio* with 5:17–20). The final section (7:13–27) well illustrates Matthew's 'moral dualism.' Like the *Didache* (*Did.* 1:1), Matthew's Jesus presents his listeners with two ways (cf. Luke 13:23–24). This leads into a treatment of true and false prophecy, a perennial problem for early Christians (cf. e.g. 1 Cor 14:26–33; 1 John 4:1–3; *Did.* 11). Like Luke's Sermon, Matthew's also concludes with a parable of Two Builders (7:24–27; Luke 6:47–49), underscoring the charge that Jesus' disciples, and subsequent readers of Matthew, are not simply to hear Jesus' words but to put them into practice.

The Interpretations

Practicing Piety (6:1–8, 16–18)

Augustine is aware of the potential conflict between Jesus' words about performing acts of piety, and his previous statement at 5:16 ('So let your light shine before …'). What Christ is forbidding here is wrong motivation: 'not if you are seen by people, but if being seen by people is the reason why you lead a righteous life,' rather than for the Father's glory (*Lord's Sermon on the Mount* 2.1.2; Augustine 2014: 69). In the words of Cornelius a Lapide, such behavior is 'vain ostentation' (Lapide 1890: 1/251).

The triad of almsgiving, prayer, and fasting recalls other Matthean triads. For the *Opus imperfectum*, there is a direct correlation between these three virtues and the three vices Christ confronted during his temptation: 'almsgiving fights against avarice, fasting against gluttony, and prayer against vainglory' (Kellerman and Oden 2010: 126). This contrasts with the *Gospel of Thomas*, which regards all three practices as sinful (*Gos. Thom.* 14). Others view Matthew's primary concern as hypocrisy. Augustine notes the original sense of the Greek *hupocritēs* as 'actor': 'Hypocrites are impersonators, mouthpieces for other characters, as in stories from the theatre' (*Lord's Sermon on the Mount* 2.2.5; Augustine 2014: 70). Similarly, Erasmus defines the hypocrites here as 'those who are actors, wearing paint and masks' (Erasmus 2008: 113).

John Chrysostom finds in the teaching about alms Christ's modification of absolute poverty implied elsewhere (e.g. 6:24–33). In his homily on this passage, he encourages those in his congregation in Antioch who can only embrace 'the middle station' of almsgiving, which presupposes some degree of wealth and possessions (Pelikan 1967: 176). Others interpret Jesus' words about the left and right hands allegorically. For Arnobius Iunior, the 'right hand' refers to orthodox Christians, who worship Christ seated at the Father's right hand, whilst the 'left hand' refers to Jews and heretics (*Expositiunculae in Matthaeum* 7).

The teaching about prayer presents disciples of Jesus as a *tertium gens*, who pray differently from both hypocritical Pharisees and verbose Gentiles. Most recognize that Jesus' words about the hypocrites are hyperbole, critiquing ostentation in public prayer ('performance for a human audience': Davies and Allison 2004: 89), although the German Pietists took them as condemning audible prayers during worship services (Chia 2006: 46). Yet, the meaning of the solution – to withdraw into one's closet or secret place (Greek *tameion*; Vulgate *cubiculum*), a command which gave the Victorian Anglo-Catholic Edward Bouverie Pusey qualms about public prayer-meetings (Larsen 2011: 20) – is widely contested. Should it be taken literally, as a physical withdrawal to a private area of one's house? Thus, for Cornelius a Lapide, it describes 'any private place such as thy bedchamber' (Lapide 1890: 1/256).

Or is it figurative, describing an interior withdrawal into the heart or the mind (e.g. Jerome; Ambrose)? Augustine finds justification for a figurative reading by appeal to the Psalter: 'What are those bedrooms if not our very hearts, which are also signified by the words of the Psalm, *What you say in your hearts, repent also upon your beds* (Ps. 4:4)' (*Lord's Sermon on the Mount* 2.3.11; Augustine 2014: 74). The author of the *Opus imperfectum* turns the saying into a full allegory: the 'inner room' is the inner mind into which the soul retreats; once there, it must 'shut out all carnal thoughts and worries' (Kellerman and Oden 2010: 120). John Calvin rejects such allegorizing as 'trifling,' though he also objects to an over-literal reading which seeks to avoid the presence of others when praying. Rather, Christ is concerned with motivation: 'whether a man prays alone, or in the presence of others, he ought to have the same feelings, as if he were shut up in his closet, and had no other witness but God' (Calvin 1949: I/312–313).

The hypocrisy of synagogal prayer is matched by a caricature of the 'empty phrases' of the Gentiles. The *Opus imperfectum* gives reason for this pagan wordiness: they are addressing, not God, but demons, who 'cannot heed them,' or 'dead kings (Jupiter, Mercury, and the rest),' or 'unfeeling idols, which cannot hear or give a response' (Kellerman and Oden 2010: 121). St. Benedict directs Jesus' words toward his monks: they will be heard by God, not by their many words, 'but in purity of heart and in tears of compunction' (*Rule of St. Benedict* 20).[1]

Later commentators will often turn this teaching against fellow Christians. The Reformers caricature Catholic, especially monastic, piety. Luther denounces the praying of the monastic Office, as driven by obligation: 'Even though a monk may have been reading or muttering his canonical times for forty years, he has not prayed from his heart for a single hour during all those years' (Luther 1956: 142). Similarly, Calvin castigates Catholicism for believing 'the efficacy of prayer to lie chiefly in talkativeness' (Calvin 1949: I/313). Such becomes part and parcel of Protestant anti-Catholic polemic. Thus the English Baptist preacher Charles Spurgeon (1834–1892) can gloss Christ's words with a sideswipe at what he regards as unscriptural devotions like the rosary: 'When ye pray, use not vain repetitions, as the papists do' (in Larsen 2007: 186).

The teaching on fasting (6:16–18) stands in tension with Christ's teaching elsewhere (e.g. 9:14–17 and parallels). However, the present teaching is for the time of the church, 'when the bridegroom is taken away.' The *Didache* provides specific regulations to differentiate authentic fasting from that of the hypocrites (though focusing less on motivation than on timing):

> But do not let your fasts coincide with those of the hypocrites. They fast on Monday and Thursday, so you must fast on Wednesday and Friday. (*Did.* 8:1; Holmes 2007: 355)

Our Father (6:9–15)

The centrality of the Our Father, often known by its Latin title Pater noster, or as 'the Lord's Prayer' (a title coined by Cyprian of Carthage) is widely acknowledged, as is the divergence between Matthew and Luke (see e.g. Chase 1891; Bahr 1965; Ayo 1992; Brown 2004; Stevenson 2004; Hammerling 2010). Origen explains the difference in terms of audience: Luke's version is delivered privately to the disciples, who do not need the more detailed explanation

1 http://www.osb.org/rb/text/rbefjo3.html#18.

offered in Matthew's public sermon (Hammerling 2010: 16). The Lord's Prayer rivals the Beatitudes for the claim to encapsulate Christian doctrine. Tertullian, who provides one of the earliest commentaries on the prayer (probably written 200–206 CE), describes it as 'a summary of the whole Gospel' (*On Prayer* 1; Stewart-Sykes 2004: 42). Others emphasize its superiority as the model for Christian prayer, a 'method of prayer' (Lapide 1890: 1/258), to be prayed three times a day, according to the *Didache* (*Did.* 8:3). Luther also urges that the Lord's Prayer should be prayed frequently, as an 'excellent and brief formula' for those who otherwise would not know how to pray (Marty 1983: 36). However, he also laments the fact that it 'is prattled and chattered so irreverently all over the world!' (in Arand 1995: 42). Others stress the prayer's performative character. The Antiochene exegete Theodore of Mopsuestia (350–428) views its brevity as an indication that 'the prayer does not consist so much in words as in good works, love and zeal for duty' (O'Donnell 1960: 13–14).

By the fourth century, the Our Father has become one of those 'symbols' of the Faith not to be divulged to outsiders. For Ambrose, the Lord's Prayer is only to be taught to the baptized, on the Friday following their baptism at Easter. A similar practice is advocated in the *Mystagogic Catecheses* attributed to Cyril of Jerusalem. Ambrose's disciple Augustine allows it to be taught to catechumens prior to baptism, as does the fifth-century bishop of Ravenna, Peter Chrysologus (Hammerling 2010: 45–46, 59–77). This may also be implied by the late fourth-century *Apostolic Constitutions*, which presumes that the newly baptized are able to utter the prayer immediately following the post-baptismal anointing (*Apostolic Constitutions* 7.45; Stevenson 2004: 66). Others, including the fourth-century Spanish Christian poet Juvencus, see its evangelistic potential. Thus, while not revealing its precise wording to outsiders, Juvencus presents a paraphrase in his verse harmony of the Gospels (c. 330), imitating Virgil's style to convince Roman contemporaries of the superiority of the Christian message:

> O Most High Father, we pray
> that our veneration of your
> name may be made holy in us:
> May the peaceful and bountiful
> light of your kingdom come
> and shine forth in the world.
> (Juvencus, *The Four Books of the Gospels* 1.591–593; Hammerling 2010: 48)

The Lord's Prayer is not just for new initiates, however, but for mature Christians. Indeed, according to the popular *Expositio Orationis Dominice* by the Saxon Augustinian Jordan of Quedlinburg (c. 1300–1370/1380), its brevity is designed to facilitate memorization, thus aiding frequent repetition by the laity (*Lecture* 3; Saak 2015: 99). Augustine's *Enchiridion* presents the Christian faith as summarized in the Creed (faith) and the Our Father (hope and love: Hammerling 2010: 89). The Lord's Prayer is important for Luther's Small and Large Catechisms (Arand 1995), and structures the teaching about prayer in both the 1564 *Catechism of the Council of Trent* and the 1992 *Catechism of the Catholic Church* (*CCC* 2759–2865). It also functions, along with the Ten Commandments and the Apostles' Creed, as an important catechetical text for early Anabaptists (Snyder-Penner 1994). That it is a prayer for all Christians is visualized in the Church of the Pater Noster on the Mount of Olives, whose cloister contains ceramic plaques of the Our Father in more than a hundred languages.

Unsurprisingly, the prayer has had particular importance for the Christian mystical tradition (reflected already in Origen's *On Prayer*, c. 234). The German mystic Magdalene Beutler (1407–1458) wrote a 332-page *Erklärung des Vaterunsers*, a 'stream-of-consciousness devotional monologue' (Winston-Allen in Taylor and Choi 2012: 70). The Spanish Carmelite Teresa of Avila (1515–1582) devoted a substantial section of her *Way of Perfection* to instructing her fellow nuns on the benefits of praying the Our Father: 'I tell you that it is very possible that while you are reciting the Our Father or some other vocal prayer, the Lord may raise you to perfect contemplation' (*Way of Perfection* 25; Teresa of Avila 1980: 131).

Our Father in Heaven (6:9)

The opening address is the great leveler, placing rich and poor on an equal footing before God (Augustine, *The Lord's Sermon on the Mount* 2.4.16). Francis of Assisi found it especially meaningful when he renounced his earthly father, Pietro di Bernardone, stripping naked before him and returning his clothes:

> He said to his father: 'Until now I have called you father here on earth, but now I can say without reservation, "*Our Father who art in heaven,*" since I have placed all my treasure and all my hope in him.' (Bonaventure, *Major Legend of St. Francis* 2:4 in Armstrong, Hellmann, and Short 2000: 538)

For Cyprian of Carthage, a bishop concerned for the unity of the church, the Matthean 'Our' is particularly significant. It means that, even when prayed by individuals, it is a prayer for the whole church (*On the Lord's Prayer* 8).

Moreover, as a window onto Christ's own prayer to his Father, the first two words have proved a potent source for speculative theology. The Greek monastic theologian Maximus the Confessor (c. 580–662) meets the objection that only the Father is addressed in this prayer, by appeal to New Testament references to the Son bearing the Father's Name (e.g. John 5:43; Phil 2:9) and the Spirit's dynamic role in establishing the Kingdom:

> For the *name* of God the Father exists in substantial form as the only-begotten Son. Again, the *kingdom* of God the Father exists in substantial form as the Holy Spirit. (Maximus the Confessor, *On the Lord's Prayer*, in Dumitraşcu 2013: 351)

Gerard Applemans (c. 1250–1325), a hermit of Brabant in the Low Countries, uses his *Gloss on the Our Father* to examine what the reference to the Father reveals about the Son, and about humanity's relationship to the God:

> The Father, in the fecundity of his nature, is speaking that word to himself, engendering the Son, another Person of his own nature, in all-perfect likeness to himself, and, in a fatherly way, recognizing the other Person as Son. But the Father, as creator, is also appropriately 'a Father to all creatures.' (van Nieuwenhove, Faesen, and Rolfson 2008: 67)

In the modern period, feminist criticism has provoked new questions about the masculine title 'Father' (for a thoughtful discussion, see Thompson 2000). Patristic and medieval interpreters often found a different aspect of the prayer problematic: the fact that the Father is said to be 'in heaven.' This might imply limitations on the Deity, a possibility rejected by Dante: 'Our Father Who in Heaven dost abide, | not there constrained but dwelling there because | Thou lovest more Thy lofty first effects' (*Purgatorio*, Canto 11:1; Dante 1995: 118). Origen objects to a literal interpretation on the grounds that God neither has a body nor resides in a particular location (*On Prayer* 23.2), while Ephrem the Syrian regards the phrase as contrasting God, who is the Lord of nature, with earthly fathers who are such 'according to nature' (*C. Diat.* 6:16a–17; Hogan 1999: 100–101).

Prayer for the Coming Kingdom (6:10)

The Our Father also expresses the centrality of 'the kingdom of the heavens' (Matthew's preferred phrase for the 'kingdom of God'). As Augustine recognizes, it is not that God does not already reign. Rather the prayer refers to God's reign being revealed to all humanity (*Lord's Sermon on the Mount* 2.6.20). The *Opus imperfectum* distinguishes between being a king (which God is by nature) and the act of reigning; God does not yet reign among all people, because not all wish to do his will, thereby acknowledging the devil's reign over them. These two kingdoms will give way to one Kingdom of God only at the judgment.

Tertullian, writing against the backdrop of martyrdom in North Africa, also understands the coming Kingdom as an eschatological promise (*On Prayer* 5; also Cyprian, *On the Lord's Prayer* 13: see Kwon 2012: 65–66). It is hastened by Christians performing God's will on earth, especially manifest in the endurance of the martyrs (Stevenson 2004: 30). This connection with the martyrs had already been made in the second-century *Martyrdom of Polycarp*, which records Polycarp's prayer on his arrest as 'May God's will be done' (*Mart. Pol.* 7).

Origen, by contrast, treats the coming Kingdom as personal and immanent, God's present reign in the individual believer (*On Prayer* 25.1). The personal impact of this petition is also central to John Wesley, Anglican priest and co-founder of Methodism, who himself underwent a dramatic conversion experience in Aldersgate Street, London, in 1738: the Kingdom 'comes to a particular person when he "repents and believes the gospel" (Mark 1:15)' (Wesley in Stevenson 2004: 192). Similarly, for the German Lutheran theologian Adolf von Harnack (1851–1930), the Kingdom 'is the rule of the holy God in the hearts of individuals' (Harnack 1957: 56). William Tyndale retains the present dimension of the petition, but emphasizes its implications for the secular, political sphere:

> That is, seeing thou art king over all, make all to know thee; and make the kings and rulers, which are but thy substitutes, to command nothing but according to thy word, and to them make all subjects obey. (in Duffield 1965: 260)

Our Daily Bread (6:11)

The precise meaning of the Greek term *epiousios*, apparently unattested prior to the Gospels (see Origen, *On Prayer* 27.7), remains 'an unresolved puzzle' (Davies and Allison 2004: 94; for the various solutions see e.g. BDF 123; Rordorf 1976; Hultgren 1990; Nolland 2005: 289–290; Luz 2007: 319–321). The problem is twofold: the derivation of the term, and its interpretation within the prayer. Alternative etymological explanations propose the translations 'bread for today,' 'bread for the coming day,' and 'bread needful for existence.' The second option is known to the sixteenth-century Italian grammarian Angelus Caninius: 'tomorrow's bread,' recalling the Sabbath's manna collected on Friday (in Lapide 1890: 1/269). Jerome knows the reading *mahar* in the Gospel 'according to the Hebrews,' meaning 'tomorrow's, that is, future, bread' (Jerome 2008: 88–89). A variation of the third option (*ousia* = 'being' or 'substance') accounts for Jerome's choice of the adjective *supersubstantialis*, 'supersubstantial,' in the Vulgate of 6:11 (replacing the Old Latin's *quotidianus*, 'daily,' which he retains for Luke's version). The text known to Ephrem reads 'Give us our constant/trustworthy bread of the day' (Hogan 1999: 106; also Syriac version of *Acts of Thomas* 12), while the fifth-century Peshitta version has 'bread of our need' (Stevenson 2004: 44).

Finding its etymology is only part of the solution, however. Origen interprets the bread as the bread 'of the divine substance,' i.e. the bread of the Word which nourishes the soul (*On Prayer* 27.7). This spiritualizing interpretation leads to a widespread identification of this bread with the Eucharist (e.g. Cyprian; Cyril of Jerusalem, *Catech.* 5), enhanced by the recitation of the Lord's Prayer prior to the reception of communion in both east and west. The fifth-century Armenian Elishe, possibly bishop of Amatunik, gives a eucharistic interpretation of Ephrem's reading 'constant bread': 'he gave himself as bread in the Upper Room and continually gives himself now as bread in the Churches on the holy altar' (in Stevenson 2004: 57). The nineteenth-century Anglican priest John Keble provides a similar interpretation:

> Give us this day our daily bread: Thou in whom we being many are One bread and One body; grant that we, being all partakers of that one bread, may day by day be more One in thee. (in Stevenson 2004: 196)

Erasmus also interprets the bread in a figurative, albeit non-eucharistic sense, as 'the bread of your heavenly teaching' (Erasmus 2008: 117).

Others emphasize its material dimensions: it is a prayer for natural bread, as a symbol of our bodily requirements: 'everything necessary for the preservation of this life, like food, a healthy body, good weather, house, home, wife, children, good government, and peace' (Luther in Marty 1983: 37–38; also Theodore of Mopsuestia; John Calvin; William Tyndale; Juan de Valdés). Gregory of Nyssa views this petition as a restraint on luxury: 'So we say to God: Give us bread. Not delicacies or riches, nor magnificent purple robes, golden ornaments, precious stones, or silver dishes' (*On the Lord's Prayer, Sermon* 4; Gregory of Nyssa 1954: 63).

Augustine favors a range of meaning, both material and spiritual (the latter incorporating both God's word and the Eucharistic bread: *The Lord's Sermon on the Mount* 2.7.25–27). Augustine is widely followed in the West (e.g. Aquinas; Lapide). More complex is the late medieval interpretation of Jordan of Quedlinburg, which combines the literal meaning (material bread) with a series of spiritual meanings: doctrinal bread ('of understanding,' see Sir 15:3), sacramental bread, and heavenly bread 'of glory,' which will be eaten in the Kingdom of God, where we 'will also be fed by the delicious contemplation of humanity in Christ' (*Lecture* 6; Saak 2015: 133–147). In a later revision of his *Expositio*, he adds a fourth: the bread of sorrow, or 'tearful bread' (Saak 2015: 37–38).

Forgive Us Our Debts (6:12)

Matthew's petition for forgiveness of 'debts' ('sins' at Luke 11:4) reflects the Aramaic understand of debt as both literal and a metaphorical reference to sin (Luz 2007: 311). Patristic authors often find reassurance in this petition that sin committed after baptism can be forgiven (e.g. Chrysostom). Thus, Augustine asserts: 'Baptism was instituted on account of all sins; for venial sins, without committing which it would be impossible to live, prayer was instituted' (Augustine, *De symbolo sermo ad catechumenos* 1, 7, 15–16: Kraszewski 1999: 283).

The importance of this petition for Christian communal life explains its prominence in monastic ritual. The *Rule of St. Benedict* prescribes recitation of the Lord's Prayer at Lauds and Vespers to overcome dissensions within the community:

> The Morning and Evening Offices
> should never be allowed to pass
> without the Superior saying the Lord's Prayer
> in its place at the end
> so that all may hear it,
> on account of the thorns of scandal which are apt to spring up.
> Thus those who hear it,
> being warned by the covenant which they make in that prayer
> when they say, "Forgive us as we forgive,"
> may cleanse themselves of faults against that covenant
> (*Rule of St. Benedict* 13).[2]

Deliverance from Evil (6:13)

Although Augustine treats verse 13 as containing two petitions ('lead us not …'; 'deliver us from …'), earlier commentators regard them as two parts of the same (Fitzmyer 2003: 25). Thus the 'reality of the evil that lies behind the temptation' is emphasized (Luz 2007: 323). This somewhat mitigates the concern that God actively leads humanity into temptation (a position explicitly rejected in Jas 1:13–14). As Tertullian writes: 'God forbid that the Lord should be supposed to tempt, as though he were either ignorant of each man's faith or desirous of overthrowing it' (*On Prayer* 8.4–6; Brown 2004: 250). Cyprian and Ambrose know the reading 'and do not suffer us to be lead into temptation' (*ne nos patiaris induci in tentationem*: Higgins 1945: 179–180), acknowledging God's permissive will but avoiding making him the direct agent of temptation.

2 http://www.osb.org/rb/text/toc.html.

Juvencus avoids the difficulty by shifting responsibility to demonic activity: 'Remove far away from us the fierce temptation of the vile demon, and may your right hand lift us up into the light away from all evil' (Juvencus, *The Four Books of the Gospels* 1.599–600; Hammerling 2010: 48).

Origen interprets this petition, not as a prayer against being tempted or tested (which is integral to earthly life) but 'so that we should not be overcome when we are tested' (*On Prayer* 29.9; Stewart-Sykes 2004: 196). God provides his people with the strength not to give up. Similarly, for Augustine and Jerome, it is a prayer that God not allow us to be tempted beyond our strength (Ayo 1992: 88; see 1 Cor 10:13). In the Middle Ages, Jordan of Quedlinburg distinguishes between being tempted, falling into temptation, suffering temptation, succumbing to temptation, and being led into temptation. The last two are to be avoided, the last being the worst, being 'when man knowingly consents to the temptation and enjoys it' (*Lecture* 8; Saak 2015: 165).

Modern commentators regularly interpret the 'temptation' or 'testing' not as ongoing temptation to sin but specifically as the eschatological trial (cf. 24:8; Mark 13:19; Rev 3:10: e.g. Brown 1961). The influence of this interpretation is found in some modern translations: 'and do not subject us to the final test …' (NABRE); 'do not bring us to the time of trial, …' (NRSV).

The final phrase is ambiguous: it could refer to 'evil' in the abstract (see 2 Tim 4:18; *Did.* 10:5) or specifically to 'the evil one,' i.e. Satan (e.g. *Ps-Clem. Hom.* 19:2). The former is preferred by Latin Fathers (e.g. Augustine), while the Greeks (e.g. Chrysostom) favor a reference to the Devil (see 13:19, 28; Brown 1961: 206–207). In the Roman Mass, the 'embolism' prayer immediately following the Our Father offers an explanatory gloss on what deliverance from evil might mean: the gift of peace, freedom from sin, and safety from disturbance or distress (*perturbatio*). Calvin views the divergence between Eastern and Western commentators of no great consequence: 'for the meaning remains nearly the same, that we are in danger from the devil and from sin, if the Lord does not protect and *deliver* us' (Calvin 1949: 329).

Other Teachings (6:19–7:12)

Mammon (6:24)

The single-mindedness demanded of disciples is perhaps best exemplified by the teaching about 'mammon,' a Semitic word designating property, wealth, or possessions (see e.g. Jerome). For the *Opus imperfectum*, this does not rule out having riches, only the possibility of being enslaved to both God and wealth.

The same point is made by Cornelius a Lapide, aware that Abraham and Isaac, King David and King Solomon, and many Christian saints were wealthy. For Jerome, almsgiving can act as a remedy against enslavement to riches. Unsurprisingly, given his 'two kingdoms' doctrine, Luther denies that Jesus' words rule out dual allegiance, to God and to prince or emperor: 'He is referring to two masters that are opposed to each other, not to those that govern together' (Luther 1956: 186).

The power of mammon to enslave explains its frequent personification. In Edmund Spenser's epic poem *The Faerie Queen*, first published in 1590, Mammon ('God of the world and worldlings I me call, | Great Mammon, greatest god below the sky') tempts Sir Guyon, the Knight of Temperance, in a manner reminiscent of Christ's temptation by the devil. Spenser's description of Mammon recalls the warning against treasures on earth in this section of the Sermon on the Mount:

> His iron coat all overgrown with rust
> Was underneath envelopèd with gold,
> Whose glistering gloss, darkened with filthy dust,
> Well yet appearèd to have been of old
> A work of rich entail and wild imagery.
> And in his lap a mass of coin he told
> And turnèd upside down, to feed his eye
> And covetous desire with his huge treasury.
> (*The Faerie Queene* 2.7.4; Spenser 1965: 300–301)

For John Milton (1608–1674), Mammon is one of the fallen angels, already fixated on material wealth while still in heaven, and who will later be active on earth tempting humans to avarice (Fox 1962):

> Mammon, the least erected Spirit that fell
> From Heav'n, for even in Heav'n his looks and thoughts
> Were always downward bent, admiring more
> The riches of Heav'n's pavement, trodden gold,
> Than aught divine or holy else enjoyed
> In vision beatific.
> (*Paradise Lost* 1.679–684; Milton 1999: 161)

Trust in Providence (6:25–34)

This radical demand is understandable as addressed to itinerant disciples in the rural Galilean context of Jesus' ministry. Indeed, it has often spoken powerfully to radical groups across the centuries. It is crucially important for Francis of Assisi, who even finds justification in verse 26 for his preaching to the birds:

> My brother birds, you who are noble among all creatures are especially bound to love and praise your Creator who clothes you in feathers, lifts you up from the earth by your wings, and provides purer mansions for you in the air. Though you neither sow, reap, nor *gather into barns*, he nourishes you without any trouble to you, and abundantly provides you with everything that's good for you.
>
> (Julian of Speyer, *Life of Saint Francis* 8.37 in Armstrong, Hellmann, and Short 1999: 396)

Martin Luther also understands 'the birds of heaven' as attentive to the divine message, at least metaphorically. A helpless sparrow can become 'a theologian and a preacher to the wisest of men,' while the lilies of the field 'are to become our theologians and masters and to embarrass us still further.' The birds and flowers teach us because they have learned what it means to trust in God (Luther 1956: 197–199). Cornelius a Lapide notes the particular suitability of birds for teaching humans 'that they ought to be heavenly, and be like birds, and fly away in spirit from earth to heaven' (Lapide 1890: 1/284). For the Anglican priest-poet George Herbert (1593–1633), the lilies of the field are signs of God's revelation written in the book of nature (*A Priest to the Temple* 15:23).

Many, however, are aware of the potential for misinterpretation. Theophylact of Ochrid rejects the suggestion that this places trust in providence at odds with the biblical command to work (e.g. Gen 2:15; 3:19; 2 Thess 3:6–15): 'Jesus does not forbid us to work, but rather He forbids us to give ourselves over entirely to our cares and to neglect God' (Theophylact 1992: 61).

There is also a tendency to allegorize. Jerome knows of some who hold that 'the birds of heaven' mean the angels and other heavenly powers, although he rejects this view by appeal to verse 26: 'Are you not more than they?' The *Opus imperfectum* understands Jesus' exhortation not to be anxious about tomorrow figuratively: 'tomorrow' means 'what is superfluous to our need' (Kellerman and Oden 2010: 138). Cornelius a Lapide interprets the lilies increasing as a reference to consecrated virgins, 'who, by increasing in virtues, grow in God, and are clothed with the garments of grace now and of glory hereafter' (Lapide 1890: 1/288).

On Not Judging (7:1–5)

The absolute command 'Do not judge' (v. 1) is widely regarded as problematic, not least given Jesus' later instructions about correcting an erring 'brother' (18:15–17). Thus Chromatius of Aquileia understands the phrase 'it will be measured to you' to mean that the Lord, far from prohibiting passing judgment, simply rules out judging rashly (*Tractatus in Matthaeum* 33.1; Kraszewski 1999:

288). Theophylact makes a distinction between condemning others, which is forbidden, and reproving others, which is permitted. Thus 7:1 critiques 'one who, despite his own great sins, condemns others who have lesser sins of which God will be the judge' (Theophylact 1992: 63). The Jamaican singer-songwriter Bob Marley also uses the passage to expose hypocritical judgment of others – 'Don't you look at me so smugly | And say I'm going bad' – in his 1962 single 'Judge Not' (Dowling Long and Sawyer 2015: 129):

> Judge not
> Before you judge yourself.
> Judge not
> If you're not ready for judgement.

For Cornelius a Lapide (following Jerome, Augustine, and Basil), Christians should avoid private judgments which damage another's reputation: in such cases, the true situation is known only to God. However, judgment is permissible 'concerning things which are open and public evils,' though this should still be exercised 'with charity and love' (Lapide 1890: 1/295).

The ecclesial connotations of 'my brother' allow both Catholic and Protestant commentators to reject the claim that Christ's words also prohibit judgment in the secular courts. By contrast, Menno Simons forbade fellow Anabaptists from holding the office of a judge (Luz 2007: 351).

Dogs and Swine (7:6)

This 'provocatively obscure' saying (Boring 1995: 212) invites allegorical interpretation. One of the earliest, recognizing that 'what is holy' refers to sacrificial food (e.g. Exod 29:37; Lev 2:3), finds a warning against allowing the unbaptized to share in the Eucharist (*Did.* 9:5; see also Chrysostom). Its effects are still felt in the solemn dismissal of catechumens during the Orthodox Divine Liturgy. Later commentators will expand this prohibition to heretics (e.g. John of Damascus, *Exposition of the Orthodox Faith* 4.13), or as a warning not to baptize rashly (Tertullian, *De Bapt.* 18).

Alternatively, the holy things are Gnostic mysteries or Christian doctrines, which are not to be shared with pagans, or those not ready to receive them (e.g. Elchasai in Hippolytus, *Ref.* 9.12; Gregory of Nazianzus, *Orat.* 2.79; Cyprian, *Treatise* 5; Evagrius of Pontus, *Praktikos*, prologue 9). Erasmus provides a similar definition of the 'pearl' that is not to be thrown before swine, on the basis of the 'pearl of great price' at 13:45–46. It denotes 'the gospel riches,' 'the secrets of heavenly teaching,' 'the gospel philosophy' (Erasmus 2008: 130–131). For Cornelius a Lapide, it is not necessary to adjudicate between the various options: 'what is holy' and the pearls symbolize 'the precious and heavenly doctrine of the Gospel, of faith and truth, and, by consequence, the holy sacraments' (Lapide 1890: 1/298).

Methodius of Olympus (d. c. 311) maintains that the apostolic charge to preach the Gospel (e.g. 28:19; Mark 16:15) demands an alternative interpretation of this saying:

> we must take the pearls to mean virtues, with which the soul is adorned as with precious pearls; and not to cast them before swine, as meaning that we are not to cast these virtues, such as chastity, temperance, righteousness, and truth, that we are not to cast these to impure pleasures, for these are like swine, lest they, fleeing from the virtues, cause the soul to live a swinish and a vicious life. (Methodius, *On Created Things*: *ANF* 6:379)

John Calvin, by contrast, sees no contradiction with the missionary charge: the 'dogs' and 'swine' are specifically 'those who, by clear evidences, have manifested a hardened contempt for God, so that their disease appears to be incurable' (Calvin 1949: 349–350).

Other commentators differentiate more clearly between the 'dogs' and the 'swine.' Hilary interprets the 'dogs' as pagans and the 'pigs' as heretics. Similarly, for Theophylact, the 'dogs' are unbelievers, while the 'swine' are degenerate believers, who emulate swine in leading 'a filthy and shameful way of life' (Theophylact 1992: 63). Jerome knows some who propose the reverse: the 'dogs' are converts who 'turn back to the vomit of their sins' (2 Pet 2:22), whereas the pigs are unbelievers, who 'are wallowing in the mud of unbelief and in vices,' to whom the pearl of the Gospel should not be entrusted (Jerome 2008: 93). The English Reformer and Bible translator William Tyndale finds a contemporary manifestation of 'the dogs' in church authorities: 'The dogs are those obstinate and indurate, which for the blind zeal of their leaven, wherewith they have soured both the doctrine and also the works, maliciously resist the truth, and persecute the ministers thereof' (in Duffield 1965: 290). Tyndale's comment is ironic, given that the same verse was used to ban vernacular Bibles during the Middle Ages (Clarke 2003: 90).

The Golden Rule (7:12)

For many, the Golden Rule (a title given to this saying since the eighteenth century) is the 'first principle of moral philosophy' (Chrysostom in Lapide 1890: 1/302), in which Christ 'shows us the way to virtue' (Theophylact 1992: 64). In fact, it is not unique to Jesus, but widely attested in different forms in Judaism and paganism (e.g. Tobit 4:15; Sir 31:15 LXX; *Ep. Arist.* 207; Hillel in *b. Šabb* 31a; *T. Naph.* 1; *2 En.* 61:1; Dio Cassius 52:34).

However, the saying can be read in a self-serving manner, as well as a 'rule of empathy' with the other (Reiner in Luz 2007: 364). Avoidance of the former might explain the addition of 'good' to 'Whatever you wish' in certain Latin manuscripts. Augustine concludes that 'good' was added for clarification, to rule out the application of the Golden Rule to an immoral desire (*Lord's Sermon on the Mount* 2.22.74). In fact, this is already excluded by Matthew's explanatory gloss – 'for this is the Law and the prophets' – which presents it as another form of the twofold commandment, to love God and neighbor, on which all the Law and the prophets hang (22:40).

Conclusion to the Sermon (7:13–27)

The Two Ways (7:13–14)

Presenting an ethical challenge in terms of two ways is common in the Judaeo-Christian tradition (e.g. Deut 11:26; 30:15; Jer 21:8; Sir 2:12; *T. Ash.* 1:3–5; *2 En.* 20:15; 1QS 3:20; *Did.* 1–6). Matthew combines this with the motif of two gates (also *T. Ab.* 8 recension B). Because the gates and ways lead to 'life' and 'destruction' respectively, the image is probably that of two gates, to a city or temple, at the *end* of two contrasting roads (so Luz 2007: 372). However, this passage has often been visualized as two gates providing entrance to the two paths.

One of the most famous examples is the lithograph *Der breite und der schmale Weg*, originally designed in Stuttgart for the German Pietist Charlotte Reihlen in 1862 (Massing 1988), and reproduced in several languages. An English version (*The Broad and Narrow Way*; Figure 8) was used in open-air preaching, and lithograph versions were popular among English-speaking evangelical Christians. The wide gate, flanked by statues of Bacchus and Venus, opens onto a broad road lined by buildings offering worldly pleasures (a brothel, tavern with a ballroom, theater, and gambling-house), ascending a hill toward fallen Babylon and the lake of fire (Rev 18:2; 20:10). A tiny narrow gate on the right opens onto a narrow path which meanders past a fountain beneath a crucifix (symbolizing Christ the spiritual rock of 1 Cor 10:4), a church, Sunday school, and charitable institutions, toward the heavenly Jerusalem. The rocks, thorns, and precipices signify the tribulations facing those who embrace the narrow way. Both wide and narrow paths are peppered with relevant biblical references, functioning respectively as warnings and encouragement.

Though sometimes interpreted as particularly addressed to monastics (e.g. *Sayings of the Desert Fathers*; *Rule of St. Benedict* 5), the challenge is more widely acknowledged as for all Christians. For Jerome, the broad road

Figure 8 *The Broad and Narrow Way*, the picture accompanying Mr. G. Kirkham's lecture on 'The Broad and Narrow Way.' Cambridge University Library 1886.12.19. Source: Reproduced by kind permission of the Syndics of Cambridge University Library.

refers to 'the pleasures of the world'; the narrow road is opened 'by means of labors and fasting' (Jerome 2008: 94). Similarly, for John Calvin, following the narrow way requires rejecting 'the allurements of a licentious and dissolute life' (Calvin 1949: 356). John Wesley offers more positive advice on how to enter the narrow gate: 'The way of poverty of spirit, the way of holy mourning, the way of meekness, and that of hungering and thirsting after righteousness' (quoted in Noll 2007: 173). Cornelius a Lapide, meanwhile, finds Old Testament types for followers of the narrow way: Lot and his daughters escaping from Sodom, Noah and his family rescued from the deluge, and Caleb and Joshua entering the Promised Land. The alternative 'broad way' lends itself to polemical usage. The English Baptist preacher Charles Spurgeon finds the liberal Anglican 'Broad Church' an obvious target (in Larsen 2007: 186).

True and False Prophets (7:15–23)

The early Christian conviction that prophecy had been renewed (e.g. Acts 2; 1 Cor 14) made the discernment of true and false prophecy a burning issue. While Matthew's first audiences may have identified a specific group being targeted (e.g. Pauline Christians or other antinomians), later commentators have often explored this passage in search of perennial advice for the church's discernment. The longer recension of Ignatius of Antioch's letter to the Ephesians (possibly fourth century) uses this passage to critique those who separate themselves from the bishop:

> For if the prayer of one or two possesses such power that Christ stands in the midst of them, how much more will the prayer of the bishop and of the whole Church, ascending up in harmony to God, prevail for the granting of all their petitions in Christ! He, therefore, that separates himself from such, and does not meet in the society where sacrifices are offered, and with "the Church of the first-born whose names are written in heaven," is a wolf in sheep's clothing, while he presents a mild outward appearance. (Ignatius, *Eph.* 5; *ANF* 1:51)

The 'wolves' are commonly understood as Christian heretics, who clothe themselves in the 'sheep's clothing' of biblical texts (Vincent of Lérins, *Commonitorium* 36), or in a veneer of piety (Jerome). For Aquinas, they also include evil teachers and prelates. The *Opus imperfectum* has a broader definition: false Christians, on the grounds that all Christians are anointed as prophet, priest, and king. Jesus' words have also been prone to satirical reworking, as in Winston Churchill's description of his political opponent Clement Attlee (prime minister of the United Kingdom 1945–1951) as 'a sheep in sheep's clothing' (in Clarke 2003: 92).

Every age is prone to find false prophets in its ecclesial opponents (as Luz [2007: 381] notes, the saying 'could be used by everyone and against everyone'). Thus for Cornelius a Lapide, the false prophets 'teach that we need not fast, nor go to confession, nor preserve virginity, nor religious vows,' veiling their errors with such 'sheep's clothing' as their use of scriptural quotations, and their claim to be reforming the church's morals (Lapide 1890: 1/306). On the other side of the Reformation divide, John Calvin knows that 'the Papists' cite this passage in order 'to induce ignorant people to avoid us' (Calvin 1949: 364).

Yet reading Matthew 7:15–23 as a unit, the characteristic of false prophecy is not heretical teaching, but failure to bear fruit in right action. Thus neither correct Christology (saying to Christ, 'Lord, Lord') nor performing exorcisms is sufficient. As Augustine recognizes, 'trees' and 'fruits' signify the human soul and the person's actions respectively. Discernment between good and bad trees is provided by Paul's list of works of the flesh and fruits of the Spirit in Galatians 5:19–23 (*Lord's Sermon on the Mount* 2.24.79–81). The *Didache* proposes that the criterion for discernment is whether the prophet seeks to gain from his ministry: staying three days, or asking for money (*Did.* 11:5–6). William Tyndale advocates the same: 'Take heed to thy preacher therefore, and be sure, if he be covetous and gape for promotion, that he is a false prophet' (*Exposition on Matt V–VII*: Duffield 1965: 195).

Jesus' words about good trees not producing bad fruit (vv. 17–19) have served as an important proof text for various groups, such as the Manicheans (dividing humanity according to two natural principles, good and bad), the Pelagians (against original sin, on the grounds that the evil of sin cannot be produced from a good person), and the Donatists (who rejected the efficacy of baptism by wicked priests: Lapide 1890: 1/308). Jerome objects to the Manichean view that good trees can *never* produce bad fruit, appealing to 'good trees' such as Moses, David, and Peter, who nonetheless sinned, 'bad trees' capable of good, such as Jethro, Achior, and Menander (quoted by Paul at 1 Cor 15:33), and 'good trees' who became bad (Judas Iscariot) or vice versa (e.g. Paul). Arnobius Iunior looks to salvation history to find the key: the 'bad tree' is the old Adam, yielding sin, lust, and avarice; the 'good tree' is the wood of the cross (*Expositiunculae in Matthaeum* 10; Kraszewski 1999: 29).

Some find the suggestion that wicked people can prophesy or perform exorcisms problematic, though the Anglican theologian Daniel Whitby (1638–1726) finds biblical examples of each in Balaam and Judas Iscariot respectively (Whitby in Cornwallis 1820: 28). Aquinas is concerned about the proposition that demons can work miracles: 'I say that they cannot; but they do some things which seem to be miracles, and yet are not miracles.' He notes the alternative solution of Jerome: that certain gifts of the Spirit are given freely to both good and evil people, and that the children of God and of the devil are distinguished only by charity (Aquinas 2013a: 247).

Building on the Rock (7:24–27)

The concluding parable continues the motif of eschatological judgment, a fact recognized by the Spanish Jesuit Juan de Maldonado (1533–1583): the 'rain,' 'wind,' and 'flood' are 'meant to describe the same day of judgment as a terrible tempest' (Maldonado 1888: 1/253). However, its contrast between a 'wise' or 'prudent' and 'foolish' builder (cf. Luke 6:47–49) also lends itself to allegorical interpretation, to describe Christian life in the present. For Jerome and Theophylact, the rain symbolizes the devil, the floods those who think contrary to Christ, the winds 'the spiritual wickedness in the heavenly places' (Eph 6:12) or evil spirits. Augustine finds an allegory of moral degeneration, the rain, winds, and floods representing 'dark superstitions,' 'the gossip of men,' and the river of life 'with its lusts of the flesh' respectively (*Lord's Sermon on the Mount* 2.25.87; Augustine 2014: 113–114). Aquinas, by contrast, proposes that each house faces a different threat, interpreting the 'rain' as teaching, which can be either good or bad. Hence, the house of the foolish man is threatened not by demonic activity but by the good: the rain of good teaching, floods symbolizing good teachers, the winds who are angel-spirits (Ps 103:4). Its fall is the fall of great Babylon (Rev 14:8).

The tropological sense is clear to many interpreters: the wise builder is a Christian who not only hears Christ's commandments but also acts on them (e.g. Hilary; Theophylact; Maldonado). Erasmus elaborates on this point effectively: the person who really listens to Christ's words is 'like a thoughtful and prudent man who, in order to construct a solid and strong building, first of all looks to find a solid and unmovable foundation to which to entrust a substructure that will withstand all the assaults of storms' (Erasmus 2008: 138). Religious activities such as fasting and almsgiving, Erasmus continues, are a splendid building, but will come crashing down unless one is 'fixed on the teaching and promises of the gospel.'

Given Matthew 16:18, the house founded on rock is sometimes understood as the church (e.g. Jerome), built upon Christ the 'rock' (e.g. Hilary; Augustine; Arnobius Iunior; Theophylact; Aquinas; Luther; cf., e.g. Rom 9:32–33; 1 Cor 3:11; 10:4; 1 Pet 2:6). A sixteenth-century ecclesiological variant is Cornelius a Lapide's interpretation, which contrasts the spiritual house of the soul, founded on 'faith solidified by good works,' with the (Protestant) house built on sand, i.e. on faith without works (Lapide 1890: 1/314; so also Maldonado on Calvin). An unusual alternative reading is provided by John of Parma, early minister general of the Franciscans, for whom the rocky foundation is holy poverty, 'the foundation and guardian' of all other virtues (in Stoddart 1914: 60).

Matthew 8–9

Ancient Literary Context

The Matthean Jesus now descends from the mountain, accompanied by crowds. Discourse gives way to narrative once again, in a carefully crafted section emphasizing Jesus' miraculous power (8:1–9:8; 9:18–34), as well as growing conflict from his contemporaries (9:1–17). Matthew's thematic arrangement of this section is clear by comparison with Mark and Luke, who

Matthew Through the Centuries, First Edition. Ian Boxall.

order these stories very differently (Mark 1:40–45; 1:29–34; 4:35–5:20; 2:1–22; 5:21–43; Luke 5:12–16; 7:1–10; 13:28–29; 4:38–41; 9:57–62; 8:22–39; 5:17–39; 8:40–56).

Indeed, many modern commentators find strong support in this section for Markan Priority. They point, for example, to Matthew's abbreviated form of the miracle stories (problematic for Augustine's view that Mark is Matthew's abbreviator; compare, e.g. 8:28–34 with Mark 5:1–20; 9:23–26 with Mark 5:35–43). There are also indications of Matthean 'fatigue' in his use of Mark: e.g. Jesus' command to the leper not to tell anyone (8:4) is redundant given that Jesus is surrounded by 'many crowds' (8:1: Goodacre 1998: 52).

The focus on deeds complements the Sermon's emphasis on words (the two sections are bracketed by a literary *inclusio*: 4:23; 9:35). Some scholars find a Moses typology at work, reflected not only in Jesus' mighty works (cf. Exod 7–12; *Pirke Aboth* 5.5: 'Ten wonders were done for our Fathers in Egypt'; Teeple 1957: 82–83), but also in details such as leprosy, stretching out the hand, and the use of Isaiah 53 where the Servant is portrayed in Mosaic terms (e.g. Theophilos 2013; though see Allison 1993a: 213).

Yet the miracles raise hermeneutical difficulties for many post-Enlightenment readers, leading to alternative rationalist explanations. Friedrich Schleiermacher (1768–1834) proposed that Jesus revived the official's daughter from a coma, taking literally Jesus' words at 9:24 (that the girl is not dead but sleeping). Others (e.g. Schleiermacher's contemporary Heinrich Paulus) offered a psychological explanation of the hemorrhaging woman, while in his *Das Leben Jesu kritisch bearbeitet* (1835–1836), David Friedrich Strauss emphasized the mythic character of both miracles (see Zwiep 2015: 357–360). More recent interpreters find problematic the fact that the healing stories appear to treat disabilities as conditions to be overcome (e.g. McColl and Anscough 2009; though also Horne 2005).

A triad of conflict stories in 9:1–17 makes explicit the motif of opposition from within Israel, implicit from the beginning (e.g. 2:3, 13, 16–18; 3:7; 4:12; 5:11–12). The basic sequence – the healing of a paralytic; dining with tax-collectors and sinners; the question of fasting – is shared with Mark and Luke (Mark 2:1–22; Luke 5:17–39). In its Matthean context, it prepares the way for the narrative breach between Jesus and his religious opponents in chapter 12. Moreover, for some commentators, this narrative works on two levels: opposition to Jesus' activity within Israel is 'transparent' to the story of the post-Easter community, moving from origins in Israel, through the bitter experience of separation, to a new future in the Gentile mission (so, e.g. Luz 2001: 2).

The Interpretations

The miracles of Matthew 8–9 are regularly treated as confirming Christ's teaching in the Sermon (e.g. Jerome; Aquinas; the sixteenth-century Spanish Jesuit Maldonado). Early commentators are not unaware of the differences from Mark and Luke. The anonymous author of the *Opus imperfectum* proposes that Matthew's order is thematic rather than strictly chronological: presenting Christ's miracles after sections recounting his birth, baptism, temptation, and doctrine. In the early modern period, the Flemish Jesuit Cornelius a Lapide concurs. He acknowledges the disagreement in order, and regards Mark and Luke as preserving the chronological sequence of the miracles, with the healing of Peter's mother-in-law occurring *before* that of the leper (Mark 1:29–31, 40–45; Luke 4:38–39; 5:12–16). Matthew's non-chronological order reflects his concern 'to give, at the commencement of Christ's preaching, a summary of His doctrine, and then to relate in order His miracles, both those which He wrought before His sermon, and those which He wrought afterwards, in confirmation of His doctrine' (Lapide 1890: 1/332).

Figurative interpretations are also common. Building on Christ's praise of the Gentile centurion (8:10), several find a salvation-historical dimension to other miracles in these chapters. Some are surprising, in that they transform Matthean characters who were probably Jewish into representative Gentiles. Thus the paralytic is viewed as representing all the pagans, whose sins are forgiven through Christ, the 'Son of Man' or new Adam (e.g. Hilary). For both Hilary and Jerome, the woman with a hemorrhage (9:20–22) also symbolizes the Gentiles, despite nothing being said about her ethnic origins. They present her faithful character as a contrast to the synagogue represented by the father and his daughter (9:18–19, 23–26), though overlooking the fact that Matthew describes him simply as a 'ruler,' not 'leader of the synagogue' (9:18; cf. Mark 5:22; Luke 8:41).

Nonetheless, symbolic interpretations do not override interest in the centrality of the miracles for Jesus' ministry. Characters healed by Jesus function not simply as types, but as impressive exemplars of faith in their own right. Nor is Matthew's Christ-centered focus sidelined. The miracle stories, as well as the interwoven narratives of conflict, are fertile ground for Christological exploration, debate, and apologetics.

A Triad of Healings (8:1–17)

Given that the mountain signifies for the *Opus imperfectum* 'the height of virtue, the pinnacle of the church,' it is only when Christ descends to humbler ground that the crowds are able to follow him (Kellerman and Oden 2010: 165).

Similarly, for Erasmus, the descent from the 'lofty things' allows Christ to descend to the level of the crowd, 'in which were many who were sluggish, feeble, lame, and sick, and who had to be enticed to the pursuit of heavenly things even by physical blessings' (Erasmus 2008: 139–140). Thomas Aquinas finds an additional figurative meaning: Christ's descent from the mountain refers to the incarnation, when the one 'in the form of God' emptied himself in becoming human (see Phil 2:6–11).

These first three healings are often paid specific attention. For the Dutch Protestant theologian Hugo Grotius (1583–1645), they present three kinds of divine benefits: those bestowed on us through our own bequest (the leper), those received through the prayers of others (the centurion's servant), and those granted by God 'of His own free mercy' (the mother-in-law: in Ford 1859: 149–150). Others, especially modern commentators, focus on the main characters: they are all marginal figures (a leper, a Gentile centurion and his presumably Gentile servant, a Jewish woman; e.g. Davies and Allison 1991: 8, who add the demoniacs of 8:16–17 to the initial triad).

The Leper (8:1–4)

A common interest is in the faith implied by the leper's opening words: *Kurie* 'is not simply polite speech' (Luz 2001: 6). For Aquinas, the leper manifests faith in the divinity of Christ, for he recognizes that he has the power of God to cleanse him (also, e.g. Lapide). John Calvin is less sure that the leper's prostration is an act of worship, partly given the alternative verbs used by Mark and Luke, partly given that prostration was widely used in the East as a mark of respect. Nonetheless, the leper clearly 'acknowledged a divine power in Christ' (Calvin 1949: 372–373).

This focus on faith often occurs together with an emphasis on the leper's representative character, his leprosy interpreted as a figure of sin (e.g. *Opus imperfectum*), or specifically mortal sin (e.g. Lapide). For the English Benedictine abbot Ælfric of Eynsham (c. 955–1010), the leper 'signifies all mankind who are repulsively leprous with manifold sins in the inner man, unless it submits to belief in Christ and prudently perceives that it may not receive soul cleansing except through the Lord' (*Homily for the Third Sunday After Epiphany*, in Olsen 2015: 197). In other words, all humans are lepers, in need of the divine physician's touch. The eighteenth-century hymn-writer John Newton makes a similar point in his 'The Leper,' one of the *Olney Hymns*:

> Oft as the leper's case I read,
> My own described I feel;
> Sin is a leprosy indeed,
> Which none but CHRIST can heal.
> (*Olney Hymns* 82)

For Newton, Christ is able to 'cleanse my leprous soul from guilt.' Others (e.g. Erasmus), taking a more literal approach, highlight the social dimension of leprosy in terms of community exclusion, reiterated in modern commentaries (e.g. France 2007: 305–306).

The command that the leper show himself to the priest contains the ambiguous phrase 'as a testimony to them': this could be taken either negatively (testimony 'against those who saw the miracles and did not believe') or positively (testimony to the man's cure: Aquinas 2013a: 254). The reference to the (Jewish) priest sometimes functions as support for the Catholic practice of auricular confession, the (Christian) priests pronouncing on the 'spiritual leprosy' of sin (e.g. Aquinas). Unsurprisingly, Calvin rejects such an interpretation as 'highly foolish' (Calvin 1949: 375).

The Centurion's Boy (8:5–13)

This healing at a distance highlights the encounter between Jesus and a prominent military officer. It contains at its heart a dramatic reversal of social roles: 'it is the rich, powerful and influential Roman who petitions help from a Judean lacking property and without any defined status in the Judean social system' (Esler 2014: 8). The centurion's name is not given in the text, although Cornelius a Lapide knows the tradition, which he traces to the *Chronicle of Pseudo-Dexter*, that he was the father of the centurion who confessed Christ at the cross (27:54).

The differences between Matthew's account and Luke's (Luke 7:1–10, where the centurion does not approach Jesus directly) provoke inevitable attempts at harmonization (though John Chrysostom suggests that Luke describes a different centurion). One explanation is that the centurion first sends elders of the Jews (Luke), then comes himself (Matthew: e.g. Theophylact; Lapide). Alternatively, Matthew implies in abbreviated form what Luke makes explicit, that the centurion sends through his friends (Augustine, *Agreement Among the Evangelists* 2.20.49). While Matthew and Luke agree in highlighting the centurion's faith, the former goes further, presenting him as foreshadowing those who will come 'from east and west' to participate in the messianic banquet. Though originally describing the in-gathering of Israel's dispersed tribes (e.g. Ps 107:3; Isa 43:5; Zech 8:7–8; Bar 4:37; 5:5; *1 En.* 57:1; *Pss. Sol.* 11:2–4), Matthew clearly intends those gathered 'from east and west' to refer to Gentiles (Chrysostom suggests that Christ used this circumlocution so as not to offend his hearers). Augustine gives examples of these unspecified Gentiles in a Sermon for the Epiphany (drawing on the olive tree image from Rom 11:17–24):

> For the Magi came from the East and Pilate from the West. Hence, the Magi bore witness to the King of the Jews at His rising, that is, at His birth, and Pilate at His setting, that is, at His death, so that in the kingdom of heaven with

> Abraham and Isaac and Jacob, the progenitors from whom the Jews drew their lineage, they might feast, not as legitimate offspring of these three, but as engrafted upon their stock through faith so as to prefigure the wild olive to be engrafted upon the olive tree of which the Apostle speaks. (*Sermon* 201.2; in Augustine 1959: 69)

Thus, although a minority argue for the centurion being Jewish (he had built a synagogue, Luke 7:5; see Davies and Allison 2004: 120), the context supports the majority view that he is a non-Jew. Hence he is a fitting type of the Gentiles, who are saved by faith (e.g. Hilary; *Opus imperfectum*). Remigius, fifth-century bishop of Rheims, calls him the 'first fruits of the Gentiles' (in Ford 1859: 146). For Augustine, the fact that Christ enters neither the house of the centurion nor that of the Canaanite woman (15:21–28) is of profound salvation-historical significance. Both these episodes teach that 'the gentiles to whom he does not come will be saved by his word' (*Questions on the Gospels* 1.18; Augustine 2014: 367).

This wider significance appears in visual art. In Paolo Veronese's *Christ and the Centurion* (c. 1575; Nelson-Atkins Museum of Art, Kansas City), the group comprising Christ, the disciples, and the centurion is flanked by characters in contemporary dress, signifying those coming from east and west respectively. On the far left of the canvas, a Turk is engaged in conversation with an apostle, possibly Matthew. On the right are two European males, the one on the far right being Veronese himself (Fehl 1957).

For Jerome, the centurion is also a model of humility, on the grounds of his declaration 'I am not worthy' (so also e.g. Chrysostom), and of wisdom, in seeing Christ's hidden divinity (Theophylact and Juan de Maldonado also emphasize that the centurion expresses faith in Christ as God, rather than a mere wonderworker). The centurion's words, 'Lord, I am not worthy …,' were eventually incorporated into the Roman rite of the Mass, initially as part of the priest's preparation for communion (e.g. *Missale Romanum* 1570), and eventually also recited by the people (see Jungmann 1955: 2/355–357, 372). Thus 'my servant' has become 'my soul' in need of healing, an interpretation taken up in the liturgies of other churches, e.g. the American Episcopal Church. In his homily on this passage, John Chrysostom complements a eucharistic interpretation by highlighting how his Christian congregation in Antioch can also receive Christ present in the poor:

> Let us hearken, as many as are to receive Christ: for it is possible to receive Him even now. Let us hearken, and emulate, and receive Him with as great zeal; for indeed, when you receive a poor man who is hungry and naked, you have received and cherished Him. (*Homily on Matthew* 26:1; *NPNF* 1st series 10:176–177)

Yet despite the centurion's exemplary character, some find aspects of Jesus' response problematic. Many are troubled that the divine Christ 'wondered' (8:10; see Lapide 1890: 1/327–328; Maldonado 1888: 1/263–264). Aquinas distinguishes between two kinds of marveling: astonishment, which 'does not arise in God,' and 'the apprehension of the greatness of an effect,' which can apply to Christ (Aquinas 2013a: 258). John Calvin attributes the wonder to Christ's human nature, since '*Wonder* cannot apply to God' (Calvin 1949: 382).

Christ's prioritizing the centurion's faith over that of his own people ('among no-one in Israel have I found such faith') also gives cause for concern. Calvin wishes not to absolutize this statement, on the grounds that the faith of Mary was greater than the centurion's in believing the angel's message (Luke 1:38). He proposes that the impressiveness of the Gentile's faith is twofold. First, it represents abundant fruit yielded from 'a slight and inconsiderable acquaintance' with doctrine (Calvin 1949: 382). Second, in contrast to the Jews (e.g. 12:38–42), this Gentile asks for no sign. Cornelius a Lapide believes that Christ must be speaking of 'the ordinary run of people at the time of His preaching, for there was without doubt greater faith in the Blessed Virgin, in Abraham and Moses, and John the Baptist, and others' (Lapide 1890: 1/328).

This story is also considered for its moral implications. Tertullian (*On Idolatry* 19; also *de Corona* 11; see Ryan 1952: 17–20; Gero 1970) knows some who use it in support of Christian participation in the military, though is unpersuaded, given that Christ disarmed Peter in Gethsemane (26:52; John 18:10–11). Augustine's letter to the military tribune Boniface reveals how much has changed by the fifth century. Augustine instances the centurion, along with King David, the centurion Cornelius (Acts 10), and the soldiers baptized by John (Luke 3:14), as an example of those able to please God while engaged in military service (*Ep.* 189.4; on diverse early Christian attitudes, see Kreider 2003). Doubts about Christian participation in warfare linger across the centuries, only partially ameliorated by appeals to the spiritual sense: 'the centurion is everyone who rules over his members, senses, and faculties, so that they, as it were soldiers, may fight for and serve God' (Lapide 1890: 1/332).

Those who interpret Matthew's ambiguous Greek term *pais* as 'servant' (Luke has *doulos*, 'slave': Luke 7:2) rather than 'son' (the Vulgate reads *puer*, 'son'), are forced to deal with Jesus' silence about the social stratification within the centurion's household. Some appeal to this story as reflecting the natural social order. The Anglican commentator Mary Cornwallis finds in the centurion's 'tender concern' for his servant a model for contemporary householders in the treatment of their own domestic servants (Cornwallis 1820: 31). Cornelius a Lapide goes further, finding a tropological lesson for masters and superiors in ensuring their inferiors practice the Christian faith

(Lapide 1890: 1/332). While acknowledging his personal antipathy to slavery, the Catholic bishop of Charleston, John England, appeals to this story in defense of the Roman Catholic Church's sanctioning of the institution, in a letter dated 21 October 1840:

> In the New Testament we find instances of pious and good men having slaves, and in no case do we find the Savior imputing it to them as a crime, or requiring their servants' emancipation. – In chap. viii, of St. Matthew, we read of a centurion … (England in Smith, Handy, and Loetscher 1963: 2/202)

A similar assertion is made by the Swiss-born Protestant theologian Philip Schaff: 'if the servant of the gentile centurion was a slave, as in all probability he was, we would have a strong proof from [Christ's] own mouth for the perfect compatibility of slaveholding with a high order of Christian piety' (Schaff 1861: 28).

More recently, attention has shifted to another dimension of the relationship between centurion and *pais*, exploring the possibility that the latter is his lover or 'boy-love,' and that Jesus' silence might be construed as tacit approval of a relationship considered scandalous by his Jewish contemporaries (e.g. Theissen 1987: 106; Jennings and Liew 2004; though see also e.g. Saddington 2006; Zeichmann 2015).

Mother-in-Law (8:14–15)

Following his encounter with the centurion in Capernaum, Jesus enters 'the house of Peter.' Cornelius a Lapide wonders whether Jesus has moved to another city, since John 1:44 identifies Bethsaida as the town of Andrew and Peter. While Mark's parallel describes the presence of Simon (Peter), Andrew, James, and John (Mark 1:29), even Peter is absent from Matthew's abbreviated version. The centrality given to the sick woman does not extend to giving her a name, however: she remains identified solely by her relationship to her son-in-law. Her significance is variously understood: as a suppliant, a type of the synagogue (e.g. Pseudo-Bede, matched by 'Peter's house' as signifying the circumcision; Aquinas), or, given her feverish state, 'a soul seething in the fire of concupiscence' (Aquinas 2013a: 262).

Many commentators have focused their interest instead on the reference to Peter's 'house' (8:14). The latter appears to undermine Peter's commitment to his radical call (see 4:18–20). This passage was hotly debated in the Middle Ages, particularly in the context of the Franciscan *usus pauper* controversy (see Madigan 2003: 99–101). On a plain reading, the reference appeared to support the claims of the secular clergy that Christ and the apostles owned property. The radical Franciscan theologian Peter John Olivi (1248–1298) offered an alternative reading more conducive to the Franciscan ideal of poverty. His interpretation juxtaposes the location of the house (which, in contrast to Lapide, he believes to be Capernaum, 8:5) with the statement about Bethsaida in John 1:44. Olivi's ingenious solution is that the house in Capernaum could therefore not be Peter's own, but must have belonged to his wife (in Madigan 2003: 99–100). In the sixteenth century, Juan de Maldonado also sees the problem. Maldonado rejects the view of unnamed 'heretics' that the apostles kept their houses and returned to them periodically, which he refutes on the basis of Peter's words at 19:27 ('We have left everything …'). Matthew calls it Peter's house 'because it had been such,' but had subsequently been bequeathed to his wife or mother-in-law (Maldonado 1888: 1/272).

Peter's wife (see 1 Cor 9:5) and children are also anonymous, though subsequent reception makes them Christian converts, and gives them names. Peter's wife is variously called Perpetua, Concordia, and Mary. His daughter is called Petronilla (e.g. *Golden Legend*; Lapide), traditionally identified with the virgin martyr of that name buried in the cemetery of St. Priscilla, Rome (e.g. Holweck 1924: 790, 807). According to Clement of Alexandria, Peter's wife also underwent a martyr's death (Clement of Alexandria, *Strom.* 7:11).

While those who interpreted the mother-in-law figuratively could sidestep the issue of Peter's marital status, this would become important in later debates about married clergy, especially bishops. The passage causes the Zurich Reformer Heinrich Bullinger (1504–1575) to pose the following question:

> We see here that a married man was called by Christ as an apostle … Why then is it that the Roman popes took away the wives from the bishops and the other servants of the church? (Bullinger in Luz 2001: 14)

Bearing Our Diseases (8:17)

Matthew's interpretation of Isaiah 53:4 is surprising, in part because the passage is more concerned with vicarious suffering than literal 'removal' of physical illness, in part because Isaiah 53 is normally linked to Christ's passion (e.g. Rom 4:24; 1 Pet 2:24). One early solution is to read this scene as anticipating the sufferings of the cross. For Apollinaris, bishop of Laodicea in Syria (d. 390), the quotation refers ultimately to the Savior's passion, which brought healing and life *(Frag.* 37 in Reuss 1957: 11). Hilary of Poitiers resorts to a figurative interpretation: the healings at evening are figures of Christ's post-passion activity of teaching his disciples, forgiving sins, and defeating the powers of evil. Hence 'he assumed the weaknesses of our human helplessness [witnessed] by the Passion of his body according to the words of the prophets' (Hilary of Poitiers 2012: 93).

Even when the focus on the healing ministry is to the fore, the connection with overcoming sin is often maintained. John Chrysostom explains Matthew's application of Isaiah 53 to sicknesses on the grounds that these generally come from our sins (also Theophylact). Overlooking the Hebrew parallelism between the two halves of the Isaiah quotation, Aquinas understands 'taking infirmities' and 'carrying diseases' as describing two different activities: the first pertaining to light sins which can be easily removed, the second to greater sins.

Crossing the Sea and Calming the Storm (8:18–27)

8:18–9:1a recounts a journey across the Sea of Galilee and back again. It incorporates two miracles: the calming of the storm (8:18–27), and the healing of two demoniacs (8:28–34, an exorcism proper). Matthew's version of the sea miracle is highly distinctive, for at least two reasons. First, his inclusion of material about would-be disciples (8:19–22) allows the literal 'following' into the boat to function as a metaphor for discipleship. Second, the whole tenor of the miracle recalls the post-Easter life of the community, tossed by the storms of the world, petitioning its risen Lord in a quasi-liturgical prayer, 'Lord, save' (8:25). Often associated with the twentieth-century German redaction critic Günther Bornkamm (who speaks here of 'the little ship of the Church'), this ecclesial interpretation has an ancient pedigree, as Bornkamm himself acknowledges (Bornkamm 1982: 55; see e.g. Goldammer 1941).

Would-Be Disciples (8:19–21)

Two characters approach Jesus in succession, one described as a 'scribe,' the second 'another of his disciples.' The latter reference is a probable indicator that Matthew envisages a wider body of 'disciples' than the Twelve, as noted by Hilary of Poitiers. By contrast, Clement of Alexandria brings this second character into the fold of the Twelve by identifying him with the apostle Philip (*Strom.* 3.5).

The distinction between the two is clear from their address to Jesus. For Jerome, the scribe is rebuked because he does not address Jesus as 'Lord,' but merely as 'teacher.' A similar point is often made by modern commentators, observing that addressing Jesus as 'Lord' is the preserve of actual or potential disciples (e.g. 8:2, 6, 8, 25; 14:28; 17:4; 26:22). By contrast, those hostile to Jesus, or undecided about him, call him 'teacher' (e.g. 9:11; 12:28; 17:24; 19:16; 22:16, 24, 36; Judas Iscariot calls him 'Rabbi,' 26:25, 49). For Hilary, Jesus' saying about foxes and birds clearly indicates that the scribe is an unbeliever: understood figuratively, foxes describe false prophets (e.g. Ezek 13:4), and birds of the air evil spirits. Augustine views him as pretending to have the obedience of the disciple; Christ unmasks his pretense by reference to foxes, a conventional symbol of deceit (*Seventeen Questions on Matthew* 5).

Jerome draws further implications from his scribal occupation: he is a 'man of letters' rather than a 'spiritual hearer' (Jerome 2008: 102), rendering him incapable of understanding Jesus' words. Calvin draws different conclusions from the same detail: the scribe would have been an honored figure in Jesus' society, with an easy life. Hence he functions as a warning to Christians who boast in their discipleship, while 'taking no thought of the cross or of afflictions' (Calvin 1949: 388). The Spanish theologian Juan de Valdés finds here two differing responses to Christ:

> In the book-learned scribe and theologian, I contemplate men of the world, who, seeing nothing in Christ but what is prized and esteemed by the world, with little or no reflection, resolve to follow Christ; but when they see in Christ abjectness, poverty, and humility, which are disdained by the world, they give up their resolution ... In the disciple I contemplate the children of God, predestinated to life eternal, whom Christ constrains to follow Him, causing them to desist from the fulfilment of the obligation of human generation, [of birth], to fulfil the obligation of Christian regeneration. (Valdés 1882: 140)

That the Son of Man has nowhere to lay his head was of particular significance for the Capuchin Franciscans. According to their *1536 Constitutions*, Capuchin friars are to emulate Christ by sleeping only on mats, boards, or hay.

The meaning of Jesus' command to 'leave the dead to bury their own dead' (8:22; 'an oxymoron,' Luz 2001: 18) is highly contested, not least because it is unclear whether we should understand the man's father to be still living (e.g. Theophylact) or already dead (e.g. Chrysostom; Lapide). Its literal meaning is highly offensive, potentially advocating infringement of the Law (e.g. Hengel 1981: 3–15; Sanders 1985a: 252–255). This explains regular attempts to mitigate its harsh implications (see Luz 2001: 19). For many, the 'dead' gravediggers are the spiritually dead, whether sinners (e.g. *Glossa Ordinaria*), lax Christians with a veneer of piety (e.g. Clement of Alexandria, *Paed.* 3.11), or unbelievers (e.g. Jerome; Chrysostom). Thus the faithful are urged to have no association with the 'dead' world. For John Calvin, the 'dead' are those who forget God, concerned only for the things of this world.

Whatever the precise meaning of the 'dead,' many agree that Christ is not condemning the burial of parents per se, but stressing the priority of God's call (e.g. Bockmuehl 1998). Aquinas phrases it in terms of divided loyalties: should the man return to bury his father, 'afterwards he would probably have had thoughts about his father's will; and in this way he would be wholly drawn back' (Aquinas 2013a: 265). Alternatively, it is a reminder of the Lord's Prayer, in which God is the believer's living Father. This is of particular significance if, as Hilary proposes, the earthly father is himself an unbeliever. Hilary also sees implications for Christian prayer for the departed: the words 'Leave the dead to bury their dead' encourages Christians 'not to mix the unbelieving dead with remembrances of the saints' (Hilary of Poitiers 2012: 96).

The Boat of the Church (8:23–27)

The interpretation of the boat on the sea as the church is at least as early as Tertullian, writing in maritime Carthage against the backdrop of Christian persecution (see Rankin 1995: 10–14, 67):

> But that little ship did present a figure of the Church, in that she is disquieted in the sea, that is, in the world, by the waves, that is, by persecutions and temptations; the Lord, through patience, sleeping as it were, until, roused in their last extremities by the prayers of the saints, He checks the world, and restores tranquility to His own. (*On Baptism* 12:7; *ANF* 3:675)

Tertullian presents this ecclesiological interpretation in his treatise *On Baptism*, responding to the claim of some that the sprinkling of the waters represented a kind of 'baptism' for otherwise unbaptized apostles like Peter (a reading which Tertullian rejects). Viewing this scene as a type of later Christian baptism is evident in early Christian art, e.g. the baptistery of San Giovanni in Fonte, Naples; see Jensen 2011: 182–184, 191–194).

Peter Chrysologus, fifth-century bishop of Ravenna, also views the boat as the church: 'Christ gets into the vessel of his church, always ready to calm the waves of the world' (*Sermon* 50.2 in Simonetti 2001: 169). This interpretation is often repeated across the centuries, though Hilary adds a word of warning that those churches failing to follow God's word will be 'shipwrecked' (Hilary of Poitiers 2012: 97; cf. 1 Tim 1:19–20; see also Cyprian, *Ep.* 59:6). Cornelius a Lapide sees the boat as a symbol both of the church and the individual soul in its temptations. A eucharistic interpretation – Christ present sacramentally in the midst of his church – occurs in the popular devotional hymn *Sweet Sacrament Divine* by the English Roman Catholic priest Francis Stanfield (1835–1914):

> Sweet Sacrament of rest, ark from the ocean's roar,
> within thy shelter blest soon may we reach the shore;
> save us, for still the tempest raves,

> save, lest we sink beneath the waves:
> sweet Sacrament of rest.

The Lutheran pietist scholar Johann Albrecht Bengel (1687–1752), reading Matthew's text more literally, finds in the boat buffeted by the waves evidence for the particular character of Christ's school of discipleship:

> Jesus had an itinerant school: and in that school his disciples were much more solidly instructed than if they had dwelt under the roof of a single college, without any anxiety or trial. (Bengel 1971: 143)

Some propose an additional interpretation: the boat symbolizes the wood of Christ's cross (e.g. Pseudo-Bede; Aquinas; Lapide), which Aquinas justifies by reading Matthew intertextually with the Wisdom of Solomon: 'therefore people trust their lives even to the smallest piece of wood, and passing through the billows on a raft they come safely to land' (Wis 14:5 NRSV).

The similarities between this sea story and that of Jonah (Jon 1:4–7) encourage a typological reading, with Jonah as a type of Christ asleep in the boat (e.g. Jerome; Aquinas; Lapide; see Stone 2013). It is a short step to seeing connections (e.g. Lapide) with the resurrection of Christ (the 'sign of Jonah': 12:38–42; cf. Luke 11:29–32), aided by Matthew's reference to a 'great earthquake' on the sea (8:24, anticipating 28:2), and describing Jesus being 'raised' from sleep (8:25–26; see 28:6, 7). In Jacques Tissot's *Jesus Stilling the Tempest* (1886–1894; Brooklyn Museum, NY), the entrance to the cabin from which Christ emerges resembles the entrance to a tomb (see Tissot 2009: 129).

Two Gadarene Demoniacs (8:28–34)

The precise geographical location of the miracle is unclear due to textual variants (region of the Gerasenes, Gadarenes, or Gergasenes), which Origen discusses at length, opting for 'Gergasenes' as the correct reading, albeit on the grounds of local tradition and dubious etymology (*Commentary on John* 5.41). Modern textual critics tend to prefer 'Gadarenes' (see Metzger 1994: 18–19).

Both Mark and Luke mention only one demoniac (Mark 5:2; Luke 8:27). For Augustine, Matthew has correctly preserved the memory that Jesus cured two, Mark and Luke giving priority to the one who was a 'distinguished and famous person, who was especially lamented in that area and whose health was of particular concern' (*Agreement Among the Evangelists* 2.24.56; Augustine 2014: 204; also, e.g. Calvin). Chrysostom proposes that he was fiercer because he was possessed by more demons.

Matthew's abbreviated version heightens its Christological focus. At the climax to his *Paradise Regained*, John Milton presents the miracle as a dire warning to Satan of his impending demise (see Jeffrey 1992: 298):

> ... he, all unarm'd,
> Shall chase thee with the terror of his voice
> From thy Demoniac holds, possession foul,
> Thee and thy Legions, yelling they shall fly,
> And beg to hide them in a herd of Swine,
> Lest he command them down into the deep,
> Bound, and to torment sent before their time.
> (*Paradise Regained* 4.626–632; Milton 1968: 396)

A similar point is made in the engraving *Jesus Healing the Possessed* (1851–1860) by Julius Schnorr von Carolsfeld, a member of the group of German Romantic painters known as the Nazarenes. Jesus the healer stands serenely at the center, his hand raised against the winged demons emerging from the two tortured demoniacs. It is a vivid visual representation of Christ's defeat of the forces of chaos.

Hilary offers a salvation-historical interpretation. The local city is the synagogue, descended from Shem. The two demoniacs are the two races derived from Noah's two other sons. The people from the city are the Jewish people, who reject him. But this sophisticated reading ill fits the geographical location in the Decapolis, where the citizens are likely to be pagans (evidenced by their herd of pigs). Nonetheless, the Gentile identification is applicable to the demoniacs themselves, symbols of those held captive to idolatry (so Chromatius of Aquileia, *Tractate on Matthew* 43.4). Stanley Hauerwas offers a modern symbolic interpretation which also embraces Christian readers:

> If we have to choose between a life we know, even a life possessed by demons and ruled by death, and a life of uncertainty to which Jesus calls us, a life that may well expose us to dangers in Jesus' name, we too may ask Jesus to leave our neighborhood. (Hauerwas 2006: 98)

Contemporary readers introduce a fresh set of questions. What is the moral status of a story which celebrates the violent deaths of so many animals (e.g. Linzey 1994: 121)? What economic implications would such an event have had on the herdsmen and their dependents (already raised implicitly by Jerome, *Life of St. Hilarion* 32; *Homily* 54)? How far is the story shaped by the political dimensions of Roman occupation, given the use of the Greek *agelē*, normally denoting military units, to describe the 'herd' of pigs, and the fact that one of the emblems of the Tenth Legion Fretensis stationed in Palestine was the wild boar (e.g. Boring 2006: 151; Yarbro Collins 2007: 269)? How might social psychology illuminate the story of the demoniacs (e.g. Newheart 2004)? What does recent postcolonial criticism have to say about the ethics of translation? With respect to the latter, Musa Dube finds in the 1908 Setswana translation of the Bible, widely used in Botswana, a striking example of how colonizers can utilize the language of the colonized to underscore the latter's subjection. The 'demons' which possess the two men are translated as *Badimo*, 'the High Ones' or 'ancestors,' thus depriving the Setswana tradition of its very center (Dube 1999).

Controversy in Christ's Own City (9:1–17)

Crossing the Sea, Jesus returns to 'his own city' (9:1), understood variously as Bethlehem (Sedulius, *Paschal Song* 3.87), Nazareth (Jerome), and Capernaum (the most probable meaning: Chrysostom, Theophylact, Nicholas of Lyra, Maldonado, Lapide, Calvin, Henry Hammond). Hilary's salvation-historical reading of the Gadarene story adds a figurative interpretation to this geographical reference: Christ's city is his own faithful people.

An opening healing story (the paralytic) marks the transition from miracle to conflict, in which Jesus faces opposition for declaring forgiveness of sins (9:1–8), consorting with sinners (9:9–13), and failing to promote fasting (9:14–17). Matthew (like Mark and Luke) focuses on the faith of the four bearers, though John Chrysostom includes also the faith of the paralyzed man. Cornelius a Lapide finds a moral lesson in the action of the four friends: namely, that one should care 'not only for thine own salvation, but for that of thy neighbours' (Lapide 1890/1: 351). The etymological relationship between paralysis (*paralusis*) and the verb 'to loose' or 'free' (*luō*) underscores this connection with forgiveness of sin, while the change of the man's state from the horizontal to the vertical position invites parallels with the resurrection. Both are richly utilized in patristic exegesis (e.g. Chrysostom; Augustine, *Enarrationes in Psalmos* 37:1–3), and in early Christian art, where the paralyzed man is a particular motif in baptisteries and on tombs (see e.g. Horne 2005).

The controversy over fasting contrasts with Jesus' earlier teaching on the subject (6:16–18). The rejection of fasting here reflects the time of Christ's earthly ministry, while the Sermon presupposes the time 'when the bridegroom is taken away' (hence, according to Jerome, the church prepares for celebrating Christ's passion by 40 days of Lenten fasting). Jerome adds a tropological interpretation: the bridegroom can be said to depart because of our sins, which then call for the fasting of repentance. Hilary of Poitiers interprets the time of the bridegroom figuratively. Those from whom the bridegroom is taken away are those who do not believe in Christ's resurrection; they will have to 'fast' by being deprived of the Eucharist. Likewise, the torn garment and old wineskins are those weakened by sin, who do not receive the grace of the sacraments.

These sayings about cloth and wineskins (9:17) are obscure, particularly given Matthew's unique conclusion: 'and both are preserved.' Does this refer to the preservation of both old wineskins and new wine (cf. 13:51–52), or to the new wineskins and the new wine they contain? Tertullian of Carthage rejects a radical Marcionite reading of Jesus' saying: 'How is it he has rent off the gospel from the law, when he is wholly invested with the law, – in the name, forsooth, of Christ?' (*Adv. Marc.* 3.15; *ANF* 3:334). Jerome, by contrast, reasserts the contrast between new and old: the old refers to the scribes and Pharisees, or the precepts of the Law, the new to precepts of the Gospel, which cannot be mingled with the former. Theodore, fourth-century bishop of Heraclea in Thrace, also juxtaposes Israel with the church, making a connection with baptism in the process (see Rom 6:1–11): the new wine is a new teaching which cannot be given to 'those enslaved to the letter of the old covenant,' but only to those who have become 'new wineskins,' who have put away the 'old self' (Theodore of Heraclea, *Frag.* 57; Reuss 1957: 72).

John Calvin rejects the dichotomy between Pharisaic teaching and the Gospel message. Rather, the old bottles and torn garments refer to Christ's own weak disciples. His interpretation turns hard sayings into pastoral accommodation to human frailty:

> The amount of the statement is, that all must not be compelled indiscriminately to live in the same manner, for there is a diversity of natural character, and all things are not suitable to all; and particularly, we ought to spare the weak, that they may not be broken by violence, or crushed by the weight of the burden. (Calvin 1949: 407–408)

Call of Matthew (9:9–13)

Sandwiched between the healing of the paralytic and the fasting pericope is the call of Matthew, coupled with a celebratory banquet illustrating the Matthean motif of mercy taking precedence over sacrifice (see Hos 6:6). This tale, like the call of the four fishermen (4:18–22), has universal appeal in depicting the powerful attraction of Christ. Erasmus describes how Christ's face contained 'a certain hidden force by which he drew to himself those whom he wanted, as a magnet attracts iron' (Erasmus 2008: 154).

Mark and Luke call the tax-collector Levi (Mark 2:14; Luke 5:27). For Jerome, following Origen (*Frag.* 173), this is a sign of their honor toward their fellow evangelist, not wanting to call him by the 'common name' of Matthew. As many modern commentators note, however, it is improbable that a Jew would have had two Semitic names (e.g. Luz 2001: 32; though see France 2007: 352). More likely, the evangelist has replaced an original Levi with the name of one of the Twelve, whom he later calls a 'tax collector' or 'toll collector' (10:3). Mark Kiley highlights the wordplay in this passage between Matthew (*Matthaios*), 'disciple' (*mathētēs*) and 'learn' (*mathete*). Thus naming this tax-collector Matthew presents him as the archetypal disciple or 'learner' (Kiley 1984). Some ancient interpreters propose a third, albeit implausible, alternative: that Mark and Luke describe the call of a different person (e.g. Origen, *Contra Cel.* 1.62; Heracleon in Clement of Alexandria, *Strom.* 4.9).

Matthew's call is often presented as an illustration of divine mercy (e.g. Jerome; *Ep. Barn.* 5 applies this to all the apostles). His occupation underscores his sinful status: Erasmus notes the bad reputation tax-collectors had, a consequence of their legendary greed. Hilary earlier made a similar point, explaining the etymology of the Latin term for 'tax collector,' *publicanus* (reflected in the older English translation 'publican'). It is derived from 'the life of those who abandoned the words of the Law and preferred to comport themselves according to common and public practice' (Hilary of Poitiers 2012: 103). Many medieval interpreters know Bede's articulation of the theme, in his homily for the Feast of St. Matthew:

> [Jesus] saw a publican, and because as he saw [him] he felt compassion for him and chose him [*quia miserando atque eligendo vidit*], *he said to him, 'Follow me.'* (*Homily* 21; Bede the Venerable 1991: 207)

Bede's phrase *miserando atque eligendo* was adopted by Pope Francis as his personal motto.

The scene has proved popular in visual art from the sixteenth century onwards, especially in centers of trade and finance, such as Florence and Venice, and subsequently in the Netherlands (e.g. Marinus van Reymerswaele, *The Calling of Matthew*; 1536, Musée des Beaux-Arts, Ghent). The focus, reflecting contemporary literary sources, is either on Matthew as the type of a forgiven sinner, or the personification of avarice in need of healing (Vlam 1977).

Arguably the most famous example is Michelangelo Merisi da Caravaggio's *The Calling of St. Matthew* (1590–1600), part of a cycle of three paintings for the Contarelli Chapel in San Luigi dei Francesi, Rome (on this see Hass 1988; Puttfarken 1998; Zuffi 2012). The identity of the apostle in Caravaggio's painting is disputed. Since Bellori in 1672, he has been identified with the old man at the center of the group with his hand across his breast, his face illuminated by the divine light. This would accord with the elderly Matthew in later depictions of the scene by Jan Sanders van Hemessen (1536; Alte Pinakothek, Munich) and Hendrick Ter Brugghen (seventeenth century; Le Havre Museum). However, Caravaggio's central figure is dissimilar to his other depictions of St. Matthew in the chapel (*St. Matthew and the Angel* and *The Martyrdom of St. Matthew*).

Alternatively, Matthew may be the beardless young man seated opposite Christ, his hand around a money bag (a conventional attribute of Matthew) with the older man pointing toward him. The counting table then functions as 'a notional obstacle' between Christ and the tax-collector's response (Hass 1988: 247; also Puttfarken 1998: 166–172). Either way, Christ's pointing gesture is a clear reference back to the finger of God in the Sistine Chapel's *Creation of Adam* by Caravaggio's namesake Michelangelo Buonarroti. In an act of new creation, 'Christ's finger "calls" Matthew to a new life' (Zuffi 2012: 33).

Another Cluster of Miracles (9:18–34)

Matthew's version of the hemorrhaging woman and the official's daughter (9:18–26) is characteristically succinct (cf. Mark 5:21–43; Luke 8:40–56; on the history of interpretation, see e.g. Selvidge 1990: 17–30; Zwiep 2015). Details which make Mark's account so dramatic – the crowd surrounding the woman; Jesus' question 'Who touched me?'; the transition from the daughter being in extremis to the report of her death – are lacking in Matthew (though the Holman Christian Standard Bible smooths over the last discrepancy by translating the father's words in 9:18 as 'My daughter is near death').

Yet, despite this loss of dramatic tension, something else is gained: sharpened focus on Christ the healer, which has arguably made a greater impact on the visual reception of the hemorrhaging woman, the *Haemorrhoissa*. The earliest examples, such as a third-century mural in the Catacomb of Saints Peter and Marcellinus in Rome, or an ivory relief on the *Brescia Casket* (c. 360–370; Museo Civico, Brescia), present Christ alone with the suppliant woman holding the hem of his cloak, with no crowd or even disciples present. Even the flow of blood is absent; the woman's initiative in reaching out to Christ, and Christ's healing look which dries up the blood-flow, are conflated (see e.g. Baert 2011: 35–61; Baert, Kusters and Sidgwick 2012; Sidgwick 2014).

None of the evangelists are explicit about the cause of her bleeding, leading Amy-Jill Levine to caution against the frequent assertion of modern commentators that the woman was ritually unclean (Levine 1996: 384). Yet most have interpreted her 'issue of blood' as a vaginal bleeding (Lev 12:7; 15:19–33; 20:18; see e.g. France 2007: 361). Thus the *Haemorrhoissa* has often been appealed to in support of menstruating women being allowed into church. According to Bede, Gregory the Great made just such an appeal in his response to a series of questions posed by Augustine of Canterbury (*Ecclesiastical History of the English People* 1:27; see also *Did. apost.* 26.62.5; for a contrary view, see e.g. Dionysius of Alexandria, PG 10: 1281–1282). Her image is found on exorcism charms and amulets, presenting her as a powerful protector for women against uterine bleeding (Baert, Kusters, and Sidgwick 2012: 672–678).

Although in Matthew the *Haemorrhoissa* is anonymous, her biography is filled out in subsequent reception. In apocryphal texts, she is called Berenice (*Acts of Pilate* 7.1) or Veronica (*Cura Sanitatis Tiberii*; *Mors Pilati*), thus identifying her as the woman who, in post-biblical tradition, wiped the face of Jesus on his way to the cross. According to the fifth- or sixth-century Coptic *Book of the Resurrection of Jesus Christ by Bartholomew the Apostle*, Berenice was among the women who discovered Christ's empty tomb. Ambrose of Milan, followed by Pseudo-Bonaventure, believes the woman to be Martha, the sister of Mary (Luke 10:38–42; John 11:1–44). Eusebius claims that she was from Paneas, Caesarea Philippi, and that a bronze statue of her kneeling before a man, identified as Christ, could be seen outside her house (*H.E.* 7.18; see Sidgwick 2014: 2–3). By contrast, the official's daughter (Matthew does not even name her father 'Jairus,' cf. Mark 5:22; Luke 8:41) remains largely anonymous. A rare exception is the animated film *The Miracle Maker* (2000, directed by Derek Hayes and Stanislav Sokolov), telling the story of Jesus through her own eyes, in which she is called Tamar.

That these two stories are interwoven leads many to seek a common interpretation. Hilary and Jerome propose a salvation-historical reading, which echoes Eusebius' claim that the woman was a Gentile. The delay in the raising of the young girl, caused by the healing of the hemorrhaging woman, signifies the conversion of the Gentiles prior to the salvation of the synagogue (cf. Rom 9–11). That the woman stretches out to touch Jesus allows Jerome to connect her with the psalmist's reference to Gentile Ethiopia: 'Ethiopia will hasten [to stretch forth] her hand to God' (Ps 68:32; Jerome 2008: 110). Hilary opts for a complex allegory: the girl's father is the Law, given that there is no mention of his faith; the ruler's house is the synagogue; the mourners in the house sing songs of mourning from the Law, before being expelled from the synagogue; the woman represents the Gentiles, or tax-collectors and sinners who are offered salvation by Christ. Both commentators thereby obscure the particularity of the hemorrhaging woman, and thus the potential of her story to speak to similar women within early Christian communities (see Selvidge 1990: 18). In the late Middle Ages, Peter John Olivi offers a distinctive typological reading whereby the Gospel events prefigure the establishment of the Franciscan order. For Olivi, the healing of the daughter signifies the rehabilitation of the 'carnal church' at the end of the ecclesiastical age, when another Christ comes in the person of Francis of Assisi (in Madigan 2003: 82–83).

John Greenleaf Whittier universalizes the *Haemorrhoissa*'s story in his 1866 hymn 'Immortal Love Forever Full' (see Clarke 2003: 105):

> The healing of his seamless dress
> is by our beds of pain;
> we touch him in life's throng and press,
> and we are whole again.

This section concludes with the healing of two blind men (9:27–31) and a mute demoniac (9:32–34; cf. Luke 11:14–15). Jerome emphasizes the close connection between the blind men and the preceding two healings, allowing him to read this story in terms of the 'blindness' of both Israel and the Gentiles (a view criticized by Chromatius of Aquileia, on the grounds that Gentiles would not have acclaimed Christ as 'Son of David': *Tractate on Matthew* 48:2). For the ninth-century Frankish Benedictine exegete Rabanus Maurus, the two blind men also symbolize the Jews and the Gentiles, while the dumb demoniac signifies the whole human race (in Ford 1859: 171). John Chrysostom, attentive to the literal sense, notes the men's disobedience to Christ's command to secrecy, which turns them positively into preachers of the Gospel. Hilary, meanwhile, finds in the demon-possessed man who is both deaf and mute a clear figure of the pagans, in need of an 'all-encompassing salvation' (Hilary of Poitiers 2012: 108).

Matthew 10

Ancient Literary Context

In this second Matthean discourse, Jesus prepares to send out the Twelve as laborers into the harvest (9:36–38). What Jesus has done in Matthew 8–9 (healing the sick, raising the dead, cleansing lepers, casting out demons), his ambassadors will also do as they continue his mission. Although many of the sayings are paralleled in Mark and Luke (e.g. Mark 6:8–11; 9:41; 13:9–13; Luke 6:40; 9:2–5; 10:16; 12:2–12, 51–53; 14:25–27; 17:33; 21:12–19), Matthew weaves them together into a distinct discourse majoring thematically on the mission to 'the lost sheep of the house of Israel' (10:5–15), persecution by both synagogue leaders and Gentile rulers (10:16–33), the division caused by the person of Christ (10:34–36), and the rewards promised to those who receive Jesus' emissaries (10:37–42; for alternative structural theories, see e.g. Davies and Allison 1991: 160–162; Talbert 2010: 130–137).

Unlike the post-Easter commission to evangelize 'all the nations' (28:19), this initial mission excludes Gentile and even Samaritan territory (10:5; though see 10:18). Critical scholarship has often viewed this as a relic of conservative Christian-Jewish tradition, preserved by an evangelist who brings out of his treasures things both new and old (see 13:52; e.g. Schweizer 1975: 235). An alternative narrative-critical or rhetorical-critical approach would present the tension in terms of two stages, the restoration of Israel, then the in-gathering of the nations, separated by the resurrection (e.g. Talbert 2010: 138–140).

Perhaps most striking is Matthew's positioning of material associated with Jesus' end-time teaching (Mark 13:9–13; see also Luke 21:12–19) early in the public ministry. What for Mark may well be present or even future – persecution by synagogues, governors, and kings – has now become a past reality in the evangelist's experience. The theme of hostility and controversy (9:1–17, 32–34) now becomes a leitmotif for the disciples as they prepare to take on Christ's mantle. But, unlike Mark (Mark 6:30–33), Matthew never explicitly recounts the Twelve's return from their preaching mission. Nor does he clearly differentiate in this sermon between apostolic foundations ('the twelve apostles,' sent only to the lost sheep) and ongoing Christian discipleship. The effect is to blur the boundary between the initial (pre-Easter) mission to Israel and the ongoing (post-Easter) mission. The narrative is 'transparent' to the future mission of the church (see Luz 2001: 62–63).

The Interpretations

Introducing the Twelve (10:1–4)

This second discourse is prefaced by the commissioning of 'his twelve disciples' (10:1) or 'the twelve apostles' (10:2), though Erasmus, aware that other texts treat the Twelve as a subset of Jesus' students, describes them as 'twelve principal disciples' (Erasmus 2008: 165). The Welsh Reformed minister Matthew Henry (1662–1714) designates the chapter as an ordination sermon.

The number 12 is widely acknowledged as patterned on the 12 tribes of Israel (e.g. Theophylact; Rabanus Maurus; Matthew Henry), pointing to the role of the Twelve in 'the future restoration of the Church' (Calvin 1949: 438;

see 19:28). Interest in numerology sometimes produces more speculative proposals. Aquinas begins with the obvious connection with the 12 tribes; thus the selection of 12 apostles shows the conformity of Old and New Testaments. However, he also considers it appropriate that 12 is derived from 3, the number of the Trinity, and 4, the number of the world; alternatively, it is 6 (a number he regards as perfect) doubled (Aquinas 2013a: 302).

The order of the Twelve, and some of the names, differ in the various accounts (cf. Mark 3:13–19; Luke 6:12–16; Acts 1:13); moreover, some Latin manuscripts place Philip and Bartholomew before James and John. That Matthew describes Peter as 'first' is of obvious interest. For some (e.g. Theophylact) this merely expresses the chronological priority of Peter's call, though others object, on the basis of John 1:40–41, that 'first called' is a more appropriate designation for Andrew (e.g. Maldonado). Jerome emphasizes priority of merit or qualities; alternatively, Peter's position anticipates his subsequent leadership role in the early church (e.g. Meyer 1877: 288; France 2007: 378). From the Reformation onwards, interpretation of this phrase often betrays differing views of the papacy. Thus John Calvin denies that Peter's historic priority can be extended to subsequent bishops of Rome, while the French Protestant exegete Theodore Beza wonders (in his edition of the Greek New Testament) whether 'first' might be a later gloss to promote Petrine primacy. By contrast, the Jesuit Juan Maldonado explains Peter's priority in the list on the grounds that he was 'first in dignity and authority,' just as Judas Iscariot's position at the end of the list underscores his worthlessness (Maldonado 1888: 1/325).

That Matthew is named *after* Thomas and explicitly called 'the tax-collector' (10:3; cf. Mark 3:18; Luke 6:15; Acts 1:13) is widely explained in terms of the evangelist's humility or sense of unworthiness (e.g. Jerome; Theophylact; Aquinas; Maldonado; Bengel). For John Chrysostom, the presence in the list of two tax-collectors (he identifies 'James the son of Alphaeus' as 'Levi the son of Alphaeus,' Mark 2:14), four fishermen, and a traitor is especially instructive. Christ chooses the despised and lowly to cooperate in his mission.

Harmonization is a common strategy for dealing with discrepancies. Thus Thaddaeus is treated as synonymous with Lebbaeus (a variant in some manuscripts) and Luke's 'Judas of James' (Luke 6:16; e.g. Jerome; Chrysostom; Augustine, *Agreement Among the Evangelists* 2.30.70; Aquinas, *Catena Aurea*). Because of his close association with Philip, Bartholomew is sometimes identified as Nathanael (John 1:45–51; e.g. Isho'dad of Merv; Rupert of Deutz; Meyer 1877: 289). More plausible is the concern to find meaning in their names. Simon's epithet 'the Cananean' is explained variously as a reference to his hometown ('Cana': e.g. Jerome; Aquinas), his homeland ('Canaan': e.g. Codex Sinaiticus), and his zeal (Aramaic *qan'ān*, hence 'Simon the zealot' at Luke 6:15: e.g. Jerome, who links 'zeal' etymologically with 'Cana'; Maldonado; most modern scholars). Judas Iscariot's name is explained as a derivation from his tribe of Issachar, thus pointing to the reward for his betrayal (Issachar = 'booty'), or from his home town (e.g. Jerome, Theophylact; Aquinas). Maldonado knows the etymology 'man of Carioth/Kerioth' (see Josh 16:25), preferred by many later scholars (e.g. France 2007: 378) and already reflected in the reading *apo Karyōtou* in Codex Bezae (Brown 1994: 1414). Others (e.g. Lapide) connect the name with *sicarius* or 'dagger-man,' identifying Judas as a revolutionary. Thomas Aquinas is typical of medieval exegetes in using etymology as a springboard to deeper meanings, though some (e.g. Andrew = 'manly') appear more convincing that others (e.g. Philip = 'the mouth of the torch,' making him an appropriate model for preachers: Aquinas 2013a: 303).

Commissioning the Twelve (10:5–15)

The exclusion of a mission to Gentiles or Samaritans is intelligible in its narrative context, reflecting Jesus' historical ministry, or the initial missionary focus of Matthean Christianity. However, it soon becomes historically anachronistic, and homiletically unprofitable, as the Gospel is read by Gentile communities. Perhaps closest to Matthew's text are those who explain the tension in terms of salvation history, such as Pope Gregory the Great:

> When the former [the Jews] were called but refused to be converted, the holy preachers would come in turn to the calling of the Gentiles. The preaching about our Redeemer, which had been spurned by his own people, would be extended to the Gentiles as outsiders, and what happened to the Jews by way of example would prove to be an increase of grace for the Gentiles. (*Homily* 17; Gregory the Great 1990: 120)

Others resort to allegory. For Hilary, not going in the way of Gentiles means avoiding pagan activity and a pagan lifestyle; similarly, avoidance of Samaritan towns is a command not to enter the churches of heretics.

Some early critical scholars, reading this command literally, struggle to harmonize it with Gospel passages which have Christ and his disciples enter Samaritan towns (e.g. Luke 9:51–56; 17:11–19; John 4). Johann Albrecht Bengel explains the discrepancy in terms of phases of the public ministry. Since Christ has already preached in Samaria (Bengel alludes to John 4), and the apostles will come to them later (Acts 8), 'it was less necessary that the apostles should now visit them and sojourn in them' (Bengel 1971: 156).

The fact that the mission of the Twelve, like that of Christ himself, is marked by healings and exorcisms, is regarded as problematic by those who notice the lack of such supernatural phenomena in their own day. One solution is that this charge is restricted to the apostles, equipping them with miracles to convince those who otherwise might be unpersuaded by such uneducated preachers. Maldonado points to the appropriateness of the apostles, as preachers of the New Law, having powers equal to or greater than those of Moses, who taught the Old Law.

More commonly, Roman Catholics advocated the continuation of miracles up to the present as a sign of Catholic authenticity. By contrast, the view that miracles had ceased in the early church marked the Protestant response to what was perceived as 'papist' superstition or even diabolic activity (see Shaw 2006). Closer to the Catholic position was the renewed emphasis upon the miracles listed in 10:8 among seventeenth-century Quakers and Baptists. The Particular Baptist preacher Christopher Blackwood (1606–1670) notes how Jesus' words continue to be fulfilled in his own day:

> There are many whom other adjurers, and inchanters, and your witches could not cure, very many of our own men, I say, Christians have healed and do heal, adjuring them by the name of Jesus Christ ... (Blackwood 1659: 738)

Material Support

Sent out two by two, the Twelve are to rely on divine Providence, and the material support of those among whom they labor. Having received freely, they are to give freely, a saying regularly cited in warnings against simony (that is, payment for spiritual blessings; see Acts 8:18–19: e.g. Gregory the Great, *Homily* 17; *Glossa ordinaria*; Bengel). It is central to the attack on ecclesiastical corruption by the Bohemian Reformer Jan Hus (1369–1415), in his 1413 tract *On Simony*:

> The apostles received freely, without bribery, without unworthy subservience, or material favor; therefore, they likewise gave freely, without such bribery. But since now clergy do not receive freely, they likewise do not give freely, neither absolution, nor ordination, nor extreme unction, nor other spiritual things. (in Spinka 1953: 203)

Jesus' charge in Matthew is even more demanding than the Markan parallel, which only forbids food, bag, money, and a second tunic (Mark 6:8–9). Whereas Mark's version permits the disciples a staff and sandals (perhaps recalling the Passover: Exod 12:11), in Matthew both are disallowed. The Twelve thus lack even the benefits afforded to wandering Cynic preachers, who could take a staff, a money-purse, and a double cloak (Diogenes Laertius, *Vit. phil.* 6.22–23; *Cynic Epistles*, Diogenes 7; Talbert 2010: 131). Origen finds a further contrast between Jesus' apostles, his priests, and Israel's high priest, who is permitted two tunics (*Hom. in Lev.* 6.3). According to Eusebius, Origen himself traveled for years without shoes in fidelity to Christ's command (*H.E.* 6.3.10–13).

Many offer ingenious solutions to the disagreement between Mark and Matthew over the staff (see Ahern 1943). One proposal is that the two evangelists use the same word to describe two different sticks: Matthew forbids a heavy club whilst Mark allows a simple walking stick (e.g. Ephrem in Power 1923; Calvin). Or Matthew's words are to be taken literally, whereas Mark is speaking metaphorically about the authority that the Twelve have received from the Lord (Augustine, *Agreement Among the Evangelists* 2.30.74). Maldonado claims that both convey, in their different wording, the detachment required of apostles:

> For each, expressing not the words, but the meaning, of Christ, intended to teach us that He forbade the Apostles to have anything beyond what was required for present use. S. Matthew signifies this by saying, 'Nor staff,' for even the very poorest man has his staff. S. Mark signifies it by the words, 'A staff only.' For whoever has only a staff has nothing superfluous, as Jacob said (*Gen.* xxxii. 10): 'With my staff I passed over this Jordan," that is, "I was poor and had nothing but my staff in my hand.' (Maldonado 1888: 1/333)

Some embrace Christ's radical demands enthusiastically. In the *Earlier Rule* of the Friars Minor, St. Francis makes it central to the friars' missionary activity (though it is omitted from the *Later Rule* of 1223, approved by Pope Honorius III):

> When the brothers go through the world, let them take *nothing* for the journey, *neither knapsack, nor purse, nor bread, nor money, nor walking stick.* (Chapter XIV: How the Brothers Should Go Through the World, in Armstrong, Hellmann, and Short 1999: 73)

Many, however, find ways of ameliorating its literal sense: e.g. it is applicable only for the initial mission to Israel (e.g. Chrysostom, *Hom. in Rom.* 2.16.3; Calvin), or it is simply exemplifying an underlying principle:

> Christ did not forbid two garments at once if cold or need required them, but the possession of more than is required for present use, as they who are wealthy have, and such as take care for such things. (Maldonado 1888: 332)

For Augustine (*Agreement Among the Evangelists* 2.30.73), the teaching represents a power, which the apostles are free not to use, rather than a command; this explains why Paul can work with his own hands in Corinth (1 Cor 9:12–15). Aquinas appeals to Augustine's reading to justify the right of bishops to own property (*S.T.* 2a.2ae, q. 185, a. 6).

Amelioration also occurs through allegorization. The saying about two tunics is a case in point. Origen interprets the double garment as the old Adam, and the new humanity of those baptized into Christ (Origen, *Hom. in Luc.* 23). Hilary also finds a baptismal reference, though for him it represents a rejection of rebaptism. Since Christians have already put on Christ (see Gal 3:27), they should not be clothed again with a second tunic.

Although this discourse addresses itinerant apostolic ministry, its relevance for settled parochial ministry is sometimes considered. Thus the Second Vatican Council's Decree on Priestly Life and Ministry, *Presbyterorum ordinis* (1965), advocates a priestly spirituality of voluntary poverty modeled on the practice of Christ and the apostles:

> And by their example the apostles witnessed that a free gift of God is to be freely given, with the knowledge of how to sustain both abundance and need. A certain common use of goods, similar to the common possession of goods in the history of the primitive Church, furnishes an excellent means of pastoral charity. By living this form of life, priests can laudably reduce to practice that spirit of poverty commended by Christ.[1] (*Presbyterorum ordinis* 17)

Shaking the Dust from One's Feet

In response to rejection in specific households (10:13–15), disciples are to shake the dust from their feet (see Acts 13:51–52). Almost certainly, this act is a response to a refusal of hospitality, the dusty feet manifesting the host's failure in foot-washing (e.g. Tertullian, *Adv. Marc.* 4.24; Origen, *Hom. in Gen.* 4.2; Chrysostom; see Rogers 2004: 182–183). This explains the reference to Sodom and Gomorrah, paragons of failed hospitality (see Gen 18–19; Wis 19:14; Josephus, *Ant.* 1.194–204; *m. 'Abot* 5.10). Sadly, it has sometimes been used against fellow believers. In 1054, Cardinal Humbert shook the dust from his feet as he left Hagia Sophia in Constantinople, having delivered a bull of excommunication to Patriarch Michael Cerularius (Clarke 2003: 108–109).

In the modern period, the act functioned as a ritual curse for nineteenth-century Mormon missionaries, following words dictated by Joseph Smith in July 1830:

> in whatsoever place ye shall enter in & they receive you not in my name ye shall leave a cursing instead of a blessing by casting off the dust of your feet against them as a testimony & cleansing your feet by the wayside. (Revelation, July 1830, in Weber 2013: 108)

---

1 http://www.vatican.va/archive/hist_councils/ii_vatican_council/documents/vat-ii_decree_19651207_presbyterorum-ordinis_en.html.

In a subsequent revelation dated to August 1831, Smith clarified that the cursing was to be done in secret, to avoid provoking the unbeliever (Weber 2013: 111).

Warning of Persecution (10:16–33)

Those sent to 'the lost sheep' are themselves like sheep in the midst of wolves. Matthew may be reversing traditional language which envisaged Israel's 'sheep' attacked by wolf-like Gentiles (e.g. *1 En.* 89:55; *4 Ezra* 5:18). Thus the wolves are synagogue leaders who persecute Christ's followers (Jerome identifies them as the scribes and Pharisees). Others seek to actualize the saying in the present. Francis of Assisi quotes this verse in connection with those friars inspired 'to go among the Saracens and other unbelievers.' Just as the apostles were sent out by Christ, so these friars must seek the permission of their Minister (*Earlier Rule* 16:1–3). The seventeenth-century Particular Baptist preacher Christopher Blackwood invites his audience to recognize 'wolves' by their subtlety and cruelty: 'so among the Jews were Pharisees, among the Gentiles Philosophers and Tyrants, among the Christians Hereticks' (Blackwood 1659: 755).

The animal symbolism continues: the apostolic 'sheep' are to be 'wise' as serpents and 'innocent' as doves. For the *Opus imperfectum*, this means both 'understanding deceit' and 'forgiving injuries' (Kellerman and Oden 2010: 175). The fourth-century Egyptian desert mother Amma Syncletica, shaped by her experience as a hermit, understands being like serpents as 'not ignoring attacks and wiles of the devil,' who is a serpent, and the simplicity of doves as 'purity of action' (*Saying* 18 in Ward 1975: 234). Theophylact, apparently drawing on the early Christian *Physiologus* also used by Augustine and John Chrysostom (see Porter 1987), elaborates on what serpentine shrewdness might mean:

> For just as the serpent allows all the rest of its body to be struck but guards its head, so let the Christian give all his belongings and even his body to those who would strike it; but let him guard his Head, which is Christ and faith in Him. And just as the serpent squeezes through a narrow hole and sheds its old skin, so too let us traverse the narrow way and shed the old man. (Theophylact 1992: 86)

The image thereby becomes broader than a call for wisdom. It has Christological and baptismal implications.

Jesus' words will become proverbial. They are paraphrased by the protagonist Barabas in Christopher Marlowe's 1588 drama *The Jew of Malta*, albeit to describe his negative character: 'Now will I show myself to have more of the Serpent than the Dove; that is, more knave than fool' (*The Jew of Malta* 2.3; in Clarke 2003: 109).

The words about fleeing from one town to another under persecution (10:23) are highly contested, especially by those who find themselves being persecuted. Does this saying refer only to the initial mission to 'the lost sheep' (so, e.g. Jerome; Chrysostom; Theophylact)? Or is it also applicable to subsequent generations of missionaries (e.g. Origen, *Hom. on Judges* 9; Maldonado)? If the latter, is it a dominical command, or is it a divine permission for when circumstances make flight beneficial for the spread of the Gospel? Augustine offers a nuanced approach, in which the needs of those left behind are paramount:

> Let those, therefore, who are servants of Christ, His ministers in word and sacrament, do what he has commanded or permitted. When any of them is specially sought for by persecutors, let him by all means flee from one city to another, provided that the Church is not hereby deserted, but that others who are not specially sought after remain to supply spiritual food to their fellow-servants, whom they know to be unable otherwise to maintain spiritual life. When, however, the danger of all, bishops, clergy, and laity, is alike, let not those who depend upon the aid of others be deserted by those on whom they depend. (*Ep.* 228.2; *NPNF* 1st series, 1:577)

The saying is appealed to in the sixteenth century by those who had fled their own countries to escape persecution: e.g. the Italian Reformed theologian Peter Martyr Vermigli (1499–1562) and the English Protestant Marian exiles whom Vermigli encountered in Strasbourg (see Wright 2001; Zuidema 2013). For both, flight was preferable to remaining and falling into apostasy.

Tertullian changed his view on this question. In his earlier period, he held the position that Christians should not court persecution unnecessarily, which might lead to denying the faith under torture (*Ad uxorem* 1.3.4). In his later Montanist phase, however, he maintained that flight under persecution was an exception granted only to the apostles, in that initial mission to 'the lost sheep of the house of Israel' (*De fug.* 6). It has no bearing on future generations of Christians, who find themselves 'in the way of the Gentiles.'

Equally debated is the statement (10:23) that they will not 'finish' the towns of Israel until the Son of Man comes. For Hilary, it points to the salvation of Israel at Christ's final coming, after the 'full number' of Gentiles has come in (Rom 11:23–27). Thomas Aquinas finds a reference to the resurrection, and the subsequent mission to the Gentiles. Others propose the fall of Jerusalem, an interpretation which John Calvin considers rather forced. He prefers an intermediate coming of Christ in the power of the Spirit, to comfort the apostles in the midst of their mission. The French-German theologian Albert Schweitzer (1875–1965) famously interpreted the saying as expressing the mistaken conviction of the historical Jesus that the Kingdom was to come imminently, even before the return of the Twelve:

> He tells them in plain words (Matt. 10.23) that he does not expect to see them back in the present age. The Parousia of the Son of man, which is logically and temporally identical with the dawn of the kingdom, will take place before they have completed a hasty journey through the cities of Israel to announce it ... It is equally clear ... that this prediction was not fulfilled. The disciples returned to him and the appearing of the Son of man had not taken place. (Schweitzer 2000: 327)

Not Peace but a Sword (10:34–36)

This hard saying appears to contradict both the commandment to honor father and mother (Exod 20:12) and Jesus' promise of peace (John 14:27). Thus there is a natural resistance to interpreting the sword literally, a view supported by the Lucan parallel, which refers to 'division' (Luke 12:51). Many commentators find good biblical precedent (Eph 6:17; Heb 4:12; Rev 1:16; 19:15) for treating 'sword' as a metaphor for the word of God ('the word of truth and knowledge': *Ps.-Clem. Rec.* 6.4; Aquinas), or specifically the preaching of the Gospel (e.g. Hilary; Theophylact; Calvin). Or the sword denotes the consequences of that preaching: a world divided over faith in Christ (Jerome). More specifically, it might be a symbol for persecution (10:17, 28), which would tear at the heart of families and synagogue communities (see Mic 7:6). The *Pseudo-Clementine Recognitions* envisage just such a familial division over the faith:

> For in every house, when there begins to be a difference between believer and unbeliever, there is necessarily a contest: the unbelievers, on the one hand, fighting against the faith; and the believers on the other, confuting the old error and the vices of sins in them. (*Ps.-Clem. Rec.* 2:29; *ANF* 8:105)

Patristic exegetes sometimes develop the metaphor into a full-blown allegory, which shifts the focus from social relationships to internal struggle. For Hilary, the 'father' of the body is sin, and unbelief the 'mother' of the soul and 'mother-in-law' of the human will; the believer is separated from all three through baptism, which is 'a sort of excision by God's sword' (Hilary of Poitiers 2012: 125). Augustine's figurative interpretation is closer to Matthew, in acknowledging the social dimension of the struggle. Thus the man's 'father' is the devil; the daughter against her mother symbolizes the battle of God's people against the worldly city Babylon; the daughter-in-law against her mother-in-law describes the church against the synagogue. The sword dividing them is the Word of God (*Seventeen Questions on Matthew* 3).

Yet the sword reference also has its literalist readers. The Anabaptist preacher Thomas Müntzer uses it as justification for violence against his theological foes (see Clarke 2003 : 111), in his 1524 *Sermon to the Princes*:

> O beloved, yea, the great Stone there is about to fall and strike these schemes of [mere] reason and dash them to the ground, for he says (Matt. 10:34): I am not come to send peace but a sword. What should be done, however, with the same? Nothing different from [what is done with] the wicked who hinder the gospel: Get them out of the way and eliminate them, unless you want to be ministers of the devil rather than of God, as Paul calls you.[2] (Rom. 13:4)

In the modern period, this passage has been key in attempts to present the historical Jesus as a violent revolutionary (e.g. Brandon 1967).

Demands and Rewards (10:37–42)

In the Marcan parallel (Mark 9:37), it is receiving a 'child' which is equivalent to receiving Christ and the one who sent him. Matthew, by contrast, interprets 'little ones' metaphorically. It is now a designation for the faithful (Aquinas), 'a sweet epithet for *disciples*' (Bengel 1971: 163), particularly those who are least in the church (Calvin).

The promise of the reward exceeds the worthiness of the one welcomed. Thus, Jerome speculates that even those who receive Judas Iscariot, or false prophets, would still be rewarded, for the welcome is predicated on the office of 'prophet' or 'righteous' person, not on the individuals involved.

The explicit mention of water temperature (10:42) probably reflects the Middle Eastern climate, where *cold* water would be far more refreshing than tepid. However, Thomas Aquinas, building on Jerome, offers a different explanation. Christ says this so as to include the poor, who may not have firewood to prepare hot water, or to shame those who might otherwise plead poverty. Offering cold water is, as Hilary observes, 'a light responsibility' (Hilary of Poitiers 2012: 128).

2 http://germanhistorydocs.ghi-dc.org/docpage.cfm?docpage_id=5218.

Matthew 11–12

Ancient Literary Context

As the narrative resumes, the motif of hostility running through the preceding discourse (10:14–15, 17, 23, 34–36) is heightened. It begins with John the Baptist questioning Jesus' messianic status (11:2–19), and continues with rejection in Chorazin, Capernaum, and Bethsaida (11:20–24). There follow specific stories of opposition (12:1–14), the second of which culminates in the decision

Matthew Through the Centuries, First Edition. Ian Boxall.

of the Pharisees to put Jesus to death. Thus the forthcoming passion narrative is again foreshadowed. This narrative section culminates in the shocking claim from Christ's opponents that he performs exorcisms by Beelzebul (12:22–32), and their demand for a sign (12:38–42).

Matthew utilizes a variety of literary forms (e.g. conflict stories, prophetic woes, wisdom sayings) to shape this story of growing antagonism. Much of the material in chapter 11 is paralleled only in Luke, with a return to the Markan sequence from chapter 12 onwards. Elements of distinctive Matthean redaction include prioritizing the Pharisees as primary opponents of Jesus (e.g. 12:14, 24; cf. Mark 3:6, 22; Luke 6:7; 11:15). Matthew also reiterates his conviction that Jesus' teaching fulfills rather than abolishes the Law and the prophets (see 5:17–20). Thus his redaction of the grain plucking episode provides additional support from both (the practice of the priests on the Sabbath, e.g. Lev 24:8; Num 28:9–10; the quotation from Hos 6:6, 'I desire mercy, not sacrifice'; cf. Mark 2:23–28) as justification for the disciples' practice.

The Interpretations

John and Jesus (11:2–19)

The question posed by John the Baptist ('Are you the one who is to come ...?') provides an opportunity for Matthew's Jesus to reflect on John's role. John is in prison (see 4:12), according to Josephus in the Herodian palace-fortress of Machaerus (*Ant.* 8.5.2). He sends a group of his own disciples to Jesus, the second time John's followers have questioned Jesus (see 9:14). The pericope may reflect ongoing debates between early Christians and disciples of the Baptist concerning their leaders' respective roles (see also e.g. John 1:19–28; Acts 19:1–7).

John's imprisonment readily lends itself to actualization by Christians who find themselves attacked for their own prophetic witness. The Spiritual Franciscan Peter John Olivi (1248–1298) detects a correspondence between John's imprisonment and the persecution of Francis of Assisi, probably either by the Dominicans or by the secular clergy:

> You may consider a similar allegory for the end of the ecclesiastical age (*pro fine temporis ecclesiastici*), in which another John has appeared. In him the understanding of the secrets of the gospel clearly shone, in order that the Spirit of Christ (or Christ in his spirit or the perfect life of Christ) might be introduced. (Olivi, *Matt.* 87vb; Madigan 2003: 96)

John's Question (11:3)

Christian veneration for the Baptist means that few early commentators are willing to attribute his question to genuine doubt, despite the surprising contrast between Christ's compassionate acts of healing and the 'fiery judgment' expected by John (3:11–12; see e.g. Dupont 1961; Simonetti 1980). A rare exception is Tertullian, who ascribes John's doubt to the fact that the spirit of prophecy had withdrawn from him now that the Christ had appeared (*Adv. Marc.* 4.18). The Marcionite alternative which Tertullian opposes is that John's question reveals him to be a prophet, not of the Father of Christ, but of the alien creator God (Simonetti 1980: 368).

Jerome (following Origen, *Hom. in 1 Reg.* 28.3–25) denies that John doubted Jesus' messianic identity as such. Rather, Jerome extrapolates from the form of the question: 'the one who is to come.' He interprets this as John questioning whether Christ, whom he announced in this world, should also be announced in the lower world of the dead, to which John was about to depart (see Sheerin 1976: 7–9). The same idea is taken up by Gregory the Great:

> He said, *Are you he who is to come or shall we look for another?* as if saying, 'Just as you deigned to be born on behalf of human beings, make manifest whether you will also deign to die on our behalf. Then I who was the forerunner of your birth may also become the forerunner of your death, and may proclaim you in hell as the one who is to come, as I have already proclaimed to the world that you have come.' (Gregory the Great 1990: 29)

Many prefer that John's question was spoken for the benefit of John's disciples, who needed to be persuaded of Christ's superiority (e.g. Hilary; Chrysostom; *Opus Imperfectum*; Theophylact; Pseudo-Bonaventure; Calvin; Maldonado). Erasmus sums this up well: John's question directly targets his own disciples' envy, to 'put an end to their exaggerated ideas about him' (Erasmus 2008: 182).

Modern readers are more open to the Baptist's doubt. The German exegete Heinrich August Wilhelm Meyer (1800–1873) views John's questioning as 'a temporary eclipse of his settled conviction, which owing to human infirmity, had yielded to the influence of despondency.' This was, however, no indication of the Baptist's 'want of spirituality,' as Jesus' positive assessment in 11:7–11 makes clear (Meyer 1877: 310). Charles Clifton Penick (1843–1914), Episcopal missionary bishop of Cape Palmas in West Africa, describes a shift in his own understanding from the type of explanation espoused by Meyer:

> In my earlier years I thought this message of John to Jesus disclosed something of doubting sadness, the fruit so natural to such a hard trial as that to which John was being subjected – the trial of inaction, injustice, oppression, and seeming

> neglect. But now I cannot hold the idea. The whole tone of the Baptist's life, the shape of his message, and especially the shape of our Lord's answer, all lead me to conclude that it was simply the gratifying of his deep, sympathetic love for Jesus and the work. (Penick 1881: 182–183)

The Russian Orthodox theologian Sergei Bulgakov (1871–1944) similarly rejects theories positing actual doubt, which 'denigrate the Forerunner.' Instead, he sees in this episode a window onto John's 'personal Gethsemane,' a regular part of the spiritual life (Bulgakov 2003: 91).

A Shaken Reed, Fine Clothes, and a Wilderness Prophet (11:7–10)

The metaphor of a 'reed shaken by the wind' apparently serves to contrast John with 'a fickle and irresolute man' (Meyer 1877: 312), though some have interpreted the shaken reed as a critique of John himself, now wavering over Jesus' identity (e.g. Isho'dad of Merv in Harris 1895: 55; Albright and Mann 1971: 136). The original saying probably contrasted the steadfast, ascetic prophet John with the finely dressed Herod Antipas, whose first coins bore the image of a reed, and who wavered between two capitals (Sepphoris and Tiberias), two wives (Phasaelis, daughter of Aretas IV, and Herodias), and two political powers (Rome and Nabataea: Theissen 1991: 26–42).

Earlier commentators often seek a deeper meaning. For the *Opus Imperfectum*, the reed symbolizes 'a carnal and profane person in whom there is no marrow of faith,' on the grounds that a reed is hollow (Kellerman and Oden 2010: 197). Gregory the Great likewise interprets the shaken reed as an unspiritual soul, enabling him to draw a tropological message for his audience. They are to be unwavering like John, steady in mind and heart, not easily provoked to anger (*Homily* 5).

John is both a prophet and more than a prophet. Hilary explains the latter statement in the sense that, unlike his predecessors, he both prophesied about Christ and was privileged to see him. The *Opus Imperfectum* identifies additional features of John's biography which point to his greatness over earlier prophets: recognizing God while in his mother's womb, giving 'the honor of baptism to God,' and being himself the object of prophecy (Isa 40:3; Mal 3:1), as well as seeing Christ face to face (Kellerman and Oden 2010: 198).

The quotation from Malachi (11:10; cf. Mark 1:2, where it is misattributed to Isaiah; Luke 7:27) clarifies the connection between John and one particular prophet: the returning Elijah (Mal 4:5–6; Matt 11:14; 17:13). The Greek word for 'messenger,' *angelos*, leads to questions about John's 'angelic' credentials (see Joynes 2005). The *Opus Imperfectum* finds here evidence for John's superior sanctity, achieved by virtue and grace, despite the fact that he was not an angel by nature:

> I think, if it is not too audacious to say, that John is more glorious than if he had been an angel in name and nature because he was a human being and called an angel because of the just deserts of his virtue. (Kellerman and Oden 2010: 199)

In the Byzantine and Russian iconographical traditions, John's angelic status is a prominent feature, even to the extent of portraying the Forerunner as 'The Angel of the Wilderness,' replete with angel's wings (e.g. Schwartz 1997).

John and the Coming Kingdom (11:11–15)

John's ministry marks the transition from the period of prophetic anticipation to the time of the Kingdom. This helps explain the paradox in Jesus' words, whereby the 'least' in the Kingdom are greater than John, despite none born of women being greater than he (11:11; this qualifying phrase is absent from the Hebrew Matthew in the fourteenth-century polemical treatise of Shem-Tob: Howard 1998: 6). Nonetheless, the precise nature of his greatness remains disputed. The general patristic assumption is that it lies in his personal holiness and asceticism (e.g. Cyril of Jerusalem, *Catech.* 3.6; Chrysostom; Jerome). By contrast, Reformers such as John Calvin insist that the 'greatness' refers to the office of 'prophet,' not to John's personal dignity.

That John was the greatest of all those born of women is Christologically problematic, for John cannot be greater than Christ. Several make a distinction between being born 'from a woman' (which Christ was) and 'of a woman' (which excludes Christ, since he pre-existed Mary: e.g. *Opus Imperfectum*). Another solution is that the 'least in the kingdom' is Christ himself, thus safeguarding the latter's superiority as 'greater than' John (Chrysostom; Hilary; Jerome; Theophylact). Given 10:42, however, it is more likely that 'the least' are the disciples as citizens of the Kingdom (e.g. Bengel). For Juan de Maldonado, those 'born of women' refer to the people of the Old Covenant only; the greatness of the disciples is connected to the superabundance of grace poured out in the Gospel. This would potentially exclude John from the Kingdom. Alternatively, the saying contrasts the time before the Kingdom with its arrival, without excluding John from entering: 'the least in the kingdom will be greater than the greatest is now' (Davies and Allison 2004: 178).

The Violence of the Kingdom (11:12)

Jesus' saying in verse 12 is 'one of the NT's great conundrums' (Davies and Allison 2004: 178; see Cameron 1988). Matthew's version (cf. Luke 16:16) could mean that the Kingdom of the heavens 'has been forcefully advancing' (NLT) or 'thrusts itself forward' (Bengel 1971: 167, taking the Greek *biazetai* as a middle voice) or, more likely, 'suffers violence' (passive voice, e.g. Vulgate: *regnum caelorum vim patitur*; Tyndale; AV; NRSV).

Equally disputed are the identity of 'the violent ones' who seize or snatch it. Some posit a positive identification: the Kingdom suffers violence from those seeking to enter it, achieved through their penitence and other hardships (so e.g. Irenaeus, *Adv. Haer.* 4.37.7; Clement of Alexandria, *Quis dives* 21.3; Chrysostom; Jerome), or specifically their monastic asceticism (e.g. *Apophthegmata Patrum* 1152). The Greek theologian Gregory Palamas (1296–1359) appeals to the passage to justify the constant repetition of the Jesus Prayer by fellow hesychasts (*Treatise Against Barlaam* = PG 151: 690; Cameron 1988: 24). Alternatively, it describes the violent grasping of the Kingdom by sinners impelled by grace (e.g. *Opus Imperfectum*; Calvin). In Martin Luther's words: 'These are the ones who burst in by force and press forward as if trying to break down the door, wanting to be saved' (*Annotations on Matthew* 11:12; Luther 2015: 130). This optimistic reading lies behind the title of Flannery O'Connor's 1960 novel *The Violent Bear It Away* (see Clarke 2003: 114). A variant is that the Kingdom is open to all who wish to belong, unlike the Mosaic Law which was restricted to the people of Israel. Thus specific Matthean narratives present the Kingdom being 'snatched' from the Jews by the centurion (8:5–13) and the Canaanite woman (15:21–28: e.g. Maldonado).

Others conclude from the violent description that genuine enemies are meant, who respond to the preaching of the Kingdom with violent opposition (e.g. Luz 2001: 141). The arrest and execution of John by Herod Antipas (14:1–12) is one such manifestation of the violence (14:1–12; see e.g. Reid 2004: 239–240; Bates 2013). For Dorothy Jean Weaver, this interpretation accords with a recurring motif in Matthew's narrative, whereby suffering violence is a fact of life for God's righteous throughout history, from 'righteous Abel' onwards (Weaver 2011).

Rejection in Local Cities (11:20–24)

The rejection of John and Jesus by 'this generation,' exemplified by children's street games (11:16–19), reaches a climax with a series of prophetic woes against local Jewish towns which resisted Christ's Kingdom preaching. Chorazin and Bethsaida are not mentioned elsewhere in Matthew, unlike the town of Capernaum (e.g. 4:13; 8:5). Several commentators draw conclusions about the latter without ever having visited. Thus Juan de Maldonado, aware that it was a city or town on the lakeshore ('a seaport'), finds an underlying reason for its condemnation: 'it most probably abounded in vice, as is generally the case with seaports and large cities' (Maldonado 1888: 1/376). Harmonization with John (John 1:44), who links Bethsaida with some of Christ's apostles, enables Theophylact of Ochrid to emphasize the centrality of free will:

> [Jesus] calls to mind Bethsaida, the city of Andrew, Peter, Philip and the sons of Zebedee. Evil does not come from nature, but from our own choice; for if it came from nature, these apostles too would have been evil. (Theophylact 1992: 96–97)

The prophesied fall of Capernaum, echoing that of the king of Babylon (Isa 14:4b–21), points to the arrogance of Christ's adopted home (e.g. Jerome), or a combination of pride and impenitence (e.g. Aquinas). Jerome also offers an additional interpretation which fits the variant reading 'you who have been exalted to heaven.' Such prior exaltation, he suggests, describes the city's privilege in receiving Christ's hospitality and witnessing his miracles.

The irony of Jesus uttering woes, generally addressed by Israel's prophets to Gentiles, against Jewish cities is not lost on John Calvin, who recognizes the rhetorical strategy to 'touch His own people the Jews to the quick' (Calvin 1972: II/15). Thomas Aquinas exploits the etymology of the place names to underscore the privileged position of these towns over Tyre, Sidon, and Sodom:

> Corazain is interpreted 'service unto him,' Bethsaida 'house of fruits.' To whom more is entrusted, of him more is required. (Aquinas 2013a: 349)

But the challenge of the text to contemporary audiences is often of primary concern. Thus the *Opus imperfectum* issues this warning to Christians, who can read about the powerful works of Christ in the Gospels:

> Therefore, if Christ grieves over those cities because they did not repent, although they did not see all the miracles of Christ, how do you think that he daily grieves over us Christians who daily read and hear about his acts of power in the church and yet nonetheless do not repent of our sins? (Kellerman and Oden 2010: 202)

Similar is John Chrysostom, who grounds his homiletic exposition in the interpretation of Sodom's sin as failure in hospitality, and neglect of the poor (e.g. Gen 19:1–29; Ezek 16:49–50):

> To these same things let us also listen: since not for the unbelievers only, but for us also, hath He appointed a punishment more grievous than that of the Sodomites, if we will not receive the strangers that come in unto us; I mean, when He commanded to shake off the very dust: and very fitly. For as to the Sodomites, although they committed a great transgression, yet it was before the law and

> grace; but we, after so much care shown towards us, of what indulgence should we be worthy, showing so much inhospitality, and shutting our doors against them that are in need, and before our doors our ears? or rather not against the poor only, but against the apostles themselves? (*Homily on Matthew* 37.7; *NPNF* 1st series, 10:242–243)

The 'Johannine Thunderbolt' (11:25–30)

The German theologian Karl von Hase (1800–1890) famously described this passage as 'a meteorite fallen from the Johannine sky' (von Hase 1876: 421–423). This 'Johannine thunderbolt,' as it has become more commonly called, presents a Matthean Jesus speaking with the exalted accent of John's Christ about the Son's exclusive knowledge of the Father (cf. 24:36). In the words of the sixteenth-century Spanish humanist Juan de Valdés, these words 'teem throughout with divinity' (Valdés 1882: 207).

The 'wise' and 'intelligent' are often identified as the Jews and the 'babes' as the Gentiles (*Opus Imperfectum*; Theophylact). A solution better fitting the context is that the former are the scribes and Pharisees and the latter the apostles (Chrysostom; Jerome, Maldonado), or that all followers of Christ are to become like children so as to inherit the Kingdom (Hilary). Martin Luther actualizes the text in his last sermon, preached on 15 February 1546 in Eisleben, just three days before his death. He finds the contemporary 'wise' among Anabaptists, fanatics, rebels, anti-sacramentarians and the pope and his cardinals, as well as 'emperors, kings, princes, or learned men' (Luther 1959: 387). The 'babes' are faithful evangelical Christians, who put their trust in God's word alone.

The Christological dimensions of the passage ensure that it is employed robustly in debates over the person of Christ. The statement that 'no-one knows the Father except the Son, and the one to whom the Son wills to reveal him' (11:26) was understood by gnostics and Marcion to point to Christ's revelation of a previously unknown God (Irenaeus, *Adv. Haer.* 1.20.1–3; 4.6; Tertullian, *Adv. Marc.* 4.25.1; see e.g. Houssiau 1953: 329–332; Luz 2001: 159–160). For the Arians, the passage implied a time before 'all things' were handed over to the Son (see Athanasius, *In illud omnia* 1). From the orthodox side, Hilary finds ample ammunition to refute the Arian denial of the *homoousios*: 'By this revelation he teaches that there is the same substance of both Father and Son within their mutual knowledge' (Hilary of Poitiers 2012: 137; also Tertullian, *Adv. Prax.* 22.8–11). Centuries later, Thomas Aquinas draws upon his extensive knowledge of patristic exegesis to find a dual critique of Christological heresy. Thus 11:25–27 excludes both Sabellianism, in that it clearly distinguishes the Son from the Father, and Arianism, in that Christ calling God his own Father reveals that they are of the same nature.

With the invitation to 'Come to me' (11:28), Matthew's Jesus adopts the additional accents of divine Wisdom (e.g. Prov 8:3–4; Sir 24:26; 51:31), a point acknowledged by Aquinas. Christ's 'easy' yoke and 'light' burden are often contrasted with the burden of the Law, or specifically its interpretation by the scribes and Pharisees, who 'bind heavy burdens' (23:4). A rare exception is Tertullian, who engages the passage against the penchant of wealthy Christian women for costly necklaces, contrasted with the alternative 'yoke' of martyrdom embraced by the North African martyrs:

> I fear the neck, beset with pearl and emerald nooses, will give no room to the broadsword! Wherefore, blessed (sisters), let us meditate on hardships, and we shall not feel them; let us abandon luxuries, and we shall not regret them ... But Christians always, and now more than ever, pass their times not in gold but in iron: the stoles of martyrdom are (now) preparing: the angels who are to carry us are (now) being awaited! Do you go forth (to meet them) already arrayed in the cosmetics and ornaments of prophets and apostles; drawing your whiteness from simplicity, your ruddy hue from modesty; painting your eyes with bashfulness, and your mouth with silence; implanting in your ears the words of God; fitting on your necks the yoke of Christ. (*On the Apparel of Women* 13; *ANF* 4:25)

The contrast with the Mosaic Law requires further clarification. Following Jerome, Maldonado asks rhetorically how the yoke of the Gospel can be lighter than the Law, given the rigorous demands of Christ's teaching. The answer is fourfold: (i) the Gospel only gives commands which are necessary for salvation; (ii) it removes the heavier penalties prescribed by the Law, such as the *lex talionis*; (iii) it replaces force by love and goodwill; (iv) in the Gospel, the Spirit is given to assist with the burden (Maldonado 1888: 1/383).

In the cut-and-thrust of Reformation polemics, and building on an observation in Erasmus's *Annotations*, the burden of Mosaic legislation is widely reinterpreted as the 'burden' of Roman canon law (see Clarke 2003: 118). Martin Luther's assessment is more autobiographical: those who labor and are heavy burdened are those weighed down by a conscience apart from Christ, torturing itself under the Law (*Annotations on Matthew* 11:28; Luther 2015: 142).

Many have found Christ's statement that his yoke is easy and his burden light (the Gospel of Thomas has 'yoke' and 'lordship': *Gos. Thom.* 90; see DeConick 1990) encouraging. 'By encouragement He assuages sins, reducing lust, and at the same time inspiring hope for salvation,' writes Clement of Alexandria to his early Christian audience (*Paed.* 1.10; *ANF* 2:232). In his 1546 sermon, Luther issued the following invitation in the name of Christ:

> Only come to me; and if you are facing oppression, death, or torture, because the pope, the Turk, and the emperor are attacking you, do not be afraid; it will

> not be heavy for you, but light and easy to bear, for I give you the Spirit, so that the burden, which for the world would be unbearable, becomes for you a light burden. (Luther 1959: 392)

In John Bunyan's *The Pilgrim's Progress* (1678), echoing Hilary's interpretation, the burden is the burden of sin, which Christian carries on his back, and from which he is liberated by his journey to the cross:

> He ran thus till he came at a place somewhat ascending, and upon that place stood a *Cross*, and a little below, in the bottom, a Sepulcher. So I saw in my Dream, that just as *Christian* came up with the *Cross*, his burden loosed from off his Shoulders, and fell from off his back; and began to tumble, and so continued to do, till it came to the mouth of the Sepulcher where it fell in, and I saw it no more. Then was *Christian* glad and lightsom, and said with a merry heart, *He hath given me rest by his sorrow; and life, by his death.* (Bunyan 1678: 35–36)

This image of Christian being relieved of his burden at the cross regularly illustrated editions of Bunyan's work, and was one of the images selected for his tomb in Bunhill Fields, London (Kreitzer 2005: 73–77).

The yoke saying has also been influential in Christian worship and devotion. Thomas Cranmer included it among the 'Comfortable Words' in the 1549 *Book of Common Prayer*, thus ensuring its popularity among Anglican Christians: 'Come unto me all that travell, and bee heavy laden, and I shall refreshe you.' Cognizant of this, the English essayist and lexicographer Samuel Johnson references the saying in his *Prayers and Meditations*, in preparation for receiving his Easter communion in 1761:

> Since the communion of last Easter, I have led a life so dissipated and useless, and my terrors and perplexities have so much increased, that I am under great depression and discouragement; yet I purpose to present myself before God tomorrow, with humble hope that he will not break the bruised reed. Come unto me all ye that travail. ('Entry for Easter Eve 1761,' in Tippens, Walker, and Weathers 2013: 26)

The same verse is recalled in the popular hymn 'What a Friend We Have in Jesus,' originally composed as a poem in 1855 by the Irish poet Joseph M. Scriven, where the burden is one of cares and anxieties:

> Are we weak and heavy laden,
> cumbered with a load of care?
> Precious Savior, still our refuge;
> take it to the Lord in prayer.

Growing Opposition (12:1–14)

Another group of conflict stories (plucking grain on the Sabbath; healing a man with a withered hand) continues the narrative motif of opposition and failure to repent, with the Pharisees as Jesus' main antagonists. Matthew is also keen to emphasize continuity with the Mosaic Law. Thus, the grain plucking episode emphasizes the need (the disciples' hunger), as well as multiplying arguments from both Law and prophets. Similarly, Matthew's version of the man with a withered hand is centered on a typical rabbinic debate about treatment of a domestic animal on the Sabbath (12:11–12; cf. Mark 3:1–6; see CD 11.13–14; *b. Šabb.* 128b).

Augustine explores the grain incident for its Christological significance. The biblical examples cited from David (1 Sam 21:1–7) and the Temple priests (Lev 24:8; Num 28:9–10) are appropriate for Christ who is both king and priest (Augustine, *Seventeen Questions on Matthew* 10). Christ's statement that 'there is something greater than the temple here' (12:6) is also widely interpreted Christologically. Theophylact paraphrases Christ's words thus: 'I am the Master Who is greater than the temple …' (Theophylact 1992: 101; also e.g. Aquinas; Maldonado). Alternatively, it refers to the presence of mercy, which, according to the punchline in Matthew's version (citing Hos 6:6), takes precedence over temple sacrifice (so Luz 2001: 182). Codex Alexandrinus, by including this passage as part of its twentieth *kephalaion* (i.e. 11:2–12:8), encourages its readers to interpret the incident as a practical example of Christ's statement at 11:30 ('For my yoke is easy, and my burden is light': Goswell 2009: 149).

Augustine also finds a figurative dimension to the disciples' picking ears of grain (which would have involved 'shucking' them): it describes the stripping away of the flesh required of new Christians entering the body of Christ (*Questions on the Gospels* 1.2; see Col 2:11; 3:5, 9). Hilary moves even further in this direction by reading the story as a full-blown allegory of the preaching of the Gospel: the field is the world (see 13:38), the grain crop future Gentile believers, for whose salvation the disciples hunger.

The story of the man with a withered hand is also sometimes interpreted figuratively. Jerome reads it as an allegory of salvation history, culminating in the restoration of the Jewish synagogue through the apostles (who symbolize the restoration of the 'right hand'). Aquinas's figurative reading is more universal: 'By this man is signified the human race, whose hand was withered by original sin; or any sinner whatever, whose hand and operative power has withered' (Aquinas 2013a: 362).

Others, more concerned with the story's literal sense, nonetheless exploit gaps in the narrative for the sake of fuller illumination. According to the *Gospel of the Hebrews*, the man was a stonemason by trade; hence the urgency for his hand to be restored (in Jerome 2008: 141). Others explain Jesus' motives for withdrawing (12:15), in response to the Pharisees' plot to destroy him. The verb is widely used in Matthew to denote a withdrawal in the face of opposition or threat (e.g. 2:12, 13, 14; 4:12; 15:21; 27:5; Good 1990). Sensitive to the theme of mercy, Theophylact offers an alternative explanation. Christ's withdrawal is a manifestation of his own mercy, aimed at preventing the Pharisees from actually committing murder (also e.g. *Glossa Ordinaria*; Erasmus). By contrast, Matthew's statement that the Pharisees 'departed' conveys for Theophylact not simply their physical departure, but their spiritual 'departure' from God.

Jesus the Gentle Servant (12:15–21)

A commentary on the action is now provided by a 'formula quotation,' presenting Jesus as the gentle Servant of the Lord. The precise form of the quotation (from Isa 42:1–4) diverges both from the MT and the LXX, a divergence explored in detail by many exegetes (e.g. Maldonado). Given the reference to the Servant as 'beloved,' Eduard Schweizer suggests that 'we may have here a Christian Greek targum that assimilates the text to the story of Jesus' baptism' (Schweizer 1975: 281; see 3:17). But the quotation fits the context not simply for its Christology, which reflects Matthew's wider presentation of Jesus as the meek and humble king. It contains other key Matthean motifs: 'judgment' or 'justice'; the significance of Christ's 'name'; the extension of salvation to the Gentiles.

Desiderius Erasmus finds comfort in Isaiah's stress on the Servant's gentleness, and the universal character of his mission:

> I will give him my Spirit, gentle and mild, and by its inspiration he will pronounce judgment, not only to the people of Israel, but even to all the gentiles. He will not do this by uprisings or by force, for he will not dispute or cry out against the contentious; nor will anyone hear his voice sounding in the streets in the customary manner of those who wage battles with their tongues. He will leave scope for unconquerable malice, but he will try to lead everyone to salvation. (Erasmus 2008: 197)

Erasmus's paraphrase stands in sharp contrast to the heated and often highly polemical theological controversies of his own day. By contrast, John Calvin is concerned to resist interpretations which advocate indiscriminate gentleness, noting that the passage refers only to sparing the weak, not the strong and wicked.

The general sense of the 'crushed reed' and the 'smoldering wick' or 'linen flax' is clear. As Richard France explains:

> A reed was used for measuring and for support, so that once its straightness was lost by bending or cracking it was of no further use. A strip of linen cloth used as a lamp wick, if it smokes, is of no use for giving light and is simply a source of pollution; it is in danger of going out altogether. Common sense would demand that both be replaced, the reed being snapped and discarded or burned and the wick extinguished. The imagery thus describes an extraordinary willingness to encourage damaged or vulnerable people, giving them a further opportunity to succeed which a results-oriented society would deny them. (France 2007: 472–473)

The same sentiments are conveyed by Eugene Peterson's idiomatic translation *The Message*: 'He won't walk over anyone's feelings, won't push you into a corner' (Peterson 2002).

However, the precise referents of these two phrases is less certain. For Hilary, the bruised reed refers to the fragility and weakness of the Gentiles, the smoldering wick to that spark which remains in the remnant of Israel. Theophylact understands both as the Jews, exemplifying divine patience. Thomas Aquinas offers two alternatives. First, as for Theophylact, both describe the Jews, the 'reed' symbolizing the royal power now 'bruised' by the Romans, and the 'smoldering wick' (Vulgate *linum fumigans*) the priesthood, who wore linen garments. But if the two phrases refer in a special way to the Jews, in a general sense the reed describes sinners, and the wick weak believers (Aquinas 2013a: 367).

Jesus and Beelzebul (12:22–37)

The so-called 'Beelzebul Controversy' (cf. 9:32–34) has as its narrative setting the exorcism of a blind and deaf demoniac (12:22–23). But the focus soon shifts to accusations that Jesus is the agent of 'Beelzebul, the prince of demons.' Jesus responds with a *reductio ad absurdum* argument, undermining this charge on the grounds that divided kingdoms, cities, and houses or families are doomed to fall, before presenting himself as the stronger one who binds the strong man, Satan (see Isa 49:24–25).

The metaphor of a house divided is taken up by the Bishop of Carlisle in William Shakespeare's *Richard II*, prophesying the dire consequences of the usurpation of the throne by Richard's cousin, Henry Bolingbroke, Duke of

Lancaster (thus for Shakespeare anticipating the fifteenth-century Wars of the Roses):

> O, if you raise this house against this house,
> It will the woefullest division prove
> That ever fell upon this cursed earth.
> (*Richard II* 4.1)

The name Beelzebul probably means 'lord of the temple' or 'lord of the heavenly dwelling,' although Latin and Syriac authors, along with readers of the KJV, are more familiar with the reading 'Beelzebub,' identifying this demon-ruler with Baal-zebub or 'lord of the flies,' the god of Ekron (2 Kgs 1:2, 16). Matthew's text appears to equate Beelzebul with Satan (12:26–27), an identification followed by some apocryphal accounts of Christ's descent into hell (e.g. Greek A *Acts of Pilate* 22, where Hades addresses Satan as 'Beelzebub, heir of fire and torment, enemy of the saints': Elliott 1993: 188). It is also reflected in the 1693 pamphlet 'Of Beelzebub and His Plot' by the New England Puritan minister Cotton Mather, on the Salem witch trials:

> 'Tis probable that the devil, who was the ringleader of that mutinous and rebellious crew which first shook off the authority of God, is now the general of those hellish armies; our Lord that conquered him has told us the name of him; 'tis Belzebub; 'tis he that is the devil and the rest are his angels, or his souldiers. (in Stedman and Mackay Hutchinson 1889: 117)

However, the two are regularly treated as separate characters, particularly in the dramatic and poetic tradition. In the York cycle, the demon Belsabub is Satan's second-in-command, captain of the underworld (Jeffrey 1992: 81). He plays a similar role in Christopher Marlowe's *Doctor Faustus,* along with the demon Mephistopheles, and in John Milton's *Paradise Lost*:

> There the companions of his fall, o'rewhelm'd
> With Floods and Whirlwinds of tempestuous fire,
> He soon discerns, and weltring by his side
> One next himself in power, and next in crime,
> Long after known in Palestine, and nam'd
> Beelzebub.
> (*Paradise Lost*, Book 1, lines 76–81)

By Whom Do Your Sons Cast Them Out? (12:27)

Readers of Matthew disagree over the identity of 'your sons' (KJV: 'your children'; NRSV: 'your own exorcists') who also cast out demons, and who will be the judges of Jesus' accusers. Modern commentators are virtually unanimous in identifying the 'sons' as contemporary Jewish exorcists (Shirock 1992), a view found in Jerome and later advocated by John Calvin. Yet this is not without contextual problems, for, according to the logic of Jesus' argument, exorcisms performed by other Jews would then be equally valid evidence for the coming Kingdom (see Beare 1981: 279).

A common patristic interpretation finds a reference instead to the apostles, or the disciples more widely, who may be called 'your sons' in that they were born of the Jews (e.g. Chrysostom; Chromatius of Aquileia; *Opus imperfectum*; Theophylact). Thus, the mission of the Twelve serves as testimony to Christ's divine authority ('authority over unclean spirits,' 10:1). Jerome offers both possibilities. If they are Jewish exorcists, then Jesus is using a 'clever question' to force the Pharisees to admit the true cause of his power. However, the fact that these 'sons' will be the 'judges' of Christ's accusers, supports their identification with the apostles, who will sit on 12 thrones judging the 12 tribes (19:28; Jerome 2008: 143).

Blasphemy Against the Holy Spirit (12:31–32)

Readers of Matthew across the centuries have understandably been keen to identify that unpardonable sin, the 'blasphemy of the Spirit' or 'speaking against the Holy Spirit.' The context within the Beelzebul controversy points to a very specific sin, attributing to Satan what is the action of God, as at least one manifestation of this blasphemy. As the 1582 Rheims New Testament has it, the sin against the Holy Spirit was committed by the Jews 'when of malice they attributed the euident workes of God in casting out diuels, to the diuel himself.'

Hence early commentators often identify a specific act of blasphemy. According to the *Didache*, it comprises the refusal to acknowledge as divinely inspired an itinerant prophet who manifests Christ-like conduct:

> Also, do not test or evaluate any prophet who speaks in the spirit, for every sin will be forgiven, but this sin will not be forgiven. However, not everyone who speaks in the spirit is a prophet, but only if he exhibits the Lord's ways. (*Did*. 11:7–8; Holmes 2007: 363)

The interpretation of these verses often closely parallels patristic debates over the Trinity or the person of Christ. Given that the Beelzebul controversy concerns the Pharisees' attitude to Jesus' activity, some interpret the blasphemy as a denial of Christ's divinity (e.g. Hilary). Athanasius distinguishes between the sin 'against the Son of Man,' i.e. Christ in his human nature, and a sin against Christ in his divine nature (Athanasius, *Discourses Against the Arians* 1.12.50; also Cyril of Alexandria, *Frag.* 156 in Reuss 1957: 203). The latter is committed by the Pharisees, because they attribute the action of the divine Word to the devil. For Basil the Great, the fact that the sin involves speaking 'against the Holy Spirit' means that it is a denial of the Spirit's divinity (*On the Holy Spirit* 18–20).

For some, this sin can only be committed by Christians, on the grounds that believers alone possess the Holy Spirit. This view is well expressed by Origen: 'he who has been deemed worthy to have a portion of the Holy Spirit, and who has relapsed, is, by this very act and work, said to be guilty of blasphemy against the Holy Spirit' (*De Princ.* 1.3.7; *ANF* 4:254). The Roman theologian and anti-pope Novatian (c. 200–258) interpreted the sin against the Holy Spirit more specifically as denial of the faith in face of persecution (see Heb 6:4–6), leading to his rigorist position against the *lapsi*. This is rejected by Ambrose of Milan, on the basis of his closer reading of the passage: the sin at issue is specifically speaking against the Spirit, attributing the Spirit's power to Satan, which he extends to include those who seek to undermine the ecclesial unity which the Spirit brings (*Concerning Repentance* 2.4.24; see Lammé 2012: 22–23). Jerome also opposes Novatian's view, in a letter of 385 to Marcella, albeit on the grounds that Christ attributes the sin to the Pharisees, i.e. non-Christians:

> It must be proved to Novatian, therefore, that the sin which shall never be forgiven is not the blasphemy of men disembowelled by torture who in their agony deny their Lord, but is the captious clamor of those who, while they see that God's works are the fruit of virtue, ascribe the virtue to a demon and declare the signs wrought to belong not to the divine excellence but to the devil. (*Ep.* 42; *NPNF* 2nd series, 6:56)

Augustine interprets the unforgiveable sin as the intentional and malicious rejection of the source of forgiveness, God's gift of the Spirit. However, for him it is impenitence to the end of one's life, which means it can only be determined at death (*Sermon* 71; see Luz 2001: 207–208; Lammé 2012: 25–26). Thus, in contrast to Athanasius, Augustine regards the sin of the Pharisees, not as the sin against the Holy Spirit, but against the Son of Man, Christ's words about making the tree good (12:33) implying the possibility of conversion. Moreover, like his mentor Ambrose, Augustine's interpretation has a strong ecclesiological dimension, for the Spirit is God's gift to the church. In his discussion of love of enemies (5:43–48), he defines the sin against the Holy Spirit in terms of threats to ecclesial unity, as 'the undermining of brotherly charity out of spite and envy after the grace of the Holy Spirit has been received' (*The Lord's Sermon on the Mount* 1.22, 75; Augustine 2014: 65).

Aware that Christ's harsh words refer to 'perverse and intentional malice,' some seek to downplay the possibility of this sin being committed, notably Erasmus:

> But if someone utters abuse against the Spirit of God, whose manifest power he has seen from the deeds themselves, he will not easily (*vix*) find forgiveness. And whoever utters abuse against the Son of man, casting scorn upon him because of the weakness of his flesh, will be forgiven, because where a misdeed is mixed with error and ignorance there is no perverse and intentional malice. (Erasmus 2008: 200)

In a similar fashion, the 1992 *Catechism of the Catholic Church* prefaces its essentially Augustinian definition with emphasis on divine mercy:

> There are no limits to the mercy of God, but anyone who deliberately refuses to accept his mercy by repenting, rejects the forgiveness of his sins and the salvation offered by the Holy Spirit. Such hardness of heart can lead to final impenitence and eternal loss. (*CCC* 1864)

The detrimental impact of this harsh yet ambiguous teaching has often been profound. John Bunyan describes in his 1666 *Grace Abounding* how he struggled for two and a half years under the conviction that he had committed this unforgiveable sin:

> Then was I struck into a very great trembling, insomuch that at sometime I could, for whole days together, feel my very body, as well as my minde, to shake and totter under the sense of the dreadful Judgement of God, that should fall on those that have sinned that most fearful and unpardonable sin. (in Tipson 1984: 303)

The statement that the sin against the Holy Spirit will not be forgiven even in 'the age to come' implies that some sins can be forgiven then, allowing Augustine to use this as a proof text for purgatory:

> As also, after the resurrection, there will be some of the dead to whom, after they have endured the pains proper to the spirits of the dead, mercy shall be accorded, and acquittal from the punishment of the eternal fire. For were there not some whose sins, though not remitted in this life, shall be remitted in that which is to come, it could not be truly said, 'They shall not be forgiven, neither in this world, neither in that which is to come.' (*Civ. Dei* 21.24; *NPNF* 1st series, 2:470)

This reading is unsurprisingly rejected by the Reformers. Calvin takes the phrase to refer not to an intermediate state but to absolution of sins at the last judgment.

The Sign of Jonah (12:38–45)

Whereas in Mark, Jesus refuses to provide any sign to 'this generation,' in both Matthew and Luke he offers 'the sign of the prophet Jonah' (Luke 11:29–32; cf. Mark 8:11–12; on the Christian reception of Jonah, see e.g. Bowers 1971; Sherwood 2000: 11–87). Luke seems to understand this sign as the preaching of repentance. For Matthew, by contrast, it is primarily the death and resurrection of Christ (12:40; 16:4), though several commentators are troubled by the fact that Christ was not in the tomb for precisely 'three days and three nights' (see Adam 1990). Justin Martyr resolves the problem by having Jonah emerge from the fish 'on the third day' (*Trypho* 107.2). The third-century Syrian *Didascalia Apostolorum* counts Christ's suffering at the sixth hour on Good Friday as the first 'day,' and the three hours of darkness on Good Friday as the first 'night,' followed by another three hours of 'day' between the death of Jesus and Friday sundown (*Did. apost.* 21.13). Aquinas, following Augustine, finds the solution in synecdoche, whereby part of a day is counted as a whole. Other medieval interpreters find a 'mystical' reading whereby the three days denote the three periods of salvation history: before the Law, under the Law, and under the New Law of Christ (e.g. *Glossa ordinaria*).

Matthew's version exercises the dominant influence in the subsequent reception history (Chow 1995: 175–193). For Justin, debating with the imaginary Jew Trypho, Christ's resurrection is the great indictment of Trypho's compatriots, given their evident knowledge of Jonah's story (*Trypho* 107). Irenaeus stresses how the 'sign of Jonah' also anticipates the bodily resurrection of believers, thus challenging gnostic alternatives (*Adv. Haer.* 3.20.1–2; 5.31.2). Tertullian places emphasis on Christ's death as the sign: Jonah 'suffered a typical example of the Lord's passion, which was to redeem heathens as well (as others) on their repentance' (*De Pudic.* 10:3–4; *ANF* 4:84; also Jerome, *Ep.* 53).

The bishop-martyr Methodius of Olympus (d. c. 311) finds here an extended allegory of the whole human story. The whale symbolizes time; Jonah represents Adam, the first and archetypal human, who fell from life to death, as Jonah was cast into the sea and was removed by time (swallowed by the whale), before being resurrected:

> As, then, Jonah spent three days and as many nights in the whale's belly, and was delivered up sound again, so shall we all, who have passed through the three

> stages of our present life on earth – I mean the beginning, the middle, and the end, of which all this present time consists – rise again. For there are altogether three intervals of time, the past, the future, and the present. And for this reason the Lord spent so many days in the earth symbolically, thereby teaching clearly that when the fore-mentioned intervals of time have been fulfilled, then shall come our resurrection, which is the beginning of the future age, and the end of this. For in that age there is neither past nor future, but only the present. (*On the History of Jonah* 2 = *ANF* 6:378)

The typological connection between the story of Jonah and the resurrection is popular in early Christian art, particularly in association with baptism as a dying and rising with Christ (Jensen 2012: 153–156). The connection is established through the sequential presentation of Jonah's story: being swallowed by the fish, spat out, and reclining on dry land (e.g. the late third-century 'Jonah Sarcophagus' in the Vatican's Museo Pio Cristiano). That Jonah is typically portrayed naked underscores the connection with the newly baptized, who entered the baptismal waters unclothed.

The 'sign of Jonah' also leaves its mark on the dramatic tradition. In the fifteenth-century N-Town Plays (misnamed by an early cataloguer as the *Ludus Coventriae* cycle), Jonah the prophet has a speaking part in which he explicitly prophesies the resurrection:

> I jonas sey that on the iij^de^ morn
> ffro deth he xal ryse this is a trew tall
> fyguryd in me the which longe beforn
> lay iij days beryed with in the qwall.
> (in Bowers 1971: 54)

Jesus' saying also provides the title for the early monastic journal of the American Trappist monk Thomas Merton, published in 1953 as *The Sign of Jonas*. For Merton, the sign of the resurrection is a sign which particularly marked his monastic vocation, since he originally followed the prophet Jonah in traveling in the opposite direction when God ordered him to go to his 'Nineveh,' the Abbey of Gethsemani in Kentucky:

> The sign Jesus promised to the generation that did not understand Him was the 'sign of Jonas the prophet' – that is, the sign of His own resurrection. The life of every monk, of every priest, of every Christian is signed with the sign of Jonas, because we all live by the power of Christ's resurrection. But I feel that my own life is especially sealed with this great sign, which baptism and monastic profession and priestly ordination have burned into the roots of my being, because like Jonas himself I find myself traveling toward my destiny in the belly of a paradox. (Merton 1983: 11)

The Wandering Spirit (12:43–45)

Perhaps originally a 'piece of exorcistic folk wisdom' (Luz 2001: 221), in its present Matthean context this pericope functions as a commentary on the Pharisees who ask for a sign, and the 'evil and adulterous generation' they represent (12:45; cf. Luke 11:24–26). What happens to the possessed person, likened to a house in which the demon formerly dwelt, will happen to this generation, if it continues to reject Jesus and thereby remain empty.

An early tendency is to turn the particular (the house = this generation) into the universal. For Jerome, the unclean spirit was expelled from the Jews when they received the Law, and wandered instead 'through the deserted places of the Gentiles.' When the pagans were converted, it returned to its former home among the Jews, and found the house (i.e. the temple) vacant (Jerome 2008: 149). John Calvin extends this approach further, so that the parable describes the situation of all Adam's offspring, the dwelling-place of the devil unless they are converted 'from Satan's stinking stables to His own temple.' Those who are 'empty' of God's Spirit, who cut themselves off from His grace, are ready to receive the devil again, along with his seven other demons (Calvin 1972: II/32).

Mothers, Sisters, and Brothers (12:46–50)

After conflict, the focus now returns to those who remain with Jesus, the emerging church. Though Matthew's version is less harsh on Jesus' blood relations than Mark's (cf. Mark 3:20–21, 31–35), this short 'pronouncement story' prioritizes an alternative family of disciples, defined by doing the Father's will.

According to Tertullian, Marcion interpreted Jesus' question as meaning that he had no earthly mother or relatives, somewhat implausibly given the presence of both mother and brothers in the story (Tertullian, *Against Marcion* 4.19). In his refutation of Marcion, Jerome adds that it was also proposed by Manicheus:

> He has not denied his mother, then, in the sense that Marcion and Manicheus think, as one who was thought to have been born of a phantom. Rather, he preferred the apostles to his relatives, that we too, in terms of degree of affection, might prefer the spirit to the flesh. (Jerome 2008: 150)

Jerome's exegesis contains a further twist. He believes that the person who informed Christ of the presence of his family sought to trip him up, to see whether he preferred flesh and blood to the things of the spirit. Hence Jesus' refusal to go outside reflects, not a denial of his mother and brothers, but a direct response to the one plotting against him.

Developing Mariology may partially explain the popularity of figurative readings which distance the passage from the historical figure of Mary. For both Hilary and Jerome, the mother and brothers are symbols of the synagogue, standing 'outside' the church. But even in the heat of Reformation debates, there is a general consensus across the confessional divide that, on the literal level, this story exalts discipleship over family ties. The Spanish Jesuit Juan de Maldonado expresses the sentiment well:

> For although His Mother was truly a Virgin in body, and James, Joses, Judas, and Simon were truly His brothers in kinship, yet much more perfectly and with greater merit was she His Mother, and were they His brothers, in mind, because they did the will of His Father who was in heaven. (Maldonado 1888: 1/420)

John Chrysostom sees the episode as part of the ongoing education of Mary and the brothers, leading them from reliance on blood ties ('superfluous vanity') to acknowledgment of his role as teacher and Lord:

> And this He said, not as being ashamed of His mother, nor denying her that bare Him; for if He had been ashamed of her, He would not have passed through that womb; but as declaring that she has no advantage from this, unless she do all that is required to be done. For in fact that which she had essayed to do, was of superfluous vanity; in that she wanted to show the people that she has power and authority over her Son, imagining not as yet anything great concerning Him; whence also her unseasonable approach. (*Homily on Matthew* 44; *NPNF* 1st series, 10:278–279)

Chrysostom draws an interesting parallel with Christ's response to his mother at the wedding of Cana (John 2:1–11). Both episodes contain a rebuke followed by an acquiescence to the request; in this case, Chrysostom finds significance in the statement that Christ then 'came out of the house' (13:1) to where his family were gathered.

John Calvin follows Chrysostom in finding a rebuke to 'Mary's importunity,' in interrupting her Son while he was teaching. Christ's diminishing of their physical relationship provides a lesson for all Christians. That he 'receives all His disciples and believers into the same rank of honor as if they were His closest relatives' reveals that 'he was given, not just to a few but to all the godly, who by faith compose with Him one body' (Calvin 1972: II/56). The notes to the 1582 Catholic Rheims New Testament extend the reference to general familial relationships, to assure its Catholic readers that the commandment to honor father and mother is not thereby overridden: 'The dutiful affection toward our parents and kinsfolk is not blamed, but the inordinate loue of them to the hinderance of our seruice and duty toward God' (Rheims 1582: 34).

Gregory the Great draws a distinction between the roles of 'brother or sister' and that of mother. If someone becomes Christ's brother or sister by faith, he or she becomes his mother by preaching, which is a form of 'giving birth':

> He brings forth, as it were, the Lord Jesus, whom he introduces into the heart of the person listening; he becomes his mother, if through his words the love of the Lord is produced in his neighbor's heart. (*Homily* 1; Gregory the Great 1990: 6)

Matthew 13

Ancient Literary Context

Jesus is the parabolic preacher par excellence. The term 'parable' (Greek *parabolē* meaning 'thrown alongside') is used in the LXX to translate the Hebrew *mashal*, a broad term encompassing proverbs, similitudes, and wisdom sayings (e.g. Num 23:7; Deut 28:37; Ezek 12:22). A basic working definition

Matthew Through the Centuries, First Edition. Ian Boxall.

of the Gospel parables is provided by the British New Testament scholar C.H. Dodd:

> At its simplest the parable is a metaphor or simile drawn from nature or common life, arresting the hearer by its vividness or strangeness, and leaving the mind in sufficient doubt about its precise application to tease it into active thought. (Dodd 1935: 16)

Through familiarity, many contemporary readers hear Jesus' parables as 'domesticated' moralizing stories. Yet it is precisely their strangeness, their capacity to shock, or in Dodd's words to tease the mind 'into active thought,' which may need to be recaptured (see e.g. Wilder 1964: 79–96; Levine 2014). Within the Gospels, they function as vehicles for exploring the surprising character of the Kingdom (see e.g. Blomberg 1991; Gowler 2000; Snodgrass 2008; Zimmerman 2015: 21–55).

Matthew 13 contains a substantial parables discourse, a longer version of that found in Mark 4:1–34 (cf. Luke 8:4–15; 13:18–21). Matthew shares with his fellow Synoptic authors the parables of the Sower and the Mustard Seed, together with explanations of Jesus' parabolic teaching. In addition, Matthew includes the Wheat and the Tares with its own interpretation (possibly his reworking of Mark's Seed Growing Secretly, Mark 4:26–29), the Leaven (Luke 13:20–21), and the short parables of the Treasure in the Field, the Pearl of Great Price, and the Dragnet, the latter with its own interpretation (13:44–50; cf. the version in *Gos. Thom.* 8, where the distinction is between 'small' and 'large' fish). Comparison with Mark and Luke highlights Matthew's distinctive treatment of the parables: his use of striking, rather flat characters ('wise' and 'foolish,' 'good' and 'bad'), and his tendency to allegorize (Goulder 1974: 47–69).

Some modern commentators find in this preference for allegory an early move toward the 'domestication' of the parables, 'closing down' their interpretation to a single, univocal meaning (e.g. Levine 2014: 278; see Gowler 2017: 4–8). Others argue to the contrary that allegorical interpretation can be multivalent (e.g. Lischer 2014: 48–58), particularly in contrast to historical criticism's focus on uncovering a parable's 'main point,' a procedure pioneered by the German New Testament scholar Adolf Jülicher in his 1886 classic *Die Gleichnisreden Jesu*. Still others urge that attention to Matthew's redaction of the parables in their wider narrative setting will yield a rich harvest (e.g. Drury 1985).

The particular narrative location of Matthew's parables discourse underscores the mounting tension created by the division within Israel over Jesus' Kingdom preaching. For some, it marks the 'turning-point' in Matthew's story (Kingsbury 1969; though see Luz 2001: 228–229). Christ now teaches the crowds in puzzling, enigmatic parables, whereas his own followers have been granted the privilege of understanding 'the secrets of the kingdom of the heavens' (13:11; cf. Mark 4:11). The disciples are apparently the only ones to hear the interpretation of the Sower parable (13:18–23, cf. 13:17); they are also the privileged recipients (in 'the house,' 13:36) of the interpretation of the Wheat and the Tares, and the only ones to hear the final triad of Treasure, Pearl, and Dragnet.

The motif of division and discord continues with the narrative shift at the end of this chapter. Having completed his discourse, Jesus comes to 'his own country,' where his townsfolk take offense at him. Though closely paralleling Mark 6:1–6 (cf. the longer version at Luke 4:16–30), Matthew's version smooths out Christological ambiguity (e.g. 'he did not perform many mighty works there,' 13:58; cf. Mark's 'he could not perform any mighty work there,' Mark 6:5).

The Interpretations

From the beginning, readers of Matthew's parables have disagreed over hermeneutical method. The Matthean tendency to allegorize the parables was enthusiastically embraced by various gnostic groups. This explains the rather more restrained interpretation offered by Irenaeus, who was also keen to emphasize the unity of old and new covenants, against Marcion and the Valentinians (*Adv. Haer*. 4.36.1–8; 4.40.2–41.1; see Gowler 2017: 19). This is perhaps clearest in his treatment of the two vineyard parables (20:1–16; 21:33–45) as allegories of salvation history (Minns 2012), but also in his interpretation of the Treasure in the Field. Rebuttals of gnostic readings are also evident in Tertullian (*De Pudic*. 9) and Origen, who both resist the idea that every detail of a parable has some hidden meaning (see Wiles 1958: 228–294), though Origen also observes that the evangelists were the first to establish the principle of allegorical interpretation.

The Antiochene John Chrysostom places more emphasis on the literal sense of the parables, and their moral implications for contemporary Christians (see Gowler 2017: 83). The tension between allegorical and literal continues, to varying degrees, through the succeeding centuries, with a significant decline in allegorical reading since the Renaissance and Reformation.

The hortatory aspect is a common feature of the reception of the parables, which are frequently the subject of homilies, sermons, and expository teaching directed toward ordinary Christians (e.g. Gregory the Great; Hildegard of Bingen; Luther; Calvin). For monastics (e.g. the Cappadocians Basil the Great and Gregory of Nazianzus), the single-minded devotion demanded by the Treasure in the Field and the Pearl of Great Price is readily interpreted in terms of Christian asceticism (Matz 2013).

The polemical use of the parables is also a recurring motif across the centuries. Augustine engages the Wheat and the Tares against the Donatists' insistence on a 'pure' church, devoid of any corrupting 'weeds.' In the Middle Ages, this parable plays a key role in determining the appropriate response to heresy (e.g. the differing interpretation of Wazo of Liège and Thomas Aquinas). Both sides of the Reformation divide find justification for their doctrine of salvation in parables such as the Sower, generally at the expense of their theological opponents.

Teaching from a Boat (13:1–2)

Paralleling the mountain location of Christ's first discourse, the setting of this sermon is in a boat, where again Jesus assumes the seated position of the teacher. In narrative terms, this location could serve several practical purposes. For Jerome (followed by Calvin), it is an act of the compassionate Lord, making his teaching available to the crowds who were unable to enter his house. According to the *Opus imperfectum*, Christ chose the location in order that the people could hear and see him better (also Theophylact). For John Chrysostom, the end of the previous chapter (12:46–50) provides the narrative key: Christ leaves the house to reproach his brothers, and to show honor to his mother. He then gets into the boat so that he could see the crowd, and they understand him better. By contrast, Erasmus paraphrases Jesus' action as one of withdrawal: he gets into a boat 'in order to be freer from the crowd' (Erasmus 2008: 208).

But this is often combined with a 'mystical' interpretation. Hilary finds here a symbol of the church (see 8:23–27), where God's word is preached; the crowds represent those outside the church, to whom the word comes in puzzling parables. For Aquinas, the house signifies Judea, from which Christ goes out (23:38; cf. Jer 12:7) to the sea, i.e. the Gentiles (Ps 103:25). The boat is the church gathered from among the Gentiles; those he teaches are the catechumens. Alternatively, based on a passage from Wisdom (Wis 8:16), the house is the 'interior mind,' the 'hidden place of contemplation,' from which Christ goes to 'the public place of teaching' (Aquinas 2013b: 3–4).

Several observe that there are seven parables in Jesus' discourse (Gundry 1994: 250), not counting the saying about the scribe at 13:52. The radical Franciscan theologian Peter John Olivi (1248–1298) interprets this number in light of his apocalyptic view of history. Each one points to a different period of church history, from its beginnings (the Sower and the Wheat and Tares), through its expansion (the Mustard Seed and the Leaven), the renewal of evangelical poverty (the Treasure and the Pearl), to the final conversion of the world (the Dragnet; Madigan 2003). Thus the Sower refers to the divided response in Christ's time; the Wheat and Tares to the time of the apostles; the Mustard Seed and Leaven to 'the propagation of the kingdom of God among princes and the whole human race'; the Treasure to 'the darker condition of the Church' (presumably because the treasure was hidden); the Pearl to the Kingdom 'when esteemed above all things'; the Dragnet to the mixed body of the church in the last days (Madigan 2003: 84–87). The Lutheran pietist scholar Johann Albrecht Bengel (1687–1752) detects a similar mystical significance:

> [T]hese seven parables ... have also a most hidden meaning, referring to the various periods or ages of the church; and this in such a manner that their fulfilment is consecutive, though no one is completed before the beginning of that which follows. (Bengel 1971: 183)

The Sower and Its Interpretation (13:3–9, 18–23)

Though some have attempted to explain the sower's indiscriminate scattering in terms of ancient Palestinian farming practices (that plowing followed sowing: Jeremias 1955: 9–10), it is the peculiarity of his actions which the parable emphasizes (Harrington 1991: 194). In narrative context, the apparent wastefulness of indiscriminate sowing reflects the divided response to the 'word of the kingdom' (13:19) preached both by Jesus and by the Twelve (e.g. 10:11–25; 11:16–24; 12:1–50). As John Chrysostom has it in his homily on this parable:

> For as the sower makes no distinction in the land submitted to him, but simply and indifferently casts his seed; so He Himself too makes no distinction of rich and poor, of wise and unwise, of slothful or diligent, of brave or cowardly; but He discourses unto all, fulfilling His part, although foreknowing the results; that it may be in His power to say, What ought I to have done, that I have not done? (*Homily on Matthew* 44; *NPNF* 1st series, 10:281)

The provision of a point-by-point interpretation for this parable explains the widespread tendency to read it allegorically (see Luz 2001: 238–240). Yet the interpretative grid provided by 13:18–23 contains sufficient gaps to allow a diversity of understandings. For the author of *1 Clement*, the parable functions, along with the phoenix, as a potent symbol of the resurrection:

> The sower went forth and cast into the earth each of the seeds. These seeds, falling to the earth dry and bare, decay; but then out of their decay the majesty of the Master's providence raises them up, and from the one seed many grow and bear fruit. (*1 Clem*. 24:5; Holmes 2007: 79)

For many others, the paraenetic potential of the different kinds of seeds/soils, denoting different types of hearer or response, is paramount. Typical is the *Opus imperfectum*: the soil along the path signifies worldly people, the hard, rocky ground those with hardened hearts, that among thorns those who worry over riches, and the good soil those in whom the word is able to be productive. This might imply that responses are predetermined, a reading which John Chrysostom is keen to refute:

> There is such a thing as the rock changing, and becoming rich land; and the way-side being no longer trampled on, nor lying open to all that pass by, but that it may be a fertile field; and the thorns may be destroyed, and the seed enjoy full security. (*Homily on Matthew* 44; *NPNF* 1st series, 10:281–282)

According to William Cowper's 'The Sower,' one of the *Olney Hymns*, divine grace is acknowledged as a prerequisite for the soul being fertile soil:

> Father of mercies we have need
> Of thy preparing grace;
> Let the same hand that gives the seed,
> Provide a fruitful place.[1]

Identifying the Sower (13:3)

The identity of the Sower is not spelt out explicitly in Matthew's text. He could symbolize God the Father, who comes out to sow seeds of righteousness among the Gentiles, and who from the beginning had sown his seeds both in nature and in the Mosaic Law (*Opus imperfectum*). Such an identification supports Clement of Alexandria's conviction that Greek philosophy paved the way for the preaching of the Gospel. God, the sower, has not only sown in different soils, but sown different types of seed:

> For the husbandman of the soil which is among men is one; He who from the beginning, from the foundation of the world, sowed nutritious seeds; He who in each age rained down the Lord, the Word. But the times and places which received [such gifts], created the differences which exist. Further, the husbandman sows not only wheat (of which there are many varieties), but also other seeds – barley, and beans, and peas, and vetches, and vegetable and flower seeds. (*Strom.* 1.7.1; *ANF* 2:308)

More frequently, the sower receives a Christological interpretation ('God the Word': Origen, *Comm. on Matt.* 10.2; also e.g. Aquinas). For Theophylact, Christ

1 http://www.ccel.org/ccel/newton/olneyhymns.Book1.MAT.h1_85.html.

'went forth' to sow at the incarnation (also e.g. *Glossa ordinaria*). Others (e.g. Chrysostom; Jerome; Maldonado; Calvin) understand the 'going forth' to refer specifically to Christ's teaching in parables during his ministry. Alternatively, given that in Christian preaching Christ the Word is proclaimed, the sower also symbolizes the preacher (e.g. Bede; Hugh of St. Cher; Albert the Great; references in Wailes 1987: 98). An early version of this is found in the Valentinian Ptolemy's *Letter to Flora* (second century), where Ptolemy implicitly identifies himself as the sower, who is passing on the apostolic tradition he has received (Flor. 7.9; also Justin Martyr, *Trypho* 125.1–2; see Jorgensen 2016: 163–165).

A Hundredfold, Sixtyfold, Thirtyfold (13:8, 23)

The tendency to extend Matthew's allegorical approach is particularly reflected in interpretations of the parable's conclusion, which differentiates between degrees of fruitfulness. That fructification is the climax of the parable is represented visually by the presence of female figures and a loaf of bread ('the fructified word') in Jacopo Bassano's *The Parable of the Sower* (c. 1561; Thyssen-Bornemizsa Collection, Madrid; see Berdini 1997: 75–77).

Irenaeus knows an early interpretation whereby the hundredfold, sixtyfold, and thirtyfold refer to a differentiation in eternal rewards: the heavens, paradise, and the city, presumably the new Jerusalem, respectively (*Adv. Haer.* 5.36.2; also Clement of Alexandria, *Strom.* 6.14; see Wiles 1958: 293). In the period of Christian martyrdom, pride of place is given to those who lay down their lives for the faith. Origen, whose own father Leonides died a martyr's death under Septimius Severus, explores the Sower in his *Exhortation to Martyrdom*, reminding his hearers that the parable warns against falling away when 'affliction and persecution' come (*An Exhortation to Martyrdom* 49; Origen 1979: 77). For Cyprian of Carthage, the hundredfold fruit of the martyrs is followed by the sixtyfold fruit of the virgins (*On the Dress of Virgins* 21). Augustine adds marriage as a lesser, thirtyfold degree, for those 'engaged in the battle' with the passions (*Questions on the Gospels* 1.9; Augustine 2014: 365). Thomas Aquinas will later follow Augustine's reading, regarding these three groups as achieving in differing degrees the 'perfection of justice.'

Unsurprisingly, in his treatise in praise of virginity against Jovinian, Jerome sees the 'hundredfold' promise as addressed to virgins, followed by the widows and continent, and finally the married (*Adv. Jov.* 1.3). Theophylact finds a similar justification for elevating the celibate life: Christ's words refer to the extreme asceticism of the anchorite (a hundredfold), the cenobite or monk living in community (sixtyfold), and the married (thirtyfold). Jerome's interpretation is common in medieval exegesis (e.g. *Glossa ordinaria*). It is adopted by John Wyclif (*In omnes Novi Testamenti Libros* 27d), and echoed in Geoffrey

Chaucer's *The Parson's Tale*, where a girl's virginity is described as 'thilke precious fruyt that the book clepeth the hundred fruyt' (see Siebald in Jeffrey 1992: 733). Gregory the Great takes a different tack: faith in the Trinity (thirtyfold), leading to good works (sixtyfold) and the contemplation of eternity (a hundredfold), though its suggestion of spiritual progress is ruled out by the parable's insistence that different levels of fruitfulness are found in different people (Wailes 1987: 100).

The *Opus imperfectum* finds the changing fortunes of the Old Testament patriarch Job relevant for clarifying the distinction between degrees of fruitfulness:

> The good soil is those who refrain from evil riches and do good deeds as much as they can, and their fruit is thirtyfold. But if they despise all their good deeds and approach to serve God, they have a sixtyfold fruit. But if also an infirmity of the body afflicts them and they endure it faithfully, they have a hundredfold fruit and are good soil. For also Job before his testing had a thirtyfold harvest as he lived righteously in his wealth; after the loss of his wealth and children, he had a sixtyfold harvest; but after the plague on his body, he had a hundredfold harvest. (Kellerman and Oden 2010: 246)

In the sixteenth century, the parable's conclusion becomes a battleground for opposing doctrines of salvation. Martin Luther regarded Jerome's elevation of virginity as 'utterly unchristian' (see Siebald in Jeffrey 1992: 733), and it is dismissed by John Calvin as 'foolish.' Equally, the Reformers are keen to refute any suggestion that salvation might be earned. Juan de Maldonado's interpretation of the Sower (bearing fruit refers either to doing good works, or eternal life) is a direct polemical response from the Catholic side. He regards Jesus' saying as overthrowing two 'errors of Luther and Calvin': namely, that eternal life cannot be merited, and that 'the reward of all the blessed will be equal' (Maldonado 1888: 1/434–435).

The Purpose of Parables (13:10–17, 34–35)

Twice during this discourse, an explanation is offered as to why Jesus teaches in parables. The first (13:10–17) is provoked by a question from the disciples, which Chrysostom and Calvin think reveals their concern for the crowd. Matthew's version differs significantly from its Markan parallel (Mark 4:10–12; cf. Luke 8:9–10). First, it offers a more positive portrayal of the disciples: whereas in Mark, they have been given the single 'secret of the kingdom of God,' though their narrative portrayal manifests their inability to comprehend it, in Matthew, they have been granted to *know* or understand the Kingdom's *secrets*. Second, Mark's statement that Jesus teaches in parables 'in order that' (Greek *hina*) the people may not understand, i.e. that he deliberately provokes incomprehension, in Matthew reads 'because' (or possibly 'that'; Greek *hoti*). Finally, Matthew explicitly quotes Isaiah 6:9–10 (an important passage in the early church for explaining the limited success of the Gospel within Israel, e.g. John 12:40; Acts 28:26–27).

For some modern scholars, Matthew's shift from *hina* to *hoti* results in a softening of Jesus' words (e.g. McNeile 1952: 190; BDF §369). Given that the crowds were unable to understand his previous words, Jesus begins teaching in parables in the hope that they might finally understand, whether because the parables are more understandable or, more probably, that their obscurity is meant to provoke the people to greater attentiveness. In his paraphrase, Erasmus hints at just such a possibility:

> Jesus replied to them in this way: 'Because the people show that they are not sufficiently ready for the truth to be revealed, for some of those mixed in the crowd not only are not made better by the truth, but are even incited by it to become more wicked. Therefore, the message I set before them is fashioned according to the state of mind they bring to listening. They refuse to understand the things that are most obvious; I veil my message with obscurity to incite them in this very way to the desire for learning and inquiry.' (Erasmus 2008: 209)

For most interpreters, by contrast, Matthew's version merely underscores Israel's prior lack of understanding, or that of subsequent 'hardened' hearers. The blame lies entirely with the people, not with Christ or God. Thus, for Clement of Alexandria, it was not that 'the Lord caused the ignorance'; rather, 'He prophetically exposed this ignorance, that existed in them, and intimated that they would not understand the things spoken' (*Strom.* 1.1; *ANF* 2:299). The passage, in other words, reveals Christ's foreknowledge, not his will.

On different sides of the Reformation divide, both Martin Luther and the Jesuit scholar Juan de Maldonado regard Jesus' parabolic teaching as punishment for a prior refusal to listen. Luther paraphrases the passage thus:

> This people is deplorably proud and wicked to such an extent that even when I work and speak plainly, they not only refuse to hear and to learn but even want to slander and blaspheme the acknowledged truth. Therefore, I do to them just what they want so that, since they do not wish to accept what is open, they shall hear parables that they cannot understand even if they might want to [understand]. (*Annotations* on Matthew 13:13; Luther 2015: 190)

Similarly, for Maldonado, 'because they would not believe and understand, and were, therefore unworthy of having these mysteries revealed to them,'

Christ speaks to them 'darkly' as a punishment for their unbelief, despite having witnessed his miracles and heard his teaching (Maldonado 1888: 1/423). John Calvin finds support for predestination: God by his grace alone opened up his mysteries to the disciples, while the rest were deprived of it.

The second passage (13:34–35) expands Mark's conclusion to the parables discourse (Mark 4:33–34) by again appealing to prophetic fulfillment. The quotation in question comes from Psalm 78:2 (LXX and Vulgate Ps 77:2), the psalmist being understood as a prophet. Yet some early exegetes anticipate modern textual criticism (e.g. Metzger 1994: 27–28) by discussing the reading 'through Isaiah the prophet' found in some ancient manuscripts. Both Eusebius (*Comm. in Pss.* = PG 23:901) and Jerome claim that the original read 'Asaph the prophet' (given that this psalm is introduced as 'Of Asaph'), Jerome attributing the error to a misguided scribal 'correction' (see North 2008: 270–271).

The Wheat and Tares and Its Interpretation (13:24–30, 36–43)

The second parable is also given an allegorical interpretation (to the disciples, in the house, 13:36), leading Richard of Saint Victor to observe that Jesus' words here 'are easier and plainer than others' (in Wailes 1987: 105). This sets some limits to subsequent receptions of the parable: the man who sows is the Son of Man, who sows good seed (the children of the Kingdom) in the field of the world; his rival sower is the devil, who sows weeds (his own children); both wheat and weeds are harvested (by angels) at the 'end of the age,' when the separation between weeds and wheat takes place. However, Matthew's Jesus fails to explain all details of the parable. It is left to later readers, developing the allegorical method proposed by Matthew's text, to identify the 'sleepers' and the householder's 'servants.' For Jerome, the sleeping men are the church's teachers who should have been on the lookout for heretics; by contrast, Thomas Aquinas understands them as a symbol of humanity, appointed to keep guard, yet slumbering in the sleep of death. The servants are the angels (Jerome), good people (Aquinas), or 'ardent ministers of the Church' (Maldonado 1888: 1/437).

Moreover, commentators have not always felt constrained even by the interpretation provided by Matthew's text. In the Jewish Christian Pseudo-Clementine writings, the 'enemy' is identified as the apostle Paul, and the tares his antinomian Gospel:

> For some from among the Gentiles have rejected my lawful preaching and have preferred a lawless and absurd doctrine *of the man who is my enemy*. (*Letter of Peter to James* 2.3; Schneemelcher 1992: II/494)

Many others move beyond Matthew's clear statement that the field symbolizes 'the world' (13:38). Theophylact of Ochrid understands this to have personal as well as a universal application: the field is the individual soul (Theophylact 1992: 115). Theophylact also points to the convert Paul, the penitent thief (Luke 23:39–43), and Matthew himself as warnings against prematurely harvesting the weeds:

> If, for example, Matthew had been cut down while he was a tare, the wheat of the word which was later to spring up from him would have been cut down with him. Similarly with Paul and the thief. (Theophylact 1992: 115)

The English Catholic poet Chidiock Tichborne (1562–1586) understands the 'field' as his own short life, in his *Elegy* composed while awaiting execution for treason for his involvement in the Babington Plot to assassinate Elizabeth I:

> My prime of youth is but a frost of cares,
> My feast of joy is but a dish of pain,
> My crop of corn is but a field of tares,
> And all my good is but vain hope of gain.
> The day is gone and yet I saw no sun,
> And now I live, and now my life is done.[2]

A more common elaboration identifies the field with the church (see McIver 1995). Augustine paraphrases 'the world' as 'the Church spread throughout the world.' He appeals to the consciences of his Christian hearers, as 'dearest grains of Christ,' to see whether they might in fact be weeds rather than wheat, in need of repentance (*Sermon* 73A; Augustine 1991: 295–296). This ecclesial interpretation of the parable (a 'mixed body' which cannot safely be separated until the end) has proved particularly important in disputes over church membership. Pope Callistus I appealed to it to advocate leniency toward sinners in the church, including clergy, according to his rival Hippolytus of Rome (Hippolytus, *Ref.* 9.7). Augustine himself employs it effectively against the Donatist insistence on a 'pure church' (e.g. *Sermons on New Testament Lessons* 38.21); ironically, he was influenced in this by the Donatist Tyconius, the second of whose 'rules' for biblical interpretation was 'on the Lord's twofold body' (*De domini corpore bipertito*). In the eighteenth century, the English evangelical hymnwriter John Newton similarly speaks of the division within 'the outward church': 'Though in the outward church below | The wheat and tares together grow; | Jesus ere long will weed the crop, | And pluck the tares, in anger, up' (*Olney Hymns* 86).

2 https://www.poetryfoundation.org/poems/47443/my-prime-of-youth-is-but-a-frost-of-cares.

The notion of a *corpus permixtum* is central to the magisterial Reformers (see Luz 1994: 79–82). In Calvin's words: 'So long as the Church is on pilgrimage in this world, the good and the sincere will be mixed in it with the bad and the hypocrites' (Calvin 1972: II/74–75). Martin Luther treats the parable as a challenge to those whom he regarded as the contemporary Donatists, the Anabaptists, 'who in their shared frenzy cry out that the true Church is not the Church, because they see sinners and godless people mingled together [in it], and they separate themselves from it' (*Annotations on Matthew* 13:28; Luther 2015: 199). Mirroring this, the Counter-Reformation identified the tares as Protestants, as visualized by the Italian artist Domenico Fetti in his *The Sower of Tares* (1620–1621; Courtauld Gallery, London), the evil character of the second sower conveyed by his sowing seed with his left hand, and across rather than along the plowed furrows (Askew 1961: 34–35).

The identification of the weeds (the 'children of the evil one') as heretics, or specific heresies (e.g. Clement of Alexandria, *Strom.* 7.15; Origen, *Homilies on Joshua* 21.1; Tertullian, *Adv. Prax.* 1.6; Aquinas), leads to debates about how ecclesial enemies should be treated (see Gowler 2017: 74–76, 99–102). For some, the parable clearly rules out violence against those considered heretical. In a letter to the bishop of Châlons-sur-Marne, addressing a Manichaean-type heresy in the former's diocese, Bishop Wazo of Liège (c. 985–1048) uses the Wheat and the Tares to advocate mercy, in imitation of the Lord:

> What does the Lord reveal by these words but His patience, which He wishes His preachers to display to their erring fellow men, particularly since it may be possible for those who today are cockle, tomorrow to be converted and be wheat. (Wazo of Liège in Wakefield and Evans 1991: 92)

Two centuries later, Thomas Aquinas maintains that compelling heretics and apostates to embrace the faith by force, or even uprooting them by death, is not ruled out by the parable, for in such cases the clear difference between the faithful and the heretics means that there is no danger of rooting out the 'wheat' unwittingly (*ST* IIa.IIae, q. 10, a. 8; q. 11, a. 3).

The eighteenth-century American preacher and theologian Jonathan Edwards testifies to the use of this parable in internal debates among American Puritans over admission to the Lord's Supper, and the practice of excommunication:

> It is agreed on all Hands, that adult Persons, actually admitted to Communion of the visible Church, however they may behave themselves so as to bring their spiritual State into Suspicion, yet ought not to be *cast out*, unless they are obstinate in *Heresy* or *Scandal*; lest, while we go about to root out the *Tares*, we

> should root out the *Wheat* also. And 'tis also agreed on all Hands, that when those represented under the Name of *Tares* bring forth such evil Fruit, such scandalous and obstinate Wickedness, as is plainly and visibly inconsistent with the Being of true Grace, they ought to be *cast out*. (*Humble Inquiry* 3.6; Edwards 1746: 103)

A twenty-first-century example is Cardinal Josef Ratzinger's (later Pope Benedict XVI) text for the Stations of the Cross on Good Friday 2005 at Rome's Colosseum, widely interpreted as a reference to the sexual abuse scandals in the Catholic Church:

> In your field we see more weeds than wheat. The soiled garments and face of your Church throw us into confusion. Yet it is we ourselves who have soiled them! It is we who betray you time and time again, after all our lofty words and grand gestures. Have mercy on your Church; within her too, Adam continues to fall.[3]

The Mustard Seed and the Leaven (13:31–33)

Both Matthew and Luke (Luke 13:18–21) link the Mustard Seed and the Leaven, reflecting their common theme of extraordinary results from modest beginnings. Origen classifies these two as similitudes rather than parables, presuming that they are addressed, not to the crowds, but only to the disciples (13:10). But verses 34–35 suggest a wider audience, supported by the fact that these parables receive no interpretation. Hence Johann Albrecht Bengel concludes that, like the Sower and the Wheat and the Tares, they are addressed to the crowds.

The unexpected character of the Mustard Seed is that the seed in question does not ordinarily grow into a 'tree' (13:32; Luke 13:19; cf. Mark 4:32). Thus, for John Calvin, this parable of humble beginnings confounds the irreligious who scoff at the Gospel 'because it is brought by obscure and unknown ministers' (Calvin 1972: II/79). Theophylact of Ochrid finds significance in the category of seed for what followers of Christ are called to be: like mustard, they should be 'hot, zealous, pungent, and reproving' (Theophylact 1992: 116). This line of interpretation, also found in Hilary, is frequently developed in the Middle Ages, to apply to the pungent faith of the martyrs, or the fervor of the pious soul (see Wailes 1987: 112–113).

Some nineteenth-century interpretations of the parable reflect contemporary theories of the inevitability of progress, as describing the gradual,

3 http://www.vatican.va/news_services/liturgy/2005/via_crucis/en/station_09.html.

inevitable growth of the church or the Kingdom. According to German Lutheran exegete Heinrich August Wilhelm Meyer (1800–1873):

> *The parable of the mustard seed* is designed to show that the great community, consisting of those who are to participate in the Messianic kingdom, *i.e.* the true people of God as constituting the body politic of the future kingdom, is destined to develope [sic] from a small beginning into a vast multitude, and therefore to grow *extensively*. (Meyer 1877: 365–366)

When allegorized, the mustard seed could be interpreted as the 'word of the kingdom' (as in 13:18: e.g. Jerome; Theophylact), the apostles who preach it (e.g. Theophylact), or (in light of 17:20) as faith. But many interpreters presume that it symbolizes Christ himself, the incarnate Word (e.g. Clement of Alexandria, *Paed.* 1.11; Hilary; Paschasius Radbertus). For Irenaeus, the parable anticipates Christ's death and resurrection, and the subsequent spread of the Gospel to all nations:

> He, hidden in the heart of the earth, in the grave, and grown to a great tree in three days, spread out His own branches to the ends of the earth. Reaching forth from Him, the Twelve Apostles, fair and flourishing branches, became shelters to the nations as to the birds of heaven. (Irenaeus, *Frag.* 29, in Smith 1925–1929: III/18)

This identification of the birds as Gentiles reflects the influence of Daniel 4, an intertextual connection frequently made (e.g. Aquinas; Luz 2001: 261; France 2007: 526–527). Jerome has an alternative explanation of the branches in which they shelter: they symbolize different teachings, which provide rest for the souls of believers. Aquinas's Dominican teacher Albert the Great (c. 1200–1280) interprets the branches as the major churches and bishops of Christendom (in Wailes 1987: 110).

It is not only Christians who have been captivated by Jesus' parabolic teaching, however. The Vietnamese Buddhist monk Thich Nhat Hanh, friend of both Thomas Merton and Martin Luther King Jr., offers a Buddhist reading of the parable according to which Christ is but one of many doors to the Kingdom. The Mustard Seed is about enlightenment, the 'seed of the kingdom of God' within every person, which can grow into a large bush if 'we know how to plant that seed in the moist soil of our daily lives' (Nhat Hanh in Gowler 2017: 250).

Overfamiliarity may downplay the surprising, provocative character of the Leaven. The oddity that the woman 'hid' the leaven or yeast in the flour (13:33) is obscured in many English translations (NRSV, NIV, and NABRE all translate as 'mixed'). There is also hyperbole in the 'three measures' of flour: between 40 and

60 pounds, or enough to feed 150 people (Luz 2001: 262; Levine 2014: 121). Both Martin Luther (*Annotations* on Matt 13:33) and Johann Albrecht Bengel make the intertextual connection with Genesis 18, where Sarah makes bread from three measures of flour to feed the three visitors by the oak of Mamre.

Yet the instinct of many is to allegorize every detail. Given the lack of an interpretation in Matthew's text, however, the allegorizing possibilities are almost endless, though most agree that the 'leaven,' despite negative uses of the term elsewhere (e.g. 16:6, 12; 1 Cor 5:6–8), has positive connotations in this instance. Hilary of Poitiers presumes a Christological focus. Christ is the leaven, the three measures of flour the Law, the prophets, and the Gospels, which speak in harmony now that the yeast has worked its way through them. Other interpretations of the leaven include the apostles (e.g. Chrysostom; Theophylact), charity (Augustine), or the teaching of the Gospel (Jerome). Hilary is aware of alternative interpretations of the measures of flour: either referring to the unity of Father, Son, and Holy Spirit (e.g. Tertullian, *De orat.* 25.2; *De bapt.* 6.2), or to the three races descended from the sons of Noah, thus pointing to the 'leavening' of all the nations by the Gospel. The same principle seems to underlie the identification of the flour as the three known continents of Europe, Asia, and Africa (in Clarke 2003: 127).

A reaction to such detailed allegorization is detected in Juan de Maldonado, who is predisposed to treat the 'woman' in the parable as merely incidental to the stories (from his cultural perspective, it is 'a woman's work to grind'). Nonetheless, he entertains an alternative possibility: that she signifies 'an Evangelical Doctor, who pours the Word of God into the minds of his hearers' (Maldonado 1888: 1/440). This is not dissimilar from Jerome's interpretation of the woman, as either the preaching of the apostles, or the church. An alternative identifies her as Mary, who is instrumental in reversing the 'leaven of death' brought through Eve by the 'leaven of resurrection' (Peter Chrysologus, *Sermon* 99), or who is distinguished by the leaven of her faith (Bernard of Clairvaux; see Wailes 1987: 115–116). In contrast is the negative reading suggested by Hilary, whereby the woman is the synagogue, which buried Christ, the hidden leaven (also e.g. Hugh of St. Cher).

Three More Kingdom Parables (13:44–50)

The final three parables, only found in Matthew and the Coptic *Gospel of Thomas* (*Gos. Thom.* 8; 76; 109) are directed to the privileged disciples. The first two, the Treasure in the Field and the Pearl of Great Price, explore the single-mindedness required of those who pursue the vision of the Kingdom. The final parable of the Dragnet reiterates motifs of good and bad, and final separation at the judgment, already encountered in the Wheat and the Tares. It is also the only one of the three to receive an interpretation.

The Treasure Hidden in the Field (13:44)

For Irenaeus, engaged in controversy with the Valentinians, the Treasure is a lesson in scriptural hermeneutics. The treasure is Christ himself, albeit hidden in the scriptures. It can only truly be recognized for what it is when scripture is interpreted according to the rule of faith (*Adv. Haer*. 4.26.1; see Jorgensen 2016: 56–57). For Origen, Christ is the field in which the treasure is hidden, appealing to Paul's letter to the Colossians, which speaks of Christ as the one in whom 'all the treasures of wisdom and knowledge are hidden' (Col. 2:3; see also Jerome). Theophylact finds the key to the parable in another Pauline passage, 1 Corinthians 2:7 ('We preach a wisdom that is hidden') to explain the treasure either as Christ himself, or the knowledge of Christ. Hilary treats the parable as an allegory of the incarnation, in which Christ the Word is hidden in the flesh.

All three parables receive a Christological interpretation in early Christian exegesis. In the *Acts of John*, the dying apostle, while celebrating his final Eucharist, lists 'the inexpressible Pearl,' 'the Treasure,' and 'the Net' among the Christological titles with which John glorifies the name of the Son (*Acts of John* 109; Schneemelcher 1992: II/202; also *Acts of Peter* 20). Jerome, writing to the Roman senator Pammachius, widowed husband of Paula's daughter Paulina, links the Treasure and the Pearl:

> We know that Christ is wisdom. He is the treasure which in the scriptures a man finds in his field. He is the peerless gem which is bought by selling many pearls. (*Ep*. 66.8; *NPNF* 2nd series, 6:138)

The homiletic genre lends itself to tropological interpretation. Hence in his homily on the parable, Gregory the Great proposes to his congregation that the treasure is 'heavenly delight,' and the field in which it is hidden 'the discipline of the pursuit of heaven' (*Homily* 9; Gregory the Great 1990: 63). Pursuing the treasure, in other words, requires the mastery of earthly desires central to Gregory's own monastic tradition. For the scholastic Dominican Albert the Great, the treasure is 'the study of virtue and wisdom,' 'hidden' in the sense that it can only be discovered 'within the solitude of silence, humility, and the mind's devotion to pleasing God' (Wailes 1987: 120). Such a moral challenge, however, is often more accessible when the faithful have role models to emulate. Hence, the Victorian Tractarian priest-poet John Keble finds the parable actualized in the call of Matthew the tax-collector, who 'rose and left his gold; | His treasure and his heart | Transferr'd' (Keble 1885: 247).

Francis of Assisi is another notable Christian who sought wholeheartedly for the treasure, as noted in the Divine Office of St. Francis by the German Franciscan Julian of Speyer (1228–1232):

> As soon as Francis ceased to deal
> In civic merchandising
> Into the Lord's field he withdrew
> To meditate in quiet;
> The gospel treasure he found there
> Would henceforth be his trading.
> (in Armstrong, Hellmann, and Short 1999: 333)

The Pearl of Great Price (13:45–46)

The Pearl also highlights the extreme value of the Kingdom, for, as Amy-Jill Levine observes, pearls were so luxurious that most people in the first century would never have seen one (Levine 2014: 134). In his commentary on the parable, Origen spends considerable time exploring different types of pearl and their provenance, before moving to the allegorical interpretation of the parable (the prophets, as mussels which produce Christ, the pearl of great price):

> And let the prophets be, so to speak, the mussels which conceive the dew of heaven, and become pregnant with the word of truth from heaven, the goodly pearls which, according to the phrase here set forth, the merchantman seeks. And the leader of the pearls, on the finding of which the rest are found with it, is the very costly pearl, the Christ of God, the Word which is superior to the precious letters and thoughts in the law and the prophets, on the finding of which also all the rest are easily taken. (*Commentary on Matthew* 10.8; *ANF* 9:417–418)

Identifying the pearl as Christ is a commonplace (e.g. Hilary; *Glossa ordinaria*; Richard of Saint Victor; Aquinas). Writing against both Marcionites and Manichaeans, Jerome interprets the pearls sought by the merchant as the Law, the prophets, and Christ, the latter being the most precious. Hence the former two, though good, need to be sold in order to buy Christ (Aquinas adds pagan philosophy to Moses and the prophets as good pearls surpassed by the 'pearl of great price'). The Welsh Non-Conformist commentator Matthew Henry (1662–1714) observes in his commentary that 'Jesus Christ is a *Pearl of great* price; in having him, we have enough to make us happy here and for ever' (Henry 1960: 71). A rare Christological variant is found in Pseudo-Bede, who identifies the merchant as Christ, and the pearl as the church, purchased with his own blood (PL 92:69; also Bruno of Segni, *Hom.* 141; see Wailes 1987: 123).

Others understand the pearl as the Kingdom of which Christ is King. In his poem 'The Pearl' from his 1633 collection *The Temple*, George Herbert describes how the ways that he knows well, of learning, honor, and pleasure, are as nothing compared with his love for God (hence the repeated 'Yet I love thee' at the end of the first three stanzas). These must be sold in order for him to climb to God and acquire his Kingdom (see Gowler 2017: 145–147):

> I know all these, and have them in my hand:
> Therefore not sealed, but with open eyes
> I flie to thee, and fully understand
> Both the main sale, and the commodities;
> And at what rate and price I have thy love;
> With all the circumstances that may move:
> Yet through these labyrinths, not my groveling wit,
> But thy silk twist let down from heav'n to me,
> Did both conduct and teach me, how by it
> To climbe to thee.[4]

Jerome also proposes an additional reading, whereby the pearl is prayer and earnest study of the scriptures associated with the contemplative life (e.g. *Ep.* 54:11). This is paralleled in the East in the Cappadocian Fathers Basil the Great and Gregory of Nazianzus, both of whom connect the quest for the pearl with the renunciation associated with Christian asceticism (see Matz 2013: 279–281). Jerome is widely followed by medieval exegetes, particularly the monastics, who regarded the pearl as a symbol of purity or chastity (see Jeffrey 1992: 594). Liturgically in the West, the Pearl was the Gospel reading at Mass on the feasts of virgins, a practice which may have influenced the fourteenth-century Middle English poem *Pearl*, whose central visionary character is the 'Pearl-maiden' (Bhattacharji 1995).

Jerome is an example of how allegorical interpretation need not close down interpretation to one, univocal meaning. Even more polyvalent is the interpretation of Ephrem the Syrian, whose poetic instinct in his *Hymns on the Pearl* (*Hymns on Faith* 81–87) allows him to treat the symbol of the pearl as 'a door that opens and reveals many facets of the "truth" and symbolizes not only the kingdom but also Christ, faith, the virgin birth, Christ's crucifixion, and many other things' (Gowler 2017: 50; see Brock 1992).

The parable lends its name to one of the four 'standard works' or volumes of scripture for Mormonism, *The Pearl of Great Price*, first published in Liverpool

---

4 https://www.ccel.org/h/herbert/temple/Pearl.html.

in 1851 (Smith 1851; see Clark 1955; Baldridge in Ludlow 1992: 1070–1072). Here the 'pearl' is the scriptures (the volume contains excerpts of Joseph Smith's translations of Genesis and Matthew), and the wider revelation believed to have been mediated through Smith himself.

The Dragnet (13:47–50)

The final parable also receives an explicit interpretation (13:49–50), thus providing a foundation for future allegorical interpretations, which explore details in the story left unexplained. Thus the 'vessels' in which the good fish are collected symbolize the heavenly mansions (Jerome; Geoffrey Babion = PL 162: 1376–1377); the net is the Christian Gospel, woven together from Old and New Testaments (for further examples, see Wailes 1987: 124–127).

The Dragnet's dualistic focus on good and bad fish lends itself to polemical use, in different contexts. Augustine cites it in support of the Catholic position against the Donatist insistence on the 'pure church':

> Anyone who knows the gospel will recognize these words and tremble.
> He sees that the nets are the church, he sees that this world is the sea;
> The different kinds of fishes are the just mixed up with the sinners;
> The shore is the end of the world: then is the time for separation.
> (Augustine, *Psalm Against the Donatists* 8–11; White 2000: 53)

In the sixteenth century, it is employed by the Jesuit Juan de Maldonado to contrast Catholic and Protestant doctrines of salvation:

> For, if we understand the Gospel, Christ signifies that not all who receive the Gospel, that is, the faith, will be saved, but they only who are the good fishes, that is, they who have not only faith, but also good works; for all are fishes, that is, all are Christians, all are faithful, but those are evil, these good. Against this, the heresy of the above teaches that all who have faith will be saved. (Maldonado 1888: 1/446)

In non-polemical contexts, this parable's similarity to the Wheat and the Tares, and the earlier connection between the call of fishermen and the apostolic mission (4:18–22), often suggests an ecclesial interpretation. Gregory the Great interprets the net as a metaphor for the church, entrusted to fishermen, and in which all kinds of people are drawn out of the sea of this present age, to be divided, i.e. judged, when they reach the shore which symbolizes the end of this age (*Homily* 9).

The Wise Householder (13:51–52)

The parables discourse concludes with a similitude likening the scribe 'discipled for the kingdom of the heavens' to a householder who produces things new and old from his treasure-chest. Despite the normal semantic domain of the Greek verb *ekballein* having to do with expulsion ('throw out'), the general tendency of early readers is to envisage the householder selecting carefully from his treasury rather than engaging in spring cleaning (Phillips 2008). This is reflected in the Vulgate's translation (*profert* = 'brings out'), and most English translations: e.g. 'bringeth forth' (Wycliffe; Geneva Bible; Douai-Rheims; KJV); 'brings out' (NIV; NRSV).

In narrative context, the obvious referent of 'the scribe' is the disciples, who claim to understand 'all these things' (13:51). In Matthew's Jewish context, scribes were tasked with opening up the treasures of wisdom (Luz 2001: 286). Jerome thinks this an appropriate description of the apostles, given that they are the 'scribes and secretaries of the Savior' (Jerome 2008: 165; also Aquinas; Maldonado). Origen thinks that it is a reference instead to actual Jewish scribes who have embraced the message of the Kingdom, while for Euthymius Zigabenus, Christ is the scribe. If disciples are scribes, then, by extension, the term can apply to a preacher or teacher of the Gospel, who can 'draw forth various things, now from the books of the Old Testament, now from the Gospel philosophy, according to the need of his audience' (Erasmus 2008: 218).

Erasmus's identification of the 'new' and 'old' as the two Testaments is regularly attested. In the second century, it serves Irenaeus well in his debate with those who deny the validity of the old covenant (*Adv. Haer.* 4.9–11). For similar reasons, it is used by the orthodox against the Manicheans (e.g. Augustine, *Seventeen Questions on Matthew* 15). An alternative is proposed by Gregory the Great: the new things are the 'delightfulness of the kingdom,' the old things the terrors of eternal punishment (*Homily* 9; Gregory the Great 1990: 66). His reading may be determined in part by his homiletic purpose, to persuade the members of his congregation whether by enticement or by fear. Origen also sets the 'new' and 'old' in opposition to each other, as the contrast between 'spirit' and 'letter.' Christ brings out of his treasury both new things, 'things spiritual,' and old things, written on stone and engraved on stony hearts. Thus, by comparison of the two, the disciple will prefer the former.

Occasionally, modern exegetes find in this passage the 'signature' of the evangelist, not Matthew the tax-collector but a converted scribe (e.g. Goulder 1974: 375). Others, wishing to preserve some connection between this Gospel and the tax-collector Matthew, note that the term has a wider sense of 'writer,' and therefore appropriate to one who worked in a customs office (see France 2007: 545). However, the words 'every scribe' would rule this out, at least as an exclusive identification.

Rejection in Christ's Own Country (13:53–58)

Matthew's parables discourse, replete with warnings of divided responses, concludes with Jesus' return to 'his home country' or 'home town' (Greek *patris*). Origen wonders whether this refers to Nazareth or Bethlehem, concluding that the choice of word is deliberate, and open to a 'mystic' meaning: it refers to the whole of Judaea, pointing to Christ's rejection by his people. Capernaum, as the town which Jesus made his home (4:13), makes good sense of the wider narrative context (it is an appropriate setting for the action in chapter 12, where his mother and brothers are present; its lakeside location fits Jesus' withdrawal in a boat at 14:13; see Nolland 2005: 574). Most, however, conclude that Nazareth is meant (e.g. Jerome; Chrysostom; Theophylact; Euthymius; Maldonado; cf. Luke 4:16–30).

The offense taken by his townsfolk is provoked by his 'wisdom' and 'mighty works,' which they find difficult to square with his being 'the son of the carpenter/artisan' (cf. Mark 6:3: 'Is this not the carpenter?'). By this they mean the son of Joseph, unaware of the virgin birth tradition disclosed to Matthew's audience (1:16, 18–25). Yet Aquinas, following Hilary, finds ironic appropriateness in this title (Latin *fabri filius* = 'the son of the craftsman'), given that Christ is the Son of the creator, the consummate craftsman (see Ps 73:16).

This passage, along with 1:25 and 12:46–50, features prominently in debates about Jesus' relatives, often shaped by belief in Mary's perpetual virginity. The eastern tradition generally followed the *Protevangelium of James*: namely, that the 'brothers' were step-brothers from Joseph's earlier marriage (e.g. *Coptic History of Joseph the Carpenter*; Epiphanius, *Anchoratus* 60.1; *Pan.* 28.7.6; 51.10.7–8; followed also in the West by Hilary). A variant is preserved by Theophylact: they are Joseph's children by the wife of his brother Cleopas, the result of a Levirate marriage.

Following Jerome, who fiercely contested Helvidius's assertion that they were the natural offspring of Mary and Joseph (*Against Helvidius* 19), and Augustine (*On the Work of Monks* 13.14; *Sermon* 51), western Christianity preferred a different solution: Joseph too was a virgin, and the 'brothers' were cousins (e.g. Peter Damian; Rupert of Deutz; Peter Lombard; Thomas Aquinas; Henry Hammond). This alternative account developed into a complex narrative whereby the mother of Mary, St. Anne, was married three times, to Joachim (the Virgin Mary's father), Cleopas, the brother of Joseph (the father of Mary Cleopas), and Salome (the father of Mary Salome). Mary Cleopas married Alphaeus, and was mother of James the Less and Joseph the Just (some lists add Simon and Jude, following 13:55). Mary Salome was the wife of Zebedee, thus making the apostles James and John cousins of Christ (see e.g. Haymo of Halberstadt, *Historiae sacrae epitome*; *Golden Legend*).

Figure 9 *The Holy Kinship*. South German (Swabian or Franconian), c. 1480–1490. Polychromed wood, 1280 × 1125 × 270 mm. Patrons' Permanent Fund, National Gallery of Art, Washington, DC. Source: Photo courtesy National Gallery of Art, Washington.

The so-called Holy Kinship is regularly depicted in pre-Reformation English medieval stained-glass (e.g. Holy Trinity Goodramgate, York; Antechapel of All Souls College, Oxford), and was an important subject in art, particularly in Germany and the Low Countries, from the late fifteenth century. It functioned as a potent matrilineal rival to the patrilineal focus of Matthew's genealogy and the Jesse Trees (see Sheingorn 1990). Anne and the three Marys are prominent, with the respective husbands in the background (Figure 9). Alternatively, each daughter is depicted separately with her father, husband, and children (e.g. Bernhard Strigel's *Saint Mary Salome and Her Family* and *Saint Mary Cleophas and Her Family*; c. 1520/1528; National Gallery of Art, Washington DC). Some versions, such as *The Holy Kinship* by Geertgen tot Sint Jans (c. 1490; Rijksmuseum, Amsterdam) also include Elizabeth, the mother of John the Baptist, believed to be the daughter of Anne's sister Hismeria.

Matthew 14–15

Ancient Literary Context

Matthew's narrative now continues in a sequence closely paralleling that of Mark (Mark 6:14–8:10). The theme of opposition and rejection remains to the fore. The 'flashback' to the death of John the Baptist (14:1–12), whose arrest was mentioned at 4:12, provides another foreshadowing of the cross (underscored by a number of phrases which will be used again in Matthew's

Matthew Through the Centuries, First Edition. Ian Boxall.

passion narrative: 'arrested,' 14:3; 26:50, 57; 'bound,' 14:3; 27:2; disciples taking the body for burial, 14:12; 27:57–61). Matthew's version is shorter and simpler, with hints of editorial 'fatigue' pointing to his reworking of Mark (Goodacre 1998: 46–47). It places blame for John's death squarely on the shoulders of Herod Antipas (Mark presents his new wife Herodias as the villain, Mark 6:19). This strengthens the parallel between John and Jesus, who was threatened at his birth by Antipas's father Herod the Great (2:16–18), and whose eventual execution in Jerusalem will be orchestrated by male religio-political leaders.

This section of the narrative contains three stories classified by form critics as 'nature miracles' (Bultmann 1968: 215–218) or 'non-therapeutic miracles' (Gerhardsson 2016: 52). The two feedings (14:13–21; 15:32–39) are very similar in structure and content, and may well be variants of the same event. Both recall a miracle performed by the prophet Elisha (2 Kgs 4:42–44), as well as God's gift of manna in the wilderness (Exod 16:11–36; Num 11). The feeding of the 5000 is followed immediately by the walking on the water (also Mark 6:45–52; John 6:16–21). Modern critics often categorize this water miracle as a theophany or epiphany rooted in Old Testament tradition (Exod 14:19–22; Job 9:8; e.g. Heil 1981), hearing in Jesus' 'it is I' or 'I AM' (14:27), the revelation of the divine name (Deut 32:29; Isa 41:4; 43:10; 45:18–19; 48:12; 51:12). But these Israelite traditions seem to be merged with Graeco-Roman traditions about the gods and 'divine men' (Luz 2001: 320).

In their present context the miraculous feedings function as a pair, arguably preparing for an expansion of the Messiah's role of feeding God's people (Ezek 34:23) to include the Gentiles (e.g. Gundry 1982: 321; though see Cousland 1999 and Luz 2001: 344–345). Sandwiched between them are a pair of contrasting narratives. One encapsulates the hostility toward Jesus of the Pharisees and scribes from Jerusalem, signifying the religious leadership of the evangelist's day (15:1–20). The second presents the persistence of a non-Israelite, whom Matthew identifies as a despised Canaanite (15:21–28; Mark calls her a Syro-Phoenician, Mark 7:26). Thus, the division within Christ's own people is combined with hints that the previously restricted mission 'to the lost sheep of the house of Israel' (10:6) will eventually be broadened to incorporate 'all the nations' (28:19). In both stories, the discussion revolves around food (handwashing before eating; the privilege of eating bread), thus providing the link between the two feeding miracles. In particular, attention to the words of the disciples and Jesus highlights the role played by the Canaanite woman in the transition from the first feeding to the second ('Send the crowds away,' 14:15; 'Send her away,' 15:23; 'I do not want to send them away hungry,' 15:32).

The Interpretations

Attention to the unfolding sequence of events, and their interrelationship, in this section of the story is not the sole preserve of modern narrative critics. For Hilary of Poitiers, the whole section from the arrest of John to the walking on the water has an inner coherence, albeit a figurative one in terms of the history of salvation. John's imprisonment parallels Israel's 'imprisoning' of the Law, signified in John's sharp rebuke to Herod of what the Law required. The daughter's dancing, using 'the enticements of the flesh,' recalls Israel's yielding to 'the seductions of pleasure' (probably a reference to dancing before the golden calf, Exod 32:6). The Law was buried with John, and the report of John's disciples to Jesus marks the transition from the Law to the Gospels. Christ then enters the church, symbolized by his boarding the ship, and retreats to a 'desert' place, where those who have withdrawn from the synagogue to the church follow him (Hilary of Poitiers 2012: 161–163).

The Death of the Baptist (14:1–12)

Several commentators appeal to 'ancient historians' for the story of John's demise, apparently having Josephus's account in mind (*Ant.* 18.5.2; e.g. Jerome). Few, however, deal head-on with the discrepancies between Josephus and the evangelists, at least until the modern period. A rare exception is found in the textual tradition, where the bilingual Codex Bezae and some Latin manuscripts omit the name 'Philip' in verse 3, apparently in conformity to Josephus's claim that Herodias's first husband was a different brother, also called Herod (see Metzger 1994: 28–29). In the sixteenth century, the Spanish Jesuit Juan de Maldonado itemizes all the differences between Josephus and the Gospels, though he opts in favor of the evangelists' version, on the grounds (dismissed by later commentators) that they are independent corroborating witnesses, as well as closer to the events. John Calvin also prefers the version in the Gospels, identifying Herodias's previous husband as Herod Philip rather than Herod king of Chalcis.

Matthew's correct designation of Antipas as 'Herod the tetrarch' (rather than Mark's 'king') is of significance within his wider narrative. Thomas Aquinas, following John Chrysostom, observes that this title both distinguishes him from and connects him to his father Herod the Great, who massacred the innocent firstborn (also Euthymius Zigabenus; Erasmus). Thus, Matthew presents a series of malevolent Herods, each of them anticipating Christ's passion. In the case of this story, Aquinas emphasizes its foreshadowing character: what happened to John would also be done to Jesus. Jerome, aware of Matthew's conviction that John was another Elijah (3:4; 11:14; 17:13), finds both Herod Antipas and Herodias also playing to Old Testament type, as a new Ahab and Jezebel (1 Kgs 2:18–24). He views Herod's 'grief' as crocodile tears; when the evangelist made this claim, he was merely following historiographical convention, articulating what Herod's guests *thought* was the case, the cunning Herod hiding his true opinion regarding John (an explanation also given in the *Golden Legend*). Others, such as Theophylact, believe Antipas' grief to be genuine, a recognition of John's virtue.

Antipas is also accorded a representative role. Theophylact observes, in light of Matthew's statement that Herod heard of Jesus' fame only at this point, how the powerful are little concerned with those, like the Baptist, who shine in virtue. Martin Luther similarly seeks to identify contemporary Herods in the Christian rulers of his day (and linking this story with Jesus' description of Antipas as a 'fox' at Luke 13:32):

> This is a picture of the leading men and magnates in the world, for they are all Herods. They put on a show of being well-disposed toward the Word, but in private they mock it and toss it away, but in such a way that they do not wish to appear to have had anyone put to death; no, indeed, they praise John and Christ and love them and desire to see them. O foxes, foxes! They deserve to be swallowed up by the earth. (*Annotations on Matthew* 14:1–2; Luther 2015: 222)

Herodias and Salome

In the event, despite Matthew's shifting of responsibility to Herod himself (v. 5), it is the two female characters who have fared worst in the subsequent reception of this story. Jerome's view of Herodias as a new Jezebel is but one example of her transformation into a *femme fatale* and enemy of God's prophet. The fourth-century *Life of John the Baptist*, attributed to the Egyptian bishop Serapion of Thmuis, describes how Herod's love for her was motivated both by her beauty and her 'diabolical artifices' (Mingana 1927: 250). Even the American suffragist Elizabeth Cady Stanton (1815–1902) succumbs. Writing in *The Woman's Bible*, she contrasts the villainous mother with her graceful daughter, faced with 'a great trial' in being forced to request the head of the Baptist. It is left to her co-editor Ellen Battelle Dietrick (1847–1895) to rehabilitate Herodias, reading the Gospels with a 'hermeneutic of suspicion' which leads her, in contrast to patristic and Reformation commentators, to prefer Josephus's version of events:

> In regard to the charge against Herodias, which is current among theological scandal-mongers, there is not a moderately intelligent jury of Christendom (if composed half of men and half of women) which, after examining all the available evidence, would not render a verdict in her favor of 'Not Guilty.'

> The statement that She 'paid the price of her own daughter's debasement and disgrace for the head of John the Baptist,' is an assertion born wholly of the ecclesiastical, distorted imagination. Not even a hint, much less an iota of proof, to warrant such an assertion, is found anywhere in history – sacred or profane. While some anonymous author of the early Christian centuries did put in circulation the charge that John the Baptist was put to death at the instigation of Herodias (without implicating her daughter's character, however), Josephus, on the contrary, explicitly declares that his death was wholly a political matter, with which the names of Herodias and her daughter are not even connected by rumor. (Stanton 1898: 119–120)

Herodias' daughter (identified as Salome by Josephus, *Ant.* 18.5.3) also has a checkered reception history, despite her ambivalent role in the Gospel text. Often the criticism focuses on the dance itself: Theophylact thinks it is unbefitting a princess to be such a skilled dancer. The story contributes to strictures against dancing, as in John Chrysostom's homily on the passage (*Homily on Matthew* 48:4; see also Ambrose, *On Virginity* 3.5–6). Some later Christian groups have followed suit in bans on social dancing (see Clarke 2003: 130–131).

Other interpreters cast a shadow on Salome's moral character. In a disturbing sermon on the story, Peter Chrysologus, fifth-century bishop of Ravenna, dehumanized the gyrating girl as little more than a wild animal:

> A creature enters the room, not a girl; a lynx, not a maiden, moves to the music. She has the mane of an animal, not hair, sprouting up from the crown of her head. She spreads out her limbs with twists and turns; she steadily grows in ferocity. She becomes cunning in cruelty, not in body. And this extraordinarily wild animal lets out a growl. (*Sermon* 127.9 in Simonetti 2002: 4)

Ambrose of Milan focuses on her 'loss of modesty,' attributing this to the influence of her adulterous mother (in Long 2013: 1155). Thomas Aquinas is typical of many in medieval and early modern discussions in accusing her of 'wantonness' (*lascivia*). Some medieval traditions emphasize the outworking of her crime against the Baptist in her own death. In one version, she slips on ice and is herself decapitated. The English Benedictine historiographer Matthew Paris (c. 1200–1259) knows an alternative legend, whereby the earth swallows her alive (see Jordan 2012: 8–10).

This negative portrait continues into the modern period. In the sixteenth century, John Calvin writes that for a girl of marriageable age to dance was 'a shameful mark of lasciviousness and harlotry' (Calvin 1972: II/142). For Martin Luther, she is 'the devil's instrument,' 'the dancing daughter' (*Annotations on Matthew* 14:1–2; Luther 2015: 224). His contemporary Desiderius Erasmus, whilst agreeing with older interpreters that Salome danced 'with lascivious gestures,' retains at least some sense of Herod's culpability in the matter. Antipas had 'grown hot with wine'; the girl was therefore able to 'take advantage of this lust of the royal breast' (Erasmus 2008: 222).

Salome in Art, Drama, and Literature

The figure of Salome comes to particular prominence in literature, drama, and visual art from the late Middle Ages onwards. In the Byzantine tradition, Salome is often depicted balancing the Baptist's head on her own head as she dances (as in a fourteenth-century mosaic lunette in the baptistery of San Marco, Venice). The scene was especially popular in Western art, given the liturgical celebration of the Baptist's beheading on 29 August, though with considerable diversity in this visual tradition (see e.g. Rodney 1953; Apostolos-Cappadona 2009; Long 2013). Giotto's *Feast of Herod* (c. 1320; Peruzzi Chapel, Florence) juxtaposes from left to right the headless corpse of John, Salome dancing before Herod, and Salome presenting John's head to her mother, as part of a cycle of frescoes presenting the Baptist's story. Giotto's depiction of the dancing girl controlled and virtually motionless, and her diminutive size on the right of the panel as she kneels before Herodias, produces 'an impression of the girl more as an obedient daughter than as an active agent in John's martyrdom' (Long 2013: 1164–1165). Rembrandt's pen drawing of *The Beheading of the Baptist* (c. 1660; Rotterdam) also presents a more sympathetic view. This focuses less on John and his executioner (the subject of Rembrandt's 1640 etching of the scene) than on the reaction of the bystanders, notably Salome, her face expressing 'all at once diffidence and puzzlement and curiosity and sadness' (Neufeld 1970: 178). The figure of Salome in Caravaggio's *The Beheading of St. John the Baptist* (1608; Saint John Museum, Valletta, Malta) is a peripheral figure, depicted 'as a paragon of modesty,' while in his *Salome Receives the Head of Saint John the Baptist* (1607–1610; National Gallery, London), she looks away from the head on the platter, as if distancing herself from the execution (Nutu 2009: 218, 220).

Other artists visualize Salome in more negative terms. Donatello's *Feast of Herod*, a bronze relief for the font in the Baptistery of San Giovanni, Siena (1425), presents a dancing Salome whose posture is 'slithery,' 'both pagan and erotic' like a dancing maenad (Long 2013: 1185). Alternatively, the presence of demons highlights the 'demon-inspired' character of her dance. In a thirteenth-century lintel carving at the entrance to the baptistery in Parma, Salome is literally pushed forward by the devil to begin her dance (Long 2013: 1160, Figure 3). In the early modern period, depictions of Salome often focus on the (male) exploration of female beauty, as in Andrea Solario's *Salome with the Head of*

John the Baptist (c. 1507–1509; Metropolitan Museum of Art, New York) and Titian's *Salome* (c. 1550; The Prado, Madrid). By contrast, Gustav Moreau's nineteenth-century *Salome and the Apparition of the Baptist's Head* (1876; Musée d'Orsay, Paris) presents her as the epitome of the *femme fatale*, bare-breasted and bejeweled.

Alternatively, visual representations shift the focus from Salome's dance to explore the wider symbolic character of the Herodian birthday banquet. Occasionally, it takes on eucharistic dimensions, an interpretation arguably derived from the narrative juxtaposition of John's death with the feeding of the 5000. In illuminations of the scene from Gospel books at Chartres (ninth century) and Bamberg (tenth or eleventh century), bread and fish are placed on Herod's table, while in the fourteenth century the round head of John often resembled the host at Mass (Janes 2006: 446).

The dance of Salome is also popular in literature and drama (see Stocker 2009). The fourteenth-century Florentine *Vita di San Giovanni Battista* knows the demonic version of the story, describing how Herodias consults with devils before hatching her plot against John, and Salome is taught 'new and delectable things' by one of the demons (Long 2013: 1161). Many modern audiences know the daughter as mediated through Oscar Wilde's 1893 play *Salomé*, which introduced the now-famous 'Dance of the Seven Veils' (see Becker-Leckrone 1995: 252–257), or the reworking of Wilde's play in Richard Strauss's 1905 opera of the same name (Santini 2011). Wilde presents her as sexually attracted to John, an interpretation derived from Heinrich Heine's 1841 poem *Atta Troll*. The play climaxes with her kissing the lips of the decapitated Baptist: 'Ah, Jokanaan, Jokanaan, thou wert the only man that I have loved. All other men are hateful to me. But thou, thou wert beautiful!' (Wilde in Skaggs 2002: 132). An attempt to redeem her character surfaces in the Hollywood movie *Salome* (1953; directed by William Dieterle), in which the girl, played by Rita Hayworth, dances in an attempt to save John's life, having been converted by his preaching (see Clarke 2003: 130).

Severed Head and Interred Body (14:11–12)

The burial of John's body by his disciples anticipates the burial of the dead Jesus, though without the accompanying hope of resurrection. Many assume that it was John's headless body which was placed in the tomb. According to Serapion's *Life of John the Baptist*, John's head flew over Jerusalem, where it cried out against Antipas' marriage for three years, then to the city of Homs in Syria where it was buried by the Christian believers (Mingana 1927: 252–253). Theophylact claims that the head was first buried at Emesa or Emissa (also John Rylands Coptic MS. No. 97; Dionysius Exiguus, *De inventione capitis*

Johannis Baptistae = PL 67: 421, 443). A different tradition is preserved in *The Golden Legend*. The head was originally buried close to Herod's palace in Jerusalem, at the instigation of Herodias. In the fifth century, following a revelation of John to two monks, it was rediscovered, and taken to Emissa where it remained in a cave. It was subsequently rediscovered by the monk Marcellus, following another vision of John, and reburied in the city's church. Subsequent travels would take John's head to Constantinople, and Poitiers in France (Jacobus de Voragine 1993: 2/137–138). Other Christian communities also made claims to possession of John's head, such that by the end of the Middle Ages there were no less than 12 rival skulls (Baert 2011: 65). Most prominent among the claimants are the Umayyad Mosque in Damascus, Amiens Cathedral, and the Church of San Silvestro in Capite, Rome.

The *Life of John the Baptist* also attests that John's body was originally buried in Sebaste (Nablus), despite his death taking place in Machaerus on the eastern shore of the Dead Sea. There it remained for 400 years, surviving Julian the Apostate's attempt to burn it, before being transferred under Athanasius to Alexandria, where it was eventually placed in a new church in honor of the Baptist (Mingana 1927: 253–257). Both Thomas Aquinas and *The Golden Legend* know the tradition of burial in Sebaste. The latter also describes rival traditions regarding the burning of John's body. Some assert that it was burned on the day of his death, with his followers partially recovering the remains. Alternatively, his bones were burned and pulverized under Julian the Apostate in an attempt to quash pilgrim devotion, with only his head being preserved. Yet another tradition asserts that some of the bones were rescued by monks as relics, and taken to Alexandria via Jerusalem, and subsequently to Genoa in Italy.

John's head plays a role in Reformation polemics over relics of the saints. The young Luther had venerated the head in San Silvestro in Capite while on pilgrimage to Rome, only subsequently to read traditions ('all Chronicles') claiming that John's body had been removed from its grave and burned by the Saracens. Hence it features in his subsequent polemic against the 'lies' of the pope, a vivid example of how he 'cheats' the people of Rome (Luther 1959: 314).

Two Miraculous Feedings (14:13–21; 15:32–39)

The two feeding miracles are distinguished by location (a desert place; a mountain) and numbers (of loaves, baskets, and people). The instinct of early interpreters is to explore the symbolic dimensions of these stories. Several (e.g. Hilary) anticipate modern narrative critics in finding a progression in the dual feedings from exclusive focus on Israel ('the children') to incorporation of the Gentile 'dogs,' a process in which the Canaanite woman (15:21–28) plays a key transitional role. Origen, by contrast, interprets the two miracles as signifying two different stages in Christian maturity:

> The Lord fed the multitudes twice. Those whom He first feeds, that is the beginners, He feeds with barley loaves, but afterwards, when they had now advanced in the word and teaching, He set before them wheaten loaves (i.e. higher teaching). (Origen, *Hom. in Gen.* 12.5 in Smith 1925–1929: III/97–98)

The loaves (i.e. the letter of scripture) need to be broken up, in order that something of their meaning might reach the multitudes, and what they cannot consume is gathered to prevent it from being lost.

Yet the rich texture of these feeding miracles opens up other interpretative possibilities (see Luz 2001: 312–313). Unsurprisingly, homilies and other paraenetic texts explore the moral lesson of the stories. Clement of Alexandria (*Paed.* 2.1.13) finds in the feeding miracle an example of frugality, given that Christ provided a feast with loaves and broiled fish, while for Theophylact it teaches the need to share in hospitality the little that we have. For John Chrysostom, the moral lesson is threefold:

> As well by the place therefore, as by His giving them nothing more than loaves and fishes, and by setting the same before all, and making it common, and by affording no one more than another, He was teaching them humility, and temperance, and charity, and to be of like mind one towards another, and to account all things common. (*Homily on Matthew* 49; *NPNF* 1st series, 10:306)

Such moral lessons are rooted in the recognition that, in the miracle, God is caring for his people's bodily needs. Christ multiplies the loaves and fishes to demonstrate that he is the creator, and the one who provides what humans eat (so Theophylact). Thus, there is an implicit fulfillment of the petition for 'daily bread' in the Lord's Prayer (6:11). Others draw the contrary lesson that 'Man does not live by bread alone.' John Chrysostom, reading the first miracle in light of John's version ('you seek me not because you saw signs …' John 6:26), explains why Matthew's Gospel contains only two miraculous feedings: 'Therefore neither does He work this miracle continually, but a second time only; that they might be taught not to be slaves to their belly, but to cling incessantly to the things of the Spirit' (*Homily on Matthew* 49; *NPNF* 1st series, 10:306). Erasmus interprets the bread as 'the simple gospel teaching' that 'apostolic men' were to give to the people (Erasmus 2008: 227).

Concern for spiritual food leads some to interpret the feedings eucharistically (e.g. Ambrose, *In Luc.* 6.94; Theophylact; though this seems to have been a marginal reading in the early church: Luz 2001: 313). Textual evidence for such a reading is found in scribal attempts to conform 15:35–36 and 26:25–26 (Matthew's Last Supper account) more closely to each other. The eucharistic connection is particularly evident in a liturgical context, as in the 'Kontakion on the Five Loaves,' by the sixth-century Syrian Romanos the Melodist. This appeals to the miraculous feeding in order to exhort the faithful to 'approach with fervour the mystic bread':

> Everyone has come to hear yet once again how the Gospels cry out,
> and to marvel at Jesus. For he ineffably
> once nourished five thousand in the wilderness;
> fearsome wonder, full of all amazement!
> For the Saviour took five loaves, as it is written,
> and, from them, nourished these thousands,
> and all were completely filled by the ineffable Wisdom.
> For they did not need a multitude of loaves,
> since Christ was present, who is
> *the heavenly bread of incorruption.*
>
> (Romanos the Melodist 1995: 90)

Renewed interest in the literal sense renders the stories particularly problematic in the age of Enlightenment. Heinrich Eberhard Gottlob Paulus's rationalist interpretation (proposed in 1828), whereby the production of five loaves and two fish provoked members of the crowd to share their own picnics, is widely repeated. Its influence is evident on Lloyd C. Douglas's 1942 novel *The Robe*, where an eyewitness to the original feeding later reminisces to the tribune Marcellus:

> Well – no, sir. We didn't laugh, though almost everyone smiled over such a big crowd being fed on almost nothing, as you might say. As I told you, I had been ashamed to bring out the food I had, and now I was ashamed not to; so I unwrapped my bread and fish, and broke off a piece, and offered it to the man next to me. (Douglas 1999: 282)

Albert Schweitzer rejects such a naturalistic explanation, concluding instead that the whole story is historical with the exception of the concluding remark, namely, that all were 'satisfied.' Everyone received 'a very little'; the true significance lies in 'the giving of thanks and in the fact that they had received consecrated food from' the future Messiah, i.e. they had participated unwittingly in the messianic feast (Schweitzer 2000: 338).

The Significance of Numbers

Attention to numerical symbolism is common to both ancient and modern interpreters, and often feeds into salvation-historical interpretations. For Hilary of Poitiers, the five loaves represent the five books of Torah, the two fish the preaching of the prophets and John the Baptist, and the 12 baskets the 12 apostles. The 5000 matches the number of Israelites who believed the gospel at Acts 4:4. Jerome concurs that the number five stands for the Law, though is less sure whether the two fish symbolize the two Testaments, or are another symbol for the Law (on the grounds, which he does not explain, that two is an even number). The number of baskets was to ensure that each apostle received one. Theophylact will later draw out the logical conclusion: this included Judas Iscariot, though he later failed to remember the miracle when he betrayed Jesus. Theophylact continues the earlier instinct to allegorize, albeit arriving at some different conclusions. Thus the 5000 represent those who are sick in their five senses. The two fish symbolize the words of the fishermen, i.e. the Gospel and the Epistles (presumably he means John and Peter). Thomas Aquinas distinguishes between the literal meaning of the numbers, and their mystical sense. On the literal level, the small number of loaves and fish reveal the detachment of the apostles from earthly concerns, and their wholehearted attachment to the word of God. Figuratively, he follows many of his predecessors in identifying the five loaves with the Mosaic Law; the two fish stand for the Psalms and the prophets.

The numbers associated with the feeding of the 4000 receive a similar treatment. Hilary is an early example of those who find here an anticipation of Gentile conversion. There are seven loaves and seven baskets, he argued, because the pagans do not receive salvation by the Law and the prophets, but by the sevenfold grace of the Spirit (see Isa 11:2–3). That Matthew is not specific over the number of fish in this second feeding ('a few') points to the manifold charisms that the Spirit distributes. The 4000 people represent the multitude gathered from the four parts of the earth, anticipating the future spread of the church. Jerome is less precise, although his comments also imply universality: he notes that seven is a perfect number, while four symbolizes stability, like the fourfold Gospel. For Theophylact, followed by Aquinas, the 4000 signify those who have become perfect in the four universal or cardinal virtues (courage, prudence, justice, and self-control). Like Hilary, Theophylact sees in the seven loaves and baskets the seven gifts of the Spirit. Aquinas elaborates further: the seven loaves signify the new law of Christ, formed by the sevenfold gift.

Matthew's concluding comment about the numbers present at each feeding ('without women and children,' 14:21; 15:38), unique to his Gospel, piques the interest of many. The phrase is potentially ambiguous, leading some to the unlikely conclusion that no women or children were present (an interpretation known to Origen). Jerome, widely followed by Western commentators (e.g. *Glossa ordinaria*; Aquinas) is embarrassingly dismissive: women, as the 'fragile sex,' and children as of a lesser age, are not worthy to be counted. The *Glossa* adds a figurative interpretation: these signify the weak in faith (*infirmos in fide*), who are not yet ready for battle. By contrast, Eastern commentators such as Euthymius Zigabenus read the reference in a more positive sense. The expanded number makes the miracle all the more impressive.

Walking on the Water (14:22–33)

The first feeding is closely connected to the nature miracle which follows it (surprisingly omitted by Luke). The theophanic character of the story is noted by Aquinas, who appeals to Psalm 88:10 (where the Lord rules the power of the sea), and Psalms 73:14 and 103:26 (referring to the defeat of the sea dragon). He also points to the revelation of the divine name to Moses (Exod 3:14) as illuminating Christ's 'It is I' or 'I AM' (14:27). A similar intertextual relationship is often identified by modern commentators (e.g. Heil 1981; Davies and Allison 1991: 506), though many struggle with the historical character of this story. Some follow Heinrich Eberhard Gottlob Paulus in positing alternative, rationalist explanations, based on an ambiguity in the Greek. The Scottish New Testament scholar William Barclay (1907–1978) offers this possibility in his *Daily Study Bible*:

> The truth is that there are two perfectly possible interpretations of this passage, so far as the actual Greek goes. It may describe a miracle in which Jesus actually walked on the water. Or, it may equally mean that the disciples' boat was driven by the wind to the northern shore of the lake, that Jesus came down from the mountain to help them when he saw them struggling in the moonlight, and that he came walking through the surf and the waves towards the boat, and came so suddenly upon them that they were terrified when they saw him. Both of these interpretations are equally valid. Some will prefer one, and some the other. (Barclay 1975: 105)

Yet older interpreters are often as interested in the disciples in the boat, giving the story a similar ecclesiological interpretation to the calming of the storm (8:23–27). For the fifth-century Roman monk Arnobius Iunior, the ship is the church, buffeted by persecution, the 'contrary wind' being the devil who opposes the church (*Expositiunculae in Matthaeum* 18 in Kraszewski 1999: 324). Similarly, Aquinas interprets the story as ecclesial experience after Christ's ascension, when his people are tossed about in the sea of the world. Hilary of Poitiers' reading locates the church's story at the very end of salvation history, taking a cue from the timing of Christ's appearance on the waves. The fourth watch of the night (i.e. between 3 and 6 a.m.) is an appropriate time for the Lord's final coming to his church, following the first (the time of the Law), the second (the prophets), and the third (Christ's coming in flesh). The buffeting of wind and waves describes the effect of the spirit of Antichrist, expected in the last days. The calm 'indicates the peace and tranquility of the Church eternal after his return in glory' (Hilary of Poitiers 2012: 169).

Peter Walks Toward Jesus (14:28–31)

Unique to Matthew is the vignette describing Peter's attempt to emulate his Lord. Hilary understands the story as prefiguring Peter's role in the passion narrative: initially forsaking the world (the waves) and following the Lord, but then wavering (his denial), before crying out to the Lord to save him (his repentance). Others emphasize the positive dimension of his request: it reveals his pre-eminent love for Christ (Chrysostom; Theophylact), or the fervor of his faith (Jerome; Aquinas).

In the Middle Ages, the passage often reflects Catholic conviction that Peter's role continues in his successors, the bishops of Rome. Particularly striking is Bernard of Clairvaux's *De Consideratione* 2.8.16 (PL 182: 752), whereby the sea is understood as rulers, magistrates, bishops, and churches upon which the pope treads as Peter trod water. From the Reformation onwards, receptions of this scene often closely mirror the confessional stances of their proponents vis-à-vis papal claims to continue the Petrine ministry. The Catholic tendency is to see a Peter who is 'brave and devoted,' albeit one subsequently rebuked for his doubt, while Protestants perceive Peter's actions as 'hasty, presumptuous and foolish' (Nicholls 2008: 169). Thus, the Catholic humanist scholar Desiderius Erasmus develops John Chrysostom's view:

> Peter, indeed, who always burned with a certain singular love for Jesus, believing that nothing at all that Jesus bade was difficult to do, saith: 'Lord, if it is you, bid me to come to you over the waters.' (Erasmus 2008: 229)

Peter's faith only wavered when he took his eyes off Jesus. By contrast, John Calvin reads the very same words as evidence that Peter's faith was not yet mature, and that in stepping out of the boat he was attempting to 'fly without the wings of faith' (Calvin 1972: II/153). However, his fellow Reformer Martin Luther bucks the trend. Luther finds a Peter motivated by zeal and love, only subsequently wavering in faith. He thereby fulfills an exemplary role for Christians, albeit those who have grasped the Gospel message of *sola gratia*:

> Peter is depicted for us in this way so that we might not be presumptuous, even if we have made a good start in faith, but may fear God and, despairing for ourselves and our own powers, cry out and always ask for grace alone. (*Annotations on Matthew* 14:31; Luther 2015: 232)

Peter as exemplar of faithful Christians amid the storms of life is also the dominant theme in *Olney Hymns* 87, composed by John Newton:

> To Peter on the waves he came,
> And gave him instant peace;
> Thus he to me revealed his name,
> And bid my sorrows cease.
>
> Then filled with wonder, joy and love,
> Peter's request was mine;
> LORD, call me down, I long to prove
> That I am wholly thine.
>
> Unmoved at all I have to meet
> On life's tempestuous sea;
> Hard, shall be easy; bitter, sweet,
> So I may follow thee.

The story is attested in Christian art from an early period. The scene of Peter coming to Jesus on the water is found in one of the third-century Christian frescoes which adorned the Christian baptistery at Dura Europos (Yale University Art Gallery), giving the scene a baptismal focus. However, art historians are divided over whether Peter is the lower figure of the two, raising his hand to Christ in the moment of sinking, or (as is more likely, given the Christlike clothing of the left-hand figure) the higher figure to the right, the fresco thus depicting Peter's successful walking on the water (Peppard 2011: 171). The former view may be unduly influenced by later Western depictions of the scene, the latter reflects the positive image of water in eastern baptismal theology (Nicholls 2008: 135–144).

Arguably the most famous visual interpretation is Giotto's *Navicella*, produced c. 1305–1313 for Old St. Peter's in Rome, now surviving in its reworked form by Orazio Manenti for the current St. Peter's Basilica, 1674–1675 (Köhren-Jansen 1993; Nicholls 2008: 161–170). Peter is depicted in the water to the right, reaching out to Christ. At the center is the 'little ship' of the church, steered by Paul on the left, meaning that the two apostle-martyrs of the Roman church frame the boat. Produced in the wake of the Holy Year of 1300, and around the time of Clement V's departure for Avignon, it serves to legitimate the threatened papacy. Hence the earthly Peter (or Peter's papal successor), stretching out in faith, is supported by the intercession of the heavenly St. Peter in the top right of the frame.

Dispute Over Handwashing (15:1–20)

Returning to the Galilean side of the lake at Gennesaret (14:34), the Jewish Jesus (with a 'tassel' on his prayer-shawl: 14:36) again encounters hostility from Jewish leaders, specifically the Pharisees and scribes (15:1). Yet, as the gulf between Gentile church and Jewish synagogue solidifies, readers of Matthew 15 forget the intra-Jewish character of this controversy story. Instead, it often becomes paradigmatic of the Jews' 'opposition' to the divine will, or of supposed Jewish prioritizing external over internal purity (e.g. Chrysostom).

Yet there are exegetical alternatives. This passage has often functioned as an internal critique for the Christian community. Taking its cue from Jesus' words in verse 7 ('You hypocrites'), *1 Clement* directs the quotation from Isaiah (Isa 29:13) toward hypocritical Christians:

> Therefore let us unite with those who devoutly practice peace, and not with those who hypocritically wish for peace. For somewhere it says, 'This people honors me with their lips, but their heart is far from me.' (*1 Clem.* 15:1–2; Holmes 2007: 65)

The passage is also regularly appealed to as a warning against heretics and schismatics. The longer recension of Ignatius of Antioch's *Letter to the Trallians* uses Jesus' words in verse 13 ('Every plant which my heavenly Father has not planted will be uprooted') against a succession of heretics (Simon, Menander, Basilides; the Nicolaitans), and Christians who are 'ashamed of the passion' (Ignatius, *Trallians* 11, longer version; *ANF* 1:71). For Cyprian of Carthage, Christ's warning against 'blind guides' (15:14) encompasses those who threaten the unity of Christ's people (*De unitate* 17). Theophylact knows a controversial Manichaean interpretation of the passage, whereby the 'uprooting' refers to the commandments of the Law.

The application of this controversy story to intra-ecclesial matters, and to those considered heretical, continues into the medieval and modern periods.

The Fourth Lateran Council of 1215 appeals to 15:14 in addressing the widespread ignorance of the clergy (Lateran IV, Canon 27):

> To guide souls is a supreme art. We therefore strictly order bishops carefully to prepare those who are to be promoted to the priesthood and to instruct them, either by themselves or through other suitable persons, in the divine services and the sacraments of the church, so that they may be able to celebrate them correctly. But if they presume henceforth to ordain the ignorant and unformed, which can indeed easily be detected, we decree that both the ordainers and those ordained are to be subject to severe punishment. For it is preferable, especially in the ordination of priests, to have a few good ministers than many bad ones, for if *a blind man* leads *another blind man, both* will fall *into the pit*. (Lateran IV, *Canon* 27 in Tanner 1990: I/248)

The Italian poet Dante Alighieri (c. 1265–1321) equates 'the tradition of the elders' (15:2) with ecclesiastical traditions, specifically papal decretals (a critique also made in fourteenth-century England by John Wycliffe: Levy 2007: 160), in his political treatise *De Monarchia*:

> Subordinate to the Church are the traditions called Decretals, which, while they must be revered for their apostolic authority, must nevertheless be held unquestionably inferior to the fundamental Scriptures, seeing that Christ rebuked the priests for not doing so. When they had inquired, 'Why do thy disciples transgress the tradition of the elders?' (for they had omitted the washing of hands) Christ answered, as Matthew testifies, 'Why do ye also transgress the commandment of God by your tradition?' Here the inferiority of tradition is clearly implied. (*De Monarchia* 3.3.10; Dante 1904: 146–147)

The Lutheran *Augsburg Confession* of 1530 cites this passage in support of rescinding monastic vows as 'human commandments': 'Every service of God that is instituted and chosen by men to merit justification and grace without the command of God is wicked, as Christ says, "In vain do they worship me with the precepts of men"' (*Augsburg Confession* 27:36 in Pelikan and Hotchkiss 2003: 101). John Calvin, meanwhile, finds the Pharisees and scribes actualized in the sixteenth-century papacy, which in his view places rules concerning fasting and abstinence over the weightier matters of the Law:

> The Pope, along with all the dirty rabble of his clergy, does not deny that God must be obeyed. But when it comes to the point, they detest an ordinary meal of meat as a capital crime, whereas theft or adultery is only a venial fault for them. And in this they overturn God's Law for the sake of their traditions. (Calvin 1972: II/160)

FIGURE 10 Pieter Brueghel the Elder (c. 1525–1569). *Parable of the Blind Leading the Blind*. 1568. Tempera on canvas, 860 × 1540 mm. Museo Nazionale di Capodimonte, Naples. Source: Photo Scala/Ministero per i Beni e le Attività culturali/Art Resource, NY.

Perhaps the most famous visual interpretation of the parable at the heart of this passage (15:13–14; cf. Luke 6:39) is Pieter Brueghel the Elder's 1568 *The Parable of the Blind Leading the Blind* (Figure 10). Six figures, each with a different eye condition, stumble forward in procession, with a church (identified as Sint-Anna Church in the Flemish village of Sint-Anna-Pede) in the background. The first two, who have already passed the church, stumble into a ditch. The painting has produced divergent interpretations, reflecting differing views of Brueghel's theological stance at a time of persecution of Protestants by the Spanish rulers of the Netherlands. For some, the church functions as a sign of the mediating role of the Catholic Church: the first two men are beyond redemption, but there is hope for the remaining four. The painting may contain an implicit critique of contemporary Protestant iconoclasm. Or the blind leaders may represent failing priests, their purses and staffs revealing a failure to heed Christ's command to his apostles (10:9–10). Alternatively, given the withered tree depicted outside the church, Bruegel is expressing anti-Catholic, possibly Calvinist sympathies. The Catholic Church itself would then be the 'blind guide' leading the blind (see e.g. Lindsay and Huppé 1956; Hamilton 2007).

The Canaanite Woman and Her Daughter (15:21–28)

Matthew's version of this story is more developed than the Markan parallel (Mark 7:24–30; see Good 1991; Lawrence 2009; Klancher 2013). Not only does Matthew identify the woman as a 'Canaanite,' a sworn enemy of Israel, whose predecessors were victims of divinely approved genocide (see Josh 3:10; 13:1–7). Jesus' initial rebuff occurs three times, not once, moving from silence (15:23), to the assertion of his ministry to the 'lost sheep of the house of Israel' (15:24), to his statement about not giving the children's bread to dogs (15:26; cf. Mark 7:27). Moreover, Matthew accords a role in the encounter to the disciples, who further compound the woman's difficulties by urging Jesus to 'Send her away' (15:23). On the other hand, this serves to underscore the woman's tenacity, leading to an explicit affirmation of the greatness of her faith (15:28; cf. Mark 7:29).

This faithful woman remains anonymous in the text. However, in the Pseudo-Clementine *Homilies* (2.19), she is called Justa, and, as befits the text's Jewish-Christian provenance, is depicted as the archetypal Jewish proselyte, rejecting her former life and embracing the Mosaic Law, thus appropriately sharing in the children's bread. For Origen, she symbolizes the progress of the human soul as she 'comes out' from a place of humiliation to healing. Similar sentiments are expressed by Origen's student Didymus the Blind, commenting on Zechariah 14:21 ('And there will no longer be any Canaanites in the house of the Lord Almighty on that day'):

> No one is evil by nature, as some heretics think; the proof that a change of (spiritual) state is an effect of the Will can be drawn from the Gospel, since the Canaanite woman became a woman again, from the dog that she was, when He who saved her named her his daughter in pronouncing these words: 'My daughter, your faith has saved you.' (*In Zach.* 5.210–211 in Klancher 2013: 73)

More commonly, she is interpreted not as a Jewish convert but a representative of Gentile Christianity (e.g. Ambrose; Isho'dad of Merv; Theophylact; see Klancher 2013: 81–88, 102–103). Unfortunately, this is often presented in supersessionist terms, as though the woman's acceptance now means a role reversal in which the Jewish 'children' have now become the 'dogs' (e.g. Epiphanius the Latin, *Interpretation of the Gospels* 58). Shakespeare's Shylock thus plays to type (or caricature) when he exclaims: 'Thou call'dst me dog before thou hadst a cause; / but since I am a dog, beware my fangs' (*The Merchant of Venice*, Act 3, Scene 3).

Jerome is explicit in viewing the woman as a figure of the church, called from the nations, and marked by the virtues of faith, patience, and humility (also Theophylact). Her humility is manifest not least in her willingness to accept the title 'dog.' A variant is found in Hilary, for whom it is not the woman herself (who is a proselyte), but her daughter who symbolizes the Gentiles. As an exemplar of faith, interpreters instinctively read back into the woman's story subsequent Christological developments. Thus, her address to Christ is understood as manifesting faith in his divinity ('Lord') and humanity ('Son of David': e.g. Aquinas). That a Canaanite would acclaim him by the Judean title 'Son of David' is particularly puzzling, leading Calvin to conclude that the woman must have had some knowledge of Davidic promises, their 'odour' having spread into Gentile territory. It is preeminently her faith, but also her humility and capacity to transgress boundaries, which leads Chaucer's Second Nun to compare herself to the Canaanite woman (see Dobbs 2013):

> Thynk on the womman Cananee, that sayde
> That whelpes eten somme of the crommes alle
> That from hir lordes table been yfalle;
> And though that I, unworthy sone of Eve,
> Be synful, yet accepte my bileve.
> (*Prologue* to the *Second Nun's Tale*, lines 57–63)

John Newton expresses in poetry how this 'dog' acts out of character to manifest the faith of the 'children':

> Yet although from Canaan sprung,
> Though a dog herself she styled;
> She had Israel's faith and tongue,
> And was owned for Abraham's child.
> (*Olney Hymns* 88)

Jesus' desire to draw attention to the Canaanite woman's faith, or even increase it, is one common explanation given for his initial rebuff (e.g. Ephrem, *C. Diat.* 12.13; Chrysostom; Theophylact; Aquinas). For Bede, this has an exemplary function: 'in order to demonstrate to us the perseverance of this woman that we can always imitate' (*Homilies on the Gospels* I.22; Bede the Venerable 1991: 216). Commentators are also concerned to point out that Christ does not contradict himself, hence the appeal back to his teaching about not going in the way of Gentiles (10:5; e.g. Hilary; Aquinas). The Gentile mission belongs to the apostolic period; the issue, then, is one of timing, not of divine will.

Perhaps the most surprising explanation, however, is that the delay provides an opportunity for the disciples to intercede on her behalf (Hilary;

Theophylact; Aquinas). This requires an optimistic reading of their request to 'Send her away' (Greek *apoluson autēn*; Vulgate *dimitte eam*), which ill befits the reason given ('for she is crying out after us'). Such a reading is attested in the *Hebrew Gospel of Matthew*, preserved in the fourteenth-century treatise of the Jewish scholar Shem-Tob:

> So his disciples approached him and said to him: Our master, why do you abandon the woman who is crying out after us? (Howard 1995: 75)

Aquinas is aware of the difficulty, forcing him to clarify that the disciples' actual words obscure their true concern: 'And this is a manner of speaking (*modus loquendi*), for when we intend one thing, the contrary is said' (Aquinas 2013b: 79). John Calvin is closer to the text, noting that the disciples find her a nuisance and fail to intercede on her behalf. He also dismisses Catholic attempts to use this passage in support of seeking the intercession of the saints.

Modern critics, while accepting that, like the centurion of Capernaum (8:5–13), the woman is a model of Gentile faith ('the apostolic "foremother" of all gentile Christians': Schüssler Fiorenza 1983: 138), nonetheless present more nuanced perspectives on this story. Some observe how patristic and medieval exegesis, reflecting the separation of Gentile church from Jewish synagogue, underestimates the extent to which, for Matthew, the church emerges out of and is rooted in Israel (e.g. Levine 1988; Sim 1998; Lawrence 2009: 262). Postcolonial critics resist the longstanding temptation to turn this Canaanite, with her own ancestral faith traditions, into a Christian convert (e.g. Pui-lan 1995: 71–83). Feminist critics have challenged the emphasis on the woman's humility, not least because it downplays the active role she plays in challenging Jesus (Wainwright 1994; Lawrence 2009: 269–271; Luz 2001: 341). While praising Jesus' 'patience with women,' Elizabeth Cady Stanton nonetheless highlights the woman's intellectual prowess: 'The woman of Canaan proved herself quite equal in argument with Jesus' (Stanton 1898: 121). Given the lack of reference to her husband (though see Pseudo-Clementine *Hom.* 2.19–21), some even find in her story the courage of a single mother (Dickerson 2013).

As a consequence of the Canaanite woman's persistence, the Gentiles are able to receive the children's 'bread,' variously understood as the teaching of the Gospel (Theodore of Mopsuestia, *Frag.* 83 in Reuss 1957: 126; Maldonado), the divine word spoken through Moses and the prophets (Christian of Stavelot, PL 106:1390), or the Eucharist (Tertullian, *On Prayer* 6). The latter interpretation is familiar to generations of Anglican Christians, nurtured by Thomas Cranmer's 1548 *Prayer of Humble Access*:

> We do not presume to come to this thy table, O Merciful Lord, trusting in our own righteousness, but in thy manifold and great mercies: we be not worthy so much as to gather up the crumbs under thy table: but thou are the same Lord, whose property is always to have mercy …

In Armenian Christianity, the Canaanite woman supplies the voice for the monastic poet-saint Gregory of Narek (951–1003):

> In the voice of the Canaanite woman,
> I pray from the bottom of my heart,
> like a starving dog yelping, wretched and anxious, begging for scraps,
> a few crumbs of the bread of life,
> from your bountiful table.
> (*Book of Lamentations,* Prayer 35 in Samuelian 2001: 285).

Matthew 16

Ancient Literary Context

The narrative continues with a further rupture in the relationship between Jesus and the leaders of Israel, and a stronger indication that the latter will eventually be replaced. The chapter is dominated by the much-disputed Confession of Peter (16:13–20; see Rigaux 1967; Brown, Donfried, and Reumann 1974: 83–101; Caragounis 1990; Davies and Allison 1991: 602–643; Luz 2001: 353–377; Bockmuehl 2012: 73–77), located in the district of Caesarea Philippi, the northern Gentile city of Paneas. This pronouncement story functions as a key narrative turning-point in all three Synoptic Gospels (Mark 8:27–30; Luke 9:18–21). Like Matthew's account of the Walking on the Water (14:22–33), his version of the Confession is expanded by the incorporation of special Petrine traditions. What in Mark is presented as a misunderstanding is here understood as divine revelation (16:17). Simon Peter correctly identifies Jesus as both 'Messiah' and 'Son of the living God,' recalling promises to the house of David (2 Sam 7; 1 Chron 17). In response, Simon too is given a new name (like Abraham, Gen 17:1–8; cf. Isa 51:1–2), and a new role (like Eliakim, steward of the royal house in Isa 22:22), in relation to the church which Christ is to build (recalling Solomon's building the temple, 1 Kgs 6; 2 Chron 3; Barber 2013).

The Semitic-sounding character of Jesus' words to Peter (16:17–19, e.g. 'flesh and blood,' 'rock'/'Peter,' connected to the Aramaic *kephā*'; 'gates of Hades [i.e. Sheol]') have led some to the conclusion that the whole is an authentic dominical saying, or that its origins lie in a post-Easter commissioning of Peter. Others prefer that it reflects a later reworking of originally independent Jesus sayings, together with post-resurrection traditions, whether by Aramaic-speaking or Greek-speaking Christians; still others posit Matthew's own redactional work, given the absence of these verses in Mark and Luke (see Robinson 1984; Davies and Allison 1991: 604–605; Luz 2001: 355–360). Those who posit a Syrian, and especially an Antiochene, provenance for the First Gospel locate these special Petrine traditions there, recalling Peter's earlier association with that city (Streeter 1924: 500–523; Brown and Meier 1983: 64–68).

The Interpretations

The Leaven of the Pharisees and Sadducees (16:1–12)

Two interwoven pericopae sharpen the negative characterization of the 'Pharisees and Sadducees.' The irony that two bitterly opposed groups are here united in their opposition to Jesus is not lost on commentators (e.g. Origen; Theophylact; Erasmus). Jesus' temptation by the devil is resumed as these two groups request a sign, 'testing him.' Jesus' response, as previously to the scribes and Pharisees, is to promise the sign of Jonah, i.e. his death and resurrection (on the Sign of Jonah, see above on 12:38–45). Indeed, this encounter marks a narrative breach between Christ and his opponents, as he now withdraws (16:4), not to meet either group again until his arrival in Judea (19:3; 22:23; see Luz 2001: 348).

Verses 2–3 (cf. Luke 12:54–56) are absent from many manuscripts, as Jerome notes in his commentary, though he includes them in the Vulgate (for varying text-critical assessments, see Metzger 1994: 33; Luz 2001: 347). Their absence is not due to difficulty of interpretation, however. The meaning is all too clear: though the scribes and Pharisees are skilled weather forecasters, they are incapable of discerning from the prophets about the coming of the Savior (e.g. Jerome), or the time for salvation of souls (e.g. Erasmus). The 'signs of the times' here are critical eschatological signs associated with the Messiah's coming.

In the mid-twentieth century, the phrase was famously adopted, though with a different nuance, by the Second Vatican Council's Pastoral Constitution on the Church in the Modern World, *Gaudium et Spes* (1965). Here it describes the church's task of identifying signs of God's presence (or absence) in significant historical events, as it seeks to perpetuate the mission of Christ in the world:

> To discharge this function, the church has the duty in every age of examining the signs of the times and interpreting them in the light of the gospel, so that it can offer in a manner appropriate to each generation replies to the continual human questionings on the meaning of this life and the life to come and how they are related. There is a need, then, to be aware of, and to understand, the world in which we live, together with its expectations, its desires and its frequently dramatic character. (*Gaudium et Spes* 4; Tanner 1990: II/1070)

The second section (16:5–12) functions as a warning to the disciples against the 'leaven of the Pharisees and Sadducees.' Matthew explains what Jesus means, though without amplification: their leaven is their teaching (cf. Luke 12:1: 'hypocrisy'). Interpreters seek to clarify further. For many, it is their interpretation of the Mosaic Law (e.g. Jerome; Lapide), for others the corruption of their teaching by ambition, greed, or similar vices (e.g. Erasmus). Some look for contemporary actualizations. Luther urges his contemporaries to 'Beware of the leaven of the Papists' whose desire to rule the church parallels the dominance of Pharisees and Sadducees over the synagogue (Luther 2015: 270). From the Catholic side, Juan de Maldonado sees the 'leaven' present in the unlikely alliance of Lutherans and Calvinists, who 'very widely differ among themselves, but conspire against the Catholic Church; that is, the Body of Christ' (Maldonado 1888: 2/25).

Peter's Confession (16:13–20)

This passage is one of the most disputed in the whole of scripture, given its use both in support of and opposition to the developing institution of the papacy (for its reception history, see e.g. Taheny 1961: 17–35; Cullmann 1962: 164–176;

Ramm 1962; Burgess 1976; Bigane 1981; Timiadis 1983; Froehlich 1989; Ocker 1991; Luz 2001: 373–377; Clarke 2003: 138–147; Crosby 2008). Matthew's version is fuller than in Mark or Luke. Peter acclaims Jesus not merely as the Messiah/Christ (Luke: 'Messiah/Christ of God'), but as 'the Christ, the Son of the living God,' the latter phrase contrasting Israel's God with the 'dead' gods of the Gentiles (e.g. Jerome; Calvin). The Confession has regularly functioned as a proof-text in theological debates about the Trinity and the person of Christ. The juxtaposition of 'son of the living God' and 'my Father in heaven' is cited in support of the distinction of persons in the Godhead (Tertullian, *Adv. Prax.* 21; Novatian, *Trinity* 26). Peter's confession of Christ's divinity is central to the exegesis of this passage by the fourth-century Cappadocians Basil the Great, Gregory of Nazianzus, and Gregory of Nyssa in their battles with the Arians (see Taheny 1961: 20–21). Alternatively, his two-part confession is interpreted in terms of a two-natures Christology, 'Christ' describing his humanity, 'Son of the living God' his divinity (e.g. Maximus of Turin, *Sermons* 37).

Matthew's Jesus declares Peter's words an act of divine revelation (e.g. *Ps.-Clem. Hom.* 17:18; Justin, *Trypho* 100.4), provoking a blessing of Peter in return. This is accompanied by a change of name, from Simon bar-Jona to Peter/Rock. Jerome is one early commentator who discusses the etymology of bar-Jona, which he interprets as 'son of the dove' (also e.g. Pseudo-Bede; Rabanus Maurus; Aquinas). He is also aware of ancient commentators who think this to be a corruption of 'son of John' (as in John 21:16; modern proponents include e.g. Luz 2001: 362). The positive Matthean view of Peter is challenged by the Coptic *Gospel of Thomas,* where it is Thomas, rather than Peter, who makes the correct profession (*Gos. Thom.* 13). Several note the oddity of this section's absence from Mark's account, given the traditional connection between Mark and Peter. Eusebius hints that the reason for Mark's silence regarding the latter is due to modesty on Peter's part (Eusebius, *Dem. Evang.* 3.5).

On This Rock I Will Build My Church (16:18)

In contrast to 18:17, the reference seems to be to the whole church, Christ's holy people, built as a new temple by Christ the new Solomon (cf. 1QS 8.5–10; 4QpPs 37 3.16; Gal 2:9; 1 Cor 3:9–17; Eph 2:20–22; 1 Pet 2:5). But the precise identification of the 'rock,' and the implications of this for the post-apostolic church, have proved controversial. What has become in modern times 'the Roman Catholic view' of the passage is that the pun *petra/Petros* identifies Peter himself as the rock on which the church is built. This interpretation is dramatically visualized in St. Peter's Basilica in Rome, built on the traditional site of Peter's tomb, where the Vulgate translation of 16:18 (*Tu es Petrus et super hanc petram aedificabo ecclesiam meam*) is inscribed inside the dome in letters six feet high. Yet it was only one interpretation among several in the patristic period and Middle Ages. Nor, on the other hand, have non-Roman Catholics always rejected it out of hand. Some modern Protestant New Testament scholars, such as W.D. Davies and Dale Allison, present this as the 'most natural interpretation' of the phrase, while the Lutheran church historian Karlfried Froehlich speaks of 'the clear Petrine meaning of the verse' (Davies and Allison 1991: 627; Froehlich 1989: 12). This does not, however, necessarily commit them to the further view that Peter-as-rock validates a specific Petrine ministry across the centuries.

The Petrine interpretation of the 'rock' is attested in the Jewish-Christian Pseudo-Clementine *Homilies* (possibly third century), where Peter's apostolic authority, based on direct association with Christ, is contrasted with the claim of Simon Magus (thought to be a thinly disguised *alter ego* for the apostle Paul) to visions (e.g. Gal 1:12; cf. 2 Cor 12:1–10):

> But if you were visited by him for the space of an hour and were instructed by him and thereby have become an apostle, then proclaim his words, expound what he has taught, be a friend to his apostles and do not contend with me, who am his confidant, for you have in hostility withstood me, who am a firm rock, the foundation stone of the Church. (*Hom*. 17:19 in Schneemelcher 1992: 537)

Similarly, this interpretation occurs in the *Hebrew Gospel of Matthew* preserved in Ben-Tob's medieval Jewish polemical treatise: 'I say to you: you are stone and I will build upon you my house of prayer' (Howard 1995: 81).

Peter-as-rock is attested in the patristic period (e.g. Tertullian, *De praesc. Haer*. 22.4; Hilary; Leo the Great, *Sermons* 3 and 4). Ambrose of Milan's hymn *Aeterne rerum conditor*, widely known due to its use in the Roman breviary, presents this interpretation in speaking of Peter's denial at cockcrow (albeit here emphasizing his weakness):

> Lo! e'en the very Church's Rock
> melts at the crowing of the cock.[1]

But it is perhaps most robustly defended, along with the defense of an ongoing Petrine office in the papacy, by Counter-Reformation exegetes such as the Dominican Thomas de Vio (Cajetan), and the Jesuits Robert Bellarmine, Juan de Maldonado, and Cornelius a Lapide (Bigane 1981: 105–143). This comes on the back of Reformers such as John Calvin objecting to contemporary papal use as an example of 'the Roman antichrist' perverting this passage in order 'to

1 http://www.preces-latinae.org/thesaurus/Hymni/AeterneRerum.html.

bring in some excuse for his tyranny' (Calvin 1972: II/188). Lapide responds thus to the critiques of Calvin and other Reformers:

> For before the coming of the Holy Ghost, Peter was very far from being the rock of the Church; yea through fear he denied Christ in His Passion. So then the word 'Peter,' and 'Petra,' denotes the firmness of S. Peter as a prince of the Church, and of his successors the Pontiffs, and their constancy in the faith and religion of Christ. (Lapide 1890: 2/214–215)

Yet across the centuries other interpretations have often dominated, even in Catholic circles. Indeed, another sixteenth-century Catholic exegete, Desiderius Erasmus, writes in the 1516 edition of his *Annotations* as though the use of this passage in support of the papacy were a novelty: 'Therefore I marvel that there are those who twist (*detorqueant*) this passage to refer to the Roman pontiff' (in Bigane 1981: 16).

Reading scripture in the light of scripture, many have advocated a Christological interpretation. The rock is Christ himself (1 Cor 10:4), the sole foundation (1 Cor 3:11), whose teaching provides the solid bedrock on which the wise build their houses (7:24–27). For Jerome, that Christ the rock calls Peter 'rock' is akin to Jesus the Light of the World (John 8:12) declaring his disciples to be the light of the world (5:14). Augustine, who previously proposed the Petrine interpretation, in his *Retractions* offers this as an alternative, leaving his readers to make up their own minds between the two:

> For, 'Thou art Peter' and not 'Thou art rock' was said to him. But 'the rock was Christ,' in confessing whom, as also the whole Church confesses, Simon was called Peter. But let the reader decide which of these two opinions is the most probable. (*Retractions* 1.20.1; Augustine 1968: 90–91)

Hence the Christological interpretation came to be viewed as 'the Augustinian interpretation,' which was widely influential in Latin medieval exegesis (e.g. Paschasius Radbertus; Aquinas; see Levy 2007: 169–170), and preserved by later Catholic exegetes such as the sixteenth-century Belgian Capuchin Frans Titelmans. Typical is the comment in Pseudo-Bede (whose commentary was written prior to 820): '*Upon this rock*, that is, the Saviour, whom you have confessed …' (PL 92:78D–79A). This view is famously proposed in the hymn composed in 1866 by the Anglican priest-poet Samuel John Stone, based on the ninth article of the Apostles' Creed:

> The Church's one foundation
> Is Jesus Christ her Lord,
> She is His new creation
> By water and the Word.

Occasionally, Peter is recognized as a secondary foundation (as are the other apostles, on the basis of Eph 2:20), Christ being the primary. Thus the Franciscan theologian Bonaventure can speak of Peter as 'the vicar of the rock' (in Froehlich 1989: 12). Similarly, Thomas Aquinas clarifies: 'One should say that Christ is the foundation through himself, but Peter insofar as he is his vicar' (Aquinas 2013b: 100).

Alternatively, the 'rock' is Peter's faith, or specifically the confession of Christ's messiahship he has just uttered (Gregory of Nyssa, *Encomium in S. Stephanum protomartyrem* 2; Theodore of Mopsuestia, *Frag.* 92 = Reuss 1957: 129; Chrysostom; Juan de Valdés; Calvin; Geneva Bible). For Isho'dad of Merv, the Syriac bishop and theologian of the Church of the East, *Cepha* is not 'the person of Simon, but the confession and the right faith that were in him, which the Father had caused to flow into his mouth' (Isho'dad of Merv 1911: 66). In his paraphrase, Erasmus interprets the name given to Peter as appropriate to his unwavering faith, contrasting with the diverse opinions of the crowd, and has Christ declare that he will build his church on 'the rock of your confession' (Erasmus 2008: 246). It is also reflected in the popular interpretation provided by Marcelino, a member of the basic Christian community at Solentiname in Lake Nicaragua:

> The firm rock, it seems to me, is the faith that he is the Messiah, the Liberator, the one who's going to change the world. Our community of Solentiname must also be based on that faith. If it isn't, the same thing will happen to us that happens to religion in many parts of the country. It's like an old house that's falling down, all shattered by the earthquake. (Cardenal 2010: 268)

However, these different understandings of the 'rock' were not always understood as mutually exclusive (a fact attested by the presence of all three in the *Glossa ordinaria* on Matthew). For Ambrose of Milan, the rock is Christ; yet Peter was so-called because of the solidity of his perseverance and the firmness of his faith, which Ambrose's readers are to emulate as other 'rocks' (*Exp. ev. Luc.* 9:20). While Augustine's general view was that Christ was the rock, at times he could understand it to refer to Peter, the apostles, the church, or Peter's confession of faith (Taheny 1961: 28–29). This variety is even reflected in Martin Luther's challenge to papal claims. For Luther, the rock is Christ in the primary sense. However, the confession of the true Rock by Peter the 'rock man' is also a rock who manifests rock-like faith:

> Not upon the rock ... of the Roman Church is the Church founded, as some decrees explain it, but upon the faith which Peter confessed for the entire Church. (in Cullmann 1962: 168)

An Ongoing Petrine Role?

Luther's challenge highlights an issue which has been central to the discussion of this passage almost from the beginning. What are the implications of this Petrine passage for the church in subsequent generations? Is Jesus' promise for Peter alone, or (in light of 18:18) for the wider body of his original disciples? Does it extend beyond the apostolic age, either to justify a specific 'ministry of Peter,' or to speak to some ongoing apostolic ministry among Christ's people? For some, it speaks to Peter's unique role in salvation-history, like Abraham before him: 'his faith is the means by which God brings a new people into being' (Davies and Allison 1991: 643). The parallel with Abraham is already drawn in the sixteenth century by Juan de Maldonado.

Yet the possibility that Peter's role continues is debated already in the early centuries of Christianity. In promoting a rigorist approach to sins of unchastity, Tertullian refers sarcastically to a 'bishop of bishops,' thought to be Pope Callistus I, who claims for himself and 'every church [or 'the entire church'] that is near Peter *(Petri propinquam)*' the power to bind and loose (*De Pudic.* 21). 'Near Peter' in this passage apparently refers to Rome's claim to the grave of the apostle (Cullmann 1962: 121, 165–166). Tertullian rejects this Roman view, or even that it can extend to other bishops, claiming that this power was granted to Peter personally.

By contrast, Origen's spiritual exegesis of the passage leads him to extend Christ's words to Peter to all Christians, at least potentially. Peter becomes a type of the true Christian gnostic:

> And if we too have said like Peter, You are the Christ, the Son of the living God, not as if flesh and blood had revealed it unto us, but by light from the Father in heaven having shone in our heart, we become a Peter, and to us there might be said by the Word, You are Peter, etc. (Matthew 16:18). (*Commentary on Matthew* 12.10; *ANF* 9:455–56)

A more restricted view is proposed by Origen's contemporary Cyprian of Carthage (c. 200–258). His treatise *On the Unity of the Catholic Church* was probably written in defense of Cornelius as rightful bishop of Rome against his rival Novatian. Hence, Cyprian notes that Jesus first makes promises to Peter so that the 'beginning proceeds from unity' (*De unitate* 4; *ANF* 5:422). However, after the resurrection he extends the same power to all the apostles, and thence to the bishops. In the ninth century, the Frankish Benedictine bishop Rabanus Maurus clarifies Cyprian's position, to the effect that 'all the Apostles were made with Peter equal sharers of dignity and power' (*De clericorum institutione* 1.4 in Taheny 1961: 20).

This understanding that Peter has a representative role vis-à-vis the other apostles (also e.g. Jerome), and by extension bishops and other church leaders, presents him as a 'corporate personality,' a view expressed in the ninth century by Hincmar, archbishop of Rheims:

> Although apparently given by the Lord to Peter alone, the power to loose and to bind must be acknowledged, without any doubt, as given also to the other apostles ... For as all were addressed in general, the one Peter answered for all; likewise, what the Lord answered Peter He answered all in Peter. Similarly today, the same function is given the whole church in the bishops and priests. (*Schedule for the Synod of Douzy*, 860 in Tavard 1985: 259–260)

Yet the particular association of Peter with the see of Rome manifests itself in an interpretation giving particular prominence to the bishops of that city. The Pseudo-Clementines assert that Peter passed on his teacher's chair and authority of binding and loosing to his successor as bishop of Rome, Clement (*Epist. Clem. to Jas.* 2.1). For Pope Leo the Great (pope 440–461), Peter's rock-like confession of Christ continues to be effective mystically in his successors the bishops of Rome:

> The dispensation of Truth therefore abides, and the blessed Peter persevering in the strength of the Rock, which he has received, has not abandoned the helm of the Church, which he undertook. For he was ordained before the rest in such a way that from his being called the Rock, from his being pronounced the Foundation, from his being constituted the Doorkeeper of the kingdom of heaven, from his being set as the Umpire to bind and to loose, whose judgments shall retain their validity in heaven, from all these mystical titles we might know the nature of his association with Christ. And still today he more fully and effectually performs what is entrusted to him, and carries out every part of his duty and charge in Him and with Him, through Whom he has been glorified. And so if anything is rightly done and rightly decreed by us, if anything is won from the mercy of God by our daily supplications, it is of his work and merits whose power lives and whose authority prevails in his See. (Leo the Great, *Sermon* 3; *NPNF* 2nd series, 12:117)

For Aquinas, the relationship between 16:19 (and, by implication, also 18:18) and John 20:23 ('Those whose sins you forgive, they are forgiven ...') is expressed in terms of direct and indirect commission. Here Peter is granted the authority to bind and loose 'immediately,' while the other apostles receive it from Peter. Hence the pope, standing in Peter's place, has full power *(plenariam potestatem),* the other bishops deriving their power from him.

The Gates of Hades (16:18)

The phrase 'Gates of Hades' is the Greek equivalent to the 'gates of Sheol' (or 'gates of death,' e.g. Job 38:17; Ps 9:13–14; Wis Sol 1:13). Thus it refers to the undifferentiated realm of the dead, the underworld, or, more specifically, death's destroying power (cf. Rev 6:8; 20:13–14). Some commentators identify Hades with the Greek Tartarus, that section of the underworld reserved for the punishment of the wicked (e.g. Hilary of Poitiers; Jerome; Erasmus). Early English translations (e.g. Wycliffe Bible; AV; Douay-Rheims) opt for the potentially misleading 'gates of hell,' i.e. the place of eternal punishment for the wicked. The ethics, and politics, of translation is acutely raised by the Kenyan Gĩkũyũ version of Matthew, produced by colonial missionaries. For 'Hades' they used the Gĩkũyũ equivalent 'the abode of spirits,' understood negatively so as to undermine positive indigenous beliefs about the ancestors (Kinyua 2015: 17).

Jesus' promise to Peter that these gates will not prevail against 'it' (literally 'her,' Greek *autēn*) is ambiguous. The feminine pronoun could refer to the 'rock,' a position espoused by Ephrem the Syrian, Origen, and Ambrose, and in the modern period by Adolf von Harnack (for references, see Luz 2001: 363–364; also Robinson 1984). In this case, it is a promise that Peter and the other apostles would be preserved from death, a view already dismissed by Jerome, who sees it contradicted by their subsequent martyrdoms. More commonly, it is understood as a promise that the gates of Hades will not have the upper hand against the church. Erasmus sums it up well. Christ will so fortify his church, i.e. his house and palace, 'that no force of the Tartarean kingdom will be able to take it by storm' (Erasmus 2008: 246). This view is reflected in the popular hymn 'Onward Christian Soldiers' by the nineteenth-century Anglican priest Sabine Baring-Gould:

> Gates of hell can never
> 'Gainst the Church prevail,
> We have Christ's own promise,
> And that cannot fail.

Martin Luther is more circumspect. Christ's promise refers to the power of the devil being ineffective against the church, but only when it 'stands firm in faith and without sin' (in Ramm 1962: 214; a similar view is expressed in the eleventh century by Theophylact).

Some also offer a figurative interpretation of the phrase. For Jerome (following Origen), the 'gates of Hades' signifies 'vices and sins,' or heretical doctrines which lead people into Tartarus (Jerome 2008: 192). Augustine similarly understands heresies (*On the Creed* 14; also Theodoret of Cyrus, *Ep.* 141), while Augustine's mentor Ambrose, in his commentary on the Lucan parallel, gives the phrase a moral meaning: fornication, apostasy, and mortal sin (Taheny 1961: 22).

The Power of the Keys (16:19)

The juxtaposition of 'gates of Hades' and 'keys of the kingdom of heaven' strongly suggests that the keys are given to Peter to provide access to the latter (or alternatively, to allow the heavenly realm to break into the earthly: so Marcus 1988). This explains St. Peter's traditional location at the pearly gates, welcoming the departed righteous to their heavenly home. It is central to Hilary of Poitiers' blessing of Peter:

> Worthy is the rock upon which the Church is built, against which the laws of hell and the gates of Tartarus and all the prisons of death are broken. O blessed porter of heaven, by whose decree the keys of eternity's entrance are handed over, and whose earthly judgment with heavenly authority has already been decreed. (Hilary of Poitiers 2012: 182)

The 'power of the keys' seems associated, at least in part, with the authority to 'bind' and 'loose,' a power later granted to all the disciples (18:18). As the Anglican priest and Cambridge scholar John Lightfoot recognized in his 1658 *Horae Hebraicae et Talmudicae*, binding and loosing was 'a very usual phrase in the Jewish schools,' rabbinic terminology for halakhic decisions regarding what is permitted and forbidden, believed to be recognized in the heavenly court (Lightfoot 1859: II/236–240; see also Str-B 1.741–746; Derrett 1983). Thus Peter can be understood as the church's 'supreme Rabbi' (Streeter 1924: 515), invested with teaching authority paralleling developments in Pharisaic Judaism. Joel Marcus sums this up well:

> Our passage speaks of the revelation to Peter in the earthly sphere of the interpretation of the law that has been decided in heaven. He is given total power on earth to distinguish valid from invalid prohibitions, 'binding' upon human beings the observance of certain of them – even some not explicit in the Mosaic torah – and 'loosing' them from the observance of others of them – even some enjoined by Moses. (Marcus 1988: 452)

Yet the precise definition of binding and loosing is complicated by the later reference at 18:18, in the context of a discussion of church discipline and possible excommunication, and the Johannine parallel where the risen Christ gives the disciples authority to forgive or retain sins (John 20:23).

The binding and loosing of sins is a popular interpretation (e.g. Tertullian, *De pud.* 21; Cyprian, *De unitate* 4; Firmilianus, *Ep. ad Cyprianum* 75.16; Gregory the Great, *Homilies on the Gospels* 2.26.4; Augustine, *Sermon* 149.6). Both Tertullian and Augustine regard this power to have been entrusted to the faithful corporately, acting at one with the Spirit. For Cyprian, it is a power entrusted to the bishops (e.g. *Ep.* 33). Others manage to combine all three Gospel passages (16:19; 18:18; John 20:23) in the one interpretation. The fourteenth-century English Carmelite theologian John Baconthorpe, for example, identifies three functions of the keys: to bind and loose sins in sacramental penance; to make laws and judgments (a juridical dimension); to make decisions regarding excommunication (Turley 1982: 750).

More commonly, the Latin West interprets the plural 'keys of the kingdom' as two: the key of knowledge and the key of power, sometimes connected to the spiritual and secular power of the papacy, and symbolized by the two crosskeys on papal coats of arms. This is conveyed visually by Pietro Perugino's fresco *The Delivery of the Keys* (1481–1483; Sistine Chapel, Rome), commissioned by Pope Sixtus IV (Figure 11). Sixtus's predecessor Peter kneels before Christ, who hands over two large keys. In the background is the Temple of Solomon, flanked by two Roman triumphal arches, apparently modeled on Rome's Arch of Constantine, the emperor who, according to the Donation of Constantine (now widely accepted to be a medieval forgery), granted authority over the western empire to the papacy. The presence of men in contemporary dress among the archaically attired apostles hints at the perpetuation of Peter's commission in the papacy of Perugino's day. So too does the inscription on the triumphal

FIGURE 11 Pietro Perugino (c. 1450–1523). *The Delivery of the Keys*. 1481–1483. Fresco, 3300 × 5500 mm. Sistine Chapel, Rome. Source: Photo Scala/Art Resource, NY.

arches, which explicitly connects the scene to the papacy of Sixtus: 'You, Sixtus IV, unequal in riches but superior in religion to Solomon, have constructed this vast temple.' Significantly, Perugino's fresco directly faces Botticelli's *Punishment of Korah* on the opposite wall of the chapel. This Old Testament story (Num 16:1–40), where Korah and his associates oppose the authority of Moses and Aaron, was regularly appealed to by supporters of papal claims against the Conciliarists, who ascribed supreme authority within the church to ecumenical councils (Stinger 1985: 204–207).

A satirical look at the claims of corrupt popes to possess the power of the keys occurs in the anonymous Latin dialogue *Iulius exclusus* e *coelis*, possibly composed by Erasmus. The deceased Pope Julius II (1503–1513), the so-called 'Warrior Pope,' finds the gates of heaven closed to him, and his own keys of no use:

> What the devil is this? The doors won't open? Someone must have changed the lock, or at least tampered with it. (in Jütte 2015: 117)

Martin Luther, who read this dialogue approvingly, uses his annotation on 16:19 to polemicize against the temporal power of the papacy:

> Therefore, the pope does not here possess – just as St. Peter did not – power to snatch away kingdoms, to depose kings and to put them on the throne, and to harass them at his own whim. For Christ is speaking about binding and loosing sins, that is, about eternal life and death, not about the crowns and majesties of the world. For He is discussing the Church – that is, those who faithfully confess the Rock – and not an earthly government. (*Annotations on Matthew* 16:19; Luther 2015: 285)

In sixteenth-century England, the Tudor lawyer Christopher St. German offers a rather awkward political reading of the passage, clearly designed to justify Henry VIII's position as earthly head of the Church of England. He interprets 16:19 as granting the authority to bind and loose to bishops, an authority now superseded by the subsequent conversion of Christian kings (his interpretation of the later reference at 18:18: see Rex 2014). In the following century, John Milton alludes to the passage in his 1637 poem *Lycidas*, to attack worldly Church of England bishops and clergy:

> Last came, and last did go,
> The Pilot of the Galilean lake;
> Two massy keys he bore of metals twain
> (The golden opes, the iron shuts amain).
> He shook his mitred locks, and stern bespake:

'How well could I have spar'd for thee, young swain,
Enow of such as for their bellies' sake
Creep and intrude, and climb into the fold?
Of other care they little reck'ning make
Than how to scramble at the shearers' feast
And shove away the worthy bidden guest.
Blind mouths! that scarce themselves know how to hold
A sheep-hook, or have learn'd aught else the least
That to the faithful herdman's art belongs!'

Peter, the 'Pilot of the Galilean lake' with his two 'massy keys ... of metals twain,' castigates the corrupt shepherds who have climbed like thieves and robbers 'into the fold' (see John 10:1, 8).

Taking Up the Cross (16:21–28)

With the solemn phrase 'From that time' (cf. 4:17; see Kingsbury 1976), the focus turns to the instruction of the disciples concerning the suffering of the Son of Man (cf. Mark 8:31–9:1; Luke 9:22–27). The contrast with the preceding pericope is heightened by Matthew's insertion of the word *skandalon* (16:23). Peter the rock, whose confession is praised as divine revelation, has quickly become a 'stumbling stone,' inspired by Satan. Jerome seeks to lessen the difficulty, speaking of Peter's rebuke as the words of an affectionate lover, and noting the future tense of Jesus' previous promise to Peter. Peter has not yet become the rock on which the church is built.

In response (16:24–26), Jesus teaches his disciples that following him requires taking up their cross, and, paradoxically, losing their lives (or souls) in order to find it. Ignatius of Antioch understands Christ's words as a summons to martyrdom:

> Neither the ends of the earth nor the kingdoms of this age are of any use to me [lit. 'will profit me nothing']. It is better for me to die for Jesus Christ than to rule over the ends of the earth. (Ignatius, *Rom.* 6:1; Holmes 2007: 231)

Some manuscripts of Ignatius establish the link more strongly by directly quoting from 16:26 at this point. In more settled times, the sheer radicality of Christ's teaching has been embraced through the 'new martyrdom' of monasticism and asceticism. It has also been foundational for modern martyrs, such as the German Lutheran Dietrich Bonhoeffer, whose radical discipleship would lead to his execution by the Nazis on 9 April 1945. In his *Cost of Discipleship*, Bonhoeffer provides a commentary on the Markan parallel (Mark 8:31–38) exploring the meaning of self-denial ('to be aware only of Christ and no more of self, to see only him who goes before and no more the road which is too hard for us'), and its challenge to contemporary churches:

> If our Christianity has ceased to be serious about discipleship, if we have watered down the gospel into emotional uplift which makes no costly demands and which fails to distinguish between natural and Christian existence, then we cannot help regarding the cross as an ordinary everyday calamity, as one of the trials and tribulations of life. We have then forgotten that the cross means rejection and shame as well as suffering. (Bonhoeffer 1963: 98)

Yet this passage has also been utilized in ways which seem antithetical to its plain sense (see e.g. Clarke 2003: 147–148). Pope Urban II appeals to it to promote Christian participation in the First Crusade, according to an account of his speech at the Council of Clermont (27 November 1095):

> And so Urban, Pope of the Roman see, with his archbishops, bishops, abbots, and priests, set out as quickly as possible beyond the mountains and began to deliver sermons and to preach eloquently, saying: 'Whoever wishes to save his soul should not hesitate humbly to take up the way of the Lord, and if he lacks sufficient money, divine mercy will give him enough.' Then the apostolic lord continued, 'Brethren, we ought to endure much suffering for the name of Christ - misery, poverty, nakedness, persecution, want, illness, hunger, thirst, and other (ills) of this kind.' (in Krey 1921: 28–29)

The Franks who responded to Urban's call to take up the cross 'caused crosses to be sewed on their right shoulders.' The Fourth Lateran Council of 1215 applies the same saying to Catholics who 'take the cross and gird themselves up for the expulsion of heretics,' granting them the same privileges as Crusaders who have gone to the aid of the holy land (Lateran IV, Canon 3; Tanner 1990: I/234).

The final saying (16:28) is already considered problematic by the evangelists, as the variants in Mark and Luke reveal (Mark 9:1; Luke 9:27). What event is meant by 'the Son of Man coming in his kingdom'? If it refers to the Parousia, then the statement that 'some of those standing here' will 'not taste death' is disconfirmed by the passing of the apostolic generation. A solution of sorts is known to Martin Luther, who asserts that '[n]early all' of his contemporaries believe Christ to be speaking about John (on the basis of John 21:23, a view also known to Maldonado) and Mary, both widely believed to have been assumed into heaven (*Annotations on Matthew* 16:28; Luther 2015: 302). But earlier commentators refer it to a different event: Christ's coming in the church (e.g. Gregory the Great = PL 76: 124), the ascension, which the apostles witnessed (e.g. Dionysius the Carthusian), or Christ's resurrection, which marks the defeat of death (e.g. Luther; Calvin). Perhaps most popular, and arguably most sensitive to the saying's narrative context, is to connect it to the Transfiguration which immediately follows, as prefiguring his future coming in glory (e.g. Hilary; Jerome; Chrysostom; Augustine, *Sermo* 78.1; Cyril of Alexandria = PG 72:424–425). For Juan de Maldonado, 'Christ calls His Transfiguration His kingdom, not because it was such properly, but because it was the image of it … in figure; not present, but in a glass darkly' (Maldonado 1888: 2/61). Some modern commentators also connect this saying to the Transfiguration, at least in its present context (e.g. Harrington 1991: 249). Others interested in the historicity of the logion claim that the historical Jesus was mistaken in anticipating an early coming of the Kingdom (e.g. Kümmel 1984: 40–42), or avoid the difficulty by treating the verse as an inauthentic Jesus saying (e.g. F.C. Baur in Luz 2001: 387; Bultmann 1968: 121).

Matthew 17

Ancient Literary Context

This chapter is dominated by Matthew's Transfiguration account, closely paralleled in Mark and Luke (Mark 9:2–13; Luke 9:28–36). It has been variously categorized as a displaced resurrection appearance story (Bultmann 1968: 259–261), a divine epiphany (Heil 2000), and an apocalyptic vision (Kee 1972). Ancient audiences may have heard in the Greek verb *metamorphoō* or the Vulgate's *transfiguro* echoes of pagan stories about gods changing their form

Matthew Through the Centuries, First Edition. Ian Boxall.

(e.g. Ovid, *Metamorphoses*), just as younger twenty-first-century audiences more familiar with Harry Potter might treat Professor McGonagall's transfiguration classes at Hogwarts (Rowling 1997: 100) as the interpretative key to the story. Yet the Gospel narratives depict a very specific 'change of form': a transfiguration 'from glory to glory' in which the divine presence breaks in on (or is made momentarily visible to) the bewildered disciples.

Matthew alone identifies the Transfiguration as a 'vision,' thus heightening the apocalyptic dimension of the story. This is underscored by his description of the three disciples falling to the ground, and Jesus touching them while commanding them not to be afraid (17:6–7; cf. Dan 8:17–18; 10:10, 18–19; Rev 1:17; *Apoc. Ab.* 10:1–8). Matthew also builds on the Sinai potential of Mark's version (the three disciples recalling Aaron, Nadab, and Abihu; the presence of the cloud: Exod 24:1, 9–10, 15–18) to strengthen his Moses–Jesus typology. This accounts for his reordering of Mark's 'Elijah with Moses' to stress Moses' priority (17:3; cf. Mark 9:4), and his observation that Jesus' face 'shone like the sun' (17:2; cf. Exod 34:29–35). His omission of the offensive phrase 'He [Peter] did not know what to say, for they were terrified' (Mark 9:6) is of a piece with his tendency to soften Mark's harsh portrayal of the disciples, and to raise the profile of Peter specifically. Finally, he adds a narratorial aside to the account of Jesus' descent and the dialogue concerning the returning Elijah (cf. Mark 9:11–13; absent from Luke). As a careful reader of Mark, Matthew seeks to make explicit what remained implicit in his predecessor: the identification of the returned Elijah with John the Baptist.

The descent from the mountain is followed in all three Synoptics by the healing of a possessed boy (17:14–21; Mark 9:14–29; Luke 9:37–43a). Matthew's version is a significantly abbreviated version of Mark's, with a high degree of minor agreements with Luke. The inability of Jesus' disciples to heal the 'son,' attributed to their 'little faith' (cf. 8:26; 14:31), provides the opportunity for a pronouncement about faith like a mustard seed. The final pericope, following a second passion prediction (17:22–23), continues the motif of sonship ('So the sons are free,' 17:26). This uniquely Matthean story is variously categorized as a 'nature miracle,' a 'rule miracle,' or, given that the catching of the fish is not actually recounted, a scholastic dialogue (Bultmann 1968: 34–35; Davies and Allison 1991: 738). Again, Peter is Jesus' main interlocutor, heightening the Petrine interest.

The Interpretations

The Transfiguration (17:1–13)

The Transfiguration is no stand-alone event, but a crucial link in a chain of events leading to the cross: in the words of Archbishop Michael Ramsey (1904–1988), 'a gateway to the saving events of the Gospel' (Ramsey 1949: 145).

Given the liturgical and homiletic prominence of Matthew's Gospel from early times, it is unsurprising that it is his account which dominates in the reception history (see Ramsey 1949; Luz 2001: 400–403; Lee 2004; Stevenson 2007, 2008). This did not prevent some degree of harmonization in both commentary and homily, where significant elements in the variant accounts (e.g. Mark's reference to Jesus' clothes being whiter than any earthly 'fuller' could bleach them, or Luke's attention to the conversation with Moses and Elijah about his 'departure') form part of the discussion.

The reception history also reveals a profound sensitivity to narrative context, akin to modern narrative criticism, in order to understand the meaning of this event on the mountain. The Transfiguration is set within a broad sequence of baptism, ministry, suffering, death, and glorification, functioning as a manifestation of 'the Son of Man coming in his kingdom' (a fulfillment of 16:28; e.g. Hilary of Poitiers; Theophylact), a 'preview of the future kingdom and the glory of the triumphant one' (Jerome 2008: 201), or a revelation of future glory (Aquinas). For the nineteenth-century Tractarian Isaac Williams, it 'set forth by anticipation the Resurrection and Regeneration of the flesh' (in Ford 1859: II/303).

The Mountain (17:1)

The Gospels are silent about the specific location of the mountain, which Johann Albrecht Bengel regards as fortuitous, since 'thereby superstition is prevented' (Bengel 1971: 217). Matthew's description of it as 'high' (17:1), and the proximity of the previous scene to Caesarea Philippi, might suggest Mount Hermon (9232 ft). However, early tradition identifies the place as the more modest Mount Tabor (1886 ft) in Lower Galilee. This identification is made in a scholion on Psalm 89:12 (Ps 88:13 LXX: 'Tabor and Hermon will shout for joy in your name') attributed to Origen (Hilhorst 2009: 331), as well as by Cyril of Jerusalem and Jerome (Cyril of Jerusalem, *Catech.* 12; Jerome, *Ep.* 27). John of Damascus (c. 680–750), building on Origen's exegesis, notes Tabor's appropriateness as a fulfillment of that psalm. Mount Hermon had rejoiced at the baptism, to which this event is closely linked through the heavenly voice declaring Christ's 'name' (John apparently locates the Baptist's ministry at the source of the Jordan, in the foothills of Hermon). At the Transfiguration, the fulfillment of the psalm is complete:

> Now Thabor too rejoices and its glad: the divine, holy mountain, the high mountain, now rightly shines out no less, in glory and brilliance, than it does in its physical height. (*Oration on the Transfiguration* 3; Daley 2013: 209)

Tabor becomes the accepted location for the event (e.g. Piacenza Pilgrim; Peter Comestor, *Historia Scholastica*).

Yet the symbolic significance of the mountain is often more important than its geographical location. A typological reading may already be implicit in 2 Peter's 'holy mountain' (2 Pet 1:18), recalling Mount Zion in Psalm 2:6 LXX, as well as the tendency to view the Mount of Transfiguration as a new Sinai (e.g. Maldonado). Interpreting the event allegorically, Origen views it as 'the "high mountain" of wisdom,' to which those who glimpse Christ's divinity in the Gospel can ascend (in Daley 2013: 56–57). It symbolizes a particular type of 'seeing.' Much later, Thomas Aquinas will regard the high mountain as pointing to the 'loftiness (*altitudo*) of contemplation,' accessible to all the nations (cf. Isa 2:11; Thomas Aquinas 2013b: 115).

After Six Days (17:1)

The timing of the Transfiguration is a puzzle, particularly given the tension with Luke's 'about eight days.' Both John Chrysostom and Jerome seek to resolve this by claiming that Matthew and Mark count only the days in between, whereas Luke includes the first and last. Another problem on the literal level is the six days' delay itself. The Flemish Jesuit Cornelius a Lapide (1567–1637) offers a geographical solution: the distance from Caesarea Philippi to Mount Tabor, combined with the slow pace of Jesus' ministry (Lapide 1890: 2/245–246).

However, the phrase has yielded an even richer crop of allegorical interpretations, building on the identification of the Transfiguration as an anticipation of Christ's risen glory. The six days signify that the resurrection (Rabanus Maurus) or the heavenly Kingdom (Hilary) are preceded by 6000 years (the six expected ages of the world). Origen urges that those who wish to see Christ transfigured 'must ascend above the six days, so that he may no longer gaze on "things visible" ... nor experience any worldly desire,' and seek instead 'the things that are unseen' (in Daley 2013: 55–56; cf. 2 Cor 4:18). Aquinas concurs that to reach the Kingdom of God requires being elevated over all the creatures created in those six days. In the Joachite interpretation of the Spiritual Franciscan Peter John Olivi, the time reference is a prophecy of six periods of church history, which must precede the transfiguration of Christ's mystical body (Madigan 2003: 89–91).

The Three Companions (17:1)

The choice of Peter, James, and John (also 4:18–22; 26:37) is variously explained. Many connect their privileged status with aspects of their character, or their future roles. Popular among later commentators is John Chrysostom's identification of Peter as preeminent in the intensity of his love for Jesus, John as the one whom Jesus loved, and James for his willingness to drink the cup of martyrdom (e.g. Theophylact; Aquinas). Similar is the view of John of Damascus: Peter is chosen given that he 'had received the rudder of the whole Church,' James because he was about to be martyred, John because he was 'the virgin-theologian' (*Oration on the Transfiguration* 9; Daley 2013: 217). Jerome sees the selection of these three as an illustration of the Gospel maxim: 'Many are called, few are chosen' (20:16; 22:14). For John Calvin, the number is appropriate as the required number of witnesses according to Deuteronomy 17:6.

Yet the triumvirate of disciples also provides scope for more figurative interpretations. Hilary draws an analogy between the ascent of the three disciples and the descent of the three sons of Noah:

> By the three disciples who were taken apart is shown the future election of the people who were to come from a threefold origin: Shem, Ham, and Japheth. (Hilary of Poitiers 2012: 186)

Their presence on the mountain prefigures the conversion of the Gentile world. Aquinas sees a further Trinitarian reference, noting that one can only arrive at the Kingdom of God 'in the faith of the Trinity' (Thomas Aquinas 2013b: 115).

The Nature of the Transfiguration (17:2)

The nature of Christ's transfigured form has proved theologically problematic from the beginning. Irenaeus responds to gnosticizing alternatives (similar to views expressed in e.g. *Acts of Peter* 20; *Acts of John* 90) when he presents the Transfiguration as a vision of God's glory in the incarnate Christ (*Adv. Haer.* 4.20.9–10). It is a direct answer to Moses' request to see the divine glory (Exod 33:19–23). By contrast, Origen offers a spiritual interpretation. The transfigured Jesus is the Logos as seen by those who have 'ascended the mountain' in their reading of scripture so as to know him no longer 'according to the flesh.' Those who cannot move beyond the 'letter' of the Gospels are symbolized by the remaining disciples at the foot of the mountain. Christ's dazzling white garments are the 'sayings and writings of the Gospels,' made white when a person expounds them so as to reveal the divine reality of Jesus they convey (in Daley 2013: 56–57; also Wright 2012: 254–259). Jerome may be distancing himself from Origenist tendencies when he describes the transfigured body of Jesus as not 'spiritual' or 'airy' but 'bodily and tactile' (Jerome 2008: 198).

The ongoing eastern tradition develops in a twofold manner. First, the event comes to be viewed as manifesting or anticipating Christ's coming Kingdom, in which Christ's divinity is made visible. But an equal concern of many eastern commentators is the 'transfiguration' or divinization of Christ's followers (cf. Rom 12:2; 2 Cor 3:18; see Luz 2001: 400–403). This became a major theme for the eastern hesychast tradition, whose 'prayer of the heart' enabled access to the 'uncreated light' seen by the three disciples on Mount Tabor. The interpretative key is the eschatological promise at 13:43 that the righteous will 'shine like the sun.' Gregory Palamas (1296–1359) articulates this idea in a homily for the Feast of the Transfiguration:

> and so, becoming wholly divine light, as offspring of the divine light, they shall gaze on the one who outshines them in a divine and ineffable way, whose glory, naturally coming forth from his divinity and possessed in common by his body, was revealed on Thabor through the unity of his hypostasis. (*Homily* 34.11; Daley 2013: 362)

Eastern Christianity has maintained a rich tradition of holy figures replicating in their own lives the shining 'like the sun' of Christ's transfigured face, notably St. Seraphim of Sarov (1759–1833: see Barton 2001).

Occasionally the connection is made, as in recent critical scholarship, between the shining of Jesus' face (17:2) and that of Moses on his descent from Sinai (e.g. Eusebius, *Dem. ev.* 3.2). The parallel is evoked, however, to emphasize the difference. According to Gregory Palamas, Moses 'underwent transfiguration – he did not bring it about,' whereas 'our Lord Jesus Christ had that brilliance from within himself' (*Homily* 3.11; Daley 2013: 362). A similar point was made centuries earlier by the fifth-century Syriac poet-theologian, Jacob of Sarug:

> Unlike Moses, who became radiant from without,
> our Lord is light from within himself together with His Father.
> It is written about Moses that the skin of his face became radiant,
> not that he was transfigured, shone forth and became white as our Redeemer.
> Moses indeed saw God and he was made to shine forth,
> but our Lord was God who is wholly light.
> (*Homily on the Transfiguration of Our Lord,* lines 199–204; Jacob of Sarug 2008: 28)

Although the transfiguring or divinization of the faithful is a particular emphasis of eastern Christianity, an ecclesial interpretation of the Transfiguration is also attested in the West, focusing on Christ's clothing. For Augustine, his shining white garments symbolize the church, held in place by the person it clothes (*Sermon* 78). In another sermon on the Transfiguration, Augustine makes explicit his dependence on 13:43 (as well as Phil 3:21), and employing Tyconius' rule 'Concerning the Lord and his Body' to speak of the future transfiguration of the faithful:

> Now all of us will be shining as splendidly as the sun at the end of the ages, and that is the splendor that the Lord displayed in himself. His members will shine as the head has shone. (*Sermon* 79A; Augustine 1991: 347)

This is developed further in the Middle Ages. In his *Postilla super Matthaeum*, the Dominican exegete Hugh of St. Cher (c. 1200–1263) discusses how the Transfiguration also signifies the transfiguration of Christ's mystical body (Canty 2011: 24–25). However, his allegorical interpretation distinguishes sharply between the clergy (Christ's 'face') and the laity (his 'garments').

Western exegetes also express an interest in Christ's human nature. In a Transfiguration sermon preached in 445, Leo the Great interprets the Transfiguration as a revelation of Christ's divinity *and* his glorified humanity (*Sermon* 51). This view of Christ's humanity as a 'prism' through which Christ's divinity may be perceived is also attested in Ambrose Autpert and Bede (Canty 2011: 15). The medieval scholastic theologians speculated about how Christ's transfigured humanity was related to his incarnate human nature on the one hand, and his post-resurrection state on the other. Later, Calvin reiterates the concern regarding the capacity of the disciples to see God's glory. He finds in Matthew's reference to Christ's face shining 'like the sun' an accommodation to the disciples' current state: they did not see him as he now is in heaven, where his face now 'far transcends the sun's glory,' but were given 'such a taste of His infinite glory, as they were able to receive' (Calvin 1972: II/198).

Moses and Elijah (17:3)

Early commentators already know the interpretation, common among modern exegetes, whereby Moses and Elijah represent the Law and the prophets (e.g. Origen; Jerome; Theophylact; *Glossa ordinaria*; Maldonado): in the case of Elijah, by *synecdoche*, one of the prophets standing for them all. John Chrysostom adds other reasons for their presence: Elijah's testimony to Christ's Transfiguration confirms Peter's confession against alternative views of Jesus ('some say Elijah,' 16:14). The presence of Moses the lawgiver and Elijah who was 'jealous for God's glory' also serves to refute Jewish charges that Jesus was a law-breaker and blasphemer. Further, as Old Testament exemplars of the need to 'lose one's life' in order to find it, both 'show forth the glory of the cross' so as to encourage the disciples in the face of impending suffering (*Homily on Matthew* 56.2; Daley 2013: 72). In the Middle Ages, the English Franciscan philosopher-theologian Alexander of Hales (c. 1185–1245) offers a further spiritual interpretation: Moses, as lawgiver, signifies the active life, whereas Elijah symbolizes contemplatives (Canty 2011: 69).

Many modern scholars draw on Jewish traditions which treat both Elijah and Moses as having ascended into heaven (2 Kgs 2:1–12; Josephus, *Ant.* 4.320–23; *As. Mos.* 10:12; Str-B 1.753–54; e.g. Luz 2001: 397; Puig i Tàrrech 2012). Thus they are present on the mountain as heavenly beings (Bengel). By contrast, Origen implies that both come from the resting-place of the Old Testament saints, to which they return to share what they have heard on the mountain with those who would be raised at the crucifixion of Jesus (see Daley 2013: 65). Much later, Calvin apparently espouses a similar position, for he thinks that God, who has both souls and bodies in his hand, raised them both so as to be present on the mountain.

A more pervasive view in patristic and medieval commentators is to differentiate between them: Elijah descends from heaven whereas Moses ascends from the underworld (e.g. Jerome); Moses personified 'the company of the dead,' Elijah the living (Jacob of Sarug, *Homily on the Transfiguration of Our Lord,* lines 251–52; Jacob of Sarug 2008: 34). This distinction accounts for another comment of Chrysostom's:

> That they [the disciples] might learn that he has authority over death and life, and rules both what is above and what is below. So he brings on the scene both one who is dead and one who never suffered that fate. (*Homily on Matthew* 56.2; Daley 2013: 72)

For Thomas Aquinas, their presence means that Christ receives a fourfold testimony: from heaven (the voice of the Father), from hell (Moses), from paradise (Elijah), and from earth (the three disciples). He also addresses a theological conundrum created by the belief that Moses came from the realm of the dead. In what form did he appear? Rejecting an alternative suggestion that his angel appeared in his place, Aquinas asserts that he was present in soul alone.

Several early commentators (e.g. Irenaeus, *Adv. Haer*. 4.20.9; Tertullian, *Adv. Prax*. 14.7; John of Damascus) exploit Matthew's description of the Transfiguration as a 'vision' to present it as a vision granted also to Moses and Elijah, the fulfillment of what was promised on Sinai/Horeb (e.g. Exod 33:18). In his homily on the Transfiguration, the seventh-century monk Anastasius of Sinai places the following words on the lips of Moses:

> Now I have seen you, the truly existing one … you, who said on the mountain, *I am He-Who-Is* [Exod 3:14]. … I have seen you, whom of old I desired to see, saying, *show yourself clearly to me* … I have seen you, no longer as you revealed your back and turned me away on the rock of Sinai, but made visible to me clearly on the rock of Tabor. (in Bucur 2010: 20)

Building Three Tents (17:4)

Jerome, reading Matthew in the light of the other Gospels, presents Peter as misguided in his desire to construct three tents, 'since there is one tabernacle of the Gospel' which recapitulates the Law and the prophets (Jerome 2008: 199). Others appreciate the psychological complexity of Peter's response. John

Chrysostom is a sensitive reader of Matthew (though without consciousness of Marcan priority) in detecting that evangelist's softer portrayal of the first apostle. Peter is 'the hot-headed lover of Christ,' who is consumed by love for Jesus. Peter's statement that it was good for them to be on the mountain was spoken, not out of concern for his own welfare but for that of the Lord. His subsequent offer to build three tents may be out of keeping with his previous confession of Jesus as the unique Son of God. But this was the result of fear rather than malice (*Homily on Matthew* 56.3; Daley 2013: 75–78). Similarly, for Theophylact, the fearful Peter speaks 'out of great love,' because he 'did not want Christ to suffer,' and reckons that remaining on the mountain will provide the protection of the two heavenly figures, who contended with the Egyptians and called down fire from heaven respectively (Theophylact 1992: 146). By contrast, Origen sees demonic activity at play in Peter's 'It is good for us to be here,' just as he had previously been called 'Satan' at Caesarea Philippi.

The tension inherent in the story – an understandable longing to remain on the mountain, together with the need to descend to complete the journey to Jerusalem – is well expressed in the hymn *'Tis Good, Lord, to Be Here* by Joseph A. Robinson, clearly inspired by Matthew's version ('Thy face and garments, like the sun, | Shine with unborrowed light'):

> Before we taste of death,
> We see Thy kingdom come;
> We fain would hold the vision bright
> And make this hill our home.
> 'Tis good, Lord, to be here.
> Yet we may not remain;
> But since Thou bidst us leave the mount,
> Come with us to the plain.
>
> (*Lutheran Hymnal* #135)

The close correlation between divine glory and the human suffering of the passion seems to be grasped by Florence Nightingale (1820–1910), in a letter dated 14 November 1854, less than two weeks after her arrival with a group of nurses in war-torn Crimea: 'in the midst of this appalling Horror (we are steeped up to our necks in blood) there is good, and I can truly say, like St Peter, "It is good for us to be here"' (Nightingale in Larsen 2011: 126).

The Transfiguration in Liturgy and Visual Art

The liturgical reception of the Transfiguration is very rich. In the East, the Feast of the Transfiguration or *Metamorphosis* (one of the Twelve Great Feasts) has been celebrated on 6 August since the fourth or fifth century (Daley 2013:

19–23). This is 40 days prior to the Exaltation of the Cross on 14 September, possibly reflecting an ancient tradition that the Transfiguration occurred exactly 40 days before the crucifixion (Stevenson 2007: 13). The origins of the feast are obscure: variously attributed to the Armenian Gregory the Illuminator (d. 390), to the practice of the church of Jerusalem, and to the dedication of a fourth-century church on Mount Tabor. Reflecting eastern exegesis, and especially the theology of the festal sermons (e.g. by Proclus of Constantinople, John of Damascus, and Gregory Palamas), the liturgical celebration of the *Metamorphosis* has emphasized 'the mystical and hope-filled participation of the believers in the reality of Christ's resurrection' (Luz 2001: 401). This is reflected in hymns for the feast:

> Splendidly celebrating the day of the forefeast of the glorious and awesome transfiguration of Christ today, O ye faithful, let us cry aloud together: Transform our nature, O Savior, illumining it with Thy divine flesh, and impart to it its original dignity of incorruption, in that Thou art compassionate, that we may all glorify Thee, our one God. (Matins of the Forefeast in Lambertsen 1997: 62)

By contrast, the Transfiguration feast appears only sporadically in the West: it is attested in Spain in the ninth century, and later in England, particularly in monasteries of the Cluniac congregation, the twelfth-century abbot of Cluny, Peter the Venerable, being one of the feast's keenest promoters. But it was only declared a universal feast by Pope Callistus III in 1457, linked to the Christian victory over the Turks at Belgrade the previous year (Pfaff 1970: 13–39).

More pervasive (and probably earlier than the 6 August feast) is the practice of reading Matthew's Transfiguration Gospel during Lent. By the time of Leo the Great, it was read on 'Ember' Saturday (when new priests were ordained) preceding the Second Sunday of Lent (Leo the Great, *Sermon* 51; Pfaff 1970: 13; Cavalcanti 2001: 371). Recent Anglican and Lutheran practice has located the reading of the Transfiguration story on the Sunday before Lent, though still retaining its proximity to the penitential season. This Lenten location emphasizes the fundamental connection between Transfiguration and the cross: 'there is no short-cut to glory' in the Christian life (Barton 2001: 246).

If commemoration of the Transfiguration invited participation, particularly in its eastern form, this was aided by visual depiction (on visual reception, see, e.g. Schiller 1971: 145–152; Anthony 2014: 268–329). Early representations are often figurative, such as the mosaic in Sant' Apollinare in Classe, Ravenna (c. 549). The transfigured Christ is represented as a bejeweled cross, containing a small medallion of Christ, set against a backdrop of gold stars. The three apostles are depicted as three lambs in paradise below. The prominence of the cross links the event with the passion which is about to unfold, though given its depiction as a 'cross of light,' also with the last judgment and Christ's return in glory (Schiller 1971: 148).

The apse mosaic at St. Catherine's Monastery, Mount Sinai (between 548 and 565) is more conventional, presenting Christ and the other characters in bodily form. It is possible that the Transfiguration sermon of Anastasius of Sinai referenced above was preached in full view of this mosaic. The transfigured Christ stands at the center within a dark blue mandorla, probably symbolizing the divine presence in the cloud, rays of light emanating from his body. Details such as the representation of the disciples awaking from sleep suggest particular influence of Luke's account (Luke 9:32; see Elsner 1994: 111–114; Anthony 2014: 276–277). Nonetheless, potential echoes of Matthew's version are found in the heightened Mosaic typology present in the monastery church, albeit a typology which emphasizes Christ's superiority to Moses. The mosaic is framed by two scenes from the life of Moses on the triumphal arch above the apse conch: Moses removing his sandals at the burning bush (the traditional site of which is incorporated into the monastery), and Moses in the cleft of the rock on the summit of Sinai (Exod 3:1–6; 33:18–23). Thus the Transfiguration is presented as a third theophany, greater than the other two in that it makes possible the full vision of God 'face to face' which was earlier denied to Moses. This is no less the case for the monastic or pilgrim viewer of the mosaic, inviting further progress in the mystic ascent to the divine light (see Elsner 1994).

The possibility not only of vision but of the transfiguration or 'divinization' of the worshipper, signified by the rays of light penetrating the human witnesses, is prominent in Byzantine icons of the *Metamorphosis*, such as the panel icon painted c. 1403 by Theophanes the Greek (Figure 12). This suggests particular dependence on Matthew's narrative, given the posture of the disciples, prostrate before the transfigured Christ (17:6). Theophanes' icon breaks with iconographical tradition by including both the ascent and descent of Christ and the three disciples, thereby connecting the event to the wider story of the Gospel (Stevenson 2007: 1–5). In the West, Fra Angelico's fresco (c. 1440–1445) in the Dominican priory of San Marco, Florence, emphasizes the Transfiguration as preparation for the Passion. The transfigured Christ stands in cruciform pose, as if already hanging from the cross, in line with the note of penitence which marks many of the frescoes of San Marco (Hood 1993: 221).

The Exorcism of the Son (17:14–20)

Matthew interprets this boy's condition as due to the phases of the moon (cf. Mark 9:17): he is 'moonstruck' (17:15; Vulgate *lunaticus*), hence the translation 'lunatic(k)' in early English translations such as the Wycliffe Bible, the Douay-Rheims, and the KJV. Origen, for whom each of the diseases cured by Christ symbolizes a different sickness of the soul, interprets the boy's seizures in a spiritual sense:

> Similar disorders you may find in certain souls, which are often supposed to be healthy in point of temperance and the other virtues; then, sometimes, as if they were seized with a kind of epilepsy arising from their passions, they fall down from the position in which they seemed to stand, and are drawn away by the deceit of this world and other lusts. (Origen, *Commentary on Matthew* 13.4; *ANF* 9:477)

Origen's influence leads Jerome to interpret the boy's disease tropologically as a warning to those who periodically fall into vice. Augustine (*Questions on the Gospels* 1.21) specifically allegorizes the 'fire' and 'water' into which he falls, as anger and carnal desires respectively.

Those who focus on the literal sense often detect a tension between the boy's 'moonstruck' condition and Matthew's reference to a demon (17:18). Thus, Theophlyact of Ochrid, following John Chrysostom, concludes that the demon would take advantage of the full moon to attack his victim. The motive here may well be theodicy, to distance God himself from the origin of the sickness (see Davies and Allison 1991: 722, n. 10). In the sixteenth century, John Calvin proposes a mediating position. He regards the boy's condition as natural epilepsy, even though he allows that Satan was responsible for his 'deaf and dumb spirit' (Mark 9:25). Modern exegetes, by contrast, often offer a straightforward biomedical diagnosis, albeit at the risk of ignoring the social dimensions of the story and 'domesticating' the seizure (see the critique in Lawrence 2013: 98–123).

When the father approaches Jesus, explaining the inability of the disciples to cure his son, Jesus' response is a negative one to a 'faithless and perverse generation' (17:17; cf. 12:39; 16:4). The phrase suggests a general reference, to the crowds, or to Jesus' contemporaries. Alternatively, it might include the failing disciples, who will soon be rebuked for their 'little faith' (17:19–21; cf. 6:30; 8:26; 14:31; 16:8). Yet several commentators seek to exonerate the disciples, and instead implicate the boy's father. For John Chrysostom, Christ's words are addressed first to the father, who is 'exceedingly weak in faith' (Chrysostom seeks support here from Mark's version), and then through him to all the Jews. Jesus thus dismisses the 'complaints' of the man and those who thought badly of the disciples. Theophylact follows Chrysostom, adding the faithlessness of the boy himself.

Yet, as Theophylact admits, the disciples are also rebuked for their 'little faith.' Hilary attributes this to a 'kind of torpor' which came upon them while the Lord was on the mountain, weakening their faith (Hilary of Poitiers 2012: 188).

Figure 12 Theophanes the Greek (c. 1330–1410). *Transfiguration from Pereslav*. c. 1403. Icon on panel. Tretyakov Gallery, Moscow. Source: Photo Scala/Art Resource, NY.

The remedy is for them to move from having 'little faith' to faith 'like a grain of mustard seed,' although the distinction between the two is far from clear, given the tiny size of the seed in question (13:32; see Luz 2001: 409–410). This faith can move mountains (also 21:21), which many explain by appeal to a similar saying in Paul ('and if I have all faith so as to remove mountains,' 1 Cor 13:2; e.g. Origen; Jerome). For Jerome, 'all faith' means that it is large, not small. Utilizing another passage in the same Pauline letter (1 Cor 12:9), Cyril of Jerusalem differentiates between 'dogmatic faith,' necessary for all Christians, and a specific charism of faith given only to some which is able to effect extraordinary things (*Catech.* 5.11; also Calvin). Others find the clue in the category of seed, noting that mustard has a strong and pungent taste, thus symbolizing an ardent faith (e.g. Augustine, *Tractates on John* 40.8). Luz argues strongly that, contextually, the faith spoken of here must include faith in healing, and the extraordinary power of God (Luz 2001: 410).

Still, the notion of humans literally moving mountains raises questions (Calvin detects hyperbole in Jesus' words). Theophylact takes it literally, concluding that the apostles at a later date must also have moved mountains, although their locations have not been recorded. There are certainly legends about others sufficiently rich in faith to perform this miracle (e.g. Gregory Thaumaturgos). The fourteenth-century explorer Marco Polo recounts the story of a Christian shoemaker whose intense prayer resulted in a mountain being moved, thus saving the Christian population from being executed by the local caliph in Baghdad (*Description of the World* 1.26–29; Marco Polo 2016: 21–24). Jerome, by contrast, argues that 'this mountain' is not to be interpreted literally, but refers to the corruption which Jesus has removed from the epileptic son, referencing Jeremiah 51:25 ('I am against you, O destroying mountain, says the LORD, that destroys the whole earth ...,' NRSV).

Given the juxtaposition of two stories of two sons (the transfigured Jesus and the healed boy), linked together by the descent from the mountain (17:9–13), it is surprising how few interpreters exploit the Christological potential. A rare exception is Raphael's 1518–1520 *Transfiguration* (Figure 13), his last and largest painting, which explicitly reads the two scenes in parallel (Schiller 1971: 152; Kleinbub 2008, 2011). Commissioned by Cardinal Giulio de' Medici (the future Pope Clement VII) as an altarpiece for his cathedral in Narbonne, the fine character of Raphael's painting meant it never left Rome. In the upper register, Christ hovers transfigured, as if already risen and ascended, Peter, James, and John shielding their faces from the divine light. The lower register depicts the failure of the nine remaining apostles to heal the epileptic boy, i.e. the stage just prior to the one described by Matthew.

The boy's posture suggests he is being pulled in two directions, his right side upwards toward the vision of Christ, his left side down toward the earth by the opposing demon. His resulting 'cruciform' posture provides an interesting foil to the figure of Christ. The two parts of the altarpiece are also connected by the pointing figure of one of the nine apostles on the left, whose lowered head suggests that he is contemplating the Transfiguration not physically but, to use Origen's phrase, with the 'eyes of the heart' (Kleinbub 2008: 374–375). Thus, the external vision of the three on the mountain is juxtaposed with the internal vision of some of those below. This is complemented by the face of Christ, which seems to be gazing beyond the painting itself, contemplating the divine essence he possesses, which, according to medieval theologians, could only be 'viewed' intellectually. Raphael thus presents for his viewers a progression through the three stages of vision, from the corporeal through the internal or 'imaginary,' to the summit of intellectual vision (Kleinbub 2008: 384).

The Coin in the Fish's Mouth (17:24–27)

The final pericope again heightens Peter's role (in the second-century *Epistula Apostolorum*, the command to catch the fish is given to all the apostles: *Ep. apost.* 5). Many interpreters from earliest times (e.g. Melito, *Peri Pascha* 86; Hilary; Apollinaris of Laodicea, *Frag.* 87; Cyril of Alexandria, *Frag.* 212; Calvin; Baronius; Bengel) have understood this pericope to concern payment of the temple tax (Exod 30:11–16; Josephus, *Ant.* 18.312; *War* 7.218). This leaves the way open to figurative, typological readings. For Hilary, given that the temple tax was established for the redemption of soul and body, it foreshadows the offering Christians should make to Christ, the true Temple.

But different taxes have also been proposed. Origen, Chrysostom, and Theophylact connect the passage with the money to be paid to the tribe of Levi at the birth of firstborn sons (Num 3:43–50). Hence Christ, as firstborn Son, also appropriately pays. Others propose a Roman civil tax (e.g. Irenaeus, *Adv. Haer.* 5.24.1; Clement of Alexandria, *Paed.* 2.1.14; Jerome; Gregory of Nazianzus, *Orat.* 29.20; Erasmus; Lapide; Maldonado; see Cassidy 1979). Jerome connects this with the fact that Judea had become a tributary state under the Emperor Augustus. The issue then concerns the grounds on which Christians 'render to Caesar' (cf. 22:15–22). Aquinas engages the passage in a nuanced fashion against claims that it exempts Christians from obedience to secular powers, arguing that the children are 'free' from the authority of tyrants (*Commentary on the Sentences* 2, Dist. 44, q. 2, a. 2), while the Reformers relate it to the doctrine of two Kingdoms (see Luz 2001: 419). Roman Catholic canonists appeal to this passage to justify clerical exemption from civil taxation by divine right (see Luz 2001: 419), though Catholic exegetes such as Cornelius a Lapide reject such an application.

Such attempts to interpret this pericope's implications for ecclesial life presume that the statement 'the sons are free' refers not simply to Christ himself. For Jerome, Christians can also be treated as sons of the king, exempt from taxation metaphorically, given that Christ has paid the tribute on their behalf through his passion. Paul's distinction between what is lawful and what is expedient (1 Cor 10:23–33) is often in the background. Theophylact treats it as an example of an action which, though not required, does not harm us. In such

FIGURE 13 Raphael (1483–1520). *The Transfiguration*. 1518–1520. Oil on wood, 4100 × 2790 mm. Pinacoteca Vaticana, Rome. Source: Photo Scala/Art Resource, NY.

cases, one should not cause offense. Yet such generalizations risk downplaying the political, and potentially subversive, dimensions of Jesus' response to Peter (e.g. Carter 1999).

Matthew does not recount the actual discovery of the fish by Peter. Nonetheless, it is presumed, as a 'manifold miracle of omniscience and omnipotence' (Bengel 1971: 223). Early commentators frequently give it an ecclesiological twist, building on other passages connecting fishing with the mission and expansion of the church (e.g. 4:19; Luke 5:1–11; John 21:1–14). Cyril of

Alexandria reads the story as teaching a deep mystery about Christians, now saved and bearing the image of Christ through the apostolic preaching:

> For we are the fish snatched from the bitter disturbances of life. It is just as if we have been caught out of the sea on the apostles' hooks. In their mouths the fish have Christ the royal coin, which was rendered in payment for two things, for our soul and for our body. (*Frag.* 212; Simonetti 2002: 66)

Similarly, Apollinaris of Laodicea views the fish as a type of the church, rescued from 'the brine of faithlessness and superstition' and now 'raised up by the apostles' hook of teaching and the fishing nets of the Word to the knowledge of God' (*Frag.* 88; Simonetti 2002: 65).

Christology also comes into play, notably in allegorical interpretations of the coin. For some, it symbolizes the two natures of Christ (e.g. Theophylact), given that is it sufficient to pay the tax for both Jesus and Peter. Alternatively, since a stater is the equivalent of four drachmas, it signifies the preaching of the good news as presented in the four Gospels (e.g. Hilary). From the Enlightenment, the miracle aspect is viewed as particularly problematic. According to the rationalizing exegesis of Heinrich Eberhard Gottlob Paulus (1761–1851), the story presents Jesus instructing Peter to depend on nature, by raising enough money by fishing to pay the tax (in Baird 1992: 205).

The most famous representation of the scene in visual art is *The Tribute Money* by the Italian Renaissance painter Masaccio (1425; Brancacci Chapel, Santa Maria del Carmine, Florence). Part of a cycle from the life of St. Peter, patron saint of the chapel's founder, Pietro Brancacci, the story is recounted in three scenes presented synchronically: Peter in dialogue with Jesus (center); Peter finding the coin in the fish's mouth (left); Peter giving the coin to the tax-gatherer (right). The fresco is variously interpreted against the backdrop of contemporary debates in Florence over proposed tax reform, Pope Martin V's recent decree that the church of Florence be liable to state taxation, and the Brancaccis' specific cultivation of papal support for Florence against Milan. The latter would account for the presence of all the apostles in the scene (against the biblical text), heightening the prominence among them of Christ and Peter. The wider narrative structure of Masaccio's frescoes in the Brancacci Chapel also suggests a broader theological message. *The Tribute Money* symbolizes salvation through Christ's church, or the resurrection (in the fish) as counterpart to the preceding fresco of *The Expulsion of Adam and Eve from Eden* (see Casazza 1990: 25–26; Baldini and Casazza 1992; Clarke 2003: 153; Alkholy 2008: 440–441).

Matthew 18

Ancient Literary Context

Having turned his attention in the preceding narrative (13:53–17:27) to Jesus' new community, Matthew sets some parameters to that community's internal life in his fourth, and shortest, major discourse. Variously referred to as the 'Ecclesiological Discourse' (Thompson 1970: 2), 'The Community Discourse' (Luz 2001: 421; Schnackenburg 2002: 170), or 'Concerning Church

Administration' (Bacon 1930: 297), it nonetheless lacks the literary coherence of Matthew's other discourses.

The opening section (18:1–9) contains material also found at the same point in Mark and Luke (Mark 9:33–37, 42–48; Luke 9:46–50; cf. Luke 17:1–2), though Matthew omits the maverick exorcist (Mark 9:38–41; Luke 9:49–50), perhaps because it ill-suits his concern for ecclesial cohesion. This omission ensures a smooth transition from the pronouncement about 'children' to the warning of setting stumbling blocks before 'these little ones who believe in me.' Thus, the child functions more clearly as a metaphor for church members.

The central section comprises double-tradition material, including the Lost Sheep (18:10–20; Luke 15:3–7; 17:3; *Gos. Thom.* 107). The differing literary contexts in which Matthew and Luke locate this parable result in divergent interpretations. Whereas for Luke it concerns God's embrace of marginal 'tax collectors and sinners' (Luke 15:1), in Matthew the issue is wayward or lapsed members of the church. The broad motif of protection of wanderers and reconciliation of sinners provides the occasion for discussing disciplinary structures, related to the community's authority to 'bind' and 'loose' (18:18; cf. 16:19). The section concludes with a statement about Christ's presence with those gathered in his name (see 1:23; 28:20), reminiscent of Jewish statements about the Shekinah (*m. 'Abot* 3.2, 6; *b. Sanh.* 39a). The concluding parable of the Unforgiving Servant (18:21–35) returns to the theme of sin and forgiveness, though with a distinctively Matthean twist in terms of eschatological judgment. The parable's assumption that being forgiven presupposes a willingness to forgive recalls the Lord's Prayer (especially 6:12).

The Interpretations

Children and the Kingdom (18:1–9)

Becoming Like Children (18:2–4)

To illustrate his point about greatness in the Kingdom, Christ calls a little child, variously identified as the young Ignatius of Antioch (Bengel), 'Blessed Martial' (probably the third-century St. Martial of Limoges, whom legend transformed into a first-century disciple of Peter: Aquinas; Lapide), and the beloved disciple (John 13:23; Ephrem the Syrian in Salvesen 2006: 312). Bengel sees in the choice of the diminutive noun *paidion* ('*little* child') a conscious response to the disciples' quest for greatness.

Jesus' words are familiar but obscure, and differing interpretations reflect the changing cultural status of children, often tinged with sentimentality. Common explanations are that Jesus is speaking about their simplicity (Clement of Alexandria, *Paed.* 1.5; Hilary), their innocence (Herm. *Sim.* 9.29), or their unassuming humility (Theophylact; Calvin; Lapide). Some find the key in the Beatitudes, equating the childlike character demanded by Christ with being 'poor in spirit' (Theophylact), while, in a sermon for the Epiphany, Leo the Great links the reference to the childhood Christ took up in the incarnation, where the Magi encountered humility, innocence, and gentleness (*Sermon* 37.3). Jerome observes that a child doesn't remain angry, harbor grudges, or fall into sexual temptation, while Bengel points to their 'wonderful degree of humility, simplicity, and faith' (Bengel 1971: 224). Erasmus has a rather idealized view: 'a little child and still foreign to all feelings of ambition and envy, simple, pure, living under the guidance of nature alone' (Erasmus 2008: 259). John Calvin is more realistic, knowing that children have their faults. Nonetheless, he believes that they do not yet know the rivalry present in Christ's adult disciples. In more recent popular piety, it is children's openness to wonder which often comes to the fore. The German poet Matthias Claudius (1740–1815) exemplifies this view in his 'Evening Hymn':

> Let us become simple
> and here on earth
> like children be pious and joyful.
> (in Soelle and Schottroff 2000: 55)

Early Syriac commentators are more concerned to interpret Jesus' words in the light of other scriptural texts about children (Salvesen 2006), notably Genesis 2–3. Thus becoming like a child is to regain the childlike status Adam possessed before the Fall. The late fourth- or early fifth-century Syriac *Book of Steps* or *Liber Graduum* describes the perfect state of the celibate as a return to Adam's original state, where neither he nor Eve experienced desire nor were aware of their nakedness. This is explained by reference to Christ's words in 18:3 (Mimra 15.3; Salvesen 2006: 315–316).

Modern scholars often opt for humility, on the grounds that Jesus speaks in verse 4 of 'humbling oneself' or 'making oneself small' (like children, who are physically small: Luz 2001: 428), though with some clarification:

> The point, of course, is not that children are self-consciously humble but that they are, as part of society at large, without much status or position. (Davies and Allison 1991: 757)

Moreover, commentators both ancient and modern are quick to clarify that becoming childlike doesn't lead to moral or spiritual immaturity: 'For we must be as children in the humility of our mind, not be infantile in our thoughts; and we must be as children in guilelessness, but not in foolishness' (Theophylact 1992: 153).

An alternative route, proposed by Origen alongside the 'simpler' reading of the passage, is to interpret the 'child' allegorically, as the Holy Spirit, to whom disciples of Jesus must be conformed:

> Now consider if you can say that the little child, whom Jesus called, was the Holy Spirit who humbled Himself, when He was called by the Saviour, and set in the midst of the reason of the disciples of Jesus; if, indeed, He wishes us, being turned away from everything else, to be turned towards the examples suggested by the Holy Spirit, so that we may so become as the little children, who are themselves also turned and likened to the Holy Spirit. (*Commentary on Matthew* 13.18; *ANF* 9:485)

In later centuries, the discussion revolves less around would-be believers becoming 'like' children than the passage's implications for children themselves. The passage becomes a particular battleground (along with 19:13–15; Mark 10:13–16; Luke 18:15–17: 'let the little children come to me ...') in arguments between Anabaptists and other Christians over the legitimacy of infant baptism (see, e.g. Heinrich Bullinger in Stephens 2002: 186).

Causing Little Ones to Stumble (18:6–7)

Verse 6 clarifies that the 'children' function as a metaphor for the 'little ones who believe in me,' i.e. members of the church (Theophylact). But what kind of church members? The warning against causing one of these to stumble seems to be addressed to 'greater' or 'stronger' members. Thus the 'little ones' are regularly understood as a subgroup among Christians. For Theodore of Heraclea, they are 'those imperfect in their knowledge or those recently baptized' (*Frag.* 105; Simonetti 2002: 73). The modern scholar David Orton posits something similar: they are 'the newer recruits' in Matthew's scribal community, 'the undergraduate disciples of the gospel who join with prophets and mature scribes in the mission to make more disciples' (Orton 2003: 501). Such are not to be despised or lead to stumble.

The 'stumbling stone' (Greek *skandalon*) seems to be a reference to apostasy, akin to Peter's rejection of a suffering Messiah at 16:23 (cf. 11:6; 13:57; 15:12; 26:31, 33). Yet interpreters have often found this passage pertinent to other 'scandals.' *1 Clement* applies it to the schism within the church in Corinth (*1 Clem.* 46). St. Benedict uses it in his Rule to warn the cellarer of the monastery against withholding food, the 'little ones' referring to the members of the monastic community who are literally dependent, like children, on the cellarer's provision, and the 'scandal' the sin of irritation (Kardong 1996: 265):

> He should give the brothers their established allotment of food without arrogance or delay so as not to scandalize them. He should remember the Lord's saying about the fate of anyone *who should scandalize one of these little ones.* (*Rule of St. Benedict* 31.16; Kardong 1996: 259)

The Flemish Jesuit Cornelius a Lapide provides a comprehensive list of possible 'scandals':

> persecutions, derision, injuries of the righteous; also evil examples, false doctrines, things done or said unseasonably; for there are many things which are good and lawful in themselves, but by reason of inopportuneness of time, or place, when they are done before the uninstructed, become an occasion of scandal. (Lapide 1890: 2/288)

Jesus' words have also made an impact in the secular world. President Abraham Lincoln famously cites them in his Second Inaugural Address (4 March 1865), delivered in the final stages of the American Civil War, applying them to the offense or 'stumbling block' of slavery:

> The Almighty has His own purposes. 'Woe unto the world because of offenses; for it must needs be that offenses come, but woe to that man by whom the offense cometh.' If we shall suppose that American slavery is one of those offenses which, in the providence of God, must needs come, but which, having continued through His appointed time, He now wishes to remove, and that He gives to both North and South this terrible war as the woe due to those by whom the offense came, shall we discern therein any departure from those divine attributes which the believers in a living God always ascribe to Him?[1]

The Lost Sheep (18:10–14)

This parable continues the application to 'these little ones,' whose angels 'continually behold the face of my Father in heaven' (18:10; Irenaeus is aware that the Marcosians reverse the direction, by having the Father continually keeping the angels before his face: *Adv. Haer.* 1.13.3). Matthew alludes here to the Jewish belief that individuals, and not simply nations, have angels appointed for them

1 http://avalon.law.yale.edu/19th_century/lincoln2.asp.

by God (for references, see Davies and Allison 1991: 770, n. 82). He apparently claims that the angels of the 'little ones' are closer than others to the throne of glory (Rowland 1994: 510–511).

Their identification as guardian angels is attested early (Origen; Chrysostom; Jerome; Basil, *Adv. Eunom.* 3.1), and regularly repeated (e.g. *Opus imperfectum*; Maldonado; *Catechism of the Catholic Church* 336). Liturgically, 18:1–5, 10 is the Gospel for the Roman feast of the Guardian Angels on 2 October. Theophylact of Ochrid gives a reason for the particular proximity of the guardians of the 'little ones' to the divine throne:

> The angels of those who are little and humble in Christ are so intimate with God that they always stand before Him and behold His face. From this it is apparent that although we all have angels, the angels of us sinners are ashamed on account of our lack of boldness, and neither do they have boldness to behold the fact of God and perhaps even to pray for us. (Theophylact 1992: 155)

Their ability to behold the face of God 'in heaven' suggests a reference to a particular class of 'higher' angels, e.g. the angels of the Face or angels of the Presence (see Bucur 2007), although Aquinas treats the guardian angels as belonging to a lower order of angels, whose activity is largely confined to earth (*ST* Ia. 113, art. 3). What it means for them to see the face of the invisible God is widely debated. According to Cyril of Jerusalem, the angels do not see God as he is, but only according to their capacity (*Catech.* 6.6; see John 6:46). Cornelius a Lapide explains that they see 'the beauty and the brightness of the Divinity,' which makes them blessed, 'for otherwise, strictly speaking, God has not a face, even as he has not a body' (Lapide 1890: 2/293). Alternatively, Christology provides the key. For Clement of Alexandria, the face of the Father is Christ, the Word (*Strom.* 7.58.3–6), an interpretation followed by the Cappadocian Gregory of Nyssa, who equates the divine 'face' with the 'imprint' (*charaktēr*) of God's being at Hebrews 1:3 (in Bucur 2007: 228).

The reference to the angels leads into the parable proper (18:12–14), suggesting a fairly straightforward identification between the 'little ones' and the sheep that goes astray. For Origen, the parable specifically addresses the responsibility of bishops and pastors (*Hom. in Josh.* 7.6; also *Did. Apost.* 7), whereas John Chrysostom views it as speaking paraenetically to all members of the church.

Yet almost from the beginning, this parable has been the object of complex and sophisticated allegorization, such as by Simon Magus (Irenaeus, *Adv. Haer.* 1.24.2; Hippolytus, *Ref.* 6.19) and the Valentinian gnostics (Irenaeus, *Adv. Haer.* 1.8.4; see Gregg 1976: 87–91; Jorgensen 2016: 85–155; Gowler 2017: 16–20).

The Valentinians read the story as an allegory of the cosmic accident which led to this created world in which souls find themselves imprisoned:

> For they explain the wandering sheep to mean their mother, by whom they represent the Church as having been sown. The wandering itself denotes her stay outside of the Pleroma in a state of varied passion, from which they maintain that matter derived its origin. (Irenaeus, *Adv. Haer.* 1.8.4; *ANF* 1:327)

The version in the *Gospel of Thomas* also betrays gnostic tendencies. The sheep which goes astray is the 'largest' or 'greatest,' and is told that the shepherd loves it more than the 99 (*Gos. Thom.* 107): i.e. the largest sheep is arguably 'the Gnostic who has gone astray and has been brought to knowledge by Christ' (Luz 2001: 444).

Opponents respond by redirecting the allegory, in a way which ensures continuity between the God of Israel and the Father of Jesus. Thus for Irenaeus, the shepherd is the Logos who comes to deal with the sin of Adam by an act of recapitulation, rather than by facilitating a 'gnostic' flight from materiality (*Adv. Haer.* 3.19.3; Gregg 1976: 91–95; Jorgensen 2016: 114–120; see Rom 5:12–19). Irenaeus' salvation-historical reading is flexible enough to incorporate the salvation of the individual, Christ seeking out the 'carnal person' (*Adv. Haer.* 5.9–12; Jorgensen 2016: 120–122). More complex variations of Irenaeus' reading are regularly found in the ensuing centuries (e.g. Paschasius Radbertus; CCCM 56B: 882–888). The shepherd is Christ, who left the 99, i.e. the angels in heaven, and came to seek the one lost sheep, i.e. Adam as representing fallen humanity (Hilary), taking the form of a servant (Theophylact; see Phil 2:6–11). The identification of the shepherd with Christ is strengthened by manuscripts which include the interpolated verse 11 ('For the Son of Man came [to seek and] to save the lost'), regarded as original by Chrysostom, Hilary, and Chromatius of Aquileia. The angelic interpretation of the 99 may have been suggested by the mention of angels in verse 10. Indeed, some interpreters may have found the idea of angels being left to fend for themselves more plausible than humans being neglected (Bishop 1962: 47–48).

Jerome, who knows this interpretation, prefers a simpler one: the 99 sheep are the number of the just, the one sheep the number of sinners (also Rabanus Maurus; Aquinas). Augustine posits the reverse: the one sheep represents the humble, the 99 the proud, who are left 'on the mountains' or, following Luke's version, 'in the desert,' i.e. in their arrogant self-sufficiency (*Questions on the Gospels* 2.32; see Wailes 1987: 130). Nor is he alone in speculating about numbers. Hilary adds Abraham and Sarah to the mix, playing on the numbers 1 and 99, and their sum, 100. In Greek, the numeral 1 is denoted by the letter *alpha* and a hundred by *rho*, the letters added to names of Abram and Sarai to produce Abraham (Greek *Abraam*) and Sarah (*Sarrah*) respectively. Hence he concludes: 'We are all in the one man, Abraham, and we are all together, those in whom the number of the heavenly Church will be accomplished' (Hilary of Poitiers 2012: 196: Sarah is a type of the heavenly church).

Peter Chrysologus appeals to the contemporary system of finger counting, whereby 100 is the first number reckoned using the right hand. Thus the rehabilitation of the one sheep marks a return from the left hand to the right (*Sermon* 168; PL 52:640C–641A). A similar point had already been made in the Valentinian *Gospel of Truth* (*Gos. Truth* 31.28–32.30; Jorgensen 2016: 144).

Forgiveness and Community Discipline (18:15–20)

This section bears the characteristics of a 'church rule' (Luz 2001: 448), and it has been incorporated across the centuries, suitably adapted for local circumstances, into monastic rules of life, such as the Rule of St. Basil *(Long Rule* 36) and the Rule of St. Benedict, which envisages that faults of a brother will be admonished by his monastic seniors, leading to possible exclusion from the common table and monastic choir, and, in extreme cases (*Rule of St. Benedict* 28), expulsion from the monastery:

> If any brother is found to be defiant or disobedient or arrogant or a murmurer, or if he is in any way opposed to the Holy Rule or disdains the directions of his seniors, let him be admonished privately once and a second time by his seniors according to the command of our Lord. If he does not change his ways, let him be publically upbraided in the presence of all. If he still does not amend, and if he appreciates the penalty, let him undergo excommunication. But if he is insensible to it, let him undergo physical punishment. (*Rule of St. Benedict* 23: 'Excommunication for Faults'; Kardong 1996: 230)

Procedures for expulsion from the community for serious reasons, though apparently for a remedial purpose, are reflected elsewhere in the New Testament (1 Cor 5:1–5; 2 Cor 2:5–11; cf. *Did.* 15:3; for a Jewish parallel, see 1QS 6.24–7.25). The remedial aspect has often been to the fore in Christian applications of Matthew's passage (for texts, see, e.g. Luz 2001: 455). The mid-second-century *Epistula Apostolorum* combines reference to the procedure in Matthew (though without the third public stage before the church), with a warning against giving credence to slander (*Ep. apost.* 48–49). In a sermon interpreting the 'binding' and 'loosing' of verse 18 as disciplinary, Augustine reminds his hearers that holding 'your brother as an outsider to the covenant community' has as its ultimate aim loosing, that is, reconciliation following admonishment (*Sermon* 82.7 in Simonetti 2002: 79). John Chrysostom repeatedly refers to the therapeutic purpose of the process, like that of a physician seeking a cure, and emphasizes that both parties – the offender and the offended – suffer 'a common loss from the enmity' (*Homily on Matthew* 60; *NPNF* 2nd series, 10:372). The practice of forgiveness of sins is an important dimension of early Anabaptism which continues to the present, often related to conflict resolution, as in the Mennonite Conciliation Service's *Mediation and Facilitation Manual.*

Martin Luther is also concerned to avoid the public maligning of the sinner through gossip, which would transgress the Eighth Commandment. In his *Large Catechism* of 1529, he distinguishes between secret or private sins, and public sin (i.e. those already widely known, including doctrinal error). The whole process of 18:15–17 is only required in the case of the former, directed toward the 'great and excellent work' of gaining one's brother (in Mayes 2006: 37).

Like the monastic communities, various ecclesial communities have developed the disciplinary procedure in different ways. The medieval Catholic Church developed complex structures which differentiated between major and minor excommunications, the former public and often with consequences in the secular realm, the latter involving exclusion from communion (see Luz 2001: 455). The practice of 'the ban' is central to early Anabaptists and their descendants (Kuepfer 2007). One classic Anabaptist articulation of 'the ban' is found in the 1527 'Brotherly Union of a Number of Children of God Concerning Seven Articles' or *Schleitheim Confession of Faith*, emerging from a meeting of Swiss Brethren and South German Anabaptists presided over by a former Benedictine monk, Michael Sattler (Wenger 1945; Akin 1988; Snyder 1989). The ban is to be employed, not with force, but with love, aimed at maintaining the purity of Christ's body in the baptized community, prior to observing the Lord's Supper:

> Second. We are agreed as follows on the ban: The ban shall be employed with all those who have given themselves to the Lord, to walk in His commandments, and with all those who are baptized into the one body of Christ and who are called brethren or sisters, and yet who slip sometimes and fall into error and sin, being inadvertently overtaken. The same shall be admonished twice in-secret and the third time openly disciplined or banned according to the command of Christ. Mt. 18. But this shall be done according to the regulation of the Spirit (Mt. 5) before the breaking of bread, so that we may break and eat one bread, with one mind and in one love, and may drink of one cup. (*Article 2 on the Ban* in Wenger 1945: 248)

By 'the ban' is meant excommunication, rather than the later practice of 'shunning,' associated with Amish communities.

The precise meaning of 'tell it to the church' (18:17) is contested. For Jerome, this means the whole community. Others (Chrysostom; Theophylact;

Euthymius Zigabenus) restrict it to bishops and pastors. Such divergence comes to a head in the sixteenth century, with the Council of Trent upholding the latter view in the face of Protestant alternatives:

> Concerning the ministry of the sacrament [of penance], however, the holy council declares false and completely alien to the truth of the gospel all teachings which destructively extend the ministry of the keys to all persons indiscriminately, in addition to bishops and priests, and maintain against the institution of this sacrament that those words of the Lord, *Whatever you bind on earth shall be bound in heaven, and whatever you loose on earth shall be loosed in heaven*, and, *If you forgive the sins of any they are forgiven; if you retain the sins of any, they are retained*, were spoken to all Christ's faithful without distinction and discrimination, so that anyone has the power to forgive sins, public sins by reproof if the one reproved agrees to this, secret sins by a voluntary confession made to anyone. (Trent, Session 14, Chap. 6; Tanner 1990: II/707)

The matter is further complicated in contexts where the whole population is Christian, and the distinction between ecclesiastical and secular authorities is thereby blurred. Thus, Luther envisages that bringing the sin before the community can be achieved either through the civil or church tribunal (Mayes 2006: 38).

Pope Pius XI employs Christ's subsequent words ('if he does not listen to the church') with considerable force in his 1937 encyclical *Mit brennender Sorge* ('With burning concern'), reasserting human rights and fundamental Christian values against Nazi abuses:

> Faith in Christ cannot maintain itself pure and unalloyed without the support of faith in the Church, 'the pillar and ground of the truth' (1 Tim. iii. 15); for Christ Himself, God eternally blessed, raised this pillar of the Faith. His command to hear the Church (Matt. xviii. 15), to welcome in the words and commands of the Church His own words and His own commands (Luke x. 16), is addressed to all men, of all times and of all countries.[2] (*Mit brennender Sorge* 18)

Where Two or Three Are Gathered in My Name (18:20)

The promise of Christ's presence 'where two or three are gathered in my name' (18:20) provokes considerable speculation. The reconstructed original reading in P. Oxy. 1.23–27 ('Where there are three, they are without God, and where there is but a single one I say that I am with him': Attridge 1979) is possibly a

2 http://w2.vatican.va/content/pius-xi/en/encyclicals/documents/hf_p-xi_enc_14031937_mit-brennender-sorge.html.

Christian anchorite alternative to defend the Christian solitary life (Davies and Allison 1991: 791; cf. *Gos. Thom.* 30), while Origen individualizes by interpreting the words as agreement of body, soul, and spirit. Yet the literal level speaks of two or three Christians: for Tertullian, three are sufficient for the church to be present, even if all are laity (*Exhortation to Chastity* 7.3). Chromatius of Aquileia understands it to speak of Christian brothers and sisters gathered in prayer and unity, detecting intertextual echoes of Psalm 133:1 and the three men in the furnace (Dan 3). Therefore, it does not apply to schismatics, who have abandoned the peace of the church. The Latin hymn *ubi caritas est vera*, traditionally sung during the washing of the feet ritual on Maundy Thursday, also emphasizes the necessity for unity in charity as assurance of the divine presence:

> WHERE charity and love are, God is there.
> As we are gathered into one body,
> Beware, lest we be divided in mind.
> Let evil impulses stop, let controversy cease,
> And may Christ our God be in our midst.[3]

Others use Jesus' saying as a springboard to further deductions. For Ignatius of Antioch, it provides the foundation for his appeal to the Ephesian church to be united around its bishop at the Eucharist:

> Let no one be misled: if anyone is not within the sanctuary, he lacks the bread of God. For if the prayer of one or two has such power, how much more that of the bishop together with the whole church! (*Eph.* 5 = Holmes 2007: 187)

A similar logic leads to conclusions about the superiority of bishops gathered in council. In his letter to the Council of Ephesus of 431, Pope Celestine I argues that, if the Spirit can assure Christ's presence to two or three, how much more so when 'such great multitudes of the saints' are gathered together into one (*Ep.* 18.1; PL 50:505). A similar sentiment is expressed by the Council of Chalcedon to Pope Leo the Great in 451:

> For if where two or three are gathered together in His name, He has said that there He is in the midst of them, must He not have been much more particularly present with 520 priests, who preferred the spread of knowledge concerning Him to their country and their ease? (Leo the Great, *Ep.* 98.1; *NPNF* 2nd series, 12:72)

---

3 http://www.preces-latinae.org/thesaurus/Hymni/UbiCaritas.html.

In the sixteenth century, John Calvin will challenge the conviction, based on such a reading of verse 20, that councils cannot err, maintaining that Christ's assurance only extends to those who truly meet in Christ's name, i.e. in true piety, faith, and doctrine.

The Unmerciful Servant (18:21–35)

The parable is introduced by a question addressed to Jesus by Peter, regarding how often a sinning brother should be forgiven. Indeed, Erasmus suggests that Peter's question is provoked by Jesus' previous words about expulsion from the community, seeking clarification on how many times forgiveness should occur before excommunication ensues. Peter's apparent generosity (seven times, a perfect number), is shown wanting by Jesus' response:

> Peter's breast was narrow as yet, carnal, and bounded by the flesh. He could not understand the infinite abyss of mercy which there was in the Divine nature of Christ. (Lapide 1890: 2/309)

Christ is speaking of infinite forgiveness, 'not setting a number here, but what is infinite and perpetual and forever' (John Chrysostom, *Homily on Matthew* 61; *NPNF* 1st series, 10:375). This central point is clear, even allowing for the translation dispute about the number. Does Christ urge Peter to forgive 77 times (e.g. Origen; Bengel; NRSV; NABRE; BDF §248), or 70 times 7, i.e. 490 times (e.g. Jerome; Theophylact; Erasmus; Geneva Bible; Douay-Rheims; KJV; RSV)? Several find an intertextual echo of Genesis 4:24, where the vengeance of Cain is said to be avenged 7 times, and Lamech 77 times. This is reversed by the limitless forgiveness offered by Christ (Tertullian, *De Orat.* 7.2; Origen).

Such divine generosity is underscored by the exaggerated figure of the first servant's debt: 10 000 talents, which interpreters convert into contemporary equivalents. The marginal note to the Geneva Bible clarifies that it is 'a very great sum of threescore hundred thousand crowns.' In the following century, Cornelius a Lapide calculates it as a 120 million French crowns. The NIV paraphrases effectively as 'ten thousand bags of gold' (further clarifying that just a single talent was the equivalent of 20 years' labor for a regular worker). By comparison, *The Message*'s 'a hundred thousand dollars' (Peterson 2002) appears meager.

Some readers find additional symbolism in the number. Augustine links it to the 77 generations from Christ to Adam according to Luke's genealogy, which Luke presents immediately after recounting Jesus' baptism (Luke 3:23–38):

> So then if no generation was omitted, there is no exemption of any trespass that ought not to be forgiven. For therefore did he reckon up his seventy-seven generations, which number the Lord mentioned as to the forgiveness of sins; since he begins to reckon from the baptism, where all sins are remitted. (*Sermon* 83.5; Simonetti 2002: 83)

The interpretative key to the parable is provided by the punchline in verse 35: the unforgiving servant's fate is that of all those who fail to forgive 'from their heart.' It is a sentiment espoused by the Duke in Shakespeare's *The Merchant of Venice*, in words addressed to Shylock: 'How shalt thou hope for mercy rend'ring none?' (Act 4, Scene 1, line 88). The parable also leaves its mark on Leo Tolstoy's novel *Resurrection*, where the hero Nehlúdof advocates unlimited forgiveness, in light of his experience of Russian prisons and legal system, where '[v]icious men were trying to reform other vicious men':

> The answer he had been unable to find was the same that Christ gave to Peter. It was to forgive always, every one, to forgive an infinite number of times, because there are none who are not themselves guilty, and therefore none who can punish or reform. (Tolstoy 1966: 496)

Given Christ's clear punchline, Hilary sees little need to elaborate further, despite his usual preference for allegorization (similarly Chrysostom; Paschasius Radbertus; Rupert of Deutz). Origen does explore potential allegorical dimensions, including identifying the one owing 10 000 talents as the devil, a reading later rejected by Jerome as 'no ecclesiastical interpretation' (Jerome 2008: 214). But even Origen recognizes the difficulties of a figurative reading, with the disclaimer that 'with regard to the interpretation of the loftiest type, we make no profession' (*Commentary on Matthew* 14.6; *ANF* 9:498). Augustine also resorts to some mild allegorizing, relating both the 10 000 talents and the 100 denarii to sins against the Decalogue, and interpreting the king's threat to sell his servant as damnation, and the servant's wife and children as cupidity and evil works respectively (*Questions on the Gospels* 1.25; see Wailes 1987: 133).

Full-blown allegorical interpretations are more common in the Middle Ages. The ninth-century Frankish Benedictine scholar Rabanus Maurus allegorizes the parable in terms of the Jews, who transgressed the Decalogue (= 10 000 talents), and the Gentiles, from who the Jews demanded circumcision and Torah observance. The apostles and preachers are the fellow-servants (see Wailes 1987: 135–136; also Pseudo-Bede; Dionysius the Carthusian). In the East, Theophylact also resorts to complex allegory: the king is the Word, who became incarnate, and as judge settles his servants' accounts. The wife is the flesh as partner of the soul, and the children evil works performed by both body and soul. The flesh is given over to Satan, with the ultimate purpose that the spirit may be saved (see 1 Cor 5:3–5).

Counter-Reformation realism is visible in *The Unmerciful Servant* (c. 1620; Gemäldegalerie Alte Meister, Dresden) by the Roman Baroque artist Domenico Fetti. Fetti vividly portrays the failure of mercy on the part of the servant forgiven the huge debt. It depicts him in a dark space at the bottom of a staircase, probably meant to represent the entrance to the prison, seizing his fellow servant by the neck. The superior status of the former over the latter is represented by his greater age, and his larger size. The younger servant gazes out of the painting at the viewer, as if pleading for forgiveness, while the older man looks directly at his victim, failing in his duty to forgive as he has been forgiven (see Askew 1961: 28; Gowler 2017: 141–142).

Matthew 19–20

Ancient Literary Context

19:1 marks a key stage in the journey to Jerusalem, as Jesus leaves Galilee and moves swiftly to the region of 'Judea beyond the Jordan' (cf. Mark 10:1), before arriving in Jerusalem at 21:1–11. The mention of this specific location ('a stop along the way on a pilgrimage journey': Verseput 1994: 114), as well as repeated references to crowds (19:2; 20:29), reminds the readers that the Passover pilgrimage to Jerusalem has begun, albeit one which will end in Jesus' death.

Matthew Through the Centuries, First Edition. Ian Boxall.

The basic shape and content of the narrative follows closely Mark 10 (partially paralleled in Luke 18:15–43). It combines several literary forms: a conflict story in which the Pharisees reappear to 'test him' (19:3; cf. 4:1–11); didactic dialogues with the disciples over marriage (19:10–12) and wealth (19:23–30), the latter preceded by another dialogue between Jesus and a wealthy would-be disciple (19:16–22); two stories in which Jesus instructs about the nature of the Kingdom (19:13–15; 20:20–28); a third passion prediction (20:17–19); a healing (20:29–34).

Matthew's version contains several distinctive features. First, he appends to the discussion regarding marriage a saying about eunuchs 'for the kingdom' (19:12). This has been variously interpreted as advocacy for celibacy (Kleist 1945), a specific reference to those who have divorced wives for reason of *porneia* and find themselves unable to remarry as a consequence (Quesnell 1968), or a warning to Jesus' male disciples that, in Jesus' egalitarian view of marriage, they must 'symbolically sever their testicles as the symbolic bases of kyriarchy' (Talbott 2006: 40). Second, Matthew's Jesus gives the Twelve an eschatological role as judges (19:28; cf. Luke 22:28–30). Third, Matthew inserts the parable of the Workers in the Vineyard (20:1–16), unique to his Gospel, illustrating the saying at 19:30 that 'many who are first will be last, and those who are last will be first.' He also attributes the request of James and John to their mother (20:20; cf. Mark 10:35–45), and transforms the healing of blind Bartimaeus into a healing of two blind men, reflecting his penchant for doublets (20:29–34; also e.g. 9:27–31; cf. Mark 10:46–52; Luke 18:35–43).

The Interpretations

Marriage, Divorce, and Eunuchs (19:1–12)

Jesus' response to the Pharisees shifts the focus from intra-Jewish debates about divorce (reflected in the views of Hillel and Shammai over Deut 24:1; see e.g. *m. Giṭ* 9.10) to the creator's design 'from the beginning' (Gen 1:27; 2:24), which overrides the later Mosaic 'permission' to Israelite males to divorce. Early interpreters often appreciate the broader cultural context of Jesus' words. Divorce, as Gregory of Nazianzus observes, 'is hard on women.' The Genesis passage cited by Jesus, by contrast, acknowledges that the two have 'equal honour' (*Orat.* 37.6–7; *NPNF* 2nd series, 7:340). It also represents a criticism of polygamy (cf. CD 4.20–5.1; Instone-Brewer 2006: 17–18), a point noted by the *Opus imperfectum*. As in the Sermon on the Mount, Jesus again provides an exception to the otherwise uncompromising prohibition on divorce (see above on 5:32).

Some move beyond the literal level of the dialogue, driven by biblical use of marital imagery to describe God's relationship with Israel, or Christ's with his people. The Carolingian Benedictine theologian Remigius of Auxerre (c. 841–908) detects a Christological pattern: Christ left his Father (in his descent from heaven) and his mother (the unbelieving synagogue), and cleaved to his wife (the church), so that he and the church are now one body (in Ford 1859: II/334–335).

Jesus' saying about eunuchs for the sake of the Kingdom (19:12) is particularly disputed. This group is the last of three mentioned, the other two (those born eunuchs, those who make themselves eunuchs) closely resembling rabbinic discussions, which distinguish between 'eunuchs of the sun/of heaven' (i.e. those so born) and 'eunuchs of men' (i.e. the castrated: Str-B 1.805–7; Luz 2001: 501). The literal background to the third type may well be pagan priests such as those of Cybele, who castrated themselves out of devotion to the mother goddess, and whose presence is attested in Samaria (Harvey 2007: 7–11). Eunuchs generally were the victims of ridicule in the Roman world, perceived as 'fat and beardless in physique, yellow and wrinkled in complexion, effeminate and touchy of character' (Harvey 2007: 8). They were especially despised by Jews given their inability to fulfill the command to 'go forth and multiply' (see, e.g. Deut 23:1–2; Josephus, *Ant.* 4.290–291), though Isaiah attests to a more positive reversal of their fortunes (Isa 56:3–5; cf. Wis 3:14). It is possible that underlying Jesus' usage here is the memory of an accusation laid against him during his public ministry.

What constitutes a eunuch 'for the sake of the kingdom of heaven'? Is it metaphorical, or, like the first two types of eunuchs, to be taken literally? A minority have understood it in a literal sense. Eusebius famously claimed that the young Origen castrated himself in response to Jesus' words (see Markschies 2009):

> At this time while Origen was conducting catechetical instruction at Alexandria, a deed was done by him which evidenced an immature and youthful mind, but at the same time gave the highest proof of faith and continence. For he took the words, 'There are eunuchs who have made themselves eunuchs for the kingdom of heaven's sake' (Matthew 19:12) in too literal and extreme a sense. And in order to fulfill the Saviour's word, and at the same time to take away from the unbelievers all opportunity for scandal – for, although young, he met for the study of divine things with women as well as men, – he carried out in action the word of the Saviour. (Eusebius, *H.E.* 6.8.1; *NPNF* 2nd series, 1:254)

Jerome makes the same claim (*Ep.* 84.8, albeit almost certainly dependent on Eusebius), while Epiphanius of Salamis reports even more elaborate stories along similar lines (*Pan.* 64.3.11–2). Doubts exist, however, regarding the reliability of Eusebius' report. Most significant is Origen's own exegesis of the passage in his *Commentary on Matthew*, where he rejects a literal in favor of a figurative interpretation of all three categories of eunuch, referring to the moral person. The eunuch for the sake of the Kingdom is someone who cuts off 'the passionate faculty of the soul without touching his body' (Heine 2013: 124).

However, others have interpreted Christ's words literally, notably the Russian sect known as the Skoptsy or 'castrated ones,' which flourished between the late eighteenth and early twentieth centuries. The Skoptsy took Christ's words to heart by practicing ritual castration, as a mark or seal of the 144 000 followers of the Lamb (Rev 7:4; 14:1; see Engelstein 1999).

Most Christians have rejected such a literal interpretation. Indeed, the Council of Nicaea (325) declares self-castration as incompatible with the clerical state:

> If anyone in sickness has undergone surgery at the hands of physicians or has been castrated by barbarians, let him remain among the clergy. But if anyone in good health has castrated himself, if he is enrolled among the clergy he should be suspended, and in future no such man should be promoted. (Nicaea I, *Canon 1*; Tanner 1990: I/6)

Instead, this third category of eunuchs has been widely understood figuratively, albeit not in a monochrome fashion. It is understood by the Basilidians as promoting an extreme asceticism (in Clement of Alexandria, *Strom.* 3.1), an interpretation downplayed by their opponents. Clement himself understands Christ's words as an exhortation to control the passions, even within marriage: 'For it is a praiseworthy thing to castrate oneself because of the kingdom of heaven from every concupiscence and to purify our conscience of dead works to serve the living God' (*Strom.* 3.7 in Arendzen 1919: 237). This seems to underlie the rendering of the saying in the *Hebrew Gospel of Matthew*:

> Because there are eunuchs from their birth; these are those who have not sinned. (There are eunuchs made by man) and there are self-made eunuchs who subdue their desire for the sake of the kingdom of heaven; these are (those who enter) into great prominence. (Howard 1995: 95)

Others find a reference here to voluntary celibacy, 'in hope of living in closer communion with God' (Athenagoras, *Leg.* 33; *ANF* 2:146; cf. Jerome; Augustine, *Confessions* 8.1; Theophylact). For Tertullian, the saying reveals Christ's preference for continence over marriage (*Monog.* 3.5). Thus Christ agrees with the disciples' assertion that it is better not to marry.

In the Greek East, there is a tendency, following Origen, to interpret all three categories allegorically (see Luz 2001: 498). Gregory of Nazianzus understands eunuchs from birth as those who 'seem by nature to incline to good,' and eunuchs made so by others as people 'whom reason cleanses, by cutting them off from the passions' (*Orat.* 37.20). The third type are those who have cultivated virtue unaided by human teachers:

> Others, too, who have not met with teachers, have been laudable teachers to themselves. No father nor mother, no Priest or Bishop, nor any of those commissioned to teach, taught you your duty; but by moving reason in yourself and by kindling the spark of good by your free will, you made yourself a eunuch, and acquired such a habit of virtue that impulse to vice becomes almost an impossibility to you. (*Oration* 37.21; *NPNF* 2nd series, 7:344)

The understanding of the third type as celibates, who have embraced a higher state than marriage, informs views of the religious life throughout the Middle Ages. According to *The Golden Legend*, Francis of Assisi once threw himself in the snow, and made a family out of seven snowballs (a wife, two sons, two daughters, a maidservant, and a manservant), in order to quash his burning passions (Jacobus de Voragine 1993: II/223).

The Reformers, while for the most part accepting that this saying refers to celibacy, nonetheless challenge the priority of celibacy over the married state, emphasizing Christ's clarification that this 'word' is not for everyone. In a sermon on Matthew 19 preached in 1537, Martin Luther praises the virginity of the 'true eunuchs' who 'castrate themselves spiritually,' i.e. who are 'chaste willingly and have the grace to remain a virgin voluntarily. Is it also very good and fine for them to live chastely in this way, yet not so as to make it into a service to God or an act of superiority.' Yet, he is keen to remind his hearers that it is a charism granted to some only, and not to be imposed: 'In short, people like this have a golden treasure and precious jewel, and to these belongs the answer which the Lord Christ gives the apostles here. However, I do not let this be said of all people – rather, only if one has this gift' (Luther 2014: 16). Moreover, this should not be turned into a 'work,' a 'service to God or an act of superiority' (Luther 2014: 16–18). Similarly, a marginal gloss to the 1599 version of the Geneva Bible ('and there be some eunuchs, which have gelded themselves for the kingdom of heaven') clarifies the meaning of 'gelded' (i.e. 'castrated') so as to emphasize that this is a divine gift: 'Which abstain from marriage, and live continently through the gift of God.'

The Catholic response to the Reformers is articulated formally by the Council of Trent, which reasserts the priority of celibacy for the sake of the Kingdom over marriage: 'If anyone says the married state is to be preferred to that of virginity or celibacy, and that it is no better or more blessed to persevere in virginity or celibacy than to be joined in marriage: let him be anathema'

(Trent, Session 24, Canons on the sacrament of marriage 10; Tanner 1990: II/755). Counter-Reformation exegetes such as Lapide and Maldonado also respond directly to the Protestant critique. For Maldonado, verse 11 should not be interpreted as 'Not all are able to do what you say – abstain from marriage,' but 'All men take not this word,' i.e. not all understand it (Maldonado 1888: 2/135–136; the Vulgate has *non omnes capiunt verbum*).

The Rich Youth (19:16–30)

Following a brief pericope concerning Jesus' encounter with children (19:13–15; on Children and the Kingdom, see above on 18:1–9), this dramatic story encapsulates the radical demands of discipleship. Matthew's version justifies the traditional title of this passage as 'The Rich Young Man,' for he alone identifies the questioner as a youth (19:20; cf. Mark 10:21; Luke 18:18). Matthew also confronts the Christological ambiguity in Mark's version ('no one is good but God alone'), highlighted by the Arians (see e.g. Epiphanius, *Pan.* 69; Hilary, *De Trin.* 1.29), which might be read as Jesus distancing himself from the 'good God' (Mark 10:17–18). Though he retains the phrase, Matthew rephrases the man's question, so that the conversation revolves around 'the good thing,' thus lessening the potential contrast between God and Jesus (19:16–17; though see Luz 2001: 511, n. 20).

Many early interpreters interpret this story's critique of riches figuratively. One classic exposition is Clement of Alexandria's *Quis dives salvetur?* which blends the Matthean and Markan versions. Clement moves beyond a literal focus on giving up material possessions to the soul's detachment from possessions and anxiety. Reading the story intratextually in the light of the Matthean Beatitudes, Clement proposes that the man is invited to become 'pure in heart' and 'poor in spirit' rather than materially poor (*Quis dives* 16–17):

> He does not, as some conceive off-hand, bid him throw away the substance he possessed, and abandon his property; but bids him banish from his soul his notions about wealth, his excitement and morbid feeling about it, the anxieties, which are the thorns of existence, which choke the seed of life. (*Quis dives* 11; *ANF* 2:594)

The disciples' question ('Who then can be saved?') is an indicator that they have grasped this spiritual, parabolic dimension of Jesus' words, for they were not themselves materially rich, but nonetheless recognized that they still clung to the 'riches' of the passions (*Quis dives* 20). Origen similarly understands wealth figuratively, as symbolizing evil deeds.

Other patristic exegetes opt for a full-blown allegory. For Hilary, the young man represents the Jewish people, who were 'rich' on the Law, and therefore unable to enter the Kingdom except with difficulty. The *Opus imperfectum* concurs, adding that the camel, who can pass through the eye of a needle more easily, though still with difficulty, signifies the Gentiles. Just as a camel's hump weighs its head down and prevents it from lifting its neck, so the Gentiles are bent down by idolatry and therefore unable to 'lift the head of their souls upward or come to the knowledge of God' (*33rd Homily*; Kellerman and Oden 2010: 265; also Paschasius Radbertus). The fifth-century Roman monk Arnobius Iunior has a similar allegorical reading, although viewing the 'camel' more positively (*Expositiunculae in Matthaeum* 19; Kraszewski 1999: 340). The 'rich man' symbolizes the Jews, who 'exited Egypt with riches,' the 'camel' Christians who 'have now put aside the burdens of our sins and have entered through the "needle's eye," that is, the strait and narrow gate that leads to life' (see 7:14).

But the story's power lies especially in its impact on the literal level. Its focus on 'being perfect' has led to the story justifying a 'higher' perfection for certain groups, such as monks and other religious (it is a key text for Aquinas's distinction between 'precepts' and 'evangelical counsels': *ST* IIa.IIae. q. 186, a. 3). According to Athanasius' *Life of St. Antony*, it was hearing this Gospel which inspired Antony of Egypt, the 'father of monasticism,' to take his first radical steps. Antony had already been contemplating the sharing of possessions by the apostles in the early church (Acts 4:34–35), following the death of his parents:

> Pondering these things, he went into the church; it happened that the Gospel was being read at that time and he heard the Lord saying to the rich man, 'If you want to be perfect, go, sell all your possessions and give to the poor, and come follow me, and you will have treasure in heaven.' When Antony received from God the remembrances of the saints and realized how that passage had been read for his sake, he immediately left the church, and the possessions that he had inherited from his ancestors (there were three hundred fertile and very prosperous acres) he freely gave away to people from his village so they would not bother him or his sister about anything. He sold all his remaining possessions and, collecting a considerable amount of money, distributed it among the poor, keeping a little for his sister. (*Greek Life of Antony* 2.3–5; Athanasius of Alexandria 2003: 59)

Several centuries later, Bernard of Clairvaux will look at the history of Christian monks and anchorites as the radical outworking of Christ's invitation:

> These are the words which in all the world have persuaded men to a contempt of the world, and to voluntary poverty. They are the words which fill the cloisters with monks, the deserts with anchorites. These, I say, are the words which spoil Egypt, and strip it of the best of its goods. (cited in Lapide 1890: 2/341)

Jesus' response to the rich man also inspired Francis of Assisi and his early companions, as expressed in his Rule of 1221:

> The Rule and life of the friars is to live in obedience, in chastity and without property, following the teaching and footsteps of our Lord Jesus Christ who says: 'If you will be perfect, go sell what you have, and give to the poor, and you shall have treasure in heaven; and come follow me' (Matt. 19:21). (quoted in Muessig 2009: 138)

Others insist that it is addressed to all Christians, especially the rich, even if the demand to sell 'all' is sometimes mitigated (e.g. Origen; Chrysostom), or the saying about a camel passing through the eye of a needle is occasionally blunted (e.g. Theophylact suggests that *kamēlos* should be rendered not 'camel' but 'ship cable,' while the *Glossa ordinaria* posits a low gate in Jerusalem called 'the camel,' because those entering had to stoop camel-like in order to pass through). This broader interpretation even informs contemporary Roman Catholic discussion, as in John Paul II's 1993 encyclical *Veritatis Splendor*:

> This vocation to perfect love is not restricted to a small group of individuals. The invitation, 'go, sell your possessions and give the money to the poor,' and the promise 'you will have treasure in heaven,' are meant for everyone, because they bring out the full meaning of the commandment of love for neighbour, just as the invitation which follows, 'Come, follow me,' is the new, specific form of the commandment of love of God. (*Veritatis Splendor* 18)[1]

Whether this young man was ultimately able to make the heroic response to Jesus' invitation is not made clear in the Gospel text, and the version in the *Gospel of the Nazarenes* (as cited in Origen's commentary) has the rich man scratch his head at Jesus' words. Most commentators have assumed his failure due to the fact that he leaves this encounter 'sad' (19:22). Thus, for Clement of Alexandria, 'he did not truly wish life, as he averred, but aimed at the mere reputation of the good choice' (*Quis dives* 10; *ANF* 2:594). This conclusion is somewhat ironic, given Clement's warning later in his treatise that his readers not judge who is worthy and who unworthy (*Quis dives* 33; see Clarke 2009: 451). But many others concur, or even question the man's motives. Hilary castigates him for the haughty manner of his question, and his overconfidence in the Law. For Jerome, the man is lying when he claims to have kept the commandments; moreover, as he departs he manifests the worldly sorrow which, according to Paul, leads to death (2 Cor 7:10). These generally negative

---

1 http://w2.vatican.va/content/john-paul-ii/en/encyclicals/documents/hf_jp-ii_enc_06081993_veritatis-splendor.html.

portraits explain why the rich young man has been proposed as one possible candidate for the shade Dante sees in Hell, who 'made through cowardice the great refusal' (*Inferno* 3.60; see Clarke 2009: 447).

The Workers in the Vineyard (20:1–16)

The primary focus of this parable may well have originally been on its climax, thus emphasizing God's extraordinary generosity (Luz 2001: 533–535). This reading has left some traces on the story's reception history. For Hilary of Poitiers, the central message is God's free gift of grace granted through justification by faith. In the fourteenth-century anonymous poem *Pearl*, the deceased daughter of the dreamer tells her father in a vision that her queenly status in heaven is due, not to any meritorious acts of her own, but to sheer divine graciousness. She does so by connecting this parable with the earlier parable of the Pearl (13:45–46). Hence, although she died as a young child, she is one of the workers called at the eleventh hour, who received full wages despite only having labored in the vineyard of this world for a short time before her untimely death (Wilcox 2011). *Pearl* thereby undercuts human attempts to quantify salvation in human economic terms:

> So poor men take their portion too,
> Though late they came and puny they were,
> And though they make but little ado,
> The mercy of God is much the more.
> (*Pearl,* lines 573–576 in Wilcox 2011: 12)

Nonetheless, readers across the centuries have detected layers of complexity which resist reducing the parable's meaning to a simple point, as the twelfth-century Cistercian abbot Isaac of Stella noted:

> Take this parable of our text. It seems a straightforward piece of Scripture if ever there was one, and yet it is rightly explained and commented on by many different authors in many different ways, but no one can so get to the bottom of it that all possible interpretations are exhausted, that posterity cannot add a word to what has already been said. (*Sermon* 16; Isaac of Stella 1979: 129)

That Matthew connects this parable to the saying about first and last at 19:30 (reiterated in a different form at 20:16) explains an early tendency to interpret it in salvation-historical terms. The first are the Jews, and the last the Gentiles, who also share in the vineyard owner's generosity, albeit at the end (cf. Rom 1:16; 11:25–26), and who receive their wages first. Some explicitly link the complaints of those called at the first hour with the jealousy Paul expects will be felt by Jews at the conversion of the Gentiles (Rom 11:11, 14; e.g. Jerome).

The basic pattern is set by Irenaeus, driven by a theological concern for continuity between the Testaments. According to Irenaeus, the Ptolemaean Valentinians rooted their cosmology, consisting of 30 invisible aeons, in the observation that this number was the sum of the hours mentioned by the parable: 1, 3, 6, 9, and 11 (*Adv. Haer.* 1.1.3). By contrast, his rather restrained allegorical interpretation describes the phases of history from the creation until the end:

> Also by the parable of the workmen who were sent into the vineyard at different periods of the day, one and the same God is declared (Matthew 20:1, etc.) as having called some in the beginning, when the world was first created; but others afterwards, and others during the intermediate period, others after a long lapse of time, and others again in the end of time; so that there are many workmen in their generations, but only one householder who calls them together. (*Adv. Haer.* 4.36.7; *ANF* 1:518)

This historical interpretation is frequently repeated, albeit with some variation (e.g. different temporal divisions; Christ rather than the Father as the owner of the vineyard), through to the Middle Ages (e.g. Origen; Hilary; Jerome; Cyril of Alexandria, *Frag.* 226; *Opus imperfectum*; Paschasius Radbertus; Albert the Great; Aquinas; Nicholas of Lyra; see Wailes 1987: 137–144; Steinmetz 1980: 33–35; Tevel 1992: 362–369; Gowler 2017: 33–34, 66–68, 87–89). Typical is Pope Gregory the Great (c. 540–604), for whom the vineyard symbolizes God's people, ruled by God the Creator (the owner), which produces many saints from Abel down to the end of time (the branches of the vines). The hired workers cultivating his vineyard are preachers (the patriarchs, then teachers of the law, prophets, and finally apostles), preaching at various times of the day. The morning signifies the period from Adam to Noah, the third hour from Noah to Abraham, the sixth hour from Abraham to Moses, the ninth hour from Moses to Christ's coming, and the eleventh hour from Christ to the end of the world, when the apostles have received full pay although they came late. But Gregory then broadens the definition of the workmen, to include everyone 'who had the right faith with good works': first, the Hebrews, then the Gentiles at the eleventh hour (*Homily* 11; Gregory the Great 1990: 83).

The radical Franciscan Peter John Olivi is influenced in his reading of the parables by the twelfth-century abbot Joachim of Fiore. Therefore he adds a correspondence between these five periods and New Testament history: the first hour corresponds to the call made by Christ and his apostles, the third hour the time of the general councils of the church, the sixth the time of the wisdom of Greek and Latin Fathers, represented by Augustine and Gregory the Great, the ninth the Greek schism and the rise of the Saracens (which was matched more positively by the proliferation of monasticism), and the eleventh the coming of Francis of Assisi (Madigan 2003: 103–104). An Islamic variant of the historical reading is found in various forms in the *hadith*, whereby the Jews and then the Christians work for the first two parts of the day, while the Muslims work from the time of 'Asar prayer until sunset, and receive a double wage (in Gowler 2017: 72–73).

In a sermon preached in 1525, Martin Luther notes that he does not object to those who read the parable in the manner expounded by Gregory the Great. However, his preference is to treat the parable as concerned specifically with the history of Israel, rather than the longer history from Adam. The vineyard is the Jewish people, the laborers the prophets, and the parable culminates in the coming of Christ, and his sending the apostles to make Jews and Gentiles into one vineyard. He also finds here support for salvation by grace, despite the parable's explicit focus on payment: 'To everyone, regardless of whether he worked much or little, He gives the afore-promised coin, that is, His Son, Jesus Christ, forgiveness of sins, redemption from death and every affliction' (Luther 2014: 71–72).

In an earlier sermon, preached in 1517, Luther had attempted to link merit with reward, by claiming that the greater humility of those hired at the eleventh hour meant that their 1 hour was worth 12 hours of the earlier grumblers (Steinmetz 1980: 35). Patristic and medieval exegetes had used similar arguments in order to avoid charges of divine injustice. For Gregory of Nazianzus, the greater faith of those who came at the eleventh hour made up for their lesser works (*Orat.* 40;20). Ironically, Luther's younger contemporary Juan de Maldonado will appeal to the same idea that some complete a day's work in the single hour of activity, an interpretation directed in part against the Lutherans.

Origen, followed by many of his successors, combined the salvation-historical reading with other interpretations, regarded as complementary (see Tevel 1992: 358–362). For example, building on the historical relation of the parable to the periods from Adam to Christ, Origen also interprets it as a description of the spiritual senses from Adam (touch, given that Adam was told not to touch the tree, Gen 3:3) to Christ (sight, given that the disciples were able to see him). More commonly cited is Origen's third, moral interpretation, again well-articulated by Gregory the Great. This applies the various times of the day to an individual's life: the morning is childhood; the third hour, youth; the sixth, young adulthood; the ninth, old age; the eleventh, the very old. People are called into the Lord's vineyard at different stages of their life; yet all receive the same pay of a denarius, i.e. 'an equal recompense of life' (*Homily* 11; Gregory the Great 1990: 77–85). Jerome provides biblical examples to illustrate the point: Samuel, Jeremiah, and John the Baptist are among those who served in the vineyard from their mother's womb. This interpretation makes room for the kind of 'deathbed conversion' envisaged by the Oxford scholar Robert Burton (1577–1640): 'Thou mayest in the Lord's good time be converted; some are called at the eleventh hour' (*Anatomy of Melancholy* 3.4.2.6. in Siebald in Jeffrey 1992: 430). The phrase 'eleventh hour' (20:6, contemporized in the NRSV as 'about five o'clock,' given that the hours were counted from 6 a.m.) has for this reason entered into popular culture, as 'the latest possible moment' (OED). This explains the title of the 2007 documentary *The 11th Hour*, narrated by Leonardo DiCaprio, warning of the dire consequences of global warning. Perhaps even more famous is the timing of the Armistice, which brought to an end the First World War: 11 a.m. on 11 November 1918, or 'the eleventh hour of the eleventh day of the eleventh month.'

A different kind of moral interpretation is proposed by Isaac of Stella. Focusing on the central motif of the vineyard and its vines, Isaac presents it as symbolic of a person's spiritual growth: 'For my part, I view my whole self, soul and body both and not just my soul, as the one vine that I may not neglect, but must dig about it and cultivate it to prevent it being overrun by unwelcome weeds and by the roots of other plants or be smothered by its own offshoots' (*Sermon* 16; Isaac of Stella 1979: 131).

Most traditional interpretations follow Matthew's general hermeneutic of reading parables allegorically, thus focusing on the vineyard owner as a benevolent and generous God. By contrast, some contemporary exegetes, particularly those who read the parable from the social location of exploited, especially Hispanic, day laborers in the United States, propose a more complex relationship between the parable and the Kingdom. They challenge common perceptions of day laborers regularly found in New Testament scholarship, typified by Joachim Jeremias's assertion that the last to be hired have only themselves to blame, on the grounds that 'they sit about in the market-place gossiping till late afternoon' (Jeremias 1955: 26), an interpretation belied by Matthew's own text ('Because nobody has hired us,' 20:7). As Pablo Jiménez writes:

> These commentators ignore that seasonal workers usually have to attend several 'work calls' during the day. They go from job site to job site until they are hired. They may even go to a new job site after completing an assignment. In short, these sad remarks advance one of the main tenets of the ideology of the powerful: the idea that the poor are lazy. (Jiménez 1997: 37)

For Jiménez, the landowner thus acts unlike other landowners in that he pays wages based not on merit but on need, manifesting 'interhuman' justice. A similar point is made by William, a member of the basic Christian community at Solentiname in Lake Nicaragua: 'Not according to the work but according to the need' (Cardenal 2010: 381). Others by contrast, such as Jean-Pierre Ruiz, argue that, through his arbitrary use of money, the landowner is showing not his generosity but his power, and the dependence of his workers on him, which overrides such considerations as 'a fair day's wage for a fair day's work.' Thus the face of God in this parable is to be sought, at least from the perspective of immigrant day laborers, not in the landowner, but in the 'least of these my brothers and sisters' (25:37–40), the owner's exploited workers (Ruiz 2007: 22–23). Such economically focused interpretations are anticipated in John Ruskin's 1860 essay 'Unto this Last' (whose title comes from the KJV translation of this parable, and was subsequently published in book form), which critiqued capitalist economics, and was a major influence on the philosophy of Gandhi.

The Mother of the Sons of Zebedee (20:20–28)

Matthew gives a central role to the unnamed mother of the sons of Zebedee, James, and John, who asks for seats in the Kingdom on behalf of her sons (cf. Mark 10:35–45). She is one of several anonymous females whom Matthew introduces by reference to their male relatives (e.g. 'the wife of Uriah,' 1:6; Pilate's wife, 27:19). She will appear again as one of three women, along with Mary Magdalene and Mary 'of James,' at the crucifixion (27:56). Harmonization with Mark has given her the name Salome (Mark 15:40), leading to etymological speculation. The *Opus imperfectum* clearly connects the name with the Hebrew *shalōm*, thus presenting her as 'a peaceful woman.'

Her naming is just the beginning of a complex process whereby her family tree will be closely entwined with that of Christ. This is most evident in the western medieval tradition of the Holy Kinship, whereby she is known as 'Mary of Salome,' one of three daughters of St. Anne, the mother of the Virgin Mary, each daughter fathered by a different husband. (On the Holy Kinship, see above on 13:53–58.) Salome is now the name of her father, Anne's third husband, rather than her personal name. Highly popular in the Middle Ages, the traditions of the Holy Kinship are later dismissed by Martin Luther as 'vulgar, filthy obscenities, … nothing but lies and fables' (Luther 2014: 63). By contrast, Juan de Maldonado suggests that the fact that question may come from Jesus' aunt makes it all the more compelling.

Commentators are divided as to whether the mother deserves praise or blame for her intervention, though their observations are illuminating for changing (and predominantly male) perceptions of women. The author of the *Opus imperfectum* views her positively, and regards it a shrewd move on the part of the sons to send their mother in their stead. If what they seek is inappropriate, it will be easier to forgive a woman; if appropriate, then Christ can be expected to listen more readily to a mother. But in fact, the mother is praiseworthy in her own right, because she is placing commitment to the Kingdom above earthly considerations, having left her own husband behind. The latter claim is interesting, and may be a deduction from Matthew's statement that she was among the women who had 'followed' Jesus from Galilee (27:55). Gregory of Nazianzus also praises her for asking 'in an impulse of parental affection, … through the excess of her love and of the kindness due to her children' (*Orat.* 37.14; *NPNF* 2nd series, 7:342).

Jerome is less effusive, but still gives her the benefit of the doubt. Her question betrays 'a feminine eagerness,' though he regards her as mistaken in thinking that the coming of the Kingdom will be immediately consequent on Christ's resurrection. Yet her 'womanish error' is similar to that of Peter, who asks about building three tents on the mount of Transfiguration (Jerome 2008: 226).

Martin Luther's chauvinistic comment presents James and John as using their mother to get what they want, though there is no indication that he disagrees with their imagined assessment of how a woman operates:

> Even if we fail, He will think that our mother acted as a foolish woman, but if we succeed, we will come out with our honor. And He probably will be unable to refuse our mother easily, as it is commonly the case that women get what they request more easily than men, since they are really canny in such matters. (Luther 2014: 64)

More surprising, perhaps, is the negative assessment provided by Elizabeth Cady Stanton in *The Woman's Bible*, which neglects the fact that in the Markan parallel it is the sons who are angling for key positions in Christ's Kingdom:

> A mother's ambition to lift her sons over her own head in education and position, planning extraordinary responsibilities for ordinary men, has proved a misfortune in many cases … Mothers are quite apt to overestimate the genius of their children and push them into niches which they cannot fill. (Stanton 2002: 122)

Hilary suggests that the places on right and left are reserved for such as Moses and Elijah, who had already flanked him at the Transfiguration; Euthymius Zigabenus opts for Peter and Paul. Jerome is insistent, by contrast, that they have been allocated, not to specific persons, but to those who embrace a particular kind of life: that of public confession and martyrdom. He thus sees a smooth transition to Jesus' invitation that James and John drink the cup that he will drink (20:22–23). The most obvious verbal link, as Maldonado observes, is with the cup of Christ's suffering and death (26:39; cf. 26:27–28). Therefore many commentators find here a prophecy of future martyrdom, the two brothers sharing in Christ's cup through laying down their own lives. The martyrdom of James is explicitly mentioned in Acts (Acts 12:2). More problematic is viewing John as a martyr, given the dominant tradition that he survived to a great age. In his commentary, Jerome offers one solution: that John underwent a 'virtual martyrdom' when he was plunged into boiling oil in Rome, prior to his exile to Patmos (see also e.g. Tertullian, *De praesc.* 36.3; Origen). Cornelius a Lapide expands this by noting that John's long life was a continual martyrdom, and that in particular he shared in Christ's cup of suffering by standing with Mary at the foot of the cross (John 19:26–27). An alternative, albeit minority, view is that both sons of Zebedee died a martyr's death (see Culpepper 2000: 170–174).

The cup of which Christ speaks seems to have inspired the early second-century martyr Polycarp of Smyrna. In the prayer attributed to Polycarp in the account of his martyrdom, he cries:

> I bless you because you have considered me worthy of this day and hour, so that I might receive a place among the numbers of the martyrs in the cup of your Christ, to the resurrection to eternal life, both of soul and of body, in the incorruptibility of the Holy Spirit. (*Mart. Pol.* 14.2; Holmes 2007: 321–323)

Two Blind Men at Jericho (20:29–34)

At this climactic stage of the journey toward Jerusalem, where the other Synoptic evangelists recount the healing of a single blind man (whom Mark names Bartimaeus), Matthew describes the healing of two blind men. Augustine is persuaded that all three evangelists describe the same event, but that Bartimaeus was more prominent, explaining why he alone is mentioned by Mark and Luke (*Agreement Among the Evangelists* 2.65, 125).

For Jerome, who lived for many years in nearby Bethlehem, the rugged terrain of Jericho and the prevalence of dangerous bandits in the area is of significance. Oddly, however, he seems to assume, against the plain sense of the narrative, that Christ descended from Jerusalem to Jericho rather than viewing the latter as the last stop of the journey up to the holy city. Thus he finds a fulfillment of Isaiah 9:2 (explicitly cited by Matthew at 4:15–16), whereby Jesus performs an act of rescue: 'If he had remained in Jerusalem and had not descended to the lowly places, the crowds would have sat in darkness and in the shadow of death until today' (Jerome 2008: 229). Jerome's comment implies a figurative interpretation of the two men, as representatives of the Jewish people, now brought from darkness to light by the presence of Christ. The crowd which rebukes them are pagans, grafted artificially onto the olive tree, and therefore warned by St. Paul against resenting the salvation of the original tree (Rom 11:18). Jerome may be influenced here by Origen, who identified the two men as Judah and Israel.

The same interpretative strategy leads other patristic exegetes to very different conclusions. Hilary views them as a figure of the Gentiles, descended from Noah's sons Ham and Japheth, paralleling the sons of Zebedee who signify the people of Israel, descended from Shem. Ironically, despite their blindness, they have 'seen' Christ's route and request the restoration of their sight. Those who try and prevent them are the people of the Law, who fail to see what these blind Gentiles see, that Christ is the Son of David. For Augustine, the two blind men symbolize people from both Israel and the Gentiles (*Questions on the Gospels* 1.28; also Rabanus Maurus).

Sophisticated intertextual readings lead to Christological observations. The *Opus imperfectum* exploits hints elsewhere in Matthew that Christ is the personification of heavenly Wisdom (e.g. 11:19, 28–30), to identify Christ as the rose to which Wisdom likens herself in Ben Sira: 'I grew tall like a palm tree in Engedi, and like rosebushes in Jericho' (Sir 24:14 NRSV). Thus the blind men of Jericho smelt the 'fragrance of his divinity' even before they saw him (Kellerman and Oden 2010: 291).

The men's blindness is often given a figurative meaning, with moral implications for the reader. Cornelius a Lapide proposes that 'by the two blind men we may understand the twofold blindness of the affections and of the understanding' (Lapide 1890: 392). Similar is Erasmus's comment: 'Thus by his touch Jesus heals the mind blinded by worldly desires, and light is given so that we might follow his footsteps' (Erasmus 2008: 290).

One striking feature of the story is that Jesus 'stopped' or 'stood still' before calling the two men (20:32). Jerome explains this in terms of the rugged terrain, especially dangerous for those who were blind: 'In Jericho there are many pitfalls, many cliffs and precipices that fall into bottomless depths. For that reason the Lord stops, so that they may be able to come' (Jerome 2008: 230). This moment is vividly visualized by the French artist Philippe de Champaigne, who may have known Jerome's comments through Cornelius a Lapide's *Great Commentary*. In his *Christ Healing the Blind* (c. 1660; The Putnam Foundation, Timken Museum of Art, San Diego), Champaigne has depicted Christ standing at a distance from the two men, surrounded by a crowd, with Jericho set in the context of a rugged landscape. The blind men stand to the left, clothed as hermits, arguably recalling Augustine's proposal that they manifest the ascetical discipline of crucifying the flesh by perseverance and prayer. Christ points to them, recalling his hand gesture in Caravaggio's *Calling of St. Matthew* and, more importantly, his *Raising of Lazarus*. Champaigne's Christ too is calling forth a miracle at the moment of pointing, enabling the men to 'see' with spiritual insight in their response to his audible call, even before they come to see physically (Clifton 2017).

Matthew 21–22

Ancient Literary Context

The journey now concludes with the arrival in Jerusalem. The narrative setting – the climax to a Passover pilgrimage – heightens the sense of festivity and expectation. The basic sequence of events, and much of the content, closely parallels Mark. It begins with Jesus' so-called 'triumphal entry' (21:1–11; Mark 11:1–11; Luke 19:28–38; John 12:12–19). Early audiences might recall the entry into Jerusalem by Solomon, after being anointed as king (1 Kgs 1:32–53).

Matthew Through the Centuries, First Edition. Ian Boxall.

This is followed by the temple episode (21:12–17; Mark 11:15–19; Luke 19:45–48; cf. John 2:13–22), and the cursing of the fig tree (21:18–22; Mark 11:12–14, 20–24).

Nonetheless, there are differences in Matthew's version. Most notably, he has Jesus ride on two animals, thus offering a literal fulfillment of his formula quotation from Zechariah (21:5, citing Zech 9:9; cf. Isa 62:11). He has also decoupled the temple and fig tree episodes, sandwiched together in Mark. The effect is to emphasise the unique significance of each separate event, which now occur on two separate days. Matthew's redactional changes also extend to a reference to blind and lame people approaching Jesus in the temple (21:14), and to the children's praise in fulfillment of Psalm 8:2 LXX, both additions emphasizing the fidelity of marginal characters.

These three dramatic, prophetic actions at the beginning of the Jerusalem section prepare for Jesus' return to the Temple the next day. Here his teaching provokes a series of controversy dialogues, and several parabolic responses (21:23–22:46; cf. Mark 11:27–12:37; Luke 20:1–21:4). The rhetorical effect is to heighten once again the opposition to Jesus, as he is questioned in turn by the chief priests and elders (21:23), the Pharisees and Herodians (22:15), some Sadducees (22:23), and a Pharisaic lawyer (22:34). Jesus responds not only with typical one-liners, but also with some longer parables: the uniquely Matthean parable of the Two Sons (21:28–32), the triple-tradition Vineyard Tenants (21:33–46; Mark 12:1–12; Luke 20:9–19), and the Marriage Feast (22:1–14, loosely paralleled in Luke 14:15–24, and *Gos. Thom.* 64). The series of events climaxes with a dialogue which revisits the Christological issue at the heart of Jesus' entry into Jerusalem: the identity of the Son of David (22:41–46; cf. 21:5, 9).

The Interpretations

The King's Humble Entry (21:1–11)

The Flemish Jesuit Cornelius a Lapide draws attention to the sequence of geographical locations which mark the final stage in Christ's ascent to the holy city: 'from Bethany through Bethphage, the Mount of Olives and the valley of Jehoshaphat was the road to Jerusalem' (Lapide 1890: 2/397). Following older exegetes such as Jerome, Lapide explores the etymology of Bethphage, as 'house of the mouth' or 'at the mouth of a valley.' He notes that this etymology is likely topographical, given the village's location in a cleft or 'mouth' at the foot of Mount Olivet, and at the entrance to the valley. He also accepts as probable the claim of his contemporaries Cornelius Jansen (1585–1638) and Christianus Crucius Adrichomius (1533–1585) that Bethphage was a priestly village (a claim previously made by Jerome), which provided sacrificial animals for the temple. Hence its appropriateness as a stopping-place for Christ, the true sacrificial lamb. Lapide also thinks it significant that Jesus' journey takes him through the valley of Jehoshaphat (though this is not explicit in Matthew's text), the traditional location of the last judgment (Joel 3:2, 12), given that he will judge the nations. More recent exegetes provide a more probable etymology ('house of (unripe) figs'), though they also draw conclusions from the narrative location. For Davies and Allison, this name prepares the audience for Jesus' subsequent cursing of an unfruitful fig tree in Jerusalem (Davies and Allison 1997: 115).

The two disciples sent by Jesus to locate the donkey and colt are unnamed. Hilary of Poitiers identifies them as Peter and Philip (also Pseudo-Bede; *Glossa ordinaria*; the medieval York 'Entry into Jerusalem' play), Cornelius Jansen as Peter and John, given that, according to Luke 22:8, these two will later make preparations for the Passover meal (in Lapide 1890: 2/399). For Origen, these two unnamed disciples are types of Peter and Paul, the apostles to the Jews and the Gentiles respectively (also Jerome; Theophylact). Later exegetes will find further symbolism in the two, such as the active and contemplative life (e.g. Aquinas).

Matthew's focus on two animals rather than one unsurprisingly provokes interest (it is relatively late commentators, such as John Calvin, who detect Hebrew parallelism at play). Jerome objects that the literal sense – that Jesus straddled two animals simultaneously – is impossible, thus calling for a figurative interpretation. He develops a salvation-historical solution already proposed by Justin (*Trypho* 53.1), Origen and, in part, Fortunatianus of Aquileia, and widely repeated in the subsequent reception history. The yoked donkey is a figure of the synagogue, yoked to the Law; Jesus sits instead on the donkey's colt, a figure of the untamed Gentiles (for Fortunatianus, the colt symbolizes those from the synagogue who come to believe). For Hilary, the donkey and colt came from the Samaritans, a wild pagan people, and therefore both symbolize the pagans. This explains his identification of the two disciples as Philip and Peter, who were responsible for the conversion of Samaria (Acts 8:5–8; also e.g. *Glossa ordinaria*).

Arnobius Iunior focuses on the younger colt, as a symbol of the church born from the mother. The event thus signifies the fulfillment of Isaiah 1:3, which contrasts Israel's lack of knowledge with the ass's ability to recognize its master's manger:

> By 'ass's colt' He signifies the new people, that is, us, who know the stable of our Lord, i.e. the altar, where we receive our nourishment. (*Expositiunculae in Matthaeum* 21; Kraszewski 1999: 344)

An alternative reading of the literal sense, attested already in Origen, is that Christ sits not on the two animals but on the garments which have been placed on them by the disciples (for modern discussion, see e.g. Gundry 1994: 409–410; Coppins 2012). According to Pseudo-Bonaventure's *Meditations on the Life of Christ*, he rode first on the ass, then on the colt. However, as the nineteenth-century German theologian David Friedrich Strauss would later observe in his classic *Das Leben Jesu kritisch bearbeitet*, changing animals on such a short journey would have been inconvenient (Strauss 1973: 553; see Instone-Brewer 2003: 98). Many, like Juan de Maldonado, harmonize all four Gospels by envisaging Jesus riding only the colt.

The exegetical problem is addressed by visual artists in different ways. Sometimes, Christ rides on the mother, the small colt walking underneath (e.g. Pietro Lorenzetti, *Entry of Christ into Jerusalem*, c. 1320; Basilica of St. Francis, Assisi; Fra Angelico, *The Entry into Jerusalem*, 1450; San Marco, Florence) or closely following (e.g. Duccio, *The Entry into Jerusalem*, 1308–1311; Museo dell'Opera del Duomo, Siena; Jean-Hippolyte Flandrin, *Christ's Entry into Jerusalem*, 1842–1848; Saint-Germain-des-Prés, Paris). Only occasionally is Christ portrayed straddling both animals (e.g. Master of San Baudelio de Berlanga, *Entry of Christ into Jerusalem*, 1125; Indianapolis Museum of Art). More frequently, artists sidestep the problem by depicting the single donkey of Mark, Luke, and John.

The dramatic approach to Jerusalem has had a rich and wide-ranging impact. Jesus riding into the city is regularly reenacted, both in the annual Christian liturgy of Palm Sunday, featuring processions involving the waving of palm and olive branches, and in dramatic performances. In medieval Europe, Palm Sunday processions often included life-sized wooden images of Christ on a donkey. While this practice generally died out in northern Europe following the Reformation, the so-called *Palmesel* or 'Palm donkey' survived in southern Germany, Austria, and Switzerland until the late eighteenth century (Harris 2012). Examples in drama include the York 'Entry into Jerusalem' play (Napolitano 2009), and the famous passion play performed every ten years at Oberammergau, Bavaria, where Christ's entry is the opening scene, accompanied by acclamations from the Chorus:

> Hail to Thee! Hail! O David's Son!
> Hail to Thee! Hail! The father's throne
> Belongs to Thee
> Who comest in the name of God,
> Whom Israel onward throngs to meet,
> Thy praise we sing.
> (Community of Oberammergau 1960: 16)

Thus 'Jerusalem' is made present everywhere Christians gather to remember this event.

The fourth-century pilgrim Egeria provides an eye-witness description of the annual Palm Sunday procession from the Mount of Olives into Jerusalem itself. It begins with a reading of the Gospel passage about 'the children who met the Lord with palm branches' (Egeria appears to be conflating two events in Matthew's narrative, the entry into Jerusalem and the children in the temple, 21:15–16):

> At this the bishop and all the people rise from their places, and start off on foot down from the summit of the Mount of Olives. All the people go before him with psalms and antiphons, all the time repeating, 'Blessed is he that cometh in the name of the Lord.' The babies and the ones too young to walk are carried on their parents' shoulders. Everyone is carrying branches, either palm or olive, and they accompany the bishop in the very way the people did when once they went down with the Lord. (*Egeria's Travels* 31.2–3; Wilkinson 1981: 133)

This connection between the crowds and children is already established by the time of Clement of Alexandria, who connects the scene with the childlike vocation of Christians, learning from Christ the divine educator: 'The prophetic spirit also distinguishes us as children. Plucking, it is said, branches of olives or palms, the children went forth to meet the Lord, and cried, saying, Hosanna to the Son of David! Blessed is He that comes in the name of the Lord' (*Paed.* 1.5; *ANF* 2:212).

The children regularly appear in visual art. Byzantine tradition emphasizes the children laying their clothes on the path. The Western preference is to depict boys climbing trees in order to cut branches. A prominent example of the later is Giotto's *The Entry into Jerusalem* (c. 1305; Scrovegni Chapel, Padua). In William Blake's *Christ's Entry into Jerusalem,* painted for Thomas Butts (1800; oil on copper; Pollok House, Glasgow, B422), Christ is surrounded by children with the demeanor of adults (or 'child-like adults,' Rowland 2010: 221–222), while his own disciples follow behind. The children are also mentioned in Theodulph of Orleans's ninth-century hymn *Gloria laus et honor,* sung on Palm Sunday by many English-speaking Christians in John Mason Neale's nineteenth-century translation:

> All glory, laud, and honor
> to you, Redeemer, King,
> to whom the lips of children
> made sweet hosannas ring.

Yet the entry itself remains inherently ambiguous. Many see a manifestation of Christ's kingly authority, provoking the acclamations of the crowds. In a sermon preached in 1538, Martin Luther emphasizes how Christ 'rode into Jerusalem with His glorious splendor and stirred up the entire city' (Luther 2014: 75). However, the scene is one of profound humility, the choice of a donkey and its foal standing in marked contrast to the triumphal entry of victorious monarchs on powerful warhorses. For Eusebius, this is proof of Christ's taking on our humanity in the incarnation (*Dem. ev.* 9.17). John Calvin considers the borrowed ass and the lack of a saddle 'a sign of terrible and shameful poverty' (Calvin 1972: II/291). Moreover, Zechariah's prophecy about the king being 'meek' or 'humble' (Zech 9:9, quoted at 21:5) recalls the third Beatitude (5:5), and Jesus' self-designation as 'meek and humble in heart' (11:29). The Puritan Matthew Henry is impressed by this humility:

> Sion's King comes riding, not on a prancing horse, which the timorous petitioner dares not come near, or a running horse, which the slow-footed petitioner cannot keep pace with, but on a quiet ass, that the poorest of his subjects may not be discouraged in their access to him. (Henry 1960: 106)

In his *Entry into the City* (2012; Center of Continuing Education, University of Notre Dame), the US artist John August Swanson interprets the scene as a grand protest march encapsulating the hopes of those working for peace and social justice. The disciples are marchers, and both they and the crowds wave colorful banners. Swanson describes his intentions thus:

> I wanted to convey my feelings from being in marches for peace and justice. This scene has been repeated countless times in the lives of heroic and selfless leaders who have fought for love, peace, and social justice. It is relived in the lives of Martin Luther King, Mahatma Gandhi, Oscar Romero, and Cesar Chavez.[1]

The peaceable, non-warrior-like characteristics of Christ are powerfully conveyed in Byzantine iconography, where he is depicted riding side-saddle (Davies and Allison 1997: 120). A similar posture appears in Blake's *Christ's Entry into Jerusalem*. Blake has combined this with a hand-gesture which suggests not triumph but blessing, as Christ moves toward a distant Jerusalem, which may suggest the heavenly, eschatological city rather than its earthly counterpart. An alternative is that Blake is making a plea that Jerusalem be 'builded here' (see his 1810 Preface to 'Milton'), rather than in some transcendent realm.

Blake's interpretation hints at the capacity of this scene to work on several different levels, reflecting the multivalent associations of Jerusalem in the

1 http://www.johnaugustswanson.com/default.cfm/PID%3d1.2.30.2-7.html.

fourfold senses of scripture found in medieval exegesis. On the literal level, Christ enters historical Jerusalem, initiating the chain of events that will end at Golgotha. The Italian poet Giambattista Marino (1569–1625) sees the entry into Jerusalem as an anticipatory triumphal procession, preceding the victory of the cross it celebrates:

> Where thy victorious feet, Great God, should tread,
> In honor this green tapestry is spread;
> And as all future things are past to thee,
> The triumph here precedes the victory.
> (trans. T. Stanley, in Atwan, Dardess, and Rosenthal 1998: 358)

Yet Jerusalem is also interpreted allegorically as the church, as in Matins for Palm Sunday in the Byzantine liturgy, which proclaims how Christ 'weds the New Zion' as he enters the city (in Baggley 2000: 97). A tropological or moral interpretation is provided in a homily for Palm Sunday preached by the eleventh-century Benedictine reformer Peter Damian: the journey into Jerusalem symbolizes the conversion of the sinners, humbly confessing their sins (*Homilia VII in dominica palmarum*; PL 144:545). Blake's painting hints at the anagogical level, describing the ultimate destination of Christians. Antecedents for this latter view include the Carolingian theologian Paschasius Radbertus (785–865), for whom Matthew's whole narrative sequence from Jericho via the Mount of Olives into the holy city signifies the Gentiles' journey from the world via the church to the heavenly Jerusalem (see Luz 2005a: 8).

Matthew's statement that the whole city was 'shaken' (21:10, a verb connected to the noun 'earthquake') is puzzling. This tends to be interpreted as inward emotion, the crowds moved by the sight of what they saw, though not fully understanding it (e.g. *Opus imperfectum*; Chrysostom). Some treat it as an implicit example of prophetic fulfillment: the 'quaking' of the city recalling the earthquake of Zechariah 14:4–5. Aquinas interprets the statement that the whole city was 'moved' (*commota*) to mean that it 'wondered' or 'marvelled' (*admirata*); this enables him to see the event as a fulfillment of both Psalm 60:4 (Vulgate Ps 59:4, which speaks of the earth being rocked) and Isaiah 60:5 (which prophesies Zion's marveling at the eschatological pilgrimage of the Gentiles). By contrast, Juan de Maldonado interprets the phrase negatively, paralleling the disturbance of Jerusalem at the arrival of the Magi at 2:3:

> But the city was not moved now by joy, or wonder, or fear, but by envy and malignity, at seeing Christ received with such honour; as the following words seem to signify. (Maldonado 1888: 2/200)

The Temple Incident (21:12–17)

The temple episode marks a transition from Jesus as king to Jesus as prophet (21:11), who attacks the transformation of God's house into a 'den of bandits.' The precise meaning of the event is disputed, particularly for those seeking to get behind the Gospel narratives to the historical ministry of Jesus. It is variously interpreted as protest against the economic corruption of the priesthood, an attempt to purify the cult, and an enacted prophecy of the present temple's destruction (e.g. Sanders 1985a: 70–71; Theissen and Merz 1998: 432–433).

Matthew's version prioritizes certain aspects of the story. By omitting 'for all the nations' (21:13; cf. Mark 11:17), he highlights the temple's role as a 'place of prayer,' as well as possibly avoiding the embarrassment that the expected eschatological pilgrimage (Isa 60) failed to materialize. He also makes explicit reference to the presence of the blind and lame (21:14), thus reversing a ban attributed to Christ's ancestor David (2 Sam 5:6–8 LXX). Some (e.g. Theophylact) regard them as symbols of the Gentiles. The motif of inclusion is continued by Matthew's statement about children crying out in the temple (21:15–16). This recalls earlier descriptions of Christians as children or 'little ones' (e.g. 18:4, 6, 10, 14), an observation made by Hilary.

Many early readers are sensitive to this ecclesial interest, reading the episode as concerned not only with the second temple destroyed by the Romans, but also with the new temple of the church built by Christ, the new Solomon (16:18). Jerome describes this as the 'mystic' meaning of the passage, hinting at the sin of simony, that is, buying or selling divine blessings or ecclesial offices for monetary gain (attributed to Simon Magus at Acts 8:9–24):

> Jesus daily enters the Temple of the Father and expels from his own Church all such bishops, priests, and deacons, as well as laymen and the whole crowd. He holds them all guilty of a single crime, namely, of selling and buying. For it is written: 'Freely you have received, freely give.' (Jerome 2008: 237)

Hilary is explicit about the simony connection: the selling of doves refers to benefitting financially from the gifts of the Holy Spirit (who appears as a dove at 3:16; also Bruno of Segni; Theophylact; Aquinas; John Hus, 'On Simony'); the 'chairs' of the sellers symbolize the seat of priestly office. The same point is made by Gregory the Great in a letter to Bishop John of Corinth:

> Furthermore, it has come to our ears that in those parts no one attains to any sacred order without the giving of a consideration. If this is so, I say with tears, I declare with groans, that, when the priestly order has fallen inwardly, neither will it stand long outwardly. For we know from the Gospel what our Redeemer in

> person did; how He went into the temple, and overthrew the seats of them that sold doves (Matthew xxi:12). For to sell doves is to receive a temporal consideration for the Holy Spirit ... (*Ep.* 5.57; *NPNF* 2nd series, 12:186)

Dante recalls the temple episode in his prayer (*Paradiso* 18) that Christ be angry with the temple merchants once again, alluding to ecclesiastical abuses during the pontificate of Pope John XXII (Swindell in EBR 5: 409). Cornelius a Lapide broadens the application in considering the episode's moral implications: the money-changers are 'simoniacal persons, indeed all sinners, who profane their soul, which is the temple of God, by lusts and sins' (Lapide 1890: 2/415).

The temple-as-church exegesis could extend to attitudes regarding church buildings. According to his biographer Stephen of Ripon, the Northumbrian bishop St. Wilfrid (c. 633–709) used the story as an interpretive lens through which to view the decrepit state of a stone church in his new diocese of York. For Wilfrid, 'the house of God and the house of prayer had become like a den of thieves; so, forthwith, in accordance with the will of God, he made a plan to restore it' (Stephen of Ripon, *Vita sancti Wilfridi* 16 in O'Brien 2015: 202).

Ecclesial interpretations are found on either side of the Reformation divide. The Reformers appeal to the passage against what they regard as Catholic abuses, including private masses and the selling of indulgences. For Luther, Christ's anger in the temple finds its contemporary counterpart in divine anger against the papacy, 'which has falsified God's Word and made the forgiveness of sins into a den of robbers and a business' (Luther 2014: 86–87). For the Council of Trent, the episode was a crucial weapon in its desire to root out abuses in the celebration of the Eucharist, whether slackness, irreverence, or 'the taint of simony': 'so that the house of God may truly be called and be seen to be a house of prayer' (Session 22, 'Decree on things to be observed and avoided in celebrating mass'; Tanner 1990: II/737).

Trent's desire to reform the church influenced the interpretation of this scene by visual artists, such as El Greco's *Christ Driving the Traders from the Temple* (c. 1600; National Gallery, London), one of several versions he painted of this subject. Here Christ's anger contrasts with the irreverence of the traders. A more Protestant version, equally concerned with the purification of the church, is Rembrandt's *Christ Driving the Money Changers from the Temple Cloisters* (1626; Pushkin Museum of Fine Arts, Moscow). Rembrandt's interpretation, which portrays the action taking place within the Romanesque arches of a church building, accords with John Calvin's conviction that what Christ says about the temple is actually said about the church (Perlove and Silver 2009: 250–255).

As well as its popularity in visual art, the scene's dramatic character has been captured effectively in film. A striking actualization occurs in *Jesus of Montreal* (1989; directed by Denys Arcand). Daniel, the actor playing Jesus in the passion play which provides the setting for the film, drives film directors out of a theater with a 'whip' made of electric cords (Nichols 2008: 165). The American singer-songwriter Johnny Cash also explores contemporary parallels in his musical documentary *Gospel Road* (1973). The scene of his hippie-like Jesus driving out the merchants is accompanied by Cash's own narration, describing Jesus' 'public exposé' of the 'religious establishment' (Baugh 1997: 36).

Jesus and the Fig Tree (21:18–22)

The story presupposes that Jesus is hungry, which for Jerome reassuringly underscores the reality of Christ's humanity. Others, however, assert that Christ only feigned hunger to provide an opportunity for the miracle (Chrysostom; Euthymius Zigabenus; Maldonado), or that the evangelist describes his 'hunger' for the salvation of his own people (Fortunatianus of Aquileia). Matthew's omission of 'For it was not the season for figs' (Mark 11:13) avoids one of the problems in Mark's account, namely, why the tree was cursed for not bearing fruit outside its natural cycle. Nonetheless, even Matthew's version strikes many readers as out of character with his broader portrayal of Jesus. The nineteenth-century Anglican commentator Mary Cornwallis protests:

> None but the bitterest enemies of Christ can for a moment imagine that the curse pronounced upon the barren fig tree was the result of disappointment or revenge: could he, whose life evinces one continued series of mildness, patience, and forgiveness; who with his last breath prayed for his murderers; be betrayed into an act of pitiful vengeance upon an unoffending tree, to which his own providence had denied fecundity? (Cornwallis 1820: 69)

Rather, Cornwallis emphasizes the story's instructional character: to strengthen the faith of the disciples in the forthcoming trial, and, in addition, to teach a general moral lesson: 'it teaches the danger of being unprofitable servants, and the displeasure likely to be incurred by those, who, supported and cherished by Divine bounty, make no suitable return.'

The emphasis on the power of faith is underscored by Matthew's statement that the fig tree withered 'immediately' following Christ's words (21:19). Nonetheless, the biblical associations of figs with Israel's fruitfulness (e.g. Jer 8:13; 24:1–10; Hos 9:10; Mic 7:1–6) encourage patristic and medieval commentators to discern a deeper meaning. Hilary views the tree as a figure of the synagogue, while Fortunatianus of Aquileia explicitly connects the withering with Vespasian's destruction of Jerusalem in 70 CE. Theophylact of Ochrid interprets the tree's having leaves but lacking fruit according to the letter/spirit distinction: the synagogue has only the letter of the law, not the fruit of the Spirit. For Jerome, the tree's location 'by the road' or 'way' is a parable of Israel's failure to follow the Way, despite its possession of the Law.

The Two Sons (21:28–32)

Debate over the respective authority of Jesus and John the Baptist (21:23–27) leads into the uniquely Matthean parable of the Two Sons (21:28–32), which explores different responses to John's ministry. Again, Matthew seems to invite readers to allegorize his parable. Its main lines are clear: the son who changes his mind and ultimately obeys the father (i.e. God) represents the tax-collectors and prostitutes; the son whose actions do not match his positive words symbolizes the chief priests and elders. This meaning is evident, even allowing for the complex textual variations (see Metzger 1994: 44–46). Codex Sinaiticus (preferred in UBS and NA, and in many English translations) has the first son carry out the father's will. Codex Vaticanus inverts the order of the two sons, perhaps reflecting a salvation-historical interpretation whereby the unreliable Jews are succeeded by the obedient Gentiles. In Codex Bezae and many Old Latin texts, the order of Sinaiticus is retained, but the answer as to which does the father's will (21:31) is given as 'the last' or 'the newest' (Greek *ho eschatos*; OL *novissimus*). For many commentators, this latter reading is 'obvious nonsense' (Beare 1981: 424). Jerome, however, defends it as pointing to the Jewish leaders' perversity: they spoil Jesus' point (a similar point is made by Hilary, whose complex exegesis reflects the complexity of the textual tradition: Doignon 1985). It may also be the text underlying Irenaeus' salvation-historical interpretation (Minns 2012).

Jerome's interpretation of the parable is typical of patristic, medieval, and early modern exegetes (e.g. Chrysostom; *Opus imperfectum;* Nicholas of Lyra; Dionysius the Carthusian; Aquinas; Maldonado), although it jars with Matthew's text which 'does not assign ethnic categories to the characters in the parable' (Levine 1988: 205). The first son symbolizes the Gentiles, who initially received the natural law, which they rejected through pride, though ultimately repented at the coming of Christ. The second son represents the Jews, who failed to keep their vow of obedience (see Wailes 1987: 145). Jerome closely connects this with the Tenants which immediately follows, the Jews regarded as having killed Christ, the son and heir, as well as Luke's alternative parable of the Prodigal Son, in which one son is temperate, the other 'luxurious' (Luke 15:11–32).

Arguably, the parable also addresses a word of warning to Matthew's own readers, which can be obscured by the Jewish–Gentile distinction, or even the narrative concentration on the 'chief priests and elders of the people.' Thus the *Opus imperfectum* actualizes the parable in a contemporary distinction between priests and laity, hinting at the dangers of clerical superiority in the author's own day. The Italian Benedictine Bruno of Segni (c. 1045–1123) broadens the identification of the disobedient son from Jewish leaders to include 'others who pretended that they were just' (PL 165:247D–248A), i.e. to critique spiritual hypocrisy. Such sentiments are powerfully expressed by the eighteenth-century Anglican poet Christopher Smart in his *Parable XI: The Father and His Two Sons*:

> Christ in the parable decries
> A mere professor's life of lies,
> Who's bold to preach and reprimand
> In words magnificent and grand,
> The pompous self-applauding saint,
> All inward filth and outward paint.

The Vineyard Tenants (21:33–46)

Matthew's allusions to Isaiah 5 suggest that this parable is an allegory of Israel (the vineyard), and the rejection of the prophets (the servants, see e.g. Jer 7:25; 35:15) and then Jesus (the son) by the leaders of the people (the tenants). It is even possible that the evangelist, like the authors of the Targum on Isaiah, identified the 'tower' as the temple (Davies and Allison 1997: 176, n. 8). Thus the allegorical interpretations of the early church differ from Matthew only in degree, not in kind. Irenaeus of Lyons provides the classic interpretation, springing from his apologetic concern to show the unity of the two Testaments, and the progression from Israel to the (Gentile) church:

> It is therefore one and the same Father who planted the vineyard, who led forth the people, who sent the prophets, who sent His own Son, and who gave the vineyard to those other husbandmen that render the fruits in their season. (*Adv. Haer.* 4.36.2; *ANF* 1:515)

Irenaeus' theological interest in Christ's recapitulating Adam's story means that he understands the vineyard to be a symbol not of Israel specifically, but of humanity. However, God only began to let it out to tenants under Moses, when he installed the hedge (instructions regarding worship), built the tower

(Jerusalem), and dug the winepress (to receive the Holy Spirit). Thus the tenants are the Jewish people, to whom prophets are sent both before and after the exile, until the sending of God's Son, when the vineyard is entrusted to the Gentiles who now form 'the illustrious Church.'

Many follow Irenaeus's basic pattern, though with greater emphasis on Israel as the vineyard (e.g. Hilary, Jerome, Epiphanius the Latin, *Interpretation of the Gospels* 31; Aquinas, Erasmus), and increasing allegorization of the details (Wailes 1987: 147–153). The hedge refers to the prayers of the saints, or of angels (Aquinas), or the faith (Arnobius Iunior, *Expositiunculae in Matthaeum* 22); the tower is Christ (Epiphanius the Latin); the winepress is the altar (Jerome), the prophets, or the martyrs who shed their blood (Aquinas).

However, the sharp distinction between the Jews and the Gentiles, or Israel and the church, betrays the changed circumstances in which these Christian exegetes write. In his commentary, Origen sees the problem, acknowledging the difference between Isaiah's blaming of the vineyard and the Gospel's blaming the tenants (i.e. those entrusted with care of the vineyard). He finds the solution in 21:43 (unique to Matthew): the vineyard represents not Israel but the 'mysteries of the kingdom' (the Law, prophets, and other scriptures) first entrusted to the Jews (Wailes 1987: 149–150). Others, e.g. Fortunatianus of Aquileia, Theophylact, and Aquinas, are even more sensitive to Matthew's narrative context, where the chief priests and Pharisees recognize themselves as the parable's target (21:45), as well as the Isaiah intertext. The Jewish people are the vine, or the vineyard, while the chief priests and Pharisees, or the leaders of the people in general, are symbolized by the tenants. God's complaint, at least in this parable, is therefore not against the people so much as the rulers. A similar interpretation is found in the ninth-century Syriac bishop Moses Bar-Kepha, probably dependent upon Ephrem. Moses explains the allegory thus, rooting it historically in the circumstances of Jesus' day, and particularly the activity of the priesthood:

> [Christ] calls God the man, and his people the vineyard; the hedge is the observance of laws, or the help of God; the tower is the temple, the wine-vat is the altar on which the blood of the sacrifices is shed; the husbandmen are the band of priests; the servants that were sent are the prophets; the sending of the son at the last he calls his own coming; and that they cast him out of the vineyard and killed him means that he perished at their hands. (in Harris 1895: 73)

For the majority of exegetes, however, verse 43 denotes a clear shift from the leaders alone to the whole nation, the Kingdom of heaven being taken from them and given to another 'nation,' the church or the Gentiles. Yet Calvin reminds his Christian readers that the parable is also addressed to them, and that the Kingdom will be removed from them too, if it is not 'rooted in true godliness' (Calvin 1972: III/22).

Modern critical scholarship, both Christian and Jewish (e.g. Levine 1988: 206–211; Sim 1998: 148–149), appeals to the ancient cultural context of Matthean Christian Jews. Far from envisaging the replacement of God's people Israel by a new Gentile church, the parable speaks of the replacement of the tenant-leaders of the people by others. The vineyard, however, remains in God's possession, albeit cared for by a new *ethnos*, understood as 'people' rather than 'nation' (Peter and the disciples).

The Marriage Feast (22:1–14)

Whereas many modern commentators regard the Marriage Feast as a parallel to Luke's Great Banquet (Luke 14:15–24, a link already made by Theophylact and Maldonado), older exegetes often treat the two as distinct (e.g. Augustine, *Agreement Among the Evangelists* 2.71; Paschasius Radbertus; *Glossa ordinaria*; Aquinas; Nicholas of Lyra). For Gregory the Great, Matthew's version is concerned with ecclesiology, the church in the present age (on the grounds that no-one can be expelled from the heavenly eschatological banquet), whilst Luke's deals with soteriology. The mixed character of the wedding banquet after the final invitation, containing both good and bad, indicates that the parable describes the church in the present age (*Homily* 38).

Many read the parable as concerned with the Son's marriage to the church, announced by the prophets. Some give additional weight to the fact that servants are sent twice (in vv. 3 and 4), interpreting them as the prophets followed by the apostles, or the apostles and their successors (e.g. Origen; Jerome; Chrysostom; Maldonado; see Wailes 1987: 153–161). A marginal note in the Geneva Bible finds support in the parable for a distinctly Puritan ecclesiology:

> Not all of the whole company of them that are called by the voice of the Gospel are the true Church before God; for the most part of them had rather follow the commodities of this life, and some do most cruelly persecute those that call them, but they are the true Church, which obey when they are called, such as for the most part they are, whom the world despiseth.

The ecclesial interpretation shapes the tradition of visualizing the parable in Byzantine iconography. Dionysius of Fourna's *Painter's Manual* provides the following description of how the banquet should be painted. It is to be set within a church building, flanked by Jews rejecting the invitation on one side and the apostles teaching Gentiles, tax-collectors, and harlots on the other:

> In the midst of the church is a table on which are a cup and a plate, and in a circle round this are ranged the orders of the angels and choirs of all the saints, dressed in white and holding lamps. In the midst of them is one man in filthy clothes, and his hands and feet are being bound by demons and he is being dragged by them into Hell. Christ stands near him, clothed in regal and patriarchal clothes, and says to him on a scroll: 'Friend, how camest thou in hither not having a wedding garment?' (Hetherington 1996: 42)

Others (e.g. Theophylact) understand the nuptial joy to refer to the resurrection on the last day. The hostile reception of the servants by the Jewish people leads to an opening to the Gentiles – those subsequently found in the highways or main streets – through the preaching of the apostles. For Hilary, the excuses of those first invited, that they must tend to farm or business, betray the vices of human ambition and greed respectively.

Two features of Matthew's parable are especially odd. The first is the extreme reaction of the king, provoked by the equally extreme reaction of some of the wedding guests: killing the murderers and burning their city (22:6–7). The modern instinct to find a reference to the fall of Jerusalem in 70 CE is anticipated by several earlier exegetes (e.g. Jerome; Chrysostom; Euthymius Zigabenus; Theophylact; Aquinas; Erasmus; Maldonado). Jerome juxtaposes this with another possibility: that the armies of the king are the angels at the last judgment. Gregory the Great sees in those who kill the servants a prophecy of the persecution of the church, the servants signifying the martyrs (*Homily* 38).

A second oddity is the expulsion of the guest without a wedding garment (22:11), brought in at short notice. This provoked the eighteenth-century French philosopher and controversialist Voltaire to ask why the king failed to provide one himself (in Clarke 2003: 179). The problem is often side-stepped by allegorizing. In the *Pseudo-Clementine Homilies*, the wedding garment is baptism, which brings people to the wedding-banquet through repentance (*Hom.* 8.22). More specifically, it is the garment worn at baptism (Tertullian, *Scorp.* 6; probably also Hilary). Cyril of Jerusalem comments on this parable in a baptismal context, as he addresses catechumens (though Cyril seems to regard the garment as symbolizing the appropriate disposition of repentance):

> Begin at once to wash your robes in repentance, that when called to the bride-chamber you may be found clean. For the Bridegroom invites all without distinction, because His grace is bounteous; and the cry of loud-voiced heralds assembles them all: but the same Bridegroom afterwards separates those who have come in to the figurative marriage. O may none of those whose names have now been enrolled hear the words, Friend, how did you come in hither, not having a wedding garment (Matthew 22:12)? (*Catech.* 3.2; *NPNF* 2nd series, 7:14)

Gregory the Great identifies the obvious flaw in the baptismal interpretation, at least for those who, like him, interpret the marriage feast as a description of the church:

> What do we think is meant by the wedding garment, dearly beloved? For if we say it is baptism or faith, is there anyone who has entered this marriage feast without them? No, all at the feast have come to believe. What then must we understand by the wedding garment but love? (*Homily* 38; Gregory the Great 1990: 347)

Alternatively, the garment symbolizes the good works produced by love, or by the Holy Spirit (Irenaeus, *Adv. Haer.* 4.36.6; Jerome), or the virtues (Origen), or true faith and justice (*Opus imperfectum*; Hugh of St. Cher; see also Luz 2005a: 58–59), or the newness of life which faith demands (Geneva Bible). For Erasmus, the man who is expelled symbolizes those who lack moral conversion, or who, having professed the gospel, now 'return to the squalor of their former lives' (Erasmus 2008: 303). In the background here may be Revelation 19:8, in which the bridal gown of the Lamb's bride is 'the righteous deeds of the saints.' Reading in the light of other scriptural passages leads to other possibilities. For some, the garment is the resurrection body, on the basis of 2 Cor 5:4 (see Davies and Allison 1997: 204, n. 55). Others find the solution in Paul's exhortation to 'Put on the Lord Jesus Christ' (Rom 13:14, e.g. Aquinas).

Modern commentators tend to appeal to a specific cultural practice, whereby wedding garments were provided by the host. The early nineteenth-century Anglican commentator Mary Cornwallis is typical:

> But in order to see the complete beauty of the parable, we should understand the nature of an eastern entertainment. In these, the guests are supplied with outward garments by the master of the entertainment, according to their rank; and sumptuous wardrobes are kept for the purpose: consequently it was an insult to him, when any one appeared without the robe presented. In like manner, the graces of the Holy Spirit are as munificently dispensed to all who seek them in sincerity; and, at the last day, it will be found that no guests will be admitted to the wedding supper of the Lamb, but those who appear clothed in this spiritual attire: consequently those who have it not must share the fate of the man in the parable, for their rejection of proffered grace. (Cornwallis 1820: 71)

The evidence for this practice is, however, debatable. As Heinrich Meyer observes, the claim is a deduction from the later 'Oriental custom of presenting handsome caftans to those who are admitted to the presence of royalty' (Meyer 1879: 80).

A Series of Debates (22:15–46)

This section concludes with four controversy debates, involving both Pharisees and Sadducees, which reveal their shared antagonism toward Jesus (seeking to trap him, 22:15; testing him, 22:35). Their hostile response presents them as exemplars of those in the preceding parable who reject the invitation to the wedding banquet (22:5).

Render to Caesar (22:15–22)

The first dialogue (Mark 12:28–34; Luke 10:25–28) seeks to force Jesus either to oppose or support the payment of Roman taxation, probably both the agricultural *tributum soli* and the *tributum capitis* imposed on personal property (Davies and Allison 1997: 214). Aquinas draws attention to the futility of their desire to entrap Jesus 'in a word,' given that he is himself the Word of God.

The Pharisees come with the Herodians. The identity of the latter is disputed, not least because Jerusalem and Judea were directly governed by Rome. They are variously understood as Herod Antipas' soldiers (Jerome) or courtiers (Luther), or specifically the servants who gathered the Roman taxes on behalf of the Herodian rulers (Aquinas), or that political party which promoted the interests of the dynasty (Meyer 1879: 84). Some early exegetes even claim that the Herodians believed Herod, probably Herod the Great rather than Antipas, to be the Messiah prophesied in Genesis 49:10 ('The sceptre shall not depart from Judah': Epiphanius, *Pan.* 40.1; Apollinaris of Laodicea, *Frag.* 112; Theophylact). A sixteenth-century alternative is the marginal note in the Geneva Bible, which views them as representatives of a new religion patched together from Judaism and paganism. Most likely, they represent the opposing view to the Pharisees over paying tribute to Caesar, accentuating the trap laid against Christ.

Jesus' punchline (22:21) is as ambiguous as it is brilliant, provoking not only the amazement of the Pharisees, but a rich crop of diverse and occasionally mutually exclusive interpretations across the centuries (see Giblin 1971; Rowland 1989: 367–370; Clarke 2003: 179–183; Luz 2005a: 63–65). For many, what needs to be rendered to Caesar and what to God is clearly, if not always easily, differentiated. Some focus on the element of payment in coins, denoted by the denarius bearing the image and inscription of the emperor ('Tiberius Caesar Augustus, son of the divine Augustus,' a not unproblematic inscription for Jews and Christians). Therefore Roman tribute is among Caesar's dues; the temple tax is included among the 'things of God' (Hilary). Jerome similarly sees the distinction in terms of what people are called to pay or offer. Hence the things of Caesar including tribute money, the things of God sacred offerings such as tithes, first fruits, and sacrificial victims.

However, the phrase is widely understood as encompassing more, thus setting significant boundaries on what can be rendered to the emperor, with greater emphasis on rendering to God (Luz 2005a: 63–65). Tertullian, who seeks to reassure the emperor that Christians pay their taxes (*Apol.* 42), understands the 'things of God' to refer to human beings, bearing God's likeness (*Adv. Marc.* 4.38; Gen 1:26). Aquinas distinguishes between what is natural (such as bread and wine), given by God, and what is artificial (such as this denarius), which comes from Caesar. He also follows Tertullian in a 'mystical' interpretation, interpreting the 'things of God' as the human soul, while Theophylact makes a similar distinction between external things and that which is inner and spiritual. Juan de Maldonado articulates the difference in terms of the virtues, particularly the theological virtues: 'The things that are God's are faith, hope, charity, obedience' (Maldonado 1888: 2/235). The sixteenth-century Geneva Bible advocates obedience even to immoral public officials, though within very precise limits:

> The Christians must obey their Magistrates, although they be wicked and extortioners, but so far as the authority that God hath over us may remain safe unto him, and his honor is not diminished.

Christ's words, then, are an invitation to moral reflection: 'a challenge that looks to man's discerning his relationship to God in moral conduct' (Giblin 1971: 527).

Politically, therefore, the division between what is God's and Caesar's can be contested. Hincmar, ninth-century Archbishop of Rheims, acknowledged the right of the Frankish kings to profits from church land to support military activity, on the grounds that a bishop 'ought to render to Caesar what is Caesar's.' Nonetheless, he insisted that such land remain under ecclesiastical control, with the primary purpose of care for the poor, as well as supporting the financial needs of the clergy ('what is God's': in Moore 2011: 374).

The early Anabaptists also take a nuanced view, despite accusations from the magisterial Reformers that they are opposed to the state. The Moravian Anabaptist leader Balthasar Hübmaier responds to charges of sedition by asserting that he recognizes the authority of the civil government, and approves paying taxes and tithes. Nonetheless, like his fellow Anabaptists, obedience to the government depends upon it functioning in harmony with the Gospel. Thus he is happy to accept the charge of sedition: '… that I am accused of being a seditious person, thank God, it is the same name that was given to Christ my Saviour' (Hübmaier in Schaff 1932: 41).

Others see a more overtly positive position accorded to the Roman state (see also Rom 13:1–7; 1 Tim 2:1–4; 1 Pet 2:13–17), and therefore to subsequent civil authorities, particularly when the latter are Christian. Thus Christ's teaching plays a key role in later Western political thought, perhaps most famously in Luther's 'two kingdoms' doctrine. Calvin also adopts the distinction between 'the spiritual and civil government,' which leads him to reject rebellion against civil authorities as rebellion against God himself. Even this is not without limits, however: 'if in return the leaders usurp the rights of God they are to be denied obedience as far as possible short of offence to God' (Calvin 1972: III/27).

King James I of England (James VI of Scotland) observes in his 1598 *The True Law of Free Monarchies* how Christ's words endorsed the payment of taxes even to an idolatrous and persecuting Roman system, thus justifying their applicability to obedience to Christian kings like himself (see Clarke 2003: 182). From the Catholic side, Cornelius a Lapide also reflects the concern to render temporal things to the civic power. Yet the precise division between God's and Caesar's remains contested. The solution of the English philosopher Thomas Hobbes, in his 1651 book *Leviathan*, is to render all things to Caesar, by subordinating ecclesiastical power to the civil ruler, even restricting to the sovereign the authority to interpret scripture. For Hobbes, the second half of Jesus' saying is tautologous: 'That which belongs to God belongs to Caesar' (Pabel 1993: 334).

Still others find Jesus' response politically provocative, noting that he possesses no Roman coinage of his own, whereas his opponents, who have the coin, are firmly declaring themselves on Caesar's side. The differentiation between God's people and structures of governance among the nations is evident in the section of 'Political Authority' in the 1540 *Biblical Concordance of the Swiss Brethren*. The concordance sets this passage alongside a range of other scriptural texts (e.g. Exod 18; Deut 17; Isa 1, 3; Jer 27; Matt 17:25–27; 20:25–28; Acts 5:29; 18:12–16; Rom 13; 1 Tim 1:8–10) which suggest that believers are to be governed differently. Particularly telling is the use of Sirach 17:17, as applied to the Brethren as the Israel of God: 'For every nation he has provided a ruler, but Israel is the Lord's portion' (Fast and Peters 2001: 99–100). In the modern period, this view eschews such binary distinctions as spiritual/temporal or religion/politics, as well as the attractions of civic religion. As the title of an article by the American Catholic theologian William Cavanaugh puts it: 'If you render unto God what is God's, what is left for Caesar?' (Cavanaugh 2009). For Mahatma Gandhi, Christ's words are deliberately evasive, and tend toward civil disobedience, whilst revealing those who question him to be politically compromised:

> Jesus evaded the direct question put to him because it was a trap. He was in no way bound to answer it. He therefore asked to see the coin for taxes. And then said with withering scorn, 'How can you who traffic in Caesar's coins and thus receive what to you are benefits of Caesar's rule refuse to pay taxes?' Jesus' whole preaching and practice point unmistakably to noncooperation, which necessarily includes nonpayment of taxes. (Gandhi 1930)

The episode has had visual and musical as well as political impact. One of the earliest examples in visual art is Titian's *The Tribute Money* (c. 1516; Gemäldegalerie Alte Meister, Dresden), commissioned by Alfonso I d'Este, Duke of Ferrara. Alfonso had a particular interest in this pericope, given the division of his territories between the Holy Roman Empire ('the things of Caesar') and the Papal States ('the things of God'). That Christ's finger points at the coin may be directed against ecclesiastical, i.e. papal interference in his secular affairs (the coin should be rendered to Caesar, not to God's representative, the pope). By contrast, Titian's much later version for Philip II of Spain (c. 1543–1568; National Gallery, London) has Christ point in a heavenwards direction, thus prioritizing 'the things of God,' while his questioner holds out the coin. In his 1997 anthem *Tribute to Caesar*, the Estonian composer Arvo Pärt breaks his own composition rules in order to make certain theological points, e.g. to highlight the deceit of the Pharisees and Herodians, and to suggest that 'the things that should be given "unto God" are the sinful souls of the Pharisees and Herodians' (Hehn 2016: 38).

Marriage and the Resurrection (22:23–33)

The Sadducees' question involves attempted ridicule by bringing the tradition of Levirate marriage (Deut 25:5; cf. Gen 38:8) into dialogue with the resurrection doctrine they reject as non-Mosaic. Their *reductio ad absurdum* concerns seven brothers, each of whom marries the first brother's wife, and each dying childless. Whose wife will she be at the (for them non-existent) resurrection? The question is not only posed in such a way as to ridicule Jesus; it also perpetuates the view that wives are mere possessions of husbands (an objection noted by feminist critics: e.g. Schüssler Fiorenza 1983: 143–145). The story itself is so ridiculous that Martin Luther admits that he would not have believed it were it not in the Bible (Luther 2014: 135).

Some interpreters conclude that the number seven must have been chosen for some symbolic reason. Arnobius Iunior proposes that the seven brothers symbolize the seven patriarchs, and also the 'seven' books of Moses. Their wife signifies the synagogue 'into whom the seven patriarchs spilled the seed of Christ's name, yet she conceived no faith' (*Expositiunculae in Matthaeum* 24; Kraszewski 1999: 350).

Christ's withering response is that these aristocratic Jewish leaders know neither the scriptures nor 'the power of God.' Jerome concludes, employing the patristic principle that 'Scripture interprets Scripture,' that the latter phrase is Christological (Paul calls Christ 'the power of God' at 1 Cor 1:24). Marriage is not appropriate to the resurrection, where those raised will be 'like the angels in heaven.' The precise likeness to angels is never spelt out, however. Methodius of

Olympus (d. c. 311) rejects any suggestion that Christ's words undermine belief in the resurrection of the flesh. He draws his readers' attention to the fact that Jesus utters a simile: the raised are not angels but only like angels. Like the angels, they are incorruptible and, at least implicitly, have no need to procreate in marriage. In addition, the *telos* of the resurrected righteous is the vision of God:

> And He speaks of our being near the angels in this respect, that as the angels in heaven, so we also in paradise, spend our time no more in marriage-feasts or other festivities, but in seeing God and cultivating life, under the direction of Christ. For He did not say they shall be angels, but like angels, in being, for instance, crowned, as it is written, with glory and honour; differing a little from the angels, while near to being angels. (*Resurrection* 1.12; *ANF* 6:367)

The idea that those who share immortality with the angels no longer need to perpetuate the human species is sometimes repeated by later commentators (e.g. Maldonado). So too is the conviction that resurrected humans are still embodied, and differentiated by sex. Jerome is insistent: Christ does not say that they are incapable of marriage, but only that they do not marry. For Aquinas, the reason why marriage is ruled out is that sexual passions make humans more beastlike (*bestiales*). It was only in the later Middle Ages, possibly due to the interest in courtly love, that theologians began to consider the possibility of sexual intercourse in heaven (e.g. Andrew the Chaplain, twelfth-century author of the treatise *On Love*; Davies and Allison 1997: 230, n. 67).

Some Christian authors envisage the angel-like existence of the resurrection as already anticipated in this present world, particularly by those whose Christian life is marked by profound asceticism. In his biography of his sister Macrina the Younger (c. 330–379), who eschewed marriage following the tragic death of her betrothed, Gregory of Nyssa speaks of how she 'led her angelic and heavenly life' of prayer, sanctity, and good works (Gregory of Nyssa 1916: 42).

Rooting the doctrine of the resurrection in Exodus 3:6 ('I am the God of Abraham …,' 22:32) strikes many modern exegetes as 'very tendentious exegesis of an Old Testament passage' (Robinson 1997: 530). This is not merely post-Enlightenment bias, however. It embarrassed several of the early Fathers, who realized that this verse was far from the most compelling proof-text for the resurrection. Jerome would have preferred Isaiah 26:19 and Daniel 12:2, though supposes that Christ's choice was limited given that the Sadducees only accepted the authority of the Pentateuch (a claim rejected by some later scholars, e.g. Meyer 1879: 2/90). John Chrysostom stresses the present tense of God's words to Moses, but, as Juan de Maldonado later observes, something more is required. Maldonado paraphrases as follows: 'I am the God who made a covenant with

Abraham, Isaac, and Jacob to perpetuate their seed, and I therefore wish to keep it, because they still live and urge Me daily by their prayers to deliver their children from captivity of Egypt' (Maldonado 1888: 2/238).

The Two Greatest Commandments (22:34–40)

Jesus' response to the hostile Pharisee's question (22:36) is to link two commandments, concerning obligations to God and neighbor respectively (Deut 6:5; Lev 19:18). These are sometimes understood to summarize the two tablets of the law given to Moses on Sinai (Exod 31:18; 34:1: e.g. Calvin; Maldonado).

The distinction between loving the Lord with 'heart' and 'soul' and 'mind' is keenly felt by some. Theophylact finds here a reference to the animal, vegetative, and rational parts of the human person. Thomas Aquinas distinguishes between love arising from passion (loving with the heart) and that which springs from the judgment of reason (with the soul). Maldonado cautions against such over-precision: 'The meaning simply appears to be that we should love God with all our strength, and look to Him for everything' (Maldonado 1888: 2/241).

Yet readers of Matthew have often found it easier to imagine loving neighbors whom they can see, than God whom they cannot. Theophylact thus begins with the second love commandment, to show how the two are 'welded together.' If one loves one's neighbor, then one fulfills the commandments; if one does the latter, then one loves God. For many, the definition of neighbor is broad, encompassing those in need (under the influence of the Lukan parallel, which introduces the Good Samaritan, Luke 10:25–37). Yet the precise definition of loving one's neighbor 'as oneself' sometimes divides along denominational lines. Catholic theology distinguishes between 'self-love' and 'selfishness,' the former describing loving oneself not for one's own sake, but for God's sake, i.e. for the glory of God (e.g. Aquinas). Luther, by contrast, understands loving 'as oneself' as the self-love of sinful humanity, 'curved in upon yourself' (see Luz 2005a: 39). The distinction is not hard-and-fast, however. For the German Lutheran exegete Johann Albrecht Bengel, 'He who loves God will love himself in a proper degree without selfishness' (Bengel 1971: 258–259).

Who Is the Son of David? (22:41–46)

The final question comes not from opponents but from Jesus himself, who initiates the dialogue over the implications of Psalm 110:1 (cf. Mark 12:35–37a; Luke 20:41–44). The issue is clearly Christological, although Matthew's preference for the title 'Son of David' elsewhere (e.g. 1:1; 9:27; 15:22; 20:30–31) makes clear that he does not want to deny it to Jesus here. Rather, it is supplemented by the title 'Lord,' interpreted here as addressed by David as psalmist to the

Christ. Many commentators take as their starting point the recognition that 'Messiah' in Jewish understanding describes a human figure, anointed by God for a particular purpose. Yet the move they then make is to critique the Jews for their failure to acknowledge Christ's divinity, reading the passage as a clear articulation of a two-natures Christology (e.g. Origen; Chrysostom; Hilary; *Opus imperfectum*; Dionysius the Carthusian; Euthymius Zigabemus; Maldonado). As the marginal note to the Geneva Bible puts it: 'Christ is David's son touching his manhood, and his Lord, concerning his Godhead.' John Calvin goes so far as to find in this encounter the beginnings of all Christological heresies, which either deny Christ's divinity so as to reduce his power to save, or his humanity so as to close off his natural affinity with his people.

Some commentators betray knowledge of alternative Jewish exegetical traditions for reading Psalm 110, to which they are forced to respond. These attribute the psalm, not to David himself, but to Abraham's servant Eliezer of Damascus (Gen 15:2; see Jerome), or Melchizedek, or some other psalmist contemporary with David (see Maldonado 1888: 2/243). Hence 'my Lord' refers not to Christ but to Abraham, or David, or King Hezekiah (on the latter, see Justin Martyr, *Trypho* 33; Tertullian, *Adv. Marc.* 5.9).

Sitting 'at my right hand' is, as John Calvin notes, not a literal statement but a metaphor for Christ sharing God's authority. Long before Calvin, however, this meant that the passage became an important proof text for the Trinity. This takes visual form in many medieval illuminated psalters and Books of Hours. The image of the Son seated at the Father's right hand, with the dove-like Spirit between them, is often contained within the initial D of *Dixit Dominus*, the opening words of Psalm 110/Vulgate Psalm 109 (e.g. British Library, Royal 2 B VIII, f. 101v). The popularity of such images is the result of this psalm being recited in the western office of Vespers, where its Christological interpretation is clear. Its musical impact continues throughout the Middle Ages and into the modern period, with significant compositions of *Dixit Dominus* by Monteverdi (1610), Handel (1707), and Mozart (1779).

Matthew 23

Ancient Literary Context

The fifth and final dominical discourse (Matt 24–25) is preceded by a shorter speech of Jesus directed toward the scribes and Pharisees, distinctly Matthean in its present composition. Mark's Gospel contains at this point a brief denunciation of the scribes, for their love of privilege and external piety (Mark 12:38–40; also Luke 20:45–47). In Matthew, it has become a substantial

Matthew Through the Centuries, First Edition. Ian Boxall.

speech (combining Markan material with Matthean redaction and sayings paralleled in Luke 11:39–52), containing seven woes (23:13–36; cf. *Gos. Thom.* 39; 102; for seven in a context of judgment, see Gen 4:24; Lev 26:18; Prov 6:31; Rev 8–9; 16).

In the macro-structure of Matthew's Gospel, these woes arguably mirror the Beatitudes at the beginning of the Sermon on the Mount (5:3–12; cf. the combination of beatitudes and woes at Luke 6:24–26). For some, this strengthens the argument for seeing this chapter as the opening section of Matthew's fifth discourse rather than a separate section (e.g. Hood 2009). For others, this is the last of a series of shorter discourses which advance the narrative plot (along with 11:7–15; 12:25–45; 19:23–20:16; 21:28–22:14; Luz 2005b: 22–24).

Yet the tenor of this discourse sits awkwardly alongside the teaching of the Sermon on the Mount, advocating humility and love of enemies (e.g. 5:5, 44), and condemning those who describe their brother as 'fool' (5:22; Jesus calls his opponents 'blind fools' at 23:17). Many contemporary readers find the vehemence of Jesus' attack 'malevolent and offensive' (Saldarini 1992: 659), making Matthew 23 'the unloveliest chapter in the Gospel' (Viviano 1990: 3). Two scholarly moves attempt to locate this jarring language in a historically intelligible context. The first is to view the prominence given to the scribes and Pharisees as a reflection of mutual hostility and tensions between Matthean Christians and local Pharisee-dominated synagogues (e.g. Davies 1964; Sim 1998). In the case of 'the scribes,' the reference appears to be to Torah experts closely associated with the Pharisaic movement, rather than all Jewish scribes (cf. 13:52; 23:34).

Secondly, commentators locate Matthew's language alongside stock polemic used against religious and philosophical opponents in the ancient world. Matthew's polemic against the scribes and Pharisees would have sounded far more conventional to ancient audiences, and indeed, by comparison with other texts, remarkably mild (see Johnson 1989; Davies and Allison 1997: 258–263; Simmonds 2009). Its primary function would probably have been to legitimate the early Christian readers, and delegitimate their main Pharisaic rivals (Saldarini 1992). A secondary function of the warnings may well have been internal: encouraging self-critique on the part of those exercising leadership responsibility within the community of disciples.

The chapter climaxes with Christ's famous lament over Jerusalem (23:37–39; cf. Luke 13:34–35). It is replete with memorable feminine imagery in which Jesus likens his desire for the city to that of a mother bird gathering her chicks for protection. The profound pathos of the saying looks to the future desolation of Jerusalem's 'house' (according to the scholarly consensus over this Gospel's dating, a prophecy which has already been fulfilled in the Roman destruction of the temple).

The Interpretations

Woes Against the Scribes and Pharisees (23:1–36)

Despite qualifications expressed by historical critics, many have treated Christ's condemnation as a straightforward historical description of scribes and Pharisees, 'concerned only with externalism, triviality, and legalistic observance' (Sanders 1985b: 360). This is a very different portrait of Pharisaism than that of Matthew's contemporary Josephus (*War* 2.162–63; *Ant.* 18.12–15). Though Josephus has his own biases (he claimed to follow the Pharisaic way), other sources both within the New Testament itself (e.g. Luke 7:36–50; 13:31–33; John 3:1–2) and in the later rabbinic sources urge a more nuanced understanding. Matthew, by contrast, shows no awareness of the well-documented self-critique and warnings against hypocrisy found in Jewish texts from Pharisaic–rabbinic circles (see Luz 2005a: 105).

Sadly, it is the Matthean portrait which has stuck in imaginations shaped by the Christian tradition, informing even contemporary dictionary definitions of Pharisees as hypocritical, legalistic, and self-righteous. However, the fact that the woes were not read in the lectionary, and often only briefly commented upon, limited their impact on ordinary Christians and their Jewish fellow-citizens (see Luz 2005a: 133). Many, on the other hand, have been more sensitive to the text's original rhetorical function as delegitimating rival teachers, or actualized its potential for warning Christian audiences of the perennial dangers of hypocrisy and privilege. Jerome recognizes that Jesus' condemnation of binding heavy burdens (23:4) has a broader moral application to all who exercise the office of teacher. Aquinas follows him in this, noting that such a practice adds the sin of malice to that of hypocrisy, and contrasting this with the 'light' burden which Christ imposes (11:30). Despite his reputation for anti-Jewish sentiments, it is general ecclesial hypocrisy which is to the fore in John Chrysostom's homily on the passage. Commenting on 23:27 ('You are like white-washed tombs …'), Chrysostom asserts that, whatever Christ's words held for his original hearers, they are even more biting for his Christian congregation in fourth-century Antioch, whose baptismal vocation brings with it greater responsibilities:

> But that 'they' should be such persons is not 'so' dreadful a thing (although it be dreadful), but that 'you,' that have been counted worthy to become temples of God, should of a sudden have become sepulchres, having as much ill savor, this is extreme wretchedness. He in whom Christ dwells, and the Holy Spirit has worked, and such great mysteries, that this man should be a sepulchre, what wretchedness is this? What mournings and lamentations does this call for, when the members of Christ have become a tomb of uncleanness? (*Homily on Matthew* 73.3; *NPNF* 1st series, 10:442)

In the Middle Ages, William of Ockham finds in the warning against laying heavy burdens (23:4) a clear indictment of the medieval papacy:

> For some called Roman pontiffs, abounding in luxuries, glorying in pomp and honors, enriching their relations and trying to enoble them, have attempted to impose heavy and unbearable burdens on emperors, kings, prelates, and churches, and on all the faithful. Indeed they have wickedly labored to reduce everyone to slavery. (*Brev. prin. tyr.* 2.17; William of Ockham 1992: 56)

A nineteenth-century example comes from the African-American abolitionist and social reformer Frederick Douglass (1818–1895). Douglass sees the religion of the scribes and Pharisees actualized in the American Christianity of his day, heavily implicated as it was in the slave trade. The appendix to his *Life* contains an extended reflection upon the 'woes' of Matthew 23. Though he too assumes the Matthean portrait of Pharisaic 'externalism' to be historically correct, his application hits the target of contemporary hypocrisy:

> Dark and terrible as is this picture, I hold it to be strictly true of the overwhelming mass of professed Christians in America. They strain at a gnat, and swallow a camel. Could any thing be more true of our churches? They would be shocked at the proposition of fellowshipping a sheep-stealer; and at the same time they hug to their communion a man-stealer, and brand me with being an infidel, if I find fault with them for it. They attend with Pharisaical strictness to the outward forms of religion, and at the same time neglect the weightier matters of the law, judgment, mercy, and faith. They are always ready to sacrifice, but seldom to show mercy. (Douglass in Tippens, Walker, and Weathers 2013: 70)

Some would see a similar tendency to contemporize, and in the process de-Judaize, in Pier Paolo Pasolini's depiction of the scribes and Pharisees in his 1964 film *Il Vangelo secondo Matteo*. According to one critic, in Pasolini's portrayal they are 'not so much specifically Jewish Pharisees and scribes as they are the bureaucrats, owners, and bosses of every age and culture' (Aichele 2002: 531). For others, however, Pasolini further compounds the problem, despite his stated aim of using the Gospel conflict to comment on religious conflict in twentieth-century Italy. Not only does the film present the woes of Matthew 23 in their entirety, it further villainizes the Jewish authorities by differentiating them from other characters by their preposterously exaggerated headgear (see Reinhartz 1998). Less problematic, perhaps, is Denis Arcand's *Jesus of Montreal* (1989), where the modern-day Pharisees are clergy of the Catholic Church in Quebec. The parallels are drawn without the term 'Pharisee' ever being mentioned (the invective of Matthew's woes is directed toward 'reverend fathers').

If certain readers of Matthew 23 remind their contemporaries of the universal potential for hypocrisy, others exploit the dimension of Christ's attack which delegitimizes rival teachers. Matthew 23 has frequently functioned as a critique of ecclesiastical opponents in times of theological controversy. In Reformation polemics, 'the Pharisees' often functioned as a cipher for Catholic opponents, the woes being viewed as actualized in sixteenth-century church life (see Edwards 2015). John Calvin, for whom the neglect of the weightier matters of the Law in favor of the minutiae is a disease that 'has afflicted virtually every generation and race,' finds a prime example in the Catholic Church:

> Look at the Papists today. They transgress the chief commandments of God and spend all their energies on feeble ceremonies. This is the fiction Christ reproves in the scribes, who strenuously and scrupulously pay tithes, yet take no care for the chief articles of the Law. (Calvin 1972: III/57)

One Catholic response, that of Juan de Maldonado, is to historicize, underscoring that Christ is speaking to scribes and Pharisees in his own first-century context. Juan de Valdés makes a similar exegetical step, arguing that, if Christ's words in this chapter pertain not simply to his own contemporaries but to subsequent generations, then Christians should be obliged to keep the Mosaic Law along with the Gospel, a proposition 'which has been condemned from the time of the apostles' (Valdés 1882: 400). This historicizing move parallels sixteenth-century Roman Catholic exegesis of the Book of Revelation, such as that of Maldonado's fellow Jesuit Luís de Alcázar (1554–1613), who read the text in reference to first-century imperial Rome against the Reformers' actualizing tendencies which identified the contemporary 'Babylon' as papal Rome (see Kovacs and Rowland 2004: 20).

The chapter also functions polemically in debates between Quakers and Puritans in seventeenth-century England. In his 1655 *The Quakers Catechism*, the English Puritan Richard Baxter attempts to address a number of queries from Quakers, including one which categorizes the Puritans as contemporary Pharisees: 'Whether they that stand praying in the Synagogues or Idols Temples, and love greetings in the markets, and bindes heavy burthens on the people, and are called of men Master, be not out of Christs Doctrine?' Baxter's response is to accuse the Quakers of confusing external religious practices with hypocrisy:

> If you are not willfully blinde you may perceive that it is not all the external actions mentioned (Matt. 23) that Christ condemneth, but the pride and hypocrisy which the Pharisees manifested in them. Mark first that he bids men even hear the hypocriticall Scribes and Pharisees, and observe and do what they bid men observe and do, because they sate in Moses chair. It is not therefore all the faults there charged on them that will acquit men from observation of their

> doctrine. Is this agreeable to your practice who damn men that despise not and reject not Christs most upright and faithful ministers? Their sin is laid down in the fifth verse [All their works they do to be seen of men.] Prove this by us if you can? (Baxter in Boggs 2008: 5)

In less polemical times, shaped not least by the horrors of the Holocaust and sensitivity to Jewish–Christian relations, modern historical critics have paralleled Maldonado's interpretative move in contextualizing this chapter historically against the backdrop of late first-century formative Judaism. This more sympathetic reading has come to shape the official positions of mainstream Christian churches vis-à-vis the Jewish community. The 1985 document of the Pontifical Commission for Religious Relations with the Jews ('Notes on the correct way to present Jews and Judaism in preaching and catechesis in the Roman Catholic Church') highlights more nuanced portrayals of Pharisees elsewhere in the New Testament (e.g. Mark 12:34; Luke 7:36; 13:31; 14:1; Gamaliel in Acts 5:34–39), criticism of hypocrisy found in rabbinic sources, and the closeness between Jesus and the Pharisees on doctrines such as the resurrection, practices of piety, and teaching methods.

Sitting on Moses' Seat (23:1–3)

There is a tension running through this description of the 'scribes and Pharisees.' On the one hand, their teaching authority is apparently acknowledged. They have sat down 'on Moses' seat' (23:1; the aorist tense could be a reference to their sitting down at Jamnia, now a past event: Viviano 1990: 11). Moses' seat (*kathedra*) may refer to a physical seat in the synagogue, on which the scribes and Pharisees sat to teach (e.g. Chrysostom; Aquinas; for archeological evidence, see Luz 2005a: 99). A chair or throne is clearly envisaged by the Egyptian monk Macarius of Alexandria (d. 395) in his comment about the high priest Caiaphas:

> Caiaphas, who crucified our Lord, sat on the seat of Moses, the seat which our Lord greatly honoured. (*Ep.* 1 in Davies and Allison 1997: 268, n. 18)

Alternatively, the seat might refer to the platform from which the Law was read (Euthymius Zigabenus). By extension, it could be a metaphor for the scribes' and Pharisees' teaching authority (Jerome), specifically their spiritual descent from Moses (Chrysostom). The latter is a derivation from the fact that they indeed sat on chairs to teach (the 'best seats' in the synagogue: Renov 1955).

On the other hand, their actions are out of kilter with their words (23:2–7). More problematically, there is a tension between this pericope and other sections of Matthew's narrative, where Jesus directly challenges Pharisaic *halakah* (e.g. over Sabbath observance, handwashing, and divorce, 12:1–14; 15:1–2, 10–20; 19:3–9; see Powell 1995: 421–444). Some modern scholars therefore see Jesus' words about Moses' seat as an ironic statement (e.g. France 2007: 859–860). Alternatively, Mark Allen Powell has proposed, on the basis of the widespread illiteracy of the ancient world and the difficulty of access to Torah scrolls, that sitting on Moses' seat refers, not to their teaching authority, but to the fact that they possess the scrolls and are able to read from them:

> In saying that the scribes and Pharisees sit on Moses' seat, Jesus may be simply acknowledging the powerful social and religious position that they occupy in a world where most people are illiterate and copies of the Torah are not plentiful. Since Jesus' disciples do not themselves have copies of the Torah, they will be dependent on the scribes and the Pharisees to know what Moses said on any given subject. (Powell 1995: 431–432)

In other words, disciples should listen to and act upon their citation of the Law of Moses ('whatever they speak'), but reject their subsequent interpretations, which bind heavy burdens, and their hypocritical practice.

Earlier interpreters deal with the tension in different ways. In the Jewish-Christian Pseudo-Clementine *Homilies*, Peter teaches how Christ only condemned some of the Pharisees for hypocrisy:

> Therefore He made use of this memorable expression, speaking the truth with respect to the hypocrites of them, not with respect to all. For to some He said that obedience was to be rendered, because they were entrusted with the chair of Moses. However, to the hypocrites he said, 'Woe to you, Scribes and Pharisees, hypocrites, for ye make clean the outside of the cup and the platter, but the inside is full of filth.' (*Hom.* 11.29; *ANF* 8:291)

Others find the distinction in the Mosaic Law itself. John Chrysostom and Euthymius Zigabenus limit 'everything they tell you' to the moral law, while the ceremonial law is no longer binding. Origen, Theophylact, and Juan de Maldonado differentiate between the Mosaic Law itself and those Pharisaic traditions which 'were either wholly contrary to Scripture, or certainly not necessarily to salvation' (Maldonado 1888: 2/247). Examples of the latter include the broadening of phylacteries (23:5), and the categorization of oaths (23:16–17). A similar distinction is made by Hilary, who is concerned 'lest their human customs and unbelief nullify the teaching of the Law' (Hilary of Poitiers 2012: 240). This is in accord with Jesus' earlier debates with the Pharisees, where he criticizes them for breaking the Torah for the sake of their own traditions (15:3).

Christ's concern for the dignity of the Pharisees' office has obvious implications for the understanding of office-holders within the church (John Chrysostom applies it to teachers and priests). More specifically, the passage is read as ensuring the validity of sacraments despite the unworthiness of the minister, as in the Lutheran *Augsburg Confession* of 1530:

> Although the Church properly is the congregation of saints and true believers, nevertheless, since in this life many hypocrites and evil persons are mingled therewith, it is lawful to use Sacraments administered by evil men, according to the saying of Christ: The Scribes and the Pharisees sit in Moses' seat, etc. Matt. 23:2 (Article VIII).[1]

Broad Phylacteries and Long Tassels (23:5)

Despite the unusual terminology, it is generally accepted that the 'phylacteries' (i.e. amulets) are *tefillin* (Tigay 1979), bound to the arm and forehead in obedience to the divine command (Exod 13:9, 16; Deut 6:8). The fringes or tassels are likewise those commanded at Numbers 15:38–39 and Deuteronomy 22:12. This is the almost unanimous interpretation of commentators on Matthew (e.g. Justin Martyr, *Trypho* 46.5; Origen; Chrysostom; Jerome; Theophylact; Euthymius Zigabenus; Maldonado). A rare exception is Epiphanius, who misunderstands the broadening of phylacteries as referring to the broad purple stripes on scribal garments (*Pan.* 15.1.3; Tigay 1979: 46; Lieu 1988: 513). He is followed in this mistake by the twelfth-century Syriac Orthodox commentator Dionysius bar-Salibi.

Christ's concern is not that *tefillin* are worn, but that they are exaggerated in size so as to draw attention to the wearer. Jerome's point is slightly different: that the scribes and Pharisees carried the words of Torah on their bodies but not in their hearts. In addition, he claims that they bound sharp thorns into their tassels, which pricked them as they walked so as to remind them of their duty toward God. He also draws an analogy with Christian practice in his own day, bordering on the superstitious: the wearing of little copies of the Gospels and relics of the true cross as amulets by Christian women. John Chrysostom refers to something similar in Christian Antioch:

> And what are these phylacteries, and these borders? Since they were continually forgetting God's benefits, He commanded His marvelous works to be inscribed on little tablets, and that these should be suspended from their hands (wherefore also He said, They shall be immoveable in your eyes), which they called phylacteries; as many of our women now wear Gospels hung from their necks. And in

1 http://bookofconcord.org/augsburgconfession.php.

> order that by another thing again they may be reminded, like as many often do, binding round their finger with a piece of linen or a thread, as being likely to forget, this God enjoined them as children to do, to sew a ribbon of blue on their garments, upon the fringe that hung round their feet, that they might look at it, and remember the commandments; and they were called borders. (*Homily on Matthew* 72; *NPNF* 1st series, 10:437)

Theophylact, who normally follows Chrysostom closely, understands the fringes to be not blue but blood-red. This allows them to function symbolically for Christians, as a sign that 'we must be signed with the blood of Christ' (Theophylact 1992: 196).

Actualizations of this Pharisaic exaggeration are detected by critics across the centuries. In the twelfth century, the French theologian Alain of Lille (c. 1128–1202/1203) finds a parallel to the Pharisees' broad phylacteries in preachers who pepper their sermons with too many stories, jokes, and even songs (in van Liere 2014: 233).

Love of Titles (23:6–10)

The condemnation of the scribes and Pharisees further extends to their love of honorific titles: rabbi, father, and master (Greek *kathēgētēs*, 'instructor,' 'guide,' or 'tutor': Winter 1991). The warning against teachers being called 'Rabbi' seems to reflect developments within post-70 Judaism as the proximate background to the Gospel. Yet the wider application of the discussion is evident almost from the beginning. Origen sees the warning as addressed to those who exercise ecclesiastical office. In the thirteenth century, the warning against being called rabbi is taken with particular seriousness by Francis of Assisi, who refers to it in the Rule of 1221.

That Jesus' words describe the perennial temptation to seek honor or reputation is reflected in a number of English translations of the passage. For the Geneva Bible, the term *kathēgētēs* (23:10) is translated as 'doctor,' while both Wycliffe and KJV opt for 'master.' The later translation causes difficulties for educated Protestant pastors, such as the Puritan Richard Baxter, who is forced to defend his use of the title to Quaker critics (Boggs 2008: 5–6). Eugene Peterson's *The Message* gives verse 10 a very contemporary feel: 'And don't let people maneuver you into taking charge of them. There is only one Life-Leader for you and them – Christ' (Peterson 2002).

Richard Baxter is not alone in having to defend the use of certain titles. Jerome, aware of the use of 'father' in Palestinian and Egyptian monasteries, defends this as a usage which reflects honor due to age, not detracting from the acknowledgment of the Creator as one's true Father. For Theophylact, it is not the titles themselves which are problematic, but the desire to be called by them, while failing to recognize that their dignity belongs to God alone. To take these words too literally would risk offending against the commandment to honor father and mother (Exod 20:12). Thomas Aquinas makes the distinction between God, who alone is master or teacher properly speaking, and human teachers who are such 'by service' (*ministerio*: Aquinas 2013b: 263).

More surprising, perhaps, is the way in which some of the Reformers respond to this passage. John Calvin juxtaposes it with Paul's words about being a 'father' to his converts (1 Cor 4:15; cf. Phil 2:22) as an example of those who are given this name by God rather than assuming it for themselves. Hence, for Calvin, not only is it permitted that certain men on earth be called 'father,' it is wrong for them to be deprived of that name. Luther also holds back from the total abandonment of titles, in a sermon preached in 1538:

> Christ distinguishes here these various estates: rabbis, fathers, and lords. So there are three estates: under the rabbis are disciples, under the parents are children, under the lords are subjects. The entire world is comprised in these estates. Christ Himself distinguishes these estates and does not want them dispensed with. Instead, everything should be done so that the rabbi, father, and lord direct you to the one God … (Luther 2014: 160)

For both Luther and Calvin, the destabilizing possibility of rebellion through disrespect to those in authority may be driving their response.

Straining Gnats and Swallowing Camels (23:24)

The ridiculous portrayal of the scribes and Pharisees is particularly exemplified in the image of them straining a gnat yet swallowing a camel. The first reference almost certainly alludes to the practice of straining wine through a sieve to prevent unclean insects getting in (*m. Šabb.* 20.2; *b. Ḥul.* 67a; see Lev 11:41). Like the gnat, the camel is also an unclean animal (Lev 11:4), as well as being incredibly large. Yet they avoid swallowing the tiny insect, only to devour an even greater source of defilement.

Fortunatianus of Aquileia complicates the camel reference by connecting it to Abraham's ten heavy-laden camels (Gen 24:10). He interprets these as a symbol of the Decalogue, the Law's 'written burdens' (Fortunatianus of Aquileia 2017: 81). Jerome is more straightforward. Jesus is making a contrast between their attention to the details of tithing (the gnat) and their swallowing or neglecting justice, mercy, and faith (the camel). Thomas Aquinas proposes Jerome's as one possible reading in his lecture on the passage. He sets beside it another, which provides a moral application for his Dominican students: that both the gnat and the camel refer to sins, the former lesser and the latter greater.

English-speaking commentators have often been diverted by a typographical error in the KJV, whereby 'strain out' becomes 'strain at' (Davies and Allison 1997: 296).

Whitewashed Tombs (23:27)

An equally striking description is of the scribes and Pharisees as 'whitewashed' or (perhaps better) 'plastered' tombs, which appear beautiful on the outside but whose interiors are full of bones, i.e. ritually unclean. The former translation presupposes the Jewish practice of marking graves with lime prior to Passover to avoid inadvertent contact with corpses (Theophylact; Henry Hammond). Against that is the lack of evidence that whitewashing was considered making something beautiful (see Davies and Allison 1997: 300–302). Jerome thinks that covering the outside of tombs with chalk was just the first stage in beautifying them, as preparation for them being covered in marble and painted. Either way, the point is clear, as in the following paraphrase by the seventeenth-century English commentator Henry Hammond:

> Even so are ye the fairest in outward guise and show, but in your hearts, designs, and actions that flow from thence, the most noisome and polluted that can be, nothing but contrariety to your professions, and instead of justice and charity, which ye pretend, the most greedy and ravenous oppressors. (Hammond 1845: 110)

This imagery very quickly enters into standard Christian polemic against Jews and Judaizing Christians. Thus, whether alluding to Matthew directly or utilizing common tradition, Ignatius of Antioch describes Judaizers and others who do not speak about Jesus as Christ as 'tombstones and graves of the dead' (*Philad.* 6.1; Holmes 2007: 241).

However, many are sensitive to its universal application, and its particular warning to professing Christians. The contrast between the outer and the inner is picked up by Dante in his description of the 'Moat of the Hypocrites,' whose inhabitants are the 'painted people,' echoing the painted tombs of Matthew's polemic. They wear monk-like garments which externally are gilded, but whose bright exterior conceals the fact that they are made of heavy lead and cannot be cast off (*Inferno* 18). Dante thereby reveals the tragic truth about a lifetime of hypocritical concealment, as one of his commentators puts it:

> Although the souls in this Moat see through one another and know that all are false, not one lays aside the gilded cloak in consequence; their doom is to wear it even among their fellow-hypocrites. They have acted a part so long that they have lost for ever the power of being themselves. (John Smyth Carroll in Stoddart 1914: 96–97).

The wording of the KJV ('whited sepulchres') has been particularly influential in the English-speaking world. In Joseph Conrad's 1899 novella *The Heart of Darkness*, the narrator, Charles Marlow, describes the Brussels of King Leopold II as a 'city that always makes me think of a whited sepulchre,' a pointed attack on Belgian colonial influence in the so-called 'Congo Free State' (Conrad 1995: 37).

The Blood of Zechariah Son of Barachiah (23:35)

The reference to tombs provides a verbal connection to the final woe, implicating the scribes and Pharisees of Jesus' generation in the deaths of the prophets, despite their adorning the prophets' tombs in the present (23:29–32). The woe presupposes both biblical and post-biblical traditions about the persecution and martyrdom of Israel's prophets (e.g. Jer 26:10–24; 38:4–13; 2 Chron 24:20–22; *Lives of the Prophets*). The connection with the ancestors' shedding prophetic blood is made by Christ's statement that his contemporaries kill, crucify, or otherwise mistreat the 'prophets and wise men and scribes' he himself sends to them (23:34). Patristic commentators typically understand a reference to the disciples or apostles (see Luke 11:49: 'prophets and apostles'). Jerome lists Stephen, Paul, and Peter as among the exemplars of those killed, and connects the saying to 1 Corinthians 12, where prophecy and wisdom are among the gifts granted to the early church. Similarly, Theophylact explains how the apostles are made scribes, i.e. teachers, and wisdom-filled prophets, by the Holy Spirit. Thus, despite their apparent veneration for the prophets of old, their treatment of Jesus and his followers implicates them in the blood of the righteous. As John Calvin succinctly asserts: 'This is the way of hypocrites' (Calvin 1972: III/61).

Calvin's real target, however, is not the first-century scribes and Pharisees, but the papacy of his own day. Rome venerates the tombs of the apostles and martyrs in its midst, yet in Calvin's view persecutes those who hold to the apostolic doctrine. 'Let them adorn the images of the saints as they please,' he continues, 'with incense, candles, flowers and pomp of all sorts; if Peter were alive today they would tear him to ribbons, they would stone Paul to the ground' (Calvin 1972: III/62).

The precise identity of 'Zechariah son of Barachiah' is a frequent topic of discussion, as this appears to conflate the prophet of that name with another Zechariah, son of Jehoiada, who was killed in the temple court by King Joash of Judah (Zech 1:1; 2 Chron 24:26; the Old Greek of 2 Chronicles has the alternative reading 'Azarias son of Iodae': Gallagher 2014: 123). The debate is further complicated by the second-century *Protevangelium of James*, which understands the reference to John the Baptist's father, struck down by Herod's soldiers sent to search for his young son during the massacre of the innocents after Jesus' birth:

> And Herod searched for John, and sent officers to Zacharias, saying: Where have you hid your son? And he, answering, said to them: I am the servant of God in holy things, and I sit constantly in the temple of the Lord: I do not know where my son is. And the officers went away, and reported all these things to Herod. And Herod was enraged, and said: His son is destined to be king over Israel. And he sent to him again, saying: Tell the truth; where is your son? For you know that your life is in my hand. And Zacharias said: I am God's martyr, if you shed my blood; for the Lord will receive my spirit, because you shed innocent blood at the vestibule of the temple of the Lord. And Zacharias was murdered about daybreak. (*Prot. Jas.* 23; *ANF* 8:366)

A variant is found in the Amharic commentary tradition of the Ethiopian Orthodox Church, combined with the claim that Zechariah's blood bubbled for 70 years, until seven of Herod's relatives were executed by the emperor Titus (Cowley 1985a: 293–294). Origen (whose text of 2 Chron 24:26 reads 'Azarias son of Iodae') also identifies Zechariah with the father of the Baptist, though citing a parallel tradition to the *Protevangelium*, which attributes Zechariah's murder to his advocating the admission of Mary (a married woman) into the area reserved for virgins in the temple. Theophylact also opts for the father of the Baptist, thinking it plausible that, just as this Zechariah was named after the prophet, so his own father bore the name of the prophet's father (also Epiphanius, *Pan.* 26.12.1–4). In its favor is the second-person verb used in Jesus' words: 'whom you killed …,' suggesting a contemporary of his interlocutors.

Various commentators (e.g. Jerome; Chrysostom; Aquinas; Maldonado) debate the merits of all three candidates. Jerome dismisses Origen's preference for the father of John the Baptist on the grounds that it comes from an apocryphal writing. This makes all the more ironic his own position. He opts for Zechariah son of Jehoiada, on the grounds that this, rather than 'son of Barachaiah,' is the reading in the Gospel used by the Nazarenes (another non-canonical text!). He also notes that Barachaiah means 'blessed of the Lord,' and suggests it is an appropriate second name for a righteous priest such as Jehoiada (Jerome is followed in the West, e.g. by Bede, *Homily* 1.3, Rabanus Maurus, Paschasius Radbertus, Aquinas, and Calvin).

Modern scholars frequently understand the evangelist to be 'book-ending' the Hebrew canon in his naming of Abel and Zechariah (Genesis to Chronicles), identifying the latter with the son of Jehoiada (e.g. Nolland 2005: 946–947; France 2007: 880; Byron 2011: 751). The fact that the Fathers failed to make this connection may suggest that it owes more to the impact of the printing press, producing Hebrew Bibles concluding with Chronicles from the fifteenth century onwards, than ancient perceptions of canonical shape (see Gallagher 2014).

A Lament for Jerusalem (23:37–39)

Jesus' speech climaxes with his double-lament 'Jerusalem, Jerusalem.' Many commentators are moved by the emotion in Christ's words. For Jerome, Jesus weeps like a father over the holy city, while John Chrysostom regards the repetition of the name as underscoring Christ's mourning, and his great love for the city. Yet, *pace* Jerome, the Gospel image is not that of a father, but of a mother bird with protective wings. The Christian apocryphon *5 Ezra* (second to fifth century CE) reflects a heightened Christology by identifying the speaker as 'the Lord Almighty' (*2 Esdras* 1:28–30). Chrysostom sees the appropriateness of the mother hen image:

> And His affection He indicates by the similitude; for indeed the creature is warm in its love towards its brood. And everywhere in the prophets is this same image of the wings, and in the song of Moses and in the Psalms, indicating His great protection and care. (*Homily on Matthew* 74.3; *NPNF* 1st series, 10:447)

Chrysostom seems to be thinking here of texts such as Isaiah 31:5, Psalms 17:8, 36:7, and 91:4, as well as the image of God as an eagle bearing the Israelites on his wings at Deuteronomy 32:11.

The Christological image is particularly important for the eleventh-century Benedictine philosopher, theologian, and archbishop of Canterbury, Anselm, who combines Christ's maternal language with that used by the apostle Paul in his 'Prayer to St. Paul':

> And you, Jesus, are you not also a mother?
> Are you not the mother who, like a hen,
> gathers her chickens under her wings?
> Truly, Lord, you are a mother,
> for both they who are in labour
> and they who are brought forth
> are accepted by you.
> (Anselm 1979: 153)

Anselm goes on to envisage his soul as a dead chick in need of the revivifying and justifying action of the mother (see Bynum 1982: 114). If Anselm emphasizes the protective embrace of Christ, Erasmus's paraphrase stresses Christ's anxiety for his offspring: 'as an anxious hen fearing for her chicks gathers them under her wings and comforts them' (Erasmus 2008: 323).

The metaphor is sometimes applied to the church as the body of Christ (e.g. Fortunatianus of Aquileia; *Opus imperfectum*), and by extension to ecclesiastical leaders, called to model their lives on the pattern of Christ, as in the reprimand of the bishop of Le Mans by Adam, Cisterican abbot of Perseigne (c. 1145–1221):

> Besides, in what way are you yourself named father or mother of little ones, you who do not jealously watch over your chicks with tender affection as a hen does, or like an eagle provoking her chicks to fly flutter over them and bear upwards in your wings both by word and example those little ones commended to you? (in Bynum 1982: 125)

The image is not common in visual art, although a modern mosaic of Christ as mother hen, wings outstretched over seven chicks, adorns the altar of the Church of *Dominus Flevit* ('The Lord Wept') on the Mount of Olives overlooking Jerusalem.

Christ's closing words (23:38–39) point beyond the rejection of the mother hen by her chicks, and the consequent desolation of their 'house' (cf. Jer 12:7–8), to a time when they will greet the returning Son of Man with the words 'Blessed is the one coming in the name of the Lord' (Ps 118:26, quoted by the Palm Sunday crowds at 21:9). The desolate house could be a reference to the temple (e.g. Jerome; *Opus imperfectum*), the city of Jerusalem, or the whole 'house of Israel' (in favor of all three, see Garland 1979: 198–200). Fortunatianus of Aquileia understands it to refer to the synagogue, deserted by the Holy Spirit, while the *Opus imperfectum* allows that it refers, not only to the physical temple, but to Christian heretics.

The precise meaning of 23:39 is contested, particularly when it comes to be spoken, not as in Matthew by Christ the Jewish prophet to his own people, but in a situation of radical separation between Jew and Christian (especially where the latter have become the persecuting majority). Origen reads it positively, in connection with Paul's conviction that 'all Israel will be saved' (Rom 11:26; Origen, *Frag.* 464; also e.g. Cyril of Alexandria, *Frag.* 264 in Reuss 1957: 243), meaning that the loss of the temple is not the last word for God's ancient people. Jerome also hears words of hope, though it presupposes some kind of conversion. There remains a 'time' of repentance for the Jews, in order that they may 'see the face of Christ' when he comes at the End (Jerome 2008: 269; see also e.g. Gundry 1994: 474). Cornelius a Lapide expects that the conversion will come about prior to the Parousia through the preaching of Elijah. Others, by contrast, consider that the confession will be uttered unwillingly, under compulsion (e.g. Chrysostom; Euthymius Zigabenus; Maldonado). Hilary reads the harsh polemic of Matthew 23 as pointing to persistent 'obstinacy'; thus, he cryptically comments that 'they bless him through the confession of stubborn unbelief' (Hilary of Poitiers 2012: 247). For Theophylact, Israel will utter the blessing at the Parousia whatever, whether willingly or unwillingly. John Calvin is even clearer that this is an oracle of judgment: 'He says that He will not come to them until they cry out in fear – too late – at the sight of His terrible Majesty, "truly He is the Son of God"' (Calvin 1972: III/71).

In the modern period, Davies and Allison suggest a third, conditional interpretation, albeit one rooted in Old Testament promises of redemption, which focuses on the phrase 'until you say':

> The text means not, when the Messiah comes, his people will bless him, but rather, when his people bless him, the Messiah will come. (Davies and Allison 1997: 323)

Different readings of these final verses reflect deeper theological differences. In the sixteenth century, the passage is key to the debate between Desiderius Erasmus and Martin Luther over free will (see Clarke 2003: 186–187). The issue of free will over divine compulsion is also explored in the eighteenth century by John Wesley. In a sermon on free grace preached in Bristol in 1740, Wesley cites the passage as one among many scriptural passages which clarify why not all are saved, despite the Lord's desire to the contrary:

> So our Lord expressly: 'They will not come unto me that they may have life;' 'The power of the Lord is present to heal them,' but they will not be healed. They 'reject the counsel,' the merciful counsel, 'of God against themselves,' as did their stiff-necked forefathers. And therefore are they without excuse; because God would save them, but they will not be saved. This is the condemnation, 'How often would I have gathered you together, and ye would not.' (*Sermon* 110.22; Wesley 1986: 553–554)

Matthew 24–25

Ancient Literary Context

The final Matthean discourse (Mark 13; Luke 21; cf. *Did.* 16:3–6) begins with a geographical transition from the temple (24:1–2) to the Mount of Olives, traditional location of the last judgment (24:3; see e.g. Zech 14:1–5). The speech which Jesus now delivers is variously called 'the Eschatological Discourse,' 'the Olivet Discourse,' and 'the Synoptic Apocalypse.' The first two titles describe its subject matter (prophecies of end-time events) and location (the Mount of

Matthew Through the Centuries, First Edition. Ian Boxall.

Olives) respectively. However, although eschatological events are certainly included, the discourse disappoints in its failure to provide a full account of the eschatological scenario, including the resurrection and precision over the coming new age.

The descriptor 'Synoptic Apocalypse' (sometimes 'Little Apocalypse') reflects a theory originally proposed by Timothée Colani in 1864 that underlying Matthew 24 and parallels is a Jewish-Christian apocalyptic document written prior to Jerusalem's fall (see e.g. Brown 1979; Theissen 1991: 123–165; Beasley-Murray 1993; Moloney 2002: 248–251; France 2007: 333–336). The passage is full of stock eschatological language, including the wars, earthquakes, and famines typically associated with the 'messianic woes' (e.g. *2 Bar*. 70:8), and cosmic signs affecting sun, moon, and stars (Isa 13:10; cf. e.g. *1 En*. 80:4; Rev 6:12–13; *Sib. Or*. 2194, 200–202; 5.152). Decisions as to whether these should be understood literally, or as more figurative descriptions of dramatic transitions within history, affect the interpretation of the whole.

Scholars have understood its function in several complementary ways: providing a clearer perspective on the readers' own post-Easter experience (including suffering and persecution), giving meaning to historical events such as Jerusalem's destruction, encouraging hope and watchfulness, and completing the earthly story of Jesus in the future coming of the Son of Man. Matthew's version has its own distinctive features. For example, Matthew has already used the material about being handed over to synagogues and rulers (Mark 13:9–12; Luke 21:12–16) at 10:17–22, perhaps to highlight its fulfillment in the persecution of missionary disciples by the time of his first audiences. He also clarifies certain ambiguous features (e.g. that the 'abomination of desolation' was spoken of by the prophet Daniel [Matt 24:15], and that it refers to a thing rather than a person: cf. Mark 13:14; see Dan 9:27; 11:31; 12:11). For modern exegetes, Matthew's greater clarity is often cited in support of dating his Gospel after the temple's destruction.

Matthew's discourse, moreover, is considerably longer than Mark's and Luke's, through the addition of several other parables. Some of these are paralleled elsewhere in Luke (e.g. the Thief in the Night: 24:43–44; Luke 12:39–40; the Wicked Servant: 24:45–51; Luke 12:41–46). The Talents is a probable variant of Luke's parable of the Pounds (25:14–30; cf. Luke 19:11–27). Others are unique to Matthew: the Wise and Foolish Virgins (25:1–13) and the Sheep and the Goats (25:31–46). At this climactic moment, therefore, the hostility toward the Messiah Jesus sharpens into focus on the eschatological judgment, both of God's people Israel and of the nations. The particular revelation that it is the Son of Man who will sit on the throne of glory (25:31), prepares the reader for the story of the humiliated, tortured, and crucified Son of Man in the passion narrative which immediately follows.

The Interpretations

Jesus Leaves the Temple (24:1–2)

Matthew's statement that Jesus had already departed from the temple when he uttered the prophecy of its destruction (cf. Mark 13:1: 'As he was departing from the temple') is viewed as significant by careful readers of the text. For Theophylact, it symbolizes his departure from the Jews, such that their house is left desolate (23:38). Similarly, Thomas Aquinas thinks that Christ's physical departure shows that he has left the temple spiritually. This has a modern variant among those Matthean scholars who read the Gospel as, in part, an allegory of the departure of Matthean Christian Jews from the Jamnian-dominated synagogues (e.g. Luz 2005a: 166–167).

Several also read Jesus' saying about the stones being thrown down in verse 2 on two levels. Hilary reads it both as a prophecy of the temple's destruction by the Romans and a reminder that believers are to be worthy temples of God. Similarly, for Theophylact, it speaks literally of the fall of Jerusalem. However, anagogically, it also draws the disciples (and readers) away from attachment to earthly things, toward their ultimate destination, the new Jerusalem.

From the Birthpangs to the Parousia (24:3–31)

According to the *Acts of John* 97 (probably late second century), there was a cave on the Mount of Olives associated with the teaching of Jesus, especially his final discourse. As part of Constantine's building project, a church was constructed over this cave, known as Eleona or 'of the olives' (Murphy-O'Connor 2008: 143). It also came to be identified as the place where Jesus taught his disciples the Lord's Prayer (linking Luke 10:38–11:4 with Mark 11:12–25); hence its current name of the Church of the Pater Noster. Commentators find other associations beside the obvious connections with the last judgment. Jerome draws significance from its name, given the use of olive oil in lamps: the Mount is 'where the true light of knowledge was arising' (Jerome 2008: 269). Origen connects the location, planted with olive trees, to Psalm 52:10 (Ps 51:10 LXX) which speaks of the righteous as like an olive tree flourishing in God's house. Hence the Mount of Olives becomes an allegory of the Gentile churches.

Having left the temple, Jesus sits in typical teacher's posture, in full view of the city. Matthew widens the audience by replacing Mark's Peter, James, John, and Andrew (Mark 13:2, the first four called: Mark 1:16–20) with all the disciples. On this mountain associated with eschatological judgment, they ask Jesus a series of questions which provoke his lengthy eschatological discourse.

How many questions interpreters enumerate, and decisions as to whether Jesus chooses to answer all or only some, affect how the discourse is divided, and interpretations of its subject-matter. Do the disciples ask three questions (the time when no stone will be left upon another, the sign of the Son of Man's coming, the sign of the end of the age: e.g. Jerome; Peter John Olivi in Burr 2016: 24; Maldonado), or only two (the coming of the Son of Man being equated with the end of the age: e.g. Chrysostom)? If so, how much of the discourse is past history for the evangelist's first audiences? Or, more pertinently for subsequent readers, where should they locate their own time in the unfolding eschatological process? Alternatively, does Jesus sidestep, or only partially answer, the first of the disciples' questions? If the latter is the case, then is the discourse predominantly, or entirely, about the ultimate future? Or does he answer all the questions, but not in strict order (so e.g. Maldonado, who suggests that this confusion was to ensure 'that no one might know of the end of the world': Maldonado 1888: 2/271).

These uncertainties mean that commentators have come to widely differing conclusions as to whether Matthew 24 is predominantly concerned with events now past (especially connected to the events of 70 CE), events still to come, or a combination of both (Luz 2005a: 184–189). For several early exegetes, the emphasis is upon the future, arguably reflecting an early Christian response to the delay of the Parousia. The *Didache* links various sections of the discourse (e.g. 24:6, 15, 23–24, 30) with other New Testament passages, as a prophecy of the future 'world-deceiver' immediately prior to the end:

> And then the deceiver of the world will appear as a son of God and will perform signs and wonders, and the earth will be delivered into his hands, and he will commit abominations the likes of which have never happened before. Then all humankind will come to the fiery test, and many will fall away and perish; but those who endure in their faith will be saved by the accursed one himself. And then there will appear the signs of the truth: first the sign of an opening in heaven, then the sign of the sound of a trumpet, and third, the resurrection of the dead … (*Did.* 16:4b–6; Holmes 2007: 369)

The 'deceiver' appears to be a composite figure, combining false Christs who perform signs and deceive many (24:5, 24), the second beast of the Apocalypse (Rev 13:13–14), and the 'man of lawlessness' (2 Thess 2:3–4). Irenaeus explicitly links Matthew 24 with 2 Thessalonians as a prophecy of the future reign of the Antichrist prior to the ultimate end. The Antichrist will sit in the temple in Jerusalem, 'endeavouring to show himself as Christ,' which Irenaeus views as a direct fulfillment of 24:15–21 (*Adv. Haer.* 5.25.2; *ANF* 1:553). Hippolytus (170–235), in a fragment preserved by the twelfth-century Syrian Dionysius bar-Salibi, similarly sees everything at least from 24:15 onwards as referring to the future time of the Antichrist, and the Parousia which will swiftly follow (Gwynn 1889).

Other exegetes give more weight to past historical fulfillment. Hilary makes a clear break at verse 15, though explicitly identifies what precedes as answering the disciples' first question: 'When will these things be?' 'These things' have already happened in history, in the destruction of Jerusalem by the Romans. John Chrysostom gives a historicizing interpretation to an even greater part of the discourse. 24:4–28 refers to what has already passed, including the 'end' of Jerusalem (24:13–14). He appeals to Josephus' graphic descriptions of the Jewish War to show how history has already confirmed the truth of Christ's words that the tribulation will be greater than anything previously known (24:21). Theophylact of Ochrid differs only marginally. The destruction of the temple and Jerusalem's Roman 'captivity' covers 24:4–22. The future time of the Antichrist begins with 24:23 ('Look, here is the Christ'), and culminates with signs of the Son of Man's coming, and his arrival to bring in the end of the age (24:29–31).

The distinction between past and future eschatological consummation is complicated further by Jerome's commentary and the *Opus imperfectum*, which treat certain verses as describing both. Jerome's reading of the warning against false messiahs and false prophets (24:24) is actually threefold. It refers simultaneously to the past (the Roman siege of Jerusalem in 70 CE), the present (heretics and antichrists battling against the church), and the future (the end of the age). Alternatively, given the hortatory character of so many verses (e.g. 24:4, 6, 16–18, 20, 23, 26, 32), the Latin Fathers prioritize moral readings of the discourse (see Williams 2014: 91). At an earlier stage, Origen had introduced a further complication, by combining a historical reading with a spiritual and individualized interpretation, in which the Parousia describes the 'appearance of the Word in the soul,' which is then confronted with battles, spiritual famines, and the false word in the 'sacred place' of scripture (in Luz 2005a: 189).

The mixture of past historical fulfillment and expectation of the Antichrist's imminent coming is pervasive throughout the Middle Ages, especially due to the influence of Augustine's letter to Hesychius, bishop of Salona. In response to Hesychius's concern over the nearness of the end, Augustine links the disciples' three questions to the fall of Jerusalem, the present 'coming' of Christ in his body the church, particularly its battles with the people of the devil, and his final coming at the end of the age. Different parts of the discourse are related specifically to one of these three (*Ep. ad Hesychium* 199; Augustine 2004: 327–354). In its later medieval configuration, however, the same verses are interpreted as referring simultaneously to different realities, whether an event of past history, the ecclesial present, or eschatological future, or, eventually, seeing earlier events as types of events still to come (see Luz 2005a: 187). So for Aquinas, the coming of Christ has a twofold meaning: his ultimate coming at the end of the age, and his 'coming as the one who comforts the minds of men, to whom he comes spiritually' (Aquinas 2013b: 287–288). In addition, the interpretation of the eschatological discourse is sometimes linked to the Apocalypse of John (e.g. Victorinus of Pettau interprets the last three horsemen of Revelation 6 as the wars, famines, and pestilence of 24:14: see Kovacs and Rowland 2004: 79).

Historicizing interpretation becomes more prominent in the early modern period, particularly among Protestants (e.g. Hugo Grotius). This could be explained by a number of factors: humanism's interest in history and historical sources; a waning of interest in eschatology, and, particularly since the Enlightenment, an aversion to a Jesus who reveals heavenly mysteries (Luz 2005a: 186). Particularly striking is the Cambridge scholar John Lightfoot, who in his *Horae Hebraicae*, understands the entire discourse as concerned with the fall of Jerusalem, noting that 'the destruction of Jerusalem is very frequently expressed in Scripture as if it were the destruction of the whole world.' The coming of the Son of Man with his angels after Jerusalem has been 'reduced to ashes' refers to the sending out of his ministers 'with the trumpet of the gospel,' to gather a new church out of the Gentiles (Lightfoot 1859: II/318, 320).

The Abomination of Desolation (24:15)

The ominous Danielic phrase 'the abomination of desolation' originally described the pagan statue, or, more likely, altar to Olympian Zeus, set up in the Jerusalem temple by the Greek king Antiochus IV Epiphanes (Dan 9:27; 11:31; 12:11; 1 Macc 1:54; see Ford 1979; Theophilos 2012). Readers of Matthew are therefore invited to identify the new 'abomination,' presumably also in the Jerusalem temple (Matthew specifies 'in the holy place'). Interpreters are generally divided over whether it is still future, or refers to an event now past.

Hippolytus of Rome expects 24:15 to be fulfilled only at the coming of the Antichrist (so also Irenaeus, *Adv. Haer.* 5.25.2; Hilary). According to a summary preserved in the twelfth-century Apocalypse commentary of Dionysius bar-Salibi, Hippolytus understands that 'it is not concerning the Jews, and the laying waste of Jerusalem, that these things are said, but concerning the end of Antichrist' (in Gwynn 1889: 137–138). Both Hippolytus and bar-Salibi read Matthew in the light of Revelation 11:1–2, regarding both as referring to the time of the Antichrist prior to the future end, when the church will be persecuted for 'forty-two months' or three and a half years (the 'half week' of Dan 9:27; see Gwynn 1889).

For many others, however, the abomination of desolation is now past history. Most commonly, it is linked to the Roman destruction of the city, whether the fall of the temple in 70 CE or the construction of a pagan temple on the site by Hadrian c. 130 CE. Luke already connects it to the former ('when you see

Jerusalem surrounded by armies ...,' Luke 21:20). Eusebius of Caesarea also links it with the Roman siege of Jerusalem, although he traces the beginning of the end to Pilate's placing imperial standards in the holy city (*Dem. ev.* 8.2), a view also discussed by Jerome. Others are more specific: the 'abomination' refers to the Roman armies (Chrysostom; John Lightfoot in Lightfoot 1859: II/313–314), the statue of Titus (Theophylact; Euthymius Zigabenus), or the arrival of the Roman standards on the Mount of Olives, a location sanctified by the frequent presence of Christ (Bengel 1971: 271).

Jerome considers three options for the literal sense, though without expressing a clear preference between them. The abomination refers either to the image of Caesar placed in the temple by Pilate, the equestrian statue of Hadrian, which supposedly stood on the site of the Holy of holies to Jerome's day, or the future arrival of the Antichrist, standing in the temple of God (see 2 Thess 2:3–4). John Cassian also connects the abomination with Hadrian, although to an idol of Jupiter the emperor set up in Jerusalem rather than his own statue, and claims that it will be set up in the church once again at the final coming of the Antichrist (John Cassian, *Conf.* 8.4; Daryn 2015: 165). The connection with Hadrian's equestrian statue is also made by Nicholas of Lyra, the *Glossa ordinaria* (which gives Pilate's action as an alternative), and the nineteenth-century German biblical scholar Ferdinand Christian Baur (Theophilos 2012: 13).

Martin Luther, noting that Daniel refers to the abomination more than once (Dan 9:27; 12:11), concludes that Matthew refers to the first here, linking it to Caligula's failed attempt to set up a statue of himself in the temple (Josephus, *Ant.* 18.261). The Daniel 12 reference then refers to the ultimate destruction under Hadrian (Luther 2014: 283). John Calvin thinks interpreters who find a fulfillment of Daniel 9 mistaken, and that Christ is referring to the second Danielic passage. By contrast, the Jesuit Juan de Maldonado argues, against Calvin, that Daniel 9:27 is here evoked as referring to Jerusalem's fall, and Daniel 12:11 to the time of Antichrist. A modern variant of Luther's Caligula thesis, proposed by the German theologian Otto Pfleiderer in 1868, is regularly cited by modern commentators (see Theophilos 2012: 15–16). However, for Luther, the Caligula reference does not exhaust the meaning of Christ's words: 'Nonetheless, He is simultaneously pointing to our destruction and the desolation of the whole world, which the Turk is now beginning' (Luther 2014: 283).

The prophecy is occasionally given a figurative meaning, referring to the armies of the Antichrist in the 'holy place' of the church: i.e. the various Christian heresies which 'stand' claiming to be the word of truth, or, for Jerome, 'all perverted doctrine' (Jerome 2008: 272). William Blake identifies the abomination is 'the Holy Reasoning Power,' and its offspring, such as state religion and a codified morality which stifles the imagination (*Jerusalem* 10.15; *Milton* 41.1.25; see Schell in Jeffrey 1992: 9).

In the Middle Ages, the expected future coming of the Antichrist is widespread, particularly due to the influence of Adso of Montier-en-Der's 'Letter on the Origin and Time of the Antichrist':

> As we said above, he will be born in the city of Babylon, will come to Jerusalem, and will circumcise himself and say to the Jews: 'I am the Christ promised to you who has come to save you, so that I can gather together and defend you who are the Diaspora.' At that time all the Jews will flock to him, in the belief that they are receiving God, but rather they will receive the devil. Antichrist also 'will be enthroned in God's Temple,' that is, in Holy Church, and he will make all Christians martyrs. (McGinn 1979: 94)

A modern variant of the Antichrist figure is Nicolae Carpathia, the Romanian secretary general of the United Nations who becomes supreme potentate of the Global Community during the post-rapture tribulation, in the *Left Behind* series of novels by Tim LaHaye and Jerry Jenkins (see especially LaHaye and Jenkins 1997).

Flight to the Mountains (24:16–21)

Modern scholars often link the command to those in Judea to 'flee' to the mountains (24:16) to the 'revelation' mentioned by Eusebius which led the Jerusalem church to flee to Pella prior to the destruction of the city in 70 CE (Eusebius, *H.E.* 3.5.3; Epiphanius, *Pan.* 29.7.7–8; 30.2.7; see Koester 1989; Verheyden 1990). Bengel is one early modern commentator to make the connection. There may, however, be earlier hints of such a reading. Theophylact is clear that the flight refers to the time of the Jewish War, although he thinks it is addressed to the (non-Christian) Jews rather than the apostles, for the latter will have departed the city prior to this. Jerome, by contrast, is unsure whether the flight refers to the time of Jerusalem's fall, or to the end of the world.

However, there is also a common tendency to read the passage figuratively, often with a tropological dimension, urging Christian readers to prepare for their personal 'flight' from this world in death. This is especially the case with the prayer that the flight should not happen in winter (or 'stormy weather') on a Sabbath (24:20). In its original context, the addition of 'a Sabbath' probably reflects the concerns of Matthew's predominantly Jewish-Christian audiences. Later Christians, no longer concerned with Sabbath observance, need to find an alternative interpretation. Thus the Sabbath alludes to a time of 'idleness' or rest from doing good or practicing virtue (Hippolytus in Gwynn 1889: 138; Jerome; Theophylact). 'Not in winter' is a warning against being troubled by cares and sins, as if caught in a winter's storm (Hippolytus), faith and love growing cold (Jerome), or a time lacking in good fruits (Theophylact).

Others extend the figurative reading to additional details. Origen understands the roof to be the Word, from which one never needs to descend. For Hilary, the pregnant women are a symbol of souls burdened by sin. Epiphanius the Latin understands the pregnant to be 'those who have conceived suffering and begotten iniquity by neglecting the faith' (*Interpretation of the Gospels* 33; Simonetti 2002: 195). But this seems strained compared with the obvious literal sense, that pregnant and nursing mothers would find flight particularly difficult (so Jerome; Chrysostom; Aquinas; Maldonado).

Erasmus foregrounds the historical meaning: winter travel is harsh; Sabbath observance would prevent Jesus' followers traveling very far. Bengel also reflects on the historical circumstances. Although it would not have been unlawful for Christians to flee on the Sabbath, it would have been 'very sad, on that day of joy, to break off public worship.' In addition, their preparations would have been further hindered by the crowds at the doors of the synagogues and the city gates (Bengel 1971: 272).

False Christs and False Prophets (24:24)

Warning of false messiahs and prophets is a repeated motif throughout this discourse (24:5, 11, 24). Readers of Matthew regularly treat these as prophecies of figures arising in their own time, whether as precise fulfilled prophecies or as contemporary actualizations of a recurring type. Justin Martyr identifies contemporary heretics, bearing the name of Christ but in reality being false prophets: 'Some are called Marcians, and some Valentinians, and some Basilidians, and some Saturnilians, and others by other names' (*Trypho* 35; *ANF* 1:212). Hilary and Jerome cite Simon the Samaritan, i.e. Simon Magus, as one example of a false Christ (24:5), acclaimed as 'the Power of God called Great' (Acts 8:9; according to Epiphanius, *Pan.* 21, Simon made additional claims such as 'I am the Word of God'). Hilary also gives the example of Nicolaus of Antioch, one of the seven 'deacons' (Acts 6:5), whom patristic tradition identifies as the originator of the Nicolaitan sect (see Rev 2:6, 15; e.g. Irenaeus, *Adv. Haer.* 1.26.3).

Simon Magus is a popular exemplar for many readers of Matthew, including those who think that Jesus' words about those claiming to be the Christ will find ultimate fulfillment in the future Antichrist (e.g. Epiphanius the Latin, *Interpretation of the Gospels* 33; Aquinas; Maldonado; Bengel). Theophylact adds another Samaritan, Dositheus, as a false prophet, given that he claimed to be the prophet like Moses (Deut 18:15). Bengel, paying close attention both to Acts as the 'history' of the early church, and the works of Josephus, adds to the list Theudas, the Egyptian, and 'another pretender mentioned by Josephus,' presumably Judas the Galilean (Bengel 1971: 269; Acts 5:36–37; 21:38; Josephus, *Ant.* 18.1–10; *War* 2.433).

Martin Luther, preaching on this passage in 1539, finds Christ's end-time warning being fulfilled in contemporary Anabaptists and 'Sacramentarians' (the followers of Zwingli and Karlstadt who rejected the real presence of Christ in the Eucharist), as well as in the errors of the papacy (Luther 2014: 265–266, 293). On the Catholic side, Juan de Maldonado hints at contemporary Protestant 'heretics' in warning against the false Christs and false prophets of 24:24. Nor do sixteenth-century authors only direct these verses against members of other churches. Erasmus humorously employs verse 23 to caricature rivalries between Roman Catholic religious orders:

> The Observantines say, *Christ is here*, not with the Coletines or the Conventuals. The Jacobines say, *Here is Christ*, not with the Augustinians. Again, the Benedictines clamor, *Here is Christ. Christ is not with the secular clergy who wear no cowl.* (quoted in Clarke 2003: 189)

Gathering Eagles (24:27–28)

The proverbial saying about eagles (sometimes translated 'vultures,' e.g. NRSV; NABRE, though see Carter 2003: 469–70) gathering around a corpse is frequently given a positive interpretation, despite its ominous sound (e.g. Irenaeus, *Adv. Haer.* 4.14.1; Hilary). The 'carcass' is widely identified as Christ, the public nature of whose second coming cannot be hidden. This Christological reading may partly explain the claim of David Koresh (Vernon Wayne Howell), messianic leader of the Branch Davidians of Waco in the 1990s, that he was the prophesied 'carcass' (see Clarke 2003: 188). In his commentary, Jerome observes that eagles, like vultures, are drawn to carcasses from great distances. This leads him to view them as an appropriate symbol of Christians who ought to 'hasten' to Christ, and especially his cadaver, i.e. his passion, whenever they read it in the scriptures. In line with the broader subject matter of the eschatological discourse, Theophylact finds a more specific reference to the Parousia, when the saints who are still alive will come to Christ, and be snatched up like eagles (1 Thess 4:17). Fortunatianus of Aquileia (who also connects the passage with 1 Thessalonians) interprets the body as a figure of the church.

Others propose that the 'eagles' are those blessed who are already with Christ prior to the Parousia, or specifically the angels and martyrs (e.g. Chrysostom; Euthymius Zigabenus), or all of humanity. Apollinaris of Laodicea even knows of some who claim that, at the second coming, the eagle-like righteous will 'leave paradise behind and be gathered to that place where the fall of Adam occurred,' presumably the earthly Garden of Eden (*Frag.* 126; Simonetti 2002: 200). In his sixteenth-century commentary, Juan de Maldonado reviews several of these possibilities, eventually opting for the broadest: 'for Christ signifies that all men will fly together to where He is, to be judged' (Maldonado 1888: III/284).

The specific choice of eagles leads early modern commentators to a less optimistic reading, in line with a renewed historicized reading of the discourse. In the LXX, the eagle sometimes symbolizes empires and their leaders (e.g. Hos 8:1; Ezek 17:3–4, 17), and it has particular associations with imperial Rome (e.g. *4 Ezra* 11–12; Josephus, *War* 3.123; Carter 2003). The Anglican scholar Henry Hammond (1605–1660) finds a reference here to the ensigns of the Roman armies (Hammond 1845: 115), while Johann Albrecht Bengel views the 'eagles' as a combination of the deceptive false Christs and false prophets, and the gathering Roman armies, who 'bore an eagle on their standards' (Bengel 1971: 274).

The Sign of the Son of Man (24:29–31)

The 'tribulation' just described will be followed 'immediately' by cosmic signs, then the specific 'sign of the Son of Man' heralding his coming. For those who see the whole of 24:4–28 as describing the historical fate of Jerusalem, 'immediately' requires some explanation. Bengel has an ingenious explanation for those who object that the chronological distance between the first century and the world's end is too great. The prophet is like a landscape artist:

> I reply, a prophecy resembles a landscape painting, which represents distinctly the houses, paths, and bridges in the foreground, but brings together, into a narrow space, most widely severed valleys and mountains in the distance. Such a view should they who would study prophecy have of the future to which the prophecy refers. (Bengel 1971: 274)

Jesus' words provide 'foreground' clarity about the most immediate things (such as Jerusalem's fall), whereas the 'distance' is more obscure, and (because no-one yet knows the day nor the hour, 24:36), is initially described as being close at hand (brought together 'into a narrow space'). With historical hindsight, however, the distance separating these spatially narrow 'valleys and mountains' becomes clearer.

The nature of 'the sign of the Son of Man' is not made clear, though it will appear in heaven. Origen understands it to refer to Christ coming in the glory he gained on the cross, which will leave humanity in no doubt that he is the world's judge. Jerome speaks vaguely of the sign of the cross, or 'the banner of victory of the triumphant one' (Jerome 2008: 276). For Chrysostom, Christ brings his cross with him 'that their sin may be self-condemned, as if any one who had been struck by a stone, were to show the stone itself, or his garments stained with blood' (*Homily on Matthew* 76.4; *NPNF* 1st series, 10:460).

Theophylact believes that a shining cross will appear in heaven, which Christ will then display as a reproof to his own people. The *Opus imperfectum* rejects this view; since the other Gospels speak simply of 'the Son of Man,' that 'sign' must be Christ's body. Instead, Christ himself will come bearing 'the tokens of his passion in his body, that is, the wounds of the spear and nails,' in fulfillment of Revelation 1:7 ('Every eye will see him, even those who pierced him': Kellerman and Oden 2010: 394).

Particularly striking is the interpretation of Christ's coming in the clouds offered by the radical English theologian and activist Gerrard Winstanley (1609–1676). In his *Saints Paradice*, Winstanley apparently understands this to refer to Christ-likeness appearing in humanity at the eschaton:

> And as the body of flesh in his Ascension, so called, went out of the Apostles sight, in a cloud of the Skies, so shall the same mighty man rise out of the earth, that is, from under the earthy imaginations and lusts of the sons of men; for mankind is the earth that containes him buried, and out of this earth he is to arise, and appear in the clouds, that is, as he begins to shew himself in a man or a woman, the fleshly powers in those enslaved souls will and do rise up to darken the light of that sun as long as he can, till he, the flesh, who is the wicked man, or the cursed thing that dwells within (man-kind) be taken away. (*Saints Paradice* VI in Corns, Hughes, and Loewenstein 2009: 1/356)

A Call to Watchfulness (24:32–51)

The description of Christ's coming leads into a series of parabolic sayings about the need for careful discernment and watchfulness. Bengel speculates that this recurring theme explains the popularity in the early church of the Greek name Gregory and the Latin name Vigilantius, both derived etymologically from the verb 'to watch.'

The lesson of the fig tree (24:32–33) provides a potent image for the discernment required for recognizing that 'he is near.' Several interpreters link the parable to the cursed fig tree at 21:18–19, widely understood as a symbol of Israel, or the synagogue. In contrast to the earlier withering, however, this parable is understood to point to the future conversion of the Jewish people at the end, in accordance with Paul's words that 'all Israel will be saved' (Rom 11:25; *Glossa ordinaria*). The connection with the Jews enabled some twentieth-century evangelical Christians to draw conclusions for the timing of the end from the establishment of the modern state of Israel – the 'blossoming' of the fig tree – in 1948 (in Clarke 2003: 190).

The warning from the days of Noah (24:37–41) highlights the need for permanent alertness. As John Chrysostom warns his comfortable congregation in the Great Church in Antioch, Christ's words reveal that 'He should come on a sudden, and unexpectedly, and when the more part were living luxuriously' (*Homily on Matthew* 77.2; *NPNF* 1st series, 10:464). In Noah's time, people were going about their daily business – two men in the field, two women grinding at the mill – until their world was shaken by the flood. The general interpretation is that it is better to be 'taken' than to be 'left' (e.g. Hilary; Jerome; Erasmus; Davies and Allison 1997: 383), though patristic and medieval commentators often further allegorize the details.

For Hilary of Poitiers, the saints are taken and the faithless left. The two men in the field symbolize believers and unbelievers. The two women grinding at the millstone (which Hilary interprets as the works of the Law) represent different groups of Jews. The woman who is 'taken' symbolizes those Jews who believed through the preaching of the apostles, and whose faith produces the heavenly bread of good works. Jerome understands the two women to represent the church and the synagogue, both 'grinding together at the Law.' The latter will be left or 'forsaken' (an apparent reference back to 23:38). Alternatively, this second woman symbolizes heretics who 'grind the flour of their doctrines' either from both Old and New Testaments or just from one of them (Jerome 2008: 279; the latter example probably refers to Marcionites). Some link the taken/left saying with 1 Thessalonians 4:17 (in which the saints still alive at the Lord's coming will be 'snatched up' to meet the Lord in the air: e.g. Theophylact; Bengel). Thus the passage becomes an integral part of doctrine of the rapture. A minority modern reading, emphasizing the explicit connection to the story of Noah, reads the saying in the opposite sense. Those left (like Noah and his sons) are the saved, while the taken are thrown into the fire (Merkle 2010).

The thief who breaks in during the night (24:43–44) might be expected to refer to Christ, whose coming is described in similar terms elsewhere (1 Thess 5:2; 2 Pet 3:10; Rev 3:3; 16:15). John Chrysostom recognizes this main point. Yet readers of Matthew have regularly gone in a different direction. The *Gospel of Thomas* uses Jesus' words to warn its hearers to be on their guard against the world (*Gos. Thom.* 21). Origen's allegorical interpretation is popular: the thief is the devil who tempts a person (also e.g. Fortunatianus of Aquileia; Hilary; *Opus imperfectum*; Paschasius Radbertus). Even more common is the identification of the burglar with death, especially sudden death. A different kind of warning is proposed by the thirteenth-century French Dominican Hugh of St. Cher: Christians should beware of sudden attacks by heretics, 'and so a man should guard the domicile of his mind very carefully' (in Wailes 1987: 172).

The subject-matter of the Wicked Servant (24:45–51), in which one servant appears to have authority over others, is unsurprisingly applied to those exercising authority and leadership within the Christian community (Wailes 1987: 173–177). For Origen and Hilary, it represents a warning to bishops, a reading which has impacted liturgical use. One example is an extant Anglo-Saxon lectionary (BL Cotton Tiberius A.ii), which appoints a section of Matthew including this parable (24:42–47) for the feasts of various popes and bishops (Olsen 2015: 230). Others take it in a broader sense, to include priests and other church leaders (e.g. Fortunatianus of Aquileia; Rabanus Maurus; Hugh of St. Cher; Calvin). John Chrysostom, living in a society which was at least nominally Christian, proposes that the parable 'would suit rulers in the state also, for every one is bound to make full use of what he has for the common advantage' (*Homily on Matthew* 77.3; *NPNF* 1st series, 10:466). Given that the wicked servant is also entrusted with the master's property, Chrysostom extends the application to the wealthy in his congregation, while for Nicholas of Lyra it is a warning to all Christians.

The Son's Lack of Knowledge (24:36)

Jesus' statement that not even the Son knows the day or the hour is Christologically problematic, and in apparent contradiction to 11:27 ('All things have been handed over to me by my Father'; see Davies and Allison 1997: 377–379; Luz 2005a: 213–214). For many, a ready solution is provided by the absence of 'nor the Son' in many manuscripts of Matthew. Jerome testifies in his commentary that the phrase is missing from the Greek manuscripts available to him, although he knows of Latin manuscripts which contain it. Its inclusion, he observes, is a cause of joy for Arius and Eunomius, given that it could support their belief in the inferiority of the Son. Ambrose of Milan is even more explicit: the phrase is an Arian interpolation (*De fid.* 5.16).

On the other hand, its inclusion in some of the best Greek manuscripts, as well as the words 'but the Father *alone*,' makes it more likely that scribes omitted it for doctrinal reasons than introducing it by way of harmonization to Mark 13:32 (see Metzger 1994: 51–52). Indeed, Irenaeus appeals to the saying in order to challenge the presumption of those who seek full understanding of the mysteries of God:

> But, beyond reason inflated [with your own wisdom], you presumptuously maintain that you are acquainted with the unspeakable mysteries of God; while even the Lord, the very Son of God, allowed that the Father alone knows the very day and hour of judgment, when He plainly declares, But of that day and that hour knows no man, neither the Son, but the Father only. (*Adv. Haer.* 2.28.6; *ANF* 1:401)

The fifth-century Syriac theologian Philoxenus of Mabbug makes a distinction between the degrees of Christ's knowledge prior to his ascension and afterwards, when he came to share the Father's wisdom and authority (in Davies and Allison 1997: 379).

For others, it must mean something other than its plain sense, in the light of broader considerations (both intratextual, such as 11:27, and doctrinal). Origen wonders whether 'the Son' here refers to Christ's body the church, or whether the Son has inner knowledge. Jerome reasons from what is said elsewhere about Christ the Word – namely, that he made all time and that everything has been handed over to him by the Father (11:27; John 1:3) – that he does indeed know the hour. However, he chose to keep hidden from the disciples what was not expedient for them to know (also e.g. Augustine, *De Trin.* 1.12.1; Theophylact). Jerome finds support here from Colossians 2:3 ('in whom all the treasures of wisdom and knowledge are hidden'). John Chrysostom also appeals to Colossians 2:3, as he boldly asserts that 'neither is the Son ignorant of the day, but is even in full certainty thereof' (*Homily on Matthew* 77.2; *NPNF* 1st series, 10:463).

In his Matthew commentary, Jerome's predecessor Hilary seems to have accepted the plain sense of the phrase. Hilary cautiously proposes that, although the Word has certainty about what has happened, this does not extend to the future. In light of Arian appeals to this verse, however, he subsequently changed his mind. In his treatise *On the Trinity*, he appeals to the same Colossians passage as Jerome in order to show that the real ignorance is the necessary ignorance of Christians, in order that they may remain continually alert:

> We can now understand why He said that He knew not the day. If we believe Him to have been really ignorant, we contradict the Apostle, who says, In Whom are all the treasures of wisdom and knowledge hidden (Colossians 2:3). There is knowledge which is hidden in Him, and because it has to be hidden, it must sometimes for this purpose be professed as ignorance, for once declared, it will no longer be secret. In order, therefore, that the knowledge may remain hidden, He declares that He does not know. But if He does not know, in order that the knowledge may remain hidden, this ignorance is not due to His nature, which is omniscient, for He is ignorant solely in order that it may be hidden. (*De Trin.* 9.67; *NPNF* 2nd series, 9:178)

Cyril of Alexandria addresses the problem in a different way: the statement that the Father knows should be taken to include all persons of the Trinity (*Frag.* 274 = Reuss 1957: 247; also e.g. Dionysius the Carthusian). Alternatively, a distinction is made between what Christ knew according to his divine nature, and what according to his human nature, possibly echoed in Erasmus's sixteenth-century paraphrase: 'and even the Son of man does not know' (Erasmus 2008: 331).

The primary focus of the saying, however, is not to speculate about the nature of the Son, but rather to discourage eschatological calculations on the part of the disciples. This does not put an end to such speculations, however (particularly when read in parallel with texts like Daniel with its fairly specific time references). The justification given is that, even if the time of the end is currently unknown as Jesus speaks to his followers prior to his death, greater precision might eventually be given. For Johann Albrecht Bengel, what was unknown when Jesus spoke these words prior to his death could become known more precisely following the ascension and the reception of John's Apocalypse.

The Wise and Foolish Virgins (25:1–13)

A series of three parables now heighten the motif of preparedness for the coming judgment. Some seek to differentiate between them. According to Nicholas of Lyra, the Virgins is a parable about contemplatives, the Talents about prelates, and the Sheep and the Goats about the laity (Kealy 1997: 1/177). The two unique to Matthew manifest the moral dualism typical of Matthean parables elsewhere (the division between 'wise' virgins and 'foolish' virgins, and between 'sheep' and 'goats'). The first envisages attendants of the bride awaiting the arrival of the bridegroom at the bride's house. A variant, widely known by western Christians given that Jerome includes it in the Vulgate, adds 'and the bride.' This may have been introduced to conform the text to the more frequent practice whereby the groom brings his bride to his own home for the wedding (Metzger 1994: 52–53). Alternatively, a scribe omitted this phrase because it appeared to contradict other New Testament passages where Christ the bridegroom comes to fetch his bride (Eph 5:29–32; Rev 21:2; Jerome 2008: 281, n. 137).

According to Tertullian, the Valentinians interpreted the two groups of virgins in terms of the five bodily senses and the intellectual faculties respectively (an interpretation he blames on the corrupting influence of Plato: Tertullian, *Treatise on the Soul* 18 = *ANF* 3:198). Jerome knows of some who take the parable literally, to refer to actual virgins. The theme of virginity and chastity is germane to the reading of Methodius of Olympus (d. c. 312). 'The Virgins' Hymn to Christ,' attached to his *Symposium*, includes the following antiphon:

> My purity intact for you, my lamp alight in my hand,
> Bridegroom, I come out to meet you.
> (Atwan, Dardess, and Rosenthal 1998: 272)

For Clement of Alexandria, the wise virgins signify true Christian gnostics, who are virgins 'in respect of their abstaining from what is evil,' and wise 'in respect of their waiting out of love for the Lord and kindling their light for the contemplation of things' (*Strom.* 7.12; *ANF* 2:544).

Jerome offers a typical reading of the parable as a complex allegory, giving a Christological interpretation to the bridegroom. He understands the virgins as a symbol of all who appear to believe, whether members of the church, Jews, or heretics, who have not lost their 'virginity' to idolatry. The narrative encompasses the period between the first and delayed second coming of Christ, during which many Christians have 'fallen asleep' in death, awaiting the resurrection when the bridegroom comes. Then the time for buying oil will be past, and the time of judgment present. The fifth-century Latin exegete Arnobius Iunior pays most attention to the number five. The five wise virgins are the virtues of hope, faith, charity, purity, and mercy; the five foolish virgins represent their opposites: credulity, infidelity, lovelessness, lust, and barrenness (*Expositiunculae in Matthaeum* 27; Kraszewski 1999: 356).

Allegorical readings focus particularly on the meaning of the oil (Wailes 1987: 177–184). One common interpretation is that the foolish virgins have faith (lamps) but not works (oil, e.g. Hilary; Jerome; Paschasius Radbertus; Aquinas; Maldonado; Erasmus). John Chrysostom gives even more precision about the works required: 'humanity, almsgiving, succor to them that are in need' (*Homily on Matthew* 78; *NPNF* 1st series 10:470). Fortunatianus of Aquileia regards the oil as a symbol of mercy, the wise virgins signifying 'everyone who lives chastely and simply and piously and religiously, who is merciful' (Fortunatianus of Aquileia 2017: 88). An alternative is that the oil symbolizes not good works (given that even the 'foolish' perform acts of charity), but motivation or intention, the 'inner oil of conscience' (Augustine, *Sermon* 93; Ælfric of Eynsham; Olsen 2015: 227–234). As Gregory the Great warns his hearers in his homiletic exposition:

> And there are many who afflict their bodies through abstinence, but in this abstinence they are seeking for human approval. They are devoted to teaching, they bestow much on the needy; but they are foolish virgins, because they seek only the recompense of fleeting praise. (Gregory the Great 1990: 70)

The Reformers' concern about meritorious works leads Martin Luther to interpret the oil as faith. A variant is provided by the Lutheran Bengel, who notes that the foolish had some oil in their lamps initially, but not enough to stop them going out: 'The burning lamp is faith; the lamp with oil besides is faith abounding' (Bengel 1971: 281). John Newton's hymn 'The Foolish Virgins' interprets the oil as divine grace:

> When descending from the sky
> The Bridegroom shall appear;
> And the solemn midnight cry,

Shall call professors near:
How the sound our hearts will damp!
How will shame o'erspread each face!
If we only have a lamp,
Without the oil of grace.
(*Olney Hymns* 90)

Some modern commentators urge (in the tradition of Adolf Jülicher) that the parable be interpreted parabolically, i.e. seeking its single main point, rather than allegorically. Douglas Hare insists that the oil is merely incidental to the story: 'The main point of the story is that the foolish virgins are not ready when the great moment finally arrives' (Hare 1993: 285).

Most interpreters of this parable dominated by female characters have been men. There have, however, been exceptions. Anne Vaughan Lock (1534–c. 1602), a Protestant exile during Mary Tudor's reign, wrote a commentary on the passage (Felch in Taylor and Choi 2012: 333–338). A more contemporary reading is offered by Elisabeth Cady Stanton in the *Woman's Bible*. The contemporary foolish virgins are women who 'sacrifice themselves to educate the men of their households, and to make of themselves ladders by which their husbands, brothers and sons climb up into the kingdom of knowledge, while they themselves are shut out from all intellectual companionship, even with those they love best' (Stanton 2002: 235). By contrast:

> The wise virgins are they who keep their lamps trimmed, who burn oil in their vessels for their own use, who have improved every advantage for their education, secured a healthy, happy, complete development, and entered all the profitable avenues of labor, for self-support, so that when the opportunities and the responsibilities of life come, they may be fitted fully to enjoy the one and ably to discharge the other. These are the women who to-day are close upon the heels of man in the whole realm of thought, in art, in science, in literature and in government. (Stanton 2002: 126)

Their marriage feast is not the marriage feast of the Lamb, but 'the marriage feast of science and religion,' held in 'the temple of knowledge,' the door to which is no longer shut.

This memorable parable has left its imprint in liturgy, music, visual art, poetry, and drama (on the latter, see Tydeman 2001: 395–400). From the Middle Ages, it provided the Gospel reading for feasts of virgin martyrs, thus giving specificity to a story which otherwise would apply to Christians in all states of life. But liturgical usage also allowed the more universal interpretation, through a responsory for Matins on the Feast of All Saints. Perhaps most famous is the Sarum version, *Audivi vocem de caelo* ('I heard a voice from heaven,' combining 25:6 with Jer 40:10), which survives in settings by the sixteenth-century English composers Thomas Tallis and John Taverner (Dowling Long and Sawyer 2015: 20–21). The popular Advent hymn *Wachet auf, ruft uns die Stimme* ('Awake, the voice is calling us') by the German Lutheran hymnwriter Philipp Nicolai (published in 1599; English translation by F. Crawford Burkitt), is also inspired by 25:1–13:

> Wake, O wake! With tidings thrilling
> the watchmen all the air are filling,
> arise, Jerusalem, arise!
> Midnight strikes! No more delaying,
> 'The hour has come!' we hear them saying,
> 'where are ye all, ye virgins wise?
> The Bridegroom comes in sight,
> raise high your torches bright!'
> Alleluia!
> The wedding song swells loud and strong:
> go forth and join the festal throng.

The division into wise and foolish is prominent in visual art (e.g. fourth-century fresco in the Cyriaca Catacombs, Via Tiburtina, Rome: Luz 2005a: 236). The Gothic sculptures of the virgins at Notre Dame in Paris differentiate between the wise, who hold their lamps high, and the gloomy expressions of the foolish, whose lamps are pointed down to the ground (Jantzen 1984: 148). At Amiens Cathedral, they are juxtaposed with the good and bad trees (7:17–20); at Chartres, with virtues and vices (Luz 2005a: 242). William Blake produced several watercolor versions of the 'The Wise and Foolish Virgins' (e.g. c. 1799–1800, Metropolitan Museum of Art, New York; 1825, Yale Center for British Art, New Haven), and several copies of his originals also survive (Figure 14). The basic visualization contrasts the ordered row of wise virgins to the left, standing shoulder to shoulder with each other, with the animated 'disarray' of the foolish virgins on the right. In the sky above, an angel blows the last trumpet, heralding the judgment and the coming of the bridegroom, or alternatively gathering the elect, the spires of the New Jerusalem in the background (24:31; see Rowland 2014: 319). Two virgins look left, apparently toward the approaching bridegroom, the second from the left looks ahead, as if to warn the viewer; the fourth looks upwards to the right, either to the angel of judgment or to what follows. The final virgin looks to her foolish sisters, pointing dramatically to the top right as if in warning of their impending exclusion from the wedding (Gowler 2017: 165–168).

By contrast, 'Les cinq Vierges,' a 1966 poem written in French by the American Trappist monk Thomas Merton (and dedicated to 'Jacques,' i.e. the French Catholic philosopher Jacques Maritain), allows all 10 virgins to find a

FIGURE 14 After William Blake (1757–1827). *The Wise and Foolish Virgins.* Watercolor and gouache on paper, 400 × 333 mm. Bequeathed by Miss Alice G.E. Carthew 1940. Source: Tate Gallery, London. © Tate, London/Art Resource, NY.

place in the wedding banquet. The foolish are 'Rowdies' who arrived for the wedding on motor scooters with 'their gas tanks | Empty,' but permitted to stick around because they could dance:

> So that's it there were
> Five rowdy virgins
> Without gas
> But really caught up
> In the action
> There were then ten virgins
> At the Wedding of the Lamb.
> (Merton in Rosenblatt 1993: 115)

Is this an optimistic reading of the parable by Merton, without the division of judgment, akin to the rewritten ending in Nikos Kazantzakis's novel *The Last Temptation of Christ*, in which the bridegroom opens the door to the foolish virgins (see Luz 2005a: 245)? Or is it a broader social comment 'on our consistent refusal to take responsibility for ourselves or to expect responsibility in others, even in preparation for Christ's presence?' (Daggy 1996: 24)?

Shallow by contrast is the crass use of the parable in 1964 by US Senator Robert Byrd of West Virginia, in a filibuster aimed at derailing President Lyndon Johnson's civil rights bill:

> If all men are created equal, ... how could five of the virgins have been wise and five foolish? (quoted in Branch 1998: 336)

The Talents (25:14–30)

The parable of the Talents, or the 'Unprofitable Servant,' combines motifs of watchfulness and stewardship. In line with Matthew's own tendency to allegorize Jesus' parables, his readers generally treat this story as an allegory of the judgment, even if they differ in the details. The man who goes on a journey is Christ, ascending to heaven, eventually to return at the Parousia (e.g. Jerome; Gregory the Great; Theophylact). The period between departure and return is to allow humanity to repent (Hilary), and for his servants to use what has been entrusted to them. The hymn 'Will Jesus Find Us Watching?' by the American teacher and hymnwriter Fanny Crosby (1820–1915) highlights the theme of the Lord's return, combining this parable with the similarly themed Wise and Foolish Virgins ('Faithful to Him will He find us watching | With our lamps all trimmed and bright?'):

> If, at the dawn of the early morning,
> He shall call us one by one,
> When to the Lord we restore our talents,
> Will He answer thee–Well done?
> (in Gowler 2017: 181)

The three servants are variously interpreted. Some differentiate between them, on the grounds that they have been entrusted with different amounts. A salvation-historical reading is found in Hilary, though rarely repeated by others. The servant with five talents signifies God's faithful people under the Law (five corresponding to the Pentateuch; the final total of ten talents to their obedience by grace to the precepts of the Decalogue). The one with two talents is a symbol of the Gentiles, who profess both the Father and the Son, and believe in Christ's divinity and humanity. They double what was given to them by adding works to faith. The servant with one talent is a figure of those who live under the Law though without spiritual understanding, and who hide the talent out of jealousy over the salvation of the pagans. Bengel knows of a Flemish preacher called Ruimer, who thought that five talents had been given to the Reformed Church, two to the Lutheran, and one to the Roman Catholic, to which Bengel responds: 'What has the Greek? What other churches, ancient and modern? What posterity?' (Bengel 1971: 282). Other interpreters identify all three as a specific group, whether the apostles to whom was entrusted the teaching of the Gospel before his ascension (Jerome), specifically their successors the bishops, doctors, or other prelates (*Opus imperfectum*; Dionysius the Carthusian; Nicholas of Lyra), or a broader group of clergy or preachers (Theophylact).

A similar diversity is found among those who allegorize the different numbers of talents granted to each servant. A talent, weighing between 50 and 75 pounds of silver, would have been the equivalent of approximately 20 years' wages (Davies and Allison 1997: 405; Clarke 2003: 193). Origen interprets the talents as different levels of ability in interpreting scripture, from those granted spiritual understanding (five talents) down to those unable to move beyond the letter (one talent). In his homily on the parable, Gregory the Great begins with the observation that there are five senses, sight, hearing, taste, smell, and touch:

> The five talents represent the gift of the five senses, that is, knowledge of externals; the two talents signify theory and practice; the one talent signifies theory alone. (*Homilies on the Gospels* 18; Gregory the Great 1990: 127)

The second gift ('theory and practice' or 'understanding and action,' *intellectus et operatio*) is greater than the first. The person who hides the one talent uses it for purely earthly purposes, not putting the theory into practice. That the third servant is said to be 'afraid' (25:25) refers to his fear 'to attempt a better way of life,' a besetting vice of many in the church of Gregory's day.

The basic outline of Gregory's exegesis is already found in Jerome, who also links the five talents to the five senses. The first servant uses his earthly senses to understand heavenly things, thereby doubling his share. The one with two talents understood what he had learned in the Law of Moses, and doubled it in the Gospel. The one who received one talent ('reason') allowed it to be hidden by mundane works and worldly pleasure.

Alternatively, the different weights of talents signify the different gifts of grace spoken about by Paul (1 Cor 12:4; Eph 4:7: Theophylact; Aquinas). John Chrysostom, ever sensitive to the needs of the poor, understands the talents in a broader sense, and the parable's challenge to use whatever we have been given, whether riches, rhetorical skill, or physical ability, 'both for our salvation, and for our neighbor's advantage':

> Knowing then these things, let us contribute alike wealth, and diligence, and protection, and all things for our neighbor's advantage. For the talents here are each person's ability, whether in the way of protection, or in money, or in teaching, or in whatever thing of the kind. Let no man say, I have but one talent, and can do nothing; for you can even by one approve yourself. (*Homily on Matthew* 78; *NPNF* 1st series, 10:472)

In English usage, the Authorized Version of the Bible plays a key role in the transition from 'talent' as a measurement of weight to 'talents' as a term for gifts or abilities (see Clarke 2003: 193).

A very different interpretation of the parable is given by some contemporary scholars, reading from the perspective of the exploited poor, and sensitive to the social dynamics of ancient Jewish Palestine (e.g. Rohrbaugh 1993; Ukpong 2012). Resisting an allegorical interpretation whereby the master is God or Christ, they propose that it is the third, so-called 'unprofitable' servant who 'represents the "prophetic" voice of the gospel and is the role model for Christians.' The master, by contrast, manifests the very exploitative practices which God's Kingdom opposes (Ukpong 2012: 191).

The Judgment of the Nations (25:31–46)

The Sheep and the Goats is closely related thematically to the preceding two parables, although Matthew's readers have differed over whether this too should be read as a parable, with the interpretive strategy that entails (Paschasius Radbertus; Nicholas of Lyra), as 'an actual description of the final judgment' (Gray 1989: 167: e.g. Anselm of Laon), or as an apocalyptic unveiling of the meaning of true justice (Donahue 1986). Whatever its genre, it has often been considered the 'classic' expression of the Christian Gospel (Donahue 1986: 3).

The passage describes the separation of 'all the nations,' in the manner of a shepherd dividing his flock (see Ezek 34:17, 20–21), when the Son of Man sits on his throne of glory accompanied by his angels. The animals are normally classified as 'sheep' and 'goats,' although John Chrysostom understand the latter as 'kids,' noting that kids, like the wicked, are unfruitful. The righteous, by contrast, are appropriately called 'sheep' because they are gentle, and because, just as sheep provide useful products such as wool and milk, so the saints bear good fruit (so also Theophylact). Jerome emphasizes that the word means 'he-goats,' an appropriate symbol for those to be condemned, given that it is 'a lascivious animal, apt to butt, and always burning for intercourse' (Jerome 2008: 290; so also Paschasius Radbertus; *Glossa ordinaria*; Aquinas). The *Glossa* also notes that goats were offered as sacrifices for sin, underscoring its fittingness as a description of sinners.

Diverse concerns determine which aspects of the story are prioritized. Christological controversy explains the focus of certain interpreters, not on the sheep and goats, but on Christ, his majesty, and his equality with the Father (e.g. Justin, *Trypho* 76.5). Some allegorize the throne on which Christ sits, whether as the church (Paschasius Radbertus) or the cross (Bonaventure). Others debate the identity of 'all the angels.' According to Isho'dad of Merv (d. c. 850), the Antiochene exegete Theodore of Mopsuestia maintained that this could only refer to the angels below the firmament, i.e. guardian angels, and not also the angels who minister at God's throne. Dionysius bar-Salibi, by contrast, asserts that the literal sense holds: 'all the angels' will accompany the returning Christ (see Gray 1989: 155–156).

The basic point of the parable seems obvious: judgment of humanity on the basis of its response, through six acts of charity (see Isa 58:7; Ezek 18:7, 16; Job 22:7; 31:32; Tob 4:16), to the poor and needy identified as 'the least of these my brothers.' These six actions, together with the burial of the dead (Tob 1:17 LXX), will form the basis for Lactantius's seven works of mercy (*Ep.* 65), which come to play an important role in theology and piety. A visual example is Caravaggio's *The Seven Works of Mercy* (1607; Church of Pio Monte della Misericordia, Naples).

Yet Origen for one cautions against a perfunctory reading which views salvation as the consequence of charitable works alone, irrespective of other virtues or sins (Wailes 1987: 196). A more precise concern emerges in the sixteenth century, with John Calvin objecting to a causal link between positive judgment and acts of charity on the basis of the word 'for' (25:35):

> If this were a debate on the cause of our salvation the Papists might well infer that our eternal life was merited by good works; but all that Christ was intending was to encourage His people to care for good and right conduct, and it is wrong to squeeze any meaning out of His words on the value of the merits of works. They insist on the causal particle – a weak argument: we know that it does not always signify cause, but consequence rather, when eternal life is promised to the just. (Calvin 1972: III/115)

In fact, the story is full of uncertainties, as its complex history of reception makes clear (see Wailes 1987: 194–200; Gray 1989; Luz 2005a: 267–274). Who precisely are 'all the nations'? This has implications for the identity of the 'sheep' and the 'goats.' What of the 'least'? Does this term embrace anyone in need, irrespective of their commitment to Christ? Or do other passages in Matthew suggest a narrower definition?

The judgment of the nations is widely understood to refer to the universal judgment (e.g. Cyril of Jerusalem, *Catech.* 15.24; Leo the Great, *Sermon* 9.2; Erasmus; Lapide), although some restrict it to Christians, or to that part of humanity still alive at the Parousia (see Gray 1989: 19). Universal judgment is presumed by the ninth-century Old Saxon epic *The Heliand*: 'all the sons of heroes, all the people of different clans, all people living, anyone ever raised by humans in this light, will be summoned together to Him' (Murphy 1992: 143). Similarly, Desiderius Erasmus paraphrases 'all the nations' as 'the whole race of mortals' (Erasmus 2008: 339). A modern alternative, apparently first proposed by the eighteenth-century Anglican scholar John Heylyn, is that the Sheep and the Goats describes the judgment of 'the Heathen,' the judgment of the church having already been described in the two preceding parables (see Gray 1989: 345–346). Matthew's passage is an important influence on visual interpretations of the last judgment, where the wicked appear below Christ's left hand, and the righteous below his right. Famous examples include Giotto's *Last Judgment* (1306; Scrovegni Chapel, Padua), Fra Angelico's *Last Judgment*, which includes at least one cardinal among the damned (c. 1431; San Marco, Florence), and William Blake's *A Vision of the Last Judgment* (1808; Petworth House, West Sussex), inspired by Michelangelo's Sistine Chapel fresco. In the case of Blake's version, the judgment is envisaged as occurring throughout a person's life (according to his notes, 'whenever any Individual Rejects Error & Embraces Truth a Last Judgment passes upon that Individual').

The identity of the 'least of these my brethren' falls broadly into three types, although the question is complicated in the case of those Christian authors writing in contexts where the church is largely coterminous with society. Some, either explicitly or implicitly, identify them as any poor and needy human beings, in whom Christ is present, albeit hidden (Irenaeus, *Adv. Haer.* 4.18.6; Cyril of Jerusalem, *Cat.* 15.26; Gregory of Nyssa, *On the Beatitudes* 5; Chrysostom; Pelagius, *Ad Demetriadem* 22; Peter Chrysologus, *Sermon* 42; Dionysius the Carthusian). For the Pseudo-Clementine *Homilies*, care to those in need is a recognition that human beings are made in the image of God, even if they do not all yet bear his likeness:

> Therefore it behoves you to give honour to the image of God, which is man – in this wise: food to the hungry, drink to the thirsty, clothing to the naked, care to the sick, shelter to the stranger, and visiting him who is in prison, to help him as you can. (*Hom.* 11.4; *ANF* 8:285)

For John Chrysostom, who either quotes from or alludes to this parable nearly 400 times in his extant writings, this 'sweetest passage of Scripture' represents a specific indictment of the wealthy inhabitants of Antioch, especially those who give priority to purchasing precious eucharistic vessels and vestments over caring for the beggars in their midst:

> Would you do honour to Christ's body? Do not neglect Him when naked; do not, while here you honor Him with silken garments, neglect Him outside. For He that said, 'This is my body' and by His word confirmed the fact, this same said: 'You saw me hungry and perishing with cold and nakedness and did not feed me' and 'Inasmuch as you did not do it for one of the least of these, you did not do it for me.' (John Chrysostom in Brändle 2008: 133–134)

Such a universal understanding is popular in the modern period. In a letter to his parents dated to 13 April 1738, the young Benjamin Franklin appeals to this parable to justify his conviction that 'vital Religion' suffers when virtue is overwhelmed by doctrinal orthodoxy:

> And the Scripture assures me, that at the last Day, we shall not be examin'd what we *thought*, but what we *did*; and our Recommendation will not be that we said *Lord, Lord*, but that we did GOOD to our fellow Creatures. See Matth. 2[5]. ('Benjamin Franklin to Josiah and Abiah Franklin,' quoted in Nichols 2008: 47)

For the former slave and abolitionist Frederick Douglass (c. 1818–1895), the parable is a particular indictment of Christian leaders who are indifferent to the injustices suffered by American slaves (in Gowler 2017: 174).

The impact of this broad interpretation of the 'least' on mainstream Christian thinking is forcefully represented by the Second Vatican Council's Pastoral Constitution on the Church in the Modern World, *Gaudium et Spes* (1965):

> In our times a special obligation binds us to make ourselves the neighbor of every person without exception and of actively helping him when he comes across our path, whether he be an old person abandoned by all, a foreign laborer unjustly looked down upon, a refugee, a child born of an unlawful union and wrongly suffering for a sin he did not commit, or a hungry person who disturbs our conscience by recalling the voice of the Lord, 'As long as you did it for one of these the least of my brethren, you did it for me' (Matt. 25:40). (*Gaudium et Spes* 27)[1]

It is also a dominant interpretation among twentieth- and twenty-first-century liberation theologians (see the discussion in Watson 1993).

1 http://www.vatican.va/archive/hist_councils/ii_vatican_council/documents/vat-ii_const_19651207_gaudium-et-spes_en.html.

Other readers of Matthew restrict the 'least' to needy Christians (Hilary; Aquinas; Calvin; Bengel). Several find intratextual support for this more restricted interpretation. Clement of Alexandria points to the similar 'these little ones' at 10:42 (*Quis dives* 30). Jerome, who identifies the 'least' as the 'poor in spirit,' cites Jesus' earlier statement that his 'brothers' are those who do the will of his Father, i.e. disciples (12:50). Paschasius Radbertus connects them to the 'perfect' of 19:21, 28. According to the second-century *Didascalia apostolorum*, Christians condemned as martyrs are particularly in view as those hungering, thirsting, and in prison (*Did. apost.* 19). Persecution also seems to be an issue in the testament of the Anabaptist Anna Jansz of Rotterdam, later reworked as a hymn by an anonymous poet. Stanza 17 interprets the 'least of my brethren' as the poor and needy 'who profess Christ,' probably reflecting the harsh treatment meted out to Anabaptists (Gowler 2017: 122–123).

Some are even more restrictive. In the third century, the Syriac theologian Aphrahat identifies the 'least' specifically as apostles (*Dem.* 20.16). The apostolic interpretation explains how Christ's words provide the language for the apostle Thomas to speak of his own Christ-like ministry in the apocryphal *Acts of Thomas* (*Acts Thom.* 125). For the sixteenth-century Jesuit Cornelius a Lapide, the 'least' in a primary sense are those at the forefront of the church's mission: apostles, religious and apostolic men (though he allows a wider application to all Christians in a secondary sense). A modern extension of this identifies the 'least' as Christian missionaries (Michaels 1965). Monastic readers of Matthew unsurprisingly think of 'the least of these my brothers' as brethren within the community (e.g. John of Gaza, *Questions and Answers* 124). The Rule of St. Benedict combines a specific monastic interpretation with a more general one. On the one hand, those who visit sick monks are ministering to Christ (*Rule of St. Benedict* 36). On the other, all visitors to the monastery are to be received as Christ, even if special honor is given to Christians among them:

> Let all guests who arrive be received like Christ,
> for He is going to say,
> "I came as a guest, and you received Me" (Matt. 25:35).
> And to all let due honor be shown,
> especially to the domestics of the faith and to pilgrims
> (*Rule of St. Benedict* 53).[2]

Occasionally, the precise referent is ambiguous. In *The Heliand*, the 'least' are those 'who because of humility were poor people carrying out my will'

2 http://www.osb.org/rb/text/rbeaad1.html.

(144), which could mean all Christians, or specifically vowed ascetics. Other interpreters are themselves uncertain, as in the case of Theophylact:

> He means either His own disciples or, simply, all the poor. For every poor man is Christ's brother for the very reason that Christ, too, spent His life in poverty. (Theophylact 1992: 219)

A complex reworking in hymnody is Fanny Crosby's hymn 'Have You Sought?' which combines this parable with that of the Lost Sheep (Gowler 2017: 181–183). Christians will be judged (and therefore divided into sheep and goats) on the basis of how they have emulated 'the tender Shepherd' in seeking out 'the sheep that have wandered,' i.e. sinners. Their ministering to them will include witnessing to the Gospel (a reversal of those interpretations which treat the parable as about the nations ministering unwittingly to hungry and imprisoned Christians):

> Have you been to the sad and the lonely,
> Whose burdens are heavy to bear?
> Have you carried the name of Jesus,
> And tenderly breathed it in prayer?
> Have you told of the great salvation
> He died on the cross to secure?
> Have you asked them to trust in the Savior,
> Whose love shall forever endure?
>
> Have you knelt by the sick and the dying,
> The message of mercy to tell?
> Have you stood by the trembling captive
> Alone in his dark prison cell?
> Have you pointed the lost to Jesus,
> And urged them on Him to believe?
> Have you told of the life everlasting,
> That all, if they will, may receive?

Those Christians who can answer yes to these questions posed to them by the Shepherd-King will receive his positive judgment: 'Inasmuch as' twas done for My brethren, | Even so it was done unto Me.'

Matthew 26–27

Ancient Literary Context

A basic narrative of the death and resurrection of Jesus was central to the earliest Christian kerygma (e.g. 1 Cor 15:3–7: that 'Christ died for our sins,' 'was buried,' and 'was raised on the third day according to the scriptures'), and developed versions appear in all four canonical Gospels (Mark 14–15; Luke 22–23; John 18–19). The coherent character of these passion narratives has

Matthew Through the Centuries, First Edition. Ian Boxall.

convinced many that at least one written version existed prior to the Gospels themselves, perhaps composed for liturgical performance (see Trocmé 1983).

Matthew's passion narrative has particularly close verbatim agreement with Mark, making it easy to identify those elements unique to Matthew. Some are elements of emphasis and redaction. Matthew heightens the negative portrait of Jewish authorities (e.g. they seek 'false' testimony against Jesus, 26:59; cf. Mark 14:55; both the chief priests *and* the elders persuade the crowd to ask for Barabbas' release, 27:20; cf. Mark 15:11). Matthew also heightens Mark's focus on fulfillment of scripture. For example, he adds a comment about Jesus' silence before Pilate, recalling Isaiah's Servant who 'does not open his mouth' (27:14; cf. Isa 53:7 LXX). The mocking at the cross recalls the mocking of the righteous one in the Wisdom of Solomon (27:38–44; Wis 2:18; cf. Mark 15:27–32). Mark's 'wine mixed with myrrh' has become 'wine mixed with gall,' conforming the act more closely to Psalm 69 (27:34; Ps 69:21 LXX; cf. Mark 15:23).

However, there are also events unique to our evangelist, for which he may have drawn upon popular Christian folk traditions (Brown 1994: 59–61, 755). He expands the story of Judas Iscariot to include the 'thirty pieces of silver' (26:15), and Judas' remorse and suicide (27:3–10). He alone among the evangelists mentions the dream of Pilate's wife (27:19), and Pilate's action of washing his hands, leading to the declaration of the people: 'His blood be/is on us and on our children' (27:24–25). Matthew's description of the effects of Christ's death is also far more dramatic: an earthquake, opening of tombs, and the resurrection of the saints (27:51b–53). Matthew also introduces the story of a guard at the tomb (27:62–66; 28:4, 11–15), perhaps for apologetic purposes.

Whatever Matthew's sources, his account of Christ's passion and death is carefully interwoven into his Gospel as a whole (Heil 1991a; Allison 1994). He provides regular foreshadowings of the passion: e.g. allusions to the sacrifice of Isaac, 'son of Abraham' (1:1, 2; 3:17); Herod's murderous plans to destroy him (2:16); the 'handing over' and eventual death of John the Baptist (4:12; 14:1–12); plots against Jesus by the religious authorities (e.g. 12:14); a series of passion predictions (16:21; 17:22–23; 20:17–19); a prophesy of the 'cup' that he must drink (20:22; cf. 26:39). The reader has been carefully prepared for the passion story that now unfolds.

The Interpretations

The reception of Matthew's passion narrative, albeit often harmonized with the other three, is as rich and diverse (Clarke 2003: 202–243; Luz 2005a: 303–328). Whether or not the pre-Matthean passion narrative was originally composed for early Christian worship, a major context for its reception has been liturgical.

The fourth-century pilgrim Egeria testifies to well-established liturgies commemorating the events of the passion, associated with locations in and around Jerusalem. Specifically with regard to Matthew, she mentions the reading of a section from the Eschatological Discourse (beginning at 24:4) on the Tuesday of Holy Week (*Egeria's Travels* 33.2; Wilkinson 1981: 134). She also notes substantial readings from the Passion story throughout the week, including several from Matthew's version, a usage confirmed by the fifth-century Armenian Lectionary. Outside of Palestine, there is evidence for the liturgical recitation of the passion narratives as early as Gregory of Nazianzus in the fourth century. In fifth-century Rome, Pope Leo the Great (pope 440–461) attests to the reading of the passion account on Palm Sunday, and it is clear from the seventh-century *Comes* of Würzburg that it should be Matthew's account, supplemented by Luke's on Wednesday of Holy Week and John's on Good Friday (Morin 1911: 304). This became standard practice in the West until the mid-twentieth century. Exceptions include the Ambrosian rite of Milan, where Matthew's passion narrative was read from Wednesday of Holy Week, with Matthew 27 as the Gospel for Good Friday.

In the Byzantine liturgy, substantial sections of Matthew's passion came to be read during the Great Week, from the Liturgy on the morning of Great Thursday through to Great Friday Vespers (Vaporis 1993). In the Maronite Church, Matthew's passion is read on Monday and Tuesday of Passion Week, 27:27–45 on Great Friday, and 27:57–66 (the burial and placing of the guard) on Great Saturday (Gemayel 1984). The Armenian tradition reads 27:1–56 on Great Friday (Ashjian 1978: 49).

The liturgical use of Matthew's passion narrative is reflected in Holy Week homilies, a genre particularly lending itself to moral exhortation, often highlighting the role of specific characters within the story. This didactic function of characterization is also highlighted by textual divisions. The chapter divisions in Codex Alexandrinus, which include breaks at 26:48, 26:69, and either 26:75 or 27:3 (together with the respective titles 'Concerning the betrayal of Jesus,' 'Concerning the denial of Peter,' and 'Concerning the remorse of Judas') serve to highlight the negative examples of both Judas Iscariot and Simon Peter, contrasting both with Joseph of Arimathea, whose act of kindness opens the final section at 27:57 ('Concerning the request for the body of the Lord,' Goswell 2009: 152–153).

But the reception of Matthew's passion narrative frequently occurs indirectly, through harmonized retellings of the Gospel accounts, supplemented by apocryphal and imaginative embellishment. The *Gospel of Nicodemus* (possibly fifth or sixth century) is particularly relevant to Matthew given its interest in Pilate's wife (27:19), and in the impact of Christ's death on the dead saints in Hades (see 27:52–53). The *Book of the Cock* (surviving in an Ethiopic translation of a possibly fifth- or sixth-century original) is another expansion of the Gospel narrative, read liturgically during Holy Week in the Ethiopian Orthodox Church (Cowley 1985b; Piovanelli 2003). Western texts from the late twelfth and early thirteenth centuries onwards reflect the greater focus on compassion for and imitation of Christ's sufferings, associated with Anselm of Canterbury, Bernard of Clairvaux, and Francis of Assisi. English accounts of the Passion survive from the fourteenth century, heavily influenced by Pseudo-Bonaventure's *Meditations on the Life of Christ*, a classic work of Franciscan spirituality (see Herbert 1968: xxix). The latter introduces its section on the passion of Christ with the general exhortation that 'He who wishes to glory in the Cross and Passion must dwell with continued meditation on the mysteries and events that occurred' (*Meditation* 74; Ragusa and Green 1961: 317). Visionary texts also contribute to the mix, notably the *Revelations of St. Birgitta of Sweden* (1303–1373), in which Birgitta as Christ's 'bride' receives visions of Christ's passion and is exhorted to imitate him.

Outside of the liturgy, popular reception of the passion narrative primarily occurred through drama (e.g. the Corpus Christi play cycles in medieval York and Chester, or Passion and Easter plays in continental Europe) and visual art. Visual representation of Christ's sufferings on the cross, and of the crucifixion itself, emerges relatively late (Schiller 1986; Jensen 2000: 130–155; Harries 2004; Luz 2005a: 321–328). However, scenes from the passion already appear in early Christian art, including at least two scenes unique to Matthew: Pilate washing his hands (27:24: mid-fourth-century sarcophagus from the Catacomb of Domitilla, Museo Pio Cristiano, Vatican) and Judas hanging from a tree (27:5: fifth-century ivory panel, British Museum). The passion story becomes increasingly popular through the Middle Ages, represented in fresco cycles, altarpieces, Books of Hours, and illustrated Bibles (e.g. the *Biblia pauperum*, which juxtaposes Gospel scenes with Old Testament types). With the exception of the latter, the general tendency toward harmonization is evident. Nonetheless, specific Matthean motifs do occur. Besides Pilate's handwashing, prominent examples include Judas' remorse (27:3–5: e.g. Rembrandt, *Judas Returning the Thirty Pieces of Silver*; 1629, Mulgrave Castle, North Yorkshire), the reed in Christ's hand at his mocking by Roman soldiers (27:29: e.g. Giotto, *Christ Mocked*; c. 1305, Scrovegni Chapel, Padua), and the dramatic events surrounding Christ's death (27:51–53: e.g. Jacques Tissot, *The Earthquake*; 1886–1894, Brooklyn Museum, New York).

The liturgical use of Matthew's passion is also reflected in its musical reception. Originally chanted by a single voice, the transition in the Middle Ages to having different voices for evangelist, Christ, and other characters resulted in more complex polyphonic musical settings (e.g. Francisco Guerrero, 1528–1599; Orlande de Lassus, 1532–1594). From the modern period, most famous is Johann Sebastian Bach's *St. Matthew Passion*, with libretto by Christian

Friedrich Henrici, known as Picander (see e.g. Savage 1980; Stapert 1993; Paffenroth 1995; Dowling Long and Sawyer 2015: 206–208; Franklin 2015). First performed in 1727, Bach's work was composed for a liturgical setting, thus making it the most famous example of German Lutheran passion devotion. The broader passion story, and devotion to the sufferings of Christ, have also left their mark on hymnody, from the poems of the sixth-century Latin poet and bishop Venantius Fortunatus (e.g. 'Sing my tongue the glorious battle,' and 'The royal banners forward go') to the influential seventeenth-century Lutheran passion hymns (e.g. the *Passíusálmar* by the Icelandic minister Hallgrímur Pétursson, and the German Paul Gerhardt's 'O Haupt voll Blut und Wunden').

The reception of Matthew's passion narrative, especially in art, drama, and preaching, tragically combines often profound Christian devotion with its darker potential for anti-Jewish sentiments and anti-Semitic caricature (Schreckenberg 1996: 157–192). 27:25 ('His blood be on us and on our children') has had particularly chilling effects, not only in the repeated Christian charge of 'deicide' ('killing God') directed against Jews, but the justification from this for violence against Jewish people. Its impact can even be felt in music. The American-Jewish composer David Lang describes his ambivalent reaction as a Jew to Bach's *St. Matthew Passion*, leading him to compose his own *Little Match Girl Passion*, first performed in 2009:

> It's a work I love so much, but it's always very strange listening to it, because the Jews aren't the heroes of this piece, so it's something very disconcerting for Jews to listen to this music. And so I imagined what it would be like to tell that same story with that same text and that same awe and sense of wonder and belief, but somehow replacing the suffering of Jesus with the suffering of something else. The Little Match Girl of Hans Christian Andersen seemed appropriate because of its Christian spirit [...], and I thought maybe I could take the story of the St Matthew Passion and take the story of Jesus out and plug this little girl's suffering in. (Lang in Wells 2013: 42)

Given the vast amount of material on the reception of Matthew's passion narrative, whether in its own right or in harmonized versions, space permits only a representative selection. The approach taken here will be to combine broad coverage of the narrative with closer attention to those elements which are either unique to Matthew, or where Matthew makes a significant contribution to shared material.

From Plot to Arrest (26:1–56)

With the conclusion of Jesus' fifth and final discourse ('When Jesus had completed *all* these sayings,' 26:1), the story of the handing over of the Son of Man now begins. Codex Alexandrinus highlights the close connection with the

Sheep and the Goats parable by marking out 25:31–26:5 as a single unit, with the title 'Concerning the coming of Christ' (Goswell 2009). In the thirteenth century, the Franciscan Bonaventure makes a similar connection:

> he himself in his most blessed Passion hungered greatly for our justice, and had a spiritual thirst on the cross, together with a corporal hunger and thirst ... feed him in yourself and in your heart or at least in the poor. He was a stranger since when his death was imminent he said: My kingdom is not of this world ... let us welcome this stranger inside ourselves or in his members. (in Gray 1989: 175)

Anointing at Bethany (26:6–13)

The flow of the narrative slows momentarily, as the evangelist describes the anointing of Jesus by an unnamed woman at Bethany (26:6–13; Mark 13:39). The rich texture of this story leads to different assessments of its primary significance. For some, the key lies in the anointing of Jesus' head. Early exegetes often read this story in the light of the Pauline understanding that Christ is the 'head' of the church (e.g. Eph 1:22; 5:23; Col 1:18). For Ignatius of Antioch, Christ allowed his head to be anointed so that he might 'breathe incorruptibility upon the church,' leading Ignatius to warn the Christians in Ephesus: 'Do not be anointed with the stench of the teaching of the ruler of this age' (*Eph.* 17.1; Holmes 2007: 197). That the woman recognizes Christ as her 'head' develops into a figurative interpretation whereby the woman herself symbolizes the church (e.g. Jerome). Harmonizing this story with that in Luke 7:36–50, Euthymius Zigabenus offers an explanation: the church is comprised of former sinners. The changed circumstances of a predominantly Gentile church unfortunately de-Judaize this anonymous female disciple who was almost certainly Jewish. Hilary understands her as prefiguring the Gentiles who will glorify God in Christ's passion. Theophylact develops this into a detailed allegory, whereby the woman (the church of the Gentiles) pours out myrrh (faith) on Christ's head (his divinity).

Jesus' words at 26:12 offer a different focus: she anticipates Christ's burial. For the Geneva Bible, the act of this 'sinful woman' enables Christ to point to his forthcoming death by which he will 'bring life to all sinners who flee unto him.' Others are more interested in Jesus' saying about the poor, notably John Chrysostom, known for his critique of urban poverty in Antioch. Although he does not object in principle to money being spent on church furnishings, he would rather the money be directed toward the needy. Christ said what he did to the woman so as not to discourage her; if he had been asked prior to her act, he would, however, have declined it:

> Do thou then likewise, if you should see any one provide sacred vessels and offer them, and loving to labor upon any other ornament of the church, about its walls

> or floor; do not command what has been made to be sold, or overthrown, lest you spoil his zeal. But if, before he had provided them, he were to tell you of it, command it to be given to the poor; forasmuch as He also did this not to spoil the spirit of the woman, and as many things as He says, He speaks for her comfort. (*Homily on Matthew* 80.2; *NPNF* 1st series, 10:482).

In the cut-and-thrust of sixteenth-century polemics, John Calvin is scathing about how 'the papists' read the lavishness of the anointing as justification for liturgical expenditure: 'When they hear how Christ was willing to be anointed by Mary they reckon that He is delighted with incense, candles, splendour in vestment, and like ceremonial' (Calvin 1972: III/123). Christ, however, is not present in visible form anymore, to 'accept earthly honours.' Therefore the money should be given instead to the poor. Roman Catholic exegetes meet like with like, emphasizing that there is a 'great difference' between the person of Christ and the poor. Hence Juan de Maldonado responds that 'many things which heretics and profane persons think absurd and useless are regarded by Christ as pious and full of charity,' including 'ornaments of churches instituted in honour of Christ' (Maldonado 1888: 2/369).

Thirty Pieces of Silver (26:14–16)

The woman at Bethany is juxtaposed, by way of contrast, with Judas' request for money. Although one could read Matthew's statement as Judas' recognition of Jesus' worth (the wages of the shepherd, Zech 11:12), Judas is generally regarded as motivated by greed (e.g. Chrysostom; Calvin). Nonetheless, some see the amount of money as surprisingly meager for handing over the Savior. 'He is sold, and very cheap,' exclaims Gregory of Nazianzus (*Orat.* 29.20; *NPNF* 2nd series, 7:309). Ambrose of Milan contrasts this amount with Judas' calculation of the price of the ointment (harmonizing 26:15 with John 12:5):

> O traitor Judas, thou valuest the ointment of His Passion at three hundred pence, and sellest His Passion for thirty pence. Profuse in valuing, mean in selling. (*On the Holy Spirit* 3.17.128; *NPNF* 2nd series, 10:153)

Juan de Maldonado calculates the amount as the equivalent of 30 French francs in sixteenth-century currency, sufficient to buy a field in Christ's day, though not in his own. Bengel makes the link with Exodus 21:32: Christ is sold for 'the value of a slave' (Bengel 1971: 289).

The money reference also encourages typological interpretations. The 'thirty pieces of silver' offered to Judas/Judah recalls the 20 pieces of silver which Joseph's brothers received from the Ishmaelites, at the instigation of Judah (Gen 37:28; e.g. Rabanus Maurus; Paschasius Radbertus; *Glossa ordinaria*). The Old

Testament Joseph is then a type of Christ, a connection expressed by Romanos the Melodist, sixth-century liturgical poet of Constantinople, in his Kontakion 'On Judas':

> You received thirty gold coins.
> Count them, wretch and think, which of the prophets was sold like that?
> The Joseph who was a type of Jesus, whose price you are receiving,
> and through it you receive hell with the noose for hanging.
> (Romanos the Melodist 1995: 123)

Romanos's 'gold coins' are derived from the LXX of Gen 37:28 (see also e.g. *T. Gad* 2:3). However, as Jerome had previously noted in his commentary, the 'Hebrew truth' reads 'silver,' thus making the connection with the patriarch Joseph even clearer. Aquinas, aware that only 20 pieces were given for Joseph, explains the increase to 30 symbolically: it is produced by multiplying 5 (the books of Moses, or the 5 senses) by 6 (salvation was expected to come in the sixth age).

The Last Supper (26:17–30)

Judas' decision to hand Jesus over now hangs over the impending Passover celebration. Greek exegetes often assume that the term *Pascha* (a transliteration into Greek of the Hebrew *Pesah*, 'Passover') is derived from the similar-sounding Greek verb *paschein* ('to suffer': e.g. Melito of Sardis, *Peri Pascha*; Theophylact). The Latin Father Jerome corrects the error from his knowledge of Hebrew: it means 'passing' (*transitus*). Thomas Aquinas will later summarize the four senses of the term. Historically, it refers to the original Passover in Egypt; allegorically to Christ's Passover through death; morally, to the passing from a 'carnal' to a 'spiritual' way of life; anagogically, to the passing away of heaven and earth at the end (Aquinas 2013b: 359).

Despite the continuity implied in 26:26 ('While they were eating'), many have wanted to draw a clear distinction between the Passover meal itself and what Christ then does, understood as establishing a new Passover (e.g. Jerome; Chrysostom; Calvin). The distinction is famously expressed in Thomas Aquinas's hymn *Pange lingua*: 'Types and shadows have their ending, for the newer rite is here.' Sixteenth-century Catholic exegetes even identify three stages of the supper: the Passover celebration, an ordinary meal to satisfy hunger, and Jesus' words over the bread and the cup (e.g. Maldonado; see Luz 2005a: 373).

The latter are understood by a wide variety of Christian communities as instituting the Eucharist or Lord's Supper ('an aetiological cult narrative': Davies and Allison 1997: 465), even as they disagree vehemently over the sacramental theology these words imply. Given the eucharistic connection, several commentators have found Judas' presence at the meal problematic. Matthew makes no reference to Judas leaving the table before the end (cf. John 13:30), though Hilary proposes that he departed before Jesus took the bread, suggesting the Iscariot's unworthiness to receive Holy Communion.

The evangelists have preserved the 'words of institution' in different forms (Matthew's are closest to Mark 14:22–26; Luke 22:14–23 has close parallels with Paul: 1 Cor 11:23–25). The forms used in the eucharistic prayers of different Christian denominations diverge from each other and from the canonical Gospel texts (Aquinas explains the divergence as due to the evangelists' concern to keep the 'form of the sacraments' secret: Aquinas 2013b: 383). Nonetheless, it is striking that Matthew's version, with its more liturgical feel (e.g. the explicit commands to 'eat' and 'drink'), is a substantial source for many eucharistic liturgies. Common Matthean phrases include 'take, eat,' 'drink from it,' 'all of you,' 'poured out,' 'for many,' and 'for the forgiveness of sins' (e.g. Roman rite; Book of Common Prayer of the Church of England and thence of other Anglican/Episcopal churches; Maronite rite; Byzantine Divine Liturgy of St. John Chrysostom).

Perhaps most noticeable is the Matthean phrase 'for the forgiveness of sins' (said twice in the Maronite liturgy, over the bread as well as the cup: 'for the forgiveness of sins and eternal life'). Unlike Mark, for whom John's baptism is 'for the forgiveness of sins' (Mark 1:4), for Matthew this is only achieved by Christ's death. Thus 'Jesus' lives up to his name (see 1:21): 'Jesus saves his people from their sins by dying for them and so permits a new relationship with God' (Davies and Allison 1997: 474). The *Glossa ordinaria* cross-references Hebrews 10:4, which asserts the inadequacy of animal sacrifices under the Mosaic covenant ('For it is impossible for the blood … of goats to take away sins').

Struggle in Gethsemane (26:36–56)

All three Synoptic Gospels describe Jesus' prayer in Gethsemane. He tells his disciples to sit while he goes 'over there to pray,' suggesting to Aquinas Abraham's words to his servant as he goes to sacrifice Isaac (Gen 22:5). Christ's threefold coming to the sleeping disciples after each of his three prayers (26:40, 43, 45) is read figuratively by Hilary of Poitiers as alluding to different 'comings' of the risen Christ. First Christ comes at Easter, when he rebukes the fearful disciples. Second, he visits them when he sends the Spirit. Third, he will come in glory, to give them ultimate rest. Thus Gethsemane extends into the lives of Christian readers.

This scene of Christ's distress has often proved challenging. Pagan critics used it to attack Christian claims about Christ's divinity (e.g. Origen, *Cels.* 2.23–24).

But Christological debaters across the centuries have also treated this narrative as a battleground, whether responding to the Manicheans (Christ did not really suffer), the Arians (Gethsemane confirms the Son's subordination to the Father), or the Monothelites (Christ lacked a separate human will).

One frequent response is to regard Gethsemane, and the crucifixion itself, as a cunning ruse. Most widely associated with Gregory of Nyssa, this uses the metaphor of the fishhook of divinity carrying the bait of Christ's humanity (Constas 2004). According to a fourth-century *Homily on the Passion and the Cross* attributed to Athanasius, the devil wholly misunderstood Christ's saying about the spirit being willing, but the flesh weak: 'he [mistakenly] thought that the Word was weakened together with the body, and not rather that the body was strengthened by the power of the Word' (PG 28:212 in Constas 2004: 152). The duped devil is thereby caught on the 'fishhook,' fastened to the cross, and made into a mockery.

The orthodox conviction of Christ's two natures often comes into play, grounded in the conviction that the divinity is impassible. For Leo the Great, the 'certain fear' that Christ experienced in Gethsemane exemplifies that 'wondrous exchange' by which Christ takes on human weakness in order to transform it:

> In our Nature, therefore, the Lord trembled with our fear, that He might fully clothe our weakness and our frailty with the completeness of His own strength. For He had come into this world a rich and merciful Merchant from the skies, and by a wondrous exchange had entered into a bargain of salvation with us, receiving ours and giving His, honour for insults, salvation for pain, life for death: and He Whom more than 12,000 of the angel-hosts might have served for the annihilation of His persecutors, preferred to entertain our fears, rather than employ His own power. (*Sermon* 54.4; *NPNF* 2nd series, 12:166)

Jerome develops an idea in his Matthew commentary which will become popular, grounded in the statement that Jesus '*began* to be sorrowful' (26:37). He understands this to be *propassio* or pre-passion (the 'anticipation of disease' rather than the disease itself: Simonetti 2002: 255), allowing him to distinguish between sorrow as the result of fear, which Christ does not possess, and sorrow motivated by compassion or affection. Jerome's pre-passion idea is picked up by high-medieval theologians (e.g. Peter Lombard; *Glossa ordinaria*; Aquinas). The Franciscan theologian Bonaventure can therefore assert that Christ experienced 'real sorrow' (*vera tristitia*), though not 'precisely the way that it is in us,' given that his was subject to reason rather than emerging from the 'sensitive part' of the soul (in Madigan 1995: 167). In the East, Theophylact is keen to treat Christ's sorrow in the face of death as evidence of his true humanity, while simultaneously retaining Gregory of Nyssa's idea that the devil was deceived.

Bonaventure reflects the Franciscan focus on Christ's sufferings. Being 'with Christ' in Gethsemane is an important dimension of subsequent spirituality. Pseudo-Bonaventure's *Meditations on the Life of Christ* exhorts its readers to 'Have compassion for Him and marvel at His most profound humility' as they contemplate Christ kneeling in prayer (*Meditation* 75; Ragusa and Green 1961: 320). The 'Agony in the Garden' also serves as the first of five 'Sorrowful Mysteries' of the Rosary, the Roman Catholic prayer devotion which emerged during the late Middle Ages. The didactic dimension of the episode also comes to be important. Matthew's version strongly echoes the words of the Lord's Prayer which God's people are to pray ('My Father'; 'pray that you may not enter into the trial'; 'your will be done'). Thomas Aquinas therefore sees Christ instructing his disciples in filial prayer. The seventeenth-century Anglican spiritual writer Jeremy Taylor encourages meditation on Gethsemane, in mindfulness of one's sins, as a spiritual exercise when one wakes during the night:

> Meditate on the agonies of Christ in the garden, his sadnesse and affliction all that night; and thank and adore him for his love that made him suffer so much for thee: and hate thy sins which made it necessary for the Son of God to suffer so much. (*Holy Living* 1.3; Taylor 1989: 1/56)

By contrast, post-Enlightenment receptions of the Gethsemane story idealize Christ's heroic courage, or alternatively explore his experience of divine absence (see e.g. Luz 2005a: 405–408). This interest in the human experience of Jesus has its own appeal. Its universal and character-forming dimensions are foregrounded by the Swedish lyric poet Nils Ferlin (1898–1961):

> For he who's afraid of Gethsemane
> Shall never nor giving nor getting see.
> ('Gethsemane' in Atwan, Dardess, and Rosenthal 1998: 407)

The Two Trials (26:57–27:31)

The arrest of Jesus in Gethsemane (26:47–56) leads to two judicial proceedings: before the Jewish Sanhedrin (26:57–68; 27:1–2) and the Roman prefect Pontius Pilate (27:11–26). Matthew names the high priest, who was anonymous in Mark, as Caiaphas (26:3, 57). Caiaphas will become a major character in medieval mystery plays, as personifying the Old Law, a caricature of those who insist on literalism and justice over mercy (see Jeffrey 1992: 120). William Blake expresses this sentiment succinctly:

> Caiaphas was in his own Mind
> A benefactor to Mankind:
> Both read the Bible day and night.
> But thou read'st black where I read white.
> (*The Everlasting Gospel* 2a; Jeffrey 1992: 120)

Critical scholarship is particularly conscious of historical difficulties regarding the Sanhedrin trial. Comparison with Mark reveals Matthew's tendency to shift the balance of responsibility for Jesus' death from Roman to Jewish authorities. While earlier commentators tended to assume historical accuracy, the scholarly awareness that the evangelist's narrative is shaped by his own hostile experience of synagogue authorities has influenced contemporary church doctrine and practice. In its 1985 'Notes on the correct way to present the Jews and Judaism in preaching and catechesis in the Roman Catholic Church,' the Vatican's Commission for Religious Relations with the Jews carefully lays out the complex process by which the Gospel tradition developed, with the potential consequence that 'some references hostile or less than favourable to the Jews have their historical context in conflicts between the nascent Church and the Jewish community.'[1]

The Repentance of Judas (27:3–10)

Judas' change of mind, indicated by his returning the 30 pieces of silver and subsequently hanging himself, is highly contested (Besserman in Jeffrey 1992: 418–420; Klassen 1996: 96–115, 160–176; Paffenroth 2001; Luz 2005a: 478–490; Saari 2006). It is difficult to unravel the receptions of this distinctive Matthean passage from the overwhelmingly negative perception of Judas resulting from harmonizing all four Gospels and Acts, given a more sinister turn by apocryphal embellishments. Consequently, in preaching, drama, commentary, and visual art, the guiding hermeneutical keys appear to be John (Judas 'is a devil': John 6:70; cf. Luke 22:3; John 13:27), and the damning description of Judas' demise in Acts (Acts 1:15–20). This continues until the advent of historical criticism, when more sympathetic assessments of Judas' motives come to the fore, impacting both literature (Besserman in Jeffrey 1992: 420) and film (Walsh 2010; Hebron 2016).

Matthew states that Judas returned the money after 'having repented' or 'changed his mind' (*metamelētheis*). Many commentators conclude from this verb, a different one from that used by both John the Baptist and Jesus

1 http://www.vatican.va/roman_curia/pontifical_councils/chrstuni/relations-jews-docs/rc_pc_chrstuni_doc_19820306_jews-judaism_en.html.

(*metanoeō*: 3:2; 4:17), that Judas' was not true repentance. For Augustine, the fact that Judas killed himself proves that he doubted divine mercy (*Civ. Dei* 1.17). Leo the Great (pope 440–461) similarly accuses Judas: 'And hence, Judas, thou art proved more criminal and unhappier than all; for when repentance should have called thee back to the Lord, despair dragged thee to the halter' (*Sermon* 54.3; *NPNF* 2nd series, 12:165). Others too have denied that Judas' repentance was a 'good' repentance, either because he fled from life through his suicide (Theophylact), or because he lacked hope (Aquinas). John Calvin understands Matthew to be saying only that Judas was 'touched with repentance,' not that he actually repented (Calvin 1972: III/175). Dante places Judas in the lowest circle of hell, along with Julius Caesar's assassins Brutus and Cassius (*Inferno*, Canto 34, lines 61–63).

Hence Judas frequently functions as a negative moral example. In an antiphon for the Orthodox Orthros (Matins) of Great Tuesday, the faithful are urged to pray that their fate not be that of Judas:

> Impious Judas moves with avaricious plots against the Master and deliberates and meditates betrayal. He falls from the light, and accepts darkness. He agrees to the terms, and sells the priceless One. Therefore, he, the most miserable man, finds a noose and a terrible death as the reward for his deed. Redeem us from such a fate, O Christ our God, granting remission of sins to those who celebrate with desire your most pure passion. (Vaporis 1993: 32)

In Bach's *St. Matthew Passion*, a contrast is drawn between the respective responses of Peter and Judas, highlighted by the two arias sung following Peter's weeping and Judas' remorse. The former includes the refrain 'Have mercy, my God, have mercy,' a prayer which Judas is unable to pray. The latter offers the audience, though not apparently Judas himself, the possibility of change, with the repeated phrase 'Give me back my Jesus!' (Paffenroth 1995: 132–134).

Yet the verb *metamelomai* is used positively elsewhere in Matthew. In the parable of the Two Sons it describes the action of the son who changed his mind and went into his father's vineyard despite his initial refusal. It thus functions to differentiate the tax-collectors and prostitutes positively from the chief priests and elders, who fail to change their mind (21:29, 32). Paradoxically, despite the tendency to downplay Judas' change of heart, its seriousness is implied in a wide variety of English translations: 'repented' (Wycliffe Bible; RSV; NRSV); 'repenting himself' (Douay-Rheims); 'repented himself' (Geneva Bible; KJV); 'deeply regretted' (NABRE); 'Overcome with remorse' (*The Message*). Origen struggles with the dialectic between Judas' free will and the devil's possession of him, as well as the necessity of the passion in the divine plan (see e.g. Laeuchli 1953; Paffenroth 2001: 118–119). In response to Celsus's charge that Jesus' betrayal by his disciples undermines his divinity, Origen gives a nuanced reading of 27:3–10:

> But if this covetous Judas, who also stole the money placed in the bag for the relief of the poor, repented, and brought back the thirty pieces of silver to the chief priests and elders, it is clear that the instructions of Jesus had been able to produce some feeling of repentance in his mind, and were not altogether despised and loathed by this traitor. Nay, the declaration, 'I have sinned, in that I have betrayed the innocent blood,' was a public acknowledgment of his crime. Observe, also, how exceedingly passionate was the sorrow for his sins that proceeded from that repentance, and which would not allow him any longer to live; and how, after he had cast the money down in the temple, he withdrew, and went away and hanged himself: for he passed sentence upon himself, showing what a power the teaching of Jesus had over this sinner Judas, this thief and traitor, who could not always treat with contempt what he had learned from Jesus. (*Cels.* 2.11; *ANF* 4:435)

In his Matthew commentary, Origen attributes Judas' coming to his senses as the result of the devil departing from him after his act of betrayal (Laeuchli 1953: 259). He leaves open-ended the question of Judas' ultimate redemption. A modern variant is U2's 1991 song 'Until the End of the World,' a song of love and betrayal framed as a post-mortem conversation between Christ and Judas (Dowling Long and Sawyer 2015: 248). Describing his death, Judas speaks of a combination of waves of 'regret' and 'joy' as he reached out for Christ whom he had betrayed, remembering his promise: 'You, you said you'd wait till the end of the world.'

Moreover, in the narrative dynamic of 27:3–10, Judas functions positively as a foil for the chief priests, whose concern about not putting the money into the treasury is seen as an extreme example of 'straining out a gnat and swallowing a camel' (23:24: e.g. Jerome; Aquinas). In medieval visual depictions, this contrast is often made by having the negotiating priest, though not Judas, wearing the medieval Jewish hat (thereby also burdening medieval Jews with the guilt of their priestly ancestors: see Schreckenburg 1996: 191). John Ruskin, who annotated a tenth-century Greek Gospel Lectionary with his own marginal comments, even detected a typological relationship, and contrast, between the chief priests in the temple treasury of first-century Jerusalem and the contemporary Treasury of nineteenth-century Britain: '*Our* priests don't even warn our Chancellor of the Exchequer of such unlawfulness' (in Bennett 2011: 585).

Even those like Jerome, who ultimately emphasize Judas' personal responsibility for his actions, and the impossibility of his sin being forgiven, detect this dimension of the text:

> But if he who handed over just blood sinned, how much more did they sin who had paid for the just blood and who had provoked the disciple by offering a price for the betrayal? (Jerome 2008: 309)

For Jerome, what prevents Judas being forgiven is that he then adds another sin (that of suicide) to his original act of betrayal.

The concern to emphasize that Judas' sin was an act of free will is specifically directed against alternative anthropologies treating him as evil by nature. This more sinister view of Judas, as evil from the beginning (a devil, or possessed by Satan: see John 6:70), appears frequently in Christian apocrypha, legend, and medieval drama. The *Arabic Gospel of the Infancy* describes how Judas was possessed by the devil as a child, when he first encountered Jesus (*Arab. Gos. Inf.* 35). In the entry for Saint Matthias (Judas' replacement, Acts 1:26) in *The Golden Legend*, Judas' mother is already warned in a dream about his wickedness before his birth, and his parents abandon him in a basket on the sea, whence he is carried to the island of Scariot (hence his surname). In the Chester and York plays, the *topos* of Judas' greed or avarice is reiterated. The dramatic tradition also heightens anti-Jewish dimensions of his story, as does medieval visual art, where Judas is depicted in crude caricature: 'red hair and beard, ruddy skin, yellow robe and money bag, large, hooked nose, big lips, and bleary eyes' (Besserman in Jeffrey 1992: 419).

Judas Hangs Himself (27:5)

The ambivalence of Judas' character is especially evident in receptions of his death. Generally, these harmonize Matthew's suicide with the Acts account of Judas falling headlong, understood as a sign of divine punishment (Acts 1:18; cf. 2 Chron 21:12–19; Josephus, *Ant.* 9:99–104; see Hornik and Parsons 2017: 34–36). Thus in the rather confused account provided by the *Golden Legend*, after Judas hanged himself, he burst open in the middle 'as the gospel tells us' (Jacobus de Voragine 1993: 1/168). Sometimes, the death is further embellished with a tradition attributed to Papias, claiming that Judas's body became bloated because of his impiety, and a lingering stench remained at the place of his death (*Frag.* 4.2–3).

The more optimistic reading of Judas' suicide is taken up explicitly by the Dominican St. Vincent Ferrer, in a sermon preached in 1391:

> Judas who betrayed and sold the Master after the crucifixion was overwhelmed by a genuine and saving sense of remorse and tried with all his might to draw close to Christ in order to apologize for his betrayal and sale. But since Jesus was accompanied by such a large crowd of people on the way to the mount of Calvary, it was impossible for Judas to come to him and so he said to himself: Since I cannot get to the feet of the master, I will approach him in my spirit at least and humbly ask him for forgiveness. He actually did that and as he took the rope and hanged himself his soul rushed to Christ on Calvary's mount, asked for forgiveness and received it fully from Christ, went up to heaven with him and so his soul enjoys salvation with all elect. (in Klassen 1996: 7)

Others hint at such a desire on Judas' part, only to deny its fulfillment. Hilary may be responding to a similar tradition when he asserts that Judas was 'neither visited among the dead nor had he an opportunity to repent among the living after the Lord's Resurrection' (Hilary of Poitiers 2012: 284–285). An alternative found in Theophylact is that, although Matthew states that Judas 'hanged himself,' the attempted suicide was not successful, thus frustrating Judas' desire to reach Hades before Christ, so as to receive pardon. Theophylact claims that God caused the tree to bend and that Judas survived, 'either so that he could repent, or to make an example of him and to shame him' (Theophylact 1992: 240). Judas subsequently became bloated (as in Papias), and then burst open (as in Acts).

Things get worse for this tragic figure. In the twelfth century, the French theologian Peter Comestor argues that no place was willing to let Judas in, leaving him in a perpetual state of exile (in Braswell 1995: 305). Judas as a tortured soul, albeit with some temporary respite, features in various versions of the *Voyage of St. Brendan* (Besserman in Jeffrey 1992: 419). In the poem *Judas* by the English poet Harold Monro (1879–1932), Judas' eternal punishment includes counting the 30 pieces of silver. This tragic Judas also appears visually, as in the seventeenth-century etching of *The Death of Judas* by the French artist Jacques Callot (Figure 15). As Judas' corpse hangs on the tree, in full view of the chief priests at the temple, two devils hover above, dragging his soul away to hell.

Specific trees are associated with Judas's hanging, among them the fig tree, the elder, or the oak, the latter also associated with the death of David's rebellious son Absalom (2 Sam 18:9–17; Braswell 1995: 306). The fig (Latin *ficus*) may be derived from the name of the field, 'the potter's field' (*agrum figuli* in the Vulgate of 27:7). Juan de Maldonado explains this by a tradition that the fig-tree was the tree of forbidden fruit in Eden (Gen 3:3, 7). The fifth-century British Museum ivory panel has Judas hanging from a holm oak or ilex tree.

Developing devotion to the passion of Christ among early Franciscans led to increased interest in the figure of Judas, and an interesting example of actualization. The Passion cycle in the lower church of St. Francis, Assisi, attributed to Pietro Lorenzetti, contains 'a substantial subplot' concerned with Judas' life, and a particularly gruesome depiction of his death (Robson 2004). In part, the image seems to be didactic: reflecting the medieval view of Judas as representing the sins of avarice and of despair. But it seems also to have a distinctive Franciscan flavor. St. Francis came to be viewed as another Christ, and his friars therefore as other disciples. In the fourteenth-century Franciscan *Fioretti* or 'Little Flowers of St. Francis', the saint has his own 'Judas', a 'failed friar' who like Judas longed for money rather than embracing evangelical poverty:

FIGURE 15 Jacques Callot (1592–1635). *The Death of Judas*. c. 1634–1635. Etching. Rosenwald Collection (Lieure, no. 1400, State ii/iv), National Gallery of Art, Washington, DC. Source: Photo courtesy National Gallery of Art, Washington.

> And just as one of the twelve Apostles, the one called Judas Iscariot, became an apostate from the apostolate, betraying Christ, and hanging himself by the neck; so one of the twelve companions of Saint Francis, who was named Brother John of Cappella, became an apostate and finally hanged himself by the neck. (in Robson 2004: 35)

One feature shared by both Matthew and Acts is the association of Judas with a place near Jerusalem known as the Field of Blood (27:8; Acts 1:19).

Matthew claims that the chief priests bought this field, originally 'the potter's field,' with the blood money as a burial place for foreigners. The location was identified by Eusebius as on the lower south side of the Hinnom Valley (Murphy-O'Connor 2008: 136). Although it is not clear that Gentiles are meant by 'foreigners' (it could have been for diaspora Jews who died on pilgrimage to Jerusalem), this is how it is often interpreted. This allows Jerome to add a figurative interpretation: through the blood of Christ the Potter, Gentiles are now at rest. More specifically (in line with interpretations of the Treasure in the Field, 13:44), the field is a figure of the church (e.g. Aquinas).

Matthew's concern for scriptural fulfillment is expressed by the only formula citation in the whole passion narrative (27:9–10), which the evangelist claims had been spoken 'through Jeremiah the prophet.' This is a rather loose quotation, which combines Zechariah 11:12–13 with elements of Jeremiah 18–19 (the problem is acknowledged by some scribes, hence the variant readings 'Zechariah,' 'Isaiah,' or simply 'the prophet': see Metzger 1994: 55). Jerome notes the similarity with Zechariah, and thinks the quotation was taken from there. However, he also claims to have been shown a Hebrew apocryphon of Jeremiah by a member of the Nazarene sect, which contained this text 'written word for word' (Jerome 2008: 310). Johann Albrecht Bengel also identifies Zechariah 11:12–13, noting: 'The Evangelist observes the substance of this, and gives a paraphrase' (Bengel 1971: 301). Eusebius wonders whether the passage had been maliciously removed from the text of Jeremiah, or whether a careless scribe replaced 'Zechariah' with 'Jeremiah' when copying the Gospel (*Dem. ev.* 10.4). Others look elsewhere in Jeremiah for a solution, whilst acknowledging that the precise words are substantially from Zechariah. Aquinas points to Jeremiah 17:1, which refers to the 'sin of Judah,' i.e. the 'sin of Judas.'

The Dream of Pilate's Wife (27:19)

This single verse has had a surprisingly varied afterlife (see e.g. Kany 1995; Baudoin 2010; Dodson 2010; van der Bergh 2012; Boxall 2018). The text already hints at a wider narrative, and some modern scholars have proposed that Matthew draws here on early Christian folklore, or has been influenced by Roman traditions such as the dream of Julius Caesar's wife Calpurnia, warning of Caesar's impending assassination (Dio Cassius 44.17.1; Suetonius, *Julius* 81.1, 3; Appian, *B. Civ.* 2.16; see e.g. Gillman 1992: 163–164; Brown 1994: 755, 803–807). Matthew's careful wording also points to a possible representative role. She has 'suffered many things' because of Christ, modeling Christ himself (16:21). Like the Magi (2:12), she is a Gentile who receives revelation 'in a dream.'

Matthew does not preserve the wife's name, nor do extant Roman sources. Tradition, however, obligingly fills the gap. In the *Acts of Pilate*, part of the

Gospel of Nicodemus (possibly fifth or sixth century, though containing earlier Pilate traditions), she is Prokla in the Greek version and Procula in the Latin. This is expanded to Claudia Procula in the 1619 *Chronicle of Pseudo-Dexter*, leading to an identification with the Claudia of 2 Timothy 4:21, and connection to the Julio-Claudian imperial family (Kany 1995). The twelfth-century Syriac theologian Dionysius bar-Salibi calls her Longina, though probably due to confusion with the Roman soldier Longinus, who traditionally pierced Jesus' side with a lance (Baudoin 2010: 145).

Patristic commentators regularly stress her role as a righteous Gentile and even as a Christian convert. For Origen, the fact that she suffering much on account of Christ meant that God 'desired to convert Pilate's wife in a dream' (Simonetti 2002: 280). For Hilary, she is 'faithful' (*fidelis*), already believing in Christ as she seeks to convert her husband. Thus she is an image (*species*) of the pagans. Augustine comes close to identifying her as a New Eve, a role traditionally accorded to Mary:

> In the beginning of the world the wife leads the husband to death, in the Passion she leads him on to salvation. (Augustine in Lapide 1890: III/264)

This view of Prokla/Procula as a representative faithful Gentile is developed imaginatively in the *Acts of Pilate*:

> And while he was still thinking of rising up, his wife sent to him saying, 'Have nothing to do with this righteous man. For I have suffered many things because of him by night.' And Pilate summoned all the Jews, and stood up and said to them, 'You know my wife is pious (Greek *theosebēs*) and prefers to practise Judaism with you.' They answered him, 'Yes, we know it.' Pilate said to them, 'See, my wife sent to me saying, "Have nothing to do with this righteous man. For I have suffered many things because of him by night."' The Jews answered Pilate, 'Did we not tell you that he is a sorcerer? Behold, he has sent a dream to your wife.' (*Acts of Pilate* 2.1; Elliott 1993: 172)

Her description as 'pious' or a 'God-fearer,' i.e. already sympathetically disposed toward Judaism, echoes Josephus's description of Poppaea, the wife of the emperor Nero (*Ant.* 20.195; cf. *Life* 16; see Brown 1994: 806).

In eastern Christianity, the positive portrayal of Pilate's wife leads to her canonization as a Christian saint. Eastern Orthodox Christians celebrate her as St. Prokla on 27 October. In the Ethiopian Orthodox Church, both Pilate and his wife are honored as saints, their common feast day being 25 June. An Ethiopian liturgical text exonerates both from culpability in Christ's death:

> Salutation to Pilate who washed his hands
> so he himself was pure of the blood of Christ
> and salutation to Procula, his wife,
> who sent him the message: Do not condemn Him
> because that man is pure and just.
> (Cerulli 1973: 10)

In the *Book of the Cock*, also read liturgically in the Ethiopian Church, Pilate and Procla are joined in their defense of Jesus by other members of their family, all of whom pledge their willingness to die for him. In turn, Christ promises them that they will be rewarded in the Kingdom (*Book of the Cock* 8:114; Piovanelli 2003: 430).

By contrast, receptions of this verse by women often contrast Pilate negatively with his wife. The 1611 poem on the passion of Christ, 'Salve Deus Rex Judaeorum' by the English poet Aemilia Lanyer approaches the passion story from the wife's perspective, appealing to her husband 'to beg her Saviours life,' while Pilate and the other male characters variously betray Jesus, deny him, or condemn him to death (Woods 1993). The Victorian novelist and poet Charlotte Brontë offers an imaginative retelling which hints at an unhappy marriage (Pearson 2012). Her 26-stanza poem 'Pilate's Wife's Dream' recounts what transpired when she woke from her dream, which she believes to have been inspired by the Roman gods, to see Christ's cross being constructed outside. Her words express no sympathy for her husband:

> How can I love, or mourn, or pity him?
> I, who so long my fettered hands have wrung;
> I, who for grief have wept my eye-sight dim;
> Because, while life for me was bright and young,
> He robbed my youth–he quenched my life's fair ray–
> He crushed my mind, and did my freedom slay.
> (Brontë, Brontë, and Brontë 1846: 3–4).

The majority view (e.g. Hilary; Chrysostom; Bruno of Segni; Christian of Stavelot; Erasmus; Calvin) is that Procula's dream is a vehicle of divine revelation. For Ephrem the Syrian, Christ himself has inspired the dream, a sign of his divinity: 'And if he wasn't God, who frightened the wife of Pilate with a dream?' (in van der Bergh 2012: 75). Theophylact even imagines that Christ sends her the dream while simultaneously appearing before Pilate. The Victorian Baptist Charles Spurgeon suggests that the divine choice of Pilate's wife, to whom her husband was affectionately disposed, to receive the dream was 'no doubt made by infinite wisdom and tenderness, that if possible Pilate might be stopped in his career of crime and strengthened to the performance of an act of justice' (*Sermon* 1647).[2]

There is, however, a potential theological problem: if Pilate were to listen to his wife and spare Christ, then humanity's salvation would be in jeopardy. This provoked a minority tradition, whereby the dream was not of divine origin but from the devil (e.g. Pseudo-Bede; Rabanus Maurus; Peter Comestor, *Historia Scholastica* 167). Interestingly, it is sometimes proposed side-by-side with the positive view of Pilate's wife as a type of the Gentiles, without any attempt to adjudicate between the two interpretations (e.g. *Glossa ordinaria*; Aquinas). John Calvin knows of it, though rejects it on the grounds that it is the chief priests and scribes who are demonically inspired in their desire to destroy Jesus.

This negative interpretation is particularly pervasive in popular literature (e.g. the ninth-century Old Saxon poem *The Heliand*, and William Langland's *Piers Plowman*) and drama. The medieval Cornish *Passio Christi* play has Lucifer send Beelzebub to Pilate's wife with this message:

> Greetings and salutations, great lady! To be brief, send a messenger to Pilate, warning him that if the innocent prisoner is destroyed, unsparing vengeance will be exacted from you and from your children, as will shortly become only too clear. (Harris 1969: 137).

The diabolic dream is not, however, acted upon by Pilate. In the York Cycle, the diabolic dimension has even tarnished Pilate's wife herself (named Percula). Percula has become a sorceress, contrasted negatively with her husband's more complex character (Fonzo 2013). The motif occasionally appears in visual form. One example depicts the devil standing over Pilate's wife's bed as she dreams (Herrad von Landsberg, *Hortus deliciarum*, fol. 143r: Scheidgen 2002: 327).

Most receptions in visual art and other media are overwhelming positive, however. Though her dream is rarely a subject for artists, she often appears in depictions of Christ before Pilate, whether to the side of her husband (e.g. fifteenth-century Book of Hours, Bodleian Library, Oxford; MS. Auct. D. inf. 2. 11, fol. 72v) or peering out from a window (e.g. eleventh-century nave fresco, Abbey of Sant'Angelo in Formis, Capua). The nineteenth-century French artist Gustave Doré painted the scene, reproduced in an 1877 engraving by Alphonse François (Figure 16). Pilate's wife stands on a marble staircase, her bedroom visible at the top of the stairs. An angel whispers in her ear, apparently explaining the contents of her dream, which are visible to the right of the canvas: Christ, surrounded by a multitude including kneeling Roman soldiers,

2 https://spurgeongems.org/vols28-30/chs1647.pdf.

and figures from later centuries. Some look accusingly at her as they point toward Christ.

Doré's painting is explicitly recalled in the 1899 poem by Archibald Taylor, 'Claudia Procula, or The Dream of Pilate's Wife.' Noting that 'surely angels speak to us in dreams,' Taylor then refers directly to Doré's painting, in which an angel speaks the truth to Pilate's wife on the marble staircase of Herod's palace, suggesting that Doré himself had received similar divine inspiration:

> A famous painter once, himself inspired
> By dreams perchance, his genius bent to limn
> On canvas, and in colors chaste and rare,
> That dream of Procula.
>
> (Taylor 1899: 8)

In the modern period, Pilate's wife has been the subject of several novels, most famously Gertrud von le Fort's 1970 *Die Frau des Pilatus*, in which Claudia Procula's 'suffering' consists of dreaming of a large multitude, across the centuries, praying the words of the Nicene Creed: 'Suffered under Pontius Pilate, was crucified, died and was buried' (von le Fort 2015). In the literary imagination, she is a Christian convert, although initially a secret admirer of Jesus, and sometimes a martyr. She also appears as a character in certain Jesus films: e.g. Cecil B. DeMille's 1927 *The King of Kings* and Mel Gibson's 2004 *The Passion of the Christ*. In the latter, based on a scene from the visions of the German mystic Anne Catherine Emmerich (1774–1824), Pilate's wife gives Mary a linen cloth while Jesus is being tortured prior to his crucifixion. By contrast, in the 1970 stage musical *Jesus Christ Superstar* by Tim Rice and Andrew Lloyd-Webber, she is entirely upstaged by her husband, who becomes the recipient of the dream ('I dreamed I met a Galilean').

Pilate Washes His Hands (27:24)

The Ethiopic canonization of Pontius Pilate reflects a positive assessment of his character, which several modern scholars also find reflected in Matthew's text (e.g. Gundry 1994: 562). The interpretation of the handwashing plays a crucial role here. By performing a Jewish ritual (Deut 21:1–9) and declaring himself 'innocent' of Christ's blood, Pilate arguably functions as a positive foil, not only to the chief priests and elders (27:20) but now also to 'the whole people' (27:25). In the words of the *Gospel of Nicodemus*, by performing this Jewish act Pilate is 'circumcised in heart' (*Gos. Nic.* 12; Elliott 1993: 178).

This contrast is heightened in the second-century *Gospel of Peter*, which emphasizes that 'of the Jews none washed their hands, neither Herod nor any of his judges' (*Gos. Pet.* 1.1; Elliott 1993: 154). Hilary views Pilate as a positive

Figure 16 Alphonse François. *The Dream of Pilate's Wife*. c. 1879. Engraving after Gustave Doré. Source: Photo from Library of Congress, Prints & Photographs Division, LC-DIG-pga-01296.

symbol of the pagans, while Jerome asserts that Pilate's handwashing cleanses the work of the Gentiles, estranging them from 'the impiety of the Jews' (Jerome 2008: 312). Tertullian, anticipating the Ethiopic veneration of Pilate, even has him become a Christian (*Apol.* 21). In the (probably eastern) *Paradosis Pilati*, Pilate confesses his innocence before the Emperor Tiberius, before being beheaded. His dying words are those of a Christian martyr, whose prayer is subsequently heard when an angel receives his head:

> You know that I acted in ignorance. Therefore do not destroy me because of this sin, but pardon me, Lord, and your servant Procla, who stands with me in this hour of my death, whom you taught to prophesy that you must be nailed to the cross. (*Paradosis Pilati* 9; Elliott 1993: 210–211)

By contrast, the Jewish leadership is increasingly demonized, reflecting the changed context within which the originally Jewish-Christian Matthew is being read, by exclusively Gentile-Christian audiences. The *Acts of Thaddaeus* (seventh to tenth century) removes all responsibility from the Romans, even to the extent of having the chief priests carrying out the (Roman) punishment of crucifixion.

The developing anti-Jewish sentiment is most immediately felt in drama and in visual art, where Jewish bystanders are sometimes depicted using crudely anti-Semitic caricature. In Martin Schongauer's late fifteenth-century engraving *Christ Before Pilate*, their grotesque faces contrast not only with the serenity of the Roman Pilate, his servant, and his guards, but with the beauty of the Jewish Christ (Figure 17).

Yet it is far from clear that Matthew lets Pilate off so lightly. Readers both ancient and modern (e.g. Stock 1994: 421; Carter 2000: 524; Callon 2006)

Figure 17 Martin Schongauer (1450–1491). *Christ Before Pilate*. c. 1480. Engraving. Gift of W.G. Russell Allen, National Gallery of Art, Washington, DC. Source: Photo courtesy of National Gallery of Art, Washington.

regard his handwashing as a cynical act. For Ambrose, Pilate is a judge who condemns the innocent (in van der Bergh 2012: 79), while Theophylact accuses him of duplicity, washing his hands 'as if to show that he was clean of defilement' while entertaining evil thoughts (Theophylact 1992: 243). John Calvin observes dismissively that the 'childish performance he goes through is no lessening of his guilt' (Calvin 1972: III/187), while Mary Cornwallis calls out his action as 'a mere subterfuge, which could not cleanse his soul from the guilt it had incurred' (Cornwallis 1820: 93). In her 'Salve Deus Rex Judaeorum,' Aemilia Lanyer has the accusation come directly from Pilate's wife:

> Washing thy hands, thy conscience cannot cleare,
> But to all worlds this staine must needs appeare.
> (lines 935–936; Woods 1993: 91)

Even the dramatic and artistic tradition is multifaceted. Pilate's character varies hugely in the medieval English cycles: a philosophical if ultimately weak character in the Chester and *Ludus Coventriae* Plays, manifestly evil in the Towneley Play, or more complex, as in the York Cycle (Brawer 1972: 301–302). Visual artists sometimes depict Pilate turning his head away as he washes his hands, as if unable to look at Christ directly (e.g. Jacopo Tintoretto, *Christ Before* Pilate; 1566–1567; Scuola Grande di San Rocco, Venice). A very different Pilate is portrayed by the Polish artist Piotr Naliwajko. Painted in 1990, his Pilate, seated across from Jesus in shirt and tie, is in Luz's words 'the functionary, the bureaucrat, the citizen who "cannot help it" and who washes his hands in innocence' (Luz 2005a: 511).

'His Blood Be on Us and on Our Children' (27:25)

The response of 'all the people' to Pilate's declaration of innocence has echoed down the centuries, often with dire consequences for Jewish people. In context, Matthew's words almost certainly link the crucifixion of Jesus c. 30 CE to the Roman destruction of Jerusalem in 70 CE, i.e. to events witnessed by the children of those present at Christ's trial. Thus the evangelist looks back to limited judgment already taken place, not forward to ongoing responsibility by indeterminate generations. Moreover, his passion narrative has already linked the shedding of Christ's blood with the forgiveness of sins (26:28; Heil 1991b). Such contextualization, however, has rarely been evident in what this brief verse has effected.

Instead, it has often functioned as confirmation of, and sometimes justification for, the suffering of the Jewish people down through the centuries. In choosing Jesus Barabbas instead of Jesus the Christ, the Jewish people are choosing the devil (Jerome), or the Antichrist (Hilary). The responsibility for the death of Christ holds for Jews universally, and until the end (Origen, reading 27:25 in light of 23:35–36). Jerome even links this passage to Isaiah 1:15, in which the Lord declares that he will not listen to his people, because their hands are full of blood (though Jerome ignores the following verses, which offer the hope that they can make themselves clean and pursue justice, Isa 1:16–18).

Similar examples can be adduced across the centuries, and across Christian denominations, often fueling accusations of ritual murder and blood-libel (see Michael 2006: 82–87). Aquinas asserts that 'in this way it came about that Christ's blood is demanded of them even to this day' (Aquinas 2013b: 431). The Geneva Bible's marginal note similarly asserts: 'This curse taketh place to this day.' In a sermon preached on the radio for Good Friday in 1930, the German theologian Paul Althaus, professor at the University of Erlangen, espouses a view not dissimilar to Origen's and Jerome's:

> Until the end of history the terrible word of an unsuspecting realization [looms] over Israel like a thunderstorm: 'His blood come over us and over our children.' (in Probst 2012: 32)

Although there is some nuance in Althaus's sermon (it is the 'rebel-blood of all mankind' that revolts against Christ), it is not clear that this would have been detected by radio audiences in 1930s Germany.

Nonetheless, one occasionally hears an alternative, ameliorating voice. John Chrysostom finds evidence from the mass conversions in the early history of the Jerusalem church, and from the conversion of Saul, that the merciful God refused to confirm the people's acceptance of blood guilt:

> Nevertheless, the lover of man, though they acted with so much madness, both against themselves, and against their children, so far from confirming their sentence upon their children, confirmed it not even on them, but from the one and from the other received those that repented, and counts them worthy of good things beyond number. (*Homily on Matthew* 86.2; *NPNF* 1st series, 10:513)

Aquinas's lecture on this passage also hints at the wider narrative thread of Christ's redeeming blood. Having first cited Genesis 4:10 about Abel's blood crying out for vengeance, he then quotes Hebrews 12:24, which speaks about Christ's blood being more efficacious than that of Abel. The precise theological implications, however, are not spelled out. In the sixteenth century, Erasmus seeks to balance 27:25 with Christ's mercy and offer of forgiveness of sins, noting that many in the crowds later 'adored the cross of Christ': 'Christ, however, more merciful to them than they were to themselves, refused no one forgiveness, provided each repented' (Erasmus 2008: 367). Erasmus's focus here is specifically on Jesus' generation, and their children. He says nothing explicitly about ongoing bloodguilt or need for later generations of Jews to repent of the deeds of their first-century ancestors.

Theophylact partly anticipates modern scholarship by suggesting a particular fulfillment of this verse in the Roman destruction of Jerusalem (a connection already made by Origen). Yet even for him, this does not put an end to matters: 'But even to this day, the Jews, who are children of those who slew the Lord, have His blood upon them' (Theophylact 1992: 243). In the early nineteenth century, Mary Cornwallis is less equivocal when she links 'His blood be on us and on our children' with 'the signal retaliation' when Titus crucified many after Jerusalem's capture (Cornwallis 1820: 93). For David Friedrich Strauss, historical criticism moves in a different direction, exposing this verse as unhistorical Christian fiction (see Luz 2005a: 507).

An alternative line of reception is to locate responsibility for the death of Christ, not primarily with those historically involved, still less with millions of subsequent Jewish generations far removed from those events, but with human sinners, especially Christian sinners. The Catechism of the Council of Trent summarizes:

> This guilt seems more enormous in us than in the Jews, since according to the testimony of the same Apostle: *If they had known it, they would never have crucified the Lord of glory* (I Cor.ii. 8); while we, on the contrary, professing to know Him, yet denying Him by our actions, seem in some sort to lay violent hands on him. (*Catechism of Trent*, Part I, Article IV; McHugh and Callan 1972: 57)

This is reiterated in the 1965 decree of the Second Vatican Council, *Nostra Aetate*, prefaced by a clear rejection of the 'blood-guilt' tradition and a denunciation of anti-Semitism:

> True, the Jewish authorities and those who followed their lead pressed for the death of Christ; still, what happened in His passion cannot be charged against all the Jews, without distinction, then alive, nor against the Jews of today. Although the Church is the new people of God, the Jews should not be presented as rejected or accursed by God, as if this followed from the Holy Scriptures. All should see to it, then, that in catechetical work or in the preaching of the word of God they do not teach anything that does not conform to the truth of the Gospel and the spirit of Christ. Furthermore, in her rejection of every persecution against any man, the Church, mindful of the patrimony she shares with the Jews and moved not by political reasons but by the Gospel's spiritual love, decries hatred, persecutions, displays of anti-Semitism, directed against Jews at any time and by anyone. (*Nostra Aetate* 4)[3]

3 http://www.vatican.va/archive/hist_councils/ii_vatican_council/documents/vat-ii_decl_19651028_nostra-aetate_en.html.

The responsibility of sinners has also entered deeply into the Christian psyche through dramatic reenactment (e.g. playing the role of the crowds exclaiming 'Crucify him!' in liturgical reading or in passion plays) and hymnody. A potent example of the latter is the sixteenth-century German hymn:

> Ah twas our great sins and serious transgressions
> Nailed Christ, the true son of God to the Cross
> For this, let us not sorely scold poor Judas
> Not the company of Jews; the guilt is ours!
> (in Klassen 1996: 21)

The Crucifixion of the Messiah (27:32–56)

Closely following Mark (Mark 15:21–41), Matthew briefly describes the journey to the place of execution, followed by the crucifixion and death in more detail. Slight changes in wording heighten the element of scriptural fulfillment, while the mocking 'if you are the Son of God' (27:40) links this event with Jesus' temptation in the wilderness, where the devil twice addressed him in these terms (4:3, 6). In a profound sense, as the title of the 1955 Greek novel by Nikos Kazantzakis suggests, the passion is *The Last Temptation of Christ.*

The brief appearance of Simon of Cyrene (27:32) has fascinated many. The Valentinian Basilides suggested that Christ and Simon exchanged forms, such that it was the latter rather than a heavenly being who died on the cross (in Irenaeus, *Adv. Haer.* 1.24.4). But most interpreters are more interested in Simon's action of taking up the cross (see 16:24). Thus he is widely regarded as an example of discipleship (e.g. Origen; Aquinas). More specifically, he is viewed as another figure of Gentile faith (Leo the Great, *Sermon* 46.5), despite the fact that his name suggests he was a North African Jew visiting Jerusalem (Maldonado). Hilary goes so far as to claim that Simon did what the Jews were unworthy to do. Jerome also asserts his Gentile status, though without Hilary's anti-Jewish sentiments. Others draw significance from the etymology of his name (Simon means 'obedient': Theophylact; Aquinas).

Johann Albrecht Bengel reiterates Simon's outsider status, though distinguishing him from the Roman soldiers no less than the Jewish crowds: 'There was neither Jew nor Roman who was willing to bear the burden of the cross.' He then develops an additional motif: Simon as a type of those who shoulder the burden of others. Since the crucifixion there have been many other 'Simons' willing to assist others, even 'in the remotest regions' (Bengel 1971: 304). Indeed, the Cyrenian has given his name to charitable organizations, such as the Simon Community and the Cyrenians, working with homeless people in Britain and Ireland.

Unusual is Gregory the Great, who emphasizes that Simon was 'compelled' to carry Christ's cross rather than embracing it willingly (DelCogliano 2011). Therefore he is an example of hypocritical disciples, who perform external actions without the appropriate interior intention (*Moralia* 8.44; *Homilies on the Gospels* 32). Gregory is followed by Paschasius Radbertus, and Bernard of Clairvaux, who draws the following tropological meaning from the character of Simon in a sermon for the feast of St. Benedict:

> Trees that bear fruit but not their own are hypocrites, carrying along with Simon of Cyrene a cross that is not their own. Since they lack a religious intention, they are compelled, and they are forced to do what they do not love by love of the glory they desire. (*Sermo in natali sancti Benedicti* 6 in DelCogliano 2011: 324)

Simon's African origins are often forgotten in discussions of his significance. In her 1901 poem 'Simon's Countrymen,' the African-American abolitionist Frances Ellen Watkins Harper emphasizes them to indict white American Christians implicated in racial injustice:

> And yet within our favored land,
> Where Christian churches rise,
> The dark-browed sons of Africa
> Are hated and despised.
>
> Can they who speak of Christ as King,
> And glory in his name,
> Forget that Simon's countrymen
> Still bear a cross of shame?
> (Harper 1901: 58–59)

A century or so later, the African-American theologian JoAnne M. Terrell still needs to critique the decision to cast a white actor in the role of Simon in Mel Gibson's *The Passion of the Christ*: 'At worst this glaze-over of Simon's African identity says of and to black people that we have little or no historical investment in his or Jesus' story' (Terrell 2005: 62).

The place of crucifixion, Golgotha or 'the place of a skull' (27:33), invites symbolic interpretations. Its significance is explored by an anonymous early Christian Latin poet:

> There is a place, we believe, at the centre of the world,
> Called Golgotha by the Jews in their native tongue.
> Here was planted a tree cut from a barren stump.
> (*De Ligno Crucis*; White 2000: 137)

The poet apparently combines the Jewish view of Jerusalem as the navel of the earth with Isaiah's prophecy about a shoot from the stump of Jesse, understood as foretelling the coming Davidic Messiah (Isa 11:1). In his commentary, Jerome shows knowledge of an alternative theory, found already in Origen: that the place is so named because Adam had been buried there (also Chromatius of Aquileia; Theophylact). This is reflected in the sacred topography of the Church of the Holy Sepulchre in Jerusalem, where the Chapel of Adam is directly below Golgotha.

Though attractive, Jerome refutes this explanation (his Vulgate translation of Josh 14:15 located Adam's grave at Hebron). Rather, the place is so called because it is littered with the skulls of those who had been beheaded there (a more mundane explanation which is repeated by the *Glossa ordinaria* and Erasmus). Bengel suggests instead that the name was derived from the shape of the hill, skull-like. Popular history also has it that the identification of a skull-shaped hill outside the current walls of the Old City led the Victorian British general Charles Gordon to propose an alternative location both for Calvary ('Skull Hill') and for the tomb of Christ (the historical reality is more complex: see Frantzman and Kark 2008: 126–127).

Matthew's version of the *titulus* on the cross differs from Mark and Luke by explicitly naming the crucified: 'This is *Jesus*, the king of the Jews' (27:37; cf. Mark 15:26: Luke 23:38). Those who see the reading as significant refer back to the etymological explanation of this name at 1:21 ('for he will save his people from their sins'). Examples include Albert the Great, the Welsh Nonconformist Matthew Henry, and the English Baptist theologian John Gill, who comments thus on Matthew's *titulus* in his 1746–1748 *Exposition of the New Testament*:

> Jesus was his name, by which he was commonly called and known, and signifies a Saviour, as he is of all the elect of God; whom he saves from all their sins. (Gill in Ferda 2013: 225)

The plausibility of this reading is strengthened by the multiple references to 'save' in 27:38–44 (see Ferda 2013: 229–230).

The Dawn of a New Age (27:51–54)

Jesus' dying words are the opening verse of Psalm 22 ('My God, my God, why have you forsaken me?'), followed by a loud cry (27:46, 50; Mark 15:34, 37). But is Christ's question answered within the narrative? Mark hints at an affirmative answer: first by describing the tearing of the temple veil ('from top to bottom,' i.e. by heaven's action), then by the declaration of a Gentile centurion. In Matthew, God's response reverberates even more loudly. Besides the tearing of the veil, and the declaration (now by a group), there are additional apocalyptic motifs as heaven is temporarily laid open: an earthquake, the opening of the tombs, and the raising of departed saints (27:51b–53). For the medieval German mystic Hildegard of Bingen, the earthquake is the natural world's response to the shedding of Christ's innocent blood, to which heaven replies:

> Blood that bled into a cry!
> The elements
> felt its touch and trembled,
> heaven heard their woe.
> O life-blood of the maker,
> scarlet music, salve our wounds.
> ('Antiphon for the Redeemer'; Atwan,
> Dardess, and Rosenthal 1998: 494)

There are diverse interpretations in the early church regarding the temple veil (de Jonge 1986; Gurtner 2006: 105–111). Several attribute its tearing to an angel living in the temple (e.g. Melito of Sardis, *Peri Pascha* 98; Pseudo-Cyprian, *Adv. Iud.* 4) or the Spirit departing (e.g. *T. Ben.* 9; *Did. apost.* 23; Tertullian, *Adv. Iud.* 13.15). The angelic tradition is preserved in the *Transitus Mariae*, which recounts how the women ministering in the temple sought refuge in the holy of holies, as a response to the darkness surrounding the crucifixion:

> There they see an angel come down with a sword to rend the veil in two and hear a loud voice uttering woe against Jerusalem for killing the prophets. When they see the angel of the altar fly up into the altar canopy with the angel of the sword, they know 'that God has left His people.' (*Transitus Mariae* 10 in Brown 1994: 1115, n. 41)

Alternatively, the tearing is as if the temple itself were lamenting (Pseudo-Clementine *Recog.* 1.41.3).

The earthquake is a favorite of film directors, and required particular special effects in Cecil B. DeMille's 1927 *The King of Kings*. In art, it is effectively portrayed by Jacques Tissot in *Le tremblement de terre* (1886–1894; Brooklyn Museum, New York). Viewed from a low point behind Christ's cross, cracks are beginning to appear in the surrounding rocks, while the women and the centurion prostrate themselves on the ground, ostensibly out of awe and veneration.

Given that the veil restricted visibility in the actual temple, it is frequently understood figuratively. For Origen, the curtain obscured the view from the Court of the Gentiles. Hence its tearing allowed the Gentiles to see holy things, which in turn 'makes symbolically clear that the hidden things of the law were revealed in Christ, through his suffering' (*Frag. on Matt.* 560 in de Jonge 1986: 77). Patristic and medieval authors regular move from the literal to the figurative in explaining other elements of this passage. Origen continues his theme of biblical hermeneutics in interpreting the splitting rocks. They signify the Law and the prophets, rent so that their spiritual mysteries might be made clear. For Theophylact, the rocks represent the stony hearts of the Gentiles, now open to the truth. This idea of moral change is tied by Jerome to the earthquake and the opening of the tombs. These symbolize the transformation of believers, leaving their tomb-like existence behind through conversion. The entry of the saints into the 'holy city' is understood by Theophylact to refer to those dead to sin rising to the heavenly Jerusalem (both Jerome and Aquinas are ambivalent as to whether the terrestrial or the celestial city is meant; Maldonado thinks the former). While keeping the passage grounded in the literal sense (Christ's death has real and immediate effects), Aquinas finds in the opening graves a dramatic symbol of Christ's bursting the bonds of death.

The Harrowing of Hell (27:52–53)

Matthew's skeletal description of opening graves and resurrected saints echoes several earlier texts, including Ezekiel 37:12–13, Zechariah 14:4–5, Isaiah 52:1–2 (and its Targumic expansion: Wardle 2016), and *1 En.* 93:6 (Troxel 2002). It is one key ingredient (along with Eph 4:8–10, 1 Pet 3:18b–20; 4:6, and the *Gospel of Nicodemus*) in a developing tradition about Christ's Descent into Hades or Hell, an article of faith found in the Apostles' Creed. It is also referred to in the West as the Harrowing (i.e. plundering) of Hell, a title found in the homilies of the tenth-century Anglo-Saxon monk Ælfric of Eynsham, and the Descent into Limbo, specifically the 'Limbo of the Fathers,' that section of the underworld occupied by righteous Old Testament patriarchs and prophets. As a vivid mythological description of the effects of Christ's saving death 'from the inside,' it has produced rich receptions in popular devotion, drama, hymnody, and visual art, in both East and West (see MacCulloch 1930; Kartsonis 1986; Tamburr 2007; Paulsen, Cook, and Christensen 2010). In the medieval western church, the Harrowing of Hell was particularly associated with ceremonies surrounding the Easter sepulcher (Young 1933: I/149–177).

Matthew has contributed the conviction that some of the departed saints were raised as a consequence of Christ's death, as well as the uncertainty as when precisely they emerged from their graves, and how this relates to Christ's resurrection on the third day. Both issues are debated by commentators, many of whom assume a descent to the underworld at some point between Christ dying and his emerging from the tomb. The term 'saints' or 'holy ones' suggests deceased Israelites, although Clement of Alexandria maintains that 'many' points to Christ preaching both to Jews and Gentiles in Hades (*Strom.* 6.6).

Others are more specific. They are the prophets (Ign., *Magn.* 9), an interpretation suggesting an intratextual allusion to 23:29–36 (Herzer 2012). Or they are the saints from all the tribes of Israel, 'who died either long before the birth of Christ, or not much after' (Bengel 1971: 307; see John 11:25). Bengel is keen to include suffering Job among them, given the addition to the end of the biblical Book of Job in the LXX and Theodotion: 'But it is written that he shall rise again with those whom the Lord raises' (Bengel 1971: 307). According to the Spanish Jesuit Francisco Suarez, one of those to emerge from the tombs is Joseph, the now-departed husband of Mary (in Lapide 1890: I/13).

Hints of the Descent into Hades are found in a wide variety of early Christian texts (e.g. *Od. Sol.* 42.11–20; *Ep. apost.* 27; *Gos. Bart.* 1) and early Christian commentators (e.g. Melito of Sardis, *Peri Pascha* 101–102; Clement of Alexandria, *Strom.* 6.6; Origen, *Cels.* 2.43; Cyril of Jerusalem, *Catech.* 4.11). The most developed narrative appears in the later part of the apocryphal *Gospel of Nicodemus*, known as *Christ's Descent into Hell.* The description is attributed to the two sons of Simeon (Luke 2:25), identified in the Latin versions as Karinus and Leucius, who are among the 'saints' raised at Christ's death (27:53). The dramatic arrival of Christ, illuminating the dark gloom of the underworld, is anticipated by a succession of Old Testament figures (e.g. Adam's son Seth, Isaiah, King David, John the Baptist), recounting their own prophecies of Christ's coming. The climax is announced by a voice like thunder, intoning words from Psalm 24:7 ('Lift up your gates, O rulers, and be lifted up, O everlasting doors, and the King of Glory shall come in'). Personified Hades has his demons bolt the gates in vain, as they burst open of themselves to allow Christ to enter. Christ then begins the process of rescuing the righteous dead, beginning with Adam:

> While Hades was thus speaking with Satan, the King of Glory stretched out his right hand, and took hold of our forefather Adam and raised him up. Then he turned to the rest and said, 'Come with me, all you who have died through the tree which this man touched. For behold, I raise you all up again through the tree of the cross.' With that he sent them all out. And our forefather Adam was seen to be full of joy, and said, 'I give thanks to your majesty, O Lord, because you have brought me up from the lowest Hades.' Likewise all the prophets and the saints said, 'We give you thanks, O Christ, Saviour of the world, because you have brought up our life from destruction.' (Greek version of *Christ's Descent into Hell* 8; Elliott 1993: 189)

Byzantine and Latin Christianity have their separate artistic traditions. In the East, the focus is on the Resurrection, the *Anastasis* (Kartsonis 1986). In the latest form of this iconographical tradition, the risen Christ pulls both Adam and Eve out from their graves, the gates of Hades trampled under his feet, as in the fourteenth-century fresco in the Chora Church, Istanbul (Harries 2004: 80–82). Its meaning is eloquently expressed in the Orthodox Vespers for Holy Saturday:

> Today Hell groans and cries out:
> My power has been destroyed.
> I received a mortal man
> As one of the dead.
> But I am completely unable to keep him prisoner,
> And with him I shall lose all my subjects.
> I held in my power
> The dead of all the ages.
> But look, he is raising them all.
> (in Harries 2004: 40)

Western art tends to focus on the Descent itself. Eleventh-century English examples depict a gigantic Christ, trampling the devil as he pulls Adam and Eve out from the mouth of Hades (e.g. *The Harrowing of Hell*, c. 1050; stone relief, Bristol Cathedral), or bending down to reach them (e.g. *The Harrowing of Hell*, c. 1050; Cotton Psalter, MS BL Cotton Tiberius C. VI, fol. 14r: see Tamburr 2007: figs. 2 and 3). It is also a popular scene in medieval and Renaissance passion and resurrection sequences. *Christ in Limbo*, painted c. 1490 by the fifteenth-century Sienese artist Benvenuto di Giovanni (Figure 18), now in the National Gallery of Art, Washington, DC, was probably part of a predella for his altarpiece of the Ascension, commissioned for the Monastery of Sant'Eugenio near Siena. Four other predella panels are also in Washington (*The Agony in the Garden*; *Christ Carrying the Cross*; *The Crucifixion*; *The Resurrection*); the main *Ascension* panel is in the Pinacoteca Nazionale, Siena. The viewer witnesses the scene from behind Christ, looking into the Limbo of the Fathers at the moment after the gates have been burst open (one of which now squashes the devil on the ground). The righteous saints are crowded expectantly at the entrance, waiting to be led out. Christ grasps Adam, standing next to Eve, with his left hand, and an unidentified figure, standing next to John the Baptist, with his right.

Despite its popularity, the Descent into Hell was not without its critics. It was potentially problematic for the Reformers, given its lack of explicit support in scripture, and its use to promote the existence of limbo and purgatory. Luther maintained a literal descent as an article of the Creed, though asserted that it was not a bodily descent, as Christ's corpse remained in the tomb for three days. Moreover, he personalized it, allowing it to refer to the salvation of the sinner:

> He has snatched us, poor lost creatures, from the jaws of hell, won us, made us free, and restored us to the Father's favor and grace. He has taken us as his own, under his protection, in order that he may rule us by his righteousness, wisdom, power, life, and blessedness. (*Large Catechism* in Tamburr 2007: 171)

FIGURE 18 Benvenuto di Giovanni (1436–1517). *Christ in Limbo*. c. 1491. Tempera on panel; 421 × 466 mm. Samuel H. Kress Collection, National Gallery of Art, Washington, DC. Source: Photo courtesy of National Gallery of Art, Washington.

Calvin, by contrast, interpreted the descent psychologically, not locally, as part of Christ's experience of the fearful pains of death (Tamburr 2007: 172–173). Yet it was not only sixteenth-century Protestants who were anxious about its implications. In the wake of the Council of Trent, the *Gospel of Nicodemus* was placed on the 1564 Index of Forbidden Books, while Trent's Catechism located the Descent theologically with the Resurrection (see Tamburr 2007: 175–178).

The Burial (27:57–66)

Matthew's account of the burial seeks to distance Joseph of Arimathea from the Jewish authorities. No longer identified as a member of the council (cf. Mark 15:43), he is explicitly identified as 'discipled' to Jesus (27:57). Moreover, he is a 'rich man,' whose veneration for Jesus leads him to place his corpse in his own new tomb (27:60). Modern scholars often link Joseph's wealth to Isaiah 53:9

('They made his grave with the wicked, and his tomb with the rich,' NRSV). Thomas Aquinas suggests a different intertextual connection, to Sirach 31:8 ('blessed is the rich man who is found without blemish: and who has not gone after gold, nor put his trust in money nor in treasures,' Aquinas 2013b: 450). This text is arguably more appropriate to Matthew's definition of discipleship (see e.g. 6:19–21; 13:44; 19:16–30).

The reception history of this rich man is, appropriately, also very rich, with the inevitable textual 'gap-filling' resulting in a more complete biography (see Lyons 2014). The *Gospel of Peter* hints, arguably on the basis of Matthew's claim that Joseph was a disciple (also John 19:38), of Joseph's involvement in Jesus' public ministry:

> And the Jews rejoiced and gave his body to Joseph that he might bury it since he had seen all the good deeds that he (Jesus) had done. (*Gos. Pet.* 23; Elliott 1993: 155)

The earlier part of the *Gospel of Nicodemus* (the so-called *Acts of Pilate*) continues Joseph's story post-Easter, including an appearance to him by the risen Lord (*Acts of Pilate* 15.6). Medieval English tradition claims that he traveled to England, and visited the site of Glastonbury (Lyons 2014: 72–104), a tradition reflected in William Blake's 1773 engraving *Joseph of Arimathea Among the Rocks of Albion*.

Matthew associates two other sets of characters with the burial, both of whom will provide a crucial link to the empty tomb: the women and the guards. Matthew pairs Mary Magdalene with 'the other Mary,' previously identified as the mother of James and Joseph (27:56). Harmonization with John 19:25–27 frequently leads to the identification of 'the other Mary' with the mother of Jesus (two of Jesus' brothers are named James and Joseph at 13:55). Thus for John Chrysostom, it is '[h]is mother, for she is called the mother of James'; similarly, for Theophylact, it is 'the Theotokos,' James and Joses being sons of Joseph by his previous marriage. Juan de Maldonado identifies her instead as the mother's sister, Mary the wife of Clopas/Cleophas (John 19:25).

The harmonization is generally present in artistic representations of the deposition and burial. In Rogier van der Weyden's *Descent from the Cross* (c. 1435; Museo del Prado, Madrid), the corpse of Jesus is framed on the left by his swooning mother, supported by the beloved disciple and two of her sisters, Mary of Clopas and Mary Salome (John 19:25–27; Mark 15:40), and on the right by Mary Magdalene, a servant, and Nicodemus (John 19:39), who holds Christ's feet. The central role is given to the richly dressed Joseph of Arimathea, supporting Christ's upper body and wrapping it in a burial shroud (Lyons 2014: 50–55).

The guard for the tomb, provided by Pilate at the request of the chief priests and Pharisees (27:62–66), is unknown to the other Gospels. Modern scholars, following the German Deist Hermann Samuel Reimarus (Reimarus 1985: 153–171), often treat this as an unhistorical motif, functioning apologetically against rival claims that Jesus' disciples stole the body: 'Surely one of the most extravagant of inventions' (Beare 1981: 539; on the motif, see Brown 1994: 1310–1313). Older commentators, by contrast, assume its historicity.

The burial itself concludes the story for those skeptical about the resurrection of Jesus. It is the last scene in Thomas Jefferson's *The Life and Morals of Jesus of Nazareth*. Yet both the women and the guard point to a continuation of the story, directing the reader forward to the final section of the Gospel. Moreover, many pre-critical interpreters also understand the story as working at a deeper level. That Joseph's is a 'new' tomb suggests to Jerome that it is a figure of Mary's virginal womb. This pairing is also found in the seventeenth-century English metaphysical poet Richard Crashaw:

> How Life and Death in Thee
> Agree!
> Thou had'st a virgin wombe
> And Tombe
> A Joseph did betroth
> Them both.
> (in Davies and Allison 1997: 656)

Hilary interprets the tomb differently. Given that it is hewn out of rock, it symbolizes the apostolic teaching whereby Christ is received by stony pagan hearts, 'hewn out by the labor of teaching' (Hilary of Poitiers 2012: 292).

Matthew 28

Ancient Literary Context

All four Gospels contain a narrative in which Jesus' tomb is discovered empty by female followers on the third day (28:1–8; Mark 16:1–8; Luke 24:11–12; John 20:1–13). Despite this shared tradition, however, there are noteworthy disagreements in detail: the timing and reason for the visit; the number of women (ranging from one in John to a group of at least five according to Luke 24:10); the number and identity of the characters they encounter; what they were told

Matthew Through the Centuries, First Edition. Ian Boxall.

to do. Matthew, Luke, and John (together with the various additional endings of Mark) also contain resurrection appearance narratives, associated with different geographical locations, whether the Jerusalem area (Luke 24; John 20) or Galilee (Matthew 28; John 21). Both sets of narratives represent a complex interweaving of historical memory, theological reflection, and early Christian belief in the ongoing presence of the risen Lord in communal worship (see, e.g. Heil 1991a: 91–112; Moloney 2013).

Matthew's narrative falls into three parts (vv. 1–10, vv. 11–15, and vv. 16–20). The first describes the discovery of the empty tomb by the two women mentioned at the burial (Mary Magdalene and 'the other Mary'), culminating in a brief appearance of the risen Jesus as they leave the tomb (28:9–10). As elsewhere in this apocalyptic Gospel, this narrative is marked by dramatic heavenly unveiling, as an angel of the Lord descends to roll back the stone, accompanied by an earthquake (28:2). The guards also become unwitting witnesses to the apocalyptic unveiling, their 'shaking' (28:4) paralleling the seismic activity provoked by the angel's descent. The second section focuses renewed attention on these guards, who become instruments of a great deception instigated by the chief priests, seeking to undermine the resurrection story by a rival story of grave-robbery involving Jesus' disciples (28:13). The bribing of the soldiers with silver parallels the silver coins paid to Judas Iscariot at the beginning of the passion story (26:14–16). The climactic section is a resurrection appearance to the 'eleven disciples' (the Twelve minus Judas Iscariot) on a mountain in Galilee. It is striking for its rehabilitation of the disciples, some of whom still doubt (28:17), an extension of the mission from 'the lost sheep of the house of Israel' to 'all the nations' (28:19a), and a distinctive triadic formula for baptism (28:19b). As if book-ending the whole Gospel, the final promise that 'I am with you all the days' (28:20) picks up on the interpretation of Immanuel as 'God-with-us' at the beginning of Matthew's story (1:23).

The Interpretations

The Discovery of the Tomb (28:1–8)

It has become customary to speak of 28:1 as the beginning of Matthew's resurrection narrative. However, given the movement from the place of crucifixion to the tomb a few verses earlier at 27:57, the Old Greek Divisions (found in Codex Alexandrinus), make the break at that point. Thus the burial and the resurrection are more closely connected (Edwards 2010: 424).

Matthew's time reference ('Late on the sabbath, at the dawning into the first day of the week,' 28:1) is puzzling. While the other evangelists are clear that the women visited the tomb early on Sunday morning (Mark 16:2; Luke 24:1; John 20:1), Matthew's complex wording might suggest Saturday evening instead. Jerome understands it in this way, though he is keen to refute claims of a discrepancy between the evangelists. The different time references can be reconciled, he argues, on the basis of the women's piety: they were returning to the tomb frequently during the night. Juan de Maldonado concludes instead that Matthew, like the other evangelists, referred to the early morning. Thomas Aquinas finds an additional symbolic dimension: Matthew's 'towards the dawning' points to the mystery of the resurrection, illuminating the darkness of night.

Despite Matthew's apocalyptic features (the earthquake; the descent of 'an angel of the Lord' with an appearance 'like lightning'; the angelic rolling away of the stone), he shares the reserve of the other evangelists concerning the resurrection event itself. It is described allusively, by its effects in this world. By contrast, the *Gospel of Peter* exhibits no such reservations. The knowledge of Matthew, perhaps via liturgical reading (Brown 1994: 1334–1335; Luz 2005a: 303), is evident in the guards as witnesses, and the descent of the angel to the tomb. Prior to the angel's descent, however, the *Gospel of Peter* describes the resurrection itself, witnessed publicly by the guards and the Jewish elders, as the risen Christ emerges from the tomb, accompanied by two angelic figures and followed by his victorious cross:

> Now in the night in which the Lord's day dawned, when the soldiers were keeping guard, two by two in each watch, there was a loud voice in heaven, and they saw the heavens open and two men come down from there in great brightness and draw near to the sepulchre. That stone which had been laid against the entrance to the sepulcher started of itself to roll and move sidewards, and the sepulchre was opened and both young men entered. When those soldiers saw this they awakened the centurion and the elders, for they also were there to mount guard. And while they were narrating what they had seen, they saw three men come out from the sepulchre, two of them supporting the other and a cross following them and the heads of the two reaching to heaven, but that of him who was being led reached beyond the heavens. And they heard a voice out of the heavens crying, 'Have you preached to those who sleep?,' and from the cross there was heard the answer, 'Yes.' Therefore the men decided among themselves to go and report these things to Pilate. And while they were still deliberating the heavens were again seen to open and a man descended and entered the tomb. (*Gos. Pet.* 9–11; Elliott 1993: 156–157)

The voice from the cross presupposes the Descent into Hades tradition, while the rolling of the stone 'by itself' opens the tomb for Christ and his companions to come out (in Matthew's briefer version, as Aquinas and Maldonado recognize, the angel rolls back the stone so that the women can enter).

The same tension between describing the resurrection directly and visualizing it more symbolically, or by allusion to its effects, is present in visual art (see e.g. Schiller 1986; Harries 2004; Luz 2011). Early examples convey Christ's resurrection by symbols, such as the victory wreath or garland crowning the cross (e.g. fourth-century sarcophagus from the Catacombs of Domitilla, Museo Pio Cristiano, Vatican) or the phoenix (e.g. sixth-century apse mosaic, SS. Cosmas and Damian, Rome). Alternatively, they allude to the resurrection through Old Testament types, such as Jonah (see 12:39–40; e.g. third-century fresco from the Catacomb of SS. Marcellinus and Peter, Rome). The depiction in the sixth-century East Syrian Rabbula Gospels follows Matthew's empty tomb narrative fairly closely (Figure 19). The Rabbula Gospels depict the scenes of crucifixion and resurrection on the same page, with the cross and empty tomb in perfect alignment, highlighting that death and resurrection are two sides of an integral whole. The artist also allows several moments from the narrative to be viewed synchronically. In the lower panel, the central image depicts the tomb (probably modeled on that in the Church of the Holy Sepulchre in Jerusalem), its doors blown open by the power of the resurrection, the guards lying on the ground 'like dead men' (28:4). The empty tomb is flanked on the left by the angel addressing the two women, and on the right by the encounter between the two women and the risen Christ. Harmonization with John 19 in the crucifixion scene means that 'the other Mary' at the tomb is clearly identified (as for Chrysostom and Theophylact) as the Mother of God, who stands with the beloved disciple to the left of the cross in the top panel.

The Byzantine tradition presents the resurrection in a more allusive way, the victorious Christ trampling the gates of hell, drawing Adam and Eve out from their tombs. Western artists of the later Middle Ages often return to Matthew's scene of the guards 'like dead men,' albeit responding not to the angel but to Christ himself as he rises from the tomb (e.g. Piero della Francesca, *The Resurrection*, 1460s, Museo Civico, Sansepolcro). Benvenuto di Giovanni's *Resurrection* panel (Figure 20) depicts the risen Christ standing outside the tomb, holding a victory banner, the guards lying at his feet. A single guard looks up in awe or terror. Yet Benvenuto retains some of the older ambiguity. The risen Christ remains larger than the other characters, pointing to his heavenly character. Moreover, it is not clear that the guard who looks up can see the rising Christ himself, or is simply responding to the evidence for the resurrection in the accompanying events. The visual similarity between the tomb and the entrance to Hades in Benvenuto's *Christ in Limbo* highlights the extent to which the guards now belong to the 'realm of the dead.'

FIGURE 19 *Crucifixion* and *The Women at the Tomb*, from the Rabbula Gospels. Zagba on the Euphrates, Syria, c. 586 CE. Ms. Plut. 1,56, f. 13r. Biblioteca Laurenziana. Source: Photo from Scala/Art Resource, NY.

The focus on external signs of the resurrection is much clearer in Pieter Brueghel the Elder's pastel *The Resurrection of Christ* (c. 1560; Museum Boijmans van Beuningen, Rotterdam). Though Brueghel depicts the risen Christ floating above the tomb, neither the women nor the guards look directly at him, but respond to the traces of the resurrection event provided by the angel

FIGURE 20 Benvenuto di Giovanni (1436–1517). *The Resurrection*. c. 1491. Tempera on panel; 421 × 474 mm. Samuel H. Kress Collection, National Gallery of Art, Washington, DC. Source: Photo courtesy of National Gallery of Art, Washington.

seated at the center: the rolled stone, the broken seal, the empty tomb, the angel's brightness. Christ himself, his risen glory shrouded by clouds, points the viewer to the sun as another witness to the resurrection (Melion 2017). The idea that the angel 'expresses the glory of the triumphant one' (Jerome 2008: 325) is a common understanding.

Other details of Matthew's narrative also provoke interest. For Hilary, the earthquake symbolizes the power of the resurrection, destroying the sting of death. Its function on a literal level is variously explained. It may serve to wake up the women who might have fallen asleep during the night (Chrysostom), or to ensure that the guards too would witness the events (Theophylact; Euthymius Zigabenus), or to convince both that those they encountered at the tomb were angels, given that earthquakes symbolize the divine presence (Maldonado). Aquinas draws a mystical meaning from the fact that Matthew describes two earthquakes, one at the death and the other at the tomb. The first signifies the shaking of human hearts, freed from sin by the death of Christ. The second symbolizes the glory brought by the resurrection, which prefigures the trembling of the earth at the final resurrection.

Grasping Christ's Feet (28:9–10)

The tendency to harmonize leads the author of *The Golden Legend* to identify 10 Gospel resurrection appearances, which it seeks to organize chronologically. The appearance to the two women as they leave the tomb is the second, differentiated from John's story about Mary Magdalene as the first (John 20:1–18; Mark 16:9). In addition, the *Golden Legend* adds a further three, not attested in the Gospels: to James (1 Cor 15:7), to Joseph of Arimathea (*Gospel of Nicodemus*), and to Christ's mother, which 'is believed to have taken place before all the others' (Jacobus da Voragine 1993: I/221).

That the women grasp Jesus' feet has been variously understood (see Allison 2005: 107–116). Peter Chrysologus emphasizes the women's joy in encountering the risen Lord (*Sermon* 76.3), while Hippolytus finds an intertextual echo of the Song of Songs, placing the two women in the role of the bride: 'They held him by the feet, saying, "I will not leave you until I bring you into my heart"' (*Comm. Cant.* 15 in Allison 2005: 109). Alternatively, their grasping combined with prostration suggests submission, or specifically an act of reverence or veneration (e.g. Jerome; Theophylact). The thirteenth-century Dominican Albert the Great brings this verse into dialogue with Psalm 132 ('let us worship at his footstool,' Ps 132:7b NRSV), and the prostration of the Magi (2:11), to find an act of worship (Allison 2005: 109).

Theophylact also points to an alternative and popular proposal, perhaps informed by the widespread observation that ghosts often lack feet: 'Some say that they grasped His feet purposely to ascertain if He had truly risen, and was not only an apparition or a spirit' (Theophylact 1992: 255; see e.g. Origen; Rabanus Maurus; *Glossa ordinaria*; Dionysius bar-Salibi; Euthymius Zigabenus; for other references, see Allison 2005: 110, n. 13). Put positively, as by John Chrysostom, the ability to touch provides 'an infallible proof, and full assurance of the resurrection.' Offering his congregation the possibility of actualizing the women's experience, Chrysostom makes a connection with taking hold of the risen Lord in the Eucharist:

> Perchance some one of you would wish to be like them, to hold the feet of Jesus; ye can even now, and not His feet and His hands only, but even lay hold on that sacred head, receiving the awful mysteries with a pure conscience. (*Homily on Matthew* 89.3; *NPNF* 1st series, 10:527)

Bribing the Guards (28:11–15)

The story of the guards ends very differently from that of the women, despite both groups leaving the tomb to tell others a story about Christ's resurrection. Knowing the truth about why the tomb is empty, they go instead and circulate a falsehood, receiving money in return. Jerome, assuming that the bribe is drawn from the temple treasury, finds a moral lesson here against those who misappropriate church funds.

The majority of interpreters assume, surely correctly, that the claim that the disciples stole the body was the story circulating among Jews until Matthew's day (28:15). However, Juan de Maldonado ponders a different possibility: that the 'word' circulating was that soldiers had been bribed by the Jewish authorities, i.e. that 'the falsehood of the priests did not escape the knowledge of the Jews themselves' (Maldonado 1888: 2/631). Some post-Enlightenment interpreters have preferred the historicity of the priestly version, notably Hermann Samuel Reimarus:

> From these many contradictions we now see that the guard whom Matthew posted before the tomb will not bear investigation and cannot be accepted by a rational mind. Thus, these fancies that were intended to divert suspicion of fraud from Jesus' disciples on the contrary strengthened that suspicion. (Reimarus 1985: 171–172)

The didactic function of characters in the passion story, often aided through imagining their afterlives, has occasionally extended to the guards. The American poet Edwin Markham (1852–1940) hypothesizes about the impact on one of them, looking back through years of shame produced by his being so easily corrupted by money:

> Years have I wandered, carrying my shame;
> Now let the tooth of time eat out my name.
> For we, who all the wonder might have told,
> Kept silence, for our mouths were stopt with gold.
> ('A Guard at the Sepulcher'; Atwan,
> Dardess, and Rosenthal 1998: 543–544)

The Encounter on the Mountain (28:16–20)

The final scene (the eighth Gospel appearance according to *The Golden Legend*) looks back to Jesus' teaching ministry, and forward to the post-resurrection time of the church. Harmonization of the resurrection appearances provokes a question: why does this take place in Galilee, given that the risen Christ appeared first in Jerusalem? Aquinas draws together several patristic answers. First, a Galilean appearance emphasizes continuity with the public ministry: the risen one is the one who first ministered in Galilee. Second, the disciples were safer in Galilee than in Judea, the location of Jesus' arrest. Third, following Augustine, Aquinas interprets the name 'Galilee' as 'transmigration.' Thus this appearance marks the passing over to the Gentiles (Aquinas 2013b: 461).

The mountain's precise location is not stated, though one possible translation of 28:16 identifies it as the location of the Sermon on the Mount ('where Jesus gave them commands': Davies and Allison 1997: 681). A marginal gloss in MS 1424 (ninth or tenth century) identifies the mountain as Tabor, traditional site of the Transfiguration, as does the sixth-century *Topography of the Holy Land* by Theodosius, and a Georgian text from c. 600 (Hilhorst 2009: 330). The *Golden Legend*, which also makes the connection with Tabor, claims that this resurrection appearance symbolizes contemplatives, given that it was on this mountain that Christ appeared in heavenly glory. Alternatively, the mountain 'is not to be located on a map – it is the place of revelation' (Beare 1981: 544). In the Gnostic *Sophia of Jesus Christ*, which expands the scene into a revelatory dialogue between the Savior and his disciples (Luttikhuizen 1988; Falkenberg 2013), the mountain is called 'Divination and Joy.'

Uncertainty exists over who 'doubted' (28:17). Matthew's wording could refer to 'some' of the Eleven, all of them ('When they saw him, they worshiped, but they doubted,' NABRE), or some others. John Chrysostom assumes the former, as does Johann Albrecht Bengel, who finds their stumbling faith an asset to their future ministry: 'The slower they were to believe, the greater credit is due to them afterwards as witnesses' (Bengel 1971: 311). Theophylact considers two possibilities: first, that all the Eleven worshiped him, while the 'some' were some of the 70. Alternatively, it could be a reference to the fact that Thomas (John 20:24–29), or all of the Eleven (Luke 24:41), had previously doubted in Jerusalem.

The 'Great Commission' (28:19–20a)

Christ's charge to his disciples forms an important climax to this Gospel. The manuscript tradition is relatively stable over his words, although Eusebius of Caesarea knows a shorter form: 'Go, make disciples of all the nations in my name, teaching them to observe all that I have commanded you' (Conybeare 1901). The baptismal formula is also absent from the Hebrew Matthew preserved by the medieval Jewish author Shem-Tob, as is the charge to evangelize the Gentiles, the latter reflecting this text's Jewish-Christian theology: 'Go and (teach) them to carry out all the things which I have commanded you forever' (Howard 1995: 151).

This so-called 'Great Commission' (a title probably dating from the nineteenth century) has become 'the foundational text of the modern missionary movement,' especially among Protestants (Cronshaw 2016: 110). Its influence is generally traced to the 1792 treatise by the Baptist missionary William Carey, *An Enquiry into the Obligations of Christians to Use Means for the Conversion of the Heathens* (see Parris 2015: 112–134). Carey's pamphlet challenges his fellow Protestants to embrace Christ's final charge to his apostles as addressed also to them:

> There seems also to be an opinion existing in the minds of some, that because the apostles were extraordinary officers and have no proper successors, and because many things which were right for them to do would be utterly unwarrantable for us, therefore it may not be immediately binding on us to execute the commission, though it was so upon them. (Carey 1891: 8)

Something of this reserve is found among early readers of Matthew, preoccupied with survival in the face of persecution, especially in the pre-Constantinian period, or defining and defending the doctrines of Christ and the Trinity (Parris 2015: 112–116). The commission to make disciples of all nations is often understood as a specific charge for the apostolic generation (e.g. Eusebius, *H.E.* 3.5.2). The ongoing growth of the church in the post-apostolic age occurs mainly through the attraction of Christian lives rather than through concerted evangelistic strategies (see Kreider 2016). Athanasius of Alexandria (c. 296–373) articulates well this conviction that the commission was fulfilled in the apostolic age:

> And then, from Dan to Beersheba was the Law proclaimed, and in Judaea only was God known; but now, unto all the earth has gone forth their voice, and all the earth has been filled with the knowledge of God, and the disciples have made disciples of all the nations. (*Discourses Against the Arians* 1.13; *NPNF* 2nd series, 4:341)

The apostolic success is understood as fulfillment of Old Testament prophecy.

Furthermore, the early emphasis is often theological rather than missiological. Irenaeus uses the baptismal formula (28:19b) to refute docetic claims that the heavenly Christ, rather than the Holy Spirit, descended upon Jesus at his baptism (*Adv. Haer.* 3.17.1). Tertullian appeals to the same passage against Monarchian denials that the Father and Son were distinct persons (*Adv. Prax.* 36). Basil the Great cites it against those who deny that the Holy Spirit should 'be ranked with the Father and Son, on account of the difference of His nature and the inferiority of His dignity' (*De Spiritu Sancto* 10.24; *NPNF* 2nd series, 8:16). Even later authors will look back to earlier debates: for Theophylact, this passage should shame both Arius (given that the Son shares the same name as the Father) and Sabellius (given that three distinct persons are mentioned). The Arians had previously used the passage to deny Christ's divinity, given that he had been 'given' all power and authority. In the nineteenth century, the

Methodist New Connexion theologian William Cooke can dismiss a Unitarian reading as implying that 'baptism is to be administered in the Name of the Father, and of a creature, and of an attribute,' which he refutes as against the plain, Trinitarian meaning of the text (in Larsen 2011: 95).

Unsurprisingly, the same passage becomes an important proof text for baptism. The *Didache* urges that baptism be administered 'in the name of the Father and of the Son and of the Holy Spirit,' preferably in running water (*Did.* 7.1; Holmes 2007: 355). The Trinitarian formula eventually becomes a requirement for sacramental validity in many churches, taking priority over alternative baptismal formulae (e.g. Acts 2:38; 8:16; Rom 6:3; Gal 3:27). At the Reformation, the Anabaptists appeal to its sequence (making disciples precedes baptizing) as an argument against infant baptism. Both magisterial Reformers and Roman Catholics are forced to respond. The Jesuit Juan de Maldonado denies that Christ forbids those who cannot be taught (i.e. babies) to be baptized, 'but that He only commands all who have been taught before to be baptised' (Maldonado 1888: 2/639).

There are a few examples of 28:19–20 being understood as a commission to ongoing missionary activity. Gregory the Great (c. 540–604) seems to be influenced by this passage in sending Augustine to England, and Gregory's influence persists throughout the Middle Ages (Parris 2015: 117–118). In the Middle Ages and especially the early modern period, Roman Catholics had highly developed missionary strategies, although other texts were often appealed to (notably Luke 14:23: 'Go out into the roads and lanes, and compel people to come in,' NRSV). The magisterial Reformers were more ambivalent as to whether the commission had been fulfilled by the apostles (e.g. Luther), or the responsibilities of the Apostolate continued (e.g. Calvin). By contrast, the Anabaptists enthusiastically embraced the commission as binding on all believers. It was also regularly cited by Puritan settlers in America (Clarke 2003: 252).

In the modern period, the 'Great Commission' has come under scrutiny, especially from postcolonial critics, who highlight its use in legitimating colonial expansion in distant lands (for differing assessments, especially of William Carey's role, see Dube 1998; Sugirtharajah 1998; Levine 2006; Bosch 2011: 57–84; Smith and Lalitha 2014; Chung 2015; Cronshaw 2016). Such concerns are anticipated to some degree by the sixteenth-century Catholic humanist Erasmus, whose paraphrase reminds his readers of the character of discipleship set out in Matthew as a whole, which should inform the subsequent making of other 'disciples':

> You will not claim them with weapons or by war, but by those same methods by which I gained this sovereignty for myself: by sacred teaching, by a life worthy of the gospel, by freely bestowing blessings, by patiently enduring wrongs. Go, therefore, as ambassadors, men of good faith, and, relying on me as your author, teach first the Jews, then those in neighbouring regions, and then all the peoples of the entire world. (Erasmus 2008: 377)

That the mission is directed toward *panta ta ethnē*, which could mean 'all the nations' or 'all the Gentiles,' has also had implications for Christian–Jewish relations. If one translates as 'all the Gentiles,' then does this mean that the Jewish people are no longer part of God's plan? If 'all the nations,' then does this require that Gentile Christians convert their Jewish brothers and sisters? Different answers have been given at different times. The 2015 statement of the Vatican's Commission for Religious Relations with the Jews, marking the fiftieth anniversary of *Nostra Aetate*, reads 'all the nations,' yet concludes that the distinctive place of the Jewish people requires that they be viewed differently vis-à-vis evangelization:

> In concrete terms this means that the Catholic Church neither conducts nor supports any specific institutional mission work directed towards Jews. While there is a principled rejection of an institutional Jewish mission, Christians are nonetheless called to bear witness to their faith in Jesus Christ also to Jews, although they should do so in a humble and sensitive manner, acknowledging that Jews are bearers of God's Word, and particularly in view of the great tragedy of the Shoah. (*The Gifts and the Calling of God Are Irrevocable* 40)[1]

A more positive rendering of 'all the Gentiles' is offered by the American Jewish New Testament scholar, Amy-Jill Levine:

> I read Matthew's Great Commission as emphasizing the evangelization of the Gentiles, not the Jews, and I read Paul as suggesting that the Jews obtain salvation not from human evangelistic efforts but from divine fiat (Rom 11). Both points might lead Christians inclined to target Jews for conversion to direct their attention elsewhere. (Levine 2006: 152)

Abiding Presence (28:20)

Differing theological presuppositions affect interpretation of Christ's parting words. For Augustine, Christ is speaking here about his divine presence (*Tractate on St. John* 60), although, as Maldonado later notes, this would be promising the disciples nothing that is not already given to all people and even inanimate objects. Or Christ is present in both his divinity and humanity (Chrysostom; Euthymius Zigabenus). John Calvin is concerned to avoid any suggestion that Christ's presence is corporeal:

---

1 http://www.vatican.va/roman_curia/pontifical_councils/chrstuni/relations-jews-docs/rc_pc_chrstuni_doc_20151210_ebraismo-nostra-aetate_en.html.

> The nature of the presence that the Lord promises His people must be understood spiritually. To help us, there is no need for Him to come down from heaven, since the grace of His Spirit may help us, as by a hand stretched out from heaven. (Calvin 1972: III/255)

This appeal to the Holy Spirit is a common one, albeit understood with varying nuances. Calvin's Catholic contemporary Erasmus paraphrases in such a way as to highlight Christ's more powerful presence: 'For when I have ceased to be with you in body, then I will be with you more effectively by my Spirit' (Erasmus 2008: 380).

The abiding presence is sometimes also linked to the Eucharist, perhaps most famously in 'Alleluia! Sing to Jesus!' by the Anglican hymn-writer William Chatterton Dix (1837–1898), composed as a communion hymn for Ascension Day (harmonizing Matt 28:20 with Acts 1):

> Alleluia! Not as orphans
> are we left in sorrow now;
> Alleluia! He is near us;
> faith believes nor questions how.
> Though the cloud from sight received him
> when the forty days were o'er,
> shall our hearts forget his promise,
> "I am with you evermore"?

Such interpretations are less conducive to non-Trinitarians. The Harvard Unitarian theologian Henry Ware Jr. (1794–1843), interprets 'I am with you always' of Christ's presence continuing in the words of Scripture:

> Yet, through the abundant goodness of our Heavenly Father, who, in ways so marvelous, has preserved for us the record of that holy revelation, and made it now accessible to every heart, we, of this remote clime, and in this distant period, hear the blessed words as if they were sounded in our ears … How near is my Saviour to me when I read records of his life. (Ware in Larsen 2011: 156)

Biographies and Glossary

Aelfric of Eynsham (c. 955–1010) English Benedictine monk, abbot, and spiritual writer, and important witness to monastic interpretation of Matthew.

Aelred of Rievaulx (1110–1167) English Cistercian monk, Abbot of Rievaulx, and spiritual writer.

Africanus, Sextus Julius (c. 160–240) Early Christian historian who influenced Eusebius. His solution to the discrepancies between the genealogies of Matthew and Luke was widely adopted.

Albert the Great (c. 1200–1280) Dominican theologian, teacher of Thomas Aquinas at the University of Paris, and later bishop of Regensburg.

Matthew Through the Centuries, First Edition. Ian Boxall.

Alighieri, Dante (c. 1265–1321) Florentine poet, statesman, and political theorist, best known for his *Divine Comedy*.

Allison, Dale C., Jr. (born 1955) Professor of New Testament at Princeton Theological Seminary, and co-author of the International Critical Commentary on Matthew.

Althaus, Paul (1888–1966) German Lutheran theologian and professor of theology at the University of Erlangen.

Ambrose of Milan (c. 333–397) Aurelius Ambrosius, governor of Liguria and Emilia, who became bishop of Milan in 374. He was the teacher of Augustine of Hippo.

Anabaptists A Christian tradition emerging out of the Radical Reformation in the sixteenth century (including groups such as the Mennonites, Hutterites, Swiss Brethren, and Amish), which emphasized believer's baptism and rejected the baptism of infants.

Anastasius of Sinai (seventh century) Greek monastic writer and abbot of St. Catherine's Monastery, Sinai.

Andrew the Chaplain (twelfth century) Also known by his Latin name Andreas Cappellanus. Best known for his treatise *On Love*.

Andrewes, Lancelot (1555–1626) English scholar, bishop, and renowned preacher, who oversaw the translation of the Authorized Version (AV), also known as the King James Version (KJV).

Angelico, Fra (c. 1395–1455) Fra Giovanni da Fiesole, an Italian Dominican friar and influential Renaissance artist, beatified by Pope John Paul II in 1982.

Anselm of Canterbury (c. 1033–1109) Important medieval theologian, philosopher, and saint, born in Aosta, and abbot of the Monastery of Bec, Normandy, before becoming archbishop of Canterbury in 1093.

Anselm of Laon (d. 1117) French biblical scholar and founder of the exegetical school at Laon in France, famous for its production of the *Glossa ordinaria*.

Apollinarianism The view attributed to Apollinarius of Laodicea that Christ possessed only a divine, not a human, mind.

Apollinaris of Laodicea (c. 310–390) Bishop of Laodicea in Syria. Fragments of his commentary on Matthew, used by Jerome, have survived.

Applemans, Gerard (c. 1250–1325) Hermit from the province of Brabant in the Low Countries, who wrote a *Gloss on the Our Father*. Little is known about this figure.

Aquinas, Thomas (c. 1225–1274) Dominican friar, and foremost systematic theologian of the medieval church. His interpretation of Matthew is preserved in his *Lectures on Matthew*, delivered in Paris, and his collection of patristic authorities, the *Catena aurea*.

Arcand, Denys (born 1941) French-Canadian film director, who directed the 1989 film *Jesus of Montreal*.

Arianism An early Christian heresy named after Arius (c. 256–336), priest of the church of Alexandria, which denied the full divinity of Christ.

Arnobius Iunior, or the Younger (fl. c. 460) A Christian monk, who resided in Rome from c. 432, and opposed Augustine of Hippo's doctrine of grace.

Athanasius of Alexandria (296–373) Bishop of Alexandria, theologian, and fierce opponent of Arianism.

Athenagoras (c. 133–190) Early Christian apologist of Athens, who wrote a defense of Christianity for the emperors Marcus Aurelius and Commodus.

Augustine of Canterbury (d. 604) Roman monk sent by Pope Gregory the Great on mission to England; first archbishop of Canterbury.

Augustine of Hippo (354–430) North African convert to Christianity, philosopher, preacher, and major theologian of Latin Christianity, and bishop of Hippo Regius.

Bach, Johann Sebastian (1685–1750) German Lutheran composer and cantor of the Church of St. Thomas, Leipzig from 1723. While at Leipzig he composed his influential *St. Matthew Passion* (1727).

Barbauld, Anna Letitia (1743–1825) English poet, children's author, literary critic, and educationalist, who was also a fierce opponent of the slave trade.

Basil the Great (c. 329–379) Also known as Basil of Caesarea, one of the three Cappadocian Fathers (along with his brother Gregory of Nyssa and his friend Gregory of Nazianzus). He was a strong defender of the divinity of the Holy Spirit.

Basilides (fl. 117–138) A Christian gnostic leader from Alexandria. His followers, the Basilidians, were still known to Epiphanius of Salamis in the fourth century.

Bassano, Jacopo (c. 1510–1592) Also known as Jacopo del Ponte, an Italian artist of the Venetian school, famous for his religious paintings, including several Gospel scenes.

Baur, Ferdinand Christian (1792–1860) German professor of church history, responsible for the 'Tübingen Hypothesis' which viewed the New Testament church in Hegelian terms as a struggle between a Petrine Jewish-Christian 'thesis' and a Pauline 'antithesis,' resolved in a Lucan 'synthesis.'

Baxter, Richard (1615–1691) An English Puritan theologian, whose ministry spanned the English Civil War and the Restoration.

Bede, the Venerable (673–735) Northumbrian monk of the double-monastery of Wearmouth-Jarrow, historian of the English people and biblical exegete. His interpretation of Matthew survives in his *Homilies on the Gospels*.

Benedict of Nursia, or simply St. Benedict (c. 480–543) Influenced by the monastic writings of John Cassian, he founded monastic communities, first at Subiaco and then on Monte Cassino. He is often viewed as the Father of western monasticism, and was declared patron saint of Europe by Pope Paul IV in 1964.

Bengel, Johann Albrecht (1687–1752) German Lutheran biblical scholar, whose 1742 annotations on the New Testament, the *Gnomon Novi Testamenti*, were very influential.

Benvenuto di Giovanni (fifteenth century) Benvenuto di Giovanni di Meo del Guasto, a Sienese artist and probable student of Vecchietta.

Bernard of Clairvaux (1090–1153) A French Cistercian monk, first abbot of Clairvaux, and spiritual writer. He was canonized by Pope Alexander III in 1174.

Bernardino of Siena (1380–1444) Italian Franciscan friar and popular preacher, canonized by Pope Nicholas V in 1450.

Beutler, Magdalene (1407–1458) Also known as Magdalena of Freiburg, late medieval German nun and mystic.

Beza, Theodore (1519–1605) French Protestant Reformer, who became John Calvin's successor in Geneva.

Birgitta of Sweden (1303–1373) Swedish nun, mystic, and founder of the Brigittines, canonized by Pope Boniface IX in 1391, whose *Revelations* provide important visionary insight into the Gospel passion narratives.

Blackwood, Christopher (1606–1670) English Particular Baptist preacher, who ministered in England and Ireland.

Blake, William (1757–1827) English poet, artist, author, and mystic, and profound interpreter of biblical texts.

Bonaventure (1221–1274) Giovanni di Fidanza, Italian Franciscan philosopher-theologian, minister general of the Franciscan Order and cardinal bishop of Albano. He was canonized by Pope Sixtus IV in 1482.

Bonhoeffer, Dietrich (1909–1945) German Lutheran theologian, and founding member of the Confessing Church, who was executed by the Nazi regime.

Bordone, Paris (1500–1571) Italian painter, briefly apprenticed to Titian in Venice. His work is influenced by Mannerism.

Bossuet, Jacques-Bénigne (1627–1704) French theologian, preacher, and orator, who became bishop of Meaux in 1681.

Botticelli, Sandro (c. 1445–1510) Born Alessandro di Mariano di Vanni Filipepi. Important Florentine painter, under the patronage of the Medici, who later in life was influenced by the Dominican preacher Savonarola.

Brontë, Charlotte (1816–1855) English novelist and poet, and eldest of the three Brontë sisters, who published under the pseudonym Currer Bell.

Brown, Raymond Edward (1928–1998) Influential American Roman Catholic New Testament scholar.

Brueghel the Elder, Pieter (c. 1525–1569) Dutch Renaissance painter from Brabant, who worked in Antwerp and Brussels.

Brugghen, Hendrick Ter (1588–1629) Important Dutch painter of the Dutch Golden Age, influenced by Caravaggio.

Bruno of Segni (c. 1045–1123) Italian Benedictine monk, bishop of Segni, abbot of Montecassino, and biblical commentator, canonized by Pope Lucius III in 1181.

Bucer, Martin (1491–1551) German Protestant Reformer, and former Dominican friar, active in Strasbourg.

Bulgakov, Sergei (1871–1944) Russian Orthodox theologian and priest, and head of the St. Sergius Orthodox Theological Institute in Paris.

Bullinger, Heinrich (1504–1575) Swiss Reformer and follower of Zwingli, active in Zurich.

Bunyan, John (1628–1688) English Puritan preacher, particularly famous for his classic work *The Pilgrim's Progress*.

Burkitt, Francis Crawford (1864–1935) English biblical scholar and textual critic, and Norris Professor of Divinity at the University of Cambridge.

Burton, Robert (1577–1640) Oxford scholar, vicar of St. Thomas the Martyr, Oxford, and author of *The Anatomy of Melancholy*.

Caesarius of Arles (468/470–542) Bishop, ascetic, and popular preacher in Gaul, influenced by John Cassian and Augustine of Hippo.

Callistus I, Pope (d. c. 222) Martyr and saint, also known as Callixtus I, he became bishop of Rome c. 218. He was opposed to Hippolytus over supposed laxity regarding sinners.

Callot, Jacques (1592–1635) French artist and printmaker, who studied engraving in Rome and was active in both Italy and France.

Calvin, John (1509–1564) French Protestant theologian and leader of the Reform in Geneva. Influenced by humanism in his biblical interpretation.

Caravaggio, Michelangelo Merisi da (1571–1610) Italian painter, often controversial for the realism of his religious subjects. Especially famous for his three scenes from the Life of St. Matthew.

Carey, William (1761–1834) English Baptist and missionary in India, widely recognized as the father of the modern Protestant missionary movement.

Carracci, Lodovico (1555–1619) Italian painter of the early Baroque, active in Bologna.

Cash, Johnny (1932–2003) Best-selling American singer and song-writer, whose writing reflects his Christian beliefs.

Cassian, John (c. 360–435) Monk, ascetic, and saint whose *Conferences* introduced eastern monastic rules into western Christianity.

Caswall, Edward (1814–1878) English Anglican priest and convert to Roman Catholicism, whose translations of early Christian hymns continue to be widely sung.

Catechumens Those under instruction in the Christian faith in preparation for baptism.

Celestine I, Pope (d. 432) Bishop of Rome whose papacy was devoted to combatting various heresies, including Pelagianism, Novatianism, and Nestorianism.

Celsus (second century) Pagan philosopher and opponent of Christianity, whose views were refuted by Origen in his *Contra Celsum*.

Champaigne, Philippe de (1602–1674) French painter of the Baroque period, who painted a large number of religious subjects.

Chatterton Dix, William (1827–1898) English hymnwriter, whose hymns continue to be widely sung.

Chaucer, Geoffrey (1837–1898) English poet, philosopher, and astronomer, best known for *The Canterbury Tales*.

Christian of Stavelot (ninth century) Benedictine monk of Corbie, who subsequently taught the Bible at the Abbey of Stavelot-Malmedy in Liège.

Chromatius of Aquileia (d. c. 407) Bishop of Aquileia in northern Italy. His homilies on Matthew were influenced by the commentary of his predecessor Fortunatianus.

Chrysologus, Peter (c. 380–450) Bishop of Ravenna, and influential preacher of the Latin church (Chrysologus = 'golden-worded').

Chrysostom, John (345–407) Influential preacher of the church in Antioch (Chrysostom = 'golden-mouthed'), and subsequently patriarch of Constantinople. He preached a series of homilies on Matthew.

Chytraeus, David (1530–1600) Lutheran theologian and biblical scholar, professor at the University of Rostock.

Clarke, Arthur C. (1917–2008) British science-fiction writer and underwater explorer.

Claudius, Matthias (1740–1815) German poet and journalist, who wrote under the pseudonym Asmus.

Clement of Alexandria (c. 150–215) Titus Flavius Clemens. Prominent Christian theologian and philosopher of the catechetical school in Alexandria.

Codex Alexandrinus Important fifth-century manuscript of the Greek Bible, containing most of the Septuagint and the New Testament.

Codex Bezae, or Codex Bezae Cantabrigensis Fifth-century manuscript of the New Testament in both Greek and Latin, containing most of the Four Gospels and Acts.

Codex Washingtonianus, or Codex Washingtonensis Fourth- or fifth-century manuscript of the Gospels, in the order Matthew–John–Luke–Mark.

Colani, Timothée (1824–1888) French liberal Protestant scholar, who proposed the theory of a 'Little Apocalypse' underlying Mark 13.

Comestor, Peter (d. c. 1178) French theologian at the University of Paris, famed for his voracious appetite for knowledge (Comestor = 'Devourer'). His most famous biblical work is his biblical paraphrase the *Historia Scholastica*.

Conrad, Joseph (1857–1924) Polish-British novelist and short-story writer.

Cooke, William (1806–1884) English minister and theologian of the Methodist New Connexion, and president of the Methodist New Connexion Conference, who worked for Methodist reunion.

Cornwallis, Mary (1758–1836) Evangelical Anglican and wife of the rector of Wittersham, Kent, she wrote what is probably the earliest commentary on Matthew by a woman author.

Cowper William (1731–1800) English poet and hymnwriter, who collaborated with John Newton on the *Olney Hymns* collections.

Crashaw, Richard (c. 1613–1649) English metaphysical poet, Anglican priest, and Roman Catholic convert.

Cranmer, Thomas (1489–1556) Leader of the English Reformation and archbishop of Canterbury from 1532, responsible for the first two editions of the *Book of Common Prayer*. Executed in Oxford and celebrated as a Reformation martyr.

Crosby, Fanny (1820–1915) American educator and hymnwriter, who composed over 8000 hymns and gospel songs.

Cyprian of Carthage (200–258) Bishop of Carthage in North Africa, and important theologian of the Latin church, martyred during the persecution of Valerian.

Cyril of Alexandria (c. 376–444) Important Greek theologian, patriarch of Alexandria from 412 to 444, and fierce opponent of Nestorius at the Council of Ephesus in 431.

Cyril of Jerusalem (c. 315–386) Bishop of Jerusalem, and author of the influential *Catechetical Lectures*.

David, Gerard (c. 1460–1523) Early Netherlandish painter, active in Antwerp and Bruges.

Davies, William David (W.D.) (1911–2001) Welsh Congregational minister, New Testament scholar, and professor at Duke Divinity School and Princeton University. Major twentieth-century interpreter of Matthew.

della Francesca, Piero (c. 1415–1492) Italian early Renaissance painter, famous for his biblical scenes including the Baptism and Resurrection of Christ.

DeMille, Cecil B. (1881–1959) American actor and film director, who directed *The King of Kings*, a film version of Christ's life, in 1927.

Diatessaron A harmony of the Four Gospels, produced c. 160–175 by the Assyrian Christian apologist Tatian.

DiCaprio, Leonardo (born 1974) American actor, film producer, and environmental campaigner.

Dickson, Andrew Flinn (1825–1879) American Presbyterian minister and writer.

Didymus the Blind (c. 313–98) Alexandrian exegete, pupil of Origen, and head of the Catechetical School in Alexandria.

Dieterle, William (1893–1972) German actor and film director, who directed the Hollywood movie *Salome* in 1953.

Dietrick, Ellen Battelle (1847–1895) American suffragist, and co-editor with Elizabeth Cady Stanton of *The Woman's Bible*.

Dionysius bar Salibi (d. 1171) Also known as Jacob bar Salibi, he was a prominent theologian and bishop of the Syriac Orthodox Church, who wrote commentaries on Matthew and the Apocalypse.

Dionysius the Carthusian (1402–1471) Also known as Denys van Leeuwen. Carthusian monk, theologian, and mystic, who wrote commentaries on the whole Bible.

Dionysius of Fourna (c. 1670–after 1744) Monk of Mount Athos, and compiler of *The Painter's Manual*, a manual of Byzantine iconography.

Dix, Otto (1891–1969) German Expressionist painter and printmaker, who produced a lithograph series on Matthew's Gospel.

Donatello (c. 1386–1466) Also known as Donato di Niccolò di Betto Bardi. Italian Renaissance sculptor from Florence.

Donne, John (1572–1631) English Anglican priest and metaphysical poet, who became Dean of St. Paul's Cathedral, London in 1621.

Doré, Gustave (1832–1883) French artist, cartoonist, and printmaker, famous for his 1866 engravings for *La Grande Bible de Tours*.

Dostoyevsky, Fyodor (1821–1881) Russian philosopher, novelist, and short-story writer.

Douai-Rheims Bible English Catholic translation of the Vulgate Bible, produced by members of the English College in Douai (New Testament published in Rheims in 1582; whole Bible in Douai in 1609–1610).

Double Tradition Material (mainly sayings of Jesus) found only in Matthew and Luke. Also known as Q.

Douglas, Lloyd C. (1877–1851) American Lutheran pastor, subsequently Congregational minister, and novelist.

Douglass, Frederick (1818–1895) Prominent African-American abolitionist, social reformer, orator, and author.

Dube, Musa (born 1964) Influential African New Testament scholar from Botswana, who brings postcolonial and feminist perspectives to bear on the interpretation of Matthew.

Duccio di Buoninsegna (c. 1255–c. 1319) Important Sienese painter regarded as the originator of the Trecento style regarded as the beginnings of the Italian Renaissance.

Ebionites Jewish-Christian group in the early church, which advocated observance of the Mosaic Law, and read a Hebrew version of Matthew's Gospel.

Egeria (late fourth century) Also known as Etheria or Aetheria. Pilgrim to the holy land, whose detailed description is an important source for sacred sites and the liturgical life of the Jerusalem church.

Elgar, Edward (1857–1934) English Roman Catholic composer.

Eliot, Thomas Steans (T.S.) (1888–1965) American poet and essayist, who converted to Anglicanism and became a British citizen in 1927.

Emmerich, Anne Catherine (1774–1824) German mystic and stigmatist, whose visions, transcribed by the poet Clemens Brentano, influenced Mel Gibson's *The Passion of the Christ*. Beatified in 2004 by Pope John Paul II.

Ephrem the Syrian (fourth century) Deacon, poet, and theologian, one of the most important theologians of Syriac Christianity.

Epiphanius the Latin (late fifth or early sixth century) Author of a Latin *Interpretation of the Gospels*, which draws heavily on earlier patristic sources.

Epiphanius of Salamis (c. 310–403) Bishop of Salamis in Cyprus. His *Panarion* is an important source for the writings of heretical groups of the early centuries.

Erasmus, Desiderius (1469–1536) Dutch humanist classical scholar and priest, who remained a member of the Roman Catholic Church despite critical views, and influenced both the Reformers and the Catholic Counter-Reformation.

Eusebius of Caesarea (260–339) Bishop of Caesarea, adviser to the emperor Constantine, exegete, and polemicist, best known for his *Ecclesiastical History*.

Euthymius Zigabenus (twelfth century) Monk of Constantinople, imperial adviser, and commentator on the Gospels, influenced by the exegetical tradition of John Chrysostom.

Ferlin, Nils (1898–1961) Swedish poet, actor, and lyricist.

Ferrer, Vincent (1350–1419) Dominican friar and missionary from Valencia, canonized by Pope Callixtus III in 1455.

Fetti, Domenico (c. 1589–1623) Italian Baroque painter, famous for his set of paintings on the Gospel parables.

Fortunatianus of Aquileia (d. 368) African exegete, bishop of Aquileia in northern Italy, who composed a commentary on Matthew which was used by Jerome.

Fox, George (1624–1691) English religious figure, who founded the Religious Society of Friends (also known as the Quakers).

Francis of Assisi (1181/1182–1226) Giovanni di Pietro di Bernardone, Italian deacon, preacher, and founder of the Franciscan Order, famed for his radical living out of gospel principles. He was canonized by Pope Gregory IX in 1228.

Franck, César (1822--1890) Organist and composer, born in Liège, who became organist of Saint-Clotilde in Paris and professor at the Paris Conservatoire.

Franklin, Benjamin (1706–1790) Statesman, politician, scientist, and author, considered one of the founding fathers of the United States of America.

Gandhi, Mahatma (1869–1948) Mohandas Karamchand Gandhi, Indian lawyer, activist, and politician, whose principles of non-violence were influenced by the Sermon on the Mount.

Geertgen tot Sint Jans (c. 1465–1495) Early Netherlandish painter, active in Haarlem.

Geneva Bible English Protestant Bible, produced by English exiles in Geneva (New Testament published in 1557; whole Bible in 1560), with annotations of a Calvinist and Puritan theological viewpoint.

Gentile da Fabriano (c. 1370–1427) Italian painter and representative of the International Gothic style, active mainly in Tuscany.

Gerson, Jean (1363–1429) French scholar, theologian, poet, and chancellor of the University of Paris.

Ghiberti, Lorenzo (1378–1455) Lorenzo di Bartolo, Florentine painter of the early Renaissance.

Ghirlandaio, Domenico (1448–1494) Florentine Renaissance painter, and teacher of Michelangelo.

Gibson, Mel (born 1956) American actor and film director, brought up in Australia, who directed the 2004 film *The Passion of the Christ*.

Gill, John (1697–1771) English Particular Baptist theologian and biblical scholar, who wrote an *Exposition of the Old and New Testaments*.

Giordano da Rivolto (1260–1311) Also known as Blessed Jordan of Pisa, a Dominican friar and renowned preacher, who was beatified in 1838.

Giotto di Bondone (c. 1267–1337) Influential Italian painter and architect from Florence.

Gordon, General Charles George (1833–1885) Also known as Gordon of Khartoum, British army officer, associated with the Garden Tomb in Jerusalem.

Gozzoli, Benozzo (c. 1421–1497) Florentine Renaissance artist, who painted the frescoes for the Magi Chapel in the Palazzo Medici in Florence.

Gracían, Jerónimo (1545–1614) Spanish Carmelite friar and spiritual director of St. Teresa of Avila.

Gregory the Great, or Gregory I, Pope (c. 540–604) Roman patrician, monk, liturgical reformer, and influential theologian, who became pope in 590.

Gregory of Narek (951–1003) Armenian monk, mystical theologian, and poet, best known for his poem 'The Book of Lamentations.'

Gregory of Nazianzus (c. 329–390) Greek theologian, Cappadocian Father, patriarch of Constantinople, and close friend of Basil the Great.

Gregory IX, Pope (c. 1145–1241) Ugolino di Conti, educated in Paris and Bologna, who became pope in 1227.

Gregory of Nyssa (c. 335–395) Cappadocian Father, brother of Basil the Great and bishop of Nyssa.

Gregory Thaumaturgos (c. 213–270) Gregory the Wonderworker, converted to Christianity by Origen, subsequently bishop of Neocaesarea in Pontus, Asia Minor.

Grotius, Hugo (1583–1645) Hugo de Groot, Dutch Protestant jurist and theologian, known for his historicizing approach to scripture.

Grünewald, Matthias (c. 1470–1528) German Renaissance painter, best known for his Isenheim Altarpiece.

Haimo of Auxerre (d. c. 865) Benedictine monk of Auxerre, Burgundy, and biblical exegete.

Hammond, Henry (1605–1660) Anglican priest and theologian, who supported the Royalist cause during the English Civil War. Author of the *Paraphrase and Annotations on the New Testament* (1653).

Handel, George Frederick (1685–1759) German composer who spent much of his career in London, famous for his 1742 oratorio *The Messiah*.

Hardouin, Jean (1646–1729) Breton Jesuit classical scholar and exegete, with eccentric views about the interpretation of the New Testament.

Harper, Frances Ellen Watkins (1825–1911) African-American poet, abolitionist, and suffragist from Baltimore.

Harrington, Daniel J. (1940–2014) American Jesuit New Testament scholar, whose commentary on Matthew emphasizes its Jewish-Christian origins.

Heine, Christian Johann Heinrich (1797–1856) German essayist and poet, famous for his lyrical poems.

Helvidius (fourth century) Author of a work which denied the perpetual virginity of Mary, strongly opposed by Jerome.

Henry, Matthew (1662–1714) Welsh Non-Conformist minister, who wrote an influential commentary on the whole Bible.

Herod Antipas (first century CE) Son of Herod the Great and Malthrace, tetrarch of Galilee and Peraea between 4 BCE and 39 CE, responsible for the death of John the Baptist.

Herod the Great (74/73–4 BCE) Roman client king of Judea, who reigned from 37 to 4 BCE; king at the time of Jesus' birth and responsible for the slaughter of the innocents.

Hilary of Poitiers (c. 315–367/8) Gallic theologian and bishop of Poitiers, strong opponent of Arianism, who wrote an important commentary on Matthew.

Hildegard of Bingen (1098–1179) Benedictine abbess, mystic, and preacher, whose *Homilies on the Gospels* have survived. Named Doctor of the Church by Benedict XVI in 2012.

Hippolytus of Rome (170–235) Roman theologian, schismatic bishop, and martyr.

Hugh of St. Cher (c. 1200–1263) French Dominican friar, biblical scholar, and cardinal.

Hugh of St. Victor (c. 1096–1141) Saxon Augustinian canon and mystical theologian, associated with the Abbey of St.-Victor, Paris.

Humbert, Cardinal (c. 1000–1061) Humbert of Silva Candida, Benedictine monk and cardinal who delivered the papal bull of excommunication to the patriarch of Constantinople in 1054, leading to the Great Schism between eastern and western Christianity.

Hus, Jan (c. 1369–1415) Czech theologian, church reformer, and rector of the Charles University in Prague, regarded as a precursor of the Protestant Reformation.

Ignatius of Antioch (c. 35–107) Bishop of Antioch in Syria and Christian martyr; author of letters to Christians in Asia Minor.

Irenaeus of Lyons (c. 125–200) Greek theologian from Smyrna, who became bishop of Lugdunum (Lyons) in Gaul, and a strong defender of the fourfold Gospel against Marcion and the Gnostics.

Isaac of Stella (c. 1100–1170) English Cistercian monk and preacher, abbot of the Monastery of Stella near Poitiers.

Isho'dad of Merv (ninth century) Bishop of Hdatta on the Tigris, important biblical scholar, and theologian of the Church of the East.

Isidore of Pelusium (c. 350–435) Egyptian ascetic, desert father, and prolific letter writer.

Isidore of Seville (c. 560–636) Scholar, archbishop of Seville, most famous for his encyclopedic *Etymologiae*.

Jackson, Donald (born 1938) British calligrapher and scribe, artistic director and illuminator of The Saint John's Bible.

Jacob of Edessa (c. 640–708) Syriac Orthodox monk, scriptural scholar, and metropolitan of Edessa.

Jacob of Serugh (c. 451–521) Also known as Mar Jacob, important poet-theologian of the Syriac church.

Jansz, Anna (1509–1539) Also known as Anneke Esaiasdochter and Anna of Rotterdam, a Dutch Anabaptist, author, and martyr.

Jefferson, Thomas (1743–1826) American founding father, lawyer, and third president of the United States, whose revisionist view of Jesus and the Gospels is preserved in his *The Life and Morals of Jesus of Nazareth*.

Jenkins, Jerry B. (born 1949) American novelist, and co-author with Tim LaHaye of the *Left Behind* series of novels.

Jerome (c. 345–420) Perhaps the most important western biblical scholar, Bible translator, and author of numerous commentaries.

Joachim of Fiore (c. 1135–1202) Italian abbot and mystic, whose complex biblical exegesis influenced the interpretation of Matthew by the radical Franciscan Peter John Olivi.

John of Damascus (c. 675–749) Syrian monk of Mar Saba near Jerusalem, theologian, hymnwriter, and strong defender of icons.

John of Hildesheim (1310/1320–1375) German Carmelite friar and author, most famous for his *Historia Trium Regum* (*History of the Three Kings*), a collection of legends about the Magi.

John of La Rochelle (c. 1200–1245) French Franciscan friar and theologian, who taught at the University of Paris.

John Paul II, Pope (1920–2005) Born Karol Wojtyła in Poland, he was pope from 1978 to 2005 and was canonized in 2014.

Jordan of Quedlinburg (c. 1299–1380) Also known as Jordan of Saxony, an Augustinian theologian and historian, who wrote an *Exposition of the Lord's Prayer*.

Josephus (37–c. 100) Jewish historian and apologist; important source for knowledge of Palestine and Judaism in the first century CE.

Juan de Flandes, i.e. John of Flanders (c. 1460–1519) An Early Netherlandish painter, born in Flanders, who became court artist for Queen Isabella I of Castile.

Julian the Apostate (331/332–363) Roman emperor from 361 to 363, philosopher and author, who supported the restoration of paganism as the state religion.

Julian of Speyer (d. c. 1250) German Franciscan friar, poet and composer, who wrote an Office for the Feast of St. Francis.

Jülicher, Adolf (1857–1938) German biblical scholar, professor at Marburg, best known for his interpretation of the Gospel parables.

Julius II, Pope (1443–1513) Giuliano della Rovere, who became pope in 1503, patron of arts and so-called 'Warrior Pope.'

Justin Martyr (c. 100/110–165) Pagan convert to Christianity from Samaria, apologist, and early Christian martyr.

Juvencus (fourth century) Gaius Vettius Aquilinus Juvencus, Latin Christian poet from Spain.

Kazantzakis, Nikos (1883–1957) Greek novelist, philosopher, and poet, whose novel *The Last Temptation of Christ* was published in 1955.

Keble, John (1792–1866) Anglican priest, poet, leader of the Oxford Movement, and author of *The Christian Year*.

Kepler, Johannes (1571–1630) German astronomer and mathematician, famous for his laws of planetary motion.

King James Version Also called the Authorized Version, a classic English translation of the Bible, published in 1611 at the instigation of King James I.

Koresh, David (1959–1993) Born Vernon Wayne Howell, leader and self-proclaimed final prophet of the Branch Davidian sect, who died during the siege of the sect's compound in Waco, Texas.

Lactantius, Lucius Caecilius Firmianus (c. 250–325) Early Christian theologian and apologist, and adviser to the Emperor Constantine.

LaHaye, Tim (1926–2016) American evangelical pastor and writer, and co-author with Jerry B. Jenkins of the *Left Behind* series of novels.

Langland, William (c. 1332–1386) Author of the Middle English poem *Piers Plowman*.

Lanyer, Aemilia (1569–1645) Early modern English poet, who published her volume of poetry *Salve Deus Rex Judaeorum* in 1611.

Lapide, Cornelius a (1567–1637) Cornelis Cornelissen van den Steen, a Flemish Jesuit famous for his posthumously published *Great Commentary* on scripture.

Latimer, Hugh (c. 1487–1555) Bishop of Worcester and then chaplain to King Edward VI; one of the three Oxford Protestant martyrs (along with Thomas Cranmer and Nicholas Ridley).

Leo the Great or Leo I, Pope (c. 400–461) Roman aristocrat who became pope in 440; his Christology, as set out in the Tome of Leo, was an important influence on the Council of Chalcedon in 451.

Levine, Amy-Jill (born 1956) Jewish feminist New Testament scholar who has published widely on Matthew; professor of New Testament and Jewish Studies at Vanderbilt Divinity School.

Lippi, Fra Filippo (c. 1406–1469) Florentine Carmelite friar and painter.

Lloyd Webber, Andrew (born 1948) English composer who collaborated with the lyricist Tim Rice on the 1970 rock opera *Jesus Christ Superstar*.

Lochner, Stefan (c. 1410–1451) German painter who worked in the International Gothic style, also known as the Dombild Master.

Lombard, Peter (c. 1096–1160) Influential scholastic theologian and author of the Sentences, who later became bishop of Paris.

Lorenzetti, Pietro (c. 1280–1348) Sienese painter, responsible for the Passion cycle of frescoes in the Lower Church of St. Francis, Assisi.

Ludolph of Saxony (c. 1295–1378) Carthusian monk and spiritual writer, best known for his *Vita Christi* or *Life of Christ*.

Luther, Martin (1483–1546) German Augustinian friar, theologian, and professor, who became the leader of the Reformation in Germany.

Luz, Ulrich (born 1938) Swiss Reformed New Testament scholar and commentator on Matthew, professor emeritus at the University of Bern.

Macaulay, Rose (1881–1958) English writer and novelist, whose novels explore theological and religious ideas.

Macrina the Younger (c. 330–379) Nun and ascetic, elder sister of Basil the Great and Gregory of Nyssa.

Maldonado, Juan de (1533–1583) Spanish Jesuit exegete, also known as Maldonatus, whose *Commentary on the Holy Gospels* emphasizes the historical and grammatical sense.

Manicheans Religious sect founded by the Iranian Mani, which believed in a complex cosmic dualism.

Marcion of Sinope (c. 85–160) Early Christian figure active in Rome and Asia Minor, who rejected the God of the Old Testament and whose views were strongly refuted by Irenaeus.

Maritain, Jacques (1882–1973) French Catholic philosopher and author, and important interpreter of Thomas Aquinas.

Markham, Edwin (1852–1940) American poet, lecturer, and essayist.

Marley, Bob (1945–1981) Born Robert Nesta Marley, Jamaican Rastafarian singer and songwriter.

Marlowe, Christopher (1564–1593) English poet and playwright, and major influence on William Shakespeare.

Maronites A Christian community of Syriac tradition in full communion with Rome, with its patriarchal see in Lebanon, whose name is believed to derive from the third-century Saint Maron.

Martial of Limoges (third century) First bishop of Limoges, also known as the Apostle of the Gauls.

Martynov, Vladimir (born 1946) Russian composer, with religious and philosophical interests.

Masaccio (1401–1428) Born Tommaso di Ser Giovanni di Simone, Florentine painter who painted a series of frescoes for the Brancacci Chapel in Santa Maria del Carmine, Florence.

Mather, Cotton (1663–1728) American Puritan minister and pamphleteer, active in New England, who was influential in the Salem witch trials.

Maurus, Rabanus (c. 780–856) Saxon Benedictine exegete who studied under Alcuin at Aachen, and subsequently became archbishop of Mainz.

Maximus the Confessor (c. 580–662) Greek monk and theologian, who opposed Monothelitism.

Maximus of Turin (fifth century) Bishop, theologian, and preacher; a significant number of his homilies have survived.

McCabe, Herbert (1926–2001) English-born Dominican philosopher and theologian, who taught for many years at Blackfriars, Oxford.

Melito of Sardis (d. c. 180) Bishop of Sardis in Asia Minor, best known for his treatise *Peri Pascha*.

Merton, Thomas (1915–1968) American Trappist monk, poet, spiritual writer, and social activist.

Methodius of Olympus (d. c. 311) Greek author, bishop, and martyr, influenced by Plato and allegorical in his interpretation of scripture.

Meyer, Heinrich August Wilhelm (1800–1873) German Lutheran pastor and biblical scholar, who published a critical handbook on Matthew's Gospel.

Milton, John (1608–1674) English civil servant and poet, author of the epic poem *Paradise Lost*.

Modalism The belief that the Father, Son, and Holy Spirit were three modes of God's self-disclosure, rather than three distinct persons. Also known as Sabellianism and Patripassionism.

Monothelitism The view that, although Christ had both a human and divine nature, he only had a single, divine will.

Monro, Harold Edward (1879–1932) English poet, editor of *The Poetry Review*, and founder of the Poetry Bookshop in Bloomsbury, London.

Monteverdi, Claudio Giovanni Antonio (1567–1643) Italian composer and choirmaster at the Basilica of San Marco, Venice.

Monty Python British group of comedy actors known for their surrealism, which produced a number of films including the 1979 *Life of Brian*, set at the time of Jesus.

Moreau, Gustav (1826–1898) French painter and illustrator, an exemplar of the Symbolism movement in art, who painted a number of biblical themes.

Mozart, Wolfgang Amadeus (1756–1791) Important and prolific composer, active in Salzburg and Vienna.

Muller, Harmen Jansz (1539–1617) Netherlandish engraver and publisher, active in Amsterdam.

Müntzer, Thomas (c. 1485–1525) Radical Reformer and opponent of Luther, whose radical mysticism led him to participate in the Peasants' Revolt, following which he was executed.

Nag Hammadi Town in Upper Egypt, and location of the discovery of a library of early Christian and Gnostic writings in 1945 (known collectively as the Nag Hammadi library).

Naliwajko, Piotr (born 1960) Polish artist, who has exhibited widely in Europe and the United States.

Newton, John (1725–1807) English Evangelical Anglican priest, curate of Olney in Buckinghamshire, and prolific hymnwriter, who collaborated with the poet William Cowper in the collection called *Olney Hymns* (1779).

Nicholas of Lyra (c. 1270–1349) French Franciscan biblical scholar, whose *postillae* on scripture emphasized the literal sense.

Nightingale, Florence (1820–1910) Pioneer in modern nursing and social reformer, especially prominent during the Crimean War.

Novatian (c. 200–258) Early Christian theologian and antipope, noted for his rigorist position regarding Christians who had renounced the faith during persecution and wished to repent.

Olivi, Peter John (1248–1298) French radical Franciscan theologian, whose biblical exegesis was strongly influenced by Joachim of Fiore.

Origen (c. 185–235) Prolific and influential Greek theologian, ascetic, and biblical exegete, who taught at the Catechetical School in Alexandria, and afterwards at Caesarea.

Palamas, Gregory (c. 1296–1357) Saint of the eastern church, monk of Mount Athos and archbishop of Thessalonica, and important mystical theologian.

Papias (c. 60–130) Bishop of Hierapolis in Asia Minor. Papias is one of our earliest witnesses to the authorship of the Gospels.

Paris, Matthew (c. 1200–1259) An English Benedictine monk of St. Alban's Abbey, historian, and artist.

Pärt, Arvo (b. 1935) Estonian composer, and convert from Lutheranism to Russian Orthodoxy, whose musical compositions include a setting of the Beatitudes.

Pasolini, Pier Paolo (1922–1975) Italian intellectual, writer, and film director, who directed *Il Vangelo secondo Matteo* (*The Gospel According to St. Matthew*) in 1964.

Paulus, Heinrich Eberhard Gottlob (1761–1851) German rationalist biblical critic and professor of theology, who offered a non-supernatural interpretation of the Gospel miracles.

Penick, Charles Clifton (1843–1914) American Episcopal missionary bishop of Cape Palmas in West Africa.

Percy, William Alexander (1885–1942) American lawyer and poet, author of the popular hymn about the disciples of Jesus, 'They Cast Their Nets in Galilee.'

Perugino, Pietro (c. 1450–1523) An Umbrian artist, who became one of the foremost painters in Florence. He painted the fresco *The Delivery of the Keys* (1481–1483) in the Sistine Chapel, Rome.

Peterson, Eugene (born 1932) American Presbyterian minister, scholar, and author, particularly well known for his Bible translation *The Message*.

Pfleiderer, Otto (1839–1908) German Protestant professor who held the Chair of Systematic Theology at Berlin, and was a leading exponent of liberal theology.

Philoxenus of Mabbug (d. 523) Syriac theologian and biblical scholar, robust defender of Miaphytisim (the view that Christ's divinity and humanity are united in a single nature), who revised the Syriac biblical versions to produce the Philoxenian version.

Photius I of Constantinople (c. 810–893) Prominent patriarch of Constantinople, who played a key role in the conversion of the Slavs.

Pius XI, Pope (1857–1939) Born Ambrogio Damiano Achille Ratti, he became pope in 1922; famous for his encyclical letter against Nazism *Mit brennender Sorge* (1937).

Pius XII, Pope (1876–1958) Born Eugenio Pacelli, he served in various Vatican diplomatic capacities before becoming pope in 1939. His role during the Second World War remains a matter of historical debate.

Polo, Marco (1254–1324) Venetian explorer and writer, who traveled to China and other Asian countries.

Polycarp of Smyrna (c. 69–155) Bishop of Smyrna in Asia Minor, and early Christian martyr.

Porphyry (c. 234–305) Neoplatonic philosopher, whose work *Against the Christians* provoked responses from several Christian apologists, including Jerome and Augustine.

Poussin, Nicolas (1594–1665) French painter associated with the French Baroque, who spent most of his career in Rome.

Pseudo-Bonaventure (fourteenth century) Anonymous Franciscan author of the popular *Meditations on the Life of Christ.*

Puritans English Reformer Protestants, especially of the sixteenth and seventeenth centuries, so-called because of their desire to 'purify' the Established Church from remaining Catholic elements so as to complete its Reformation.

Q A hypothetical sayings-source, used independently by both Matthew and Luke, according to the popular Two Source hypothesis. Q is thought to be derived from the German *Quelle* = 'source.'

Quadragesima From the Latin meaning 'fortieth,' Quadragesima Sunday is the First Sunday of Lent (40 days before Good Friday).

Radbertus, Paschasius (785–865) Theologian of the Carolingian period and abbot of Corbie in Picardy, whose commentary on Matthew was an important source for the *Glossa ordinaria*. Canonized by Pope Gregory VII in 1073.

Ralph of Laon (twelfth century) Brother of Anselm of Laon, with whom he taught at the cathedral school in that city. He is now believed to be the author of the *Glossa ordinaria* on Matthew.

Ramsey, Michael (1904–1988) English Anglican scholar and ecumenist, professor at Durham and Cambridge, and successively bishop of Durham and archbishop of Canterbury.

Rank-Broadley, Ian (born 1952) British sculptor, among whose major commissions is a statue of St. Matthew for St. Matthew's Church, Northampton, UK.

Raphael (1483–1520) Raffaello Sanzio da Urbino, Italian Renaissance painter and architect, famous for his frescoes in the Vatican Palace.

Ratzinger, Joseph (born 1927) German theologian, theological adviser at the Second Vatican Council, bishop, and cardinal. He reigned as Pope Benedict XVI from 2005 until his resignation in 2013.

Reihlen, Charlotte (1805–1868) Founder of the Deaconess Institute in Stuttgart, who devised the famous German print *Der breite und der schmale Weg.*

Reimarus, Hermann Samuel (1694–1768) German Deist historian and philosopher, whose posthumously published *Fragments* are often viewed as the beginnings of the quest for the historical Jesus.

Rembrandt Harmenszoon van Rijn (1606–1669) Innovative Dutch painter, whose art reflects his profound religious beliefs.

Remigius of Auxerre (c. 841–908) Benedictine monk and scholar, who taught at both Auxerre and Rheims.

Rice, Tim (born 1944) English lyricist who collaborated with the composer Andrew Lloyd Webber on the 1970 rock opera *Jesus Christ Superstar*.

Richard of St. Victor (c. 1173) Scottish Augustinian canon, theologian, and exegete, and prior of the Abbey of St. Victor, Paris.

Romanos the Melodist (c. 490–556) Byzantine hymnwriter, born in Syria but active in Constantinople, who composed a large number of *kontakia* (liturgical hymns).

Romero, Óscar (1971–1980) Óscar Arnulfo Romero y Galdámez, Roman Catholic priest, bishop, and martyr, who became archbishop of San Salvador in 1977. He was assassinated while celebrating Mass, and was beatified in 2015.

Rosselli, Cosimo (1439–1507) Florentine painter, who was one of the artists commissioned by Sixtus IV to paint frescoes on the walls of the Sistine Chapel in Rome.

Rufus of Shotep (late sixth century) Bishop of Shotep in Upper Egypt, and author of Coptic homilies on Matthew.

Rupert of Deutz (c. 1075–1129) Benedictine monk and biblical exegete, abbot of the Abbey of Deutz near Cologne, originally from Liège.

Ruskin, John (1819–1900) English painter, art critic, essayist, and philanthropist, champion of the Pre-Raphaelites and professor of fine art at Oxford.

Sayers, Dorothy L. (1893–1957) English Anglican novelist, poet, and crime writer, who wrote a radio play based on the life of Christ, *The Man Born to Be King* (broadcast in 1941–1942).

Schaff, Philip (1819–1893) Swiss Reformed theologian and church historian, who taught in the United States; editor of the *Nicene and Post-Nicene Fathers* series.

Schleiermacher, Friedrich (1768–1834) German Protestant theologian and biblical scholar, regarded as the Father of Liberal Theology.

Schongauer, Martin (c. 1445–1491) Painter, printmaker, and engraver, from Colmar in Alsace.

Schweitzer, Albert (1875–1965) French-German Lutheran theologian, biblical scholar, medical doctor, and philanthropist, author of the influential *Quest of the Historical Jesus*.

Scorsese, Martin (born 1942) Sicilian-American film director, who directed the film version of Kazantzakis's *The Last Temptation of Christ* (1988).

Scriven, Joseph Medlicott (1819–1886) Irish poet and émigré to Canada, author of the lyrics for the hymn *What a Friend We Have in Jesus*.

Sedulius, Caelius (fifth century) Christian Latin poet and hymnwriter, well known for his poetic reworking of the four Gospels, *Carmen paschale*.

Seraphim of Sarov (1759–1833) Russian Orthodox monk, hermit, mystic, and saint.

Serapion (fourth century) Coptic Bishop of Thmuis in the Nile Delta, supporter of Athanasius, believed to be the author of the Coptic *Life of John the Baptist*.

Severus of Antioch (c. 459–538) Also known as Severus of Gaza, patriarch of Antioch and saint of the Syriac Orthodox Church.

Shakespeare, William (1564–1616) Legendary English playwright, actor, and poet.

Simons, Menno (1496–1561) Anabaptist leader from Friesland, whose followers came to be called Mennonites.

Smaragdus of Saint-Mihiel (c. 760–840) Benedictine monk, writer, and homilist, who belonged to the Abbey of Saint-Mihiel in northwest France.

Smart, Christopher (1722–1771) English Anglican poet, and close associate of Samuel Johnson and Henry Fielding.

Smith, Joseph (1805–1844) American religious leader, who published *The Book of Mormon* in 1830, and founded the Church of Jesus Christ of Latter Day Saints.

Smyttan, George Hunt (1822–1870) Anglican priest and hymnwriter, who wrote the lyrics for the Lenten hymn *Forty Days and Forty Nights.*

Solario, Andrea (1460–1524) Milanese Renaissance painter, influenced by Leonardo da Vinci and Antonello da Messina.

Spenser, Edmund (1552/1553–1599) English Tudor poet, and author of *The Faerie Queene.*

Spurgeon, Charles Haddon (1834–1892) English Particular Baptist minister and renowned preacher, pastor of a congregation in London, and founder of Spurgeon's College.

Stanfield, Francis (1835–1914) English Roman Catholic hymnwriter, and priest of the Archdiocese of Westminster.

Stanton, Elizabeth Cady (1815–1902) American feminist, suffragist, and abolitionist, main author of *The Woman's Bible.*

Stone, Samuel John (1839–1900) English Anglican priest, poet, and hymnwriter, ministering mainly in London.

Strauss, David Friedrich (1808–1874) German Protestant theologian and biblical scholar, whose *Das Leben Jesu* (1835–1836) was a ground-breaking work in historical Jesus studies.

Strigel, Bernhard (c. 1461–1528) German painter, famous for his portraits and altarpieces.

Suárez, Francisco (1548–1617) Influential Spanish Jesuit philosopher and scholastic theologian.

Swanson, John August (born 1938) American artist of Mexican and Swedish parents, well known for his biblical subjects.

Tallis, Thomas (c. 1505–1585) English Roman Catholic composer of church music, who composed for a succession of English monarchs from Henry VIII to Elizabeth I.

Tatian (c. 120–180) Syrian Christian scholar, who composed a harmony of the four Gospels which came to be known as the Diatessaron.

Taverner, John (c. 1490–1545) Important Tudor organist and composer of church music.

Taylor, Archibald Alexander Edward (1834–1903) Presbyterian minister, poet, and president of the College of Wooster, Ohio.

Taylor, Jeremy (1613–1667) Anglican cleric, spiritual writer, associate of Archbishop William Laud, and subsequently bishop of Down and Connor, Ireland.

Teresa of Avila (1515–1568) Spanish Carmelite nun, reformer, mystic, and spiritual writer; canonized by Pope Gregory XV in 1622.

Tertullian (c. 155–240) Quintus Septimius Florens Tertullianus, North African theologian, apologist, and polemicist, often considered the father of Latin theology.

Theodore of Mopsuestia (c. 350–428) Important biblical exegete of the Antiochene School, bishop of Mopsuestia in Cilicia.

Theodoret of Cyrus (c. 393–458) Antiochene biblical scholar, and bishop of Cyrus or Cyrrhus.

Theophylact of Ochrid (1050–1107) Greek biblical exegete, active in Constantinople, before becoming archbishop of Ochrid in Bulgaria.

Tichborne, Chidiock (c. 1562–1586) English Roman Catholic poet, executed following his involvement in the Babington Plot against Queen Elizabeth I.

Tintoretto (1518–1594) Born Jacopo Comin, an influential Venetian painter, influenced by both Michelangelo and Titian.

Tissot, Jacques Joseph (1836–1902) French illustrator and painter, who produced a set of 265 illustrations from the Life of Christ (originals bought by the Brooklyn Art Museum).

Titian (c. 1488–1576) Tiziano Vecellio, a prominent Italian artist of the Venetian School.

Tolstoy, Leo (1828–1910) Russian aristocrat, playwright, and novelist, who came to espouse views of Christian non-violence, influenced by a literal reading of the Sermon on the Mount.

Torres, Camilo (1929–1966) A Colombian Catholic priest and academic who left the active ministry to join the National Liberation Army.

Triple Tradition Material found in all three Synoptic Gospels.

Tropological interpretation In medieval exegesis, a concern for the moral sense (i.e. the action required of the Christian reader).

Tyconius of Carthage (fl. 370–390) North African theologian and Donatist Christian, whose biblical hermeneutics influenced Augustine of Hippo.

Tyndale, William (c. 1494–1536) English scholar and Bible translator, who became an influential figure of the Protestant Reformation, before being executed on a charge of heresy.

U2 Irish rock band, formed in 1972 in Dublin; its lead vocalist is Bono.

Unitarianism Religious movement which rejects the Christian doctrine of the Trinity.

Valdés, Juan de (c. 1490–1541) Controversial Spanish Catholic humanist, whose commentary on Matthew focuses on the Gospel's literal sense and its moral implications.

Valentinians A prominent strand of early Christian Gnosticism, founded in the second century by Valentinus.

van Cleve, Joos (c. 1485–1540/1541) Artist who was active in Antwerp, famous for his religious paintings.

van den Bergh, Regardt (born 1952) South African film and television director, who directed *The Visual Bible: Matthew* in 1993.

van der Weyden, Rogier (1399/1400–1464) Early Netherlandish painter, influential figure of the Northern Renaissance, active in Brussels.

van Eyck, Jan (c. 1390–1441) Famous Early Netherlandish painter, active in Bruges, who painted the famous Ghent Altarpiece along with his brother Hubert.

van Haeften, Benedict (1588–1648) Benedictine monk of the Abbey of Affligem in Flemish Brabant, and spiritual writer.

van Hemessen, Jan Sanders (c. 1500–1566) Flemish Renaissance painter, influenced by the Italian Renaissance, active in Antwerp.

van Honthorst, Gerrit (1592–1656) Also known as Gerard van Honthorst, a Dutch artist of the Golden Age, influenced by Caravaggio during his time in Rome.

van Reymerswaele, Marinus (c. 1490–1546) Dutch painter, trained in Antwerp.

Venantius Fortunatus (c. 530–609) Early Christian Latin poet, hymnwriter, and bishop, whose hymns remain popular.

Vermigli, Peter Martyr (1499–1562) Italian Protestant Reformer and theologian, who taught in Strasbourg, Oxford, and Zurich.

Veronese, Paolo (1528–1588) Born Paolo Caliari in Verona, an Italian Renaissance painter who worked in Venice.

Victorinus of Pettau (d. 304) Bishop of Pettau or Poetovio in Pannonia, martyred during the persecution of Diocletian. Most famous for his commentary on the Apocalypse, he also wrote a commentary on Matthew, used by Jerome but now lost.

Vignon, Claude (1593–1670) French printmaker and painter, trained in Paris and Rome, famous for his religious subjects.

Vincent of Lérins (d. c. 445) Early Christian writer and monk in Gaul, born in Toulouse.

von Carolsfeld, Julius Schnorr (1794–1872) German Lutheran painter and illustrator, particularly known for his Bible illustrations.

von Harnack, Adolf (1851–1930) German Lutheran church historian and university professor.

von Hase, Karl (1800–1890) German Protestant church historian, professor of theology at the University of Jena, and great-grandfather of Dietrich Bonhoeffer.

von le Fort, Gertrud (1876–1971) German baroness, poet, novelist, and convert to Roman Catholicism.

Voragine, Jacobus de (c. 1230–1298) Also known as Giacomoda Varazze, Italian Dominican, compiler of *The Golden Legend*, and archbishop of Genoa, beatified by Pope Pius VII in 1816.

Waldo, Peter (c. 1140–1205) Also known as Pierre Vaudès, a French merchant and preacher who was leader, and possibly founder, of the medieval spiritual movement known as the Waldensians.

Ware, Henry, Jr. (1794–1843) American Unitarian theologian, and professor at Harvard Divinity School.

Wazo of Liège (c. 985–1048) Theologian and bishop of Liège, whose interpretation of the Wheat and the Tares led him to urge leniency toward suspected heretics.

Weiss, Johannes (1863–1914) German biblical scholar and university professor, who emphasized the eschatological dimension of Jesus' preaching about the Kingdom of God.

Wesley, John (1703–1791) English Anglican priest, Fellow of Lincoln College, Oxford, and co-founder of Methodism with his brother Charles.

Whitby, Daniel (1638–1726) English Anglican priest and biblical exegete, best known for his *Paraphrase and Commentary on the New Testament* (published in 1700).

Whitefield, George (1714–1770) Evangelical Anglican and close associate of John and Charles Wesley, who was active both in Britain and in the American colonies.

Whittier, John Greenleaf (1807–1892) American Quaker poet and hymnwriter.

Wilde, Oscar (1854–1900) Irish poet and playwright, whose 1893 play *Salomé* explores the Gospel story of the beheading of John the Baptist.

Wilfrid (c. 633–709) Northumbrian abbot and bishop of York, venerated as a saint after his death.

William of Ockham (c. 1287–1347) English Franciscan friar, philosopher, and scholastic theologian.

Wilson, Andrew Norman (A.N.) (born 1950) English writer, novelist, and newspaper columnist.

Winstanley, Gerrard (1609–1676) English Protestant theologian and radical, active during Oliver Cromwell's Protectorate, whose followers were known as the Diggers or True Levellers.

Winthrop, John (1587/1588–1649) English Puritan who became third governor of the Massachusetts Bay Colony.

Wyclif, John (1320–1384) Oxford theologian and Bible translator, who translated the Gospels from Latin into Middle English. He is considered a precursor of the Reformation.

Yeats, William Butler (1865–1939) Irish poet and playwright, and important literary figure.

Zeffirelli, Franco (born 1923) Italian film director and politician, who directed the television mini-series *Jesus of Nazareth* in 1977.

Zell, Katharina Schütz (c. 1498–1562) Protestant Reformer from Strasbourg, and one of the few female writers of the Reformation period.

Zwingli, Huldrych (1484–1531) Swiss Reformed theologian, influenced by the writings or Erasmus.

Bibliography

Primary Sources

Aelred of Rievaulx, 1987. *Quand Jésus eut douze ans*. Trans. J. Dubois. SC 60. Paris: Éditions du Cerf.

Ambrosiaster, 1968. *Ambrosiastri qui dicitur commentarius in Epistulas paulinas*. Ed. H.J. Vogels. CSEL 81/2. Vienna: Hoelder-Pichler-Tempsky.

Ammassari, A. (ed.), 1996. *Bezae Codex Cantabrigiensis: copia esatta del manoscritto onciale greco-latino dei quattro Vangeli e degli Atti degli Apostoli scritto all'inizio del 5.*

Matthew Through the Centuries, First Edition. Ian Boxall.

secolo e presentato da Theodore Beza all'Università di Cambridge nel 1581. Vatican City: Libreria Editrice Vaticana.

Andrewes, L., 1632. *XCVI Sermons by the Right Honourable, and Reverend Father in God, Lancelot Andrewes, Late Lord Bishop of Winchester*. 2nd edition. London: Richard Badger.

Anselm, 1979. *The Prayers and Meditations of Saint Anselm*. Trans. B. Ward. New York: Penguin.

Aquinas, T., 1995. *Catena Aurea: Commentary on the Four Gospels Collected out of the Works of the Fathers. Volume I–Part I: St. Matthew*. Trans. J.H. Newman. Albany: Christian Publications.

Aquinas, T., 2013a. *Commentary on the Gospel of Matthew, Chapter 1–12*. Trans. J. Holmes and B. Mortensen. Lander: Aquinas Institute.

Aquinas, T., 2013b. *Commentary on the Gospel of Matthew, Chapters 13–28*. Trans. J. Holmes. Lander: Aquinas Institute.

Armstrong, R.J., J.A.W. Hellmann, and W.J. Short (ed.), 1999. *Francis of Assisi: Early Documents. Volume I: The Saint*. New York, London, and Malina: New City Press.

Armstrong, R.J., J.A.W. Hellmann, and W.J. Short, 2000. *Francis of Assisi: Early Documents. Volume II: The Founder*. New York, London, and Malina: New City Press.

Ashjian, M., 1978. *The Great Week in the Armenian Tradition*. New York: Armenian Apostolic Church of America.

Athanasius of Alexandria, 2003. *The Life of Antony: The Coptic Life and The Greek Life*. Trans. T. Vivian and A.N. Athanassakis. CSS 202. Kalamazoo: Cistercian Publications.

Atwan, R., G. Dardess, and P. Rosenthal (eds.), 1998. *Divine Inspiration: The Life of Jesus in World Poetry*. New York and Oxford: OUP.

Auden, W.H., 1991. *Collected Poems*. Ed. E. Mendelson. New York: Vintage.

Augustine, 1959. *Sermons on the Liturgical Seasons*. Trans. M.S. Muldowney. FC 38. New York: Fathers of the Church, Inc.

Augustine, 1968. *The Retractions*. Trans. M.I. Bogan. FC 60. Washington: Catholic University of America Press.

Augustine, 1991. *Sermons III (51–94) on the New Testament*. Trans. E. Hill. Ed. J.E. Rotelle. The Works of Saint Augustine: A Translation for the 21st Century. Brooklyn: New City Press.

Augustine, 2004. *Letters 156–210 (Epistulae)*. Trans. R. Teske. Ed. B. Ramsey. The Works of Saint Augustine: A Translation for the 21st Century, II/3. Hyde Park: New City Press.

Augustine, 2014. *The New Testament I and II*. Ed. B. Ramsey. The Works of Saint Augustine: A Translation for the 21st Century, I/15 and I/16. Hyde Park: New City Press.

Barbauld, A.L., 2002. *Selected Poetry and Prose*. Ed. W. McCarthy and E. Kraft. Peterborough, ON: Broadview.

Bede the Venerable, 1991. *Homilies on the Gospels. Book One: Advent to Lent*. Trans. L.T. Martin and D. Hurst. CSS 110. Kalamazoo: Cistercian Publications.

Belfour, A.O. (ed.), 1909. *Twelfth Century Homilies in MS. Bodley 343. Part I: Text and Translation*. Early English Text Society: Original Series 137. London: Kegan Paul, Trench, Trübner & Co./Henry Frowde, OUP.

Bengel, J.A., 1971. *Bengel's New Testament Word Studies. Volume 1: Matthew–Acts.* Trans. C.T. Lewis and M.R. Vincent. Grand Rapids: Kregel Publications.

Blackwood, C., 1659. *Expositions and Sermons upon the Ten First Chapters of the Gospel of Jesus Christ, According to Matthew.* London: Henry Hills for Francis Tyton and John Field.

Block, K.S. (ed.), 1922. *Ludus Coventriae or The Plaie Called Corpus Christi. Cotton MS. Vespasian D. VIII.* Early English Text Society, Extra Series 120. London, New York, and Toronto: OUP.

Bonhoeffer, D., 1963. *The Cost of Discipleship.* Revised edition. Trans. R.H. Fuller. New York: Macmillan.

Brontë, C., E. Brontë, and A. Brontë, 1846. *Poems by Currer, Ellis, and Acton Bell.* London: Aylott and Jones.

Bruderhof, 2012. *Foundations of Our Faith and Calling.* Rifton and Robertsbridge: The Plough Publishing House.

Budge, E.A.W. (ed.), 1935. *The Contendings of the Apostles, Being the Histories of the Lives and Martyrdoms and Deaths of the Twelve Apostles and Evangelists. Translated from the Ethiopic Manuscripts in the British Museum.* London: Humphrey Milford for OUP.

Bunyan, J., 1678. *The Pilgrim's Progress from This World to That Which Is to Come.* London.

Calvin, J., 1949. *Commentary on a Harmony of the Evangelists, Matthew, Mark, and Luke.* Trans. W. Pringle. 3 vols. Grand Rapids: Eerdmans.

Calvin, J., 1972. *Calvin's New Testament Commentaries: A Harmony of the Gospels Matthew, Mark and Luke.* Trans. T.H.L. Parker and A.W. Morrison. Ed. D.W. Torrance and T.F. Torrance. 3 vols. Grand Rapids: Eerdmans.

Carey, W., 1891. *An Enquiry into the Obligations of Christians, to Use Means for the Conversion of the Heathen.* London: Hodder and Stoughton.

Chapman, G., J. Cleese, T. Gilliam, E. Idle, T. Jones, and M. Palin, 1979. *Monty Python's The Life of Brian (of Nazareth).* New York: F. Jordan.

Christian of Stavelot, 2008. *Expositio super librum generationis.* Ed. R.B.C. Huygens. CCCM 224. Turnhout: Brepols.

Clement of Alexandria, 1954. *Christ the Educator.* Trans. S.P. Wood. FC 23. Washington: Catholic University of America Press.

Community of Oberammergau, 1960. *The Passion Play at Oberammergau: A Religious Festival Play in Three Sections with 20 Tableaux Vivants. Written in 1860 by J.A. Daisenberger on the Basis of Old Texts.* Oberammergau: Gemeinde Oberammergau.

Conrad, J., 1995. *Heart of Darkness and Other Stories.* Wordsworth Classics. Ware: Wordsworth Editions.

Corns, T.N., A. Hughes, and D. Loewenstein (ed.), 2009. *The Complete Works of Gerrard Winstanley.* 2 vols. Oxford: OUP.

Cornwallis, M., 1820. *Observations, Critical, Explanatory, and Practical, on the Canonical Scriptures, Volume IV.* 2nd edition. London: Baldwin, Cradock, and Joy, pp. 1–109.

Daley, B.E. (trans.), 2013. *Light on the Mountain: Greek Patristic and Byzantine Homilies on the Transfiguration of the Lord.* Popular Patristics Series. Yonkers: St. Vladimir's Seminary Press.

Dante Alighieri, 1904. *The De Monarchia of Dante Alighieri*. Ed. and trans. A. Henry. Boston and New York: Houghton, Mifflin and Co.

Dante Alighieri, 1995. *The Divine Comedy. Volume II: Purgatory*. Trans. M. Musa. New York and Harmondsworth: Penguin Classics.

Douglas, L.C., 1999. *The Robe*. Boston and New York: Houghton Mifflin Co.

Duffield, G.E. (ed.), 1965. *The Work of William Tyndale*. Philadelphia: Fortress.

Edwards, J., 1746. *An Humble Inquiry into the Rules of the Word of God, Concerning the Qualifications Requisite to a Compleat Standing and Full Communion in the Visible Christian Church*. Boston: S. Kneeland.

Elgar, E., 1903. *The Apostles (Parts I. & II.): An Oratorio (Op. 49)*. London: Novello and Company.

Eliot, T.S., 1965. *Collected Poems, 1909–1962*. New York: Harcourt.

Elliott, J.K. (ed.), 1993. *The Apocryphal New Testament*. Oxford: Clarendon Press.

Elliott, J.R., and G.A. Runnalls (ed. and trans.), 1978. *The Baptism and Temptation of Christ: The First Day of a Medieval French Passion Play*. New Haven and London: Yale University Press.

Ephrem the Syrian, 1989. *Hymns*. Trans. K.E. McVey. CWS. New York and Mahwah: Paulist.

Ephrem the Syrian, 1993. *Saint Ephrem's Commentary on Tatian's Diatessaron: An English Translation of Chester Beatty Syriac MS 709 with Introduction and Notes*. Trans. and ed. C. McCarthy. Journal of Semitic Studies Supplement 2. Oxford: OUP.

Epiphanius, 2013. *The Panarion of Epiphanius of Salamis. Books II and III. De Fide*. Trans. F. Williams. Nag Hammadi and Manichaean Studies. Leiden and Boston: Brill.

Erasmus, D., 1986. *Erasmus' Annotations on the New Testament: The Gospels*. Ed. A. Reeve. London: Duckworth.

Erasmus, D., 2008. *Collected Works of Erasmus 45: Paraphrase on Matthew*. Trans. D. Simpson. Ed. R.D. Sider. Toronto, Buffalo, and London: University of Toronto Press.

Eusebius of Caesarea, 2008. *Questions Évangéliques*. Ed. C. Zamagni. SC 523. Paris: Éditions du Cerf.

Fast, G., and G.A. Peters (trans.), 2001. *Biblical Concordance of the Swiss Brethren, 1540*. Anabaptist Texts in Translation. Ed. C.A. Snyder. Kitchener: Pandora.

Ford, J., 1859. *The Gospel of S. Matthew, Illustrated (Chiefly in the Doctrinal and Moral Sense) from Ancient and Modern Authors*. 2nd edition. London: Joseph Masters.

Fortunatianus of Aquileia, 2017. *Commentary on the Gospels*. Trans. and intro. H.A.G. Houghton, in association with L.J. Dorfbauer. Berlin and Boston: de Gruyter.

Gandhi, M.K., 1930. 'Render unto Caesar,' *Young India* 12/13 (March 27): 1.

Gemayel, B. (ed.), 1984. *The Prayer of the Faithful According to the Maronite Liturgical Year. Volume 2: Season of Great Lent, Passion Week, Season of Easter*. Brooklyn: Diocese of Saint Maron.

Gregory of Nazianzus, 2008. *Festal Orations*. Trans. N.V. Harrison. Popular Patristics Series 36. Yonkers: St. Vladimir's Seminary Press.

Gregory of Nyssa, 1916. *Life of St. Macrina*. Trans. W.K. Lowther Clarke. London: SPCK.

Gregory of Nyssa, 1954. *The Lord's Prayer; The Beatitudes*. Trans. H. Graef. Ancient Christian Writers 18. New York and Mahwah: Paulist.

Gregory the Great, 1990. *Forty Gospel Homilies*. Trans. D. Hurst. CSS 123. Kalamazoo: Cistercian Publications.

Hammond, H., 1845. *A Paraphrase and Annotations upon All the Books of the New Testament, Briefly Explaining All the Difficult Places Thereof, Volume I*. Oxford: OUP.

Harris, J.R., 1895. *Fragments of the Commentary of Ephrem Syrus upon the Diatessaron*. London: C.J. Clay and Sons.

Harris, M. (trans.) 1969. *The Cornish Ordinalia: A Medieval Dramatic Trilogy*. Washington, DC: Catholic University of America Press.

Henry, M., 1960. *Commentary on the Whole Bible by Matthew Henry: New One Volume Edition*. Ed. L.F. Church. Grand Rapids: Zondervan.

Hilary of Poitiers, 1978. *Sur Matthieu* I–II. Ed. J. Doignon. SC 254 and 258. Paris: Éditions du Cerf.

Hilary of Poitiers, 2012. *Commentary on Matthew*. Trans. D.H. Williams. FC 125. Washington, DC: Catholic University of America Press.

Hildegard of Bingen, 2011. *Homilies on the Gospels*. Trans. B.M. Kienzle. CSS 241. Collegeville: Liturgical Press/Cistercian Publications.

Holmes, M.W. (ed. and trans.), 2007. *The Apostolic Fathers: Greek Texts and English Translations*. 3rd edition. Grand Rapids: Baker Academic.

Howard, G., 1995. *Hebrew Gospel of Matthew*. 2nd edition. Macon: Mercer University Press.

Hussey, A., 1975. *The Chester Mystery Plays: Seventeen Pageant Plays from the Chester Craft Cycle Adapted into Modern English*. 2nd edition. London: Heinemann.

The Hymnal, 1982: According to the Use of the Episcopal Church. New York: Church Hymnal Corporation.

Isaac of Stella, 1979. *Sermons on the Christian Year: Volume One*. Trans. H. McCaffery. CFS 11. Kalamazoo: Cistercian Publications.

Ishoʿdad of Merv, 1911. *The Commentaries*. Ed. M.D. Gibson. Horae Semiticae 5. Vol. 1.Cambridge: CUP.

Jacob of Sarug, 2008. *Jacob of Sarug's Homily on the Transfiguration of Our Lord*. Trans. T. Kollamparampil. Texts from Christian Late Antiquity 13. The Metrical Homilies of Mar Jacob of Sarug. Piscataway: Gorgias Press.

Jerome, 1965. *Dogmatic and Polemical Works*. Trans. J.N. Hritzu. FC 53. Washington: Catholic University of America Press.

Jerome, 2008. *Commentary on Matthew*. Trans T.P. Scheck. FC 117. Washington: Catholic University of America Press.

John of Hildesheim, 1955. *The Story of the Three Kings: Melchior, Balthasar and Jaspar, Which Originally Was Written by John of Hildesheim in the Fourteenth Century and Is Now Retold by Margaret B. Freeman*. New York: Metropolitan Museum of Art.

Johnson, T.J. (trans.), 2008. *The Works of Bonaventure: The Sunday Sermons of St. Bonaventure*. St. Bonaventure: Franciscan Publications.

Kardong, T.G., 1996. *Benedict's Rule: A Translation and Commentary*. Collegeville: Liturgical Press.

Keble, J., 1885. *The Christian Year: Thoughts in Verse for the Sundays and Holydays Throughout the Year*. London and Newcastle-upon-Tyne: Walter Scott.

Kellerman, J.A. (trans.) and Oden, T.C. (ed.), 2010. *Incomplete Commentary on Matthew (Opus imperfectum)*. Ancient Christian Texts. 2 vols. Downers Grove: IVP Academic.

Kraszewski, C.S. (trans.), 1999. *The Gospel of Matthew with Patristic Commentaries*. Studies in Bible and Early Christianity 40. Lewiston, Queenston, and Lampeter: Edwin Mellen Press.

Labriola, A.C., and Smeltz, J.W. (trans.), 1990. *The Bible of the Poor [Biblia Pauperum]: A Facsimile and Edition of the British Library Blockbook C.9 d.2*. Pittsburgh: Duquesne University Press.

LaHaye, T., and J. Jenkins, 1997. *Nicolae: The Rise of the Antichrist*. Wheaton: Tyndale House.

Lake, K. (trans.), 1912. *The Apostolic Fathers, Volume I*. LCL. London: William Heinemann.

Lambertsen, I.E. (trans.), 1997. *The Menaion of the Orthodox Church. Volume XI: August*. Liberty: St. John of Kronstadt Press.

Lambertsen, I.E., 2000. *The Menaion of the Orthodox Church. Volume V: January*. Liberty: St. John of Kronstadt Press.

Landau, B., 2010. *Revelation of the Magi: The Lost Tale of the Wise Men's Journey to Bethlehem*. New York: Harper Collins.

Lapide, C. a, 1890. *The Great Commentary*. 4th edition. Trans. T.W. Mossman. 5 vols. Catholic Standard Library. London: John Hodges.

Lapide, P., 1986. *The Sermon on the Mount: Utopia or Program for Action?* Trans. A. Swidler. Maryknoll: Orbis.

Lightfoot, J., 1859. *Horae Hebraicae et Talmudicae*. 4 vols. Oxford: OUP.

Luther, M., 1956. *Luther's Works. Volume 21: The Sermon on the Mount (Sermons) and The Magnificat*. Trans. J. Pelikan. St. Louis: Concordia.

Luther, M., 1959. *Luther's Works. Volume 51: Sermons I*. Ed. and Trans. J.W. Doberstein; general editor H.T. Lehmann. Philadelphia: Muhlenberg.

Luther, M., 2014. *Luther's Works. Volume 68: Sermons on the Gospel of St. Matthew Chapters 19–24*. Ed. B.T.G. Mayes. Saint Louis: Concordia Publishing House.

Luther, M., 2015. *Luther's Works. Volume 67: Annotations on Matthew Chapters 1–18. Sermons on the Gospel of St. Matthew Chapter 18*. Ed. C.B. Brown. St. Louis: Concordia Publishing House.

Macaulay, R., 1921. *Dangerous Ages*. New York: Boni and Liveright.

Maldonado, J. de, 1888. *A Commentary on the Holy Gospels. S. Matthew's Gospel*. Trans. G.J. Davie. 2 vols. London: John Hodges.

Marco Polo, 2016. *The Description of the World*. Trans. S. Kinoshita. Indianapolis and Cambridge: Hackett Publishing Company.

Marty, M.E., 1983. *The Place of Trust: Martin Luther on The Sermon on the Mount*. San Francisco: Harper & Row.

McGinn, B. (trans.), 1979. *Apocalyptic Spirituality*. CWS. New York: Missionary Society of St. Paul.

McHugh, J.A., and C.J. Callan (trans.), 1972. *Catechism of the Council of Trent for Parish Priests*. South Bend: Marian Publications.

Merton, T., 1983. *The Sign of Jonas*. New York: Octagon.

Milton, J., 1968. *Paradise Lost and Paradise Regained*. Ed. C. Ricks. New York and Toronto: The New American Library; London: The New English Library Ltd.

Milton, J., 1999. *The Annotated Milton: Complete English Poems*. Ed. B. Raffel. New York: Bantam.

Mingana, A., 1927. 'A New Life of John the Baptist,' in J.R. Harris (ed.), *Woodbrooke Studies: Christian Documents in Syriac, Arabic, and Garshuni*. Vol. 1. Cambridge: W. Heffer & Sons, pp. 234–287.

Mooney, M.S., 1915. *A Rosary of Mystery Plays: Fifteen Plays Selected from the York Cycle of Mysteries Performed by the Crafts on the Day of Corpus Christi in the 14th, 15th and 16th Centuries*. Albany: Frank H. Evory.

Murphy, G.R. (trans.), 1992. *The Heliand: The Saxon Gospel*. New York and Oxford: OUP.

Origen, 1979. *An Exhortation to Martyrdom, Prayer, First Principles: Book IV, Prologue to the Commentary on the Song of Songs, Homily XXVII on Numbers*. Trans. R.A. Greer. CWS. New York, Ramsey, and Toronto: Paulist.

Pelikan, J. (ed.), 1967. *The Preaching of Chrysostom: Homilies on the Sermon on the Mount*. Preacher's Paperback Library. Philadelphia: Fortress.

Pelikan, J., and V. Hotchkiss (ed.), 2003. *Creeds & Confessions of Faith in the Christian Tradition. Volume II, Part Four: Creeds and Confessions of the Reformation Era*. New Haven and London: Yale University Press.

Peterson, E.H., 2002. *The Message: The Bible in Contemporary Language*. Colorado Springs: NavPress.

Ragusa, I., and R.B. Green (ed.), 1961. *Meditations on the Life of Christ: An Illustrated Manuscript of the Fourteenth Century. Paris, Bibliothèque Nationale, Ms. Ital. 115*. Princeton: Princeton University Press.

Reimarus, H.S., 1985. *Fragments*. Trans. R.S. Fraser. Ed. C.H. Talbert. Chico: Scholars Press.

Rheims, 1582. *The Nevv Testament of Iesvs Christ, translated faithfully into English, out of the authentical Latin, according to the best corrected copies of the same, diligently conferred with the Greeke and other editions in diuers languages*. Rhemes: Iohn Fogny.

Romanos the Melodist, 1995. *Kontakia on the Life of Christ*. Trans. E. Lash. Sacred Literature Series. San Francisco, London, and Pymble: HarperCollins.

Romero, O., 2003. *The Violence of Love*. Trans. J.R. Brockman. Farmington: The Bruderhof Foundation.

Rowling, J.K., 1997. *Harry Potter and the Philosopher's Stone*. London: Bloomsbury.

Rufus of Shotep, 1998. *Homilies on the Gospels of Matthew and Luke. Introduction, Text, Translation, Commentary*. Ed. and trans. J.M. Sheridan. Unione Accademica Nazionale: Corpus dei Manoscritti Copti Letterari. Rome: C.I.M.

Rupert of Deutz, 1979. *Ruperti Tuitiensis, De Gloria et Honore Filii Hominis super Mattheum*. Ed. H. Haacke. CCCM 29. Turnholt: Brepols.

Ruskin, J., 1904. *St. Mark's Rest*. Rahway and New York: The Mershon Company.

Saak, E.L., 2015. *Catechesis in the Later Middle Ages I:* The Exposition of the Lord's Prayer of Jordan of Quedlinburg, OESA (d. 1380). Studies in Medieval and Reformation Traditions: Texts & Sources 6. Ed. F. Eisermann. Leiden: Brill.

Saïd, M.-B., and G. Perigo (trans.), 1979. *Magnificat: Homilies in Praise of the Blessed Virgin Mary by Bernard of Clairvaux and Amadeus of Lausanne*. CFS 18. Kalamazoo: Cistercian Publications.

Samuelian, T.J., 2001. *Speaking with God from the Depths of the Heart: The Armenian Prayer Book of St. Gregory of Narek*. Yerevan: Vem Press.

Sayers, D.L., 2011. *The Man Born to Be King: A Play-Cycle on the Life of Our Lord and Saviour Jesus Christ*. Eugene: Wipf & Stock.

Schaff, P., 1861. *Slavery and the Bible: A Tract for the Times*. Chambersburg: M. Kieffer and Co.

Schneemelcher, W. (ed.), 1992. *New Testament Apocrypha. Revised Edition of the Collection Initiated by Edgar Hennecke. Volume II: Writings Relating to the Apostles, Apocalypses and Related Subjects*. Trans. R. McL. Wilson. Cambridge and Louisville: James Clarke and Westminster John Knox.

Scofield, C.I. (ed.), 1917. *The Scofield Reference Bible*. New and improved edition. New York: OUP.

Simonetti, M. (ed.), 2001. *Matthew 1–13*. ACCS: New Testament 1a. Downers Grove: IVP.

Simonetti, M. (ed.), 2002. *Matthew 14–28*. ACCS: New Testament 1b. Downers Grove: IVP.

Smith, H., 1925–1929. *Ante-Nicene Exegesis of the Gospels*. Translations of Christian Literature. 6 vols. London: SPCK.

Smith, H.S., R.T. Handy, and L.A. Loetscher (ed.), 1963. *American Christianity: An Historical Interpretation with Representative Documents*. 2 vols. New York: Charles Scribner's Sons.

Smith, J., 1851. *The Pearl of Great Price: Being a Choice Selection from the Revelations, Translations, and Narrations of Joseph Smith, First Prophet, Seer, and Revelator to the Church of Jesus Christ of Latter-Day Saints*. Liverpool: F.D. Richards.

Spenser, E., 1965. *Books I and II of 'The Faerie Queene,' the Mutability Cantos and Selections from the Minor Poetry*. Ed. R. Kellogg and O. Steele. New York: The Odyssey Press.

Spinka, M. (ed.), 1953. *Advocates of Reform: From Wyclif to Erasmus*. Library of Christian Classics Volume XIV. Philadelphia: Westminster.

Stanton, E.C., 1898. *The Woman's Bible. Part II: Comments on the Old and New Testaments from Joshua to Revelation*. New York: European Publishing Company.

Stanton, E.C., 2002. *The Woman's Bible: A Classic Feminist Perspective*. Mineola: Dover Publications.

Stedman, E.C., and E. Mackay Hutchinson, 1889. *A Library of American Literature from the Earliest Settlement to the Present Time. Volume II: Later Colonial Literature*. New York: Charles L. Webster and Co.

Stewart-Sykes, A. (trans.), 2004. *Tertullian, Cyprian, Origen: On the Lord's Prayer*. Popular Patristics Series. Crestwood: St. Vladimir's Seminary Press.

Stoddart, J.T., 1914. *The New Testament in Life and Literature*. London, New York, and Toronto: Hodder and Stoughton.

Tanner, N.P. (ed.), 1990. *Decrees of the Ecumenical Councils*. 2 vols. London and Washington: Sheed & Ward and Georgetown University Press.

Taylor, A.A.E., 1899. *Claudia Procula and Other Verses*. Columbus: McClelland & Co.

Taylor, J., 1989. *Holy Living and Holy Dying*. Ed. P.G. Stanwood. 2 vols. Oxford: Clarendon Press.

Teresa of Avila, 1980. *The Collected Works of Saint Teresa: Volume 2*. Trans. K. Kavanaugh and O. Rodriguez. Washington: ICS Publications.

Theophylact, 1992. *The Explanation by Blessed Theophylact Archbishop of Ochrid and Bulgaria of the Holy Gospel According to St. Matthew*. House Springs: Chrysostom Press.

Tippens, D., J.M. Walker, and S. Weathers (ed.), 2013. *Shadow and Light: Literature and the Life of Faith*. 3rd edition. Abilene: Abilene Christian University Press.

Tissot, J., 2009. *The Life of Christ: The Complete Set of 350 Watercolors*. London and Brooklyn: Merrell and Brooklyn Museum.

Tolstoy, L., 1927. *Resurrection*. Revised edition. Trans. L. Maude. New York: Grosset & Dunlap.

Tolstoy, L., 1966. *Resurrection*. Trans. L. Maude. New York: Norton and Company.

Tydeman, W. (ed.), 2001. *The Medieval European Stage, 500–1500*. Theatre in Europe: A Documentary History. Cambridge and New York: CUP.

Valdés, J. de, 1882. *Commentary upon the Gospel of St. Matthew*. Trans. J.T. Betts. London: Trübner and Co.

van Nieuwenhove, R., R. Faesen, and H. Rolfson (ed.), 2008. *Late Medieval Mysticism of the Low Countries. CWS*. New York and Mahwah: Paulist.

Vaporis, N.M. (trans.), 1993. *The Services for Holy Week and Easter*. Brookline: Holy Cross Orthodox Press.

von le Fort, G., 2015. *The Wife of Pilate and Other Stories*. Trans. M.J. Miller. San Francisco: Ignatius.

Voragine, J. de, 1993. *The Golden Legend: Readings on the Saints*. Trans. W.G. Ryan. 2 vols. Princeton: Princeton University Press.

Ward, B. (trans.), 1975. *The Sayings of the Desert Fathers: The Alphabetic Collection*. Kalamazoo: Cistercian Publications.

Waters, C.M. (ed.), 2008. *Virgins and Scholars: A Fifteenth-Century Compilation of the Lives of John the Baptist, John the Evangelist, Jerome, and Katherine of Alexandria*. Medieval Women: Texts and Contexts. Turnhout: Brepols.

Wesley, J., 1986. *The Works of John Wesley. Volume 3: Sermons III 71–114*. Ed. A.C. Outler. Nashville: Abingdon.

White, C., 2000. *Early Christian Latin Poets*. London and New York: Routledge.

Wilkinson, J. (trans.), 1981. *Egeria's Travels to the Holy Land*. Revised edition. Jerusalem and Warminster: Ariel and Aris & Phillips.

William of Ockham, 1992. *A Short Discourse on the Tyrannical Government*. Ed. A.S. McGrade. Trans. J. Kilcullen. Cambridge and New York: CUP.

Woods (ed.), 1993. *The Poems of Aemilia Lanyer: Salve Deus Rex Judaeorum*. New York and Oxford: Oxford University Press.
Woolf, B.L. (trans.), 1953. *Reformation Writings of Martin Luther. Volume I: The Basis of the Protestant Reformation*. New York: Philosophical Library.
Zell, K.S., 2006. *Church Mother: The Writings of a Protestant Reformer in Sixteenth-Century Germany*. Ed. and trans. E.A. McKee. Chicago: University of Chicago Press.

Secondary Sources

Adam, A.K.M., 1990. 'The Sign of Jonah: A Fish-Eye View,' *Semeia* 51: 177–191.
Ahern, B., 1943. 'Staff or No Staff?' *CBQ* 5/3: 332–337.
Aichele, G., 1978. 'The Slaughter of Innocents,' *Christian Century* 95: 1262–1263.
Aichele, G., 2002. 'Translation as De-Canonization: Matthew's Gospel According to Pasolini,' *Cross Currents* 51: 524–534.
Akin, D.L., 1988. 'An Expositional Analysis of *The Schleitheim Confession*,' *Criswell Theological Review* 2: 345–370.
Albright, W.F., and C.S. Mann, 1971. *Matthew*. AB 26. Garden City: Doubleday.
Alkholy, I., 2008. 'A Re-Reading of Western Narrative Art in the Context of the Middle East Today,' *Third Text* 22/4: 439–447.
Allen, W.C., 1907. *A Critical and Exegetical Commentary on the Gospel According to St. Matthew*. Edinburgh: T. & T. Clark.
Allen, L., 1992. 'The Sermon on the Mount in the History of the Church,' *Review and Expositor* 89: 245–262.
Allison, D.C., 1993a. *The New Moses: A Matthean Typology*. Edinburgh: T. & T. Clark.
Allison, D.C., 1993b. 'Divorce, Celibacy, and Joseph (Matthew 1.18–25 and 19.1–12),' *JSNT* 49: 3–10.
Allison, D.C., 1994. 'Anticipating the Passion: The Literary Reach of Matthew 26:47–27:56,' *CBQ* 56: 701–714.
Allison, D.C., 2005. *Studies in Matthew: Interpretation Past and Present*. Grand Rapids: Baker Academic.
Allison, D.C., 2008. 'Matthew and the History of Its Interpretation,' *ExpTim* 120/1: 1–7.
Andersen, F.I., 1961–1962. 'The Diet of John the Baptist,' *Abr-Nahrain* 3: 60–74.
Anthony, P.B., 2014. Interpreting Vision: A Survey of Patristic Reception of the Transfiguration and Its Earliest Depiction, with Special Reference to the Gospel of Luke. Unpublished DPhil thesis, University of Oxford.
Apostolos-Cappadona, D., 2009. 'Imagining Salome, or How *La Sauterelle* Became *La Femme Fatale*,' in C.E. Joynes and C.C. Rowland (ed.), *From the Margins 2: Women of the New Testament and Their Afterlives*. Sheffield: Sheffield Phoenix Press, pp. 190–209.
Arand, C.P., 1995. 'The Battle Cry of Faith: The Catechisms' Exposition of the Lord's Prayer,' *Concordia Journal* 21: 42–65.
Arendzen, J.P., 1919. 'Ante-Nicene Interpretations of the Sayings on Divorce,' *JTS* 20/79: 230–241.

Argyle, A.W., 1956. 'Joseph the Patriarch in Patristic Teaching,' *ExpTim* 67: 199–201.

Askew, P., 1961. 'The Parable Paintings of Domenico Fetti,' *The Art Bulletin* 43/1: 21–45.

Ayo, N., 1992. *The Lord's Prayer: A Survey Theological and Literary*. Notre Dame: University of Notre Dame Press.

Bacon, B.W., 1930. *Studies in Matthew*. New York: Henry Holt and Company.

Baert, B., 2011. *Interspaces Between Word, Gaze and Touch: The Bible and the Visual Medium in the Middle Ages. Collected Essays on 'Noli me tangere,' the Woman with the Haemorrhage, the Head of John the Baptist*. Leuven, Paris, and Walpole: Peeters.

Baert, B., L. Kusters, and E. Sidgwick, 2012. 'An Issue of Blood: The Healing of the Woman with the Haemorrhage (*Mark* 5.24B–34; *Luke* 8.42B–48; *Matthew* 9.19–22) in Early Medieval Visual Culture,' *Journal of Religion and Health* 51: 664–681.

Baggley, J., 2000. *Festival Icons for the Christian Year*. London: Mowbray.

Bahr, G.J., 1965. 'The Use of the Lord's Prayer in the Primitive Church,' *JBL* 84/2: 153–159.

Baird, W., 1992. *History of New Testament Research. Volume One: From Deism to Tübingen*. Minneapolis: Fortress.

Baldini, U., and O. Casazza, 1992. *The Brancacci Chapel Frescoes*. London: Thames and Hudson.

Barber, M.P., 2013. 'Jesus as the Davidic Temple Builder and Peter's Priestly Role in Matthew 16:16–19,' *JBL* 132/4: 935–953.

Barclay, W., 1975. *The Gospel of Matthew: Volume 2*. Daily Study Bible Series. Revised edition. Philadelphia: Westminster.

Barton, S.C., 2001. 'The Transfiguration of Christ According to Mark and Matthew: Christology and Anthropology,' in F. Avemarie and H. Lichtenberger (ed.), *Auferstehung – Resurrection: The Fourth Durham–Tübingen Research Symposium: Resurrection, Transfiguration and Exaltation in Old Testament, Ancient Judaism and Early Christianity*. Tübingen: Mohr Siebeck, pp. 231–246.

Bates, M.W., 2013. 'Cryptic Codes and a Violent King: A New Proposal for Matthew 11:12 and Luke 16:16,' *CBQ* 75: 74–93.

Baudoin, A.-C., 2010, 'La femme de Pilate dans les *Actes de Pilate*, recension grecque A (II, 1),' *Apocrypha* 21: 133–149.

Baugh, L., 1997. *Imaging the Divine: Jesus and Christ-Figures in Film*. Kansas City: Sheed & Ward.

Bauman, C., 1985. *The Sermon on the Mount: The Modern Quest for Its Meaning*. Macon: Mercer University Press.

Beare, F.W., 1981. *The Gospel According to Matthew: A Commentary*. Oxford: Blackwell.

Beasley-Murray, G.R., 1993. *Jesus and the Last Days: The Interpretation of the Olivet Discourse*. Peabody: Hendrickson.

Beattie, T., 2007. 'Mary in Patristic Theology,' in S.J. Boss (ed.), *Mary: The Complete Resource*. London and New York: Continuum, pp. 75–105.

Becker, E.-M., 2015. 'Contemporary Approaches to Matthew: A "Lutheran" Critique,' in K. Mtata and C. Koester (ed.), *To All the Nations: Lutheran Hermeneutics and the Gospel of Matthew*. LWF Studies. Leipzig: Lutheran World Federation/Evangelische Verlangsanstalt, pp. 15–25.

Becker-Leckrone, M., 1995. 'Salome©: The Fetishization of a Textual Corpus,' *New Literary History* 26/2: 239–260.

Bedouelle, G., 2009. 'Biblical Interpretation in the Catholic Reformation,' in A.J. Hauser and D.F. Watson (ed.), *A History of Biblical Interpretation. Volume 2: The Medieval Through the Reformation Periods.* Grand Rapids and Cambridge: Eerdmans, pp. 428–449.

Bennett, Z., 2011. 'Ruskin, The Bible, and the Death of Rose La Touche: A "Torn Manuscript of the Human Soul,"' in M. Lieb, E. Mason, J. Roberts, and C. Rowland (ed.), *The Oxford Handbook of the Reception History of the Bible.* Oxford and New York: OUP, pp. 576–589.

Berdini, P., 1997. *The Religious Art of Jacopo Bassano: Painting as Visual Exegesis.* Cambridge, New York, and Melbourne: CUP.

Bertrand, G.-M., 1954. 'Un office du XIIIe siècle en l'honneur de Saint Joseph (Abbaye Saint-Laurent de Liège),' *Cahiers de Joséphologie* 2: 159–170, 289–322.

Bertrand, D.A., 1973. *Le Baptême de Jésus: Histoire de l'exégèse aux deux premiers siècles.* BGBE 14. Tübingen: J.C.B. Mohr (Paul Siebeck).

Betz, H.D., 1985. *Essays on the Sermon on the Mount.* Trans. L.L. Welborn. Philadelphia: Fortress.

Betz, H.D., 1995. *A Commentary on the Sermon on the Mount, Including the Sermon on the Plain (Matthew 5:3–7:27 and Luke 6:20–49).* Hermeneia. Minneapolis: Fortress.

Beyschlag, K., 1977. 'Zur Geschichte der Bergpredigt in der Alten Kirche,' *ZThK* 74/3: 291–322.

Bhattacharji, S., 1995. '*Pearl* and the Liturgical "Common of Virgins,"' *Medium Aevum* 64/1: 37–50.

Bigane, J.E., 1981. *Faith, Christ, or Peter: Matthew 16:18 in Sixteenth Century Roman Catholic Exegesis.* Washington: University Press of America.

Bingham, J., 1998. *Irenaeus' Use of Matthew's Gospel in 'Adversus Haereses.'* Leuven: Peeters.

Bird, M.F., 2004. 'The Case of the Proselytizing Pharisees? – Matthew 23:15,' *JSHJ* 2/2: 117–137.

Birns, N., 2008. 'Birth and Death: Eliot's *Journey of the Magi*,' *Sewanee Theological Review* 51/3: 269–279.

Bishop, E.F.F., 1962. 'The Parable of the Lost or Wandering Sheep,' *ATR* 44: 44–57.

Blomberg, C.L., 1991. 'Interpreting the Parables of Jesus: Where Are We and Where Do We Go from Here?' *CBQ* 53/1: 50–78.

Blowers, P.M., 2009. 'Eastern Orthodox Biblical Interpretation,' in A.J. Hauser and D.F. Watson (ed.), *A History of Biblical Interpretation. Volume 2: The Medieval Through the Reformation Periods.* Grand Rapids and Cambridge: Eerdmans, pp. 172–200.

Bockmuehl, M.N.A., 1989. 'Matthew 5.32; 19.9 in the Light of Pre-Rabbinic Halakah,' *NTS* 35: 291–295.

Bockmuehl, M.N.A., 1995. 'A Commentator's Approach to the "Effective History" of Philippians,' *JSNT* 60: 57–88.

Bockmuehl, M.N.A., 1998. 'Let the Dead Bury Their Dead' (Matt. 8:22/Luke 9:60): Jesus and the Halakhah,' *JTS* 49/2: 553–581.

Bockmuehl, M.N.A., 2006. *Seeing the Word: Refocusing New Testament Study*. Studies in Theological Interpretation. Grand Rapids: Baker Academic.
Bockmuehl, M.N.A., 2011. 'The Son of David and His Mother,' *JTS* 62/2: 476–493.
Bockmuehl, M.N.A., 2012. *Simon Peter in Scripture and Memory: The New Testament Apostle in the Early Church*. Grand Rapids: Baker Academic.
Boggs, C.J., 2008. '"The Jews" and "the Pharisees" in Early Quaker Polemic,' *Quaker History* 97/2: 1–18.
Böhm, O., 1910. 'The Calling of S. Matthew, by Carpaccio,' *Burlington Magazine* 16/82: 228–233.
Bonsirven, J., 1948. *Le divorce dans le Nouveau Testament*. Paris: Société de S. Jean l'Evangéliste, Desclée & Die.
Boring, M.E., 1995. 'The Gospel of Matthew: Introduction, Commentary in Reflections,' in L. Keck (ed.), *The New Interpreter's Bible: Volume VIII*. Nashville: Abingdon.
Boring, M.E., 2006. *Mark: A Commentary*. NTL. Louisville and London: Westminster John Knox, pp. 87–505.
Bornkamm, G., 1982. 'The Stilling of the Storm in Matthew,' in G. Bornkamm, G. Barth, and H.J. Held, *Tradition and Interpretation in Matthew*. 2nd enlarged edition. Trans. P. Scott. London: SCM, pp. 52–57.
Bosch, D.J., 2011. *Transforming Mission: Paradigm Shifts in Theology of Mission*. Twentieth Anniversary Edition. Maryknoll: Orbis.
Boskovits, M., and D.A. Brown, 2003. *Italian Paintings of the Fifteenth Century*. National Gallery of Art. New York and Oxford: OUP.
Bowers, R.H., 1971. *The Legend of Jonah*. The Hague: Martinus Nijhoff.
Boxall, I., 2013. *Patmos in the Reception History of the Apocalypse*. Oxford Theology & Religion Monographs. Oxford: OUP.
Boxall, I., 2014. *Discovering Matthew: Content, Interpretation, Reception*. London: SPCK.
Boxall, I., 2018. 'From the Magi to Pilate's Wife: David Brown, Tradition, and the Reception of Matthew's Text,' in C.R. Brewer, G.V. Allen, and D. Kinlaw (ed.), *The Moving Text: Interdisciplinary Perspectives on David Brown and the Bible*. London: SCM, pp. 17–36.
Branch, T., 1998. *Pillar of Fire: America in the King Years 1963–65*. New York: Simon & Schuster.
Brändle, R., 2008. 'This Sweetest Passage: Matthew 25:31–46 and Assistance to the Poor in the Homilies of John Chrysostom,' in S.R. Holman (ed.), *Wealth and Poverty in Early Church and Society*. Grand Rapids: Baker Academic, 127–139.
Brandon, S.G.F., 1967. *Jesus and the Zealots*. New York: Scribner's.
Braswell, M.F., 1995. 'Chaucer's Palimpsest: Judas Iscariot and the "Pardoner's Tale,"' *The Chaucer Review* 29/3: 303–310.
Brawer, R.A., 1972. 'The Characterization of Pilate in the York Cycle Play,' *Studies in Philology* 69/3: 289–303.
Bringéus, N.-A., 2003. 'The Rest on the Flight into Egypt: A Motif in Scandinavian Folk Art,' *Folklore* 114/3: 323–333.
Brock, S.P., 1970. 'The Baptist's Diet in Syrian Sources,' *Oriens christianus* 54: 113–124.

Brock, S.P., 1992. *The Luminous Eye: The Spiritual World Vision of Saint Ephrem.* Kalamazoo: Cistercian Publications.

Brooten, B., 1982. 'Konnten Frauen im alten Judentum die Scheidung betreiben?' *Evangelische Theologie* 42: 65–80.

Brown, R.E., 1961. 'The Pater Noster as an Eschatological Prayer,' *TS* 22: 175–208.

Brown, S., 1979. 'The Matthean Apocalypse,' *JSNT* 4: 2–27.

Brown, S., 1993. *The Birth of the Messiah: A Commentary on the Infancy Narratives in the Gospels of Matthew and Luke.* New updated edition. London: Geoffrey Chapman.

Brown, S., 1994. *The Death of the Messiah: From Gethsemane to the Grave.* 2 vols. Anchor Bible Reference Library. New York and London: Doubleday.

Brown, S., 1997. *An Introduction to the New Testament.* ABRL. New York and London: Doubleday.

Brown, D., 1999. *Tradition and Imagination: Revelation and Change.* Oxford and New York: OUP.

Brown, M.J., 2004. *The Lord's Prayer Through North African Eyes: A Window into Early Christianity.* New York and London: T. & T. Clark International.

Brown, R.E., and J.P. Meier, 1983. *Antioch and Rome: New Testament Cradles of Catholic Christianity.* London: Geoffrey Chapman.

Brown, R.E., K.P. Donfried, and J. Reumann (ed.), 1974. *Peter in the New Testament.* London: Geoffrey Chapman.

Bucur, B.G., 2007. 'Matt 18.10 in Early Christology and Pneumatology: A Contribution to the Study of Matthean *Wirkungsgeschichte,*' *NovT* 49: 209–231.

Bucur, B.G., 2010. 'Matt 17:1–9 as a Vision of a Vision; A Neglected Strand in the Patristic Reception of the Transfiguration Account,' *Neotestamentica* 44/1: 15–30.

Buhler, S.M., 1997. 'Preventing Wizards: The Magi in Milton's Nativity Ode,' *Journal of English and Germanic Philology* 96/1: 43–57.

Bulbeck, R., 1948. 'The Doubt of St. Joseph,' *CBQ* 10/3: 296–309.

Bulgakov, S., 2003. *The Friend of the Bridegroom: On the Orthodox Veneration of the Forerunner.* Trans. B. Jakim. Grand Rapids and Cambridge: Eerdmans.

Bultmann, R., 1968. *The History of the Synoptic Tradition.* Trans. J. Marsh. Oxford: Basil Blackwell.

Burgess, J.A., 1976. *A History of the Exegesis of Matthew 16: 17–19 from 1781 to 1965.* Ann Arbor: Edwards Brothers.

Burkey, B., 1971. 'The Feast of St. Joseph: A Franciscan Bequest,' *Cahiers de Joséphologie* 19: 647–680.

Burr, D., 2016. 'Olivi, Christ's Three Advents, and The Double Antichrist,' *Franciscan Studies* 74: 15–40.

Bynum, C.W., 1982. *Jesus as Mother: Studies in the Spirituality of the High Middle Ages.* Berkeley, Los Angeles, and London: University of California Press.

Byrne, B., 2004. *Lifting the Burden: Reading Matthew's Gospel in the Church Today.* Collegeville: Liturgical Press.

Byron, J., 2011. 'Abel's Blood and the Ongoing Cry for Vengeance,' *CBQ* 73: 743–756.

Calderhead, C., 2015. *Illuminating the Word: The Making of The Saint John's Bible.* 2nd edition. Collegeville: Liturgical Press.

Callon, C., 2006. 'Pilate the Villain: An Alternative Reading of Matthew's Portrayal of Pilate,' *Biblical Theology Bulletin* 36: 62–71.

Cameron, P.S., 1988. *Violence and the Kingdom: The Interpretation of Matthew 11:12.* 2nd edition. Arbeiten zum Neuen Testament und Judentum Band 5. Frankfurt am Main, Bern, New York, and Paris: Verlag Peter Lang.

Cantwell, L., 1982. 'The Parentage of Jesus: Mt 1:18–21,' *NovT* 24/4: 304–315.

Canty, A., 2011. *Light and Glory: The Transfiguration of Christ in Early Franciscan and Dominican Theology.* Washington: Catholic University of America Press.

Caragounis, C.C., 1990. *Peter and the Rock.* BZNW 58. Berlin and New York: Walter de Gruyter.

Cardenal, E., 2010. *The Gospel in Solentiname.* Trans. D.D. Walsh. Maryknoll: Orbis.

Carlston, C.E., 1988. 'Betz on the Sermon on the Mount – A Critique,' *CBQ* 50: 47–57.

Carter, W., 1999. 'Paying the Tax to Rome as Subversive Praxis: Matthew 17.24–27,' *JSNT* 76: 3–31.

Carter, W., 2000. *Matthew and the Margins: A Sociopolitical and Religious Reading.* Maryknoll: Orbis.

Carter, W., 2003. 'Are There Imperial Texts in the Class? Intertextual Eagles and Matthean Eschatology as "Lights Out" Time for Imperial Rome (Matthew 24:27–31),' *JBL* 122/3: 467–487.

Casazza, O., 1990. *Masaccio and the Brancacci Chapel.* Antella: SCALA.

Cassidy, R.J., 1979. 'Matthew 17.24–7 – A Word on Civil Taxes,' *CBQ* 41: 571–580.

Cavalcanti, E., 2001. 'The Sermon of Leo the First on the Transfiguration (*Serm.* LI Chavasse),' in M.F. Wiles, E.J. Yarnold, and P.M. Parvis (ed.), *Studia Patristica. Vol. XXXVIII/5: St. Augustine and His Opponents; Other Latin Writers.* Leuven: Peeters, pp. 371–376.

Cavanaugh, W.T., 2009. 'If You Render Unto God What Is God's, What Is Left for Caesar?' *Review of Politics* 71: 607–619.

Cerulli, E., 1973. *Tiberius and Pontius Pilate in Ethiopian Tradition and Poetry.* Proceedings of the British Academy, Volume LIX. London: Oxford University Press.

Chase, F.H., 1891. *The Lord's Prayer in the Early Church.* Cambridge: CUP.

Chia, R., 2006. *Radical Discipleship: Reflections on the Sermon on the Mount.* Eugene: Wipf and Stock.

Chorpenning, J.F. (ed.), 2011. *Joseph of Nazareth Through the Centuries.* Philadelphia: Saint Joseph's University Press.

Chow, S., 1995. *The Sign of Jonah Reconsidered: A Study of Its Meaning in the Gospel Traditions.* Coniectanea Biblica: New Testament Series 27. Stockholm: Almqvist and Wiksell International.

Chung, Y., 2015. 'A Postcolonial Reading of the Great Commission (Matt 28:16–20) with a Korean Myth,' *Theology Today* 72/3: 276–288.

Clark, K.W., 1947. 'The Gentile Bias of Matthew,' *JBL* 66: 165–172.

Clark, J.R., 1955. *The Story of the Pearl of Great Price.* Salt Lake City: Bookcraft.

Clark, D.H., J.H. Parkinson, and F.R. Stephenson, 1977. 'An Astronomical Re-Appraisal of the Star of Bethlehem – A Nova in 5 BC,' *QJRAS* 18: 443–449.

Clarke, H., 2003. *The Gospel of Matthew and Its Readers*. Bloomington and Indianapolis: Indiana University Press.

Clarke, A.D., 2009. '"Do not Judge Who Is Worthy and Unworthy": Clement's Warning not to Speculate About the Rich Young Man's Response (Mark 10.17–31),' *JSNT* 31/4: 447–468.

Clifton, J., 2014. 'Modes of Scriptural Illustration: The Beatitudes in the Late Sixteenth Century,' in W.S. Melion, J. Clifton, and M. Weemans (ed.), *Imago Exegetica: Visual Images as Exegetical Instruments, 1400–1700*. Leiden and Boston: Brill, pp. 545–578.

Clifton, J., 2017. '"Exactitude and Fidelity"? Paintings of *Christ Healing the Blind* by Nicolas Poussin and Philippe de Champaigne,' in V.K. Robbins, W.S. Melion, and R.R. Jeal (ed.), *The Art of Visual Exegesis: Rhetoric, Texts, Images*. Emory Studies in Early Christianity 19. Atlanta: SBL, pp. 337–357.

Collins, R.F., 1992. *Divorce in the New Testament*. Good News Studies 38. Collegeville: Liturgical Press.

Combrink, H.J.B., 1994. 'The Use of Matthew in the South African Context During the Last Few Decades,' *Neotestamentica* 28/2: 339–358.

Constas, N.P., 2004. 'The Last Temptation of Satan: Divine Deception in Greek Patristic Interpretations of the Passion Narrative,' *HTR* 97/2: 139–163.

Conybeare, F.C., 1901. 'The Eusebian Form of the Text Matth. 28, 19,' *ZNW* 2: 275–288.

Coolman, B.T., 2007. 'Hugh of St. Victor,' in J.P. Greenman, T. Larsen, and S.R. Spence (ed.), *The Sermon on the Mount Through the Centuries: From the Early Church to John Paul II*. Grand Rapids: Brazos, pp. 59–80.

Cope, O.L., 1976. *A Scribe Trained for the Kingdom of Heaven*. CBQMS 5. Washington: Catholic Biblical Association of America.

Coppins, W., 2012. 'Sitting on Two Asses? Second Thoughts on the Two-Animal Interpretation of Matthew 21:7,' *Tyndale Bulletin* 63/2: 275–290.

Cousland, J.R.C., 1999. 'The Feeding of Four Thousand *Gentiles* in Matthew? Matthew 15:29–39 as a Test Case,' *NovT* 41: 1–23.

Cowan, J., 2013. *Fleeing Herod: A Journey Through Coptic Egypt with the Holy Family*. Brewster: Paraclete Press.

Cowley, R.W., 1985a. 'The "Blood of Zechariah" (Mt 23:35) in Ethiopian Exegetical Tradition,' in E.A. Livingstone (ed.), *Studia Patristica*. Vol. XVIII/1: *Historica – Theol ogica – Gnostica – Biblica*. Kalamazoo: Cistercian Publications, pp. 293–302.

Cowley, R.W., 1985b. 'The So-Called "Ethiopic *Book of the Cock*": Part of an Apocryphal Passion Gospel, *The Homily and Teaching of Our Fathers the Holy Apostles*,' *Journal of the Royal Asiatic Society of Great Britain and Ireland* 1: 16–22.

Crawford, M.R., 2015. 'Reading the Diatessaron with Ephrem: The Word and the Light, the Voice and the Star,' *VC* 69: 70–95.

Cronshaw, D., 2016. 'A Commission "Great" for Whom? Postcolonial Contrapuntal Readings of Matthew 28:18–20 and the Irony of William Carey,' *Transformation* 33/2: 110–123.

Crosby, M.H., 2008. 'Rethinking a Key Biblical Text and Catholic Church Governance,' *Biblical Theology Bulletin* 38/1: 37–43.

Crossley, J.G., 2010. *Reading the New Testament: Contemporary Approaches.* London and New York: Routledge.

Cullmann, O., 1962. *Peter: Disciple, Apostle, Martyr: A Historical and Theological Study.* 2nd edition. Trans. F.V. Filson. Philadelphia: Westminster.

Culpepper R.A., 2000. *John the Son of Zebedee: The Life of a Legend.* Edinburgh: T. & T. Clark.

Daggy, R.E., 1996. 'Hurly Burly Secrets: A Reflection on Thomas Merton's French Poems,' *The Merton Seasonal* 21/2: 19–26.

Dahl, N.A., 1995. 'The Passion Narrative in Matthew,' in G.N. Stanton (ed.), *The Interpretation of Matthew.* 2nd edition. Edinburgh: T. & T. Clark, pp. 53–67.

Daryn, G., 2015. 'Early Christian Understandings of the 'Abomination That Causes Desolation',' *The Reformed Theological Review* 74/3: 162–175.

Davies, W.D., 1964. *The Setting of the Sermon on the Mount.* Cambridge: CUP.

Davies, S.L., 1983. 'John the Baptist and Essene Kashruth,' *NTS* 29: 569–571.

Davies, W.D., and D.C. Allison, 1988. *A Critical and Exegetical Commentary on The Gospel According to Saint Matthew. Volume I: Introduction and Commentary on Matthew I–VII.* ICC. Edinburgh: T. & T. Clark.

Davies, W.D., and D.C. Allison, 1991. *A Critical and Exegetical Commentary on the Gospel According to Saint Matthew. Volume II: Commentary on Matthew VIII–XVIII.* ICC. Edinburgh: T. & T. Clark.

Davies, W.D., and D.C. Allison, 1997. *A Critical and Exegetical Commentary on the Gospel According to Saint Matthew. Volume III: Commentary on Matthew XIX–XXVIII.* ICC. Edinburgh: T. & T. Clark.

Davies, W.D., and D.C. Allison, 2004. *Matthew: A Shorter Commentary.* London and New York: T. & T. Clark International.

Dawson, D., 1992. *Allegorical Readers and Cultural Revision in Ancient Alexandria.* Berkeley, Los Angeles, and Oxford: University of California Press.

Dawson, D., 2002. *Christian Figural Reading and the Fashioning of Identity.* Berkeley and London: University of California Press.

de Jonge, M., 1986. 'Matthew 27:51 in Early Christian Exegesis,' *HTR* 79: 67–79.

de Lubac, H., 1998–2009. *Medieval Exegesis: The Four Senses of Scripture.* 3 vols. Grand Rapids and Edinburgh: Eerdmans and T. & T. Clark.

DeConick, A., 1990. 'The Yoke Saying in the *Gospel of Thomas* 90,' *VC* 44: 280–294.

DelCogliano, M., 2011. 'Gregory the Great on Simon of Cyrene: A Critique of Tradition,' *ASE* 28/1: 315–324.

Derrett, J.D.M., 1983. 'Binding and Loosing (Matt 16:19; 18:18; John 29:23),' *JBL* 102: 112–117.

Dickerson, F.C., 2013. 'The Canaanite Woman (Matthew 15:22–28): Discharging the Stigma of Single Moms in the African American Church,' in N. Wilkinson Duran and J.P. Grimshaw (ed.), *Matthew.* Texts @ Contexts Series. Minneapolis: Fortress, pp. 65–80.

Dickson, A.F., 1872. *The Temptation in the Desert: Lessons from Christ's Conflict and Victory.* New York: American Tract Society.

Dobbs, E.A., 2013. 'The Canaanite Woman, the Second Nun, and St. Cecilia,' *Christianity and Literature* 62/2: 203–222.

Dodd, C.H., 1935. *The Parables of the Kingdom*. London: Nisbet & Co.
Dodson, D.S., 2010, 'Dream Magic: The Dream of Pilate's Wife and the Accusation of Magic in the Acts of Pilate,' in T. Nicklas, A. Merkt, and J. Verheyden (ed.), *Gelitten, Gestorben, Auferstanden. Passions- und Ostertraditionen im antiken Christentum*, WUNT 2/273. Tübingen: Mohr Siebeck, pp. 21–30.
Doignon, J., 1975. 'L'Argumentatio d'Hilaire de Poitiers dans l'exemplum de la tentation de Jésus (In Matthaeum, 3,1–5),' *VC* 29: 296–308.
Doignon, J., 1985. 'L'exégèse latine de la parabole des deux fils (Matth 21:28–31): Hilaire de Poitiers devant le problème de l'obéisance à Dieu,' *Revue d'histoire et de philosophie religieuses* 65/1: 53–59.
Donahue, J.R., 1986. 'The "Parable" of the Sheep and the Goats: A Challenge to Christian Ethics,' *TS* 47: 3–31.
Donaldson, T.L., 1985. *Jesus on the Mountain: A Study in Matthean Theology*. JSNTS 8. Sheffield: JSOT Press.
Dowling Long, S., and J.F.A. Sawyer, 2015. *The Bible in Music: A Dictionary of Songs, Works, and More*. Lanham, Boulder. New York and London: Rowman and Littlefield.
Drury, J., 1985. *The Parables in the Gospels*. London: SPCK.
Dube, M.W., 1998. 'Go Therefore and Make Disciples of All Nations' (Matt 28:19a): A Postcolonial Perspective on Biblical Criticism and Pedagogy,' in F.F. Segovia and M.A. Tolbert (ed.), *Teaching the Bible: The Discourses and Politics of Biblical Pedagogy*. New York: Augsburg, pp. 224–246.
Dube, M.W., 1999. 'Consuming a Colonial Cultural Bomb: Translating *Badimo* into "Demons" in the Setswana Bible (Matthew 8.28–34; 15.22; 10.8),' *JSNT* 73: 33–59.
Duling, D.C., 1975. 'Solomon, Exorcism and the Son of David,' *HTR* 68: 235–252.
Dumitraşcu, N., 2013. 'The Lord's Prayer in Eastern Spirituality,' *Dialog: A Journal of Theology* 52/4: 349–356.
Dungan, D.L., 1999. *A History of the Synoptic Problem: The Canon, the Text, the Composition, and the Interpretation of the Gospels*. ABRL. New York and London: Doubleday.
Dupont, J., 1961. 'L'ambassade de Jean-Baptiste (Matthieu 11, 2–6; Luc 7, 18–23),' *Nouvelle revue théologique* 83: 805–821.
Edwards, J.R., 2010. 'The Hermeneutical Significance of Chapter Divisions in Ancient Gospel Manuscripts,' *NTS* 56: 413–426.
Edwards, L., 2015. 'Matthew's Pharisees: Seven Woes and Seven Warnings,' in K. Mtata and C. Koester (ed.), *To All the Nations: Lutheran Hermeneutics and the Gospel of Matthew*. LWF Studies. Leipzig: Lutheran World Federation/Evangelische Verlangsanstalt, pp. 171–183.
Eklund, R., 2017. 'Blessed Are the Image-Bearers: Gregory of Nyssa and the Beatitudes,' *ATR* 99/4: 729–740.
Elliott, M.W., 2010. 'Effective-History and the Hermeneutics of Ulrich Luz,' *JSNT* 33/2: 161–173.
Elsner, J., 1994. 'The Viewer and the Vision: The Case of the Sinai Apse,' *Art History* 17/1: 81–102.
Engelstein, L., 1999. *Castration and the Heavenly Kingdom*. Ithaca and London: Cornell University Press.

Erikson, R.J., 1996. 'Divine Injustice? Matthew's Narrative Strategy and the Slaughter of the Innocents (Matthew 2.13–23),' *JSNT* 64: 5–27.
Esler, P.F., 2014. 'Reading Matthew by the Dead Sea: Matthew 8:5–13 in Light of P. Yadin 11,' *HTS Teologiese Studies/Theological Studies* 70(1), Art. 2773, 12 pages. doi:10.4102/hts.v70i1.2773.
Falkenberg, R., 2013. 'Matthew 28:16–20 and the Nag Hammadi Library: Reception of the Great Commission in the *Sophia of Jesus Christ*,' in E.-M. Becker and A. Runesson (ed.), *Mark and Matthew II: Comparative Readings: Reception History, Cultural Hermeneutics, and Theology*. WUNT 304. Tübingen: Mohr Siebeck, pp. 93–104.
Farid, S.W., 1965. *The Flight into Egypt*. Cairo: Youssef Abdalla.
Farmer, W.R., 1994. *The Gospel of Jesus: The Pastoral Relevance of the Synoptic Problem*. Louisville: Westminster/John Knox.
Fehl, P., 1957. 'Questions of Identity in Veronese's *Christ and the Centurion*,' *The Art Bulletin* 39/4: 301–302.
Ferda, T.S., 2013. 'The Soldiers' Inscription and the Angel's Word: The Significance of "Jesus" in Matthew's *Titulus*,' *NovT* 55: 221–231.
Filas, F., 1962. *Joseph, the Man Closest to Jesus: The Complete Life, Theology, and Devotional History of St. Joseph*. Boston: Daughters of St. Paul.
Fitzmyer, J.A., 1976. 'The Matthean Divorce Texts and Some New Palestinian Evidence,' *TS* 37: 196–226.
Fitzmyer, J.A., 2003. 'And Lead Us Not into Temptation,' *Biblica* 84: 259–273.
Fitzmyer, J.A., 2008. *The Interpretation of Scripture: In Defense of the Historical-Critical Method*. New York and Mahwah: Paulist.
Flaming, D.K., 2006. 'Calvin as Commentator on the Synoptic Gospels,' in D.K. McKim, *Calvin and the Bible*. Cambridge and New York: CUP, pp. 131–163.
Flanigan, C.C., 1992. 'The Apocalypse and the Medieval Liturgy,' in R.K. Emmerson and B. McGinn (ed.), *The Apocalypse in the Middle Ages*. Ithaca: Cornell University Press, pp. 333–351.
Fonzo, K., 2013. 'Procula's Civic Body and Pilate's Masculinity Crisis in the York Cycle's "Christ Before Pilate 1: The Dream of Pilate's Wife,"' *Early Theatre* 16/2: 11–32.
Ford, D., 1979. *The Abomination of Desolation in Biblical Eschatology*. New York: University of America Press.
Forsyth, P.T., 1905. *Religion in Recent Art: Expository Lectures on Rossetti, Burne Jones, Watts, Holman Hunt and Wagner*. 3rd edition. London: Hodder and Stoughton.
Foster, P., 2005. 'The Epistles of Ignatius of Antioch and the Writings that Later Formed the New Testament,' in A.F. Gregory and C.M. Tuckett (ed.), *The Reception of the New Testament in the Apostolic Fathers*. Oxford and New York: OUP, pp. 159–186.
Fox, R.C., 1962. 'The Character of Mammon in Paradise Lost,' *Review of English Studies* 13/49: 30–39.
France, R.T., 1979. 'Herod and the Children of Bethlehem,' *NovT* 21/2: 98–120.
France, R.T., 2007. *The Gospel of Matthew*. NICNT. Grand Rapids and Cambridge: Eerdmans.
Francis, H.S., 1953. 'The "Flight into Egypt" by Nicolas Poussin,' *Bulletin of the Cleveland Museum of Art* 40/10: 211–213.

Franklin, E., 1994. *Luke: Interpreter of Paul, Critic of Matthew*. JSNTSS 92. Sheffield: Sheffield Academic Press.

Franklin, D.O., 2015. 'Viewing the Poetic Texts in Bach's Matthew Passion from a New Perspective,' *BACH: Journal of the Riemenschneider Bach Institute* 46/1: 29–48.

Fransen, P., 1970. 'Divorce on the Ground of Adultery – The Council of Trent (1563),' *Concilium* 55: 89–100. BT184. C74. v. 55.

Frantzman, S.J., and R. Kark, 2008. 'General Gordon, the Palestine Exploration Fund and the Origins of "Gordon's Calvary" in the Holy Land,' *Palestine Exploration Quarterly* 140/2: 119–136.

Frey, J., 2015. 'Texts About Jesus: Non-Canonical Gospels and Related Literature,' in A. Gregory and C. Tuckett (ed.), *The Oxford Handbook of Early Christian Apocrypha*. Oxford and New York: OUP, pp. 13–47.

Froehlich, K., 1989. 'Saint Peter, Papal Primacy, and the Exegetical Tradition, 1150–1300,' in C. Ryan (ed.), *The Religious Roles of the Papacy: Ideals and Realities, 1150–1300*. Papers in Mediaeval Studies 8. Toronto: Pontifical Institute of Medieval Studies, pp. 3–44.

Gadamer, H.-G., 2012. *Truth and Method*. Second revised edition. Trans. J. Weinsheimer and D.G. Marshall. New York and London: Continuum.

Gallagher, E.L., 2014. 'The Blood from Abel to Zechariah in the History of Interpretation,' *NTS* 60: 121–138.

Garland, D.E., 1979. *The Intention of Matthew 23*. Leiden: Brill.

Garrow, A.J.P., 2004. *The Gospel of Matthew's Dependence on the Didache*. JSNTSup 254. London: T. & T. Clark.

Gerhardsson, B., 2016. *The Mighty Acts of Jesus According to Matthew*. Eugene: Wipf & Stock.

Gero, S., 1970. '"Miles Gloriosus": The Christian and Military Service According to Tertullian,' *Church History* 39/3: 285–298.

Giblin, C.H., 1971. '"The Things of God" in the Question Concerning Tribute to Caesar (Lk 20:25; Mk 12:17; Mt 22:21),' *CBQ* 33: 510–527.

Gibson, M.T., 1993. *The Bible in the Latin West*. The Medieval Book Volume One. Notre Dame and London: University of Notre Dame Press.

Gibson, J.B., 1995. *The Temptations of Jesus in Early Christianity*. JSNTSS 112. Sheffield: Sheffield Academic Press.

Gillman, F.M., 1992. 'The Wife of Pilate (Matthew 27:19),' *Louvain Studies* 17: 152–165.

Glover, R., 1985. 'Patristic Quotations and Gospel Sources,' *NTS* 31: 234–251.

Gnilka, J., 2003. 'Der Matthäuskommentar von Ulrich Luz,' *TLZ* 128: 227–233.

Goldammer, K., 1941. '*Navis Ecclesiae*: Eine unbekannte altchristliche Darstellung der Schiffsallegorie,' *ZNW* 40: 76–86.

Gonnet, G., 1986. 'L'Incidence du Sermon de la Montagne sur l'éthique des Vaudois du Moyen Âge,' *Communio viatorum* 19: 119–127.

Good, D., 1990. 'The Verb Ἀναχωρέω in Matthew's Gospel,' *NovT* 32/1: 1–12.

Good, D., 1991. 'The Canaanite Woman: Patristic Exegesis of Matthew 15, 21–28,' in *Figures du Nouveau Testament chez les Pères*. Cahiers de Biblia Patristica 3. Strasbourg: Centre d'Analyse et de Documentations Patristiques, pp. 169–177.

Good, D., 2013. 'Jesus, Mary and Joseph in Egypt,' in E. Iricinschi, L. Jenoth, N. Denzey Lewis, and P. Townsend (ed.), *Beyond the Gnostic Gospels: Studies Building on the Work of Elaine Pagels*. Studies and Texts in Antiquity and Christianity 82. Tübingen: Mohr Siebeck, pp. 335–344.

Goodacre, M., 1998. 'Fatigue in the Synoptics,' *NTS* 44: 45–58.

Goodacre, M., 2000. 'The Synoptic Jesus and the Celluloid Christ: Solving the Synoptic Problem Through Film,' *JSNT* 80: 31–43.

Goodman, M., 1989. 'Proselytising in Rabbinic Judaism,' *JJS* 40: 175–185.

Gorbunov, A.N., 2006. 'Christ's Temptations in the Wilderness (Milton and Dostoyevsky),' *Literature and Theology* 20/1: 46–62.

Goswell, G., 2009. 'Early Readers of the Gospels: The *Kephalaia* and *Titloi* of Codex Alexandrinus,' *Journal of Greco-Roman Christianity and Judaism* 6: 134–174.

Goulder, M.D., 1974. *Midrash and Lection in Matthew*. London: SPCK.

Gowler, D.B., 2000. *What Are They Saying About the Parables?* New York and Mahwah: Paulist.

Gowler, D.B., 2017. *The Parables After Jesus: Their Imaginative Receptions Across Two Millennia*. Grand Rapids: Baker Academic.

Grant, R.M., 1978. 'The Sermon on the Mount in Early Christianity,' *Semeia* 12: 215–230.

Gray, S.W., 1989. *The Least of My Brothers. Matthew 25:31–46: A History of Interpretation*. SBLDS 114. Atlanta: Scholars Press.

Greenman, J.P., T. Larsen, and S.R. Spencer (ed.), 2007. *The Sermon on the Mount Through the Centuries: From the Early Church to John Paul II*. Grand Rapids: Brazos.

Gregg, R.C., 1976. 'Early Christian Variations on the Parable of the Lost Sheep,' *Duke Divinity School Review* 41: 85–104.

Grosshans, H.-P., 2015. 'Perfection of Christian Life in the Face of Anger and Retaliation. Martin Luther's Interpretation of the Sermon on the Mount,' in K. Mtata and C. Koester (ed.), *To All the Nations: Lutheran Hermeneutics and the Gospel of Matthew*. LWF Studies. Leipzig: Lutheran World Federation/Evangelische Verlangsanstalt, pp. 99–114.

Guelich, R.A., 1982. *The Sermon on the Mount: A Foundation for Understanding*. Waco: Word.

Guelich, R.A., 1987. 'Interpreting the Sermon on the Mount,' *Interpretation* 41: 117–130.

Gundry, R.H., 1982. *Matthew, A Commentary on His Literary and Theological Art*. Grand Rapids: Eerdmans.

Gundry, R.H., 1994. *Matthew: A Commentary on His Handbook for a Mixed Church Under Persecution*. 2nd edition. Grand Rapids: Eerdmans.

Gurtner, D.M., 2006. 'The Veil of the Temple in History and Legend,' *JETS* 49/1: 97–114.

Gwynn, J., 1889. 'Hippolytus on St. Matthew XXIV. 15–22,' *Hermathena* 7/15: 137–150.

Hamilton, R., 2007. 'Bruegel's Falling Figures,' *Viator* 38/1: 385–404.

Hammerling, R., 2010. *The Lord's Prayer in the Early Church: The Pearl of Great Price*. New York: Palgrave Macmillan.

Hand, J.O., and M. Wolff, 1986. *Early Netherlandish Painting*. Washington: National Gallery of Art/CUP.
Hare, D.R.A., 1993. *Matthew*. Interpretation Commentary. Louisville: John Knox.
Harper, F.E.W., 1901. *Idylls of the Bible*. Philadelphia: 1006 Bainbridge Street.
Harries, R., 2004. *The Passion in Art*. Aldershot and Burlington: Ashgate.
Harrington, D.J., 1991. *The Gospel of Matthew*. Sacra Pagina. Collegeville: Liturgical Press.
Harris, M., 2012. 'Interpreting the Role of Christ and His Donkey: The Palmesel as Actor in the Processional Theatre of Palm Sunday,' *European Medieval Drama* 16: 1–17.
Harvey, A.E., 2007. 'Eunuchs for the Sake of the Kingdom,' *Heythrop Journal* 48: 1–17.
Hass, A., 1988. 'Caravaggio's Calling of St. Matthew Reconsidered,' *Journal of the Warburg and Courtauld Institutes* 51: 245–250.
Hauerwas, S., 2006. *Matthew*. SCM Theological Commentary on the Bible. London: SCM.
Hebron, C.A., 2016. *Judas Iscariot: Damned or Redeemed? A Critical Examination of the Portrayal of Judas in Jesus Films (1902–2014)*. Scriptural Traces: Critical Perspectives on the Reception and Influence of the Bible 9/LNTS 563. London: Bloomsbury.
Hegedus, T., 2003. 'The Magi and the Star in the Gospel of Matthew and Early Christian Tradition,' *Laval théologique et philosophique* 59/1: 81–95.
Hegedus, T., 2006. 'The Magi and the Star of Matthew 2:1–12 in Early Christian Tradition,' in F. Young, M. Edwards and P. Parvis (ed.), *Studia Patristica*. Vol. XXXIX: *Historica, Biblica, Ascetica et Hagiographica*. Leuven, Paris, and Dudley: Peeters, pp. 213–217.
Hehn, B., 2016. 'Theological and Musical Techniques in Arvo Pärt's *Tribute to Caesar*,' *The Choral Journal* 57/4: 32–42.
Heil, J.P., 1981. *Jesus Walking on the Sea: Meaning and Gospel Functions of Matt 14:22–33, Mark 6:45–52 and John 6:15b–21*. Analecta Biblica 87. Rome: Biblical Institute Press.
Heil, J.P., 1991a. *The Death and Resurrection of Jesus: A Narrative-Critical Reading of Matthew 26–28*. Minneapolis: Fortress Press.
Heil, J.P., 1991b. 'The Blood of Jesus in Matthew: A Narrative-Critical Perspective,' *Perspectives in Religious Studies* 18: 117–124.
Heil, J.P., 1993. 'Ezekiel 34 and the Narrative Strategy of the Shepherd and the Sheep Metaphor in Matthew,' *CBQ* 55: 698–708.
Heil, J.P., 2000. *The Transfiguration of Jesus: Narrative Meaning and Function of Mark 9:2–8, Matt 17:1–8 and Luke 9:28–36*. Analecta Biblica 144. Rome: Editrice Pontificio Instituto Biblico.
Heine, R.E., 2013. 'Origen and His Opponents on *Matthew* 19:12,' in M. Vinzent (ed.), *Studia Patristica*. Vol. LVI/4: *Rediscovering Origen*. Leuven, Paris, and Walpole: Peeters, pp. 123–128.
Hengel, M., 1981. *The Charismatic Leader and His Followers*. Trans. J. Greig. Edinburgh: T. & T. Clark.
Herbert, A.S., 1968. *Historical Catalogue of Printed Editions of the English Bible 1525–1961. Revised and Expanded from the Edition of T.H. Darlow and H.F. Moule, 1903*. London and New York: British and Foreign Bible Society and American Bible Society.

Herzer, J., 2012. 'The Riddle of the Holy Ones in Matthew 27:51b–53: A New Proposal for a Crux Interpretum,' in C.A. Evans and H.D. Zacharias (ed.), *'What Does the Scripture Say?': Studies in the Function of Scripture in Early Judaism and Christianity*. London and New York: T. & T. Clark, pp. 142–157.

Hetherington, P. (trans.), 1996. *The 'Painter's Manual' of Dionysius of Fourna*. Torrance: Oakwood Publications.

Higgins, A.J.B., 1945. 'Lead Us Not into Temptation: Some Latin Variants,' *JTS* 46: 179–183.

Hilhorst, T., 2009. 'The Mountain of Transfiguration in the New Testament and in Later Tradition,' in J. van Ruiten and J.C. de Vos (ed.), *The Land of Israel in Bible, History, and Theology: Studies in Honour of Ed Noort*. Supplements to Vetus Testamentum 124. Leiden and Boston: Brill, pp. 317–338.

Hogan, M., 1999. *The Sermon on the Mount in St. Ephrem's Commentary on the Diatessaron*. Bern: Peter Lang.

Holmes, J., 2005. 'Aquinas' *Lectura in Matthaeum*,' in T.G. Weinandy, D.A. Keating, and J.P. Yocum (ed.), *Aquinas on Scripture: An Introduction to his Biblical Commentaries*. London and New York: T. & T. Clark, pp. 73–97.

Holweck, F.G., 1924. *A Biographical Dictionary of the Saints*. St. Louis and London: B. Herder.

Hood, W., 1993. *Fra Angelico at San Marco*. London, New York, Sydney, and Toronto: BCA by arrangement with Yale University Press.

Hood, J., 2009. 'Matthew 23–25: The Extent of Jesus' Fifth Discourse,' *JBL* 128/3: 527–543.

Horne, S., 2005. '"These Then Let Us Emulate": The Early Church Illuminates Two Gospel Impairment Encounters,' in R.S. Sugirtharajah (ed.), *Wilderness: Essays in Honour of Frances Young*. LNTS 295. London and New York: T. & T. Clark, pp. 10–25.

Hornik, H.J., and M.C. Parsons, 2017. *The Acts of the Apostles Through the Centuries*. Wiley Blackwell Bible Commentaries. Malden, MA, Oxford, and Chichester: Wiley Blackwell.

Houssiau, A., 1953. *L'exégèse de Matthieu XI, 27 B selon saint Irénée*. Louvain: Publications Universitaires de Louvain.

Howard, G., 1988. 'A Note on the Short Ending of Matthew,' *HTR* 81/1: 117–120.

Howard, G., 1998. 'Shem-Tob's Hebrew Matthew and Early Jewish Christianity,' *JSNT* 20/70: 3–20.

Hughes, D.W., K.K.C. Yau, and F.R. Stephenson, 1993. 'Giotto's Comet – Was It the Comet of 1304 and Not Comet Halley?' *QJRAS* 34: 21–32.

Hultgren, A., 1990. 'The Bread Petition of the Lord's Prayer,' in A. Hultgren and B. Hall (ed.), *Christ and His Communities*. Cincinnati: Forward Movement, pp. 41–54.

Humphreys, C.J., 1991. 'The Star of Bethlehem – A Comet in 5 BC – And the Date of the Birth of Christ,' *QJRAS* 32: 289–407.

Hunt, W.H., 1885. *The Triumph of the Innocents*. London.

Instone-Brewer, D., 2003. 'The Two Asses of Zechariah 9:9 in Matthew 21,' *Tyndale Bulletin* 54/1: 87–98.

Instone-Brewer, D., 2006. '"The Scandal of Equality in Jesus" Ethical Teaching,' *Priscilla Papers* 20/2: 17–22.

Jacobs, P.W., 2016. *Joseph the Carpenter: His Reception in Literature and Art from the Second to the Ninth Century*. History of Biblical Interpretation Series 5. Blandford Forum: Deo Publishing.

Janes, R., 2006. 'Why the Daughter of Herodias Must Dance (Mark 6.14–29),' *JSNT* 28/4: 443–467.

Jantzen, H., 1984. *High Gothic: The Classic Cathedrals of Chartres, Reims, Amiens*. Trans. J. Palmes. Princeton: Princeton University Press.

Janzen, D., 2000. 'The Meaning of *Porneia* in Matthew 5:32 and 19:9: An Approach from the Study of Ancient Near Eastern Culture,' *JSNT* 80: 66–80.

Jeffrey, D.L. (ed.), 1992. *A Dictionary of Biblical Tradition in English Literature*. Grand Rapids: Eerdmans.

Jeffrey, D.L., 2007. 'Dante and Chaucer,' in J.P. Greenman, T. Larsen, and S.R. Spence (ed.), *The Sermon on the Mount Through the Centuries: From the Early Church to John Paul II*. Grand Rapids: Brazos, pp. 81–107.

Jennings, T.W., and T.-S.B. Liew, 2004. 'Mistaken Identities But Model Faith: Rereading the Centurion, the Chap, and the Christ in Matthew 8:5–13,' *JBL* 123/3: 467–494.

Jensen, R.M., 2000. *Understanding Early Christian Art*. London and New York: Routledge.

Jensen, R.M., 2011. *Living Water: Images, Symbols, and Settings of Early Christian Baptism*. Supplements to Vigiliae Christianae 105. Leiden: Koninklijke Brill NV.

Jensen, R.M., 2012. *Baptismal Imagery in Early Christianity: Ritual, Visual, and Theological Dimensions*. Grand Rapids: Baker Academic.

Jeremias, J., 1955. *The Parables of Jesus*. Trans. S.H. Hooke. New York: Charles Scribner's Sons.

Jeremias, J., 1961. *The Sermon on the Mount*. Trans. N. Perrin. London: Athlone.

Jeremias, J., 1967. *The Prayers of Jesus*. Studies in Biblical Theology. London: SCM.

Jiménez, P.A., 1997. 'The Laborers of the Vineyard (Matthew 20:1–16): A Hispanic Homiletical Reading,' *Journal for Preachers* Advent: 35–40.

Johnson, J.R., 1961. 'The Tree of Jesse Window of Chartres: *Laudes Regiae*,' *Speculum* 36/1: 1–22.

Johnson, L.T., 1989. 'The New Testament's Anti-Jewish Slander and the Conventions of Ancient Polemic,' *JBL* 108: 419–441.

Jordan, W.C., 2012. 'Salome in the Middle Ages,' *Jewish History* 26: 5–15.

Jorgensen, D.W., 2016. *Treasure Hidden in a Field: Early Christian Reception of the Gospel of Matthew*. Studies of the Bible and Its Reception 6. Berlin and Boston: De Gruyter.

Joyce, P.M., and D. Lipton, 2013. *Lamentations Through the Centuries*. Wiley Blackwell Bible Commentaries. Malden, Oxford, and Chichester: Wiley Blackwell.

Joynes, C.E., 2005. 'The Returned Elijah? John the Baptist's Angelic Identity in the Gospel of Mark,' *SJT* 58/4: 455–467.

Jungmann, J., 1955. *The Mass of the Roman Rite: Its Origins and Development: Volume Two*. Trans. F.A. Brunner. New York: Benzinger Brothers, Inc.

Jütte, D., 2015. *The Strait Gate: Thresholds and Power in Western History*. New Haven and London: Yale University Press.

Kany, R., 1995. 'Die Frau des Pilatus und ihr Name: Ein Kapitel aus der Gesehichte neutestamentlicher Wissenschaft,' *ZNW* 86: 104–110.

Kartsonis, A.D., 1986. *Anastasis: The Making of an Image*. Princeton: Princeton University Press.

Kealy, S., 1997. *Matthew's Gospel and the History of Biblical Interpretation*. 2 vols. New York: Edwin Mellen.

Kee, H.C., 1972. 'The Transfiguration in Mark: Epiphany or Apocalyptic Vision?' in J. Reumann (ed.), *Understanding the Sacred Text*. Valley Forge: Judson, pp. 137–152.

Kelhoffer, J.A., 2005. *The Diet of John the Baptist: 'Locusts and Wild Honey' in Synoptic and Patristic Interpretation*. Wissenschaftliche Untersuchungen zum Neuen Testament 176. Tübingen: Mohr Siebeck.

Kelly, J.N.D., 1995. *Golden Mouth: The Story of John Chrysostom, Ascetic, Preacher, Bishop*. London: Duckworth.

Kelly, J.N.D., 2000. *Jerome: His Life, Writings, and Controversies*. Peabody: Hendrickson.

Kidger, M., 1999. *The Star of Bethlehem: An Astronomer's View*. Princeton: Princeton University Press.

Kienzle, B.M., 2009. *Hildegard of Bingen and Her Gospel Homilies: Speaking New Mysteries*. Medieval Women: Texts and Contexts 12. Turnhout: Brepols.

Kilcourse, C.S., 2016. *Taiping Theology: The Localization of Christianity in China, 1843–64*. Christianities of the World. New York: Palgrave Macmillan.

Kiley, M., 1984. 'Why "Matthew" in Matt 9,9–13?' *Biblica* 65: 347–351.

Kingsbury, J.D., 1969. *The Parables of Jesus in Matthew 13: A Study in Redaction-Criticism*. Richmond: John Knox.

Kingsbury, J.D., 1976. *Matthew: Structure, Christology, Kingdom*. London: SPCK.

Kingsbury, J.D., 1986. *Matthew as Story*. Philadelphia: Fortress.

Kinyua, J., 2015. 'A Postcolonial Examination of Matthew 16:13–23 and Related Issues in Biblical Hermeneutics,' *Black Theology* 13/1: 4–28.

Kissinger, W.S., 1975. *The Sermon on the Mount: A History of Interpretation and Bibliography*. ATLA Bibliography Series No. 3. Metuchen: Scarecrow/American Theological Library Association.

Klancher, N., 2013. *The Taming of the Canaanite Woman: Constructions of Christian Identity in the Afterlife of Matthew 15:21–28*. Berlin and Boston: De Gruyter.

Klassen, W., 1996. *Judas: Betrayer or Friend of Jesus?* Minneapolis: Fortress.

Kleinbub, C.K., 2008. 'Raphael's *Transfiguration* as Visio-Devotional Program,' *The Art Bulletin* 90/3: 367–393.

Kleinbub, C.K., 2011. *Vision and the Visionary in Raphael*. University Park: Pennsylvania State University Press.

Kleist, J.A., 1945. 'Eunuchs in the New Testament,' *CBQ* 7/4: 447–449.

Klijn, A.F.J., 1992. *Jewish-Christian Gospel Tradition*. VCSup 17. Leiden: Brill.

Koester, H., 1957. *Synoptische Überlieferung bei den apostolichen Vätern*. Berlin: Akademie.

Koester, C.R., 1989. 'The Origin and Significance of the Flight to Pella Tradition,' *CBQ* 51/1: 90–106.

Koester, C.R., 2005. 'Gospels and Gospel Traditions in the Second Century,' in A.F. Gregory and C.M. Tuckett (ed.), *Trajectories Through the New Testament and the Apostolic Fathers*. Oxford and New York: OUP, pp. 27–44.

Köhler, W.-D., 1987. *Die Rezeption der Matthäusevangeliums in der Zeit von Irenäus*. WUNT 2.24. Tübingen: Mohr Siebeck.

Köhren-Jansen, H., 1993. *Giottos Navicella: Bildtradition, Deutung, Rezeptionsgeschichte*. Römische Studien der Bibliotheca Hertziana Band 8. Worms am Rhein: Wernersche Verlagsgesellschaft.

Koppen, K.-P., 1989. 'The Interpretation of Jesus' Temptations (Mt. 4, 1–11; Mk. 1, 12f; Lk. 4, 1–3) by the Early Church Fathers,' *Patristic and Byzantine Review* 8/1: 41–43.

Kovacs, J.L., 2000. 'Clement of Alexandria and Gregory of Nyssa on the Beatitudes,' in H.R. Drobner and A. Viciano (ed.), *Gregory of Nyssa, Homilies on the Beatitudes*. Supplements to Vigiliae Christianae. Leiden: Brill, pp. 311–329.

Kovacs, J.L., 2001. 'Divine Pedagogy and the Gnostic Teacher according to Clement of Alexandria,' *Journal of Early Christian Studies* 9/1: 3–25.

Kovacs, J.L., 2009. 'Clement (Titus Flavius Clemens) of Alexandria,' *ExpTim* 120/6: 261–271.

Kovacs, J., and C. Rowland, 2004. *Revelation: The Apocalypse of Jesus Christ*. Blackwell Bible Commentaries. Malden, Oxford, and Carlton: Blackwell.

Kreider, A., 2003. 'Military Service in the Church Orders,' *Journal of Religious Ethics* 31/3: 415–442.

Kreider, A., 2016. *The Patient Ferment of the Early Church*. Grand Rapids: Baker Academic.

Kreitzer, L.J., 2002. *Gospel Images in Fiction and Film: On Reversing the Hermeneutical Flow*. London and New York: Sheffield Academic Press.

Kreitzer, L.J., 2005. 'Matthew 11:28–30 and "Rest" from Heavy Burdens: Bunyan and De Niro Meet Jesus,' in G. Aichele and R. Walsh (ed.), *Those Outside: Noncanonical Readings of the Canonical Gospels*. London: T&T Clark, pp. 65–84.

Krentz, E., 1964. 'The Extent of Matthew's Prologue: Towards the Structure of the First Gospel,' *JBL* 83: 409–414.

Krey, A.C., 1921. *The First Crusade: The Accounts of Eyewitnesses and Participants*. Princeton: Princeton University Press.

Kuepfer, T., 2007. 'Matthew 18 Revisited,' *Vision* 8/1: 33–41.

Kümmel, W., 1984. 'Eschatological Expectation in the Proclamation of Jesus,' in B. Chilton (ed.), *The Kingdom of God*. Issues in Religion and Theology 5. Philadelphia Fortress and London:SPCK, pp. 36–51.

Kunzle, D., 2001. 'Spanish Herod, Dutch Innocents: Bruegel's *Massacres of the Innocents* in Their Sixteenth-Century Political Contexts,' *Art History* 24/1: 51–82.

Kürzinger, J., 1983. *Papias von Hierapolis und die Evangelien des Neuen Testaments*. Regensberg: Verlag Friedrich Pustet.

Kwon, J., 2012. 'Cyprian, Origen and the Lord's Prayer: Theological Diversities Between Latin West and Greek East in the Third Century,'*Asia Journal of Theology* 26/1: 56–87.

Laeuchli, S., 1953. 'Origen's Interpretation of Judas Iscariot,' *Church History* 22/4: 253–268.

Lammé, M., 2012. 'The Blasphemy Against the Holy Spirit: The Unpardonable Sin in Matthew 12:22–32,' *Mid-America Journal of Theology* 23: 19–51.

Landau, B., 2008. 'The *Revelation of the Magi* in the *Chronicle of Zuqnin*,' *Apocrypha* 19: 182–201.

Larsen, T., 2007. 'Charles Haddon Spurgeon,' in J.P. Greenman, T. Larsen, and S.R. Spence (ed.), *The Sermon on the Mount Through the Centuries: From the Early Church to John Paul II*. Grand Rapids: Brazos, pp. 181–205.

Larsen, T., 2011. *A People of One Book: The Bible and the Victorians*. Oxford: OUP.

Lash, N., 1986. *Theology on the Way to Emmaus*. London: SCM.

Lawrence, L., 2009. 'Crumb Trails and Puppy-Dog Tales': Reading Afterlives of a Canaanite Woman,' in C.E. Joynes and C.C. Rowland (ed.), *From the Margins 2: Women of the New Testament and Their Afterlives*. Sheffield: Sheffield Phoenix Press, pp. 262–278.

Lawrence, L., 2013. *Sense and Stigma in the Gospels: Depictions of Sensory-Disabled Characters*. Biblical Refigurations. Oxford: OUP.

Lee, D., 2004. 'On the Holy Mountain: The Transfiguration in Scripture and Theology,' *Colloquium* 36/2: 143–159.

Lee, M.E., 2010. 'Matthew: The Musical,' *Currents in Theology and Mission* 37/6: 479–487.

Levin, Y., 2006. '"Jesus," "Son of God" and "Son of David": The "Adoption" of Jesus into the Davidic Line,' *JSNT* 28: 415–442.

Levine, A.-J., 1988. *The Social and Ethnic Dimensions of Matthean Salvation History: 'Go Nowhere Among the Gentiles …' (Matt. 10:5b)*. Studies in the Bible and Early Christianity 14. Lewiston: Edwin Mellen.

Levine, A.-J., 1996. 'Discharging Responsibility: Matthean Jesus, Biblical Law, and Hemorrhaging Woman,' in D.R. Bauer and M.A. Powell (ed.), *Treasures New and Old: Recent Contributions to Matthean Studies*. SBLSymS. Atlanta: Scholars Press, pp. 379–397.

Levine, A.-J., 2006. '"To All The Gentiles": A Jewish Perspective on the Great Commission,' *Review and Expositor* 103: 139–158).

Levine, A.-J., 2014. *Short Stories by Jesus: The Enigmatic Parables of a Controversial Rabbi*. New York: HarperCollins.

Levy, I.C., 2007. 'John Wyclif and the Primitive Papacy,' *Viator* 38/2: 159–189.

Lienhard, J.T., 1999. *Saint Joseph in Early Christianity: Devotion and Theology. A Study and an Anthology of Patristic Texts*. Philadelphia: Saint Joseph's University Press.

Lieu, J.M., 1988. 'Epiphanius on the Scribes and Pharisees (*Pan.* 15.1–16.4),' *JTS* 39/2: 509–524.

Lindsay, K.C., and B. Huppé, 1956, 'Meaning and Method in Brueghel's Painting,' *The Journal of Aesthetics and Art Criticism* 14/3: 376–386.

Linzey, A., 1994. *Animal Theology*. London: SCM.

Lischer, R., 2014. *Reading the Parables*. Interpretation: Resources for the Use of Scripture in the Church. Louisville: Westminster John Knox.

Long, J.C., 2013. 'Dangerous Women: Observations on the Feast of Herod in Florentine Art of the Early Renaissance,' *Renaissance Quarterly* 66/4: 1153–1205.

Lossky, V., 1974. *In the Image and Likeness of God*. Crestwood: St. Vladimir's Seminary Press.

Lubbock, J., 2006. *Storytelling in Christian Art from Giotto to Donatello*. New Haven and London: Yale University Press.

Luchinat, C.A. (ed.), 1994. *The Chapel of the Magi: Benozzo Gozzoli's Frescoes in the Palazzo Medici-Riccardi Florence*. London and New York: Thames and Hudson.

Ludlow, D.H. (ed.), 1992. *Encyclopedia of Mormonism. Volume 3: N–S*. New York, Oxford, Singapore, and Sydney: Maxwell Macmillan International.

Luttikhuizen, G.P., 1988. 'The Evaluation of the Teaching of Jesus in Christian Gnostic Revelation Dialogues,' *NovT* 30: 158–168.

Luz, U., 1994. *Matthew in History: Interpretation, Influence, and Effects*. Minneapolis: Fortress.

Luz, U., 2001. *Matthew 8–20*. Trans. J.E. Crouch Hermeneia. Minneapolis: Fortress.

Luz, U., 2005a. *Matthew 21–28*. Trans. J.E. Crouch. Hermeneia. Minneapolis: Fortress.

Luz, U., 2005b. *Studies in Matthew*. Grand Rapids and Cambridge: Eerdmans.

Luz, U., 2007. *Matthew 1–7*. Revised edition. Trans. J.E. Crouch. Hermeneia. Minneapolis: Fortress.

Luz, U., 2011. 'The Resurrection of Jesus in Art,' *Interpretation* 65: 44–55.

Lyons, W.J., 2014. *Joseph of Arimathea: A Study in Reception History*. Biblical Reconfigurations. Oxford: Oxford University Press.

MacCulloch, J.A., 1930. *The Harrowing of Hell: A comparative Study of an Early Christian Doctrine*. Edinburgh: T. & T. Clark.

MacCulloch, D., 2004. 'Mary and Sixteenth-Century Protestants,' in R.N. Swanson (ed.), *The Church and Mary*. Studies in Church History 39. Woodbridge: Boydell, 191–217.

Madigan, K., 1995. 'Ancient and High-Medieval Interpretations of Jesus in Gethsemane: Some Reflections on Tradition and Continuity in Christian Thought,' *HTR* 88/1: 157–173.

Madigan, K., 2003. *Olivi and the Interpretation of Matthew in the High Middle Ages*. Notre Dame: University of Notre Dame Press.

Marcus, J., 1988. 'The Gates of Hades and the Keys of the Kingdom (Matt 16:18–19),' *CBQ* 50: 443–455.

Marcus, J., 2000. *Mark 1–8*. Anchor Bible. New York: Doubleday.

Markschies, C., 2009. 'Kastration und Magenprobleme? einige neue Blicke auf das asketische Leben des Origenes,' in G. Heidl, R. Somos, and C. Néneth (ed.), *Origeniana nona: Origen and the Religious Practice of His Time: Papers of the 9th International Origen Congress, Pécs, Hungary, 29 August–2 September 2005*. BETL 228. Leuven and Walpole: Peeters, pp. 255–271.

Marsh-Edwards, J.C., 1956. 'The Magi in Tradition and Art.' *Irish Ecclesiastical Record* series 5, 85: 1–9.

Martens, P.W., 2008. 'Revisting the Allegory/Typology Distinction: The Case of Origen,' *Early Christian Studies* 16/3: 283–317.

Martin, J.A., 1986. 'Dispensational Approaches to the Sermon on the Mount,' in S.D. Toussaint and C.H. Dyer (ed.), *Essays in Honor of J. Dwight Pentecost*. Chicago: Moody Press, pp. 35–48.

Martin, L., 2002. *Sacred Doorways: A Beginner's Guide to Icons*. Brewster: Paraclete Press.

Massaux, E., 1990–1993. *The Influence of the Gospel of Saint Matthew on Christian Literature Before Saint Irenaeus*. Trans. N.J. Belval and S. Hecht. Ed. A.J. Bellinzoni. 3 vols. Macon: Mercer University Press.

Masseron, A., 1957. *Saint Jean Baptiste dans l'Art*. Paris: Arthaud.

Massing, J.M., 1988. 'The Broad and Narrow Way from German Pietists to English Open-Air Preachers,' *Print Quarterly* 5/3: 258–267.

Mattison, W.C., 2013. 'The Beatitudes and Moral Theology: A Virtue Ethics Approach,' *Nova et Vetera* 11/3: 819–848.

Matz, B.J., 2013. 'Ascetic Readings of the Agricultural Parables in Matt 13:1–48 in the Cappadocians,' in H.-U. Weidermann (ed.), *Asceticism and Exegesis in Early Christianity: The Reception of New Testament Texts in Ancient Ascetic Discourses*. NTOA/StUNT 101. Göttingen: Vandenhoeck & Ruprecht, pp. 268–283.

Mayes, B.T.G., 2006. 'Does Matthew 18:15–16 Apply to Public Sins? The Steps of Admonition Today and in Lutheran Orthodoxy,' *Logia* 15/2: 37–44.

Mayeski, M.A., 2009. 'Early Medieval Exegesis: Gregory I to the Twelfth Century,' in A.J. Hauser and D.F. Watson (ed.), *A History of Biblical Interpretation. Volume 2: The Medieval through the Reformation Periods*. Grand Rapids and Cambridge: Eerdmans, pp. 86–112.

McArthur, H.K., 1960. *Understanding the Sermon on the Mount*. New York: Harper & Brothers.

McCabe, H., OP, 1991. 'The Genealogy of Christ,' in *God Matters*. Springfield: Templegate, pp. 246–249.

McCarthy, C., 1991. 'Gospel Exegesis from a Semitic Church: Ephrem's Commentary on the Sermon on the Mount,' in G.J. Norton and S. Pisano (ed.), *Tradition of the Text: Studies Offered to Dominique Barthélemy in Celebration of His 70th Birthday*. Orbis Biblicus et Orientalis 109. Freiburg and Göttingen: Universitätsverlag and Vandenhoeck and Ruprecht, pp. 103–123.

McColl, M.A., and R.S. Anscough, 2009. 'Jesus and People with Disabilities: Old Stories, New Approaches,' *Journal of Pastoral Care and Counseling* 63/3–4: 1–11.

McDonnell, K., 1995. 'Jesus' Baptism in the Jordan,' *TS* 56: 209–236.

McDonnell, K., 1996. *The Baptism of Jesus in the Jordan: The Trinitarian and Cosmic Order of Creation*. Collegeville: Liturgical Press.

McDowell, S., 2015. *The Fate of the Apostles: Examining the Martyrdom Accounts of the Closest Followers of Jesus*. Farnham and Burlington: Ashgate.

McGuire, B.P., 2011. 'Becoming a Father and a Husband: St. Joseph in Bernard of Clairvaux and Jean Gerson,' in J.F. Chorpenning (ed.), *Joseph of Nazareth Through the Centuries*. Philadelphia: Saint Joseph's University Press, pp. 49–61.

McIver, R.K., 1995. 'The Parable of the Weeds Among the Wheat (Matt 13:24–30, 36–43) and the Relationship between the Kingdom and the Church as Portrayed in the Gospel of Matthew,' *JBL* 114/4: 643–659.

McNamara, M., 2015. 'The Irish Origin of Vienna Codex 640,' *PIBA* 38: 67–84.

McNeile, A.H., 1952. *The Gospel According to Saint Matthew*. London: Macmillan.

Meier, J.P., 1980. 'John the Baptist in Matthew's Gospel,' *JBL* 99/3: 383–405.
Meier, J.P., 1991. *The Vision of Matthew: Christ, Church, and Morality in the First Gospel*. New York: Crossroad.
Meier, J.P., 1994. *A Marginal Jew. Volume Two: Mentor, Message, and Miracles*. New York and London: Doubleday.
Meinardus, O.F.A., 1986. *The Holy Family in Egypt*. Cairo: American University in Cairo Press.
Meiser, M., 2013. 'Protestant Reading of the Gospels of Mark and Matthew in the 20th Century,' in E.-M. Becker and A. Runesson (ed.), *Mark and Matthew II: Comparative Readings: Reception History, Cultural Hermeneutics, and Theology*. WUNT 304. Tübingen: Mohr Siebeck, pp. 151–167.
Melanchthon, M.J., 2015. 'The Flight to Egypt: A Migrant Reading – Implications for a Lutheran Understanding of Salvation,' in K. Mtata and C. Koester (ed.), *To All the Nations: Lutheran Hermeneutics and the Gospel of Matthew*. LWF Studies. Leipzig: Lutheran World Federation/Evangelische Verlangsanstalt, pp. 153–168.
Melion, W.S., 2017. '*Signa Resurrectionis*: Vision, Image, and Pictorial Proof in Pieter Bruegel's Resurrection of Circa 1562–1563,' in V.K. Robbins, W.S. Melion, and R.R. Jeal (ed.), *The Art of Visual Exegesis: Rhetoric, Texts, Images*. Emory Studies in Early Christianity. Atlanta: SBL, pp. 381–440.
Merkle, B.L., 2010. 'Who Will Be Left Behind? Rethinking the Meaning of Matthew 24:40–41 and Luke 17:34–35,' *Westminster Theological Journal* 72: 169–179.
Metzger, B.M., 1994. *A Textual Commentary on the Greek New Testament*. 2nd edition. Stuttgart: Deutsche Bibelgesellschaft/United Bible Societies.
Meyer, H.A.W., 1877. *Critical and Exegetical Handbook to the Gospel of Matthew. Volume I*. Trans. P. Christie and F. Crombie. Edinburgh: T. & T. Clark.
Meyer, H.A.W., 1879. *Critical and Exegetical Handbook to the Gospel of Matthew. Volume II*. Trans. P. Christie and F. Crombie. Edinburgh: T. & T. Clark.
Michael, R., 2006. *Holy Hatred: Christianity, Antisemitism, and the Holocaust*. New York and Basingstoke: Palgrave Macmillan.
Michaels, J.R., 1965. 'Apostolic Hardships and Righteous Gentiles: A Study of Matthew 25:31–46,' *JBL* 84/1: 27–37.
Miller, G.D., 2009. 'Trying the Fix the Family Trees of Jesus,' *SB* 39/1: 17–30.
Minns, D., 2012. 'The Parable of the Two Sons (Matt. 21:28–32) in Irenaeus and Codex Bezae,' in S. Parvis and P. Foster (ed.), *Irenaeus: Life, Scripture, Legacy*. Minneapolis: Fortress, pp. 55–63.
Mitchell, C., 1938. 'Poussin's "Flight into Egypt",' *Journal of the Warburg Institute* 1/4: 340–343.
Mitchell, M.M., 2005. 'Patristic Counter-Evidence to the Claim that "The Gospels Were Written for All Christians,"' *NTS* 51/1: 36–79.
Mitchell, M.M., 2007. 'John Chrysostom,' in J.P. Greenman, T. Larsen, and S.R. Spencer (ed.), *The Sermon on the Mount Through the Centuries: From the Early Church to John Paul II*. Grand Rapids: Brazos, pp. 19–42.
Molnar, M.R., 1999. *The Star of Bethlehem: The Legacy of the Magi*. New Brunswick and London: Rutgers University Press.

Moloney, F.J., 2002. *The Gospel of Mark: A Commentary*. Peabody: Hendrickson.

Moloney, F.J., 2013. *The Resurrection of the Messiah: A Narrative Commentary on the Resurrection Accounts in the Four Gospels*. New York and Mahwah: Paulist.

Moloney, F.J., 2015. 'A New Testament Hermeneutic for Divorce and Remarriage in the Catholic Tradition,' *Australasian Catholic Record* 92: 269–288.

Monneret de Villard, U., 1952. *Le leggende orientali sui magi evangelici*. Vatican City: Biblioteca Apostolica Vaticana.

Moore, M.E., 2011. *A Sacred Kingdom: Bishops and the Rise of Frankish Kingship, 300–850*. Studies in Medieval and Early Modern Canon Law 8. Washington: Catholic University of America Press.

Morgan, R., 2010. '*Sachkritik* in Reception History,' *JSNT* 33/2: 175–176.

Morin, D.G., 1911. 'Liturgie et basiliques de Rome au milieu du VIIe siècle d'après les listes d'Évangiles de Würzburg,' *Revue Bénédictine* 28: 296–340.

Muddiman, J., 1983. 'John's Use of Matthew: A British Exponent of the Theory,' *ETL* 59/4: 333–337.

Muessig, C., 2009. 'Preaching the Beatitudes in the Late Middle Ages: Some Mendicant Examples,' *Studies in Christian Ethics* 22/2: 136–150.

Mundy, E.J., 1981/1982. 'Gerard David's Rest on the Flight into Egypt: Further Additions to Grape Symbolism,' *Simiolus* 12: 211–222.

Murdoch, B.O., 1974. *The Recapitulated Fall: A Comparative Study in Mediaeval Literature*. Amsterdamer Publikationen zur Sprache und Literatur, 11. Band. Amsterdam: Rodopi N.V.

Murphy-O'Connor, J., 2008. *The Holy Land: An Oxford Archaeological Guide from Earliest Times to 1700*. 5th edition. Oxford and New York: OUP.

Mussies, G., 1990. 'Joseph's Dream (Matt 1, 18–23) and Comparable Stories,' in P.W. van der Horst and G. Mussies (ed.), *Studies on the Hellenistic Background of the New Testament*. Utrecht: Faculteit der Godgeleerdheid van de Rijksuniversiteit, pp. 86–95.

Myles, R.J., 2013. 'Echoes of Displacement in Matthew's Genealogy of Jesus,' *Colloquium* 45/1: 31–41.

Napolitano, F., 2009. 'The Relationship Between Rhetoric and Miracles in the York "Entry into Jerusalem,"' *Early Theatre* 12/2: 15–31.

Nelson, R.S., 1980. *The Iconography of Preface and Miniature in the Byzantine Gospel Book*. New York: New York University Press for the College Art Association of America.

Neufeld, G., 1970. 'Rembrandt's *Beheading of John the Baptist*,' *Oud Holland* 85/3: 177–179.

Newheart, M.W., 2004. *'My Name Is Legion': The Story and Soul of the Gerasene Demoniac*. Interfaces. Collegeville: Liturgical Press.

Nicholls, R., 2008. *Walking on the Water: Reading Mt. 14:22–33 in the Light of Its Wirkungsgeschichte*. Bibical Interpretation Series 90. Leiden and Boston: Brill.

Nichols, S.J., 2008. *Jesus Made in America: A Cultural History from the Puritans to 'The Passion of the Christ.'* Downers Grove: IVP Academic.

Nicklas, T., 2011. 'The Bible and Antisemitism,' in M. Lieb, E. Mason, J. Roberts, and C. Rowland (ed.), *The Oxford Handbook of the Reception History of the Bible*. Oxford and New York: OUP, pp. 267–280.

Nicklas, T., 2016. 'New Testament Canon and Ancient Christian "Landscapes of Memory,"' *Early Christianity* 7: 5–23.

Noble, J., 2001. 'The Genealogies of Christ and Their Musical Settings,' in B. Haggh (ed.), *Essays on Music and Culture in Honor of Herbert Kellman*. Centre d'Études Supérieures de la Renaissance: Collection 'Épitome Musical' 8. Paris: Minerve, pp. 197–209.

Nolan, K., 1996. '"Ploratus et ululatus": The Mothers in the Massacre of the Innocents at Chartres Cathedral,' *Studies in Iconography* 17: 95–141.

Noll, M., 2007. 'John Wesley,' in J.P. Greenman, T. Larsen, and S.R. Spencer (ed.), *The Sermon on the Mount Through the Centuries: From the Early Church to John Paul II*. Grand Rapids: Brazos, pp. 153–180.

Nolland, J., 1996. 'What Kind of Genesis Do We Have in Matt 1.1?' *NTS* 42: 463–471.

Nolland, J., 2005. *The Gospel of Matthew: A Commentary on the Greek Text*. NIGTC. Grand Rapids and Cambridge: Eerdmans.

North, J.L., 2008. 'Reactions in Early Christianity to Some References to the Hebrew Prophets in Matthew's Gospel,' *NTS* 54/2: 254–274.

Nutu, E., 2009. 'Reading Salome: Caravaggio and the Gospel Narratives,' in C.E. Joynes and C.C. Rowland (ed.), *From the Margins 2: Women of the New Testament and Their Afterlives*. Sheffield: Sheffield Phoenix Press, pp. 210–225.

O'Brien, C., 2015. 'The Cleansing of the Temple in Early Medieval Northumbria,' *Anglo-Saxon England* 44: 201–220.

O'Donnell, C.M., 1960. *St. Cyprian on the Lord's Prayer: An Abstract of a Dissertation*. Washington: Catholic University of America Press.

O'Kane, M., 2002. 'The Flight into Egypt: Icon of Refuge for the H(a)unted,' in M. O'Kane (ed.), *Borders, Boundaries and the Bible*. JSOTSS 313. London and New York: Sheffield Academic Press, pp. 15–60.

O'Kane, M., 2005. 'The Artist as Reader of the Bible: Visual Exegesis and the Adoration of the Magi,' *Biblical Interpretation* 13: 337–373.

O'Kane, M., 2010. '*Wirkungsgeschichte* and Visual Exegesis: The Contribution of Hans-Georg Gadamer,' *JSNT* 33/2: 147–159.

O'Keefe, J.J., and R.R. Reno, 2005. *Sanctified Vision: An Introduction to Early Christian Interpretation of the Bible*. Baltimore and London: John Hopkins University Press.

Oberdorfer, B., 2015. 'How Do We Deal with a Challenging Text,' in K. Mtata and C. Koester (ed.), *To All the Nations: Lutheran Hermeneutics and the Gospel of Matthew*. LWF Studies. Leipzig: Lutheran World Federation/Evangelische Verlangsanstalt, pp. 75–88.

Ocker, C., 1991. 'The Fusion of Papal Ideology and Biblical Exegesis in the Fourteenth Century,' in M.S. Burrows and P. Rorem (ed.), *Biblical Hermeneutics in Historical Perspective: Studies in Honor of Karlfried Froehlich*. Grand Rapids: Eerdmans, pp. 131–151.

Ocker, C., 2009. 'Scholastic Interpretation of the Bible,' in A.J. Hauser and D.F. Watson (ed.), *A History of Biblical Interpretation. Volume 2: The Medieval Through the Reformation Periods*. Grand Rapids and Cambridge: Eerdmans, pp. 254–279.

Olsen, V.N., 1971. *The New Testament Logia on Divorce: A Study of Their Interpretation from Erasmus to Milton*. BGBE 10. Tübingen: J. C. B. Mohr (Paul Siebeck).
Olsen, D.A., 2015. *Reading Matthew with Monks: Liturgical Interpretation in Anglo-Saxon England*. Collegeville: Liturgical Press.
Orton, D.E., 1989. *The Understanding Scribe: Matthew and the Apocalyptic Ideal*. JSNTSS 25. Sheffield: JSOT Press.
Orton, D.E., 2003. 'We Felt Like Grasshoppers: The Little Ones in Biblical Interpretation,' *Biblical Interpretation* 11/3: 488–502.
Pabel, H.M., 1993. '"Give to Caesar That Which Is Caesars": Hobbes's Strategy in the Second Half of *Leviathan*,' *Journal of Church and State* 35/2: 335–349.
Paffenroth, K., 1995. 'The Character of Judas in Bach's *St. Matthew Passion*,' *The Midwest Quarterly* 36/2: 125–135.
Paffenroth, K., 2001. *Judas: Images of the Lost Disciple*. Louisville and London: Westminster John Knox Press.
Parris, D.P., 2009. *Reception Theory and Biblical Interpretation*. Princeton Theological Monograph Series. Eugene: Pickwick.
Parris, D.P., 2015. *Reading the Bible with Giants*. 2nd edition. Eugene: Cascade.
Pasolini, P.P., 2012. *My Cinema*. Ed. G. Chiarcossi and R. Chiesi in collaboration with M. D'Agostini. Bologna: Edizioni Cineteca di Bologna and Luce Cinecittà.
Patella, M., 2005. *Word and Image: The Hermeneutics of The Saint John's Bible*. Collegeville: Liturgical Press.
Patte, D., M.A. Stubbs, J. Ukpong, and R.E. Velunta, 2003. *The Gospel of Matthew: A Contextual Introduction for Group Study*. Nashville: Abingdon.
Paulsen, D.L., 1990. 'Early Christian Belief in a Corporeal Deity: Origen and Augustine as Reluctant Witness,' *HTR* 83/2: 105–116.
Paulsen, D.L., R.D. Cook, and K.J. Christensen, 2010. 'The Harrowing of Hell: Salvation for the Dead in Early Christianity,' *Journal of Book of Mormon Studies* 19/1: Article 7.
Pearson, S.L., 2012. 'Charlotte Brontë's Poetics: A Study of "Pilate's Wife's Dream",' *Brontë Studies* 37/3: 194–207.
Pelikan, J.J., 1951. 'The Temptation of the Church,' *Concordia Theological Monthly* 22/4: 251–259.
Pelikan, J.J., 1997. *The Illustrated Jesus Through the Centuries*. New Haven and London: Yale University Press.
Pelikan, J.J., 2001. *Divine Rhetoric: The Sermon on the Mount as Message and Model in Augustine, Chrysostom and Luther*. Crestwood: St. Vladimir's Seminary Press.
Penick, C.C., 1881. *More Than a Prophet*. New York: Thomas Whittaker.
Pennells, S., 1983. 'The Spear Thrust (Mt. 27.49b, *v.l.* / Jn 19.34),' *JSNT* 19: 99–115.
Pennington, J.T., 2012. *Reading the Gospels Wisely: A Narrative and Theological Introduction*. Grand Rapids: Baker Academic.
Peppard, M., 2011. 'New Testament Imagery in the Earliest Christian Baptistery,' in L.R. Brody and G.L. Hoffman (ed.), *Dura-Europos: Crossroads of Antiquity*. Chestnut Hill: McMullen Museum of Art, Boston College, pp. 169–187.
Perlove, S., and L. Silver, 2009. *Rembrandt's Faith: Church and Temple in the Dutch Golden Age*. University Park: Pennsylvania State University Press.

Pfaff, R.W., 1970. *New Liturgical Feasts in Later Medieval England.* Oxford Theological Monographs. Oxford: Clarendon Press.

Philip, L.B., 1971. *The Ghent Altarpiece and the Art of Jan van Eyck.* Princeton: Princeton University Press.

Phillips, P., 2008. 'Casting Out the Treasure: A New Reading of Matthew 13.52,' *JSNT* 31/1: 3–24.

Pinckaers, S., 1998. *The Pursuit of Happiness – God's Way: Living the Beatitudes.* Trans. M.T. Noble. New York: Alba House/St Paul.

Piovanelli, P., 2003. 'Exploring the Ethiopic *Book of the Cock*, An Apocryphal Passion Gospel from Late Antiquity,' *HTR* 96/4: 427–454.

Pitkin, B., 2009. 'John Calvin and the Interpretation of the Bible,' in A.J. Hauser and D.F. Watson (ed.), *A History of Biblical Interpretation. Volume 2: The Medieval Through the Reformation Periods.* Grand Rapids and Cambridge: Eerdmans, pp. 341–371.

Porter, C., 1987. '"Wise as Serpents: Innocent as Doves": How Shall We Live?' *Encounter* 48/1: 15–26.

Powell, M.A., 1995. 'Do and Keep What Moses Says (Matthew 23:2–7),' *JBL* 114/3: 419–435.

Powell, M.A., 2000a. 'The Magi as Kings: An Adventure in Reader-Response Criticism,' *CBQ* 62: 459–480.

Powell, M.A., 2000b. 'The Magi as Wise Men: Re-examining a Basic Presupposition,' *NTS* 46: 1–20.

Power, E., 1923. 'The Staff of the Apostles: A Problem in Gospel Harmony,' *Biblica* 4: 241–266.

Swami Prabhavananda, 1964. *The Sermon on the Mount According to Vedanta.* Hollywood: Vedanta Press.

Probst, C.J., 2012. *Demonizing the Jews: Luther and the Protestant Church in Nazi Germany.* Bloomington and Indianapolis: Indiana University Press.

Puig i Tàrrech, A., 2012. 'The Glory on the Mountain: The Episode of the Transfiguration of Jesus,' *NTS* 58: 151–172.

Pui-lan, K., 1995. *Discovering the Bible in the Non-Biblical World.* Bible and Liberation Series. Maryknoll: Orbis.

Puttfarken, T., 1998. 'Caravaggio's "Story of St. Matthew": A Challenge to the Conventions of Painting,' *Art History* 21/2: 163–181.

Quesnell, Q., 1968. '"Made Themselves Eunuchs for the Kingdom of Heaven" (Mt 19,12),' *CBQ* 30: 335–358.

Ramm, B., 1962. 'The Exegesis of Matt. 16:13–20 in the Patristic and Reformation Period,' *Foundations* 5/3: 206–216.

Ramsey, A.M., 1949. *The Glory of God and the Transfiguration of Christ.* London: Longmans.

Rankin, D., 1995. *Tertullian and the Church.* Cambridge: CUP.

Réau, L., 1958. *Iconographie de l'Art chrétien. Tome III: Iconographie des saints. II: G-O.* Paris: Presses universitaires de France, pp. 927–931.

Reed, R., 2000. 'The Slaughter of the Innocents,' *Early Theatre* 3: 219–228.

Reid, B.E., 2004. 'Violent Endings in Matthew's Parables and Christian Nonviolence,' *CBQ* 66/2: 237–255.

Reinhartz, A., 1998. 'Jesus in Film: Hollywood Perspectives on the Jewishness of Jesus,' *Journal of Religion & Film* 2/2, Art. 2.

Renov, I., 1955. 'The Seat of Moses,' *Israel Exploration Journal* 5/4: 262–267.

Reuss, J., 1957. *Matthäus-Kommentare aus der griechieschen Kirche*. Texte und Untersuchungen zur Geschichte der altchristlichen Literatur 61. Berlin: Akademie.

Rex, R., 2014. 'Christopher St. German on Scriptures, Councils, and Monarchs,' *Reformation & Renaissance Review* 16/3: 266–279.

Riches, J.K., 2000. *Conflicting Mythologies: Identity Formation in the Gospels of Mark and Matthew*. Edinburgh: T. & T. Clark.

Riches, J.K., 2008. *Galatians Through the Centuries*. Blackwell Bible Commentaries. Malden, Oxford, and Carlton: Blackwell.

Rigaux, B., 1967. 'St. Peter in Contemporary Exegesis,' in R. Aubert (ed.), *Progress and Decline in the History of Church Renewal*. New York: Paulist, pp. 147–179.

Robinson, B.P., 1984. 'Peter and His Successors: Tradition and Redaction in Matthew 16.17–19,' *JSNT* 21: 85–104.

Robinson, B.P., 1997. '"They Are as Angels in Heaven": Jesus' Alleged Riposte to the Sadducees (Mark 12: 18–27; par. Mt 22:23–33, Lk 20:27–40),' *New Blackfriars* 78: 530–537.

Robson, J., 2004. 'Judas and the Franciscans: Perfidy Pictured in Lorenzetti's Passion Cycle at Assisi,' *Art Bulletin* 86/1: 31–57.

Rodney, N.B., 1953. 'Salome,' *The Metropolitan Museum of Art Bulletin* 11/7: 190–200.

Rogers, T.J., 2004. 'Shaking the Dust off the Markan Mission Discourse,' *JSNT* 27/2: 169–192.

Rohrbaugh, R.L., 1993. 'A Peasant Reading of the Parable of the Tenants/Pounds: A Text of Terror?,' *BTB* 23: 32–39.

Romero Pose, E., 1992. 'Matthew, Gospel of,' in A. di Berardino (ed.), *Encyclopedia of the Early Church. Volume I: A–M*. Trans. A. Walford. Cambridge: James Clarke, p. 543.

Rordorf, W., 1976. 'Le 'pain quotidien' (Mt. 6:11) dans l'histoire de l'exégèse,' *Didaskalia* 6: 221–235.

Rose, E., 2009. *Ritual Memory: The Apocryphal Acts and Liturgical Commemoration in the Early Medieval West (c. 500–1215)*. Leiden and Boston: Brill, pp. 163–212.

Rosenblatt, M.-E., 1993. 'Got into the Party After All: Women's Issues and the Five Foolish Virgins,' *Continuum* 3: 107–137.

Roukema, R., 2014. 'Reception and Interpretation of Jesus' Teaching of Love for Enemies in Ancient Christianity,' in A.C. Geljon and R. Roukema (ed.), *Violence in Ancient Christianity: Victims and Perpetrators*. Supplement to Vigiliae Christianae 125. Leiden and Boston: Brill, pp. 198–214.

Rowland, C., 1979. 'The Visions of God in Apocalyptic Literature,' *JSJ* 10/2: 137–154.

Rowland, C., 1989. 'Render to God What Belongs to God,' *New Blackfriars* 70: 365–371.

Rowland, C., 1994. 'Apocalyptic, the Poor, and the Gospel of Matthew,' *JTS* 45/2: 504–518.

Rowland, C., 2010. *Blake and the Bible*. New Haven and London: Yale University Press.

Rowland, C., 2014. 'Blake: Text and Image,' in S. Prickett (ed.), *The Edinburgh Companion to the Bible and the Arts*. Edinburgh: Edinburgh University Press, pp. 307–326.

Rowland, C., and I. Boxall, 2013. 'Reception Theory/Criticism,' in S. McKenzie (ed.), *Oxford Encyclopedia of Biblical Interpretation*. New York and Oxford: OUP, Vol. 2, pp. 206–215.

Ruiz, J.-P., 2007. 'The Bible and People on the Move: Another Look at Matthew's Parable of the Day Laborers,' *New Theology Review* 20/3: 15–23.

Rummel, E., 2009. 'The Renaissance Humanists,' in A.J. Hauser and D.F. Watson (ed.), *A History of Biblical Interpretation. Volume 2: The Medieval Through the Reformation Periods*. Grand Rapids and Cambridge: Eerdmans, pp. 280–298.

Ryan, E.A., 1952. 'The Rejection of Military Service by the Early Christians,' *TS* 13: 1–32.

Ryan, D., 2001. 'Womanly Weaponry: Language and Power in the Chester *Slaughter of the Innocents*,' *Studies in Philology* 98/1: 76–92.

Ryrie, A., 2011. *The Desert Movement: Fresh Perspectives on the Spirituality of the Desert*. Norwich: Canterbury Press.

Saari, A.M.H., 2006. *The Many Deaths of Judas Iscariot: A Meditation on Suicide*. London and New York: Routledge.

Saddington, D.B., 2006. 'The Centurion in Matthew 8:5–13: Consideration of the Proposal of Theodore W. Jennings, Jr., and Tat-Siong Benny Liew,' *JBL* 125/1: 140–142.

Saintyves, P., 1928. 'Le massacre des innocents ou la persecution de l'enfant predestine,' in P.L. Couchoud (ed.), *Congrès d'histoire du Christianisme: Jubilé Alfred Loisy*. Vol. 1; Paris: Rieder, pp. 229–272.

Saldarini, A.J., 1992. 'Delegitimation of Leaders in Matthew 23,' *CBQ* 54: 659–680.

Sale, J.R., 2007. 'Birds of a Feather: The Medici 'Adoration' Tondo in Washington,' *Burlington Magazine* 149/1246: 4–13.

Salvesen, A., 2006. 'Without Shame or Desire: The Pronouncements of Jesus on Children and the Kingdom, and Early Syriac Attitudes to Childhood,' *SJT* 59/3: 307–326.

Sanders, E.P., 1985a. *Jesus and Judaism*. London: SCM.

Sanders, E.P., 1985b. 'Judaism and the Grand "Christian" Abstractions: Love, Mercy, and Grace,' *Interpretation* 39/4: 357–372.

Santini, D., 2011. '"The Invisible Dance": Reflections on the "Dance of the Seven Veils" in Richard Strauss's "Salome,"' *Dance Research: The Journal of the Society for Dance Research* 29/2: 233–245.

Savage, E.B., 1980. 'The *St. Matthew Passion* as a Drama of Conversion,' *Church Music* 80: 56–69.

Sawyer, J.F.A., 1996. *The Fifth Gospel: Isaiah in the History of Christianity*. Cambridge: CUP.

Schaff, H.H., 1932. 'The Anabaptists, the Reformers, and the Civil Government,' *Church History* 1/1: 27–46.

Scharper, P., and S. Scharper, 1984. *The Gospel in Art by the Peasants of Solentiname*. Maryknoll: Orbis.

Scheidgen, A., 2002. *Die Gestalt des Pontius Pilatus in Legende, Bibelauslegung und Geschichtsdichtung vom Mittelalter bis in die frühe Neuzeit: Literaturgeschichte einer umstrittenen Figur*. Mikrokosmos Band 68. Frankfurt am Main: Peter Lang.

Schildgen, B.D., 1999. *Power and Prejudice: The Reception of the Gospel of Mark*. Detroit: Wayne State University Press.

Schiller, G., 1971. *Iconography of Christian Art: Volume I*. Trans. J. Seligman. Greenwich: New York Graphic Society Ltd.

Schiller, G., 1986. *Ikonographie der christlichen Kunst, Bd. 3: Die Auferstehung and Erhöhung Christi*. Gütersloh: G. Mohn.

Schnackenburg, R., 2002. *The Gospel of Matthew*. Trans. R.R. Barr. Grand Rapids and Cambridge: Eerdmans.

Schoedel, W.R., 1985. *A Commentary on the Letters of Ignatius of Antioch*. Hermeneia. Philadelphia: Fortress.

Schoedel, W.R., 1991. 'Ignatius and the Reception of the Gospel of Matthew in Antioch,' in D.L. Balch (ed.), *Social History of the Matthean Community: Cross-Disciplinary Approaches*. Minneapolis: Augsburg Fortress, pp. 129–177.

Schreckenberg, H., 1996. *The Jews in Christian Art: An Illustrated History*. Trans. J. Bowden. New York: Continuum.

Schreiner, S.E., 2007. 'Martin Luther,' in J.P. Greenman, T. Larsen, and S.R. Spencer (ed.), *The Sermon on the Mount Through the Centuries: From the Early Church to John Paul II*. Grand Rapids: Brazos, pp. 109–127.

Schulze, W.A., 1975. 'Zur Geschichte der Auslegung von Matth. 2,1–12,' *Theologische Zeitschrift* 31: 150–160.

Schüssler Fiorenza, E., 1983. *In Memory of Her: A Feminist Reconstruction of Christian Origins*. London: SCM.

Schwartz, S., 1975. The Iconography of the Rest on the Flight into Egypt. New York University, PhD thesis; UMI Dissertation Services.

Schwartz, E.C., 1997. 'The Angel of the Wilderness: Russian Icons and the Byzantine Legacy,' *Byzantinoslavica* 58: 169–174.

Schweitzer, A., 1914. *The Mystery of the Kingdom of God*. Trans. W. Lowrie. New York: Dodd, Mead & Co.

Schweitzer, A., 2000. *The Quest of the Historical Jesus: First Complete Edition*. Trans. W. Montgomery, J.R. Coates, S. Cupitt, and J. Bowden. Ed. J. Bowden. London: SCM.

Schweizer, E., 1975. *The Good News According to Matthew*. Trans. D.E. Green. Atlanta: John Knox.

Selvidge, M.J., 1990. *Woman, Cult, and Miracle Recital: A Redactional Critical Investigation on Mark 5:24–34*. Lewisburg: Bucknell University Press; London and Toronto: Associated University Presses.

Sharp, T., 1825. *A Dissertation on the Pageants or Dramatic Mysteries Anciently Performed at Coventry*. Coventry: Merridew and Son.

Shaw, J., 2006. *Miracles in Enlightenment England*. New Haven and London: Yale University Press.

Sheerin, D., 1976. 'St. John the Baptist in the Lower World,' *VC* 30/1: 1–22.

Sheingorn, P., 1990. 'Appropriating the Holy Kinship: Gender and Family History,' in K. Ashley and P. Sheingorn (ed.), *Interpreting Cultural Symbols: Saint Anne in Late Medieval Society*. Athens and London: University of Georgia Press, pp. 169–198.

Sherwood, Y., 2000. *A Biblical Text and Its Afterlives: The Survival of Jonah in Western Culture*. Cambridge and New York: CUP.

Shirock, R., 1992. 'Whose Exorcists Are They? The Referents of οἱ υἱοὶ ὑμῶν at Matthew 12.27/Luke 11.19,' *JSNT* 46: 41–51.

Sicari, A., 1971. '"Ioseph iustus" (Matteo 1,19): la storia dell'interpretazione e le nuove prospettive,' *Cahiers de Joséphologie* 19: 62–83.

Sidgwick, E., 2014. 'At Once Limit and Threshold: How the Early Christian Touch of a Hem (Luke 8.44; Matthew 9.20) Constituted the Medieval Veronica,' *Viator* 45/1: 1–24.

Sim, D.C., 1998. *The Gospel of Matthew and Christian Judaism: The History and Social Setting of the Matthean Community*. Studies of the New Testament and Its World. Edinburgh: T. & T. Clark.

Sim, D.C., 2009. 'The Rise and Fall of the Gospel of Matthew,' *Exp Tim* 120: 478–485.

Simmonds, A.R., 2009. '"Woe to You ... Hypocrites!" Re-Reading Matthew 23:13–36,' *Bibliotheca Sacra* 166: 336–349.

Simonetti, M., 1969. 'Note sul commento a Matteo di Ilario di Poitiers,' *Vetera Christianorum* 1: 36–64.

Simonetti, M., 1980. 'Praecursor ad inferos. Una nota sull'interpretazione patristica di Matteo 11,3,' *Augustinianum* 20: 367–382.

Skaggs, C.T., 2002. 'Modernity's Revision of the Dancing Daughter: The Salome Narrative of Wilde and Strauss,' *College Literature* 29/3: 124–139.

Slingerland, H.D., 1979. 'The Transjordanian Origin of St. Matthew's Gospel,' *JSNT* 3: 18–28.

Smit Sibinga, J., 1966. 'Ignatius and Matthew,' *NovT* 8/2: 263–283.

Smith, H., 1918. 'The Earliest Interpretations of Our Lord's Teaching on Divorce,' *The Expositor* 93: 361–366.

Smith, M.S., 1988. '"Seeing God" in the Psalms,' *CBQ* 50/2: 171–183.

Smith, M.J., and J. Lalitha (ed.), 2014. *Teaching All Nations: Interrogating the Matthean Great Commission*. Minneapolis: Fortress.

Snodgrass, K.R., 2008. *Stories with Intent: A Comprehensive Guide to the Parables of Jesus*. Grand Rapids and Cambridge: Eerdmans.

Snyder, A., 1989. 'The Influence of the Schleitheim Articles on the Anabaptist Movement: An Historical Evaluation,' *Mennonite Quarterly Review* 63: 323–344.

Snyder-Penner, R., 1994. 'The Ten Commandments, the Lord's Prayer, and the Apostles' Creed as Early Anabaptist Texts,' *Mennonite Quarterly Review* 68: 318–335.

Soares-Prabhu, G.M., 1992. 'Jesus in Egypt: A Reflection on Mt 2:13–15.19–21 in the Light of the Old Testament,' *Estudios Bíblicos* 50: 225–249.

Soelle, D., and L. Schottroff, 2000. *Jesus of Nazareth*. Trans. J. Bowden. Louisville and London: Westminster John Knox and SPCK.

Sottocornola, F., 1957. 'Tradition and the Doubt of St. Joseph Concerning Mary's Virginity,' *Marianum* 19: 127–141.

Spadafora, F., 1967. 'Matteo, Evangelista,' in *Bibliotheca Sanctorum. IX: Masabki–Ozanam*. Rome: Instituto Giovanni XXIII della Pontificia Università Lateranense, pp. 110–126.

Spence, J.D., 1996. *God's Chinese Son: The Taiping Heavenly Kingdom of Hong Xiuquan*. New York and London: W.W. Norton & Company.

Spencer, S.R., 2007. 'John Calvin,' in J.P. Greenman, T. Larsen, and S.R. Spencer (ed.), *The Sermon on the Mount Through the Centuries: From the Early Church to John Paul II*. Grand Rapids: Brazos, pp. 129–152.

Stanton, G., 1992. *A Gospel for a New People: Studies in Matthew*. Edinburgh: T. & T. Clark.

Stanton, G., 2013. *Studies in Matthew and Early Christianity*. Ed. M. Bockmuehl and D. Lincicum. WUNT 309. Tübingen: Mohr Siebeck.

Stapert, C., 1993. 'Liturgical and Theological Traditions in Bach's *St. Matthew Passion*,' *Perspectives: A Journal of Reformed Thought* 8/4: 17–20.

Steiner, M., 1962. *La tentation de Jésus dans l'interprétation patristique de saint Justin à Origène*. Études Bibliques. Paris: Librairie Lecoffre.

Steinmetz, D., 1980. 'The Superiority of Pre-Critical Exegesis,' *Theology Today* 37/1: 27–38.

Stephens, P., 2002. 'Bullinger's Defence of Infant Baptism in Debate with the Anabaptists,' *Reformation and Renaissance Review* 4/2: 168–189.

Stevenson, K.W., 2004. *The Lord's Prayer: A Text in Tradition*. Minneapolis: Fortress.

Stevenson, K.W., 2007. *Rooted in Detachment: Living the Transfiguration*. CSS 217. Kalamazoo: Cistercian Publications.

Stevenson, K.W., 2008. 'From Hilary of Poitiers to Peter of Blois: A Transfiguration Journey of Biblical Interpretation,' *SJT* 61(3): 288–306.

Stinger, C.L., 1985. *The Renaissance in Rome*. Bloomington: Indiana University Press.

Stock, A., 1994. *The Method and Message of Matthew*. Collegeville: The Liturgical Press.

Stocker, M., 2009. 'Short Story, Maximal Imbroglio: Salome Ancient and Modern,' in C.E. Joynes and C.C. Rowland (ed.), *From the Margins 2: Women of the New Testament and Their Afterlives*. Sheffield: Sheffield Phoenix Press, pp. 176–189.

Stone, T.J., 2013. 'Following the Church Fathers: An Intertextual Path from Psalm 107 to Isaiah, Jonah, and Matthew8:23–27,' *Journal of Theological Interpretation* 7/1: 37–55.

Stramare, T., 1997. *Saint Joseph, "Guardian of the Redeemer." Apostolic Exhortation of John Paul II. Text and Reflections*. Trans. P.J. Pavese. Santa Cruz: Guardian of the Redeemer Books.

Strauss, D.F., 1973. *The Life of Jesus Critically Examined*. Lives of Jesus. London: SCM.

Streeter, B.H., 1924. *The Four Gospels: A Study of Origins*. Edinburgh: T. & T. Clark.

Sugirtharajah, R.S., 1998. 'A Postcolonial Exploration of Collusion and Construction in Biblical Interpretation,' in R.S. Sugirtharajah (ed.),*The Postcolonial Bible*. Sheffield: Sheffield Academic Press, pp. 91–116.

Surtz, E.L., 1957. *The Praise of Wisdom: A Commentary on the Religious and Moral Problems and Backgrounds of St. Thomas More's Utopia*. Jesuit Studies. Chicago: Loyola University Press.

Taheny, T.T., 1961. *The History of the Exegesis of Matthew 16:18–19 in Commentaries of the Early Middle Ages*. Woodstock: Woodstock College Press.

Talbert, C.H., 2010. *Matthew*. Paideia Commentaries on the New Testament. Grand Rapids: Baker Academic.

Talbott, R., 2006. 'Imagining the Matthean Eunuch Community: Kyriarchy on the Chopping Block,' *JFSR* 22/1: 21–43.

Tamburr, K., 2007. *The Harrowing of Hell in Medieval England.* Cambridge: D.S. Brewer.

Tavard, G.H., 1985. 'Roman Catholic Reflections on Melanchthon's *De Potestate et Primatu Papae*,' *Concordia Theological Quarterly* 49: 253–266.

Taylor, M.D., 1980–1981. 'A Historiated Tree of Jesse,' *Dumbarton Oaks Papers* 34/35: 125–176.

Taylor, J.E., 1997. *The Immerser: John the Baptist within Second Temple Judaism.* Grand Rapids and Cambridge: Eerdmans.

Taylor, M.A., 2007. 'Mary Cornwallis: Voice of a Mother,' in C. de Groot and M.A. Taylor (ed.), *Recovering Nineteenth-Century Women Interpreters of the Bible.* Atlanta: Society of Biblical Literature, pp. 31–44.

Taylor, J.E. (ed.), 2015. *Jesus and Brian: Exploring the Historical Jesus and His Times via 'Monty Python's Life of Brian.'* London and New York: Bloomsbury T&T Clark.

Taylor, M.A., and A. Choi (ed.), 2012. *Handbook of Women Biblical Interpreters: A Historical and Biographical Guide.* Grand Rapids: Baker Academic.

Teeple, H.M., 1957. *The Mosaic Eschatological Prophet.* SBLMS 10. Philadelphia: Society of Biblical Literature.

Terrell, J.M., 2005. 'What Manner of Love?' in J.A. Noel and M.V. Johnson (ed.), *The Passion of the Lord: African American Reflections.* Minneapolis: Fortress, pp. 51–76.

Testa, B., 1994. 'To Film a Gospel ... and Advent of the Theoretical Stranger,' in P. Rumble and B. Testa (ed.), *Piero Paolo Pasolini: Contemporary Perspectives.* Toronto, Buffalo, and London: University of Toronto Press, pp. 180–209.

Tevel, J.M., 1992. 'The Labourers in the Vineyard: The Exegesis of Matthew 20,1–7 in the Early Church,' *VC* 46: 356–380.

Theissen, G., 1987. *The Shadow of the Galilean: The Quest of the Historic al Jesus in Narrative Form.* Trans. J. Bowden. Minneapolis: Fortress.

Theissen, G., 1991. *The Gospels in Context: Social and Political History in the Synoptic Tradition.* Trans. L.M. Maloney. Minneapolis: Fortress.

Theissen, G., and A. Merz, 1998. *The Historical Jesus: A Comprehensive Guide.* Trans. J. Bowden. London: SCM.

Theophilos, M.P., 2012. *The Abomination of Desolation in Matthew 24.15.* Library of New Testament Studies 437. London and New York: T. & T. Clark International.

Theophilos, M.P., 2013. *Jesus as New Moses in Matthew 8–9: Jewish Typology in First Century Greek Literature.* Perspectives on Philosophy and Religious Thought 4. Piscataway: Gorgias Press.

Tholuck, A., 1834. *Exposition, Doctrinal and Philological, of Christ's Sermon on the Mount, According to the Gospel of Matthew. Volume I.* Trans. R. Menzies. Edinburgh: Thomas Clark.

Thompson, W.G., 1970. *Matthew's Advice to a Divided Community: Mt. 17,22–18,35.* Rome: Biblical Institute Press.

Thompson, M.M., 2000. *The Promise of the Father: Jesus and God in the New Testament.* Louisville: Westminster John Knox.

Thompson, M.D., 2009. 'Biblical Interpretation in the Works of Martin Luther,' in A.J. Hauser and D.F. Watson (ed.), *A History of Biblical Interpretation. Volume 2: The*

Medieval Through the Reformation Periods. Grand Rapids and Cambridge: Eerdmans, pp. 299–318.

Tigay, J.H., 1979. 'On the Term Phylacteries (Matt 23:5),' *HTR* 72/1–2: 45–53.

Timiadis, E., 1983. '"Tu es Petrus": An Orthodox Approach,' *Patristic and Byzantine Review* 2/1: 5–26.

Tipson, B., 1984. 'A Dark Side of Seventeenth-Century English Protestantism: The Sin Against the Holy Spirit,' *HTR* 77/3–4: 301–330.

Townsend, R.P., and R. Ward, 1995. *Caravaggio and Tanzio: The Theme of St. John the Baptist*. Kansas City and Tulsa: The Nelson-Atkins Museum of Art and the Philbrook Museum of Art.

Trevett, C., 1984. 'Approaching Matthew from the Second Century: The Under-Used Ignatian Correspondence,' *JSNT* 20: 59–67.

Trexler, R.C., 1997. *The Journey of the Magi: Meanings in History of a Christian Story*. Princeton: Princeton University Press.

Trinchieri Camiz, F., 1990. 'Death and Rebirth in Caravaggio's *Martyrdom of St. Matthew*,' *Artibus et Historiae* 11/22: 89–105.

Trocmé, E., 1983. *The Passion as Liturgy: A Study in the Origin of the Passion Narratives in the Four Gospels*. London: SCM.

Troxel, R.L., 2002. 'Matt 27.51–4 Reconsidered: Its Role in the Passion Narrative, Meaning and Origin,' *NTS* 48: 30–47.

Tuckett, C., 1986. *Nag Hammadi and the Gospel Tradition: Synoptic Tradition in the Nag Hammadi Library*. Studies of the New Testament and Its World. Edinburgh: T. & T. Clark.

Tuckett, C.M., 2005. 'The *Didache* and the Writings That Later Formed the New Testament,' in A.F. Gregory and C.M. Tuckett (ed.), *The Reception of the New Testament in the Apostolic Fathers*. Oxford and New York: OUP, pp. 82–127.

Tugwell, S., 1980. *The Beatitudes: Soundings in Christian Traditions*. Springfield: Templegate.

Turley, T., 1982. 'John Baconthorpe on Papal Infallibility,' *Journal of Ecumenical Studies* 19/4: 744–758.

Turner, C.H., 1911. 'The Early Greek Commentators on the Gospel according to St. Matthew,' *JTS* 12: 99–112.

Turner, D.L., 2010. 'Matthew Among the Dispensationalists,' *Journal of the Evangelical Theological Society* 53/4: 697–716.

Ukpong, J., 2012. 'The Parable of the Talents (Matt 25:14–30): Commendation or Critique of Exploitation? A Social-Historical and Theological Reading,' *Neotestamentica* 46/1: 190–207.

van der Bergh, R.H., 2012. 'The Reception of Matthew 27:19b (Pilate's Wife's Dream) in the Early Church,' *Journal of Early Christian History* 2/1: 70–85.

van Liere, F., 2014. *An Introduction to the Medieval Bible*. New York:CUP.

Verheyden, J, 1990. 'The Flight of the Christians to Pella,' *ETL* 66/4: 368–384.

Verseput, D.J., 1994. 'Jesus' Pilgrimage to Jerusalem and Encounter in the Temple: A Geographical Motif in Matthew's Gospel,' *NovT* 36/2: 105–121.

Viljoen, F.P., 2012. 'Interpreting the *visio Dei* in Matthew 5:8,' *HTS Teologiese Studies/ Theological Studies* 68(1), Art. 905, 7 pages. doi:10.4102/ hts.v68i1.905.

Viviano, B.T., 1979. 'Where Was the Gospel According to St. Matthew Written?' *CBQ* 41: 533–546.

Viviano, B.T., 1990. 'Social World and Community Leadership: The Case of Matthew 23.1–12, 34,' *JSNT* 39: 3–21.

Viviano, B.T., 2009. 'Making Sense of the Matthean Genealogy: Matthew 1:17 and the Theology of History,' in J. Corley (ed.), *New Perspectives on the Nativity*. London and New York: T. & T. Clark, pp. 91–109.

Viviano, B.T., 2010. 'God in the Gospel of Matthew,' *Interpretation* 64: 341–354.

Vlam, G.A.H., 1977. 'The Calling of Saint Matthew in Sixteenth-Century Flemish Painting,' *The Art Bulletin* 59/4: 561–570.

von Harnack, A., 1957. *What Is Christianity?* Trans. T.B. Saunders. New York: Harper and Row.

von Hase, K., 1876. *Geschichte Jesu. Nach akademischen Vorlesungen*. Leipzig: Breitkopf und Härtel.

von Rad, G., 1966. *The Problem of the Hexateuch and Other Essays*. Edinburgh: Oliver & Boy.

Wailes, S.L., 1987. *Medieval Allegories of Jesus' Parables*. Berkeley, Los Angeles and London: University of California Press.

Wainwright, E., 1994. 'The Gospel of Matthew,' in E. Schüssler Fiorenza (ed.), *Searching the Scriptures II*. New York: Crossroad, pp. 635–677.

Wakefield, W.L., and A.P. Evans (ed.), 1991. *Heresies of the High Middle Ages*. New York: Columbia University Press.

Walsh, M.A. (ed.), 2003. *John Paul II: A Light for the World. Essays and Reflections on the Papacy of John Paul II*. Lanham: Sheed and Ward.

Walsh, R., 2010. *Three Versions on Judas*. London: Equinox.

Walsh, R., 2013. '*Monty Python's Life of Brian* (1979),' in A. Reinhartz (ed.), *Bible and Cinema: Fifty Key Films*. London and New York: Routledge, pp. 187–192.

Wanke, R.M., 2015. 'Text, Context and Tradition: Implications for Reading Matthew,' in K. Mtata and C. Koester (ed.), *To All the Nations: Lutheran Hermeneutics and the Gospel of Matthew*. LWF Studies. Leipzig: Lutheran World Federation/Evangelische Verlangsanstalt, pp. 59–71.

Wardle, T., 2016. 'Resurrection and the Holy City: Matthew's Use of Isaiah in 27:51–53,' *CBQ* 78: 666–681.

Watson, A., 1934. *The Early Iconography of the Tree of Jesse*. London: Humphrey Milford/OUP.

Watson, F., 1993. 'Liberating the Reader: A Theological-Exegetical Study of the Parable of the Sheep and Goats (Matt. 25: 31–46),' in F. Watson (ed.), *The Open Text: New Directions for Biblical Studies?* London: SCM Press, pp. 57–84.

Weaver, D.J., 2011. '"Suffering Violence" and the Kingdom of Heaven (Mt 11:12): A Matthean Manual for Life in a Time of War,' *HTS Teologiese Studies/Theological Studies* 67(1), Art. 1011, 12 pages. doi:10.4102/hts.v67i1.1011.

Weber, S.R., 2013. '"Shake Off the Dust of Thy Feet": The Rise and Fall of Mormon Ritual Cursing,' *Dialogue: A Journal of Mormon Thought* 46/1: 108–139.

Wells, D., 2013. 'In the Footsteps of Bach's St. Matthew Passion: The Passion Settings of David Lang and James Macmillan,' *Tempo* 67 (264): 40–51.

Wenger, J.C., 1945. 'The Schleitheim Confession of Faith,' *Mennonite Quarterly Review* 19/4: 243–253.

Widdicombe, P., 2013. 'The Patristic Reception of the Gospel of Matthew: The Commentary of Jerome and the Sermons of John Chrysostom,' in E.-M. Becker and A. Runesson (ed.), *Mark and Matthew II: Comparative Readings: Reception History, Cultural Hermeneutics, and Theology*. Tübingen: Mohr Siebeck, pp. 105–120.

Wilcox, M., 2011. 'Constructing Metaphoric Models of Salvation: Matthew 20 and the Middle English Poem *Pearl*,' *Studies in the Bible and Antiquity* 3: 1–28.

Wilder, A.N., 1964. *The Language of the Gospel: Early Christian Rhetoric*. New York and Evanston: Harper & Row.

Wiles, M.F., 1958. 'Early Exegesis of the Parables,' *SJT* 11: 287–301.

Wilken, R.L., 2003. *The Christians as the Romans Saw Them*. 2nd edition. New Haven: Yale University Press.

Wilken, R.L., 2007. 'Augustine,' in J.P. Greenman, T. Larsen, and S.R. Spencer (ed.), *The Sermon on the Mount Through the Centuries: From the Early Church to John Paul II*. Grand Rapids: Brazos, pp. 43–57.

Williams, P., 2007a. 'The English Reformers and the Blessed Virgin Mary,' in S.J. Boss (ed.), *Mary: The Complete Resource*. London and New York: Continuum, pp. 238–255.

Williams, P., 2007b. 'The Virgin Mary in Anglican Tradition,' in S.J. Boss (ed.), *Mary: The Complete Resource*. London and New York: Continuum, pp. 314–339.

Williams, D.H., 2014. 'The Gospel of Matthew in Service of the Early Fathers,' *Pro Ecclesia* 23/1: 81–98.

Williams Jackson, A.V., 1905. 'The Magi in Marco Polo and the Cities of Persia from Which They Came to Worship the Infant Christ,' *Journal of the American Oriental Society* 26: 79–83.

Willitts, J., 2007. *Matthew's Messianic Shepherd-King: In Search of 'The Lost Sheep of the House of Israel.'* BZNW 147. Berlin and New York: de Gruyter.

Wilson, R.R., 1975. 'The Old Testament Genealogies in Recent Research,' *JBL* 94: 168–189.

Wilson, A.N., 1998. 'Introduction,' in *The Gospel According to Matthew. Authorized King James Version*. London: Canongate, pp. vii–xv.

Wilson, C.C., 2001. *St. Joseph in Italian Renaissance Society and Art: New Directions and Interpretations*. Philadelphia: Saint Joseph's University Press.

Winter, B.W., 1991. 'The Messiah as the Tutor: The Meaning of καθηγητής in Matthew 23:10,' *Tyndale Bulletin* 42/1: 152–157.

Witakowski, W., 1999. 'The Magi in Ethiopic Tradition,' *Aethiopica* 2: 69–89.

Witakowski, W., 2008. 'The Magi in Syriac Tradition,' in G.A. Kiraz (ed.), *Malphono w-Rabo d-Malphone: Studies in Honor of Sebastian P. Brock*. Piscataway: Gorgias Press, pp. 809–843.

Wright, J., 2001. 'Marian Exiles and the Legitimacy of Flight from Persecution,' *Journal of Ecclesiastical History* 52/2: 220–243.

Wright, W.M., 2012. 'The Literal Sense of Scripture According to Henri de Lubac: Insights from Patristic Exegesis of the Transfiguration,' *Modern Theology* 28/2: 252–277.

Wuellner, W.H., 1967. *The Meaning of 'Fishers of Men'*. NTL. Philadelphia: Westminster.

Yarbro Collins, A., 2007. *Mark: A Commentary*. Hermeneia. Minneapolis: Fortress.

Yieh, J.Y.H., 2009. 'Jesus the "Teacher-Saviour" or "Saviour-Teacher": Reading the Gospel of Matthew in Chinese Contexts,' *HTS Teologiese Studies/Theology Studies* 65(1), Art. 317, 10 pages. doi:10.4102/hts.v65i1.317.

Young, K., 1933. *The Drama of the Medieval Church*. 2 vols. Oxford: Clarendon.

Young, F.M., 2002. *Biblical Exegesis and the Formation of Christian Culture*. Peabody: Hendrickson.

Zeichmann, C.B., 2015. 'Rethinking the Gay Centurion: Sexual Exceptionalism, National Exceptionalism in Readings of Matt. 8:5–13//Luke 7:1–10,' *The Bible & Critical Theory* 11/1: 35–54.

Zimmerman, R., 2015. *Puzzling the Parables of Jesus: Methods and Interpretations*. Minneapolis: Fortress Press.

Zuffi, S., 2012. *Caravaggio: The Stories of St Matthew*. Art Mysteries. Milan: 24 ORE Cultura.

Zuidema, J., 2013. 'Flight from Persecution and the Honour of God in the Theology of Peter Martyr Vermigli,' *Reformation and Renaissance Review* 15/1: 112–126.

Zwiep, A.W., 2015. 'Jairus, His Daughter and the Haemorrhaging Woman (Mk 5.21–43; Mt. 9.18–26; Lk. 8.4056): Research Survey of a Gospel Story about People in Distress,' *Currents in Biblical Research* 13/3: 351–387.

Index of Biblical References

OLD TESTAMENT

Genesis

Matthew Through the Centuries, First Edition. Ian Boxall.

Index

Matthew Through the Centuries, First Edition. Ian Boxall.